Sefer HaIkkarim

ספר העיקרים

BOOK OF PRINCIPLES

The Philosopher Rabbi Yosef Albo

There is no known book without mistakes. Therefore, I ask in every language of application if anyone has any questions, comments, clarifications, corrections, please send to: **simchatchaim@yahoo.com**

All material used in this section may not be used for commercial purposes, but only for study and teaching.

To get this book or books and information Email me at:

simchatchaim@yahoo.com

Copyright©All Rights Reserved to

www.simchatchaim.com

YB"S©All rights reserved to the Editor

First Edition 2023

Sefer HaIkkarim — Contents of the book

Sefer HaIkkarim

The contents of the book in detail can be found in the Forward

Page	Contents
5.	Forward
28.	Introduction

BOOK [Maamar] ONE

Page	Contents
33.	Introduction
33.	Chapter 1
36.	Chapter 2
39.	Chapter 3
43.	Chapter 4
46.	Chapter 5
47.	Chapter 6
49.	Chapter 7
50.	Chapter 8
56.	Chapter 9
58.	Chapter 10
59.	Chapter 11
58.	Chapter 12
69.	Chapter 13
71.	Chapter 14
74.	Chapter 15
77.	Chapter 16
81.	Chapter 17
84.	Chapter 18
90.	Chapter 19
91.	Chapter 20
94.	Chapter 21
96.	Chapter 22
97.	Chapter 23
100.	Chapter 24
103.	Chapter 25
105.	Chapter 26

Sefer Halkkarim
Contents of the book
BOOK [Maamar] TWO

109.	Introduction
109.	Observation
111.	Chapter 1
114.	Chapter 2
116.	Chapter 3
120.	Chapter 4
122.	Chapter 5
125.	Chapter 6
127.	Chapter 7
128.	Chapter 8
132.	Chapter 9
133.	Chapter 10
135.	Chapter 11
139.	Chapter 12
141.	Chapter 13
146.	Chapter 14
150.	Chapter 15
154.	Chapter 16
155.	Chapter 17
158.	Chapter 18
161.	Chapter 19
162.	Chapter 20
164.	Chapter 21
167.	Chapter 22
171	Chapter 23
173.	Chapter 24
176.	Chapter 25
180.	Chapter 26
184.	Chapter 27
187.	Chapter 28
194.	Chapter 29
198.	Chapter 30
203.	Chapter 31

BOOK [Maamar] THREE

211.	Introduction
211.	Chapter 1
216.	Chapter 2
220.	Chapter 3
225.	Chapter 4
227.	Chapter 5

Sefer Halkkarim — Contents of the book

Page	
230.	Chapter 6
235.	Chapter 7
238.	Chapter 8
244.	Chapter 9
247.	Chapter 10
254.	Chapter 11
258.	Chapter 12
260.	Chapter 13
263.	Chapter 14
268.	Chapter 15
272.	Chapter 16
277.	Chapter 17
280.	Chapter 18
287.	Chapter 19
293.	Chapter 20
297.	Chapter 21
299.	Chapter 22
302.	Chapter 23
305.	Chapter 24
309.	Chapter 25
322.	Chapter 26
326.	Chapter 27
329.	Chapter 28
333.	Chapter 29
338.	Chapter 30
344.	Chapter 31
347.	Chapter 32
350.	Chapter 33
353.	Chapter 34
355.	Chapter 35
360.	Chapter 36
364.	Chapter 37

BOOK [Maamar] FOUR

Page	
371.	Introduction
372.	Chapter 1
374.	Chapter 2
376.	Chapter 3
381.	Chapter 4
386.	Chapter 5
391.	Chapter 6
393.	Chapter 7
396.	Chapter 8

Sefer Halkkarim — Contents of the book

402.	Chapter 9
405.	Chapter 10
412.	Chapter 11
416.	Chapter 12
419.	Chapter 13
430.	Chapter 14
434.	Chapter 15
437.	Chapter 16
440.	Chapter 17
443.	Chapter 18
447.	Chapter 19
452.	Chapter 20
455.	Chapter 21
459.	Chapter 22
464.	Chapter 23
469.	Chapter 24
471.	Chapter 25
478.	Chapter 26
488.	Chapter 27
491.	Chapter 28
495.	Chapter 29
502.	Chapter 30
510.	Chapter 31
515.	Chapter 32
517.	Chapter 33
523.	Chapter 34
525.	Chapter 35
533.	Chapter 36
537.	Chapter 37
541.	Chapter 38
546.	Chapter 39
548.	Chapter 40
552.	Chapter 41
560.	Chapter 42
467.	Chapter 43
570.	Chapter 44
572.	Chapter 45
576.	Chapter 46
579.	Chapter 47
582.	Chapter 48
584.	Chapter 49
587.	Chapter 50
593.	Chapter 51

Sefer HaIkkarim
ספר העיקרים

BOOK OF PRINCIPLES

Forward

Human happiness depends upon theoretical knowledge and practical conduct, as the Philosopher explains in the book On the Soul. But it is not possible by the human intellect alone to arrive at a proper knowledge of the true and the good, because human reason is not capable of comprehending things as they are in reality, as will be explained later. There must therefore be something higher than the human intellect by means of which the good can be defined and the true comprehended in a manner leaving no doubt at all. This can be done only by means of divine guidance. It is incumbent therefore upon every person, out of all laws to know that one divine law which gives this guidance. This is impossible unless we know the basic principles without which a divine law cannot exist. Accordingly, the purpose of this work is to explain what are the essential principles of a divine law, and for this reason it is called The Book of Principles. The present work consists of an Introduction and four books.

The Introduction deals with the necessity of a work of this kind, outlines in a general way the topics which it is proper to investigate therein, points out the great importance of the subject under investigation, and explains the last verse of the ninetieth Psalm.

Book One discusses the number and nature of the principles of laws. It points out the difference between divine and conventional laws, and states the principles of each. It distinguishes between principles which are common to many laws and those which are peculiar to a given law. It shows that the principles which are common to divine laws are three: the existence of God, revelation, and reward and punishment, and from these other principles are derived. It is also pointed out in this book how the genuine law of God can be distinguished from the spurious, which pretends to be a law of God.

Book Two discusses the first principle, the existence of God, and the subordinate principles derived therefrom.

Sefer HaIkkarim — Forward

Book Three discusses the second principle, revelation, and the subordinate principles derived therefrom.

Book Four discusses the third principle, reward and punishment, and the subordinate principles derived therefrom and based upon it.

BOOK [Maamar] ONE discusses the principles of laws, and is divided into twenty-six chapters.

Chapter one speaks of the difficulty of investigating the principles of laws. It is pointed out that there are principles common to all laws and principles peculiar to a given law. Maimonides is criticized for listing the belief in the Messiah as a principle of the law of Moshe. Similarly, are those criticized who maintain that creation of the world is a principle of the law of Moshe.

Chapter two points out what denial of principles constitutes heresy and what denial does not. It is pointed out that neither the belief in the Messiah nor creation of the world should be regarded as principles of the law of Moshe, as many have thought.

Chapter three explains the meaning of the term principle and discusses the thirteen principles of Maimonides in order to determine whether the number is correct or not. It also discusses other principles of the divine law laid down by others and points out that none of them have the correct number.

Chapter four explains that the common principles of divine law are three, which are basic, namely, the existence of God, revelation of the Torah and reward and punishment. Then there are other principles derived from the former and dependent upon them. It is pointed out that the three benedictions in the ritual of the New Year, Malkuyyot, Zikronot, and Shofarot, bear allusion to the three principles mentioned, and that all the principles mentioned by Maimonides are derived from these three basic ones.

Chapter five explains the necessity of natural law for the existence of the human race, pointing out at the same time that natural law alone is not sufficient for the existence of, political society unless there be also another law. It is also pointed out that a country must have a judge or a king.

Chapter six decides that there must be a divine law to guide mankind to happiness.

Chapter seven explains that law is natural or conventional or divine. The meaning and purpose of each are explained and the manner in which they are distinguished.

Sefer HaIkkarim — Forward

Chapter eight points out some of the defects of conventional law which make it inferior to divine law. It points out also that some of the qualities of divine law are alluded to in Psalm nineteen, verse eight and following.

Chapter nine explains that the general principles of conventional law are freedom of the will and purpose. It also explains why freedom of the will is mentioned in the law of Moshe, seeing that it is not a principle of it insofar as it is divine.

Chapter ten explains that the general principles of divine law are three: existence of God, reward and punishment, and revelation of the Torah, and hence they are named as general roots of divine law. It is also pointed out that the Rabbis in the Mishnah, Chapter Helek, name also these three.

Chapter eleven explains that by a study of the law of Moshe we can find out what are the essential bases of divine law, seeing that all agree that it is divine. Accordingly, we infer that the three things mentioned are principles of divine law, seeing that they are laid down in the book of Genesis at the beginning, as the principles of every science are laid down at the beginning of that science. It is pointed out that the real beginning of the Torah is the first verse of chapter five. It explains also the meaning of the expression, Let us make man in our image [Gen. 1, 26].

Chapter twelve explains the reason why Maimonides does not include the dogma of creation in his list of principles, seeing that he regards it as fundamental in the law of Moshe, as he says in the twenty-seventh chapter of the second part of the Guide of the Perplexed.

Chapter thirteen explains that not every law which acknowledges the three principles mentioned is therefore certainly divine, unless it acknowledges also all the principles derived from the former, in which case it may be divine. It is also pointed out that to deny a derivative principle is tantamount to the denial of an original principle.

Chapter fourteen explains that a commandment of the Torah can not be regarded either as a fundamental or as a derivative principle. This is the reason why belief in tradition is not named as a principle even though it is essential to the existence of law. The reason is given why the unity of God is regarded as a principle although it is a particular commandment. It is also explained why all the principles are not specifically stated in the ten commandments. It is maintained that the first commandment is not a principle, as Maimonides says, but a command.

Sefer HaIkkarim — Forward

Chapter fifteen explains the principles derived from each one of the three original principles. It is also explained why we classify them as fundamental and derivative, or basic and resultant, and do not regard them all alike as fundamental principles.

Chapter sixteen deals with a certain topic necessary to divine law. It explains that one of the ancient philosophers thought that it is not possible to acquire knowledge of a thing that is not known. It explains the thirty-sixth verse of chapter thirty-eight of Job, the benediction beginning with the words, Thou in Thy graciousness givest man knowledge, and the rabbinical expression, If there is no knowledge there is no understanding [Mishnah, Abot, 3, 17]. This chapter is introductory to the following.

Chapter seventeen explains that every science has principles and points out the general principles of the sciences. This is done in order to make clear whence the Torah takes its principles. It explains verse one hundred and sixty of Psalm one hundred and nineteen and part of Psalm seventy-eight.

Chapter eighteen explains the difference between the genuine divine law and one that is spurious and pretends to be divine. It also explains the difference between a prophet who is not and a prophet who is a messenger of God for the purpose of giving mankind a law. It also explains the nature of the signs which prove directly the genuineness of a prophecy or a mission. It is also pointed out that any one not a prophet who makes use of the divine names is punished.

Chapter nineteen gives a definition of belief, shows to what things belief applies and when it is strongest.

Chapter twenty explains why the Torah was not given to Abraham or to Yitzhak or to Yaakov. It also explains the statement of the Rabbis in the Talmudic treatise 'Abodah Zarah: In the time to come, the Holy One, blessed be He, will take the Torah, put it in His bosom and say: Let every one who occupied himself with this come and receive his reward! It is also explained why the other nations will not receive reward for keeping the law which they received by tradition as the Israelites will receive reward for keeping their traditions.

Chapter twenty-one explains that belief leads man to eternal happiness more so than philosophical knowledge, pointing out that this is verified by experience.

Chapter twenty-two explains in what thing it is that belief leads to happiness, pointing out that belief in the impossible does not lead to

Sefer HaIkkarim — Forward

happiness, also that the impossible is of two kinds. It explains also how the thing is known to which belief applies.

Chapter twenty-three points out that besides the general belief in the Torah, the commandments and all the miracles which are mentioned in the Torah, it is incumbent to entertain six specific beliefs which are essential for the existence of the Torah at any time, and one who denies any one of them is called a heretic.

Chapter twenty-four inquires whether a person professing a given religion is obliged or permitted to investigate the foundations of his religious belief and the principles derived from them or whether he must rely on his tradition.

Chapter twenty-five investigates whether there may be more than one divine law at the same time among different nations or in different countries.

Chapter twenty-six sums up the book by giving a list of the fundamental and derivative principles essential to divine law as is demanded by logical theory and as is declared in the law of Moshe. Here end the topics of the chapters of the First Book, with the help of God, blessed be He.

BOOK [Maamar] TWO explains the first principle, the existence of God, and is divided into an Observation and thirty-one chapters, as follows:

[The Observation calls the attention of the reader to the method of this book.]

Chapter one explains that existence as applied to God is not used in the same sense as when applied to other existing things. It is pointed out that the existence of God is not known from His essence, but is inferred from the existing things emanating from Him. Part of Psalm one hundred and four is explained therein.

Chapter two explains that we can not apply the word Maker to God in the sense in which it is applied to any other agent, whether natural or voluntary. It is also pointed out that we can not say of God that He acts with an eternal will, as many have thought.

Chapter three explains in what sense we can say of God that He acts with will, pointing out that the verse, Isaiah 55, 8, For My thoughts are not your thoughts, etc., is intended to solve the difficulty concerning the divine will, which is greater than the difficulty concerning the divine knowledge, wisdom and the other attributes. It is explained that the divine will does not necessitate change in God as it does in us.

Sefer HaIkkarim Forward

Chapter four explains that from the statements in the Bible of the coming into being of things at different times we derive a proof of the existence of a Maker who acts with purpose and will. It also gives a scientific demonstration of the existence of God and of the principles derived from it, based upon the things perceived by our senses.

Chapter five points out that the first two proofs of the existence of God given by Maimonides in the beginning of the second part of the Guide are neither one of them worth the attention of the religionist, and that the third proof given there by Maimonides is the best of all.

Chapter six explains the formal content of the belief, which every religionist must entertain, in the fundamental principle of the existence of God and the secondary principles derived from it. It is pointed out that there is neither a definition nor a description of God enabling us to know His true essence and existence.

Chapter seven explains that from the secondary principles derived from the fundamental principle of the existence of God flow all the attributes which may be ascribed to God or which must be denied of Him. A reason is given why the number of secondary principles is four and not more.

Chapter eight begins to treat of the attributes in order to explain the principle of the unity of God. It is pointed out that an attribute applied to a thing descriptive of its activities does not necessarily imply plurality in the nature of the agent, even though the latter, be it natural or voluntary, is the author of contrary actions. The human soul, for example, is one though it is the author of contrary actions. God also may have attributes ascribed to Him from three different points of view, no one of them necessarily implying plurality in His essence.

Chapter nine explains the point of view which denies all attributes to God, whether essential or accidental, and criticizes it on the ground that He must have some attribute or attributes, such as unity and others.

Chapter ten explains the various meanings of the term one and the sense in which we say of God that He is one. It also explains the verse, Deuteronomy 6, 4, Hear, O Israel, the Lord our God, the Lord is One.

Chapter eleven explains the manner in which the many are derived from the One, and the emanation of existing things from the First Cause, according to the opinions of Ibn Sina and Maimonides. It explains the statement of the Rabbis: The Sabbath said to God, Master of the Universe, to every one Thou hast given a mate, but to

Sefer HaIkkarim — Forward

me Thou hast not given a mate. The Lord replied, My daughter, the congregation of Israel shall be thy mate. It is also pointed out that the commandment of the Sabbath is a sign.

Chapter twelve treats of the existence of angels, discusses the various opinions concerning their nature and the possibility of there being many angels.

Chapter thirteen explains the manner in which the many can be derived from the Simple One, according to the opinions of Ibn Roshd and the ancient philosophers. It criticizes this view, in the manner indicated in chapter eleven, and explains in this connection the verse, Hear, O Israel.

Chapter fourteen begins to treat of the second derivative principle, the incorporeality of God, and explains in what manner are attributed to God such corporeal affections as anger, sorrow, vengeance and bearing a grudge; also why we ascribe to Him pride, which is a bad quality. It explains also why God is called King of Glory.

Chapter fifteen explains in what way joy is ascribed to God, as is said [Ps. 104, 31]: The Lord rejoiced in His works, while the Rabbis say, Joy is in His habitation. It also explains the verses, Psalm 36, 8–9.

Chapter sixteen explains the various uses of the word laughter and the sense in which it is said of God that He laughs. It also explains the cause of laughter in every case and the reason for the statement of the philosophers that laughter is a human property.

Chapter seventeen explains in what sense it is said of God or of the glory of God that He is in a place, seeing that He is not corporeal. It inquires whether we can say of God or of an incorporeal thing that it occupies a certain position, up or down, though it does not occupy space. The Aristotelian definition of space is explained and criticized, the author maintaining, contrary to the view of Aristotle, that space is a vacuum or void, and answering Aristotle's criticism of this view.

Chapter eighteen begins to treat of the third derivative principle, that God is not subject to time, explaining the sense in which God is spoken of as eternal a parte ante and a parte post. It explains that there is another view of the nature of time besides that of Aristotle, namely that the unmeasured duration in the motion of the sphere is time. It also explains the expression [Is. 44, 6], I am the first, and I am the last.

Chapter nineteen explains that every attribute ascribed to God is eternal in both directions like Him, and that God does not change since He is not subject to time, while everything else changes. It explains Psalm 37, 25 together with the statement of the Rabbis that the Prince of the World is the author thereof. It gives a reason also for the repetition of the pronoun I in Is. 43, 11.

Chapter twenty explains the different meanings of the homonym **Kol** [all] in order to remove the difficulty arising from Psalm 9, 15, That I may tell of all Thy praise. It also explains the verse [Gen. 1, 31], And God saw all that He had made, and, behold, it was very good.

Chapter twenty-one begins to explain the fourth derivative principle, which is that God is free from defects, pointing out at the same time that we must ascribe to God some positive attributes. It explains in what sense these attributes are ascribed to Him according to the wise men learned in the Torah, maintaining that all the attributes are applicable to God in the sense only that they denote perfection.

Chapter twenty-two explains that the opinion of Maimonides is that the only attributes that may be ascribed to God are the negative or those which are derived from God's acts, like merciful, gracious, generous. It also explains who is deserving of being called generous. It explains also the meaning of the prayer of Moshe: Show me Thy ways [Ex. 33, 13], as well as the passage in the Talmud [Berakot 33b] wherein they say that if Moshe had not used the expression, the great, the mighty and the fearful God, and the Men of the Great Synagogue had not subsequently incorporated it in the prayer, we should not use it.

Chapter twenty-three explains that positive attributes, according to this opinion, are unworthy of God unless they designate His acts, and therefore God must be praised from two points of view with two kinds of attributes, in relation to Himself and in relation to His acts. It is also pointed out that these two kinds of praise are alluded to in Psalm one hundred and three.

Chapter twenty-four explains that there are attributes which clearly are ascribed to God by reason of His acts, while there are others concerning which it is doubtful whether they refer to God's essence or to His acts; in which latter case it is explained how the attributes are to be understood. It also explains the meaning of such attributes as living, wise, possessing will, powerful and the like.

Chapter twenty-five explains that from the fourth principle, namely that God is free from defects, it follows that God has an infinite number of perfections, and that every one of these attributes

Sefer HaIkkarim — Forward

is infinite in two respects, in time and in worth. It is also pointed out that this matter is alluded to in Psalm one hundred and thirty-nine.

Chapter twenty-six explains the word blessed, the several meanings which it has and the sense in which it is applied to God. It explains also Psalm one hundred and forty-five, pointing out how it is possible to praise God forever, using the method that is mentioned in the preceding chapter.

Chapter twenty-seven explains the application of the words **Emet** [truth], **Sheker** [falsehood], and **Kazab** [lie], pointing out that there is no existing thing to which the word **Emet** [truth] applies in the strict sense except God. This is why the Rabbis say that the seal of God is **Emet** [truth]. For the same reason God is called I am that I am.

Chapter twenty-eight explains why the tetragrammaton is called Shem ha-Meforash, pointing out at the same time that names are sometimes applied to things without there being any similarity between them. Thus, the Bible calls the altar Adonai-Nissi [The Lord is my banner] [Exod. 17, 15], and applies the name of God to Yerushalayim and the Messiah, also angels are called by the name of God. It is pointed out therein that the prophet thinks that the angel who speaks to him is God, and the angel too speaks in the name of God who sent him. A reason is given why Yehoshua bowed down to the angel, seeing that it is forbidden to prostrate oneself even to the angels. It is also pointed out that it is an error to mention the names of angels in the prayers.

Chapter twenty-nine explains the homonym or [light]. It gives the various meanings of the word and explains why God is called light. It explains the verse, Ezekiel 1, 28, as well as the statement of the Rabbis that if a person looks at the rainbow his eyes become weak. It is pointed out also that the senses perceive the accidents of things only.

Chapter thirty explains that wise men differ in degree according to the difference in their comprehension of the divine attributes of perfection. It also explains the superiority of some wise men to others according to the opinion of Maimonides who says that all negative judgments about God are true and all affirmative judgments are false.

Chapter thirty-one explains that from the connection of the parts of nature with each other we may infer the existence of one cause which unites all nature, which uniting agency is the necessary existent. It points out that the vision which Eliyahu saw on mount Horeb was an allusion to this. It explains the meaning of the

Sefer HaIkkarim — Forward

expression a still, small voice [I Kings, 19, 12], and the statement of the Rabbis that hashmal means Hayyot of fire speaking.

Here end the topics of the chapters of the Second Book, with the help of God.

BOOK [Maamar] THREE explains the second principle, revelation of the Torah, and contains thirty-seven chapters.

Chapter one explains that man is a more perfect creature than all the other animals, rejecting the opinion of the ancients who said that man is inferior in his formation to the lower animals. It explains also how man can learn manners and morals from the lower animals, an idea which is alluded to in Job 35, 11.

Chapter two explains that man has a special purpose different from the lower animals, namely human perfection. An explanation is given of the following verses, Cant. 2, 14; Ecc. 3, 19; Job 28, 12. It is pointed out that there are two kinds of perfection. A reason is given why in the account of the creation of man in Genesis there is no mention of the expression that it is good, or after his kind, as there is in the account of the creation of the lower animals.

Chapter three refutes the opinion of the philosophers that the purpose of the human race is the attainment of theoretical knowledge, pointing out that according to their opinion no person can realize the purpose of man and the creation of the human race would be in vain. It is pointed out that this matter is alluded to in the nineteenth Psalm.

Chapter four explains that it is easy for every existing being in accordance with its status to attain the perfection special to it according to its nature. It is pointed out that no perfection can be attained by any creature except through acts, and that the only acts which can confer perfection are those which are done with intelligence; also, that man whose status is far below that of the other beings endowed with a rational soul must do many acts in order to attain his perfection.

Chapter five proves from the spheres and the angels that only those acts which are done with the intention of serving God confer perfection, pointing out that the statements of the philosophers concerning the intentions of the spheres in their motions are utter folly and nonsense. Biblical verses are cited to prove that human perfection is not attained through knowledge alone but only through acts which are agreeable to God, namely such acts as are done with the intention of performing the will of God. Such perfection

Sefer HaIkkarim — Forward

embraces the entire human race or the greater part thereof. An explanation is given of Jeremiah 9, 22–23.

Chapter six maintains that human acts do not all lead to the realization of the purpose of man. The difficulty is pointed out of drawing a line of demarcation between those acts which do and those which do not lead to human perfection. It is explained how this can be done and it is maintained that the joy or the sorrow resulting from an act is a good criterion, as is proved from the verses Jeremiah 2, 19 and Psalm 119, 14.

Chapter seven calls attention to certain difficulties in the method above mentioned of defining good acts, pointing out that rational analysis is not sufficient for this purpose, much less can rational investigation determine what acts are pleasing to God. Hence it was necessary to have them defined by divine command. It is pointed out that there are some acts which reason shows to be bad and a person guilty of doing them is deserving of punishment even without a divine prohibition. This is why Cain was punished in that God had not respect to his offering. There are also acts which give perfection to the soul, but they can not all be completely determined by reason, and divine inspiration is necessary.

Chapter eight explains that prophecy does not come from the faculty of imagination as the philosophers thought, but that it is a divine inspiration which influences the rational faculty. A definition is given of prophecy and it is pointed out that the degree of Moshe was higher than that of all the other prophets, because Moshe' prophecy came to him without an intermediate agency, whereas the prophecy of the others came through an intermediate agency.

Chapter nine explains why the prophets see God under various forms though God is one; also, why they see different visions and give expression to different words when the subject matter is the same.

Chapter ten explains the manner in which the prophetic inspiration comes to the prophet and the conception thereof in the prophet's mind, differently from the explanation of the philosophers. It also explains how we may conceive of the different degrees of prophecy as dependent on the mode in which the imagination is combined with the reason. The difference is pointed out between the prophecy and miracles of Moshe and those of the others.

Chapter eleven points out that through the medium of a person who is fit for prophetic inspiration a prophetic message may come to one who is not fit for prophecy, as was the case when all Israel received divine inspiration at the time of the revelation on Mount Sinai

Sefer HaIkkarim — Forward

through the mediation of Moshe, and when Elisha received the prophetic mission through the mediation of Eliyahu. It is also explained why prophecy is found in Israel rather than among the other nations.

Chapter twelve explains that the purpose of the existence of prophecy in the human race is not for the sake of foretelling the future, but in order that man may attain to human perfection, pointing out that this is why prophecy is regarded as a secondary principle derived from revelation of the Torah, which is the fundamental principle, and not vice versa. It is also explained why providence is regarded as a secondary principle derived from the principle of reward and punishment, and not vice versa.

Chapter thirteen investigates whether it is possible that a divine law given to a particular nation may be changed for that same nation at different times, or whether it must be eternal.

Chapter fourteen explains that we find that divine laws do change, permitting what was formerly prohibited and prohibiting what was formerly permitted, and gives the reason therefor. The arguments of Maimonides are refuted which led him to include the immutability of the Torah as a fundamental principle. It explains the statement of the Rabbis that neither came it into My mind [Jer. 7, 31] refers to Yitzhak son of Abraham. It is also maintained that even if we should admit Maimonides' arguments, they would prove only that we may not change the Torah or add to or diminish from it on our responsibility, but they do not exclude the possibility that the Torah may be changed by the command of God through the decree of His wisdom, as the Adamite law was changed for Noah and the **Noachian law** was changed for Moshe.

Chapter fifteen gives a reason why meat was forbidden to Adam, permitted to Noah and again forbidden in part to Moshe. It is also explained in what consisted the sin of Cain when he brought an offering to God of the fruit of the ground so that God had not respect to him or to his offering.

Chapter sixteen explains the homonym olam [eternity], pointing out that the expressions 'olam [eternity], le'olamim [to eternity], hukkat 'olam [a statute forever], and 'ad 'olam [unto eternity], denote a fixed and finite, not an infinite time. It is pointed out that in the time of the second Temple they ceased counting the months from Nisan though it is one of the commandments of the Torah according to the opinion of Maimonides. It explains the statement of the Rabbis that the letters mem and samek on the tables of the

Sefer HaIkkarim — Forward

Decalogue were held up by a miracle. It is pointed out that the characters in which the Torah is written in our day are not Hebrew.

Chapter seventeen explains that the degree of the prophet and his power of comprehension determine the strength of belief in his message and its meaning. The meaning is explained of Isaiah's exclamation, Woe is me! for I am undone! [Is. 6, 5], as well as of the statement of the Rabbis that Manasseh tried Isaiah before he killed him.

Chapter eighteen points out that a message which a prophet receives from God can not be nullified by any other prophet, unless the former himself receives from God the contrary of the first message. Hence no prophet can annul any one of the ten commandments, for all Israel heard them publicly given by God. It is also explained that the statement of the Rabbis, The first two commandments were heard by Israel from the mouth of Geburah, does not mean that they heard them miraculously, as Maimonides maintains; also that the first commandment is not intended to teach the existence and unity of God as Maimonides says, but to remove the error of idolatry. It then explains the various errors of which idolaters are guilty and maintains that the Israelites heard all the ten commandments from God. It explains the difference between the first two commandments and the rest and points out under what circumstances the words of a prophet should be obeyed even against the commandment of the Torah.

Chapter nineteen explains that a person professing a divine law by tradition may not abandon it if it is clear to him that the principles upon which it is based are true, as we explained in the first book. It explains also the manner in which is proved the authenticity of the messenger and his mission. It explains why the Israelites followed the law of Moshe although it differed from the law of the Noachites which was divine. It then shows that we may not depart from the law of Moshe and believe any one who says that it is only of temporary validity, even in reference to the commandments outside of the Decalogue, unless he can prove his authenticity in the same way as Moshe proved his.

Chapter twenty explains that the Law of Moshe is eternal because it is impossible that there should arise another prophet like Moshe. This idea does not follow necessarily from the verse, And there hath not arisen a prophet since in Israel like unto Moshe [Deut. 34, 10], but rather from the answer given to Moshe when he said, So that we are distinguished, I and Thy people [Ex. 33, 16]. Maimonides is criticized for including the immutability of the Torah as a

Sefer HaIkkarim — Forward

fundamental principle when he had already named the superiority of Moshe' prophecy as a fundamental principle.

Chapter twenty-one explains why the Torah is called testimony, pointing out at the same time that it is not permissible to interpret the biblical text figuratively and reject the literal meaning. In this connection are explained Psalm 119, 85 and following.

Chapter twenty-two explains that the Torah which has been handed down to us by tradition and which we have today is the identical one that was given to Moshe on Sinai without any change, and that it was not changed in the days of Ezra. It explains also the statement of the Rabbis that certain words in the Torah were corrected by the Soferim.

Chapter twenty-three explains the necessity of an oral law accompanying a written, maintaining at the same time that no evidence concerning anything can be adduced from the consensus of the masses, but only from the agreement of wise men, for the masses often hold in common an opinion which is not the truth.

Chapter twenty-four explains that the Torah contains three parts, words, statutes and judgments, pointing to the fact that God is wise, possessed of will and of power. No conventional law can embrace those three things. It explains also part of Psalm one hundred and forty-seven.

Chapter twenty-five mentions the criticism directed by a Christian against the Torah of Moshe, maintaining that it is not perfect. The criticism is answered and it is explained that the Torah is perfect in every respect, considering all the four causes, the material, the efficient, the formal and the final. It is pointed out that Psalm 19, 8 alludes to this, and that the Christian translator erred in his rendering of the word temimah. Allusion is made therein also to the reasons for the institution of sacrifices.

Chapter twenty-six explains that the Decalogue embraces two kinds of commandments, those governing the relations between man and God and those governing the relations between man and man. For this reason, they were put on two tablets. It also explains why those particular commandments were chosen for the Decalogue and not others. An explanation is also given of the statement of the Rabbis that the words remember and keep in the two versions of the Decalogue were pronounced in one utterance.

Chapter twenty-seven points out that performance of a commandment requires intention. Hence it follows that negative commandments confer perfection upon the soul equally with positive. This is proved from the first few verses of Psalm one hundred and nineteen. It explains also why the positive commandments are 248 in number, while the negative are 365, and not vice versa.

Chapter twenty-eight points out that human perfection which depends upon the positive and negative commandments is found in every one of the three parts into which the Torah is divided, namely: opinions, judgments and statutes. Accordingly, perfection may be acquired by means of any one of these parts separately. It explains how a person may acquire perfection by means of the judgments, pointing out that perfection by means of the Torah can not be acquired through theory alone nor through practice alone. Incidentally is explained Proverbs 6, 23.

Chapter twenty-nine investigates a very important question, namely whether the Torah confers perfection as a whole only, not in its parts, or whether one of its parts is sufficient to confer perfection. The conclusion reached is that even a single act if done with the intention of serving God is sufficient to confer perfection according to the opinion of the Rabbis, and it is pointed out that this is a special principle of the Law of Moshe. It is also explained therein why the community is more under the protection of divine providence than the individual, the prayer of the community being more likely to be heard than that of an individual.

Chapter thirty explains that the degrees of perfection attained through the Torah are different in many ways. It also explains the statement of the Rabbis: David reduced them [the commandments] to eleven ... Habakkuk reduced them to one, etc. It explains the difference between Psalms twenty-four and fifteen.

Chapter thirty-one explains the expression serving God from fear, pointing out that the commandment to fear God, though it is special, includes all the commandments of the Torah. Incidentally is explained Deuteronomy 10, 12.

Chapter thirty-two defines fear of God, pointing out that fear may be of two kinds, fear of punishment, and awe by reason of the dignity and sublimity of the feared object. It is pointed out that both kinds are necessary for the attainment of human perfection.

Chapter thirty-three points out that joy gives completeness and perfection to the service of God, to the performance of a commandment and to everything else. The question is raised and solved of the compatibility of joy and fear in the service of God.

Chapter thirty-four expatiates upon the question of the compatibility of joy and fear being present together in the service of God, explaining at the same time Proverbs 2, 4; 10, 27.

Sefer HaIkkarim — Forward

Chapter thirty-five points out that the degree of the person who serves God from love is the highest of all degrees. Love is divided into three kinds, love of the good, love of the useful, and love of the agreeable. A definition is given of love and it is pointed out that all love comes to an end except the love of the good. The love of God, it is said, should embrace all the three kinds, an idea which, it is pointed out, is mentioned in Deuteronomy 6, 4 ff. It is further pointed out that the life of man is divided into three parts according to the different kinds of love and according to the division of the parts of the soul. It is maintained that the love of God must be shown in thought, speech and action, and at the same time an explanation is given of Deuteronomy 6, 4 ff.

Chapter thirty-six points out that the love of God does not disturb the soul as other loves do, but gives delight only, citing in this connection Canticles 7, 7. It is pointed out that he who serves God from love must examine the act at the time of doing it and choose it in preference to other acts, not minding the inconvenience that may be incurred, for he has no other purpose except to do the will of the beloved. Such was the service of our father Abraham, who was therefore called friend of God.

Chapter thirty-seven inquires whether it is possible that love may proceed from God to man, pointing out that there are three kinds of love, love of similarity, natural love and love of relation. God's love of man belongs to the third kind and is similar to the love of a king for his people, of a father for his son and of a husband for his wife. The love of God for Israel is like the love of a man for his sweetheart which is a peculiar love without reason. Hence it is called in the Bible heshek, The Lord did ... set His love [hashak] upon you ... choose you [Deut. 7, 7].

Here end the topics of the Third Book with the help of God.

BOOK [Maamar] FOUR discusses the third principle, reward and punishment. It contains an Introduction and fifty-one chapters.

The Introduction states that although freedom and purpose are not principles of divine law as such, nevertheless they must be explained before we treat of reward and punishment in the Torah. The order is explained in which the topics of this book are taken up for treatment.

Chapter one begins the discussion of God's knowledge, pointing out the reality of the contingent. Then the question is taken up of the compatibility of God's knowledge with the nature of the contingent. The opinions of Saadia and of some later authors are cited and found unsatisfactory.

Sefer Haikkarim   Forward

Chapter two lays down a preliminary statement for the solution of the above-mentioned difficulty. It is pointed out that the various sciences differ in their assumptions and principles, and it is maintained that the senses must be made the basis in every case.

Chapter three maintains that the theological scholar makes the senses the basis of everything even though he does not know the cause of the sense datum, in the same way as in the science of astronomy, the diurnal motion, which is visible to the senses, is taken as a basis, though we do not know the cause thereof. It is pointed out that reason is incapable of knowing the causes even of natural things. A solution follows of the above-mentioned difficulty in the problem of God's knowledge according to Maimonides.

Chapter four treats of the influence of the stars, and names two opinions on the subject neither of which is correct, then explains the correct theory.

Chapter five begins the discussion of freedom, points out how many kinds of human acts there are according to the demands of logical division, and classifies them into three kinds, compulsory, i.e., determined, free, and mixed of compulsion and freedom. What applies to one kind does not apply to the other. Job thought that everything was predetermined, while Eliphaz held that all was free.

Chapter six explains that diligence and effort are useful in all human acts even in matters which are determined. Incidentally it explains Psalm 128, 2.

Chapter seven begins the discussion of Providence, pointing out that Job denied providence because he observed the adversity of the righteous and the prosperity of the wicked. It is pointed out further that the problem of the adversity of the righteous has not the same difficulty as the problem of the prosperity of the wicked. Elihu replied to Job by showing him that the adversity of some righteous persons and the prosperity of some wicked persons are compatible with divine justice and Job acknowledged the truth of this statement before God.

Chapter eight gives two arguments in proof of providence, taken from an observation of nature as a whole. One argument is derived from the fact that dry land projects above water, and the other is taken from the fact that rain falls in a well-ordered manner and sometimes comes as a result of the prayer of the righteous.

Chapter nine gives three arguments in favor of providence, taken from particular phenomena in human circumstances and conduct. One argument is taken from the fact that the ideas of the wicked are not realized, the second is taken from punishments which

Sefer Halkkarim — Forward

correspond to the offence, and the third from the information which comes to one in a dream and vision of the night.

Chapter ten names two arguments in proof of providence, taken from reason. The one considers the point of view of the recipient, the other that of the agent. From the point of view of the recipient the argument is proved from Psalm eight. The argument from the point of view of the agent who exercises providence is based upon the words of Elihu [Job 34].

Chapter eleven points out that there are different kinds of providence for individuals of the human species as there are different kinds of providence for the various animal species.

Chapter twelve explains how to solve the problem of the prosperity of the wicked, pointing out four causes, any one of which may result in the prosperity of a wicked person.

Chapter thirteen explains how to solve the problem of the adversity of the righteous, pointing out causes which may result in the adversity of a righteous person without imputing wrong to God. It explains also the meaning of trial and of suffering of love.

Chapter fourteen explains why the prophets complained of these two phenomena, the adversity of the righteous and the prosperity of the wicked, pointing out that Asaph has the correct idea in the solution of these problems. Incidentally is explained Psalm seventy-three.

Chapter fifteen explains why Jeremiah and Habakkuk complained since they knew that Asaph had given the correct solution, as was mentioned in the preceding chapter. Incidentally it is pointed out that a person is affected more by what he sees than by what he hears.

Chapter sixteen discusses prayer, which is related to providence, pointing out that one who believes in providence must also believe that God may bestow good upon a person by way of grace as a result of prayer, whether the person be deserving or not. It points out also that all the other celestial powers except God are limited and can not bestow any benefits unless the recipient is fit to receive them. It explains also how the influence emanating from the stars is responsible for the error existing in the minds of idolaters.

Chapter seventeen explains that no other being in the world can bestow grace except God, pointing out four conditions which must exist in the one who bestows grace. Incidentally is explained Deuteronomy 32, 39, and the question is discussed whether the impulse to pray comes from reason or desire.

Chapter eighteen explains the causes which lead some persons to doubt the efficacy of prayer, pointing out that Job was one of those

Sefer HaIkkarim — Forward

who doubted the efficacy of prayer. It is pointed out also that prayer prepares a person to receive good, this being the opinion of Eliphaz.

Chapter nineteen discusses the nature of blessings which prophets or righteous men bestow upon persons, viz., whether they are prayers or announcements of future happenings. The conclusion arrived at is that blessings are intended to prepare the recipient to receive the divine influence.

Chapter twenty points out that though prayer is a particular commandment it is followed by greater reward than any other commandment. Therefore, we find that it is good for all things as theriaca is good for all diseases, even though the latter be contrary in their causes and symptoms.

Chapter twenty-one discusses a difficulty attaching to the previous statement: Why was not the prayer of Moshe granted when he asked to be admitted into the land of Canaan, as is told in Deuteronomy 3, 23 ff.? It explains the prayer of Moshe in that section and points out that Moshe' offence involved profanation of God's name and the sentence imposed was accompanied by an oath, hence Moshe' prayer was not granted.

Chapter twenty-two discusses the nature of Moshe' sin at the waters of **Meribah**, the explanations of the commentators not being satisfactory. It is pointed out that inasmuch as the sin in question involved profanation of God's name, it could not be forgiven.

Chapter twenty-three points out that some words or attributes denote good qualities, and some bad. This leads to a statement of the kind of words which may be used in prayer. Incidentally is explained the statement of the Rabbis that God has a place, called mistarim, where He weeps. It is pointed out also that prayer must have three qualities, agreeable words, intention, and a low voice. If these three conditions are satisfied, the prayer may be accepted, though not necessarily. It is also stated that some righteous men have their requests granted by God without prayer, some require prayer, while there are some righteous men who do not even have to ask.

Chapter twenty-four explains that the purpose intended by an act of man is not always necessarily realized. Thus, prayer is not necessarily always granted even if it is carried out properly, the causes being stated. The best prayer should be general in its terms and not specific.

Chapter twenty-five begins the discussion of repentance. It is pointed out that although repentance is one of the particular commandments of the Torah, nevertheless it is general in view of the reward that is attained as a result. Hence it should be treated after

Sefer HaIkkarim — Forward

prayer since it is a general commandment. It is pointed out that the acceptance of repentance is a matter of divine grace. Incidentally is explained the statement of the Rabbis that the penitent is in a privileged position because his guilt is accounted to him as merit; also, the meaning of Exodus 7, 3, the hardening of the heart of Sihon, Deut. 2, 30, as well as Hosea 14, 5, it being pointed out that divine grace comes to the recipient according to his request.

Chapter twenty-six explains the modes of repentance and gives a reason why Saul's acknowledgment of sin in the matter of Amalek was not accepted, while David's acknowledgment of sin in the matter of Bathsheba was accepted, for Nathan said to him: The Lord also hath put away thy sin … [II Sam. 12, 13]. A reason is given also why Saul was punished by having his kingdom taken away from him, while David was not so punished. It explains the qualities that a king should have and points out that David had them all, but not Saul.

Chapter twenty-seven suggests a difficulty in connection with repentance, pointing out that logically speaking repentance ought to be of no avail. The difficulty is solved on deeper consideration, a division being made between acts done under compulsion and acts done voluntarily. It also explains what is meant by compulsion and free will.

Chapter twenty-eight explains the necessity of the institution of repentance for the attainment of human perfection, explaining at the same time the statement of the Rabbis that thinking of sin is worse than sin. Isaiah 57, 16 and following verses are explained as referring to the penitent.

Chapter twenty-nine begins the discussion of reward and punishment, which is the third principle. It is pointed out that with respect to the belief in reward and punishment people are divided into four classes: Some deny reward altogether, some believe it is corporeal only, some believe it is spiritual only, and some believe it is corporeal and spiritual. The last is the opinion of the Torah. This difference of opinion, it is pointed out, follows the difference of opinion concerning the essence of the soul. Incidentally is explained the statement of the Rabbis that it was better for man not to have been born than to have been born. The chapter discusses also the topic of transmigration as taught by the Cabalists.

Chapter thirty points out that in respect to reward after death the sages of Israel are divided into two classes. The first is represented by Maimonides, who believes that reward after death is all spiritual and is bestowed upon the soul alone. This opinion, it is maintained,

Sefer HaIkkarim — Forward

is logically correct and is in agreement with the opinion of the Torah. The second is represented by **Nahmanides** and the **Cabalists**, who believe that reward after death is bestowed upon body and soul together. The chapter explains how their opinions are to be understood as Rabbi Aaron Halevi says, then it mentions the difficulties arising from this opinion.

Chapter thirty-one explains the arguments which led **Nahmanides** and his school to the belief that the world to come begins after the resurrection of the dead and not before, pointing out that they are invalid. It is explained and proved that the expression world to come embraces the two kinds of reward, that which comes immediately after death and that which comes after the resurrection.

Chapter thirty-two explains that every change from the habitual which happens to a person causes pain, hence death is painful to a person even though the soul passes to a state of wonderful delight. For this reason, we find that even righteous men find death painful. In this chapter is explained also why during life the soul is in need of the senses and the feelings.

Chapter thirty-three explains the form of reward and punishment of the soul in the world to come, pointing out that the statement of the Rabbis: God takes the soul, casts it into the body and judges them together, means that He confines it in space, not that He places it in the body. This expression is responsible for the error of those who maintain that the body and the soul are rewarded together.

Chapter thirty-four explains that in the world to come there are different degrees of punishment. The righteous are punished differently according to the number, always small, of sins of which they are guilty, while the wicked are punished in accordance with the great number of sins of which everyone of them is guilty. Allusion is made to the secret of the garment mentioned by the Cabalists.

Chapter thirty-five speaks of the belief in the resurrection of the dead and explains the various opinions entertained concerning this belief. It also discusses the question whether resurrection embraces the whole world or nation or only a part.

Chapter thirty-six inquires whether reward and punishment for good deeds and sins should, in accordance with strict justice, be temporary or eternal, pointing out that there is a difference between reward and punishment. Punishment in strict justice ought to be eternal, whereas reward in strict justice should be temporary, but it is eternal by divine grace. This was hinted to Abraham in Genesis 15, 1.

Sefer HaIkkarim
Forward

Chapter thirty-seven proves that punishment should in strict justice be eternal from the statement made to Moshe, Exodus 33, 3, and from the complaint that Moshe makes of this ruling in Psalm ninety. This and the following Psalm are explained as indicated.

Chapter thirty-eight criticizes our statement that punishment should be eternal, on the ground that if this were the case no one would merit the world to come or spiritual reward, since there is no man on earth so righteous that he does not sin. Incidentally are explained Psalm 62, 20; Micah 7, 18; Psalm 103.

Chapter thirty-nine mentions the old question which everybody asks, namely, why are there no promises of spiritual rewards in the Torah? A few solutions are mentioned and are found inadequate.

Chapter forty names the passages in the Torah in which are given promises of corporeal reward. These, it is maintained, are intended for the nation as a whole. The spiritual promises intended for the individual are mentioned in the Torah by allusion only. Passages are cited from the Torah, the Prophets and the Hagiographa bearing out this point.

Chapter forty-one mentions a theoretical argument which proves necessarily the immortality of the soul from the Torah as a whole, pointing out that from the punishment of the sinful soul mentioned in the Torah it follows that there is reward for the soul of the righteous. A reason is given why the Torah does not expatiate upon this point and it is argued that since experience testifies that the Torah can overcome and annul natural things, it is certainly able to give punishments and rewards which are the necessary results of the commandments of the Torah.

Chapter forty-two states that the belief in the coming of the Messiah is obligatory upon everyone who believes in the Law of Moshe. It discusses also the question whether the belief in the coming of the Messiah is based upon tradition or whether it follows necessarily from the biblical text.

Chapter forty-three states that there are different modes of existence of things: existence in God's knowledge, existence in the human mind, potential existence, actual existence. It is pointed out also that astrologers can not know things as they are, for two reasons, while the prophet on the other hand gets true knowledge without any doubt.

Chapter forty-four states that the tradition which we now have of the words of the prophets is true without any doubt and there is no possibility of there being any falsehood therein. It is pointed out also that this is a sign of the covenant between us and God pointing to

Sefer Haїkkarim — Forward

the redemption, and the verses Isaiah 59, 20–21 are explained in this sense.

Chapter forty-five explains the meaning of a covenant between two persons, pointing out that it denotes establishment of friendship. Incidentally is explained Psalm 55, 14–15. It is stated also that the purpose of the covenant of circumcision is in order to be saved from the judgment of Gehenna.

Chapter forty-six speaks of trust in God, pointing out that the essence of the believer's service is to trust in God at all times, in time of trouble and adversity as well as in time of quiet and tranquillity, for this is the essence of trust in God. Incidentally are explained Psalm forty-five and part of Psalm twenty-two.

Chapter forty-seven states that hope follows from trust and is essential to a believer. It is explained that hope is of three kinds, hope of mercy, hope of honor, and hope of promise; and that the best is the hope of promise which is hope of truth. Incidentally is explained Psalm 130, 4, 5.

Chapter forty-eight states that hope may be general and particular. Particular hope may be realized if the recipient prepares himself for it, but general hope is not realized unless all recipients prepare themselves for it, hence a general hope is not realized because not everybody's hope is proper.

Chapter forty-nine raises a question in connection with hope on the ground that it is contrary to human nature, for it confuses the soul and renders it dull and foolish. The question is answered by the statement that hope in God is better than any praise that one can give Him. Psalms 71, 14 and 65, 2 are explained in this sense. It is also pointed out that hope is the cause of hope and Psalm 37, 34 is explained in this sense.

Chapter fifty states that since we have explained that the adversity of the righteous affords no cause of criticism of God, the complaint in the Bible of the long duration of the exile must be explained in a different manner. The various modes of complaint are then given and Psalms one hundred twenty-three and eighty-nine are explained.

Chapter fifty-one explains what is the perfect good, pointing out that all the lower beings are constantly changing; corporeal goods are also constantly changing from one opposite to the other, hence joy always comes after sorrow and rest after motion, there being nothing stable except the spiritual. Incidentally are explained Genesis 49, 15 and Psalm 29, 11. It also explains the meaning of peace, as well as the priestly benediction and the meaning of the

Sefer HaIkkarim — Forward

word peace which is contained therein, thus concluding the book on a note of goodness and blessing and peace.
Completed and Finished Praise be to God.
This is the Gate of the Lord,
The righteous enter therein.
Let not the foot of pride overtake me,
And let not the hand of the wicked drive me away.
In God - I will praise His word -
In the Lord - I will praise His word.

Introduction

To know the fundamental principles upon which laws in general are based is both easy and difficult. It is easy, because all the people that we know of in the world to-day possess a law, and it is inconceivable that a person should be subject to or identified with a law without knowing its principles or having some notion of them sufficient to induce belief in them, as we do not call a person a physician who does not know the principles of medicine, nor do we call one a geometrician who does not know the principles of geometry or who does not at least have some notion of them. It is clear therefore that every one subject to a law should either possess a thorough knowledge of the principles of the law with which he is identified, a knowledge such as the nature of the subject demands, or should at least have a superficial understanding, such as one gets at the beginning of the subject.

It is difficult, because in the multitude of learned works dealing with the principles of laws, we find no treatment that is adequate. They agree neither in the nature of the principles nor in their number. On the contrary, they differ very widely, especially so in relation to the principles of the law of Moshe. For while they all agree that it is divine, they differ not a little concerning the number of its basic principles, some saying they are thirteen, some that they are twenty-six, and some that they are only six. But there is not one of these learned men who made any effort to explain those principles which pertain to a divine law generally, principles without which a divine law can not be conceived. Nor did they take the trouble to investigate whether there can be only one divine law, or whether there may be more than one; and if there may be more than one, whether every one of these must have principles peculiar to it as being a particular divine law or not. There can be no doubt, however, that a divine law

Sefer HaIkkarim — Forward

must have general principles pertaining to it in its character as a divine law generally, without which principles its divine character would disappear, and special and particular principles, the removal of any one of which would destroy this particular law, though divine law in general would not be destroyed.

I, Joseph Albo, residing here in the city of Soria, led hither by the providence of the Prime Mover, having in my humility realized the high importance and great value of this subject of investigation, and seeing the great confusion in the minds of those who have speculated concerning it, who dived in its deep waters without bringing up any pearls, the reason being that they explained the principles superficially, as occurred to their minds at first sight, instead of employing a proper method that would lead to a thorough clarification of the subject under discussion, - realizing this, I undertook to make an adequate investigation of the general principles of divine law. Hence, I have composed this book and called it The Book of Principles, because it investigates the principles of laws generally, and especially the principles of divine law. It also seeks to know whether there is only one divine law, or whether there may be more than one, and if there are more than one, how they differ one from the other. Then it investigates the principles of the law of Moshe, concerning the divine character of which all agree, and shows that it has general principles, appertaining to it in virtue of its character as divine, and special principles, appertaining to it as being the particular divine law that it is. It then goes on to point out that the general principles have under them other more particular principles, which may be called derivative, because they are subsumed under the general principles and are derived from them, coming out of them as branches from the stem of a tree, their relation to the former being such that if the general principles are removed, the particular disappear likewise. This book also points out that the general principles of divine law are three: the existence of God, revelation, reward and punishment. For this reason, we have divided this work into four books. The first investigates in a general way how many principles there are and what they are. The second discusses the first principle, the existence of God, and the derivative principles depending upon it. The third investigates the second principle, revelation, and the topics which are based upon it. The fourth treats of the third principle, reward and punishment, and the derivative principles which follow from it, and other matters connected therewith.

Sefer HaIkkarim — Forward

The effort expended to attain to or acquire anything must be commensurate with the value of the object it is sought to attain. If the object is of great value, a great effort should be made to attain it. If it is not of great value, the effort expended must not be great, but must bear a proper relation to the object sought. For example, we do not praise a man who makes tools worth a talent of silver for the purpose of producing one iron needle, as we praise one who makes tools worth ten thousand talents of silver in order to produce an infinite number of needles in succession.

Now the subject of our investigation, namely the principles of laws, is extremely important, for the perfection of man consists in being subject to laws - all men are subject to some law, though the laws differ. It is clear therefore that we must make the greatest effort to investigate this subject as far as in our power lies and as the nature of the subject permits.

And inasmuch as this subject is so very important, it is proper that we pray to God who grants unto man knowledge and understanding that He may graciously inspire us with knowledge, understanding and good sense, so that our work may partake of the divine graciousness which attaches to all the works of God; as Moshe our teacher said in his prayer: And let the graciousness of the Lord our God be upon us; establish Thou also upon us the work of our hands; yea, the work of our hands establish Thou it.

To understand the meaning of this expression it is necessary to point out that a work may be gracious from two aspects. The work itself may be perfect, so far as the nature of its substance permits. But it may also have an additional graciousness or perfection by reason of its relation to the agent, i.e., because it is the work of that agent. All the works of God have these two kinds of perfection. They are perfect in themselves, as perfect as the nature of their substance demands, and they have an additional graciousness and beauty, not flowing from the nature of their substance, but due to the fact that they are the work of God.

For example, the bee would not, so far as the nature of its own substance is concerned, have the intelligence to build the waxen cells containing the honey in the form of a hexagon. But it owes this intelligence to God who is the best of all agents. The advantage of the hexagonal form is that it is similar to the circle, which is the

Sefer HaIkkarim — Forward

natural form. And it is superior to the circle because in the figure of the hexagon a body that is made up of adjacent hexagons has the vacant space between them all filled and there is no empty space left, whereas if the cells were circular, in the shape of a cylinder, and placed in juxtaposition, there would remain vacant space between them that would be wasted. Therefore, they build them in hexagonal and not circular form. And the reason they do not build the cells square is because although in a body composed of adjacent squares the space between them is also filled up, the square is farther away from the circle, which is the natural figure, than the hexagon. This attribute the bee has because of its being the work of God, which gives it an advantage over and above the properties inherent in the nature of its substance. This is what is meant by the graciousness existing in divine works which is due to the agent.

Thus, Moshe prays first, Let Thy work appears unto Thy servants, and Thy glory upon their children, and then he prays that in our handiwork may appear the two kinds of graciousness which are found in God's work. Hence, he says, and let the graciousness of the Lord our God be upon us. He then indicates the graciousness and beauty which are due to the agent in the words, Establish Thou also upon us the work of our hands. Upon us means joined to us. The graciousness that is due to the work itself is expressed in the words, Yea, the work of our hands establishes Thou it.

Therefore, I pray to God who has absolute power and truth that He may grant me courage and strength to accomplish my purpose, that He may lead me in the way of truth, and teach me the paths of uprightness, for in Him I trust and for Him I wait, as the Psalmist says: Guide me in Thy truth, and teach me; for Thou art the God of my salvation; for Thee do I wait all the day.

Now I begin with the help of the Almighty.

Sefer Halkkarim   Forward

Sefer HaIkkarim
ספר העיקרים

BOOK OF PRINCIPLES

BOOK [Maamar] ONE

Introduction

Wherein is treated of the number of laws in general. It is made clear that there are three, natural, conventional and divine. The differences between them are stated, and the principles of every one of them investigated, in order that the principles of divine law may be made clear. Then is explained the test by which the genuine divine law may be distinguished from the spurious which pretends to be divine. The question is discussed whether there can be more than one divine law at the same time.

Chapter 1

The investigation of fundamental principles is extremely dangerous. For though laws agree in general matters, like the existence of God, reward and punishment, and so on, they are divided in particular matters. It follows therefore necessarily that laws have particular principles by which one divine law differs from another. And there is grave danger in investigating particular matters. For any one who denies one of the particular principles of a law is excluded from the group identified with that law. For example, one who denies the prophecy and mission of Moshe is a denier of the law of Moshe without any doubt, though it is not a general principle of divine law. Similarly, one who does not believe in the coming of the Messiah, which Maimonides counts among the principles of the Mosaic law, is, according to him, put into a class with those who deny one of the principles of the Mosaic law, who are excluded from the community under that law and have no share in the world to come. Maimonides, in the book Madda, in the third chapter of the Laws Concerning Penitence, classes such a person among unbelievers. This is very strange, for in the Talmudic treatise Sanhedrin, chapter Helek, we

Sefer HaIkkarim BOOK [Maamar] ONE

find a statement of Rabbi Hillel, one of the Jewish sages of the Talmud, that the Jews need expect no Messiah, seeing that they had enjoyed his benefits in the time of Hezekiah, king of Yehuda. According to Maimonides this sage would have to be classed as an infidel and excluded from a share in the world to come. But if this were the case, why is he mentioned in the Talmud if he was excluded from the community of Israel and did not believe in the principles of their law? We can not say that his words are cited only for the purpose of being refuted, for in that case he would not be referred to as Rabbi, nor would authoritative rules be quoted in his name anywhere.

Others explain the difficulty by saying that Rabbi Hillel did not deny the doctrine of the Messiah, far from it; but that he meant to say that this dogma does not rest on any biblical text; that all the chapters in the book of Isaiah which speak of the Messiah, like chapter eleven, beginning, And there shall come forth a shoot out of the stock of Jesse, and the like, refer to Hezekiah, king of Yehuda, in whose days those prophecies were fulfilled. The tenth verse of the same chapter, the root of Jesse, that standish for an ensign of the peoples, unto him shall the nations seek, refers to Merodach-balagan the son of Baladan, king of Babylon, who sent a letter and a present to Hezekiah. The expression at the end of the same verse, and his resting-place shall be glorious, also refers to Hezekiah. It is the wont of a hero or a king to go out to meet the enemy, to risk his life for his people and gain the victory for them. To remain quietly at home would be a great disgrace, and death would be better than such shame. Thus Saul, though he knew that he would die in the war, having been told by Samuel, and to-morrow shalt thou and thy sons be with me, nevertheless went to war to avoid disgrace.

Now Hezekiah was reproached by everybody because he had shut himself up in Yerushalayim and did not go out to fight. But when they saw the great miracle of the death of Sennacherib and the destruction of his army, it became clear to them that the reason Hezekiah had not gone out to fight was because he trusted in God to fight his battles. His resting, therefore, redounded to his glory, for the whole world knew that he was a completely righteous man, beloved by God, who gave him the desires of his heart and fought for him. Not so other kings, for whom resting is not glorious. When this miracle spread abroad, all the Jews who had been taken captive to Assyria and those who fled to Cush and Egypt and Pathros and other lands returned to Palestine. This is the meaning of the verse in Isaiah, And there shall be a highway for the remnant of His people, etc. This is the way in which the whole chapter is interpreted by Rabbi Moshe ha-Kohen, Ibn Balam and other literalists. Accordingly, it might be said that Rabbi Hillel's opinion was that the texts of Isaiah and the other prophets can not be cited to prove the coming of the Messiah, but that he believed in the coming of the redeemer on the basis of tradition and hence was not excluded from the community of Israel and not classed as a sinner.

This explanation, however, does not seem plausible. For the Talmud goes on to say that his disputants replied, May the Lord forgive Rabbi Hillel, a remark which indicates that they did regard him as guilty of sin for holding such an opinion. But this could not be if he merely denied the scriptural evidence and believed in the doctrine itself on the strength of tradition, as we shall make clear in Book Four. We must therefore conclude that Rabbi Hillel did not believe in the coming of the Messiah at all, and if despite this he was not classed as an unbeliever, it is because the dogma of the Messiah is not a fundamental principle of the Law of Moshe, as Maimonides thinks, for we can conceive of the existence of the Mosaic law without it. It is a special principle of the religion of the Christians, for their religion can not exist without it. However, it is a dogma which it behooves every one professing Judaism to believe, as creation of the world out of nothing is a dogma which it behooves every one professing a divine law to believe, though it is not a fundamental principle of divine law. One who believes that there is a prime and eternal matter out of which all existing things came to be through the will of God is not an infidel according to the opinion of Maimonides, who does not count creation ex nihilo among the fundamental dogmas. But he is nevertheless guilty of a sin. Similarly, Rabbi Hillel was guilty of a sin for not believing in the coming of the redeemer, but he was not an infidel. This is the opinion of the modern authorities, for they do not place the dogma of the Messiah and of the creation of the world in time among the fundamental principles.

The above remarks show how dangerous it is to investigate fundamental principles. For one runs the risk of denying something that is a fundamental principle of the Torah. Thus, according to the opinion of the one who regards creation in time as a fundamental principle of the Torah, Rabbi Moshe ben Maimon would be an unbeliever, God forbid! On the other hand, the one who does not regard the dogma of the Messiah as a fundamental principle, would be an unbeliever in the opinion of Maimonides, who classes it among the fundamental dogmas. The same thing applies to the other

Sefer HaIkkarim — BOOK [Maamar] ONE

matters which Maimonides classes among fundamental principles, though they are not such, as we shall see. For this reason we said that there is grave danger in the investigation of principles. For how can one tell what those things are, the denial of which, and of their fundamental character, constitutes one an unbeliever?

Chapter 2

It is proper, however, to say this in justification of those Jewish scholars who deal with this subject. Every Israelite is obliged to believe that everything that is found in the Torah is absolutely true, and any one who denies anything that is found in the Torah, knowing that it is the opinion of the Torah, is an unbeliever; as the Rabbis say in chapter Helek, that anyone who says, the whole Torah emanates from the divine Being except one verse, which Moshe said on his own authority, is liable to the imputation charged in the biblical expression, Because he hath despised the word of the Lord, and is classed among those who deny the divine inspiration of the Torah. But a person who upholds the law of Moshe and believes in its principles, but when he undertakes to investigate these matters with his reason and scrutinizes the texts, is misled by his speculation and interprets a given principle otherwise than it is taken to mean at first sight; or denies the principle because he thinks that it does not represent a sound theory which the Torah obliges us to believe; or erroneously denies that a given belief is a fundamental principle, which however he believes as he believes the other dogmas of the Torah which are not fundamental principles; or entertains a certain notion in relation to one of the miracles of the Torah because he thinks that he is not thereby denying any of the doctrines which it is obligatory upon us to believe by the authority of the Torah, - a person of this sort is not an unbeliever. He is classed with the sages and pious men of Israel, though he holds erroneous theories. His sin is due to error and requires atonement.

We find such opinions expressed by some of the ancient sages of Israel. Thus, we find a statement that temporal sequence existed before creation. What the author of this opinion meant to say is that the Torah does not oblige us to believe that time was itself created. Similarly, Rabbi Eliezer the Great, in Chapter three of his treatise, endeavors to name the material out of which the heavens and the earth were made. Now even if we should understand his words in their literal sense, as indicating, namely, that the world was not created out of nothing, but out of something, namely out of a

Sefer HaIkkarim — BOOK [Maamar] ONE

primitive matter, we should have no reason for bringing a charge against him. For his idea is that the Torah does not oblige us to believe in creation ex nihilo. He has no intention to deny anything that is in the Torah, Heaven forbid!

Maimonides also, the author of the Guide of the Perplexed, in chapter twenty-five of the second part, says that his belief in creation ex nihilo was not due to the authority of scriptural texts - texts can be interpreted - but to the fact that it is a true doctrine, and therefore the texts must be interpreted so as to harmonize with this doctrine. His meaning is that anything which is opposed to the texts must not be believed at all, provided the texts do not give expression to an absurd idea which the reason can not conceive. For the Torah does not oblige us to believe absurdities, which are opposed to first principles, or any imaginary notions which the reason can not conceive. But a thing which can be conceived by the mind, we are obliged to believe, though it is opposed to nature, for example, resurrection of the dead and the miracles of the Torah. An absurd idea, however, which can not be conceived by the mind need not be believed even if it is plainly expressed in the Torah. Thus the expression, Circumcise, therefore, the foreskin of your heart, must not be taken in its literal sense, but should be explained in accordance with the truth.

This is the method of Onkelos the proselyte, of Jonathan ben Uziel, and the other sages of Israel. They interpret all the expressions in the Torah and the Prophets which signify corporeality of the deity so as to harmonize with the truth. They reject the literal meaning because it expresses an absurdity. Their maxim is that the Torah speaks in the language of man and in order to quiet the ear.

The method we have been describing is precisely that which is used by some of the modern scholars, who interpret the speech of Balaam's ass in a manner different from the interpretation of the Rabbis of the Talmud. Their idea is that the Torah does not intend us to believe that miracle except in the manner in which they understand it. We say, therefore, that a person whose speculative ability is not sufficient to enable him to reach the true meaning of scriptural texts, with the result that he believes in the literal meaning and entertains absurd ideas because he thinks they represent the view of the Torah, is not thereby excluded from the community of those who believe in the Torah, Heaven forbid! Nor is it permitted to speak disrespectfully of him and accuse him of perverting the teaching of the Torah and class him among unbelievers and heretics.

Sefer HaIkkarim   BOOK [Maamar] ONE

Rabbi Abraham ben David has gone even further than this. He says that even if a person understands a fundamental principle of the Torah in an erroneous manner because of a speculative error, he must not be called a heretic. We find this idea of his in his Book of Criticisms on Maimonides. Commenting on the latter's statement that one who believes God is corporeal is a heretic, Rabbi Abraham ben David says: It is true that God is not corporeal; nevertheless, a person who believes He is corporeal by reason of biblical and **midrashic** expressions which he understands literally, must not be called a heretic.

This seems to be the correct view as held by the Rabbis of the Talmud. For in speaking of Elisha ben Abuya they quote the biblical expression, Return, ye rebellious children, and add by way of comment, except Elisha Aher, who knows his Creator and deliberately rebels against Him. They thus indicate clearly that that man alone who knows the truth and deliberately denies it, belongs to the class of the wicked whose repentance is rejected. But the man whose intention is not to rebel, nor to depart from the truth, nor to deny what is in the Torah, nor reject tradition, but whose sole intention is to interpret the texts according to his opinion, though he interprets them erroneously, is neither a heretic nor an unbeliever.

Accordingly, a person who believes that those who are resurrected will not live forever in the resurrected state of body and soul, but will return to dust, as is the opinion of Maimonides in his letter On the Resurrection of the Dead, can not be regarded as rejecting the dogma of resurrection, though, according to Rabbi Moshe ben Nahman, this is not the true belief. Similarly, one who believes that the real retribution in the future world is imposed upon body and soul jointly, and that the soul alone has no retribution apart from the body, this being the opinion of Rabbi Moshe ben Nahman and some of the wise men of the Cabala, is not a denier of the dogma of spiritual reward and punishment, though according to Maimonides this is not the true belief.

I had to write all this because I have seen insignificant men, who think they are wise, open their mouths wide in lengthy and unintelligent discourses against great men. It is clear now that every intelligent person is permitted to investigate the fundamental principles of religion and to interpret the biblical texts in accordance with the truth as it seems to him. And though he believe concerning certain things which the ancients regarded as principles, like the dogma of the Messiah and of the creation, that they are not fundamental principles, but merely true doctrines, which the

Sefer HaIkkarim   BOOK [Maamar] ONE

believer in the Torah is obliged to believe in the same way as he believes in the earth's opening its mouth on the occasion of Korah's rebellion, or the coming down of fire from heaven, and similar miracles and promises mentioned in the Torah, which are true without being fundamental principles of the Torah, - he is not a denier of the Torah or of its principles. For if he were, it would follow that there are as many fundamental principles in the Law of Moshe as there are miracles and promises in the Torah, an idea which has never occurred to any one.

Chapter 3

The word **Ikkar** [root] is a term applied to a thing upon which the existence and duration of another thing depends and without which it can not endure, as the root is a thing upon which the endurance of the tree depends, without which the tree can not exist or endure. The Rabbis of the Talmud use this term frequently. They speak, for example, of a thing which has an **Ikkar** [basis] in the Torah or not. Hence the term may be used of the basic principles upon which the existence of religious law depends, like the existence of God. For it is clear from the nature of this doctrine that it is fundamental and belief in it is essential to a divine law, for a divine law can not be imagined without belief in the existence of God. For this reason, we must investigate in order to know what beliefs are properly fundamental in divine law.

Maimonides enumerates thirteen, as follows: existence of God, unity of God, incorporeality of God, eternity of God, He alone should be worshipped and none else, prophecy, Moshe the greatest prophet, revelation of the Torah, immutability of the Torah, God's omniscience, reward and punishment, the Messiah, resurrection of the dead. This list is found in Maimonides' commentary on the Mishnah, chapter Helek.

Our first question concerning these principles which Maimonides laid down is, why precisely those thirteen? If it is because of the meaning of the term **Ikkar** [fundamental principle], we can see very well the reason for including such dogmas as the existence of God, prophecy, revelation, omniscience, providence in reward and punishment, because they are essential principles of a divine law, which can not be conceived without any one of them. We may also allow without difficulty the inclusion of Moshe as the greatest prophet and the perpetuity of the law, because they are special principles, essential to the law of Moshe, which can not be conceived without them. For if we assume that there may be a prophet greater than Moshe, it follows that the law of Moshe may be abolished, for the words of a greater prophet should be believed more than those of a prophet who is inferior in degree, as we shall see later. Likewise, if we do not believe in the perpetuity of the Torah, we can imagine that the law of Moshe may have been repealed after the Israelites were exiled from their land. But it is difficult to see why he includes unity and incorporeality among fundamental principles. For though they are true doctrines, which every one professing the law of Moshe is obliged to believe, they should not be counted among fundamental principles, seeing that the divine law would not disappear entirely if one believed otherwise. It is still more difficult to see why Maimonides included as a principle the dogma that God alone should be worshipped and none else. For, though it is one of the commandments of the Torah, as is written, thou shalt have no other gods before Me ... thou shalt not bow down unto them, nor serve them, nevertheless it is not a fundamental principle upon which the entire Torah depends. For if a man believes in God and His law, and introduce a mediator between himself and God, he violates, indeed, the commandment just quoted, but this does not make it a fundamental principle with which the entire law stands and falls. Why then does Maimonides count it as a principle? Likewise, if one believes in reward and punishment, but holds that the soul alone receives retribution in the future world, and denies that the body is resurrected after death, is there any reason why this should upset the Torah as a whole? We cannot see therefore why it was necessary to count resurrection as a fundamental principle of divine law, comparable to the existence of God.

If, on the other hand, we say that Maimonides did not draw up his list in accordance with the strict meaning of the term **Ikkar**, and therefore included true doctrines which every one professing the law of Moshe is obliged to believe, why did he not include the doctrine that the Shekinah dwells in Israel through the medium of the Torah, in accordance with the biblical expression, I will dwell therein among the children of Israel? And why did he not include the dogma of creation, which every one professing a divine law is obliged to believe, as Maimonides himself explains in the twenty-fifth chapter of the second part of the Guide of the Perplexed? It is just as important a doctrine as the eternity of God, which he does include. Or why did he not include the dogma that we must believe in the miracles of the Torah in their literal sense, and other particular doctrines which every one professing the law of Moshe is obliged to

Sefer Halkkarim BOOK [Maamar] ONE

believe, in the same way as he includes belief in the Messiah?
And if we say that he counts principles only and not merely true doctrines, why does he not include the principle that one should follow ancestral tradition? For it is a general principle of all divine laws, which cannot be conceived without it. Or why does he not include freedom of the will? For being a true doctrine, it is at the same time a principle, seeing that in the nature of things no law can be conceived without it. Maimonides himself, in the **Book Madda**, chapter 5 of the Rules Concerning Repentance, writes, every human being is given freedom of choice; if he desires to follow the path of goodness and to be a righteous man, he has the freedom to do so …
And then he says, this is a very important principle, and is at the basis of the Torah and the commandments, as is said, 'See I have set before thee this day life and good …', expatiating upon this principle at length in that chapter. It is very strange, therefore, that he did not include it among the principles in his commentary on the Mishnah, chapter Helek, where the thirteen dogmas are enumerated. In fine, the number of principles drawn up by Maimonides is subject to grave objections.

I have seen a statement made that Maimonides selected the number thirteen because the divine attributes are thirteen and because thirteen is the number of the hermeneutical rules by which the Torah is interpreted. But it is extremely unlikely that Maimonides would omit such a doctrine as freedom of the will, which is a fundamental principle according to his own opinion, so that the number may not exceed thirteen. Besides this does not explain why he counts among the thirteen those which are not essential principles at all, as we have explained.

There is one writer who says that there are twenty-six principles, including in his list anything that occurs to his mind, such as the eternity of God, His wisdom, His life, His power and His will, and other attributes besides which are ascribed to God. He also counts paradise as a principle by itself, and hell as another principle, and many other things which have no sense, having taken no pains to understand the meaning of the term **Ikkar** principle and the things to which it applies.

There is a recent writer who takes the word **Ikkar** strictly, and modifies the list of Maimonides by adding some dogmas and taking away some. According to this writer's opinion, the principles of divine law are the following six: omniscience of God, providence, omnipotence, prophecy, freedom of will, purpose of revelation, plus the three which Maimonides proves apodictically, namely, the existence, unity and incorporeality of God. His idea is that it is clear from the nature of the six dogmas above mentioned that they are essential to divine law, which can not be conceived without them. And taken together with the three others which are subject to scientific proof, they give a complete list of the fundamental principles of divine law.

The criticism that may be made of this view is that though it is true that these are general principles of divine law, which can not be conceived to exist without them, he should have included also other special principles, peculiar to the law of Moshe, as Maimonides did; or he should have included some general principle by which the genuine divine law may be distinguished from the spurious which pretends to be divine. For all religions existing in the world at the present day acknowledge these six principles, and would therefore have to be divine. Another objection to this number of principles is that though it is true that no divine law can exist without them, it does not follow that given all these principles we have all that is necessary to constitute a divine law. One more principle must be added for this purpose, viz., revelation. We can make this clearer by the following analogy. If one were to say that given nutrient and sentient we have man, because if you have man, you have nutrient and sentient, he would no doubt be wrong. For though it is true that you can not have man without them, or, which is the same thing, that they are necessary for the existence of man, it does not follow that given those things we have man, unless we add rational, and say that if we have nutrient, sentient and rational body, we have man. Similarly, here, revelation should be counted along with the others. For given divine omniscience, providence, power, prophecy, freedom, purpose, revelation does not follow, though it can not be without the others.

On the other hand, his inclusion of freedom and purpose among the principles of divine law is also open to criticism. For though it be true that they are essential to divine law, they are not fundamental principles of divine law qua divine, for they pertain also to conventional law, as will appear later. Nor is purpose, taken abstractly, a principle of divine law, rather a special purpose is. In fine, the knowledge of the essential principles of divine law is very difficult. And a more serious difficulty still is that we find no clear pronouncement upon this matter in the discussions of the talmudic Rabbis. And yet they should have treated of those principles which are the bases and foundations of divine law, seeing that human

Sefer HaIkkarim   BOOK [Maamar] ONE

happiness and spiritual reward are based upon them, as they have treated of torts and contracts which have to do with material interests merely, and are the basis of political and social order.

Chapter 4

It seems to me that the general and essential principles of divine law are three: existence of God, providence in reward and punishment, and divine revelation. These three embraces all the principles of the various divine laws, such as the law of Adam, the law of Noah, the law of Abraham, the law of Moshe, and any other divine laws, if there be such, at the same time or in succession. Implicit in every one of these are subordinate and derivative principles coming from that principle as a branch issue from a tree. Thus, from the existence of God is derived God's eternity, perpetuity, and so on. In revelation is implied God's knowledge, prophecy, and so on. And from providence follows physical reward and punishment in this world, and spiritual in the next.

From these three general principles issue special dogmas peculiar to the various divine laws, genuine or spurious, as follows: From the existence of God is derived His incorporeality, which is a special principle of the law of Moshe, and likewise His unity. Under revelation comes the prophecy and mission of Moshe. Under providence and reward and punishment comes the belief in the advent of the Messiah, which is a special principle of the law of Moshe according to the opinion of Maimonides. But according to our opinion the belief in the Messiah is not a principle. And if it is, it is not special to the law of Moshe, for the Christians too regard it as a principle, and that too in order to abrogate the law of Moshe. It is indeed a special principle for them, for their law can not be conceived without it. All these and similar dogmas which are special to certain religions are included in the three principles which we have mentioned. The question whether there can be more than one divine law at the same time or at different times, will be discussed later with the help of God.

That these three principles are the basis of the faith by which man attains true happiness is proved by the fact that the Men of the Great Synagogue composed three blessings which they incorporated in the Additional Service for New Year, going by the name of Kingdoms, Memorials and Trumpets. These three blessings correspond to the three principles and are intended to call our attention to the fact that by properly believing in these principles together with the dogmas

Sefer HaIkkarim — BOOK [Maamar] ONE

derived from them we shall win a favorable verdict in the divine judgment.

The blessing known as Kingdoms corresponds to the principle of the existence of God. This is proved by the words of the benediction, Therefore do we wait for Thee, O Lord our God, that we may quickly see Thy glorious strength, when the images will be removed from the earth and the idols will be completely cut off, when the world will be established under the Kingdom of the Almighty ... when all the inhabitants of the world will recognize and know that to Thee shall every knee bend, by Thee every tongue swear ... and all shall accept the yoke of Thy Kingdom.

The benediction called Memorials points to providence and reward and punishment, as is indicated by its contents: Thou rememberest the works of the universe, and visitest all the creatures from the beginning; before Thee are all hidden things revealed ...

The benediction called Trumpets alludes to the third principle, revelation. Therefore, it begins, thou didst reveal Thyself in the cloud of Thy glory to Thy holy people and didst speak unto them. From heaven didst Thou cause them to hear Thy voice ... This benediction is called Trumpets because at the time of the giving of the Law there was a very loud sound of the trumpet, such as never had been heard before in the world. Thunders and lightning like those seen at Sinai or of the same nature had been heard and seen before, but the sound of a trumpet without a trumpet had never been heard before, and will not be heard again until the time of the redemption. At that time the true law will be made known before the whole world. This is the time that is referred to in the words of the prophet, And the Lord God will blow the horn, according to some authorities.

I have seen a statement that the benediction Trumpets bears an allusion to the sacrifice of Yitzhak. But this is not correct, for if that were the case, we should expect the sacrifice of Yitzhak to be mentioned in this blessing, whereas mention is made of it in the benediction Memorials. The origin of this opinion is to be sought in the statement of the Rabbis that the ceremony of blowing the ram's horn on New Year is in memory of the ram which was substituted for Yitzhak. But this does not justify the opinion. For what the Rabbis mean is that the requirement of a ram's horn is to commemorate the ram of Yitzhak, not that the command itself to blow an instrument has that meaning, much less does it follow that the benediction Trumpets alludes to that event.

Sefer HaIkkarim — BOOK [Maamar] ONE

Isaiah refers to these three principles, which are the cause of happiness, in a single sentence: For the Lord is our judge, the Lord is our lawgiver, the Lord is our king, He will save us. The Lord is our judge, alludes to the dogma of providence, denoting the same idea that is contained in the expression, He is near that justifieth me; who will contend with me? let us stand up together ..., namely that we may win a favorable verdict. The Lord is our lawgiver **Mehoke** [lawgiver], refers to the dogma of revelation, which is the second principle. For the word **mehokek** [lawgiver] applies to a lawgiver, as we see in Deuteronomy, For there a portion of the **mehokek** [lawgiver] was reserved, a reference to Moshe through whom the law was given. The meaning is similar to that expressed in the words of the prophet, Hearken unto Me, ye that know righteousness, the people in whose heart is My law; fear ye not the taunt of men ..., namely that though the verdict may not be favorable to us in so far as He is our judge, seeing that a judge can not go against the law that is laid down by another, nevertheless we ought to win because He is also the legislator who lays down the statutes. The Lord is our king, alludes to the third principle, the existence of God, who is the king of the whole world, and is especially called the King of Israel and their Redeemer. The thought here is that even if in His capacity of legislator, He may refuse to transgress His own law, nevertheless as being our king, He must save us, for a king has the power to go against the law and to do whatever he desires in order to save his people. That is why the above text concludes with the words, He will save us. The meaning is that inasmuch as we have an advantage over the whole world in the possession of these three principles, upon belief in which depends man's true happiness, it is fitting that God should save us above all others.

It may be that Maimonides has the same idea concerning the number of fundamental principles as the one we have just indicated, and that his list consists of the three chief principles that we have mentioned, plus the derivative dogmas issuing from them, being all called by him principles. Thus, he lays down the existence of God, a fundamental doctrine, as the first principle. Then he enumerates along with it as principles four other dogmas which are derived from it, viz., unity, incorporeality, eternity, and exclusive worship. Then he lists as principles revelation, another fundamental doctrine, together with three other dogmas derived from it, viz., prophecy, superiority of Moshe, and immutability of the law. Then comes divine omniscience and providence in reward and punishment, the third fundamental doctrine, together with three other dogmas

Sefer Halkkarim   BOOK [Maamar] ONE

implied in it and derived therefrom, viz., spiritual retribution, Messiah, and resurrection.

According to this explanation it is clear why he did not include the doctrine of creation, for it does not come under any of the three which we mentioned. He did not include freedom and purpose because, though they are essential to divine law, they are not essential to it qua divine, as will appear later. The question still remains, however, why he did not include under existence of God life and power and other attributes, seeing that he included eternity and other attributes. The same criticism applies to the dogmas he derives from the other fundamental principles. All this will be made clear as we go on. We must now resume our discussion of the fundamental principles, which in our opinion consist of three chief dogmas. We must, however, first explain the principles of conventional laws, and then we will treat of the principles of divine law, with the help of God.

Chapter 5

Three modes of life are found among animals. There are certain species that can not live in aggregation, like beasts of prey. Living together would harm them, for if many of them gathered into one place, they would kill and devour one another. There are others again of whom the contrary is true. They can not live except in companies and groups. Association is essential for their continuance, like the human species. By reason of his delicate constitution and equability of temperamental mixture man is susceptible to cold and heat and other extremes. He needs therefore clothing to protect him from heat and cold and properly prepared food suitable for his temperament. These things can not be accomplished except by the aggregation and association of many individuals who assist one another. One sews, one weaves, one makes the needle, and so with the other arts, so that every individual obtains the food and clothing that he needs for existence and support. There are other species of animal beings which occupy an intermediate place, so to speak, between the two extremes. Aggregation is not injurious to their existence as it is to wild beasts and birds of prey, nor is it essential as it is for the human species. But gregarious life is better for them than life in isolation, like many species of herbivorous animals and gentle birds going about in flocks for the sake of company and convenience and for no other reason, seeing that gregarious life is not essential to them as it is to

Sefer Haikkarim   BOOK [Maamar] ONE

the human species.

It is because association and aggregation are necessary for the existence and support of the human species that the wise men have said that man is political by nature. They mean by this that it is almost necessary for man by his nature to live in a city [state] with a large group of men that he may be able to obtain what he needs for his life and support. It is clear therefore that the whole group residing in a city, or a district, or a region, or all the human beings in the world should have some order which they follow in their conduct, maintaining justice in general and suppressing wrong, so as to keep men from quarrelling in their transactions and business relations with one another. Such order would include protection against murder, theft, robbery and the like, and in general all those measures which are calculated to maintain the political group and enable the people to live in welfare. This order the wise men call natural law, meaning by natural that it is necessary for man by his nature, whether the order emanates from a wise man or a prophet.

Such a law, however, is not yet sufficient to order the needs of men and to control their social life, unless there is added to this a certain order or convention which embraces all the social and commercial relations and transactions of the people, like the laws of the Roman emperors, and the customs of countries, and the statutes enacted by the people of a district or a kingdom to maintain conventional justice. Such an order as this is called a convention or a conventional law. Conventional law can not exist unless there is a ruler, or a judge, or a king, placed at the head of the group or city, who compels the people to repress wrong and observe the law so as to secure the welfare of the group. It follows therefore that the establishment of a king or a ruler or a judge is almost imperative for the continuance of the human species, seeing that man is political by nature, as we have explained.

Chapter 6

If we reflect upon the formation of the animal species and the constitution of their organs, we find that the Creator has exhibited wonderful care in ordering their affairs and their every need in a remarkable manner. He has provided not merely those things which are required for the maintenance of the species or the individual, but also those things which are not essential for this purpose, but which make their state more perfect, for example the duplication of the sense organs in animals to enable them to order their affairs in a

Sefer Halkkarim — BOOK [Maamar] ONE

more satisfactory and complete manner, though it is not essential for the maintenance of their existence.

If we find such provision in inferior animals, how much more reasonable is it that He should provide for the noblest species, and order its affairs in accord with its higher character in an adequate manner so as to enable it to attain its perfection. If we look more carefully into this matter, we shall find that the divine influence by which those things are ordered which the human species needs for the attainment of the perfection for which it is destined, is more essential than many things which we see in the formation of the lower animals, such things as have a tendency to improve their condition, but are not indispensable for their existence. This divine influence may exist in a particular person only, yet it lends perfection to the entire species.

The meaning of this is as follows: The various species coming under the genera do not form a hierarchy of graded perfection. My meaning is that though it is true that among the various species there is one particular species that is more perfect than all the rest, yet this particular species alone is not the purpose of the whole genus, nor does it guide the genus to the perfection for which it is destined; for every species by itself contains in itself its own particular purpose and realizes its own perfection without reference to any other species. But while this is so in the relation of the species to one another under the genera, it is different within the species. It is true here again that every species contains a number of classes of differing degrees of value. Thus, the class of rulers has a greater measure of human perfection than the class of husbandmen; and the class of the wise men is more perfect than that of the rulers. And similarly, within every class some individual or individuals are more perfect than the other individuals of that class, and the superior individual or individuals or class are not the purpose for which the species as a whole exists. Nevertheless, the superior individual or individuals or class are the cause of the attainment by the species of the purpose for which it is intended, because they lead the species as a whole to its perfection. I mean that they are like an instrument by means of which the species is enabled to attain its normal end and perfection, though the parts of the species are unequal in degree. The following analogy will make it clear. Every individual has many different organs, all of them necessary for the existence of the animal being, though one is more perfect than the other, and a third is still more perfect, and so on until we reach the most important organ which is the basis of the animal's existence. This organ gives

Sefer Halkkarim   BOOK [Maamar] ONE

perfection to the animal, that is, it is an instrument by which perfect life flows to the animal as a whole. Thus, the heart is the basis of the animal's existence, and it is an instrument by which life flows to all the organs, and in particular the brain, which in turn transmits sensation and motion to all the other organs. Thus, the animal being maintains itself by the instrumentality, direct or indirect, of the heart. The same applies to mankind. All are equally human, yet human perfection reaches some individuals through the instrumentality of others. Just as all organs are necessary for the existence of the individual, and yet some stand higher in the scale than the others, and some receive their vital force through the instrumentality of others, so the class of wise men stand higher than the others, and it is from the wise man that emanates the order which arranges the affairs of mankind so as to enable them to attain human perfection. This order is called a conventional or positive law.

Now since, as we have said, it stands to reason that divine providence should assist mankind to receive this benefit, even as we find that it provides things of less importance in the lower animals, it follows that a divine influence must inspire some individual of the human race who is best fitted for it, that he may be an instrument by which mankind may attain the perfection for which they are destined - either a direct instrument during life, or an indirect after death, by inspiring the wise men who come after him to guide mankind everywhere and always according to the teaching they receive from him, or the ideas they derive from his writings. For the divine power is surely not unable to estimate this benefit so essential to the human race, and to perfect it continually and everywhere, any more than it is unable to award the benefit that is necessary to the lower animals. This guidance which mankind receives from this individual is called divine law. Its relation to other laws and customs is the same as that of the architectonic art to the other arts which are subordinate to it.

Chapter 7

The term **Dat** [law] applies to every rule or custom in vogue among a large group of people. It may be a body of rules embracing a great many commands, as in the expression, all that knew **Dat** [law] and judgment, or it may be applied to a single command, as in the expression, and a decree **Dat** [law] was given out in Shushan. It is applied to a divine law, as in the expression, At His right hand was a fiery law [dat] unto them, as well as to a positive human law, like the laws of the Medes and the Persians.

There are three kinds of law, natural, positive or conventional, and divine. Natural law is the same among all peoples, at all times, and in all places. Positive or conventional is a law ordered by a wise man or men to suit the place and the time and the nature of the persons who are to be controlled by it, like the laws and statutes enacted in certain countries among the ancient idolaters, or those who worship God as human reason dictates without any divine revelation. Divine law is one that is ordered by God through a prophet, like Adam or Noah, or like the custom or law which Abraham taught men, instructing them to worship God and circumcising them by the command of God, or one that is ordered by God through a messenger whom He sends and through whom He gives a law, like the Law of Moshe.

The purpose of natural law is to repress wrong, to promote right, in order that men may keep away from theft, robbery and murder, that society may be able to exist among men and every one be safe from the wrongdoer and oppressor. The purpose of conventional or positive law is to suppress what is unbecoming and to promote what is becoming, that men may keep away from the indecent according to human opinion. Herein lies its advantage over natural law, for conventional law also controls human conduct and arranges their affairs with a view to the improvement of human society, even as natural law. The purpose of divine law is to guide men to obtain true happiness, which is spiritual happiness and immortality. It shows them the way they must follow to obtain it, teaches them the true good that they may take pains to secure it, shows them also real evil that they may guard against it, and trains them to abandon imaginary happiness so that they may not desire it and not feel its loss. And in addition, it also lays down the rules of right that the political community may be ordered in a proper manner, so that the bad order of their social life may not prevent them from attaining true happiness, which is the ultimate end of the human face to which they are destined by God. Divine law is therefore superior to conventional or positive.

Chapter 8

Positive or conventional law is inferior to divine law in many ways. The first is the one we mentioned, namely that positive law controls human conduct in order to maintain a good political society, but it can not impart true theoretical knowledge, as we shall show in the sequel, so as to give immortality to the soul and enable it to return

Sefer Halkkarim   BOOK [Maamar] ONE

to the land of life from which it was taken, because positive law deals only with the becoming and unbecoming. Divine law is adequate for this purpose, because it includes both parts upon which human perfection is based, viz., conduct and theory. Divine law embraces the becoming and unbecoming, and it distinguishes between the true and the false, which constitutes the theoretical part. That is why David describes it as perfect, when he says, the law of the Lord is perfect, restoring the soul. The meaning is that the positive law is not perfect because it does not deal with true opinions, but divine law is perfect because it embraces perfection in morals and perfection in theory, which are the two parts upon which the perfection of the soul is dependent. Therefore, it restores the soul to God who gave it, and to the place which was its original home.

Another point of inferiority of the conventional law to divine law is that the former can not distinguish between the becoming and the unbecoming in all cases. For a thing may seem becoming or unbecoming to us without being so in reality. For just as it is impossible that a man should be born perfect in all the practical arts, though he may have a natural aptitude for some, so it is impossible that one should be born perfect in all good qualities and free from all defect, though he may have a greater tendency to certain qualities than to others. But that he should have all good qualities is impossible.

It becomes clear now that it is impossible for any author of a human code not to show a natural deficiency in some direction, and regard the becoming as unbecoming and the unbecoming as becoming. His testimony concerning the becoming and the unbecoming will therefore not be true. Thus Plato made a grievous mistake, advocating the unbecoming as though it were becoming. For his idea is that all the women of a given class should be held in common by the men of that class. Thus, the wives of the rulers should be common to all the rulers, the wives of the merchants common to all the merchants, and similarly the wives of the men of a given trade or occupation should be common to the men of that trade or occupation. This is a matter which the Torah forbid; even the **Noachian law** prohibits it, for Abimelech was told, Behold, thou shalt die, because of the woman whom thou hast taken; for she is a man's wife, and his excuse was that he did not know she had a husband. Aristotle, as is known, criticized Plato's idea in this matter. This shows that no human being is able to differentiate correctly between the becoming and the unbecoming, and his opinion on this matter can not therefore be relied upon. Not to speak of theoretical

Sefer Halkkarim   BOOK [Maamar] ONE

knowledge, where it is clear that we can not rely on a human opinion concerning profound problems, such as the creation or eternity of the world, for the human mind is not adequate to know this with certainty. But The testimony of the Lord is sure, making wise the simple, for it gives a reliable statement on the problem of the world's origin, and on other important problems, including morals.

Another point of inferiority in conventional law as compared with divine is that it can not give full satisfaction to those who follow its requirements. The reason is that when a person is in doubt whether the thing, he does is sufficient to lead him to the end intended, he can not feel satisfaction in what he does. But a person who follows the conventional law is precisely in this position. He does not know whether that which the law defines as just is really just or only apparently so. Hence, he can not find satisfaction. He, however, who lives by the divine law knows that what is defined therein as just is really just. Hence, he finds satisfaction in his conduct. This is why the precepts of the Lord are right, rejoicing the heart.

Another point of inferiority in the conventional law as compared with the divine is this. Conventional law can not define the specific acts which are proper in the several virtues. It can only make general statements, in the same way as a definition can be given of the general only, while the particular can not be defined. Similarly conventional law can not define particular acts. Thus Aristotle in his Ethics says repeatedly in connection with the different virtues that a virtuous act consists in doing the proper thing at the proper time and in the proper place, but he does not explain what is the proper time and the proper place. It is clearly a matter which not every one is capable of determining. Aristotle also says in various places in the Ethics that the proper measure must be maintained in every act, but does not tell us what the proper measure is. It would seem therefore that his opinion was that the determination of this matter must be sought elsewhere.

Now there is no doubt that if it were within the power of a human being as such to determine this matter, Aristotle would have discussed it. The reason he leaves this matter to another agency is because human nature is not capable of determining this matter, divine help alone can do it. For this reason, Aristotle speaks of the virtues in a general way only, defining temperance as a mean quality between excessive indulgence in eating, drinking, sexual and other pleasures on the one hand, and excessive abstinence on the other.

In the matter of sexual intercourse in particular, the authors of conventional codes say that one may have sexual union in the proper

Sefer HaIkkarim   BOOK [Maamar] ONE

manner, with the proper person and at the proper time, but they can not tell what is proper in a given case. Divine law specifies that the proper manner is such as will lead to procreation and the perpetuation of the species; the proper person is the particular person who is the man's wife, forbidding marriage with certain women as being incestuous; the proper time is when the woman is clean, forbidding intercourse during or near the menstrual period.

Similarly divine law prohibits certain foods and permits others. It prohibits the drinking of wine when one is about to perform divine service or say his prayers. It frowns upon excessive abstinence, as is clear from the interpretation which the Rabbis put upon the expression, and make atonement for him, for that he sinned by reason of the soul. By reason of what soul has he sinned? ask the Rabbis, and they answer, He sinned because he abstained from wine. In the same way the authors of conventional codes praise courage, and say that a person must not risk danger except when death would be preferable to life, but they can not tell when that is the case. Divine law, however, declares that the proper time to risk one's life is when the name of God will be sanctified thereby, as in the case of Hananiah, Mishael and Azariah, or in order to fight with idolaters so as to destroy them and wipe off their name from under heaven.

Similarly in relation to mercy and cruelty, human law can not determine the proper measure of each to indicate when each is proper and when not. The divine law makes clear that cruelty is proper in one's dealings with unbelievers, heretics and those who violate the religious law, who should be punished with stripes or death according to the magnitude of the offence, as the law determines; and that mercy is the proper quality to show to believers, and those who are poor and unfortunate; though it should be exercised differently according to circumstances. Thus, in some cases it is proper to give by way of gift, in others by way of loan. This variety of method is indicated in the expression, well is it with the man that Derleth graciously and landed, that ordered his affairs rightfully. Derleth graciously has reference to alms which are given to a poor man without expectation of return. Landreth refers to a loan. And the one who does these two things is characterized as one who ordered his affairs rightfully, and one who shall never be moved; the righteous shall be had in everlasting remembrance; because he confers benefits upon all men, by gift or by loan. Human law can not determine properly in particular cases. Hence, he who follows its sole guidance walks in darkness and does not know what specific acts he should do, or what way he should follow. But the

Sefer Halkkarim   BOOK [Maamar] ONE

commandment of the Lord is pure [like the sun], enlightening the eyes, and showing those who follow it the way they should go and the thing they should do.

Again, the author of conventional law is a human being, and therefore can not determine the becoming and the unbecoming at all times. For those things which pertain to general opinion may change, and that which is now regarded as becoming may be regarded later as unbecoming and vice versa. Thus, we find that in the days of Cain and Abel and the ancient times generally the marriage of a sister was not thought indecent. The same thing was true in the time of Abraham. For Abraham in excusing himself to Abimelech said, and moreover she is indeed my sister, the daughter of my father, but not the daughter of my mother. Later the marriage of sisters came to be regarded as indecent. For this reason, the aversion from the unbecoming which is acquired through the conventional law can not last forever, because it changes with the times. But the divine law, by reason of the fact that it is determined by divine wisdom, declares the becoming and the unbecoming for all time. And therefore, the aversion from the unbecoming that is acquired through the divine law is not liable to change or destruction, for it is free from all error and impurity, and can therefore exist forever like silver which is free from all dross, as the Psalmist says, The words of the Lord are pure words, as silver tried in a crucible on the earth, refined seven times.

The meaning of the verse is this. Impure silver made alchemically may stand one melting without betraying its impurity, but not two. In some cases, it may stand two melting's, or sometimes three and four and five, but finally the impurity is discovered. In some cases, the impurity is not discovered by melting it in a furnace, it requires melting in thick earth. But silver which is purified in thick earth and refined many times is free from all impurity, dross and alloy, and can never change afterwards though it be melted many times. This is why he compares the purity of the words of the Lord to pure silver which is refined in a crucible on the ground, that is to say in an open place in thick earth, refined seven times, in which there is not the slightest trace of impurity. Similarly, the aversion to the unbecoming which is acquired from the Torah, is clean, enduring forever, because it is not liable to the change and destruction to which conventional law is liable.

Again, the conventional law can not recompense every man in accordance with his conduct or mete out punishment properly, so that one receives stripes, another be stoned, another strangled,

Sefer Halkkarim   BOOK [Maamar] ONE

another pays damages double, and another pay four and five-fold, to make the punishment fit the crime. But the divine law gives every one retribution according to his wrong deed, no more and no less. And though we see apparently the righteous man perishing in his righteousness, and the wicked man living a long life despite his wickedness, this appears so only if we test punishment by the standard of the goods of this world alone. But if we combine the goods of this world which the bad man gets with the evils and punishment which he gets in the next world, and similarly the evils befalling the righteous in this world with the good things he will get in the next world, we shall find that the sum of the two gives a just result though either alone is not just. This is the meaning of the Psalmist when he says, the ordinances of the Lord are true, they are righteous altogether. True refers to the measure of punishment, righteous altogether refers to the sum of punishment in this world plus blessings in the next, and vice versa.

I have seen a commentator explain this verse differently. We find instances in the Torah where the same thing is forbidden and permitted. For example, one may not marry his brother's widow, yet if the brother died without issue, he may; the fat of cattle is prohibited, of certain wild animals it is permitted; the combination of meat and milk is prohibited, yet the udder is permitted, and so on. And one would think that two contradictories can not both be correct. Hence, according to this commentator's view, the statement of the Psalmist, that the ordinances of the Lord are true, they are righteous altogether, i.e., the permission as well as the prohibition. But the expression true is not a fitting one according to this interpretation. For true does not apply to the laying down of a law, but rather the term fitting or proper or right. The word true does apply to compensation or retribution, as we find, Execute true judgment, judgment indicating retribution, as in the expression, The Lord hath made Himself known, He hath executed judgment, the wicked is snared in the work of his own hands; or the expression, only to do justly. The word altogether is also unsatisfactory according to this explanation.

These are the defects of the conventional law, and a great many more might be mentioned. For example, human law can punish only a visible act, but not one that is secret, for man sees only what is visible to the eye, but the divine law lays down punishment for secret acts also, for God sees into the heart. The expression, the ordinances of the Lord are true, they are righteous altogether, may also be explained as referring to visible and secret acts. There is no need of expatiating upon this matter. I merely desired to enumerate those six points which are named by the Psalmist in the nineteenth Psalm, and which are contained in the expressions, The law of the Lord is perfect, the testimony of the Lord is sure, the precepts of the Lord are right, rejoicing the heart, The commandment of the Lord is pure, enlightening the eyes, The fear of the Lord is clean, enduring forever, the ordinances of the Lord are true, they are righteous altogether.

Having explained the six points of superiority of the divine law in comparison with the conventional, the Psalmist adds that the divine law not merely gives theoretical perfection in relation to the true and the false, and moral perfection in relation to the becoming and the unbecoming, as we have said, but it also gives perfection wherever perfection is imagined to exist, namely, also in the categories of the useful and the pleasurable. Hence the Psalmist continues and says by way of rhetorical figure that in the words of the Torah are also found the useful and the agreeable, more to be desired are they than gold, yea, than much fine gold. This refers to the useful. Sweeter also than honey and the honeycomb. This refers to the agreeable. The meaning is that the reward that is earned through the commandments is great, and is more beneficial than gold and much fine gold, and more agreeable than the honeycomb. This is so, provided one is careful to observe them. Hence he concludes, Moreover by them is Thy servant warned; in keeping of them there is great reward.

Chapter 9

The principles of conventional law are freedom of choice and purpose. This is clear because why should the founder of a code of laws fix a punishment for those who violate the rules of the code if the violator is not his own master to do what he likes? Similarly, how can a king or ruler of a country compel men to do good if a person is not his own master to do good or evil? Even those who deny spiritual reward and punishment admit that man has absolute freedom of choice which is not interfered with, and that by virtue of this freedom he can choose what he desires and can direct his activities to a given purpose. That is why it is said that a code of laws must be drawn up by a wise man or men, to define what is becoming and what is unbecoming, what is wrong and what is right in the relations of the people in the land. And a ruler and a governor must be placed over the people to compel them to maintain right

Sefer HaIkkarim   BOOK [Maamar] ONE

among mankind and to suppress wrong, so as to realize the welfare of political society.

We can see from this that it is a mistake to regard freedom and purpose as principles of divine law. For though the latter presupposes freedom, freedom is not a principle of divine law as divine; it is a principle of divine law by virtue of being a principle of all human acts and conventions and of legal customs by which a political community is kept in order and without which it can not exist. We do not say that the axioms are principles of divine law, though the latter presupposes them, as does any branch of learning and knowledge. In the same way though freedom is an essential dogma in divine law, it is not a principle thereof in so far as it is divine. For this reason, Maimonides does not enumerate it among the fundamental principles, though he believes that it is essential to divine law, as we said in chapter three. For only those dogmas are counted as principles, which are fundamental to divine law as divine.

Similarly, purpose as a general concept is not a principle of divine law as such, but of all voluntary human acts. It is therefore a principle of conventional law. For as every one who does anything deliberately and voluntarily does it because he intends a certain purpose [whether the purpose be really good or one that seems to the agent good], so the founder of a code of laws intends in his commands and prohibitions that the people should attain a certain object in their acts, viz., their well-being and the perfection of political society. It is clear therefore that purpose is a principle of conventional law also, and not of divine law as divine. Nevertheless, inasmuch as the purpose which results from the Torah, namely the future life, is different from the purpose resulting from conventional law and all the other purposes, Maimonides includes purpose among the principles, though he does not include freedom.

If one object that if freedom and purpose are not principles of divine law as such, why does the Torah say, See I have set before thee this day life ... therefore choose life, an allusion to freedom and purpose which is eternal life? We say again as we said before, that though freedom and purpose are not principles of divine law as divine, the latter necessarily presupposes them, as it presupposes the axioms, though they are not principles of divine law as such. Now no one denies the truth of the axioms, but there are those who deny the reality of freedom, like some astrologers, and there are also those who deny purpose in all acts, like the Epicureans, who believe that the world came by accident, and that no act has any purpose, but that

Sefer HaIkkarim   BOOK [Maamar] ONE

everything happens by chance. Then there are those who admit purpose in human acts, but not so lofty a purpose as spiritual immortality. For this reason, it was necessary that the Torah state these principles expressly, as a protest against the opinions mentioned, which are obviously unsound, because they nullify all human acts and human purpose, not to speak of undermining all laws.

Chapter 10

The principles of divine law in general are three: existence of God, divine revelation, and reward and punishment. There is no doubt that these three are essential principles of divine law qua divine. For if we assume the removal of one of them the law will fall entirely. This is obvious from the nature of the principles. Thus, if we do not believe in the existence of God who commands the law, there is no divine law. And if we do believe in the existence of God, and do not believe in divine revelation, there is no divine law. And if there is no corporeal reward and punishment in this world and spiritual in the next, what need is there of a divine law? If it is in order to maintain a proper order in human affairs and relations so as to have a perfect political society, the conventional law is sufficient for this purpose. It is clear therefore that if there is a divine law, it is for the purpose of leading mankind to such perfection as a human code can not attain to, viz., human perfection which depends upon perfection of the soul, as will appear later. It is clear therefore that spiritual reward and punishment is a fundamental principle of divine law without doubt. And the corporeal reward which the righteous man obtains from God in this world for his observance of the commandments is a proof of the future spiritual reward. It follows, then, that reward and punishment in general is a necessary principle of divine law.

Since these three are general principles of divine law, the Rabbis named them in the Mishnah in Chapter Helek, saying that one who denies any one of them is not to be reckoned among the adherents of the law, and therefore has no share in the world to come. Their words are as follows: All Israel have a share in the world to come, as is said, 'Thy people also shall be all righteous, they shall inherit the land forever.' But the following have no share in the world to come: He who says, there is no resurrection of the dead in the Torah. This refers to the person who denies divine retribution, symbolized in resurrection of the dead, which is a divine act in relation to body and soul, and represents all kinds of retribution. For the Rabbis indicate in their expressions that the term resurrection of the dead is used in a general and a particular sense. It may mean specifically the resurrection of the dead, and it may be used in a broader sense to denote the world of souls, the world to come and the day of judgment. They also make clear that the idea of the Messiah, which is a physical reward, represents all kinds of reward.

Then they specify the one who says there is no divine Torah, which is a second principle. Then they mention the Epicurean. According to the testimony of the ancients, Epicurus was a person who believed that the world came by accident, and denied the existence of God as the maker of the world. Those who followed his teaching were called Epicureans. We see therefore that they mention these three principles and say that he who denies any one of them has no share in the world to come because he is excluded from the community of adherents of the law.

It is true that in the Talmud **chapter Helek**, Epicurean is interpreted as one who holds the wise in contempt, but the reason they say so is because no man can know the existence of God by his own ratiocination. He gets this knowledge either by tradition or by demonstration, through the wise men. But he who holds in contempt the wise men who declare the existence of God to all, leaves himself no way by which he can know God, and hence is like one who denies the existence of God, and is therefore called an Epicurean. From the fact that in the Mishnah of chapter Helek these are the only ones who are denied a share in the world to come, it is clear that these are the three fundamental principles common to all divine law, which every adherent of divine law is obliged to believe. It is true that in the Talmud they name others who have no share in the world to come. But they are enumerated as being derived from the three chief ones, not as being themselves chief principles.

Chapter 11

Since all agree that the law which Moshe gave to the children of Israel is divine, it is fitting that we should make it a test for divine laws, and prove them by it. Just as we use one individual of a given species as a type if we desire to know the things which are essential and necessary to the existence and duration of every other member of the species, so it is proper that we should take the law of Moshe as a type and assume that those things which are necessary for the

Sefer HaIkkarim   BOOK [Maamar] ONE

existence and duration of the law of Moshe are also the things which give existence and duration to divine law.

Now since we find that the law of Moshe lays down in the beginning the three principles above mentioned, namely the existence of God, divine revelation and reward and punishment, it follows that they are necessary principles of divine law. The reason they are laid down in the section **Bereshit** is to indicate that they are principles of divine law. Just as in every science the principles are first laid down upon which the science turns and by which are proved all the other propositions that come in that science, so in the section **Bereshit** are recounted three matters, different from each other, every one explaining one of the principles to indicate that they are the fundamental principles of divine law upon which all its contents turn.

Thus, the passage from in the beginning to These are the generations of the heaven, deals with one subject, and the purpose of this section is to teach the first principle, which is the existence of God, who produces all things by His will, and to refute the opinion of the Epicurean sect who thought that the world came by chance and has no efficient cause. The entire narrative from In the beginning to These are the generations of the heaven turns upon this principle. For the order of succession of created things of different degrees and the successive appearance of plant, animal and man, point to the existence of a voluntary agent, as will be explained in the second book.

This section also makes clear that the human species is the choicest of all the lower existences, and that man is the main purpose of the creation of the lower world; for man is related to the other classes of being, like plant and animal, as form and entelechy is to matter. As in the arts those that are pre-requisite to a given art are in the position of preparatories and as matter to the art in question, which stands in the relation of form to the former, so all the forms of being preceding the human, are as it were preparatory to it and in the position of matter to the human species, which is to them in the relation of form.

This is the reason why the formation of man came later than that of the lower animals and is ascribed to God Himself, to show that the purpose of the Agent in creating the earlier species of plant and animal was the existence of the human forms. For man alone of the lower existences knows the existence of God. As soon as man made his appearance, creation was complete, and we read, And the heaven and the earth were finished, and all the host of them; for the purpose

Sefer HaIkkarim — BOOK [Maamar] ONE

of a thing always comes at the end of the work. Man is thus the end of creation, as the principal art is the end of all the arts which come before it and exist for its sake. This entire portion was written for no other purpose except to teach the first principle, the existence of a Being who made all existing things. This is the reason why throughout this section the name Elohim alone is used [Elohim denoting one who has power to produce all things], to show that the only purpose of the entire narrative in this section is to teach the existence of a Being who made all existing things, which is the first principle.

From These are the generations of the heaven to and the man knew Eve his wife, is another subject, intended to bring out the second principle, the existence of prophecy and divine revelation. This is why we find that the entire narrative turns about divine law. Thus, the first conversation God had with man was, And the Lord God commanded the man, saying ... Then comes the reason why man was given divine commandments rather than all the lower animals: And out of the ground the Lord God formed every beast of the field, and every fowl of the air; and brought them unto the man, to see what he would call them. The meaning is that seeing that man has an intelligence and knows the definitions of the animals better than any other creature, all the sublunar existences are subject to him and exist for his sake. But the purpose of man is to observe the commandments of his Maker. For this reason, he was placed in this world, symbolized by the Garden of Eden, that he may eat of the tree of life which is in the midst of the garden, an allusion to the Torah, concerning which it is said. She is a tree of life to them that lay hold upon her. But if he violates the command of his Maker he will be driven out of the garden.

The whole narrative of Adam and Eve and the serpent is a symbolic allusion to man's fortunes in this world. The serpent, whom our Rabbis call Samael, is the evil inclination which, with the assistance of woman, hinders man from attaining his perfection, and causes him to be driven out of the garden. This is the reason why in this narrative the expression Lord God is used. It is meant to indicate that in order for man to attain his perfection it is not sufficient that he believes in the existence of a Creator, which is the conception of an agent who brings into being the things of nature, and is designated by the word God [Elohim]. But he must also believe in prophecy and divine revelation. This is a higher conception than that of a creative agency bringing into being the things of nature. In possession of the faith that the commandments come from the Lord

Sefer HaIkkarim — BOOK [Maamar] ONE

God, man may eat of the tree of life and live forever. He can not attain to this by virtue of the first knowledge alone, namely that there is a Creator, but he must have in addition the belief in prophecy and the divine origin of the Torah, which commands the doing of those things which God wills, though natural reason may not dictate it. This is something higher than the things of nature.

To prevent the thought that the Creator and the Revealer of the Torah are two different persons, the introduction of the ten commandments reads, And God spoke all these words, saying, and the first commandment begins, I am the Lord, thy God, to indicate that He who gave the Law, who is represented by the tetragrammaton Lord God, is the same as the one who brought all things into being, and who is called God Elohim in the chapter on the Creation. This is also the reason why in Deuteronomy Moshe says, these words the Lord spoke unto all your assembly, to indicate that though the introductory words of the ten commandments in Exodus say, And God spoke all these words, the speaker is the same as is represented by the tetragrammaton. Thus, the entire narrative from These are the generations of the heaven to and the man knew Eve his wife, uses the expression, Lord God, to allude to the principle of prophecy and divine revelation. All the penalties mentioned in this section embrace the whole human race and are not confined to Adam and Eve alone.

From And the man knew Eve his wife, until This is the book of the generations of Adam, the text treats of another topic, and has an allusion to the third principle, namely individual reward and punishment and divine providence as extending to particular incidents occurring in the world, such as quarrels between man and man like those between Cain and Abel. The penalty mentioned in this chapter is of a different nature from that mentioned in the preceding chapters which deal with Adam and Eve. There Adam was punished because he violated the command of God, which is a lesson to the whole human race. The essential cause of the punishment was the transgression of the divine command, and the purpose of the story is not to tell the particular things that happened to Adam and Eve. Therefore, all the punishments mentioned in the story of Adam and Eve embrace the whole human race.

But in the section dealing with Cain and Abel, the topic is individual providence as concerned with the particular circumstances of every individual. Thus, we are told that God took account of Cain and punished him because his intention when he brought an offering was not sincere, and because he did violence to Abel, not merely because

Sefer Halkkarim   BOOK [Maamar] ONE

he violated a divine command. This is intended to show that God takes cognizance of evil doers and punishes them for their evil intentions and for their violent deeds. And though He may prolong His anger as He did in the case of Cain, ultimately, He exacts punishment from them as He did from Cain, paying him in his own coin. As Cain killed Abel and cut off his progeny, so was Cain killed and all his descendants were wiped out by the flood, not one remaining alive. And though among Cain's descendants there were great, wise and intelligent men, inventors of the arts and the sciences, as we read, the father of the forger of every cutting instrument of brass and iron, the father of such as dwell in tents and have cattle, the father of all such as handle the harp and pipe, nevertheless God showed them no favor.

This is the purpose of this third section, and for this reason the word Lord alone is used, to show that the individual providence touching all things that happen in the world, by reason of which everyone's fortune corresponds to his deeds, is not simply a natural result of the existence of a Creator who brings into being the things of nature, nor is it merely a result of the existence of a divine law, but it is due to the fact that God's perfection and goodness prompt Him to look out for the lowly and the weak, and to save them from their oppressors. The prophet alludes to this when he says, I dwell in the high and holy place, with him also that is of a contrite and humble spirit. The meaning is that because of His goodness and exalted station it is becoming in Him to look out for the lowly so as to show them His great power and to revive the heart of the contrite ones.

The story of Cain and Abel also makes clear that God's providence is pervaded by the quality of mercy, and that He opens to the wicked the ways of repentance, as He opened them to Cain, when He said, if thou do well, shall it not be lifted up? This is more than strict justice. For this reason, the name God is not used in this story at all. Having explained the three dogmas, which are fundamental principles of divine law, he now begins the narrative over again and gives a list of the sequence of the generations as before, beginning his account with the words, this is the book of the generations of Adam. The meaning is that here is the beginning of the book, all that has come before being the introduction stating the principles upon which the book is based, but not forming part of the book itself.

Every author in the beginning of his book gives its contents, so here the words just mentioned tell us that the book of Genesis deals with the generations of Adam and the descent of mankind from him. These words indicate that all that comes before is not part of the

Sefer HaIkkarim BOOK [Maamar] ONE

book, but expresses the principles of the book, in the same way as the principles of a science are laid down in the beginning of the science. Thus, the verse, this is the book of the generations of Adam, is the beginning of the Torah, and it tells us that the book of Genesis is the account of the generations of Adam. The author continues, In the day that God created man, in the likeness of God made He him; male and female created He them ... Now it would have been sufficient if he had said, In the day that God created man, male and female created He them. The reason he adds, in the likeness of God made He him, is in order to allude to an important matter which is essential for the existence of the Torah. The point is that individual reward and punishment, which we said is one of the principles of the Torah, can be attained by man by reason of his rational soul which is in the image of God. For it is by virtue of the rational soul that man attains to a permanent life as an individual and is thought worthy of reward and punishment as an individual, but not by virtue of the permanence he enjoys as a member of the species, an attribute which he has in common with the other animals. Thus, the verse in question, which is the beginning of the Torah, makes reference to the two kinds of continuity which man has. The expression, in the likeness of God made He him, alludes to the fact that man has an individual continuity like the celestial beings, because he is in the likeness of Elohim, i.e., the angels, who have individual continuity. The expression, male and female created He them, alludes to the continuity man enjoys in the species, which he shares with the lower animals.

There is an allusion to this idea in **Bereshit Rabbah**. Commenting on the verse, let us make man in our image, the Rabbis say, with whom did He consult? says Rabbi Yehoshua son of Levi, He consulted with the domains of heaven and earth. The meaning is this. Up to the sixth day, before man was created, there were two different kinds of created things in the world, the celestial things, which have permanent existence as individuals, and the sublunar things, which enjoy permanent existence in the species, but not as individuals. Then God consulted with the celestials and the sublunars and said, Let us make man in our image, according to our likeness, i.e., a being in whom both powers are combined, individual and specific permanence, individual permanence, like the celestials, due to his rational power, and specific permanence, like the sublunars, by virtue of his material side. This will explain why the singular is used in the expression, And God created man in His own image, in the image of God created He him, while in the expression, male and

Sefer HaIkkarim — BOOK [Maamar] ONE

female created He them, the pronoun is in the plural. The former refers to his permanence as an individual, which he enjoys over and above the other animals. The latter refers to the specific permanence, which is due to the union of male and female.

But there is a difficulty here. We find in **Bereshit Rabbah** the following story. When God dictated to Moshe the verse, let us make man, Moshe objected and said, why should you give the heretics an occasion for error? And God said, Write as I dictate, and if any one desires to err, let him do so. Now it is clear that a thing which is good ought to exist; a thing which is bad ought not to exist; while a thing which is composed of good and evil, should or should not exist according as the good or the evil predominates. Now from the expression attributed to God, Write as I tell you, and if any one desires to err, let him do so, it seems like a case of submitting to a small loss for the sake of a great benefit arising from the use of the expression let us make. But what can possibly be the great benefit resulting from the plural, let us make? If we say it is the moral lesson that the great should not disdain the advice of the small, as God consulted with the denizens of heaven and earth, His own creatures, though He had no need to do so, the benefit is not so great as to counterbalance the evil arising from the occasion for error which the expression furnishes to heretics. And even if we say that the benefit is the idea which we mentioned in the name of Rabbi Yehoshua son of Levi, viz., the knowledge that man has a rational faculty like the celestials and a material power like the lower existences, and that the rational faculty gives man individual permanence, namely immortality for the soul of the individual person, which doctrine is essential to the Torah, as we have seen, we must say in reply to this that although the teaching of such doctrine is indeed of great benefit, counterbalancing the harm arising from the possibility of error by heretics, the question still remains, what necessity was there for writing let us make, with the pronoun in the plural, the text might have read, And God said to the celestials and the terrestrials, I will make a man in your image? In this way the aforementioned benefits would be realized and there would be no room for heretical error.

My own opinion in the matter is, that though the benefits aforementioned would be realized if the text read, I will make man, the actual reading is let us make, in order to make allusion to another point more profound, and at the same time essential. The existence of the celestials which have individual continuity indicates that they are caused by a being who has the ability and the power to endow individual things with permanent existence, as in the case of the

Sefer HaIkkarim — BOOK [Maamar] ONE

celestial beings. The existence of the terrestrial beings shows that they are caused by a being who has power to perpetuate species but not individuals. This might give rise to the erroneous opinion that there are two creative Powers, as Elisha, surnamed Aher thought. Hence the text reads, let us make man in our image, as if the two Powers who gave existence to the two different kinds of beings, the celestial and the terrestrial, said, let us make man, meaning that they agreed to make a single creature, man, in which shall be united the two powers, the general power that gives specific permanence and the particular power that bestows individual permanence. This single being would from his combined nature make it clear to all that all existences, celestial as well as terrestrial, are the product of one being who possesses all powers. In this way we explain the expression, And God said, let us make man. God [Elohim], who has all powers, general and particular, united the two in agreement, and made man in whom are combined the two qualities, general and particular permanence, general, due to matter; particular, due to soul. This points to a single Being in whom all the powers are united absolutely, and shows that He who made the things which are permanent as individuals and the things which are permanent as species, is the same one.

This shows too that God's knowledge embraces particular things as well as general. This latter idea is also indicated in other ways. Thus, when God reveals Himself to the righteous men in the Bible, He mentions their names twice, Abraham, Abraham! Yaakov, Yaakov! Moshe, Moshe! Samuel, Samuel! to indicate that He knows the individual in his individuality. Similarly, the verse in Genesis, whoso **Sheddeth** [sheds] man's blood, by man shall his blood be shed; for in the image of God made He man, shows that God knows man as an individual. For if God's knowledge extended only to the species, as His providence in respect to the other animals extends only to the conservation of the species, what reason is it for punishing a murderer with death because in the image of God made, He man, since in killing one individual he has not destroyed the species? The Bible therefore says that because man was made in the image of God, he has permanence as an individual, and he who kills him should be punished. For God knows him as an individual by reason of the rational faculty which he possesses like the celestial beings, who also have individual permanence and are known by God individually by reason of their rational faculty. This is a reason, too, why man deserves individual reward and punishment, as is promised in the Torah.

Sefer HaIkkarim   BOOK [Maamar] ONE

Now both of these things are essential to the existence of the Torah. The one has reference to God, that there are not two gods as the heretics used to say, that the God of the heaven is not the same as the God of the earth. This is the belief in the unity of God which Abraham spread abroad in the world, as we find, And I will make thee swear by the Lord, the God of heaven and the God of the earth. The second has reference to man, that God's knowledge of generals and particulars was united in the creation of man. And therefore, man deserves reward and punishment, because God knows him as an individual, since he is in the image of God. This, too, Abraham published abroad, as we find him saying, The Lord, the God of heaven, who took me from my father's house, and from the land of my nativity. The meaning is that though He is the God of heaven, He nevertheless knew me as an individual, spoke to me and made me a promise. This is the reason for the expression, let us make man. And the statement of the Rabbis is now clear, that God said to Moshe, Write as I tell you, and if anyone chooses to make a mistake, let him do so. The meaning is, that the benefit arising from this expression is great and essential to the Torah, pointing out as it does that, He who made the individuals of the celestial world and has a knowledge of them is the same one who made the terrestrial species, and He knows them too. There are not two Powers, nor two different knowledges. With one knowledge He knows all.

This is what Rabbi Ammi meant in the passage in **Bereshit Rabbah**. In reference to the expression, let us make man, the question is asked: With whom did He consult? Said Rabbi Ammi: He consulted with His knowledge. The meaning is that He did not consult any one else, but his own general and individual knowledge, for the purpose of making a single being whose nature should clearly indicate that the divine knowledge is one. This will be accomplished by uniting in the new creature the general and the particular knowledge, in other words, by making him a human being. Being in the image of God like the celestial beings, he shows clearly that God knows him individually. And being male and female, he shows that God looks out for him as a species, also. This shows that God is absolutely one, and that man deserves individual reward and punishment, because he is in the image of God. This is why in this verse, which is the beginning of the Torah, as we said before, we read, In the day that God created man, in the likeness of God made He him.

Sefer Halkkarim   BOOK [Maamar] ONE
Chapter 12

Creation ex nihilo is a dogma which every one who professes a divine law is obliged to believe, in the same way as he who professes the Law of Moshe is obliged to believe that the earth opened her mouth and swallowed up Korah and his congregation, because they rebelled against Moshe. But it is not one of the fundamental principles of divine law, whose existence can not be conceived without it. The story of creation at the beginning of the Torah is not intended to teach that creation ex nihilo is a fundamental principle of the Torah, as many authorities have thought. It is true that if one believes in the eternity of the world after the manner of Aristotle, it follows that God can not lengthen the wing of a fly, nor create an ant having only four legs. Moreover, he who entertains such belief must deny all the miracles of the Torah. For he can not believe that God has the power to change a rod into a serpent momentarily, or water into blood, or dust into vermin. More than that, he would have to deny the existence of Moshe and the Messiah, because an individual whose existence must be preceded by the existence of an infinite number of individuals can never exist, for the infinite can never be completed. Thus, the whole Torah falls to the ground. But one may believe that there is a primary eternal matter, from which the world was created when and as God willed. Such an opinion as this does not contradict the miracles and wonders of the Torah. For all those miracles, which consist in a change of natural law and custom, are instances of something coming from something and not something from nothing, for example the rod turning into a serpent, or water, though a simple substance, changing instantaneously into blood. A simple substance can not change into blood. This is the reason why water is not nourishing to an animal. Yet God through Moshe gave to one portion of the water the form of fire, to another portion the form of air, to a third the form of earth. Then these portions were mixed together, so that they combined and were transubstantiated instantaneously into blood. The change was not merely apparent, for if it had been only in appearance and not in substance, the fish would not have died, nor the river become foul. Similarly, all the transubstantiatory miracles of the Torah and the Prophets are instances of something coming from something and not of something coming from nothing. Much more is this true of those miracles in which there is no transubstantiation but merely a change in quality or accident, like the instance of Moshe' hand turning leprous and as white as snow.

Sefer HaIkkarim — BOOK [Maamar] ONE

It follows therefore that though a person who believes in the eternity of the world as Aristotle conceives the doctrine, is a denier of the Torah and its miracles, one who conceives the doctrine of eternity in the manner mentioned before, does not deny the Torah or its miracles, for belief in the Torah and the miracles does not imply belief in creation ex nihilo. This is why we said in the preceding chapter that the purpose of the first section of Genesis is merely to teach the existence of the Maker, which is the first essential principle of the existence of a divine law, without which it can not be conceived. As to creation ex nihilo, it is indeed a dogma which every one professing the Torah is obliged to believe, as he is obliged to believe that Moshe split the rock so that the water flowed, that he caused the quails to fly and the manna to descend, but it is not one of the fundamental principles of divine law. For this reason, Maimonides did not include it among the fundamental dogmas of the Torah. This becomes even more significant if we observe that in Madda, in the third chapter of the treatise On Repentance, he enumerates five classes of heretics, one of them being the person who denies that God alone is the first and the Creator of all. For it is clear that one who believes in a primary eternal matter, by implication denies that God alone is the first, for primary matter is coeval with God according to this notion. We see then that though Maimonides calls that one a heretic who does not believe in creation ex nihilo, yet he does not include this doctrine among the fundamental principles, because it is not a principle without which divine law can not be conceived. It follows therefore that the purpose of beginning the Torah with the creation story is to teach the existence of the Maker, which is the first fundamental and essential principle of divine law, as we said before.

Chapter 13

Not every law which maintains the three principles mentioned, viz., existence of God, reward and punishment, and divine revelation, which are the general principles of divine law, as we have seen, is divine in the full sense of the word, so that a believer in it can be called a believer in divine law without qualification and has a share in the world to come. The truth of the matter is that these three are general principles of all divine law in the sense that one who denies any one of them is excluded from the class of those who profess divine law, and has no share in the world to come, because he does not believe properly in divine law. But one may acknowledge these

Sefer Halkkarim   BOOK [Maamar] ONE

principles and yet have no share in the world to come. He must in addition believe in the derivative principles which branch out of them. If he denies any of the subordinate principles, it is tantamount to a denial of the fundamental principle from which the former is derived.

Thus, one who believes in the first principle, the existence of God, must also believe that God is one and incorporeal in any sense, and other such corollaries as follow from or are dependent upon the first principle. Similarly, one who believes in divine revelation, which is the second principle, must believe in the reality of prophecy, and in the genuineness of the divine representative's mission. Likewise, one who believes in the third principle, reward and punishment, must believe in God's knowledge and providence, and in retribution, spiritual and corporeal. To deny any of the secondary principles which are derived from the fundamental principles or based upon them, is tantamount to a denial of the fundamental principle itself.

Thus, one who denies the reality of prophecy, which is a corollary of the principle of revelation, or the genuineness of the alleged divine messenger through whom the law is given, is virtually denying the principle of revelation. Similarly, one who believes that God is body is virtually denying the principle of the existence of God. For belief in the existence of God means the belief that there is a necessarily existent Being, who is the cause of all existing things, all of which receive influence from Him and are in need of Him, while He is in need of nothing outside of Himself. Now if the necessarily existing Being were corporeal, He would stand in need of another, for all body is composite, as Maimonides explains in the twenty-second proposition, and all that is composite has need of another, the composer and agent, who brings about the combination of its parts. The necessarily existing Being would therefore exist not through Himself, but through another, and would not be self-sufficient, but would stand in need of another. That other would then be greater than He and the author of the latter's being. The necessarily existing Being would then exist not through Himself but through another. But a being whose existence depends upon another is a possible and not a necessary existent. It follows therefore that one who says that God is body or a corporeal power, virtually denies the principle of the existence of God, as will be explained completely in the Second Book.

Similarly, one who denies providence or God's knowledge, or who says that all things are the result of fate, called in Arabic - **Al kada** and Al kadr, virtually denies the principle of reward and

Sefer Halkkarim — BOOK [Maamar] ONE

punishment, or else attributes to God wrong and injustice [God forbid!], since He punishes a sinner without fault, who could not do other than what he did. The same applies to all the secondary dogmas derived from the fundamental principles. To deny any one of them is to deny the principle itself. This is very important, for it is necessary in this way to examine carefully all the secondary dogmas which follow from the fundamental principles, and to guard against error. Only when one believes in these absolutely can he be called a believer in the three principles which we mentioned.

Chapter 14

We will now explain the method of deriving the secondary principles from these three fundamental principles, in order that we may be able to tell who is a denier and who is a believer. We will observe in the first place that none of the commandments of the Torah should be counted as a principle, whether fundamental or derivative. A person who violates a commandment of the Torah is called a transgressor, and is liable to the penalty prescribed in the Torah for that commandment. But he is not excluded from those who profess the Torah, and is not regarded as a denier of the Torah who has no share in the world to come; unless his violation of the commandment is due to the fact that he is in doubt whether it is a command of God, given to Moshe on Sinai, or not. If this is his attitude, he falls into the class of those who deny the divine origin of the Torah, as the Rabbis of the Talmud explain in chapter Helek. All the commandments of the Torah are alike in this respect. The command to send away the mother bird is as important as any other. If we should count specific commandments as dogmas by reason of the last consideration, we should have as many principles as there are commandments. And even if we restrict the term principle to those commandments which are based upon the three fundamental principles mentioned above, it would still follow that all those commandments which are found in the treatises on Idolatry and on the Foundation of the Torah in Maimonides' code are principles, for they are based upon the first principle, the existence of God.

The truth of the matter is that none of the specific commandments of the Torah should be regarded as principles, fundamental or derived. It follows from this that the duty to worship God alone, which is in Maimonides' list, should not be counted as a principle, primary or secondary, for it is a specific command: Thou shalt have no other gods before Me. Thou shalt not make unto thee a graven image, nor any manner of likeness ... thou shalt not bow down unto them, nor serve them; ... Hence a person who violates it, is not a denier of the Torah or of its principles, though he be guilty of a grave sin. The Rabbis, it is true, say that he who acknowledges belief in an idol is like one who denies the whole Torah. But the expression is significant - like one who denies, they say, not that he actually denies. Ahab is a good example. He was a worshipper of idols and yet did not deny the principles; for he believed Eliyahu and acknowledged that the rain was withheld because of Eliyahu's oath. For he said to Eliyahu, Is it thou, thou troubler of Israel? The explanation of his error in worshipping idols is either that he introduced a mediator between God and himself, or that he thought that God looked out only for the good and loyal like Eliyahu and the other righteous men, whereas the rest of mankind, he thought, were subject to the accidental influence of the heavenly bodies. Hence, he made statues and worshipped idols in order by means thereof to receive the influence of the heavenly bodies.

There is no doubt that the punishment of one who denies a fundamental or derivative principle is not the same as that of one who violates one of the commandments of the Torah. Thus, as long as the Cutheans were ignorant of the Torah and no doubt denied it, the lions devoured them. But as soon as they were taught the Torah, though they continued to worship idols, as the Bible testifies, the lions ceased to harm them. The same holds true of the punishments of the future world, for God uses scales and a balance of justice and inflicts punishment upon every one according to the magnitude of his disobedience. The punishments of this world may be used as proof of the mode of the punishments in the next world, as will be explained later. This may be shown, too, from the fact that our Rabbis count among those who have no share in the world to come, tale bearers, those who separate themselves from the community, and one who humiliates his neighbor in public, even as they count heretics, Epicureans and unbelievers. Now there is no doubt that the punishment of one who humiliates his neighbor is not the same as that of one who denies the Torah. In the same way it follows that the punishment of one who violates a commandment is not the same as that of one who denies a principle. It is clear therefore that none of the specific commandments of the Torah should be reckoned as principles, fundamental or derived.

For the same reason tradition is not regarded as a principle under the head of revelation. By tradition I mean the duty to follow what has been handed down by our ancestors and religious authorities. Such

Sefer HaIkkarim — BOOK [Maamar] ONE

a duty is essential to divine law, but it is a specific commandment. The same reason would lead us to say that the doctrine of the immutability of the Torah should not be reckoned as a principle if it is a specific command, as Maimonides thinks. In reality, however, it is not a command, but an opinion which is implied in the belief of the genuineness of the alleged divine messenger, as will be made clear in Book Three.

The reason the unity of God is regarded as a principle, though it is a specific command, is because the belief in unity involves two things - the belief that there is only one God and there is no second who is equal or similar to Him, and the belief that the necessarily existing Being, though He is one and without any plurality or composition whatsoever, is nevertheless our God, i.e., He is the cause of the plurality of existing things. The first conception of unity is a principle derived from the existence of God; the second is a specific command given to us, Hear, O Israel, the Lord our God, the Lord is one.

According to Maimonides, who includes specific commandments among his principles, counting in his list the first of the ten commandments, I am the Lord thy God, which he interprets as a command to believe that there is a necessarily existent Being, it is strange that the other principles are not mentioned in the ten commandments. But according to our view there is no difficulty here. For our idea is that no specific command is a principle. And the first commandment, I am the Lord, thy God, being a specific command, is not a principle. The meaning of it is that we should believe that the same God who took us out of Egypt, from the house of bondage, gave us the Torah on Mount Sinai. Or the first commandment may be introductory to what comes after: Thou shalt have no other gods before Me. And the meaning would be: Since I cared for you and took you out of the land of Egypt, from the house of bondage, you shall have no other gods before Me, i.e., you should not abandon My worship for the worship of another.

Many authorities are of the opinion that the words I am the Lord, thy God, etc, are not part of the ten commandments, but introductory to the two commandments which follow: Thou shalt have no other gods, etc, and-Thou shalt not make unto thee a graven image. The verse, thou shalt not bow down unto them nor serve them, is merely the explanation of these two. Their idea is that the reason the verse, I am the Lord, thy God… is placed at the head of the ten commandments is to encourage believers by indicating that divine providence inclines to the side of mercy, even though the recipient

Sefer Halkkarim   BOOK [Maamar] ONE

is not worthy. Thus, God took care of Israel when they were in Egypt, worshipping idols, and took them out of the house of bondage for the merits of their fathers. This is the meaning of the concluding words, showing mercy unto the thousandth generation of them that love Me and keep My commandments. We may take it then as proved that a specific command is not reckoned as a principle.

Chapter 15

The secondary principles, based upon the three primary which we have mentioned, and derived from them, are eight. From the first principle, existence of God, are derived four secondary principles, including all those things implied in the existence of God, who is a necessary existent. They are as follows: Unity, as we explained it above; incorporeality - God is neither a body nor a corporeal power; independence of time; and freedom from defects.

It is clear from the nature of every one of these four principles that they follow essentially from the principle of the existence of God. For if God is not one, without any composition, He is not a necessary existent. Similarly, if He is a body or a corporeal power. Likewise, if He is dependent upon time, existing in one time and not in another, time is either prior to Him or posterior, as we shall see later, and He is neither eternal nor perpetual. This is our reason for counting independence of time as a principle, rather than eternity, as Maimonides does, for independence of time includes both eternity and perpetuity. Maimonides, who counts eternity as a separate principle, should have counted perpetuity also as a separate principle.

God's freedom from defects we lay down as a principle in order to show that the necessary existent is not liable to sleep or forgetfulness or fatigue, and the like. Also, to indicate that all those attributes which God must have, like power, will and others, without which He would be defective, are ascribed to Him in a manner that will not result in a defect in His nature. Precisely in what way these attributes and others are to be ascribed to God, will be made clear in the Second Book.

The dogmas based upon the second principle, divine revelation, are three: God's knowledge, prophecy, and the genuineness of the divine messenger. And it is clear from the nature of these three that they necessarily follow from revelation. For if God does not know terrestrial existences, prophecy can not come from Him, nor a revealed Torah. And even assuming that God does know terrestrial existences, there will be no divine Torah unless there is prophecy and information communicated by God to man. And even if there is such a thing as prophecy by which man is informed of the future and given specific commandments to be followed by him and his descendants, like the command of circumcision given to Abraham, men would not have to obey the alleged prophet unless it is proven that he is a divine messenger sent to communicate to the people the commands of God. For this reason, belief in the genuineness of the messenger is a principle common to all divine laws. For if we are convinced that the messenger is genuine, whether he be a man of the greatest ability or not of the greatest, it is possible that a general and adequate code should be given through him by God, to lead mankind to eternal happiness. This is the meaning of divine revelation.

This is the reason why we did not include the superiority of Moshe as a prophet among the principles, primary or secondary, as Maimonides did. For nothing should be regarded as a fundamental principle unless a divine law can not be conceived without it, nor as a secondary principle, unless it follows necessarily from a fundamental principle. But the superiority of Moshe as a prophet does not necessarily follow from a belief in the genuine character of the messenger, though it may be compared to a branch issuing from it. If we are to count it at all, it would be as a special principle of the law of Moshe. But inasmuch as a conviction of the genuine character of the particular messenger of a given religion is a special dogma of the religion in question; and the intensity of belief in the given religion varies with the intensity of conviction in the genuine character of the messenger, we did not find it necessary to count the superiority of Moshe as a special principle of the law of Moshe. For as long as the genuineness of his mission has been verified, it is not necessary to verify the rank he holds among prophets. The question of the manner in which the authenticity of the mission must be verified beyond all doubt, will be discussed later on. The question why we regard divine revelation as a fundamental principle, and prophecy as a derivative principle following from the former, will be explained in the Third Book.

As to the third principle, reward and punishment, the secondary principle which is prior and essential to it is providence. For although we have already assumed God's knowledge, viz., that He knows the deeds of men and orders their affairs by means of a divine law so that their social life may be permanent and well conditioned, it might still be said that by reason of man's inferiority and little esteem in the eyes of God, the individual is ignored and not

Sefer HaIkkarim   BOOK [Maamar] ONE

recompensed for his specific conduct in relation to his Maker, and that he is taken account of merely as a part of the whole, and not as an individual. For this reason we regard providence as a principle that is prior to reward and punishment, in order to call attention to the fact that divine providence extends to every individual, and recompenses him for his individual relations to God, as we are told that God did not have respect unto Cain and his offering, and more especially for his dealings with his fellowmen, as the Prophet says, Great in counsel, and mighty in work; whose eyes are open upon all the ways of the sons of men, to give every one according to his ways, and according to the fruit of his doings.

Retribution is of two kinds, corporeal and spiritual; the principle therefore includes both. We did not think it proper to name corporeal and spiritual retribution as two separate principles, for the reason that some of our Rabbis say that the reward given for obedience to God's commandments is not in this world. Corporeal retribution, therefore, should not be counted as a separate principle, according to my opinion. Hence, I laid down reward and punishment as one principle, including both kinds. It will represent spiritual recompense to those who think that the main retribution is spiritual and not corporeal; and to those who believe in both kinds, it will stand for both together.

Thus, the number of primary and secondary principles of divine law in general, according to this, are eleven: existence of God, and the four secondary principles derived from it, viz., unity, incorporeality, independence of time, freedom from defects. Then divine revelation and the three secondary principles depending upon it, viz., God's knowledge, prophecy, and the authenticity of the prophet's mission. Finally, reward and punishment, and the secondary principle based upon it, viz., providence. If we combine divine knowledge and providence into one, as Maimonides does, the number will be ten.

It is clear that they should not all be called fundamental principles, because they are not equally essential to divine law. Thus, if one were a dualist or believed in the corporeality of God or that God is subject to time, this would not overthrow the divine law entirely; except for the fact that they are based upon the principle of the existence of God, and one who denies any one of them is virtually denying the fundamental principle, since he does not believe it in the proper manner. For this reason, we did not treat them all alike as fundamental principles, as Maimonides does.

The superiority of Moshe and the immutability of the law we regard as neither fundamental nor derivative principles, because they are

Sefer HaIkkarim — BOOK [Maamar] ONE

not essential to divine law. They are merely like branches issuing from the belief in the authenticity of the prophet's mission. If they are principles at all, primary or secondary, they are peculiar to the law of Moshe, and not common to all divine law. Thus, belief in the Messiah and in the resurrection of the dead are dogmas peculiar to Christianity which can not be conceived without them. But the law of Moshe can be conceived as existing without the belief in the superiority of Moshe and the immutability of the law. It is better to say therefore that they are like branches issuing from the belief in the authenticity of the lawgiver's mission, and not independent principles. Similarly, resurrection and the Messiah are like branches issuing from the dogma of reward and punishment, and not independent principles, primary or secondary, common to all divine law or peculiar to the law of Moshe. Nor do we count the duty of worshipping God alone as a principle, because it is a specific command, and must not be counted as a principle, primary or secondary, as we have explained in the preceding chapter. On the other hand, we count God's knowledge and providence as two separate dogmas, because they are different, as Maimonides explains in the Guide, and as all later authorities agree, though Maimonides himself combines them into one.

We do not include freedom of choice and general purpose among principles fundamental or derived, though they are essentia to divine law, which can not be conceived without them, because they are not essential to divine law qua divine, as was said before. But the special purpose of divine law, namely spiritual reward and punishment, we do count among fundamental principles, because it is essential to divine law. Freedom of choice, however, is not essential to divine law qua divine, and therefore is not counted among principles, whether fundamental or derived. Nevertheless, inasmuch as it is essential to divine law, and is presupposed by it, we will explain it in the Fourth Book. So much concerning the number of dogmas, fundamental and derivative. Blessed be the One who gives aid and determines. Amen, Amen.

Chapter 16

Some ancient thinkers have denied the possibility of knowledge. It is impossible, they say, to know a thing as it really is. And this for two reasons. First, because all knowledge comes from antecedent knowledge. But this antecedent knowledge in turn was an object of investigation and came from antecedent knowledge, and the same thing applies to the latter, and so the thing goes on ad infinitum. But where there is an infinite regress, no knowledge can comprehend it. The second reason is this. Anything that is known through syllogistic demonstration was either known before it was proved or not. If it was known before, it needs no proof. If it was not known before, how could one know that it might be ascertained by proof? For these two reasons they said that there is no such thing as knowledge, and that one can never acquire knowledge which he does not possess.

The true philosophers, however, refuted their arguments. The first argument, they say, does not hold. There is no infinite regress, as the skeptics think, for not all knowledge comes from antecedent knowledge which in turn is the result of investigation. Knowledge may come from antecedent knowledge which is not in turn acquired by investigation or deduction. It may come from knowledge which a person has inherent in his reason. Certain knowledge man has by his rational nature, and it is not derived from another knowledge. This knowledge which is rooted in reason is called first principles. They are first, because they are not derived from another knowledge, but are innate. These principles are the bases of science, and from them is knowledge derived.

The second argument they answer as follows: It is not true that what is not known can never be known. It may be ascertained by syllogistic proof. Before the syllogism is constructed, the thing is known potentially in the premises. The conclusion of the syllogism makes the knowledge actual. And reason itself declares that knowledge arrived at in this way is certain and absolute. These two ways of acquiring and perfecting knowledge are innate in human reason, and one does not know how he comes to have them.

That this is a true conception of knowledge is proven also from Job. Job complains of God's ways and finds fault with God for the imperfect order of nature, as he thinks. Wherefore is light given to him that is in misery, and life unto the bitter in soul? he exclaims. God answers Job by saying, how dare you criticize God's work and God's knowledge as if you knew more than He? And you have the hardihood to say that the order of nature would be better arranged on another plan! You do not even know the causes of those natural things which are in your own body, and you venture to speak about things higher up! You presume to pass judgment on God's knowledge and conduct, when you do not even know how you came by that power which enables you to acquire your own knowledge! This is the meaning of the words used by God in His first answer:

Sefer HaIkkarim — BOOK [Maamar] ONE

Who laid down the security of wisdom? Or who hath given understanding to the mind? I think that the bet of the word **Battuhot** [secure] is part of the root, and not a prefix, as in the expression, and they that provoke God are **Battuhot** [secure]. The word sekvi [mind] is derived from the same root as veistakke, which is the Aramaic translation of the Hebrew vayyashkef, he looked, and signifies the human mind. So, the best commentators understand the word. The first principles or axioms are called battuhot hokmah, securities of wisdom, because they are the foundations of science, giving man the assurance of acquiring knowledge which can not be gotten without them. Sekvi denotes the human intellect, the inventor of the syllogism, by which the conclusion is derived from the premises, the faculty which in Hebrew is called **Dinah** [understanding], and which the Rabbis explain as the power of inferring one thing from another. The meaning of the passage in Job is that God upbraided Job by pointing out to him that he does not even know how he came by the first principles, which are the security of knowledge, i.e., man acquires knowledge through them, but he does not know how they came to him and whence, except that he has them through the will of God, as David said, Behold, Thou desirest the truth of battuhot. This, then, is the meaning of the words in Job, Who laid down the **Battuhot** [security] of truth? i.e., who put them originally in man, or what natural law demands it that they should exist in man rather than in all the other animals? And He says further in His criticism that assuming the existence of the first principles in man, he does not know who gave the human mind intelligence to understand that the conclusion which follows from the premises constitutes knowledge. This, too, exists in man through the will of God. This is what David meant when he said, in allusion to the two kinds of knowledge, Behold thou desirest the truth of battuhot; make me, therefore, to know wisdom of the hidden. The words, thou desirest ... battuhot, refer to the first principles, which exist in man through the will of God. The words, make me ... to know wisdom of the hidden, refer to the fact that the knowledge which is acquired concerning a thing formerly hidden is also due to the will of God. Likewise, King Solomon said, For the Lord giveth wisdom, Out of His mouth cometh knowledge and understanding. The meaning is that wisdom [science] comes from God because out of His mouth, i.e., through His will, come knowledge, i.e., the first principles, and understanding, i.e., the ability to draw a conclusion from premises. These two powers exist in man, but we know not how they come to be there and whence they come. But we know that they are in man

Sefer HaIkkarim BOOK [Maamar] ONE

by divine grace, in order that by means of them man may have knowledge and understanding.

This is the meaning also of the benediction instituted by the Rabbis, beginning, Thou in Thy graciousness divest man knowledge, and teaches intelligent man understanding. The first principles are called knowledge simply. Hence it says, Thou in Thy graciousness divest **Adam** [man] knowledge, meaning that this knowledge is found equally in all mankind, requiring no learning, but exists by divine grace. The sequel, and teachest intelligent **Enosh** [man] understanding, refers to the ability to draw a conclusion from premises, this being the meaning of the term understanding. This ability, he intimates, is based upon natural learning; and it is ascribed to intelligent **Enosh** [man], to indicate that not all **Adam** [mankind] make use of understanding, but enosh alone. The benediction concludes with the words, thou who grantest knowledge, alluding to the kindness of God which includes the entire species, i.e., the gift of the first principles, and not to the special kindness, which is not shared by all. But it is proper that we should pray for more even than knowledge and understanding, we should pray also for intelligence [haskel]. This latter refers to divine things, as we read, That he understandeth [haskel] and knoweth Me. That part of the above benediction, therefore, which contains words of prayer includes all the three, and grant unto us graciously from Thee, knowledge, understanding and intelligence. We pray that the first principles may avail us so that through them we may acquire understanding and intelligence. So also, the Rabbis say, if there is no knowledge, there is no understanding, i.e., if not for the first principles, man would not be able to draw conclusions from premises. And if there is no understanding there is no knowledge. The meaning is, if man is not to make use of his understanding to infer one thing from another so as to acquire knowledge, the first principles [knowledge] are given him in vain.

This is also the meaning of Solomon when he says, for wisdom shall enter into thy heart, and knowledge shall be pleasant unto thy soul; discretion shall watch over thee ... to deliver thee from the way of evil. The meaning is, when wisdom [science], based upon true premises, shall enter into thy heart, and knowledge shall be pleasant unto thy soul, i.e., if you make proper use of the first principles, then shall discretion watch over thee, discernment shall guard thee, that thou mayest not be misled by erroneous ideas. This is expressed in the sequel, to deliver thee from the way of evil, from the men that speak froward things; who leave the paths of uprightness ... The meaning is that understanding if properly used, and based upon true premises, will guide man in the path of uprightness, and he will not stumble.

Chapter 17

Every science makes use of principles and postulates which are not self-evident, but are assumed as true and borrowed from another science in which they are proved. Upon these principles are built all the proofs of the science in question. Thus, the geometrician borrows the conception of line and point from the physicist. The arithmetician borrows the conception of unity and the physicist the conception of substance and accident from the first philosophy. The first philosophy in turn borrows from the physicist the conception of the first mover. So, every theoretical science necessarily assumes at the beginning certain principles and postulates which are proved in another science, as is explained in the Posterior Analytics. Upon these principles or upon the first principles [axioms] are built all the proofs occurring in that science.

This being so, it is proper to inquire where divine law takes its principles. An inquiry like this is more appropriate in relation to divine law than to any conventional law. For the principles of conventional law, viz., freedom and purpose, as we said above, are explained by the Philosopher in his Politics. But where does divine law take its principles? For though the existence of God is proved by the Philosopher on the basis of premises ultimately derived from first principles [axioms], the Philosopher does not believe in prophecy and providence, which are also fundamental principles of divine law. Where, then, are they proved, seeing that they are not self-evident, nor are they proved from premises derived from axioms? For the Philosopher does not believe in prophecy and providence in the manner in which the religionist believes in them. We must therefore explain where the Torah takes its principles.

There are four kinds of things which are known without proof:

    1. First principles [axioms]. For example, we know that the whole is greater than the part; that things equal to the same thing are equal to each other; and that the affirmative and the negative can not be true at the same time in reference to the same thing, in the same relation.

    2. Things perceived by the senses. For example, we know that fire makes hot, and snow makes cold; that opium makes cold, and pepper makes hot. This knowledge we get through our senses.

Sefer HaIkkarim — BOOK [Maamar] ONE

When we eat pepper, we feel hot, when we taste opium, we feel cold. We judge then that pepper heats because the fiery particles in it predominate, and that opium cools because the cold particles predominate in it.

3. Things known by experience. For example, we know that the magnet draws iron; that scammonium is a purgative, etc., because we observe it to be so, not by reason of the qualities of the elements of which these substances are composed, but by reason of their specific form.

4. Things known by the continuity of history. Thus, we know that Rome and Yerushalayim and Babylon were great inhabited cities, though they are so no longer. Things known in this way we believe even though we have not perceived them with out senses as if we had so perceived them, by reason of the reports which come from many people, and which no one disputes.

Every one of these four kinds of propositions may be used as a principle in a demonstration. Just as the proofs in geometry which are all based upon axioms, and the demonstrations in physics, which are based upon sense perception, are true without any doubt because their causes are known, so the proofs which are based upon experience, though their causes are unknown, must not be doubted, since our senses testify to their existence. To illustrate, just as it can never be that the angles of a triangle should not be equal to two right angles, or that pepper should not cause heat, as their causes are known and understood, so it can never be that the magnet should not draw iron, though the cause is not known or understood, for a thing to which experience testifies can not be other than it is.

The fundamental dogmas and principles of the Torah can not be apprehended by way of the axioms; nor are they at any time objects of sense perception like the heating of pepper and the cooling of opium, for their causes are unknown. For this reason, God in His wisdom indicated the truth of the principles of the Torah by experience, so as to remove all doubt concerning them. For that which is proved true by experience, like the property of the magnet in attracting iron, is not subject to doubt, though its cause be unknown, in the same way as there is no doubt concerning natural things observed by the senses whose causes are known.

This is the case in all divine laws. Thus, through the law which was given to Adam he became aware of the existence of God, who spoke to him, of prophecy, revelation and reward and punishment. For God revealed Himself and spoke to him and gave him a law, as we read, And the Lord God commanded the man, saying … The Rabbis say that in this verse all the commandments given to Adam are alluded to. He also verified by experience that there is retribution for obeying or disobeying the commandments. For he was punished because he violated the command of God and allowed himself to be tempted by the serpent through Eve. And the punishments of this world, as we have said, are evidence of the punishments in the world to come.

Noah, too, had evidence of prophecy and of the existence of God, who spoke to him. He realized that there is reward and punishment through the flood, when he and his sons were saved, while the others were punished. This is the reason why he received permission to eat flesh which was prohibited to Adam.

Similarly, when Abraham was given the command of circumcision, he became aware of the existence of God, who spoke to him, and through the same command he realized prophecy and revelation. When the Torah was given, all Israel became convinced of the general principles when through the prophetic spirit they observed that God was speaking to them and that He gave them a law. The exodus from Egypt proved to them that there is providence and reward and punishment. Thus, we see that the principles of the Torah were proved beyond a doubt by experience. It follows, then, that the Torah is true and everlasting, without a doubt, in the same way as in a syllogism if the premises are true, the conclusion resulting from them is true without a doubt. The Torah will never change, for truth is unchangeable.

This is the meaning of the Psalmist; the beginning of Thy word is truth; and all Thy righteous ordinance endureth forever. The meaning is, as the beginning of Thy word, i.e., the premises, which are stated first, in order to derive from them the conclusion, i.e., the ordinance, is true beyond doubt, the ordinance which comes from them is also true, and hence must endure forever, because truth never changes - All Thy righteous ordinance endureth forever. Therefore, the Torah, whose principles are proved by observation of the senses, is true and everlasting, and the tradition proceeding from it is also true without doubt.

To prevent the idea that the principles of the Torah are now known to us by tradition alone, Asaph explains in the Psalm beginning, give ear, O my people to my teaching, that some of the principles are known to us by theoretical speculation, some by the continuity of history, viz., those which no one disputes, and some are purely traditional. This is the meaning of the words in the Psalm, give ear, O my people, to my teaching [Torah], incline your ears to the words of my mouth ... I will utter dark sayings concerning days of old. That which we have heard and known, and our fathers have told us. That which we have heard alludes to the principle of revelation, which belongs to the category of the historical, heard among all nations, which no one disputes, like the former existence of Egypt and Babylon, which can not be denied, though we ourselves have not seen them. Revelation is mentioned first because the author is admonishing us to obey the Torah, Give ear, O my people, to my Torah. The expression which follows, and known, alludes to the principle of the existence of God, and the dogmas derived from it. These are acquired by theoretical investigation, based upon the observation of the senses and the axioms. Our fathers have told us points to the principle of spiritual reward and punishment, which we know by tradition alone.

To prove this principle, he cites the miracles and other instances of special providence experienced by our ancestors, as we learn by tradition; these being evidence of the reward in the world to come, as we shall explain in chapter twenty-one of this Book. He explains further that this tradition must be continuous from father to son. Therefore, he says, we will not hide from their children. He also makes clear that the basis of these principles known to us by tradition was observation by the senses. Then it was handed down to us by a continuous tradition. This is the meaning of the words, For He established a testimony in Yaakov. The meaning is, through the testimony of the senses which our ancestors had, God caused the Torah to be handed down continuously by tradition.

Chapter 18

As there are many laws called divine, and the devotees of every one of them have a continuous tradition, the problem arises how to distinguish between the genuine divine law and the spurious, which claims and pretends to be divine, but is not divine.

The divinity of a law may be proved in two ways, from the law itself and from the lawgiver. So far as the law itself is concerned, we must examine it with reference to the three principles mentioned above and the dogmas derived from them, as we have seen. If the law in question is not opposed to any of the fundamental or derived principles, it is divine; if it is, it is spurious and its claim is a pretence. Viewing the matter from the side of the lawgiver, we must prove in a direct manner that the lawgiver received a prophetic message, and that he was sent by God to give mankind a law. A

Sefer Halkkarim   BOOK [Maamar] ONE

thing may be proved in two ways, directly and indirectly. A thing is proved directly from its causes or essential properties. It is proved indirectly if the proof comes from accidents and not from the causes or the essential properties of the thing.

The following illustration will make the matter clear. Two apothecaries were charged by physicians with the preparation of the great theriaca. One said that he would make a good preparation that would protect from all poisons, warm and cold, and from all kinds of snake bites. He undertook to prove his promise by exhibiting to them the flesh of the viper and all the drugs which go into the composition of theriaca. He tested in their presence the properties and virtues of all the simple drugs, showing that there was no adulteration of any kind. Now there is no doubt that theriaca made in this manner is absolutely genuine, because the apothecary gave a direct verification of the fact. Similarly, if the apothecary undertook to prove the correctness of the preparation by showing that it cures all cases of disease and poison which are treated by theriaca, this mode of proof would also be satisfactory because it makes use of the essential properties of the thing. To be sure this proof is not as good as the first, which proves the thing from its causes, nevertheless both are direct modes of proof, showing that the theriaca is well prepared and has no adulteration.

The second apothecary also promised to make theriaca that would counteract all deadly poison, and cited as proof of his ability that he would walk through fire without being burned, or walk on the water without sinking. Now though he should do this in the presence of everybody and of great men and men of science, it is no direct proof that the theriaca which he made or will make is good. For though he walks through fire without being burned, the theriaca may not have the properties necessary to counteract deadly poisons. For the proof is not direct, and there is a possibility that the theriaca may be adulterated.

The same thing applies to the proof of the genuineness of a prophet or divine messenger. The fact that a person claiming to be a prophet can walk on the water, or divide a river and walk through it, or walk through fire without being burned, or can cure the sick or the lepers, is evidence of the fact that he is a worthy instrument for the performance of miracles. But it is not a direct proof that he is a prophet, much less is it evidence that he was chosen to give a law. For we find instances of miracles performed by incantation and magic, or by righteous men who are not prophets. See the story in in the Talmud **Baba Mezi'a**, concerning the dispute with Rabbi

Sefer HaIkkarim — BOOK [Maamar] ONE

Eliezer. He caused a bread-fruit tree to be uprooted from its place, and the water in a canal to turn back its course and other things besides. And yet the others with whom he disputed refused to make his opinion law, because those miracles did not stamp him as a prophet.

And so, we shall find that all the miracles which Moshe performed before the revelation of the Torah on Sinai, merely proved that he was a worthy instrument for the performance of miracles, but not for the transmission of a law. This is all that the Israelites believed about him. And they followed his directions because they believed that God heard his prayer and granted his requests. He did so in Marah, as we read, And the Lord showed him a tree; also, in the war with Amalek. On account of Moshe' prayer, God caused the manna to descend, and the sea to be divided, as we read, wherefore criest thou unto Me? This is the meaning of the expression used in the narrative of the division of the Red Sea, and they believed in the Lord, and in His servant Moshe. They believed that he was the servant of God, that God performed miracles through him, and that He granted all his requests. We find in the case of other good men too that God performed miracles through them, though they were not prophets. Thus, it is told of Rabbi Phinehas's son of Yair that he divided the waters of a river on three occasions. Miracles were also performed by Rabbi Hanina son of Dosa and Honi ha-Meaggel. The sun shone for Nakdimon son of Gorion, and Hananiah, Mishael and Azariah were saved from a fiery furnace.

Seeing therefore that miracles are not a direct proof of prophecy, the people doubted whether Moshe was a prophet, despite the miracles he performed, which were numerous and of a remarkable character in changing the laws of nature. It is only after the revelation on Sinai that the people said to Moshe, we have seen this day that God doth speak with man, and he liveth. This shows that until that time they were still in doubt about the reality of prophecy, though they believed that Moshe was the servant of God, and that miracles were performed by him, as we read, and they believed in the Lord and in His servant Moshe.

This is the reason why at the time of the revelation on Sinai, God said to Moshe, lo, I come unto thee in a thick cloud, that the people may hear when I speak with thee, and may also believe thee forever. The meaning is, I desire to prove to them directly the reality of prophecy, and also that you were sent by Me to give them the Torah. I will make them experience the prophetic spirit themselves. This will convince them that prophecy is a reality. And they will hear Me

Sefer HaIkkarim — BOOK [Maamar] ONE

speaking to you, and indicating a desire to give them a law through you. This constituted a direct proof of prophecy and of the authentic character of the messenger, and there could no longer be any doubt or the least suspicion of fraud after that sublime experience; for through it was verified the two elements essential to prove the reality of revelation. The reality of prophecy was proved, because they were all prophets at that time, and heard the voice of God speaking the ten commandments. The second element was proved when they heard the voice saying to Moshe, Go says to them: Return ye to your tents. But as for thee, stand thou here by Me, and I will speak unto thee all the commandments, and the statutes, and the ordinances, which thou shalt teach them, that they may do them in the land ... In this they had a direct proof that Moshe was a divine messenger through whom a perpetual law was to be given.

The difference between a prophet and a messenger is this: The veracity of a prophet is proved either when he truly foretells the future in all particulars, or when he performs miracles. If a prophecy is verified in this way, the Torah specifically commands us to obey the prophet no matter what he tells us to do, even if, as a temporary measure, he bids us violate a law of the Torah, as Eliyahu did on Mount Carmel, unless he bids us worship idols. For since he has been tried many times and has been proved reliable, whether in the performance of miracles or in unfailingly foretelling the future, the presumption is that he is a prophet and we are bidden to obey him, as we read about Samuel, and [the Lord] did let none of his [Samuel's] words fall to the ground. And all Israel from Dan even to Beersheba knew that Samuel was established to be a prophet of the Lord. It is like the case of an apothecary who prepared theriaca three times and it was found to be good. The presumption is in favor of his reliability until he is tried again and the theriak is found to be adulterated. Similarly, if a prophet foretells the future or performs a miracle to substantiate his prophecy, he should be believed so long as no untruth is discovered in what he says. The Bible tells us, when a prophet speaketh in the name of the Lord, if the thing follows not, nor come to pass, that is the thing which the Lord hath not spoken. It is possible that one may be a true prophet and yet on a particular occasion say an untruth on his own initiative, not by prophetic inspiration, for God is not man that He should lie. An occurrence of this kind happened to Hananiah the son of Azzur, who was a true prophet, as the Rabbis say in the treatise Sanhedrin. But he made a mistake and spoke untruth when he took the bar from off Jeremiah's neck, and broke it. He was punished for this, as we are told in

Sefer HaIkkarim — BOOK [Maamar] ONE

Scripture. Jeremiah said to him, The Lord hath not sent thee; but thou makest this people to trust in a lie. Then again, this year thou shalt die, because thou hast spoken perversion against the Lord. And further we read, So Hananiah the prophet died the same year in the seventh month.

A messenger, however, i.e., a person who is sent by God to communicate a law, can not say an untruth. For one is not called a messenger unless his mission is verified directly, i.e., when all the recipients are convinced of the reality of prophecy, as was the case of all Israel at the time of the revelation on Sinai, or when the genuine character of the messenger is proved, as was that of Moshe; not by foretelling the future or the performance of miracles, for the test of foretelling the future is not a direct proof of the authentic character of the messenger as a lawgiver. And he may tell an untruth sometimes, as happened to Hananiah the son of Azzur, as we saw before.

Similarly, the performance of miracles is doubtful as a test, for something like them may be performed by some natural science or device. But if his mission is authenticated as was that of Moshe, falsehood can not possibly enter, whether by his own choice or through some one else. Not by his own choice, for God would not authenticate his mission in the manner aforesaid, if he was likely to say an untruth later. Not through some one else, because as long as his mission has been authenticated directly, there is no longer room for any kind of doubt.

This is the meaning of the words of Maimonides in the book Madda in the eighth chapter of the treatise on the Foundations of the Torah. The Israelites did not believe in Moshe, he says, because of the miracles he performed. For those who believe on the ground of miracles, still have a reservation in their minds that perhaps the miracle could be performed by sorcery or magic ... The ground of their belief in Moshe was the revelation on Mount Sinai, when their own eyes saw and their own ears heard the fire and the thunder and the lightning. Moshe came near to the cloud, the voice spoke to him and the people heard: Moshe, Moshe, Go say to them: Return ye to your tents. But as for thee, stand thou here by Me, and I will speak unto thee all the commandment, and the statutes, and the ordinances, which thou shalt teach them ... That the experience at Sinai is the only real and indubitable proof of Moshe' prophecy, is shown in the words, Go, I come unto thee in a thick cloud, that the people may hear when I speak with thee, and may also believe thee forever. This shows that hitherto their belief was not an enduring one, but one that

Sefer HaIkkarim   BOOK [Maamar] ONE

is accompanied by doubt and reservation. So far Maimonides.

His meaning is that the miracles which are performed by the prophets, like the revivification of the corpse by Elisha, and the cure of Naaman's leprosy, and the passing of Hananiah, Mishael and Azariah through the fiery furnace without being burned, and Daniel's coming out of the lions' den unhurt, and Jonah's deliverance from the bowels of the fish, and all the other miracles performed by all the prophets, and the prognostication of the future - all these things are not essential proofs of prophecy, for one may foretell the future through astrologers or by means of familiar spirits. Some of the miracles could be performed for good and pious men who are not prophets, like Rabbi Hanina the son of Dosa, Rabbi Phinehas the son of Yair, and his associates; or they might be performed by means of natural devices, as the Rabbis say concerning Hezekiah, the king of Yehuda, that Ahaz his father caused him to pass through the fire, and yet he was saved, because his mother anointed him with oil of the salamander; or they might be performed by magic and sorcery, as the magicians of Egypt did, or by means of one of the sacred names of God. The divine names are like His instruments, having the virtue of performing miracles. Any one who uses them with God's permission, like the prophets, or in God's honor, like men of piety, is beloved in heaven and esteemed on the earth. He does not die before his time and does not fall into the hand of his enemies. As God said to Jeremiah, and they shall fight against thee; but they shall not prevail against thee; for I am with thee, saith the Lord, to deliver thee. But he who uses them of his own accord and not for the honor of God, will be cut off prematurely, will fall into the hand of his enemies, and his ultimate end will be bad; as the Rabbis say, He who uses the crown will perish. He is like a person who has stolen the king's ring or garments or seal for his own use, who deserves death. Even Isaiah, who was a true prophet, was punished with death because he used a divine name for his own benefit; as the Rabbis say: He pronounced a divine name and disappeared into a cedar tree. His punishment was that he was captured by his enemies and put to death.

This is worthy of notice because herein lies the test of one who uses divine names without God's permission, viz., he dies an unnatural death or is prematurely cut off. The matter has caused perplexity to many who could not understand how it is that bad men can perform miracles by means of divine names, since we are told by ancient authorities that the prophets made use of them, as is indicated by allusion in the three verses in Exodus, beginning respectively with

Sefer HaIkkarim BOOK [Maamar] ONE

the words, And the angel of God ... removed, And it came, And Moshe stretched out. The explanation is that everything depends upon the end. It is thus clear that a miracle is no real proof of prophecy, not to speak of the authenticity of the messenger. Therefore, the miracles which Moshe performed before the Sinaitic revelation were not direct evidence that he was a prophet, much less that he was sent to communicate a law. This was proven first when the people stood at Mount Sinai.

Chapter 19

Belief in a thing means a firm conception of the thing in the mind, so that the latter can not in any way imagine its opposite, even though it may not be able to prove it. Examples are, belief in the axioms, the opposite of which the mind can not conceive; or those things which a person firmly embraces in his thought; or things which he has by nature, not knowing how he came by them; or things apprehended by the senses, or verified by experience, the opposite of which the mind can not conceive though it does not understand the causes of their being as they are.

Belief also applies in relation to a thing which the believer himself did not observe with his senses, but which some one else - a popular and reliable person, or a number of prominent persons - observed at a given time, and which has come down to the believer from the man or men who observed them, by a continuous tradition from father to son. This is worthy of belief almost as much as that to which the believer's own senses testify, though he can not prove it by reason. An example is the testimony of experience to the fact that God may inspire with the prophetic spirit any person He pleases, though he does not possess those natural qualities which the Rabbis enumerate as essential for prophecy. Thus, they say in the **Treatise Nedarim** that the prophetic spirit does not rest upon a person unless he is wise, brave, rich, tall, handsome, etc. And yet experience showed at the time of the Sinaitic revelation that all Israel, the wise and the foolish, the short and the tall, the timid and the courageous, the rich and the poor, all attained the degree of the prophet and heard the voice of the living God speaking out of the midst of the fire, as Scripture testifies, These words the Lord spoke unto all your assembly in the mount out of the midst of the fire, of the cloud, and of the thick darkness, with a great voice, and it went on no more.

Moshe, calling attention to this wonderful phenomenon, says, did ever a people hear the voice of God speaking out of the midst of the

Sefer HaIkkarim   BOOK [Maamar] ONE

fire, as thou hast heard, and live? Though reason rejects it, it is absolutely true, since experience testifies to it, and it has been handed down by tradition continuously from father to son. It can not therefore be denied. For it is clear that no one loves a person more than his father. Hence a matter which has been continuously handed down from father to son properly takes such a firm hold upon the mind of the son that he can not imagine it not to be so, as if he himself perceived it with his own senses, for it is clear that no father desires to leave falsehood behind to his children. So the Psalmist says, O God, we have heard with our ears, our fathers have told us … Thou with Thy hand didst drive out the nations, and didst plant them in … For not by their own sword did they get the land in possession … Thou art my King, O God; command the salvation of Yaakov. The sequence of thought in the above is this: Since we have learned by tradition that Israel's victory over the nations was not a natural thing, that it was not by their own sword that they got the land in possession, neither did their own arm save them; and since this tradition was related to us by our fathers, and it is not possible to have any misgivings or suspicions that they would hand down to us falsehood; since, therefore, Thou wast the cause of the beginning of their success, command now also the salvation of Yaakov, since Thou art my King, O God, and canst do this. All this shows that tradition handed down from father to son should be accepted.

And since a divine law can not exist without it, Scripture commands us concerning it: Ask thy father, and he will declare unto thee, thine elders and they will tell thee. And the penalty that is set for the one who violates the tradition of the wise is death - Thou shalt not turn aside from the sentence which they shall declare unto thee, to the right hand, nor to the left. And the man that doeth presumptuously, in not hearkening … even that man shall die. We are also admonished to honor our parents and to punish the rebellious son, because that which is handed down by a father is almost as trustworthy as that which we perceive with our senses; belief therein is obligatory though to the reason it seems unlikely. Thus we see that belief applies to things which we have not perceived with our senses at the time of their occurrence, nor proved with our reason, but have only on the authority of continuous tradition.

Chapter 20

A thing perceived by an unusually popular and trustworthy person or by a number of persons of superior powers of comprehension or

Sefer HaIkkarim — BOOK [Maamar] ONE

by an unusually large number of persons, is more likely to satisfy the mind of its reality and to be firmly believed than a thing not so accredited. For this reason, God desired that the Torah should be given through Moshe with great publicity and in the presence of a mighty multitude of six hundred thousand people. For according to the wise men of the Cabala this number includes all physiognomies, hence the publicity could not be greater, though the number of persons had been multiplied many times.

According to the Rabbis, the revelation was published before the whole world. Commenting on the verse, The Lord came from Sinai, and rose from Seir unto them; He shined forth from mount Paran ..., they say, Why Seir and why Paran? The answer is, that God offered the Torah to all the world, who refused to accept it. Then Israel came and accepted it. The meaning is that since there were then seventy nations in the world and the text of the Bible mentions only Seir and Paran, it is clear that the reference is not to mount Seir and the wilderness of Paran, but to the whole world. Knowing that founders of religion were to arise in the future in Seir, i.e., the people of Edom and those associated with them, and in Paran, i.e., the people of Ishmael and those related to them, - two nations including the whole world, and both descended from Abraham, the first true believer, God published before these nations His revelation of the Torah to Israel, pointing out to them that the revelation of a divine law must be published very widely, else it is not divine. This is so because an order which passes between God and the prophet alone leaves a suspicion or doubt in the minds of others, even of those living in the same generation, not to mention those who come after. Thus even in the case of Moshe, the Israelites did not fully believe in his prophetic character until the day of the revelation on Sinai, when they heard the voice speaking to him, as we saw before.

This is the reason why the Torah was not given completely to Abraham, Yitzhak or Yaakov that they should command their children after them to keep the way of the Lord. For though the tradition should be handed down by them continuously from father to son, some suspicion or doubt might occur to those who came after in future generations, because those who received the law first were individuals. The case is different where the thing is clearly perceived by a very great number of persons embracing many wise and intelligent men, representing a great variety of opinions. This is the reason why the Torah was given through Moshe with such great publicity, in order, namely, as I said before, that no suspicion or doubt should remain in the minds of the recipients and their associates, nor in the minds of those who come after, so that the tradition may be as firm and true as it is possible to make it.

This is the meaning of the saying of the Rabbis in the treatise Abodah Zarah, In the future God will take the Torah in His bosom and say, 'Let all those who occupied themselves with this, come and get their reward.' At once all the nations of the world will come crowding before Him, pell mell, as is said, 'All the nations are gathered together, and the peoples are assembled; who among them can declare this ...?' 'This' means the Torah. The Rabbis mean to say that in the future God will bring all the idolatrous nations to justice because they did not fulfil the divine law. Then we are told in the sequel that God will say to them, wherewith have you busied yourselves? And they will reply that they concerned themselves with social welfare, as is recounted at length in the haggadic passage above cited. Finally, God says in reply, all that you did was not for social welfare, but for your own selfish ends. Is there any one among you who can declare this? i.e., is there any one among you who can say that he fulfilled the divine Torah? They will then reply in turn that as the Israelites are to be rewarded for observing the Law which they received by tradition, so they should be rewarded for fulfilling their law, which they also received by tradition. God will then reply, who among you can declare this, and announce to us former things? Let them bring their witnesses, that they may be justified the meaning is that the nations who claim that they relied on their tradition, must tell us former things, i.e., they must tell us the principles of their religion, which they accepted and upon which they relied. They must tell us whether they were perceived by the senses with great publicity, as were the principles of the Law of Moshe. Let them bring their witnesses, that they may be justified, that those who received that law may hear and say, it is truth; as those who received the Law of Moshe can produce their witnesses, because the principles of their religion were published before an assembly of six hundred thousand persons, who received the Torah. And then the text concludes, Ye are My witnesses, saith the Lord, i.e., all Israel are witnesses of the divine revelation of the Torah, for they heard the voice of the Lord God, speaking to them the Ten Words. The words, And My servant whom I have chosen, refer to Moshe, who is called the servant of the Lord. All of you are witnesses that the Torah is divine.

This is a wonderful interpretation of these verses according to the idea of the Rabbis that the text cited deals with the reward that follows upon the fulfilment of the Torah as a whole. And it is true.

Sefer HaIkkarim — BOOK [Maamar] ONE

For since the principles of the Torah were declared with great publicity, no doubt can possibly occur concerning the truth thereof. Hence one should have a firm faith in the law of Moshe, especially so since its principles are so clear that no doubt is possible, as we explained in chapters seventeen and eighteen of this book.

Chapter 21

Belief in God and in His Torah brings man to eternal happiness and causes his soul to cleave to the spiritual substance. This is proved by experience, as we know from continuous tradition. We know of no instance of a philosopher or other investigator attaining to the degree of the prophet, which means the union of the divine spirit with the human intellect. We do find that the devotees of the Torah came into such close intellectual union with God that they were able to change the laws of nature, cause the latter to do their bidding and perform miracles against the laws of nature. Thus, we find that the prophets proposed and God carried out their proposals. Eliyahu caused fire to descend, which is contrary to its own nature. He said, If I be a man of God, let fire come down from heaven ..., and it was so. He also divided the waters of the Jordan. Elisha cured Naaman's leprosy and brought a dead body back to life during his own life time and also after his death. Many such incidents happened to him and the other prophets. The same thing is true of all believers. Pious men, even if they are not prophets, can change the laws of nature by prayer. Hananiah, Mishael and Azariah were cast into the fire and were not burned. Rabbi Hanina the son of Dosa and Rabbi Phinehas the son of Yair made certain temporary changes in the nature and conduct of the world.

This shows that one who believes in God and in His Torah is above nature and not subject to natural law. On the contrary, the laws of nature are subject to him, and he can change them as he pleases.

This is strong and convincing proof that the Torah is divinely revealed, since God shelters, protects and shields those who trust in Him and who observe His covenant and commandments. This is what David meant when he said, the word of the Lord is tried; He is a shield unto all them that take refuge in Him. The meaning is that the proof of the divine Torah being pure and free from all dross and defect and suspicion is that He is a shield to those who trust in Him, that He performs the will of those who fear Him, that He hears their cry, fulfils the word of His servant, and carries out the plan of His messengers.

Sefer HaIkkarim   BOOK [Maamar] ONE

This is also a proof that the soul after death is united with spiritual beings. For union during life is a proof of union after death. Moshe alludes to this when he says, but ye that did cleave unto the Lord your God are alive every one of you this day. He is speaking with reference to the philosophers, who believe that only the perfect individual can unite with the spiritual beings, but not an entire congregation; but you, he says, do all of you cleave unto God. Moreover, the philosopher believes that such union is possible only after death in the spiritual life; whereas you have attained this union this day while enjoying material life, much more certain is it that you will attain it after death. He proves that such union is attainable during life from the fact that God accepts the prayer of those who ask Him to change the laws of nature in the conduct of existence. This is the meaning of the verse in the sequel, for what great nation is there, that hath God so nigh unto them as the Lord our God is whensoever we call upon Him? All this shows that belief in God and in His Torah gives perfection to the soul, causes it to unite with the celestial beings, and subjects' nature to its will. Through faith the soul rises high above the things of nature, and can therefore control them. This is why Abraham's faith is praised, and he believed in the Lord; and He counted it to him for righteousness. Moshe and Aaron were punished because they did not believe, because ye believed not in Me, to sanctify Me … therefore ye shall not bring … We also read in the Bible, Believe His prophets, so shall ye prosper, showing that belief is the cause of prosperity and happiness. It is also the cause of eternal life, as Habakkuk says, But the righteous shall live by his faith. This can not mean physical life, for the righteous man lives no more than the wicked. The reference is to eternal life, the life of the soul, which the righteous enjoy, and which they trust that God will enable them to attain, as we read, But the righteous, when he is brought to death, hath hope. The meaning is that the righteous hopes to attain that good when he dies, but when the wicked dies, his hope perishes, as we read in the Bible, when a wicked man diets, his expectation shall perish. For the wicked can not attain spiritual life after death, and they do not enjoy union with God during life. Therefore, they are always accounted as dead, as our Rabbis say, Righteous men are called living even after death; wicked men are spoken of as dead even while they are alive. This is why we find that miracles are performed for men of faith, and not for men of speculative knowledge, so as to show that faith stands higher than speculation and the things of nature. Therefore, one may through it attain true union with God during life and after death, which is higher than nature.

Chapter 22

All belief does not lead to happiness. Thus, belief in the impossible does not produce happiness. No one doubts that belief which makes a man happy must be belief in the truth, not belief that a non-existing thing exists or that an existing thing does not exist. The question therefore arises, how can we tell whether a thing is true and demands implicit belief or is not true and should not be believed. If we say that the question must be determined by reason, it will follow that ratiocination stands higher than faith, which contradicts what was laid down before. This is a difficult matter which we must endeavor to solve.

There are two kinds of impossibility. There is the essentially impossible, which we can not conceive that even God can make possible. For example, the whole is greater than the part, and the diagonal of a square is greater than the side. Now we can not conceive that God can make the part equal to the whole, or the diagonal of a square to the side, or the angles of a triangle equal to more than two right angles, or two contradictory propositions to be true at the same time about the same subject, or the affirmative and the negative to apply at the same time to the same thing in the same relation. Such impossibilities can never be accredited by tradition. Nor can our senses ever testify to their reality or the reality of anything similar, because the mind can not conceive the existence of any such thing. Such things therefore should not be believed. Thus, it can never be accredited by tradition that God can create another being like Him in all respects. For the one would necessarily be the cause and the other the effect, and they would no longer be similar in all respects.

There is another class of impossibility which it is conceivable that God may make possible - namely that which is merely impossible according to the laws of nature. Such things are not impossible for God, even though they are impossible according to the laws of nature, for example, resurrection of the dead, a human being who can live forty days and forty nights without food and drink, and other wonderful things of the same kind which are impossible by the laws of nature. This second kind of impossibility may be believed, since the mind can conceive of its existence. We may lay it down as a rule, therefore, that any thing which the mind can conceive, though it be impossible by the laws of nature, may be believed to have existed in the past, to be existing now, or to come to exist in the future. This is particularly true if experience testifies to the existence of the thing, though the mind denies its existence because it does not know the cause. Such a thing may be believed, for example the property of the magnet by which it attracts iron. The mind can not explain the cause, and is inclined to deny the reality of the phenomenon. But since experience testifies to it, and it is something that the mind can conceive, though it can not explain the cause, it is true without doubt. Similarly those things to which the senses testify, like the miracles of the Bible, such as the revival of the dead by Elisha during life and after death; remaining forty days and forty nights without food and drink, as Moshe and Eliyahu did; the descent of fire from heaven; the presence of the Shekinah in Israel, and the other miracles which were observed in the past, and which the mind can conceive though it can not explain them - all such things may be believed as being possible to the Omnipotent Being.

Chapter 23

There are six dogmas which every one professing the law of Moshe is obliged to believe. They are connected with the three fundamental principles that we laid down, but they are not derivative principles.

1. Creation of the world in time out of nothing. It is clear from its nature that it is a dogma common to divine law generally and belonging especially to the Law of Moshe, though it is neither a fundamental nor a derivative principle, because we can conceive a divine law in general and the Law of Moshe in particular without the idea of creation ex nihilo, as we explained in chapter twelve of this book. But it may be likened to a branch issuing from the first principle, which is the existence of God. We explained above that God is free from defects. Now if He can not create out of nothing, this would be a defect in His nature. We can not say that creation ex nihilo is ipso facto an impossibility, that creation must be out of something. For since the mind can conceive it, it may be believed, and comes within the power of the Omnipotent Being. Even those who believe in the eternity of the world, admit that God, though a simple intellect, is the cause of all things. Therefore matter is caused by God through the instrumentality of the Separate Intelligence which is also caused by God. But how can a Separate Intelligence be a cause of matter if there can be no coming into being ex nihilo? There can be no greater creation ex nihilo than this. If you say that

Sefer HaIkkarim — BOOK [Maamar] ONE

the reason they maintain the eternity of the world is because they can not conceive that He should create or produce at one time rather than at another, our answer is that this difficulty is valid only in the case of an agent who acts by necessity, but not in an agent who acts by will, for it is the nature of the will to act at one time rather than at another, as Maimonides explains in the Guide of the Perplexed, Book II, chapter 18. Now since God, being the best of agents, must act voluntarily and not through necessity, as will be explained in the Second Book, it follows that He must produce the world at a particular time; since this follows necessarily from the nature of will.

2. The second dogma is the superiority of Moshe prophecy to that of all other prophets who ever were or will be. Though this dogma is not essential to divine law in general nor the Law of Moshe in particular, nevertheless since the Torah says explicitly, And there hath not arisen a prophet since in Israel like unto Moshe [the meaning is that there has not arisen and there will not arise, indicating the high value of the law that was given through him, as we will explain in the Third Book], every one who professes the Law of Moshe is obliged to believe it as a dogma issuing like a branch from the principle of revelation.

3. The third dogma is that the Law of Moshe will not be repealed nor changed nor exchanged for another by any prophet. This dogma, too, though it is not essential to divine law in general or the Law of Moshe in particular, as we explained above, nevertheless it is like a branch issuing from the dogma of the authenticity of the messenger, and therefore it is incumbent upon every one who professes the Law of Moshe to believe it, as we will explain in the Third Book.

4. The fourth dogma is that human perfection may be attained by fulfilling even a single one of the commandments in the Law of Moshe. If this were not so, it would follow that the Law of Moshe hinders man from attaining human perfection, which the Rabbis call the life of the world to come. For mankind attained some degree of future life through the **Noachian law**, as the Rabbis say, the pious men of the Gentiles have a share in the world to come. This means that those who observe the seven Noachian commandments have a share in the world to come. Now if every one professing the Law of Moshe must fulfil all the many commandments mentioned therein before he can attain any degree of future life, then the Law of Moshe would hinder man from the acquisition of perfection rather than help him. But this can not be the purpose of the Law, as the Rabbis say, God desired to bestow

Sefer HaIkkarim BOOK [Maamar] ONE

merit upon Israel, therefore He gave them many laws and commandments. Therefore, it seems that this dogma is a special principle of the Law of Moshe, as we shall explain in the twenty-ninth chapter of the Third Book.

5. The fifth dogma is the resurrection of the dead. Some of our Rabbis say that only those who are perfect will have this privilege. According to this opinion, since it is not a species of reward promised to all mankind, since all mankind can not be perfect, one who disbelieves this dogma is like one who denies some one of the great miracles performed for righteous men, which are within the limits of logical possibility. This dogma would then come under the first principle. But if resurrection embraces all persons, as some of the authorities hold, then a person who disbelieves it is like one who denies a part of reward and punishment which is promised to all mankind or to the whole nation. In that case the dogma comes under the third principle. But it is not itself either a fundamental or a derivative principle of divine law in general or of the Law of Moshe in particular, for they can be conceived without it. As long as one believes in reward and punishment generally, whether corporeal, in this world, or spiritual, in the world to come, he does not deny a principle of the Law of Moshe if he disbelieves in resurrection. Nevertheless, it is a dogma accepted by our nation, and every one professing the Law of Moshe is obliged to believe it, as will be explained in the Fourth Book.

6. The dogma of the coming of the Messiah is of the same nature as the one before. It comes under the third principle, reward, and is an accepted dogma, which every one professing the Law of Moshe is obliged to believe, as will be explained in the Fourth Book. But it is not a principle, fundamental or derived, of the Law of Moshe, because the latter with its principles, fundamental and derivative, can be conceived without it.

We did not include among these dogmas, beliefs which are based upon specific commandments, like repentance, prayer, etc., for example the dogma that God hears the prayer of those who supplicate Him, or that He receives those who turn to Him in repentance, and other such dogmas based upon specific commandments, because no one commandment should be counted as a dogma rather than another. Nor did we include such beliefs as that the Shekinah dwelt in Israel, that fire came down from heaven upon the altar of the burnt-offering, that the priests received answers from God through the Urim and the Thumim, and so on, because they are included in the belief in the biblical miracles generally, and

Sefer HaIkkarim BOOK [Maamar] ONE

there is no reason for naming these rather than others, such as the dividing of the Red Sea, the opening of the earth and the swallowing of Korah and his congregation, their going into Sheol alive, and the still more wonderful phenomenon of the earth closing up again after they went down, as we read, And the earth closed upon them, so different from an opening made by an earthquake, which remains that way forever, - all these are included in a belief in the Torah and in the miracles told therein. We did enumerate specially the six beliefs above mentioned, because they are accepted dogmas among our people necessary for the maintenance of the fundamental and derivative principles of the Torah. The fulfilment of the Torah is dependent upon them, though they are not essential principles, since the Law can exist without them, as we explained above. He who denies them is called a heretic, though he does not deny the Torah, and has no share in the world to come.

Chapter 24

We must call attention here to a question concerning religious belief. Is a person who professes a given religion permitted, or obliged, to investigate the principles of his religion in order to see whether they are true and in agreement with what we have laid down concerning the principles of divine law or not? And assuming that he is permitted to do this, has he the right to choose that religion which seems to him the truer or not? Whichever alternative we adopt offers great difficulties.

In the first place, if we say that one professing a religion is obliged to investigate the principles of his religion, or is permitted to institute a comparison between the principles of his religion and those of another, the result will be that no religionist will be firm in his belief, and will therefore deserve no reward for belief, if he is not firm therein and free from doubt. For we can not call a thing belief except when the mind can not conceive the thing being otherwise, as we explained before. But if he investigates, he shows thereby that he is in doubt. And if we grant that he is permitted to investigate, suppose he has investigated and compared the principles of his religion with those of another, and found the principles of the other religion truer than those of his own, is he permitted to exchange his religion for the other? If he is permitted, the result will be that no man professing a religion can be made happy or be saved by his belief. For if, having compared the principles of his religion with those of the other and found the latter truer than his own, he has exchanged his religion for the other, it is still impossible for him to be firm in the belief of the other religion which he has chosen, because it is possible that after another investigation and a comparison between the second religion and a third, he may find the principles of the latter more satisfactory, and will have to change the second for the third, and in the same way the third for the fourth and the fourth for the fifth, and so on indefinitely. The result will be that no man will be firm in his belief until he has completed his investigation of all the religions in the world and chosen one in preference to all the rest. But there is the possibility that there is a religion at the extreme end of the inhabited world which is unknown to him, and which is truer than all the rest. No man therefore can be saved by his belief. For he can not have perfect faith until he has investigated all religions, and he can not investigate all religions, as we have seen. It would seem then that a person should not be allowed to investigate the principles of his religion so as to reach sure belief.

But if our conclusion is that one is not allowed to investigate the principles of his religion, then one of two things must be true. Either all religions lead to human happiness, and one has no advantage over the other in the matter of reward and punishment, since no one is allowed to investigate the principles of his religion nor to change it for another. But it is quite impossible that religions which are directly opposed, the one affirming what the other denies, the one trinitarian, the other monotheistic, should equally lead to happiness. On the other hand, if we say that they do not both lead to happiness, but one of them only, a great absurdity will follow, namely that God is guilty of injustice [Heaven forbid] in punishing those who profess a false religion, claiming to be divine, since the believer has no right to budge from his religion, or to change it for another, or to entertain any doubt concerning it. This difficulty applies to all divine religions and we must try to solve it.

Our solution of this question is as follows: If it were true that all the known religions of the world are opposed to one another, every one saying that the other is not divine, the question we raised would be a difficult one indeed and hard to solve. But since all religions agree in accepting the divinity of one of them, the only objection to it being that, according to them, it was temporary in character and its time has passed, our opinion is that every one should investigate the principles of his religious belief.

This applies without any doubt to those religions which are opposed to the one divine law, for no one should allow himself to be persuaded to believe something in opposition to the admittedly divine law, except after an investigation of the law, the second or the third, which he is inclined to believe, and the principles thereof, as we explained in the eighteenth chapter of this Book.

As for the admittedly divine law, one who professes it should also inquire whether it is temporary or eternal; and if it should turn out not to be eternal, wherein the change is likely to occur.

This is also Maimonides' reason for saying in the fortieth chapter of the second book of the Guide of the Perplexed that it behooves every one to investigate the religion which he professes. He says there that the investigation should embrace two aspects. First, the religion itself. He must examine the commands and prohibitions, and if he finds that their sole purpose is to remove wrongdoing and violence and to maintain order in the affairs of the state, he must know that it is a conventional and not a divine law. If, on the other hand, he finds that in addition to removing wrongdoing and violence, it also takes care to inculcate true ideas about God and the angels, and endeavors to enlighten mankind and to awaken them to the nature of truth in relation to all things, that shows it is divine. The second aspect of investigation is that of the founder of the law in question. The alleged prophet or messenger who claims that the law is transmitted through him by God must be examined with a view to determine whether his claim is genuine or whether the contents of his law are borrowed from some one else. The thing to examine is the man's character and conduct. The best test of genuineness is that he abstains from corporeal indulgences and holds them in contempt, especially the sense of touch, which is a disgrace to us, as Aristotle said. This is the gist of Maimonides' words in that chapter.

When he says that a test of the law itself is, if it takes pains to inculcate true ideas about God, etc., he is alluding to that religion which ascribes to God corporeality and trinity. And when he speaks of testing the moral qualities of the founder of the religion, he is alluding to that man who claimed that he was a prophet of the Arabs. According to Arab accounts he was addicted to physical and sexual indulgence. But this is not sufficient to enable us to differentiate a law laid down by a wise man, containing true principles such as a divine law might have, the founder himself being a man of noble character and conduct, from a divine law. There is no way of telling whether it is really a divine law or a human law which resembles a divine.

My opinion therefore is that the two-fold examination of which Maimonides speaks is to be understood in the following way. First, the principles of the religion in question must be examined, to see whether they agree with the principles of divine law which we have mentioned. Also, the secondary principles derived from the first must be examined, as we explained in the fifteenth chapter of this Book. If we find that the religion in question is in agreement with, or at least not in opposition to, the primary and secondary principles, and at the same time it endeavors to suppress wrongdoing and to inculcate true ideas among the people instead of the foolish fancies in vogue among women and common people, and to arouse them to a desire for human perfection, that shows it is divine.

Similarly, our Rabbis say in **Torat Kohanim**: Rabbi Akiba said - Thou shalt love thy neighbour as thyself is a great principle of the Torah. Ben Azzai said - This is the book of the generations of Adam is a greater principle of the Torah than that. By this is meant to indicate that a divine law must embrace both topics, the suppression of wrongdoing and violence among the inhabitants of the land, as alluded to in the expression, Thou shalt love thy neighbour as thyself, and the directing of the attention of the people to true ideas and to human perfection, which is alluded to in the verse beginning, This is the book of the generations of Adam, which continues with the words, In the day that God created man, in the likeness of God made He him, indicating that man has a human form which is in the likeness of God. And therefore, he must be careful not to disgrace it, either in his own person or in the person of his neighbor, and he must see to it that it should survive death and unite with the celestial beings in the place from which it originally came. All this a divine law should contain.

But it is still possible that it is the work of a wise man or wise men. We must therefore examine it from another aspect, namely the manner in which the messenger proved his authenticity, as one sent by God to transmit a law. If this matter is proved in a direct manner, as we explained in the eighteenth chapter of this book, the law is divine; if not, it is spurious and merely pretends to be divine, even though it acknowledges all principles, primary and derived, much more so if it opposes them or any one of them.

Chapter 25

We shall now inquire whether there must be one divine law for all mankind, or whether there may be more than one. It would seem that there can be only one, whether we consider the matter from the point of view of the giver or from that of the receiver. So far as the giver

Sefer Halkkarim   BOOK [Maamar] ONE

is concerned, it would seem that since God who orders all things is one in every respect, the order which comes from Him must also be one in every respect, for the relation of God to all human beings is the same. So far as the receiver is concerned, it would seem likewise that since the human species is one so far as their humanity is concerned, that order which guides them to attain their human perfection must also be one. From this it would seem that there can be only one divine law for all mankind.

However, on more careful consideration we shall find that though we may admit that so far as the giver is concerned there should be only one, the same result does not follow if we consider the receiver. It is clear that the temperaments of men are different either because of the difference of temperament in their ancestors or for some other reasons. No two men can have the same temperament and disposition, as Ibn Sina says in the first fen of the first book of the Canon. The differences are so great that we find persons whose qualities are the direct opposites of one another. One man is cruel in the extreme, going so far as to kill his youngest child, and another is so tender-hearted that he would not kill a mouse or an ant.

The differences in character and disposition are also due to difference in habitat. Different lands differ in respect to air, mountains, waters, and so on. There are lands in which the fruits are coarse and hard, because the air in which they grow is not pure. Then you find another land whose fruits are not sweet or wholesome because the water by which they grow is not good. The temperament of the animal beings who are nurtured on such fruits necessarily partakes of the character of the food on which they live. Another land whose fruits have a quality opposite to that of the other will produce animals with temperaments opposite to those of the other. This is why we find in one city or district sharper and cleverer men than in another. And it follows from this that the conventions and customs of the two lands are different as the temperaments of their inhabitants are different. The one land must therefore have a different law from the other at the same time. Since, however, the difference is due to the receiver and not the giver, it must relate to things which have to do with the receivers, namely in reference to the customs and conventions concerning what is becoming and unbecoming. What is becoming in one place will be unbecoming in another. But there can be no difference in the general fundamental principles or those derived from them, because these are things which depend upon the giver.

For this reason, you will find that the Noachian and the Mosaic laws, though differing in matters of detail, as we shall see, agree in the general matters which come from the giver. They both existed at the same time. While the Mosaic law existed in Israel, all the other nations had the **Noachian law**, and the difference was due to geographical diversity, Palestine being different from the other lands, and to national diversity, due to difference in ancestry. And there is no doubt that the other nations attained human happiness through the **Noachian law**, since it is divine; though they could not reach the same degree of happiness as that attained by Israel through the Torah. The Rabbis say, the pious men of the other nations have a share in the world to come.

This shows that there may be two divine laws existing at the same time among different nations, and that each one leads those who live by it to attain human happiness; though there is a difference in the degree of happiness attainable by the two laws. This difference in the laws can not concern fundamental or derivative principles. Therefore, the examination of the law itself is always of the same kind. But the examination relating to the messenger may undergo change. At all events the verification must be direct, though the verification of one religion may be different from that of another. The question whether a given divine law may change for the same people in the same land, we shall examine in the Third Book.

Chapter 26

The result of our discussion in this Book is that the number of fundamental principles of a divine law is three, existence of God, revelation, and reward and punishment. Without these we can not conceive of a divine law.

Subordinate to these three are other secondary principles derived from them and related to them as species are to their genera, namely that if you remove one of the derivative principles you do not remove thereby the fundamental principle, but if you remove the fundamental principle, the derivative principles disappear also, as we have explained.

The derivative principles coming under the existence of God, as demanded by reason and by the Law of Moshe, are: unity, incorporeality, independence of time, freedom from defects. Under revelation we have prophecy and authenticity of the messenger. Under reward and punishment are: God's knowledge and providence in reward and punishment, in this world or in the next, spiritual or corporeal.

There is no need of laying down any other principle of the Law of Moshe, fundamental or derived from these, except those mentioned. We have already explained that the duty to worship God exclusively is a commandment, and that a commandment is not a principle, either fundamental or derived. The irreparability of the Torah and the superiority of Moshe as a prophet come under the authenticity of the messenger, as will be explained in Book Three. The coming of the Messiah and the resurrection of the dead are implied in the belief in reward and punishment, such as every one professing the Law of Moshe should believe.

This is also the opinion of my teacher Rabbi Hasdai Crescas, that all these as well as creation are true doctrines which every one professing the Law of Moshe should believe, but they are not principles of this law, derivative or primary, general or special. One special principle of the Law of Moshe is that one single commandment is sufficient to enable one to acquire perfection and some degree of future life, as we explained in the twenty-third chapter of this Book.

The other laws, called divine, lay down other derivative principles under the fundamental ones, the removal of one of which makes the law fall. Thus, the Christians put under the existence of God trinity and corporeality. But it is clear that this is opposed to the derivative principles which follow from the existence of God. Under reward and punishment, they place the coming of the Messiah and resurrection of the dead. Without these it is clear that their religion can not exist. Similarly, the Mohammedans place fate and predestination, called in Arabic **Al Kada** and al kadr, under providence. But it is clear that if this were true, there would be an end to freedom of choice, and there would be no room at all for reward and punishment. The reason we did not include freedom of choice among the fundamental principles of divine law, though it is essential to it, is because it is not a principle of divine law qua divine, but it is necessarily presupposed in any code of law, whether human or divine.

Accordingly, the number of principles, fundamental and derived, is eleven: existence of God, unity, incorporeality, independence of time, freedom from defect, prophecy, authenticity of the messenger, revelation, God's knowledge, providence, reward and punishment. If we count God's knowledge and providence as one, as Maimonides does, the number of principles will be ten. And if we count freedom among the principles of divine law, since it is necessarily

Sefer Halkkarim   BOOK [Maamar] ONE

presupposed by it, though it is not essential to it as divine, the number of principles will be twelve or eleven. We did not include purpose in general as a principle of divine law, although it is presupposed in any system or code of law, human or divine, like freedom, because the special purpose of divine law is the reward that is promised, and that has already been included as a principle.

Here ends the First Book which inquires into the number of fundamental and derivative principles and the attributes common to divine laws. Praise be to God who has helped us thus far. This was all that I had intended to say in this work concerning the fundamental and derived principles. At the request, however, of my friends, orthodox believers as well as philosophers, who asked me to explain to them the meaning of these principles and other matters following from and related to them in a proper manner which is in agreement with the opinion of the Torah, I added the three Books which follow. Therefore, I promised at the beginning of the book to explain them, with the help of God who is above all praise. Amen.

Sefer HaIkkarim
ספר העיקרים

BOOK OF PRINCIPLES

BOOK [Maamar] TWO

Introduction

Wherein is explained the first principle, the existence of God, and the derived principles based upon it and following from it, which every one professing a religion should believe. As we said in the first book, the secondary principles which are based upon the existence of God are four: unity, incorporeality, independence of time, freedom from defect. In order that these derivative principles may be made clear, we must first explain the fundamental principle from which they are derived, namely the existence of God. Then we shall explain the derived principles one by one, that we may know how many there are.

Before doing this, however, I shall preface an Observation which is essential for every one who reads this book.

Observation

The reader of this book must bear in mind that there are many statements made in certain parts of this book representing not the true view but the views of the person quoted, while in another part of the book the statements are made in accordance with the true view. Or expressions are used in one place with one meaning and in another place with a different meaning. Maimonides does this often in the Guide of the Perplexed. Thus in the third chapter of the first part he says that the meaning of the biblical expression "And the similitude of the Lord doth he behold," is that he comprehends the true essence of God, whereas in the thirty-seventh chapter he writes that the expression, "But My face shall not be seen," means: My real essence as it is cannot be comprehended. And he calls attention to this in the fifty-fourth chapter and in other passages of the first part, viz. that God's real essence can not be understood by any one else.

For this reason, the reader of a book must be careful, and not be too hasty to criticize the words of the author, until he becomes familiar with the style and method of the book, and has read all that is said on the topic in question in other parts of the book. For sometimes a premise is left out in a given place because it seems obvious, or because it is explained elsewhere, or the omission is intentional, in order to conceal the idea from the reader, whereas the latter thinks that the author has made a mistake, and hastens to criticize him and thinks him a fool or an ignoramus.

We find frequent examples of this in logical arguments. Thus, if one were to say: Every man ought to know his creator, because every rational being ought to know his creator, a person might object to the argument as fallacious because it does not say that man is a rational being, and as long as the minor premise of the syllogism is not given, the point at issue can not be proved. This is true, but logicians know that a speaker or an author frequently suppresses the minor premise, as when one says: Every man is a sensitive being, because every animal is a sensitive being. Here the minor premise, every man is an animal, is suppressed, and without it the thing desired is not proved. But one should not therefore be called a fool or an ignoramus.

For this reason, the reader of a book must not be too hasty to criticize as things occur to him at first sight, but he must bear in mind that the author was not a light-minded person who failed to comprehend after long study what occurred to the reader at first sight. The reader should rather suspect his own understanding and say to himself that it is impossible that the author should have made such an obvious mistake. He should rather ascribe the error to his own thinking, and study carefully the words of the author until his real meaning becomes clear to him. For the author is often so engrossed in the profound theoretical problems that he does not think it necessary to explain a certain matter at length. This makes it hard for the reader to understand it. The reader must be very careful in this matter, or he will be in the position of those who criticize the Law of Moshe on the ground that it permits the profanation of the holy name, for it says, "And thou shalt profane the name of thy God;" or that it forbid one to do good to his enemy, for it says, "If thou see the ass of him that hateth thee under its burden, thou shalt refrain from helping him." The fault is their own, because they do not take pains to understand the rules of the language or to read what is said in another place, which may serve as a commentary on the passage in question, for example, "And ye shall not profane My holy name," and many others.

Chapter 1

The term **existence** which is applied to all existing things is a subject of dispute among philosophers, whether it denotes an accident of the existing thing or whether it is something essential. However, the term existence as applied to God can not denote an accident, because God is not receptive of accidents, as we shall explain. Nor can it be an essential element added to God's quiddity. For then God's essence would be composed of two things, which is impossible, as we shall see. It follows therefore that the term existence when applied to God denotes nothing else but His quiddity. But His quiddity is absolutely unknown, as Maimonides explains. For he says that this is what Moshe desired to know when he said to God, "Show me, I pray Thee, Thy glory." And the answer came to him, "Thou canst not see My face, for man shall not see Me and live." The Rabbis in Sifre, commenting on this, say, "Not even the angels, who are living beings." The meaning is that His quiddity is known to none beside Him. It follows, therefore, that His existence also is absolutely unknown, even to the angels. This being so, one may ask, how can that be a principle of divine law which no one can comprehend except God Himself?

The answer is that the existence of God is not a principle of the Torah from that side which is impossible of comprehension, namely from the side of God's quiddity, but from the side which is possible of comprehension, namely from a consideration that all existing things are due to His influence, that He is their cause and their maker. From this point of view, we can estimate God's excellence as the one who made existing things to be with extreme perfection and splendor. From this aspect one may speak of God and estimate His excellence. But we can not speak of God's essence because it is altogether ineffable. David alludes to this in the Psalm beginning, "Bless the Lord, O my soul." Alluding to the first aspect, he says, "O Lord my God, thou art very great," i.e., from the side of Thy quiddity Thou art very great, so that man can not speak about Thee, and with all this, "Thou art clothed with glory and majesty," i.e., from the side concerning which it is possible to speak about Thee, namely from the visible activities which come from Thee. They show Thy glory and Thy majesty. Therefore, he describes in the sequel the creations which come from God, and which point to

God's excellence and perfection by the perfection which is visible in them.

The excellence of an artificer can be seen in his work in two ways. It may show that he has made a wonderful piece of work out of excellent material. Everybody can see then that this excellent piece of work was made by an excellent and accomplished workman. For example, if one sees beautiful vessels made of gold and precious stones, these vessels no doubt point to the great excellence of him who made them. Or the artificer may have made beautiful vessels with fine engravings out of inferior material. A goldsmith, for example, made beautiful vessels with beautiful engravings out of iron. This surely shows the artificer's great skill and perfection, since he was able to make such beautiful figures and engravings on iron, which is an unyielding material that resists the work of the engraver. Surely, he can do wonderful work on more promising material.

So, Aristotle, in the eleventh book of his work On Animals, criticizes the ancient scientists who refused to treat of the nature of the inferior animals arising from putrefaction, and studied only those born of the union of male and female. Aristotle says that there is more reason for studying the inferior animals produced by putrefaction than the others, not because of the animals themselves, for they are very low and composed of very inferior material, being produced from putrefaction, but by reason of the divine power contained in them. For it shows the excellence and perfection of the producer, who infused the power of life into such inferior material, so that from putrefaction and without the union of male and female there arises an animal being similar to that which is born of the union of male and female. It thus redounds to the credit of the artificer.

Similarly, David praised God in both ways because of the creations of both kinds which emanate from Him. Referring to the first kind he says, "Who coverest Thyself with light as with a garment." This alludes to the creation of the world of the Separate Intelligences, which are called light, as we shall see when we speak of the homonymous use of the word light. Then he alludes to the world of the spheres when he says, "Who stretchest out the heavens like a curtain." Then he describes the enduring and great and awsome creations which are visible to all, like light and the heaven and the dry land and the creations upon the earth. He describes also the visible order imposed by God in perfection upon the works of creation, so that the animal beings may live and endure, "Who sendest forth springs into the valleys; they run between the

Sefer HaIkkarim   BOOK [Maamar] TWO

mountains; They give drink to every beast of the field ..." Then he speaks of the renewal of the moon every month, and of the order of day and night, which is the cause of the continued existence of the sublunar world and of all the animals according to their different degrees, pointing to the wisdom and excellence of the Creator, who appointed "the moon for seasons; the sun knoweth his going down." This is, the cause of day and night, for the maintenance of existing things, of the appearance of the land and the existence of the other awsome creations.

After having completed the praise of God by reason of the great and important creations, he recounts His praises from the other side, namely from the aspect of the inferior creations, produced by putrefaction, "How manifold are Thy works, O Lord. In wisdom hast Thou made them all; ... Yonder Sea, great and wide, therein are creeping things innumerable, living creatures." The Psalmist mentions here the creatures formed in the sea and those which are produced through putrefaction, which have not the power to reproduce their species, as is clear from the closing words, "Thou withdrawest their breath, they perish, and return to their dust. Thou sendest forth Thy spirit, they are created; and Thou renewest the face of the earth." Such expressions do not apply to creatures which are born of the union of male and female. To be created after returning to their dust can refer only to those which are produced through putrefaction. The reason he says in the beginning, "How manifold are Thy works, O Lord. In wisdom hast Thou made them all ..." is to indicate that the wisdom and excellence of an agent are shown when he endows with perfection a very inferior material, such as the material of those animal creatures arising from putrefaction, which God has endowed with the perfection of life. This shows the wisdom of the Maker. This is the reason why he adds, "May the glory of the Lord endure forever; let the Lord rejoice in His works ...", to indicate that even these low creatures arising from putrefaction are the cause of God's joy. He rejoices in them because they are His work and make known His wisdom.

The Rabbis, too, allude to the same thing in "Perek Shirah" when they ask, "What do the creeping things say?" and reply, "May the glory of the Lord endure forever; Let the Lord rejoice in His works." The meaning is that though it might not be becoming to God's dignity and His excellence and perfection to rejoice in such inferior creatures, nevertheless we may speak metaphorically of His rejoicing in them because they are His work. And the meaning of "May the glory of the Lord endure forever" is that without slighting in any way God's glory, which is eternal, we may say nevertheless that these creatures, born of putrefaction, low and insignificant as they are, having no permanence either as species or as individuals, give God cause for rejoicing because His wisdom is seen in them, which are His work, as we have explained. Thus the Psalmist praises God in this Psalm as the Maker of existing things in the two ways in which the excellence of the maker is seen. And it is in this way alone that we know the existence of God, i.e., as the Maker of existing things, not from His quiddity. This is why the Torah begins with the account of creation, showing the existence of God, the author of existing things, as we explained in Book One. This is the way we must understand the existence of God as a fundamental principle.

Chapter 2

There are two kinds of agents. There is one kind that does primarily and essentially only one thing, like the heat of fire, which heats, and the cold of snow, which cools. This kind is called natural agent, not voluntary or intentional. Then there is a kind which does contrary things. This is a voluntary agent, which acts from choice. It does a thing when it wants to, and then does the opposite when it wants to. Now it is clearly absurd to suppose that the work of God comes from Him as from the first kind of agent, for a natural agent is not separated from the act. Thus, light is not separated from the lamp, heat is not separated from fire, but God is something different from the act. Moreover, a natural agent is defective, doing a thing not with consciousness and understanding, but by necessity, when there is a recipient ready at hand; as fire burns if it finds an object capable of burning. But that which must necessarily act when the occasion presents itself is defective, since it has no power to refrain from the act or to do the opposite. But God can not have any defect, therefore His activity can not be of this kind.

But it seems inappropriate that God's work should proceed from Him as from an agent of the second class. For the term voluntary applies where the agent desires and does a given thing at a given time, which he did not desire before. The term voluntary does not apply to a thing which is always in the same condition. It follows therefore that the one who has will changes from a condition of not willing to a condition of willing. If so, he is affected by, and receives change from another, for a thing can not be active and passive at the same time in the same relation. But God can not change, nor be affected by another. Nor can He be affected by Himself, for He would then be composed of two elements, an element by virtue of which He acts, and an element by virtue of which He is acted upon. But there can not be any composition in God at all, as we shall see. Nor can God be active and passive at the same time. It follows therefore that God's activity can not be voluntary, since He can not change. Moreover, an agent possessed of will lacks the thing which he desires. But God does not lack anything which He desires at any time and did not have before. Similarly, one who exercises a choice chooses one of two things because that thing is more suitable to him than the other. He therefore lacks the thing which he chooses before he has chosen it. It follows, therefore, that God's activity can not be due to choose or will. But if He does not act with choice and will, nor like a natural agent, as light comes from the sun, as we explained, how can God be called an agent?

I have seen some authorities say that God does act with choice and will, but these do not arise in Him in time as they do in us, but are eternal. Accordingly, they say, God created the world when He did and not before, by an eternal will which decreed that the world should come into being when it did. We also find statements of the Rabbis indicating that they entertained a similar view. Thus, they say, God stipulated with the works of creation that the Red Sea should divide, that the fire should not burn Hananiah, Mishael and Azariah. From this it seems that their purpose was not to attribute to God a newly originated will at the time of the occurrence of the miracle. Therefore, they say that the miracle occurred when it did through an eternal will, which determined that the miracle should take place when it did.

But this opinion is far from intelligible. For if we examine the expression eternal will, we find that it is a spurious conception, and points to necessity rather than will. For the question remains as it was originally. When the world was created or when the miracle occurred through His eternal will, was it possible for God to postpone it to another time, or not? If He could postpone it, then the eternal will was nullified. For the reason He did not postpone it was not because of the eternal will, but because He did not desire at that moment to postpone it. If He had desired to do so, He would have postponed it. And if it was not possible for Him to postpone it because so the eternal will had decreed, then there is no such thing as will any more, and He becomes an agent acting by necessity and not with will, since He could not postpone the act if He would. We should have to say the same thing about all miracles and all acts proceeding from Him at any time, that they happen by necessity, and that the thing could not help being when it is, for so it has been determined by God's eternal will, which can not be changed. If this were so, man would be more perfect in his acts than God. For man can do either of two opposites equally, for example, he can paint the board black or white as he chooses whenever he chooses; whereas God can do only one of two opposites, the one that is determined by His eternal will; Heaven forbid that this should be the case!

Chapter 3

Since we understand by will the origination of a new state in the agent which leads him to do something that he did not do before the volition originated, the philosophers have said unseemly things about God, maintaining that His activity can not be voluntary. This opinion not only upsets all the principles of the Torah completely [for if God does not act with will, He can not act at one time rather than another, a supposition which leads to the doctrine of eternity in the absolute sense, and to the rejection of all the miracles in the Torah. Prayer ceases to be of any avail in time of distress, and right conduct and repentance are useless, and so on], it is also opposed to the demands of rational speculation. For it is an axiom that God must have ail perfections and be free from all defects. This is the meaning of the prophet when he says, "Thou that art of eyes too pure to behold evil, and that canst not look on mischief." Seeing that it would be a defect in God to look on mischief, the prophet says that He can not do so, meaning that nothing should be attributed to God which looks like a defect.
But it is clear that one who can not act voluntarily is deficient and can be called an agent only in a loose and figurative manner. Thus when we say, the fire burns, the sword kills, the lamp shines, these expressions are figurative. For the act of killing with the sword and of illuminating a house with a lamp can properly be attributed only to a free agent, namely the human being who killed with the sword and lit the lamp in the house. Similarly, if one throws a garment into the fire and it is burned, though it is the fire that did the burning, nevertheless we attribute the burning of the garment to the man who threw it into the fire, and say, so and so burned the garment. The reason is because man is a true agent, since he acts from choice and voluntarily; therefore, the act is attributed to him. But the other agencies, like the lamp, the sword and the fire, are deficient, for they have not the power to do or not to do, except according to the will of the man who acts by means of them. They are like instruments in

his hands, like an axe or a saw, of which the Bible says, "Should the axe boast itself against him that heweth therewith? Should the saw magnify itself against him that moveth it?" The meaning is, It is not proper that the axe which is an instrument should boast itself of being called agent against the one that heweth therewith, for the latter is the agent; nor is it right that the saw should magnify itself against him that lifts it up easily, as one lifts a rod, or magnify itself against those who lift it up easily, as one lifts a light staff, not as one lifts a heavy log. Isaiah says this about the king of Assyria, who thought that he was the agent who ruled over nations with wrath as he desired. But the prophet points out that he is nothing more than an instrument, that God acts through him, and sends him to execute judgment against a godless nation and the people of His indignation. Therefore, he says in the beginning, "O Asshur, the rod of Mine anger, ... I do send him against an ungodly nation, and against the people of My wrath do I give him a charge ... Howbeit he meaneth not so, neither doth his heart thinks so ..."

All this shows that the instrument is not the true agent, but he is the agent who wields the instrument with his will. Therefore, when we say of God that He is the maker of existing things, or that He does a particular thing, it can not be that He does them in the manner of the defective agents who have not the choice to do or not to do. For then man would be superior to God, seeing that a human being can either burn a garment or not burn it, whereas God has not this power. But how is it possible that He who has infinite power can not do what man can? It is clear therefore that the work of God must be like the work of perfect agents, i.e., those who act from choice and with will, whom we consider perfect agents.

The solution of the great difficulty which results from the assumption that God's activity is voluntary, is as follows: If the will and the choice which God exercises in His activity were of the same kind as the will and the choice of man, the difficulty above mentioned would be real, the difficulty, namely, that they would produce change in the agent. But as God's will is not of the same kind as ours, no absurdity results. For God's will follows His wisdom and His power, and as His wisdom and His power are infinite and not of the same kind as our wisdom and power, so His will is not of the same kind as our will. And as the wisdom and knowledge of God are not something added to His essence, as we shall see later, but are of His very essence, and His essence is absolutely unknown, His wisdom is also absolutely unknown. And when we attribute wisdom to God, all that we understand is that we

Sefer Halkkarim   BOOK [Maamar] TWO

deny the attribute of ignorance, which is the opposite.

In the same way we attribute will to God in the sense that we deny that He acts by necessity like the defective agents of finite power, God's activity being with infinite power. This being so, it follows that God's activity must be voluntary, as it is in perfect agents, but not that we understand the nature of His will. For His will is essential in Him, and as His essence is absolutely unknown, so is His will absolutely unknown. We say that He acts with will only that we may convey the idea that He does not act from necessity without intention and will. If you ask, how does He change from a condition of not willing to a condition of willing, we reply with another question, how does He change from the condition of knowing man before he comes into being to the condition of knowing him after he has come into existence? For there is no doubt that these are different states of knowledge.

There is no way out of this difficulty except by saying either that His knowledge is not of the same kind as our knowledge, and that it does not cause change in Him as our knowledge causes change in us, or to commit the grievous heresy of attributing ignorance to God and saying that He does not know any particular thing that originates in the world, but the universal only, that He did not know Moshe while he was in existence any more than He knew him before he existed and after he ceased to exist and that God does not know opposites, else He would have different kinds of knowledge. The best solution is to say that His knowledge follows His wisdom, and as His wisdom is of His very essence and not something added to His essence, and is absolutely unknown, so His knowledge and His will and His power, which follow His wisdom, are absolutely unknown. And the only understanding we have of them is that His activity is like that of the best agent. Now since we find that he who acts with power and intention and will is a better agent than one who has not these, we say that God acts with power and intention and will, though we have not the ability to understand the nature of the intention and will. But we do know that the will does not cause any change in Him, for change would be a defect.

As this matter of the will is an obvious difficulty, which occurs at first sight, the difficulty, namely, that will implies change from not willing to willing, we find that the prophets solve it in the manner we have indicated. Isaiah says, "Seek ye the Lord while He may be found, call ye upon Him while He is near; Let the wicked forsake his way, and the man of iniquity his thoughts; and let him return unto the Lord and He will have compassion upon him, and to our God,

Sefer Halkkarim   BOOK [Maamar] TWO

for He will abundantly pardon." And he continues, "For My thoughts are not your thoughts, neither are your ways My ways, saith the Lord. For as the heavens are higher than the earth, so are My ways higher than your ways, and My thoughts than your thoughts." The meaning is as follows: The people of Isaiah's day were in doubt about this matter. They said, how is it possible that after it has been determined that a certain wicked person shall die, he should, by repenting, annul the divine determination? If this is so, then God would change from a condition of willing to a condition of not willing, but it is impossible that God should first desire to punish the wicked person and then change His mind and no longer desire to punish him. Because of this difficulty they made up their minds that repentance is of no benefit to the wicked person. This difficulty Isaiah solved by saying, "For My thoughts are not your thoughts …" Because at first sight it might seem that there is a change in God's will, he says, "For My thoughts are not your thoughts, neither are your ways My ways …," i.e., as there is a difference between His knowledge and our knowledge, the two not belonging to the same class at all, so there is a difference between His will and our will, and between His ways and our ways, there being no similarity between them at all. This he indicates by the expression, "For as the heavens are higher than the earth, so are My ways higher than your ways …" For it is well known that we can not say about two things that the one is higher than the other unless they are both high and one is higher than the other, their difference being one of degree. For example, we say fire is higher than air, for the term high applies to both of them, but fire is higher than air. But if the one is the extreme of height, like the heaven, and the other the extreme of lowness, like the earth, to which the name high does not apply at all in any degree, we can not say that the one is higher than the other. And if we do use this expression, we mean that there is no relation or similarity between them at all, for the term high applies to the one, the heaven, but it does not apply at all to the other, the earth, which is the extreme of lowness.

The relation is the same, the Bible says, between God's thoughts and ways and our thoughts and ways. As the term height does not include heaven and earth, for the term applies absolutely to the heaven, but does not apply to the earth at all, so is the relation of God's thoughts and ways and knowledge to our thoughts and ways and knowledge. That is, there is no relation between them at all, and they do not come under the same genus. For God's knowledge is called knowledge in the absolute sense, while ours is not called knowledge at all. Therefore, the word knowledge can apply to the two figuratively only, for they do not differ merely in degree, they are not at all of the same genus, like the word height applied to heaven and earth. Height applies to heaven, but it does not apply to earth at all, rather the term low, and hence the two do not come under the same genus, height. And as we can not compare our knowledge to God's knowledge, so we can not compare our will to His will. And though our will necessitates change in us, God's will does not necessitate change in Him. This is the meaning of the sequel in Isaiah, "For as the rain cometh down and the snow from heaven, ... so shall My word be that goth forth out of My mouth: It shall not return unto Me void, except it accomplish that which I please." The meaning is that the divine desire is not like the human desire, which is sometimes not fulfilled. The divine desire is always realized, and there is no one to prevent Him from carrying out His will. This shows that the example is intended to explain the matter of the will, namely that His will and desire are not of the same class as our will and desire. Therefore, they do not cause change in God though they do cause change in us.

The upshot of all this is that God's work is done with will and desire, and yet it does not cause any change or defect in God's nature. Therefore, we can apply to Him the word agent with intention and will, which is the best kind of agent.

Chapter 4

We have already explained in the First Book that the Torah begins with the story of creation to prove the existence of the Maker. The account of the way in which the things passed from potentiality to actuality proves the existence of an agent who brought them into actuality. And the fact that they passed into actuality at different times, namely in the six days of creation, shows that the agent is one who acts with intention and will, and does things at different times as His wisdom dictates, though they could have all come into being at the same time. The reason they were produced at different times is to indicate intention and will. For these are at the basis of the Torah as a whole and of the reward and punishment mentioned therein, as we said before. And the Rabbis say also, "The world could have been created with one word. And the reason there were ten is in order to exact punishment from the wicked ... and to give reward to the righteous." The order in which the different things came into being denotes the natural priority of some creatures over others, and shows that every one of them came into being at the time that was suitable and appropriate to its nature, so that it may realize the utmost perfection of which it is capable, as the wisdom and will of the Maker had decreed. The expression, "And God saw that it was good," which concludes the account of every work of creation points to the idea just mentioned.

From the testimony of the senses in regard to the passing of things from potentiality to actuality, we can find a rational proof of the existence of God, as follows: We see things which are potential and then become actual. Now every thing that passes from potentiality to actuality must have a cause outside of it. For if the cause were within and there is no obstacle, the thing would never be potential at all, but always actual. And if, the cause being within, there was an obstacle preventing its actualization, which was removed, then that which removed the obstacle is the cause of the thing's passing from potentiality to actuality. Now that cause, which was itself potential before it became actual, was in this condition either because of an obstacle in itself, or because of the absence of a certain relation between the agent and the thing acted upon; and as soon as the relation appeared, the cause became actual. Whichever of these alternatives we adopt, there must be something that removes the obstacle, or that produces the required relation. But the same thing applies to this thing that removed the obstacle or brought about the relation, and this can not go on ad infinitum. We must therefore finally reach a cause actualizing the potential, which has no potentiality at all. For if it had it would be subject to possibility. This means to have the possibility of existing or not existing. But if so it would need another actualizing cause which would determine one of the alternative possibilities in preference to the other. This other therefore would be an actualizing cause without potentiality or obstacles, but one that does whatever it desires with its simple will, and it is a necessary existent.

It can not be material, for a material thing is subject to possibility and can not be a necessary existent. It is clear also from this that it is abstract or separate. But an abstract cause without possibility that causes things to pass from potentiality to actuality is God. It is clear that He is not body, and it is also clear that He is one, for the abstract is not susceptible of numerical quantity, except in so far as the one may be the cause and the other the effect. But the abstract without possibility is necessarily a cause and not an effect, for the effect is a possible existent, since its existence is dependent on another. It follows therefore that He is one. It is also clear that He is independent of time, for if He were dependent upon time, He would exist at a particular time and not at another, and then He would be subject to possibility. It is also clear that He is free from defects, for if He were defective, His work could not be absolutely perfect, whereas we see that all His works are as perfect as they can be, as the Bible says, "The Rock, His work is perfect." It is clear therefore that He is free from defect.

This proof of the existence of God is equivalent to the fourth proof mentioned by Maimonides in the Guide, where he treats of the existence of God and the principles which follow from it. It is a biblical proof which is in agreement with philosophy, and is alluded to in the creation story in Genesis, as we have seen.

Chapter 5

There are other philosophical proofs of the existence of God mentioned by Maimonides in the beginning of the second part of the Guide, which I will mention briefly to call the attention of the reader to those which are valid and those which are not. The first proof of Maimonides is based upon the existence of continuous and eternal motion, as is assumed by the Philosopher. But this is not admitted by any of those who profess a divine law and believe in creation. Nor can our senses testify to such a doctrine. We did not therefore trouble to mention that proof.

But the second proof given by Maimonides is very weak, because it is based on a premise cited in the name of Aristotle which is not proven to be true. The proposition is that if of a thing composed of two elements one element is found to exist also by itself apart from the composite thing, then it follows that the other element must also be found to exist by itself apart from the compound. For if their nature compelled them to exist in combination only, like matter and natural form, neither could exist without the other. The fact therefore that one element does exist by itself shows that there is no such necessity, and therefore the other too must exist by itself. An example of this is sakanjabin, a drink composed of vinegar and honey. Since honey is found by itself also, it follows necessarily that vinegar also is found by itself.

Then the argument proceeds as follows: We find many things composed of a mover and a moved. That is, they both move others and are themselves moved by others while they move the others. We also find a thing which is moved, but does not move another, viz. the last moved thing. It follows therefore that there must be a thing that moves another, but is not itself moved by another. This is the First Mover.

This proof is based upon the proposition above mentioned, which Maimonides cites in the name of Aristotle, but it is not true. For it does not follow that because one of the two elements of a composite thing exists alone, the other must exist alone also. Thus man is composed of animal and rational, and animal also exists by itself without rational. But rational does not exist by itself without animal, unless we say that angel is rational alone, i.e., actually intelligent without being body, nutritive and sentient, which is the definition of animal. To be sure, it is possible to object to this example by saying that animal does not exist alone, but in combination with some specific form, thus neighing animal, braying animal, roaring animal, but animal in the abstract does not exist by itself. And therefore it is not necessary that rational should exist by itself without any other form. But this is not the case in mover and moved. Still, inasmuch as the opponent may dispute the proposition in a way by citing animal or plant which is composed of body and soul, and yet body exists alone, whereas animality or the vegetative force does not exist alone, Maimonides did not rely on this proof and cited a third philosophical proof which is very strong and can not be disputed, as Maimonides says.

The argument is as follows: Existences must belong to one of three classes.

[1] They are all without origination and destruction.
[2] they are all subject to origination and destruction
[3] some are subject to origination and destruction and some are not.

There is no escape from this classification.

Now they can not all be without genesis and destruction, for we see with our senses many things coming into being and ceasing to be. They can not all be subject to generation and destruction, because if all existing things were subject to generation and destruction, all existing things would be possible existents, and they would all have been destroyed, and there would be no cause to compel their existence in preference to their non-existence. Nothing would therefore exist, since there is no cause to produce or maintain them or to compel their existence in preference to their non-existence. And yet we see that they exist. It follows therefore that there is an existent, not subject to generation and destruction, one that has not the possibility of being destroyed, and that this being compels the existence of those things which are subject to generation and destruction, in preference to their non-existence. This being is a necessary existent, not a possible existent. For this being is determined to exist either by virtue of itself or by virtue of its cause. If by virtue of itself, then it is God. And if by virtue of its cause, then its cause is a necessary existent by virtue of itself, and it is God, who produces all things that are subject to generation and decay. Without Him a thing can not exist, and He is not subject to generation and decay.

This is a very strong proof of the matter, because it shows the existence of God through a necessary classification, and not because existing things require a Maker, which is the essence of the first proof, as we have seen. Therefore, Maimonides says that it can not be rejected or disputed except by one who does not know the methods of proof. He points out also that it follows from this that He is not corporeal. For we have made clear that God is a necessary existent by virtue of Himself, and such a being is incorporeal. For all body is composed of two things, and the composition is the cause of its existence. Hence it can not be a necessary existent through itself, because its existence is dependent upon the existence of its parts and their composition. It is clear therefore that He is not body, nor a force residing in a body. It is easily proved also that He is one. For it is impossible that there should be two necessary existents equally, without any composition. For there must necessarily be in each one of them the element of necessary existence and another element by which it is differentiated from the other. The necessary existent would therefore be composed of two elements. But we have seen that the necessary existent can not have any composition in it at all. It is also clear that He is not subject to time. For everything that is subject to time is subject to change, and everything that is subject to change has a cause that makes it change. But the necessary existent through itself has no cause which makes it change. Nor can He be the cause and the subject of the change at the same time, for then He would consist of two elements, the element which causes the change and the element which undergoes the change, and He would be composite. It is also clear that He is free from defects. For if He had a defect, He would have need of another to make good the defect, and He would not be a necessary existent through Himself but through another.

Though this proof is valid and reliable, as we have seen, nevertheless Maimonides cites a fourth proof, which is the first one that we mentioned in the preceding chapter, because it agrees with the statements of the Torah in the account of creation. We gave it here first because it is biblical and at the same time is in agreement with

Sefer HaIkkarim — BOOK [Maamar] TWO

philosophy. We find also that Ibn Roshd relies upon this proof in the fourth question of his book - **Destructio Destructionis.** We followed it by this second proof, because it is a philosophical proof which Maimonides believes in, saying that it can not be objected to or disputed. We have proved therefore the principle of the existence of God by means of two valid demonstrations.

Chapter 6

Every one professing a religion who believes in the principle of the existence of God, as we have just proved it, must believe that there is in the world a Being, a necessary existent through Himself, having no cause, nor any one similar to Him. He is the cause of all existing things, whose continuity of existence is dependent upon Him, but His existence is not dependent upon them or upon any one else. This is God.

This statement gives a formal or conceptual understanding of that which was proved demonstratively in the preceding chapters. It is well to understand that as a definition or description gives a formal or conceptual understanding of the thing defined or described, so the word "existent" here is like the genus, which embraces all existing things, and the expression, "necessary existent through Himself," is the essential difference between it and the other existing things. The other words, namely that He has no cause, that there is nothing similar to Him, and so on, are merely the explanation of "necessary existent through Himself," for the purpose of giving us as complete a formal or conceptual understanding as can be had of God's existence.

In reality, however, it is neither a definition nor a description, God having no definition. For a definition is composed of genus and difference, but the word existent is not a genus which is predicated of all its subjects synonymously, as a genus is. For there is no genus in the world which includes God and another. The word existent is not applied synonymously to God and to other things. God's existence is real [absolute], whereas the existence of other existing things is acquired from His existence. But if existent is not a genus which includes God and other things, He has no difference. The expressions, there is no one similar to God, there is no one equal to Him, are words indicating otherness merely, i.e., that God is not the other existing things, for all of them acquire their existence from Him and have no existence without Him, but His existence does not depend upon their existence.

Sefer Halkkarim   BOOK [Maamar] TWO

From this principle follow the four secondary dogmas which we mentioned in the First Book, denial of which constitutes heresy. They are: unity, incorporeality, independence of time, and freedom from defect.

It is clear from the meaning of unity that it is an essential element in the principle of the existence of God and follows from it, as we have demonstrated. For if He were not one, but two or more, every one of them would necessarily have two elements, the element of necessary existence and an element by which he is differentiated from the other. He would then be composite, the composition would be the cause of his existence, and he would not be a necessary existent through himself.

It is also clear that incorporeality is an essential element of the principle of the existence of God and follows from it in the same way. All body is composed of matter and form. In every composite the composition is the cause of its existence. We thus get back to the proof of the unity. But even if we say that body qua body is not necessarily composed of matter and form, that body qua body has no composition at all, but is one by definition, and that the true view is that of the ancients; [in fact Ibn Roshd writes in the eleventh book of the Metaphysics that this is the opinion of Aristotle, and that there is no necessary composition in all bodies, the heavenly body being one in every respect and without any composition. The composition which we perceive in bodies, he says, comes merely from the specific form which is imposed upon body] - in which case we might say that God may be corporeal though He is one - nevertheless He must be incorporeal, because if He were corporeal, He would necessarily have to be finite, and He would then be similar to other bodies, and His power would be finite. But there is nothing similar to God, as we said before. Besides, one body can not move another body without itself being in motion while moving the other. But if so, it needs another mover outside of it which is not body. This mover then and not the body is the necessary existent.

It is also clear that independence of time is an essential element of the principle of the existence of God and follows from it. For if He were subject to time, He would not be the cause of all existing things, for time would be prior to Him. He would then have come into existence after a state of non-existence, and would require a cause to bring Him into existence, and would not be the cause of all things. And if He existed always with time, He would not be a necessary existent through Himself, but through another, viz. time, unless time is an immeasurable duration without which we can not think at all. Similarly, if He is not everlasting, He has the possibility of not-being, and that which has the possibility of not-being is not a necessary existent. In general, if He is dependent upon time and His existence is dependent upon the existence of time, He is not a necessary existent through Himself.

It is also easy to see that freedom from defect is an essential element of the dogma of the existence of God. For if He were defective, He would stand in need of another, and would not be a necessary existent through Himself, but through another.

Chapter 7

From these four secondary dogmas which follow, as we have seen, from the first principle, the existence of God, there issue many branches. Thus, from the first derivative dogma, unity, it follows that we must reject such divine attributes as wisdom, strength, generosity, etc., because they are all attributes added to the essence. But since God is one in every way, He can not have either essential or accidental attributes, for they all involve multiplicity and are inconsistent with unity.

From the second derivative dogma, incorporeality, it follows that we must not ascribe to God any corporeal emotions, such as anger and sorrow and joy and grudge, for all these are emotions associated with body or corporeal force.

From the third derivative dogma, independence of time, it follows that His power is infinite, and that He has infinite ability and infinite perfection. Therefore there can not be in Him any equality or similarity to other things. For since they all emanate from Him, their power must necessarily be finite, and having a finite power, they are dependent upon time. But God who produced them, since He is their creator, is eternal and infinite. This is the meaning of the biblical text, "I am the first and I am the last, and beside Me there is no God, i.e., since I am eternal there is no God that can be equal to Me. In the same strain is the following passage, "To whom then will ye liken Me, that I should be equal? Saith the Holy One. Lift up your eyes on high, and see; who hath created these?"

From the fourth derivative dogma, freedom from defect, it follows that we must not ascribe to God anything that looks like a defect, such as ignorance, weariness, etc.

Now there is no need of asking why we named these four dogmas as derived from the first fundamental principle, and did not mention the dogmas that God is wise, possessing will, powerful, living, and so on, in the same way as we mentioned unity. Or why we did not mention such dogmas as that God has no genus or difference, or one similar to Him, or opposition, or change, and so on, in the same way as we mentioned incorporeality. Or why we did not mention such dogmas as that God is infinitely perfect, that He is true and blessed, just as we mentioned independence of time. For the answer to all this is plain from what we have just said. They are all branches issuing from the derivative dogmas above mentioned. Thus, that God is wise, and living, and possessing will, and powerful, and so on, is all included in the fourth derivative dogma, freedom from defect. From the same source are derived such attributes as righteous, upright, faithful, kind, strong, merciful, gracious, and similar attributes which signify perfection. That God has no genus, species, or accident, that He is not in place, and so on, is all included in the dogma of incorporeality. That God does not change, that He is infinitely perfect, and so on, is all included in the dogma of independence of time. For everything that is subject to time is liable to change and is finite. That God has no one equal or similar to Him, and so on, is all included in the dogma of unity. That God is true is included in the first fundamental principle, the existence of God. For the word true real means nothing else except that His existence depends upon Himself and not upon another, as we shall make clear when we explain the word true. Blessed means nothing else except that He bestows upon all existing things all the perfection of which they are capable, as we shall explain later. In short, from these four dogmas issue like branches all those things which have relation to God, those which are attributed to Him as well as those which should not be ascribed to Him. We will now explain every one of these four derivative dogmas by itself. But we must first explain the subject of attributes, namely what attributes are to be ascribed to God and in what way.

Chapter 8

It is clear without much reflection that an attribute ascribed to a thing to denote its activities does not imply plurality in the essence of the active thing. For many different acts may proceed from one agent. And this is true of both kinds of agents, the natural as well as the voluntary.

Thus take a natural agent, like fire. Fire melts certain things, while it hardens others. It boils and it burns, and it makes black and it makes white. One who does not know the nature of fire might think that it has six different forces, from which the six different results follow, which we have mentioned. He might think that there is an element by which it boils, an element by which it burns, an element by which it makes black, an element by which it causes the opposite of blackness, namely it makes white, an element by which it melts, and another element by which it does the opposite, viz. it hardens. For he would say, it is not possible that one and the same agent should produce opposite effects. But he who knows the nature of fire, understands that with one and the same force which it has, namely heat, it does all those things, and that the results are different because of the difference in the recipients, without there being any multiplicity in the essence of fire.

The very same thing applies to a voluntary agent. Thus, the rational faculty in man, who is a voluntary agent, does many different things though the agent is one. He acquires the sciences and the arts, he governs states, he rips and he sews, he destroys and he builds, and does a great many different and opposite acts, though he is one and simple. For there is no one who holds that the rational faculty in man is composite. Similarly, the human soul as a whole is the author of many different natural activities, like nutrition, growth, sensation, and of voluntary acts, like the activities of the conative and the rational faculties. And yet there is no philosopher who maintains that the human soul is composite. But since we find the function of growth by itself in plants, the function of sensation in animals, and the function of ratiocination by itself in the Separate Intelligences, some have been led to think that the human soul is composite, as some physicians have written that man has three souls. But it is not so. The various functions and activities come from one and the same human soul.

Maimonides has explained this matter in the introduction to his commentary on the treatise "Abot." He cites as an example three dark places, one of which is illuminated by the lighting of a lamp, the second by the rising of the moon, and the third by the rising of the sun. Every one of these three places has in it light, a substance which causes sight to pass from potentiality to actuality, and the word illumination is applied to them all synonymously and not by way of priority and posteriority, and yet since the causes are not the same, they are different with respect to their causes. Similarly the faculties of growth and sensation in man are not the same as the faculties of growth and sensation in animals and plants, but the activities come from the human soul as they come from the souls of the ass and the eagle, though their causes are different. He also says there that they have nothing in common except the name. In conclusion he says: This is a matter of great importance and deserving of notice. Many of those who philosophize go astray in relation to it and derive theories and opinions which are far-fetched and untrue.

From these words of his it appears that from one existent there may come many different acts, some natural, some voluntary. He who does not understand the nature of the human soul will think that the many acts must come from so many different powers or faculties. But he who reflects upon the rational faculty and considers that though it is one and simple and without multiplicity, yet we say about a person, he built that house or that city, he destroyed it, he conquered a certain land, he invented a certain science, without all this necessitating multiplicity in the essence of the rational power, will understand that many acts may come from one agent. And if we find this to be the case in the sensible and inferior agents of our experience, how much more is this likely to be true in the First Agent, who is the cause of all acts, natural and voluntary. This is why we say that though we perceive that many different acts come from God, they do not necessitate any plurality in Him.

This is the reason why philosophers are permitted to ascribe attributes to God, different because of different acts, whether in different recipients, like the power of growth in the plant and the power of animality in the animal, or in one recipient, as for example that He is now gracious and merciful and now bearing grudge against one and the same person or one and the same people, and other attributes of the same kind which denote acts coming from Him. For this reason, we say that even though we characterize Him essentially by a given attribute because of a certain act we perceive to come from Him, this does not necessitate plurality in Him. Thus if we characterize Him as living, by reason of an act which comes from Him, namely life for all living beings, this does not necessitate multiplicity in His essence. For our meaning is that since we see life coming from Him, we judge that He is the source of life which He bestows upon all living things. This is why we describe Him as living, in the words of Scripture, "For with Thee is the fountain of life."

In the same way we judge that light is with Him, because we see that "in His light we see light," that He it is who gives us the power to see light, and causes sight to pass from potentiality to actuality. Similarly, we judge that all perfections are found in Him, because they come from Him. In the words of the Psalmist, "He that planted the ear, shall He not hear? He that formed the eye, shall He not, see?"

In the same way we describe Him as wise, by reason of the acts which we see coming from Him with wonderful wisdom and admirable order, indicating that He has wisdom. He may therefore be characterized by different attributes by reason of all the various acts which we see emanating from Him, without this necessitating any plurality in Him. In the same way He may be characterized by different attributes by reason of various relations, reciprocal and otherwise. For example, we say God is near to man or far from him, or in the words of the Bible, "The Lord is nigh unto them that are of a broken heart," "The Lord is far from the wicked." The nearness and the farness are on man's side, according as he comes near to God or keeps far away from Him, as the Rabbis say, in commenting on the expression, "The Lord, the Lord," "I am He before man sins, and I am the same after he has sinned," i.e., the change is not in God, but in man. Before he sins, he stands in a certain relation to God, after he has sinned, he stands in a different relation, he departs from Him, like a tree, which is now near to Reuben, now far from him, now east of Reuben, now west of him, not because of any change in the tree, but because of a change in Reuben. Or when the Bible speaks of God as Creator, and Maker, and King, and Lord, and uses other similar appellations. This does not necessitate any plurality or change in God, as it does not necessitate any plurality in Reuben when we say of him that he is the son of Yaakov and the brother of Simon and the father of Enoch and the partner of Naphtali and the owner of an ox and of a pit. All these attributes do not by any means necessitate any plurality in Reuben, for the plurality is not in the essence of Reuben, but the attributes are due to the things with which he stands in various relations.

In the same way God may be characterized by different attributes from different aspects. Thus when we say of God that He is possessed of will, or is wise, or powerful, we do not mean that He has one attribute by which He has power to create, another attribute with which He exercises will, another with which He creates, another with which He knows that which He has created, any more than we say that He has one attribute with which He created the elements, another with which He created the spheres, another with which He created the angels, and another with which He created man, all of which are different acts emanating from one agent, as we said before. But since a perfect agent can not do anything without having the power, the knowledge and the desire to do it, we say that

God has will and power and knowledge, these being different aspects of the agent which do not necessitate plurality in Him.

In these various ways God is characterized by various attributes by reason of acts different because of the recipients, or differing in their essence, or by reason of the relations and connections between Him and them, or because of difference in aspect. All these things do not necessitate any plurality in God, and are all permissible. This is the method of the Torah and the Prophets in relation to the attributes which are ascribed to God. The question whether God can be characterized by different attributes in respect to His own essence, will be left for later discussion.

Chapter 9

An attribute by which a thing is characterized is not the essence of the thing characterized, but something attaching to the essence. For an attribute must be either something essential or something accidental. If it is something essential, as when we say man is rational animal, it is not an attribute added to the essence, but it is like saying man is man, for man is nothing else except animality and rationality. It is merely an explanation of the name, since [by hypothesis] the attribute is the essence of the thing characterized and not something pertaining to the essence. There is no objection to ascribing to God an attribute of this sort, since it is not something added to the essence. For a plurality of words does not necessarily represent a plurality of things, but is merely used to explain the nature of the essence. Thus, if we say, body nutritive sensitive, these words do not add any plurality to the meaning of the word animal.

But we must know that God can not be characterized by two things as denoting His essence, in the way in which animality and rationality denote the essence of man. Nor can God be characterized by one word as denoting a part of His essence, for in either case God would be composed of two things. But we have already proved that God is absolutely simple. But He may be characterized by an attribute which is an explanation of the name by which He is called. This can be the case only if the attribute is something essential which explains the essence of the thing characterized. For example, if we say that the First Cause is a necessary existent and the absolute truth. Here the words are an explanation of the term necessary existent, as we shall see when we deal with the word truth.

If an attribute is something accidental, it is clear that it can not be ascribed to God. For an accident requires a subject, an accident not

Sefer Haikkarim   BOOK [Maamar] TWO

being able to exist by itself. God would therefore be a substance bearing accidents. Now if the existence of the substance and the necessity of its essence are independent of the accidents, then the accident may exist or not exist, whereas the substance exists by necessity. God would therefore be composed of two things, necessary existence and possible existence. As necessary existent He would be cause, as possible existent, effect. He would therefore be cause and effect at the same time, while being a substance depending upon itself. This is a contradiction, which is impossible. On the other hand, if His existence and the necessity of His essence are not independent of the accident, then the accident is a necessary existent, and the substance bearing the accident a necessary existent likewise, and there would be two necessary existents, or else one that is composed of two elements, substance and accident. But all this has been shown to be absurd. It is clear therefore that God can not be characterized by any attribute, essential or accidental. This would make it necessary to reject all divine attributes except those which are explanatory of God's necessary existence, as we said before.

On the other hand, it can be shown that God must have attributes, as follows: It follows from the above-mentioned proofs that if God is a necessary existent, He must be one, else He would not be a necessary existent. It is clear, on the other hand, that unity is in every thing an attribute added to the essence. For if Reuben were one qua man, a horse and a tree could not have unity, since unity is [by hypothesis] the quiddity of Reuben. Nor could whiteness or wisdom be characterized as one. Without doubt, then, unity is something added to the essence. Now since unity is something added to the essence, and God, as we have seen, can not be characterized by any attribute except such as is explanatory of His name, we must explain in what way it can be said that God is one. For unity is not, like the other attributes ascribed to God, named after God's acts. Having explained the meaning of unity, we will then discuss the same question concerning the other attributes, viz. in what way they can be ascribed to God.

Chapter 10

The term one applies to that which gives specialization and separation to an existing thing by which it is distinguished from another. Thus, the term one is applied to a collection of many different individuals, because they agree in a certain matter which singles them out and distinguishes them from others. This common element may be an accidental thing, as in the expression, "One people and one language." Because they have one accidental element in common, such as religion among the Ishmaelites [Arabs, Mohammedans], or blackness among Ethiopians, which separates them from others, we say that they are one people. Or the common element may be an essential thing, as when we say that Reuben and Simeon are one in humanity, or that man and horse are one in animality. These are called one because they have in common one essential thing which separates them from others. And the more this specializing thing singles them out from others, the more truly does the term one applies. Thus, the term one applies more truly to an individual, say Reuben, though he is composed of many visible members different in kind, than to a people.

A still more proper use of the term one is when it is applied to flesh, bone or a member composed of homogeneous parts. For though it is composed of different elements, the term one is applicable because it is hard to separate them and they are not perceptible to the senses. Still more proper is the application of the term one to a simple element, which can not be divided into the matter and form of which it is composed except mentally, and neither of them is perceptible to the senses by itself. A surface is one in a truer sense still, and a line even more so, since it has only one dimension, and is not composed of elements into which it may be resolved, actually or mentally, as a simple element is resolved into matter and form and a surface into length and breadth. A line is one simple dimension, by which attribute it is distinguished from all other existing things, and does not share it with any other thing. And yet the unity of a line is not perfect, because it may be divided into curved and straight. Moreover every line you can point to may be divided into small parts, each one of which is a line. A point is more truly one than a line. For a point can not be divided actually or mentally; it is different from all other existing things, with which it has nothing in common except position. But the unity of point is not perfect because it has position in common with other things. A truer unity is the numerical one, which has no position and has nothing in common with other things. But it has no real actual existence, only a mental one. And for this reason, the mind may conceive of a large aggregation of numerical units, constituting number, which may be defined as an aggregation of units. Therefore, it is clear that the numerical one is not a perfect unit either, since it does not single out and separate an actual existent from other existents, seeing that we can conceive many ones of the same kind.

Absolute unity is that which singles out and separates from others a thing existing actually, which can not be conceived as having others like it. Now since there is not among existing things any thing which has nothing in common with others, and to which there is nothing equal, except God, it follows that there is nothing in the world to which the term one applies in the sense that it is really different from every thing else, except God. For He alone is a necessary existent, while all other things are possible existents, and share this attribute in common. But there is no one that shares with God in the attribute of necessary existence or in anything else, including the word existent. For we have explained that there can not be two necessary existents, since the mind can not conceive of them as being equal in all respects, and that the term existence as applied to God and to other things is used in a purely homonymous sense. God's unity, therefore, is absolute, for no existing thing has anything in common with Him, or is like unto Him in any respect.

We have now shown that one in the true sense is applied to an existent to which there is nothing equal or similar. We have also shown that the Necessary Existent, whose existence has been proved demonstratively, has no like, nor anything in common with any existing thing. Hence it is clear that the term one which is applied to God is, as it were, a negative concept and not a positive, and therefore does not necessitate multiplicity in God's essence. The Torah expresses this idea clearly in the words, "Hear O Israel, the Lord our God, the Lord is one." The meaning is as follows: As being "our God," i.e., as the cause of all existing things - in allusion to our first proof - He must be a necessary existent, being alone the cause of all things and having none like Him, as the Bible says, "To whom then will ye liken Me, that I should be equal?" for all things outside of Him are effects. Similarly, in Himself he is "one," having no second similar to Him, and there is no other necessary existent - this being an allusion to our second proof above. This explains, so to speak, that the concept of unity which is predicated of God is negative and not positive, and therefore does not require plurality in God's essence, since it is not an attribute added to the essence.

Chapter 11

Existing things are divided first into two classes, those which have independent existence and those which are dependent on others. Examples of the latter class are accidents which reside in bodies, and

Sefer Halkkarim   BOOK [Maamar] TWO

forms which exist in matters. The first class of existents, the independent ones, are again divided into three classes: First, bodies, which are the lowest class of the three. Second, Separate Intelligences, having no dependence upon bodies. Third, souls, which are intermediate between the other two. They have a sort of dependence upon bodies, receiving impressions and influences from the Separate Intelligences and then influencing and producing impressions upon bodies. Thus, they are, as it were, intermediate between bodies and the Separate Intelligences.

Since plurality in existing things is perceived both by our intellect and by our senses, we must show how plurality can arise from the First Cause, which is one and of absolute simplicity. The explanation is this. There are ten or at least nine kinds of body. Nine of them are celestial, while the tenth consists of the matter which is within the concavity of the lunar sphere. The nine celestial bodies are living, and consist of bodies and souls, the latter exerting influence and producing impressions upon the world of nature. Thus we see that by their motions and inclinations to the north and the south, they order the affairs of living beings, and arrange their life in a manner suitable to the permanence of their species. But none can order the affairs of the living, who is not himself living. Therefore, we say that they are living and intelligent, and comprehend the things which are ordered by them.

Now this plurality can not come from simple unity, unless we say that the first principle caused to emanate from its absolutely simple existence one intellect, which is the first effect, and is a being existing independently, being neither body nor resident in body. And this intellect is the beginning of plurality, for since it is a caused thing we conceive a certain element of plurality in it. For it has two modes of understanding: It understands itself and its principle. By virtue of its understanding its principle as being simple, there emanates from it an intellect, and by virtue of its understanding itself as necessarily having two elements, a simple intellect and a possible existent in its essence [since its existence is dependent upon another], there emanates from it the soul of a sphere and its body. By virtue of understanding itself as a simple intellect, which is a noble concept, it causes to emanate from itself the soul of a sphere, and by the act of understanding itself as a possible existent, it causes to emanate from it the body of the smooth sphere which produces the diurnal motion.

In the same way from the second intellect there emanates a third intellect, and the soul of the sphere of the fixed stars, and the body of the sphere. Similarly, from the third there emanates a fourth intellect, the soul of the sphere of Saturn and its body. From the fourth there emanates a fifth intellect, the soul of the sphere of Jupiter and its body. From the fifth intellect there emanates a sixth intellect, the soul of the sphere of Mars, and its body. From the sixth there emanates a seventh intellect, the soul of the sphere of the sun, and its body. From the seventh there emanates an eighth intellect, the soul of the sphere of Venus, and its body. From the eighth there emanates a ninth intellect, the soul of the sphere of Mercury, and its body. From the ninth there emanates a tenth intellect, the soul of the ninth sphere, which is that of the moon, and its body. From the tenth there emanates the matter of all that is beneath the lunar sphere and all the souls of that region. This tenth intellect is called the Active Intellect.

Now it is clear that all these spheral bodies are necessarily different in kind, since their causes differ from each other as cause from effect. And as the matter of all which is beneath the lunar sphere is different from the matter of the lunar sphere, because their respective causes are different, the one being the cause and the other the effect, so all the spheres differ from each other, and have nothing in common except spherical form and circular motion. All that is above the lunar sphere is permanent individually and not subject to dissolution, while those things which are beneath the lunar sphere are subject to dissolution and have no individual permanence, but only as species. The moon, however, is intermediate, as it were, between those things which are subject to genesis and destruction and the things which have individual permanence and are not subject to dissolution, and for this reason the moon's light waxes and wanes. Inasmuch as this chain of cause and effect can not continue ad infinitum, it stops with the tenth intellect which moulds the matter of the things below the lunar sphere. Therefore, it is called the Active [moulding] Intellect. The Rabbis call it, the Prince of the World.

It will be seen that according to the order of the causal chain just described, every one of the caused intellects produces an effect, which is an intellect existing independently, and the soul of a sphere, while the tenth, the Active Intellect, does not produce an intellect existing independently, but only a soul which resides in matter, like the soul of a sphere, and thus is in the position of a female, receiving influence, but not exerting any. This is the meaning of the statement of the Rabbis, "The Sabbath said to the Lord, blessed be He, 'O Master of the world, to every one Thou hast given a mate, but to me

Sefer Halkkarim — BOOK [Maamar] TWO

Thou hast not given a mate.' God replied, 'My daughter, the congregation of Israel shall be thy mate'." The word Sabbath, which is feminine, alludes to the quality of being passive and not active, which is that of the tenth intellect. They call it Sabbath because the sages of the Cabala refer every one of the seven days of creation to one of the seven last intellects, calling them sefirot. The first three, they say, are spiritual, and they call them the incomprehensible light. The last seven they refer respectively to the seven days of creation, and call the tenth Sabbath because it is the last of the effects, with which the chain comes to an end. The meaning then is that the last intellect, namely the tenth, which is the Active Intellect, the same as the **tenth sefirah**, which they call Sabbath, complained before God because with it the chain of causation comes to an end, and it has no mate, viz. another intellect having independent existence to emanate from it as in the other intellects, with the result that it is in the position of a female, passive and not active. Then God replied, "My daughter, the congregation of Israel shall be thy mate." The meaning is, the intellect acquired through the Torah will be a separate intellect existing independently, permanently and controlling all material things, as the prophets and pious men produced signs and miracles by means of the intellect which they acquired through the Torah. This intellect is, as it were, a separate intellect, produced by the Active Intellect or by the **sefirah** called Sabbath.

According to some of the sages of the Cabala, who say that the **sefirah yesod** is called Sabbath, because they begin to count the days from the third sefirah, which is **binah**, the complaint is because the Active Intellect, which is **malkut**, the tenth sefirah, and caused by **yesod**, can not produce another separate intellect like all the other separate intellects which are produced by the sefirot. It is then like a female mate to Sabbath, i.e., passive, and not a male mate, i.e., active, like the others.

It is in allusion to what we have just said that the Rabbis say, "All agree that the Torah was given to Israel on the Sabbath." The meaning is, it was given on the Sabbath as an indication that by means of it a person can acquire an intellect produced by the quality called Sabbath, which has independent existence. This is the additional soul or oversoul of which the Rabbis say that it is given to man on the Sabbath and taken away from him at the close of Sabbath, in accordance with the expression, "Ceased from work and rested," which they interpret, by a play upon the Hebrew words, "Alas! the soul has gone."

For this reason, the Sabbath became a covenant and an everlasting sign between God and Israel, as the Bible says, "Wherefore the children of Israel shall keep the Sabbath ... It is a sign between Me and the children of Israel forever ..." The meaning is that the Sabbath is a sign that there is some divine bond remaining attached to the nation, which can not be denied - a bond through which the nation will attain eternal happiness for the soul and union with God, so that the pious men who observe the Sabbath will be able to produce changes in nature. This is the meaning of the expression, "sign of a covenant."

This is the opinion about the chain of causation from the First Cause, according to Ibn Sina, Maimonides and some of the other Mohammedan writers. Ibn Roshd has a different opinion in this matter, which follows the ancient philosophers, and which I shall state after I have treated of the existence of angels, in order to afford the believer a true picture of the manner in which the chain of causation continues and how the plurality of different existences proceeds from the First Cause, though He is one and of absolute simplicity.

Chapter 12

There is a dispute concerning the existence of angels between the philosophers and the sages of the Torah. All agree that angels exist, but they differ about their quiddity. The philosophers say that as their essence is simple intellect, we can not conceive that there should be plurality among them. For plurality in things agreeing in form can only be due to the matter, seeing that plurality everywhere is due to matter and unity to form, unity being therefore superior to duality. Now since angels, as being separate intellects, are not material, it is inconceivable how they can differ from each other except by one being the cause and the other the effect. For this reason, they say that the number of the separate intellects is ten, the same as the number of the spheres, which is nine, or ten if we include the matter which is beneath the lunar sphere, as we said in the preceding chapter.

A group of theologians who follow this idea say that the number of angels is the same as the number of spheres having different motions, each one of them having a special intellectual mover which gives it its special motion. Now since the number of spheres which it is necessary to assume in order to explain all the apparent motions of the heavenly bodies is forty-nine or fifty, the number of angels is forty-nine or fifty, the same as the number of movers. They say that

Sefer HaIkkarim — BOOK [Maamar] TWO

this is the opinion of the Rabbis, expressed in the following statement: "Fifty gates of understanding were created in the world, all of which were given over to Moshe except one, as is said, 'Thou hast made him but little lower than the angels.' " They are called gates of understanding because every one of them has a special mode of comprehension.

But all this is in opposition to the opinion of the Torah. For it would follow from the doctrine above mentioned that the angels sent down with messages to men are imaginary things and not real. But the Bible says that there are many angels, self-existent, who are not sent down to men, as the Rabbis say by way of comment on the verses, "The chariots of God are myriads, even thousands upon thousands," and, "Thousand thousands ministered unto him;" and that there are real angels who are sent down to mankind, as is said, "For He will give His angels charge over thee, to keep thee in all thy ways;" "The man Gabriel whom I had seen in the vision at the beginning, being caused to fly swiftly, approached close to me about the time of the evening offering;" also, "And there is none that holdeth with me against these, except Michael your prince." All of this shows that there are self-existent angels who are sent with messages to mankind, an opinion agreed upon by all theologians.

It seems therefore that the difference between the separate intellects is due to the difference in their intellectual contents, and depends upon the degree of understanding which they have of the attributes of divine perfection, but has nothing to do with one being a cause and the other an effect. The word intellect would then represent, as it were, the genus embracing them all, while the difference would be represented by their respective degrees of comprehension. And yet this would not necessitate plurality in the essence of any one of them. For some things are composed of genus and difference in reality, like man, who is composed of animality and rationality, which are the genus and the difference, having real existence. Therefore, man is necessarily composite. Some things again are composed of genus and difference by logical definition only, but not in reality, as for example, blackness is a color contracting the sight. "Color" is the genus, "contracting the sight" is the difference. But this does not induce plurality in the essence of blackness at all, because blackness is not really composed of two things but only by logical definition.

The same is true of the separate intellects. They are composite by logical definition, which does not induce plurality in their essence. Just as the advocates of the opinion mentioned before admit that there may be a difference among the separate intellects that is due to their different activities, as giving different motions to their respective spheres, without the one being a cause and the other an effect, so they may differ by reason of their degrees of comprehension. Thus, the one which comprehends one or two of the attributes of divine perfection, is different from the one that comprehends more attributes or other ideas, without this inducing any plurality in the essence of any one of them. And their power and influence in the world are different according to the difference in their respective intellectual contents. Just as a political head appoints certain persons to a given position of influence in accordance with their ability and intelligence, and gives other persons a higher position in accordance with their greater ability and understanding, so God assigns every one of the angels to a specific charge according to his power and understanding. This is what the Rabbis mean when they say, "An angel can not perform two missions." From this it appears that every angel is charged with a specific mission and power according to his understanding. Thus, the Rabbis speak of the prince of fire, and the prince of water.

Now since the attributes of divine perfection are many, or rather infinite, as we shall see later, it follows that there are a great many separate intellects, as many as there are different degrees of understanding God, and of power of action bestowed by God upon them, without the one being cause and the other effect, and this too despite the fact that they are absolutely simple and that God is absolutely one. This opinion is true and correct, in agreement with the Torah and with philosophy, as we shall explain in the following chapter.

Chapter 13

Difference and number of functions are due to one of three causes. They may be due to a difference in the active faculties. Thus, the activity of the faculty of desire is different from that of the faculty of anger. The difference may be due to a difference in the matter. Thus fire melts pitch and hardens salt. Finally, the difference may be due to a difference in the instruments. Thus, a tailor sews with a needle, and cuts with scissors. But the activity of God can not be multiplied through any one of these causes, because He is one and simple, in whom there is no plurality of faculties or difference of matters or variety of instruments. The multiplicity can therefore only be due to something else beside these things, namely the

Sefer Halkkarim   BOOK [Maamar] TWO

intermediate. That is, there emanates from Him first a single being; from this one there emanates another, from this other a third, as we explained in chapter eleven, so that the intermediate beings increase and plurality arises through them. Outside of this way, they say, it is impossible to conceive real plurality coming from God, who is absolutely one, for from the one only one thing can come.

But a difficulty arises against this explanation. It necessarily follows that there can not be a thing composed of different elements, but all existing things must be units, each produced by the one above it, which is its cause. But we do find that body is composed of matter and form, and man is composed of body and soul, the one not being the cause of the other [else one would not exist without the other], but the two of them being due to a third cause. Plurality can not therefore arise in this way.

Ibn Sina and other Arab philosophers have elaborated a way of producing plurality out of the series of intermediate beings, in the manner suggested above, saying that there is some plurality in every one of the emanations. Thus, understanding oneself is something different from understanding one's cause, and understanding oneself and one's cause is different from the conception of oneself as a possible existent qua one's self, since one's existence is dependent upon another. In this way they say plurality can come in, as we said in chapter eleven.

But Algazali knocked this idea on the head when he said that these are merely intellectual conceptions and not separate things able to produce other separate existents. Moreover, if plurality can arise from such conceptions, there is no need of many emanations, for we can conceive of multiplicity arising from the First Cause without the need of the others. Thus, the knowledge of Himself is something different from His necessary existence and from the knowledge that He is a principle of other things. Now if these conceptions exist in the First Cause without inducing plurality in Him, why can not the beings which emanate from Him be in the same case? Then the question arises again, whence does plurality come?

The truth is that the conceptions mentioned do not induce plurality either in the First Principle or in the beings which emanate from it, so as to account for the different existences which are caused by them. And if so, we ask again, how does plurality come from simple unity? This is the reason why among the ancients there were some who thought that there are two original principles, one good and one evil. For they said, "Out of the mouth of the Highest proceedeth not evil and good," meaning that it is impossible that the contradictory principles should be combined in one. And seeing that the most general contradictories, including all the species of contradiction, are good and evil, they said that there were two principles, one the principle of good, the other, the principle of evil. This was the opinion of a person whose name was Mani. His followers are called Manichaeans in the same way as those who follow the opinions of the philosopher Epicurus, who thought that the world has no ruler and denied the existence of God, are called Epicureans.

The philosophers have disputed this view in many ways. The best and clearest of the arguments against this dualism, so far as concerns the purpose of this book, is this: If we reflect upon the existing things of the world, we find that they all together tend to one end, namely the order which exists in the world, like the order existing in a camp, which emanates from the military commander, and the order existing in states, which emanates from the rulers. Now in these cases though there is multiplicity of various kinds, namely many different arts and activities and different offices, nevertheless we regard the state or the camp as one because the end to which they all tend is one, namely the stability and order of the state or camp, so we say that the world has in it good and evil so that existence as a whole may be good. Evil is not intended for its own sake, it arises by accident, like punishment or chastisement inflicted by the father upon the son, which is evil for the sake of good and not intended for its own sake. For since good things exist, it is imperative that a little evil should be mixed with the good. Thus, man is composed of a rational and an animal soul, which are the good and the evil inclinations. The good inclination was placed in man to secure the survival of the individual, so far as possible, in the immortality of the soul, while the evil inclination was implanted in him to secure the survival of the species without which man can not exist. The wisdom of the Highest decreed that it is fitting there should be great good even though a little evil must be mixed with it, for it stands to reason that it is better to have a great good plus a little evil than to lose the great good in order to avoid the little evil.

It does not follow therefore from the existence of good and evil that they come from different principles. For it is quite possible that from one principle good comes for its own sake and evil per accidens. Thus, fire is the cause of good to all sublunar existence in the genesis of all things, and yet evil comes from it sometimes when by accident it burns the garment of a good man.

In the same way there are things which, though in themselves bad, are tolerated for the sake of the good which may come from them, like penalties enacted by the founders of good codes of law which, though bad in themselves, are enacted for the sake of the general good which will follow for the nation or state as a whole, that men may be guided to happiness by uniting with one another in a perfect manner, and establish a perfect society, consisting of different kinds of people; like the human body, which has different members and different controlling organs and qualities opposed to one another, and yet all of them are intended for one purpose, namely the duration and unity of the body. It has also things injurious to the body which are due to the matter and can not be avoided.

The ancient philosophers were therefore all agreed, as Ibn Roshd says, that there is one principle in the absolute sense of the word one, and that by it all the various things of existence were ordered first for one purpose, viz. the permanence of all existence and the complete union of its parts so that existence may be unified into a complete unit; as the head of a state assigns certain people to do a given work and no other, that it may be done in a perfect manner, and assigns other people to do another kind of work exclusively, and so on with the different kinds of work. Thus he makes some to be tailors, some to be weavers, some to be builders, and in this way are completed all the arts needed in the state, and the order of the state is perfected. And yet all the many arts come from the one first head, though he is absolutely one.

In the same way though God is absolutely one, He is the cause of plurality, without this necessitating plurality in His essence. They say that the proposition, "from one can come only one," is a dialectical judgment, which is applicable indeed to a particular and concrete agent, whereas in the case of God who is the universal and general agent - the term agent as applied to Him and to others is a homonym - [for He can not be identified with one act rather than another, seeing that His relation is the same to all acts] we say that He does many different specific acts for the sake of perfect unity, i.e., in order that all the parts of nature may be combined into one, and that all the many existences may tend to one purpose, viz. the permanence of existence, in the same way as the rational soul in man, though one, does different acts for one purpose, the permanent existence of man. In this way God orders only one act, viz. the universal order, which contains a plurality of elements so as to unite all the parts of existence together.

These philosophers also say that though the simple existents which are independent of matter are related to each other as cause and effect, the series going back to one simple cause, the plurality of bodies arises from the plurality of these principles in order to unite all the parts of existence one to the other. If this plurality did not exist, existence would be defective and there would not be that one perfect end which is actually realized. So, we find different motions in the spheres because of the different principles from which they come. At the same time, they all have the one general motion embracing everything, viz. the diurnal motion, to show that they have one principle, that they all go back to one cause, and that all the different motions are for one end.

Ibn Roshd says that God commanded the principles to give an order to the spheres to make the motions that we see in them; and that the heaven and the earth were established by the command of God in the same way as by the command of the first ruler of a country the subjects of the king's commands and arrangements are controlled by those whom the king appoints to take charge of some political matter or some classes of men. This command and belief is a principle of command and belief which it behooves a man to hold, by virtue of his being a rational animal. This is the substance of the words of Ibn Roshd concerning this matter in his book, Destructio Destructionis.

It will be seen that after all that has been said, we must admit that the persistence of heaven and earth is due to command and admonition, and not to necessity. For it is inconceivable that a material thing should come from an absolutely simple immaterial intellect through necessity. It can come only through a command, which necessarily indicates creation in time; and this means that the world came to be and endures through the will of a being possessing a will, as we said in the third chapter of this Book. It almost seems as if the truth compelled him to make this admission.

The result we have reached, whether according to Ibn Sina and Maimonides or according to the opinion of Ibn Roshd, who writes in the name of the ancient philosophers, is that the plurality of things existing in the world is due to the series of intermediate beings and not to a plurality existing in the First Principle, whose unity is simple in the absolute sense of the word. This is the reason we are told in the Bible, "Hear, O Israel, the Lord our God, the Lord is one." The meaning is that we should believe that though He is our God, i.e., the cause of plurality, He is nevertheless one in the absolute meaning of the word. This will suffice in explanation of the dogma of unity and the other matters depending upon it, so as not to induce plurality in the essence of God. We will now begin to treat of the second dogma, incorporeality.

Sefer Halkkarim BOOK [Maamar] TWO
Chapter 14

It has already been proved demonstratively that God is neither body nor a force residing in body. It follows that we must deny God all bodily accidents and corporeal affections. It is necessary therefore to give a reason for the expressions found in all the Prophets that God is jealous, wrathful, vengeful and bearing grudge. Thus, Nahum says, "The Lord is a jealous and avenging God. The Lord avengeth and is full of wrath, The Lord taketh vengeance on His adversaries, and He reserveth wrath for His enemies." All these descriptions denote corporeal affections. Moreover, they are ignoble qualities which should not be attributed to any excellent person, not to speak of God. The Bible also attributes to Him pride, "The Lord reigneth; He is clothed in majesty"; also, the emotion of pity, "My compassions are kindled together"; as well as sorrow, "And it grieved Him at His heart"; and grief, "And His soul was grieved for the misery of Israel."

The explanation is this. The purpose of the prophets is to lead all mankind to worship God and to love Him. But the masses of the people can not be made to humble themselves for service except from fear of punishment. Therefore, it was necessary for the prophets to speak in a language understood by the generality of the people. Now since, in human phraseology, when a king punishes those who have rebelled against him and given his kingdom to another, he is said to be jealous and revengeful and full of wrath, so the prophets say of God when He punishes those who violate His will that He is a jealous and avenging God and is full of wrath, because the act which emanates from Him against those who transgress His will is the act of a revengeful, grudging and jealous person.

The attribution of sorrow to God must be explained in the same way. Just as human beings feel sorrow when necessity compels their works to be destroyed, so the Bible says, "And it grieved Him at His heart," and in the immediate sequel we read, "And the Lord said, 'I will blot out man whom I have created ... for it repenteth Me that I have made them.'" God is said to repent because He does the act of a person who repents of what he has made and desires to destroy it. And just as when a human being finds himself compelled by the requirements of justice to destroy what he has made, he looks about for a way which will enable him to save some of it from destruction, so God sought a way to prevent the destruction of all things. Therefore, the narrative concludes, "But Noah found grace in the eyes of the Lord." The meaning is that God brought it about that the world should be continued through Noah and his sons.

The expression, "And His soul was grieved for the misery of Israel," is to be explained in the same way. God did the act of a person who is in sorrow, whose soul grieves for the misery of his neighbor, and who puts himself to inconvenience in order to help him. So here, though Israel had sinned and were not deserving at that time of such great deliverance, nevertheless God saved them of His own accord as if He was affected by their trouble and misery, as we read, "I have surely seen the affliction of My people that are in Egypt ... and I am come down to deliver them out of the hand of the Egyptians." Similarly, is to be explained the expression, "My compassions are kindled together."

The other expressions of corporeal affections must be understood in the same way, as a mode of bringing to the human understanding the nature of the act which emanates from Him, in a manner consonant with human habits of perception. Thus, the Bible says expressly, "Take ye therefore good heed unto yourselves, for ye saw no manner of form," and yet it attributes corporeal members to God, speaking of the Tables of Stone, as "written with the finger of God"; and in the following expressions, "When I behold Thy heavens, the work of Thy fingers"; "Thy right hand, O Lord, glorious in power"; "Thy hands have made me and fashioned me"; and many others of the same kind. The explanation is that as a human person writes with the finger, finger is attributed to God; as strength in man comes from the right hand, right hand is ascribed to Him; as human acts are done with hands and fingers, hands and fingers are attributed to God; and as the acceptation of words in man is attributed to the hearing of the ears, the Bible says, "Let thine ears be attentive."

In the same way must be explained the saying of God in relation to the Temple, "And Mine eyes and Mine heart shall be there perpetually." The meaning is, my providence and my good will, indicating that God desires its permanent existence. Similarly, when the prophets picture God as a king sitting on a throne, as in Isaiah, "And I saw the Lord sitting on a throne"; "For mine eyes have seen the King, the Lord of hosts"; or when they describe Him as a strong man, "The Lord will go forth as a mighty man"; "The Lord mighty in battle"; - all this is done in order to bring before human understanding a picture of His mighty glory and majesty. Thus, David says, "They shall speak of the glory of Thy kingdom.... To make known to the sons of men His mighty acts, and the glory of the majesty of His kingdom." The meaning is that the only reason

Sefer Halkkarim   BOOK [Maamar] TWO

why they speak of Thee thus is in order to make known to the sons of men, but not in order to compare Thy kingdom with a human kingdom, for Thy kingdom is eternal, "a kingdom for all ages." It is done merely to bring the matter before the human understanding and for no other reason.

When the Bible attributes to Him pride, which is an ignoble quality in man, as is said, "Every one that is proud in heart is an abomination to the Lord," the meaning is that man should not boast of any excellence or good quality, for all comes from God, and a man should not boast of that which does not belong to him. As regards wisdom, the Bible says, "For the Lord giveth wisdom"; also, "That turneth wise men backward, and maketh their knowledge foolish." This explains that human wisdom is worth nothing, and that wisdom comes from God and from no one else. Nor should a man boast of wealth, for that is not his either, as David says, "For all things come of Thee, and of Thine own have we given Thee."

Similarly, kingdom and all exalted station and excellence come from God, as the Bible says, "Thine is the kingdom, O Lord, and Thou art exalted as head above all." And the Rabbis say, "Even the overseer of wells is appointed from heaven." The blessing concludes, "Both riches and honour come of Thee, and Thou rulest over all." That is, since everything comes from God, and man alone has nothing which is not due to the will of God, for in His "hand it is to make great, and to give strength unto all," he should not boast of that which does not belong to him and is not in his power. Therefore, pride is becoming only to God from whom everything comes. Hence the Bible attributes pride to God when it says, "The Lord reigneth; He is clothed in majesty," and in the words of Moshe, "I will sing unto the Lord, for He is highly exalted"; which Onkelos translates, "Because He is exalted above the proud, and pride is His."

Therefore, if a person boasts of some quality which is not his, it is proper that the quality should be taken away from him, as an indication that the honor and the excellence which he enjoys do not come to him from himself, but from God and by the divine will. Thus we find in the case of Nebuchadnezzar who boasted of glory and royal status, that the Bible expresses itself as follows: "But when his heart was lifted up, and his spirit was hardened that he dealt proudly, he was deposed from his kingly throne and his glory was taken from him … till thou know that the Most High ruleth in the kingdom of men, and giveth it to whomsoever He will … and setteth up over it the lowest of men."

The same is true of the prince of Tyre, who boasted of being a god.

Sefer Halkkarim   BOOK [Maamar] TWO

The Bible says about him, "Because thy heart is lifted up, and thou hast said: I am a god.... Wilt thou yet say before him that slayeth thee: I am God? But thou art man and not God, In the hand of them that defile thee." This shows that God punishes all those who boast of that which is not theirs. If one boasts of royalty God takes his kingdom away from him and gives it to the lowest of men, so that all may know that royalty does not belong to man and is not in his power. Similarly, if one boasts of divine power and makes himself a god, God punishes him and delivers him up to be killed. This is an appropriate punishment for one who boasts of being a god, as it exposes him to shame, since he can not save himself. For it is the way of God to revive the dead, "To deliver them that are drawn unto death and to rescue those that are ready to be slain." God is also eternal. But here it is the opposite. God hands him over into the hand of a slayer to show that he is no god since man can prevail over him to kill him and he has no power to save himself from death. But as to God, in whose hand is the soul of every living thing - He puts to death and brings back to life, He gives perfection to every existing thing, but He does not get any perfection from any one else, like kings, whose perfection comes from some one else. For the royalty of kings is exalted because of the honor which is shown them by others. If not for the honor shown him no one would know that he is a king and that he is superior to others. It is therefore as if honor ruled over them. But not so God, He rules over honor, therefore He is called, "King of glory."

The majesty of the king is dependent upon the multitude of the people, the more people the greater the glory. But God, being king over glory, is not exalted because of any one else nor does His kingship change or diminish as those subjects to Him are diminished or changed. Thus the Psalmist says, "The voice of the Lord maketh the hinds to calve, and strippeth the forests bare, and in His temple all say: 'Glory.' " The meaning is that even when God executes judgment and destroys the forests and the animals, His royalty and His glory are not diminished thereby, for in His palace, i.e., in His degree of existence, all is glory. And the proof of this is that "The Lord sat enthroned at the flood; Yea, the Lord sitteth as King forever." That is, God existed in the time of the flood, and though of the world before the flood, which was full of men and animals, all things were destroyed, Noah alone and those with him in the ark remaining, nevertheless God's kingdom did not change in extent, hence "the Lord sitteth as King forever." The reason it says "sitteth" and not "is," is because sitting better expresses the idea of permanence, as Maimonides says where he discusses the scriptural homonym **Yashab** [sit]. For this reason, the prophet, too, ascribes to God the attribute of sitting more frequently than other attributes. Thus, he says, "I saw the Lord sitting upon a throne high and lifted up," and not simply: "I saw the Lord upon a throne high and lifted up." The explanation is that since sitting implies permanence, without change, it is attributed to God, though neither standing nor sitting applies to Him, as the Rabbis say in the treatise Hagigah, that up above there is neither sitting nor standing, etc. A similar interpretation must be given to all the expressions of corporeal affections ascribed to God in the Bible. They are used in order to bring the matter before human understanding, but not to indicate that it is so in reality. The Rabbis have a general maxim in this connection, "The Torah uses human expressions."

Chapter 15

Joy is the perception of the agreeableness of a pleasant and appropriate thing. It is without doubt an affection. The Bible attributes it to God, when it says, "Let the Lord rejoice in His works." And the men of the Great Synagogue established a blessing containing the words, "in whose habitation there is joy." Joy is attributed to God to indicate a condition opposed to that denoted by the attribution of sorrow. If sorrow, which expresses a defect, is ascribed to Him, surely joy, which is a noble attribute, should be ascribed to Him, for the same kind of knowledge deals with the two opposites. As the word sorrow is applied in human language to the emotion which results when a thing happens contrary to desire, so joy is applied to the pleasure resulting from carrying out one's desires and realizing one's intentions in the accomplishment of work. Thus, by way of metaphor, joy is applied to God to describe a condition opposed to that denoted by the attribute sorrow, as we explained above. The expression, "The Lord rejoiceth in His works," indicates that He desires their endurance. Similarly, the expression, "in whose habitation is joy," means that real, i.e., individual permanence, is found among the celestial beings and not among the terrestrial, where the species alone are permanent. For this reason, this blessing is used in the marriage ceremony because joy in every case is the result of duration and permanence, while sorrow is due to destruction and privation.

It is possible, too, that the expression, "in whose habitation is joy," alludes to something more profound, namely, as the philosophers say, that God rejoices with His own essence, because He has beauty and majesty and perfection in Himself and needs no one else, while all things are influenced by Him and need Him, having no duration except through Him. The meaning is therefore: God's joy does not depend upon other existents, the temporary or the permanent, it resides in His own essence alone, hence "joy is in His habitation," which is similar to the expression, "Strength and gladness are in His place," i.e., on His own level of being; or in His essence, as in the expression, "Blessed be the glory of the Lord from His place," which we will explain later.

The following is a good illustration: as a wise man rejoices when he feels that he has perfect wisdom so that all other wise men have need of him and his influence, while he has no need of them, so God rejoices because His existence is not dependent upon another, while the existence of all things is dependent upon Him. To be sure, there is no relation at all between the two kinds of joy, for the joy of the wise man is due to something which he gets from another, namely from God and from other existents emanating from God, whereas the joy of God is inherent in His own essence without regard to another. Also, the joy of the wise man is necessarily finite because his understanding is finite. The joy is therefore limited, though it may continually increase. When a person desires to attain anything, the eagerness to attain it and the joy consequent upon attainment are proportional to the value of the thing sought. If the thing sought is finite, the desire will cease when it is attained and the joy comes to a standstill or disappears. But if the thing desired is infinite, the desire can never cease, nor the understanding be interrupted, and therefore the joy continues, though it is always limited, as the comprehension is limited.

This is why the Bible says, "Let the heart of them rejoice that seek the Lord." The meaning is that since God and His perfection are infinite, the eagerness and the joy of all those who seek the Lord, though their comprehension increases continually, will always remain, will never cease, but will increase as the understanding increases. Therefore, the Psalmist says, "Seek ye the Lord and His strength; Seek His face continually." The meaning is that your joy in what understanding you attain of Him will never be interrupted, but will always increase, because God is infinite, and as one attains a certain degree of understanding, he finds something else that he is eager to know but which he does not yet understand, a point alluded to in the expression, "And His strength." Similarly, must be interpreted the verse, "Let all those that seek Thee rejoice and be

Sefer HaIkkarim — BOOK [Maamar] TWO

glad in Thee." The meaning is that because God is infinite, the joy will be continual and will ever increase, and "Let such as love Thy salvation say continually: 'The Lord be magnified.' " For the more they understand, the better they will know that He is still greater; they will continually realize that He is infinite and will always say, "The Lord be magnified," and their joy will increase still further, though the content of their comprehension be always limited.

But the joy of God in His own essence is unlimited and continuous, because every kind of perfection that He appreciates in Himself is infinite, and because in His essence are contained an infinite number of perfections, permanent and unchangeable, and unlike any kind of perfection that we can have an idea of. And yet by divine grace a person may comprehend a certain degree of their excellence, a point referred to in the biblical passage, "How precious is Thy lovingkindness, O God! And the children of men take refuge in the shadow of Thy wings." The meaning is, How great and precious is Thy lovingkindness, which can not be attained by the understanding, and yet despite this preciousness and nobility it is a wonderful thing that men take refuge in the shadow of Thy wings. "Wing" here denotes mystery and concealment, as Maimonides explains where he deals with the homonym **Kanaf** [wing], and is related to the expression, "Yet shall not thy Teacher hide **Yikanef** [Himself] any more." The meaning therefore is that that which is infinite can not be attained, but remains hidden and concealed, and yet men find refuge in that hidden shadow, containing the mystery of God's essence and lovingkindness and the other attributes emanating from Him. The Psalmist also says that by reason of the understanding they acquire of that mystery, the understanding, namely, that all existing things emanate from Him by a chain of causation, and by comprehending the activities which flow from His lovingkindness and from the other attributes ascribed to Him, they derive wonderful pleasure and satisfaction in the spiritual world. Hence, he uses the future tense when he says, "They will be abundantly satisfied with the fatness of Thy house; And Thou wilt make them drink of the river of Thy pleasures." The meaning is that they will be fat and prosperous and filled with all good things as a result of the understanding they will acquire through the existing things emanating from God, which are called "back," as when God says to Moshe, "And thou shalt see My back." Here they are called "the fatness of Thy house." But as regards "the river of Thy pleasures," namely the flowing river which causes Thy own delight, i.e., Thy essence, and the infinite attributes and perfections in which Thou takest pleasure, - this they have no possibility of understanding and enjoying through their unaided mind alone, but Thou must make them drink of it by way of grace. This is why it says, "Thou will make them drink," and not "they will drink," to indicate that man can not attain them except as a matter of grace. He says "pleasures," in the plural, to indicate that the perfections in God are many, nay infinite, as will be explained later.

Then he continues, "For with Thee is the fountain of life; In Thy light do we see light," by which he means to say that there is no obstacle in the way of attaining this wonderful pleasure from the fact that the divine attributes and perfections are eternal, while human beings are not, for "with Thee is the fountain of life," and it is in Thy power to give them eternal life. Nor is there any hindrance in the fact that they have not the capacity to receive such mighty pleasure, for Thy great power is able to endow them with capacity and force to receive it, for "In Thy light do we see light," i.e., even the things perceived by our senses we can not know except through the lovingkindness which comes from Thee. For light itself we can not see, our vision is dimmed by it. It is the divine light which gives us the power to perceive light partially and enables our vision to pass from potentiality to actuality. This is why he says, "do we see light," and not "do we see the light," because we can see only a part of it and not the whole.

It may be that the expression, "In Thy light do we see light," alludes to intellectual comprehension and that the meaning is: From the intellect emanating from Thee, which is Thy light, we acquire a certain comprehension, which serves us as a light to give us illumination in the light of eternal life, and therefore we ask of Thee to bestow from the fountain of perfection which is in Thee some delight upon us by way of grace. The expression in the sequel, "O continue Thy lovingkindness unto them that know Thee," indicates that the grace of understanding, of which we spoke, is more properly bestowed upon those who know God than upon others, but as regards the upright in heart, viz. the mass of believers, they are entitled as of right to the reward promised in the Torah, hence the continuation of the verse reads, "And Thy righteousness to the upright in heart." Divine righteousness decrees that those who believe should obtain that degree of eternal life which is promised in the Torah, because they trust in God and believe in His Torah, though they are not able to acquire an intellectual comprehension. Thus the prophet says, "But the righteous shall live by his faith," which shows that the promise of eternal life is made as compensation for faith. It can not refer to life in the body, which the righteous believers enjoy no more than the wicked unbelievers. The prophet no doubt refers to eternal life, as we shall explain with the help of God.

Chapter 16

Sehok [Laughter] is a homonymous term. It applies to joy, as in the expression, "Then Abraham fell upon his face and laughed." Here "laughed" means "was glad," as is also the interpretation of Onkelos.

Laughter may also denote scorn, as in the expression, "I am as one that is a laughing-stock to his neighbour." And sometimes laughter and scorn are combined, and the words are used synonymously, as in the expression, "He that sitteth in heaven laugheth, the Lord hath them in derision," for laughter is often due to the feeling of contempt for that which deserves it, as when a person observes a defect in the words or deeds of another, while being conscious of superiority in himself, as not likely to err in word or deed as his neighbor has done. Thus, laughter arises from the feeling of contempt when he observes his neighbor doing or saying something that is unbecoming to human nature or the person's dignity.

In the same way, laughter and derision are ascribed to God in the expression, "He that sitteth in heaven laugheth, the Lord hath them in derision." The reason is because He hears them saying, "Let us break their bands asunder," words a human being should not use; as our Rabbis say: The reason that the Psalm of Absalom stands next to that dealing with Gog and Magog, is that if any one should say, Is it possible that a servant should rebel against his master? you say to him, Is it possible that a son should rebel against his father? And yet the latter actually happened, so the former will happen. It is clear from this that it is an unusual thing for a man to say, and that he who says it deserves derision and contempt. In such cases, then, laughter is attributed to God or man.

Sometimes a person laughs when he deceives another in a matter about which the latter should have taken caution and did not. Accordingly, the cause of laughter in all cases is a feeling of superiority in the person laughing, when he sees another commit a folly or exhibit ignorance or foolishness. When the scientists say that laughter is a human property, i.e., the cause of laughter is not known, they mean to say that we do not know why laughter is accompanied by certain bodily motions or why laughter is caused by touching the armpits or feeling other sensitive places in the body. But derision as a cause of laughter is well known, as we have shown in explaining the verse, "He that sitteth in heaven laugheth."

Chapter 17

Makom [Place] is a term applied to the thing which surrounds bodies and bounds them. An incorporeal thing can not be said to be in place, because the name place applies only to a thing which is filled by another body having dimensions, which enters place and is surrounded by it. Hence it can not be said of God or of the separate intellects that they are in place, for they are not bodies having dimensions which place can surround.

The Bible says in reference to this, "Behold, the heaven and the heaven of heavens can not contain Thee," meaning that God does not need place to stand in. Such expressions as, "And I will dwell among the children of Israel"; "Then it shall come to pass that the place which the Lord your God shall choose to cause His name to dwell there"; do not mean that God needs a place to dwell in. The explanation is this. The revelation of God's glory takes place by means of a body that is visible to the senses, like a fire or a pillar of cloud. Thus, we read: "And the appearance of the glory of the Lord was like devouring fire on the top of the mount"; "And behold, the glory of the Lord appeared in the cloud"; "And the angel of the Lord appeared unto him in a flame of fire out of the midst of a bush." The sudden appearance of the pillar of cloud or of a flame of fire out of the midst of a bush, the bush not being consumed, was an indication that the glory of the Lord, which could not be seen with the senses, was there. This is why the Bible assigns a particular place to the presence of the divine glory, not that the glory has need of a place or of a body to stay in. And inasmuch as place holds a thing in permanency, God is called "dwelling-place" [Heb. ma'on], as Moshe says, "Thou hast been our dwelling-place," meaning that God contains the world and holds it in permanency as a place holds an object. For this reason, the Rabbis call Him "place," as in "Blessed be the Place [God] who gave the Torah to Israel," also, "And wave his hand to the Place [God], that He remove the leper."

The substance of a thing is also called place, as the Rabbis say, "From its own place the matter is proved," also, "Blessed be the glory of the Lord from His place." The last expression means that the glory of the Lord which appeared to the prophets emanated from God's own essence without a mediator, and not that the glory has a place.

There is a question, however, worth noting, whether it is possible to attribute to God location. For though God is not in place, a specific location may be applied to Him, like above, as we read in the Bible, "For God is in heaven, and thou upon earth"; and all authorities agree that heaven is the dwelling of the spiritual beings, though they have no need of place. It would appear, therefore, from this that even though He is not corporeal, it is possible to attribute to Him location, without this necessitating corporeality in Him. The same is true of the soul; though she is incorporeal, nevertheless she has a certain location, viz. in the body. For since she is not outside of the body, she is identified with a certain locality, though she is not in place. Similarly, we say that the soul of the wicked is judged in Gehenna. Here again though she is not body so as to be in place, place nevertheless bounds her, and she is there to receive her punishment, in the same way as she was in the body when she sinned, though she is not corporeal. In this way it is possible to say of God that though He is not in place, He is in a certain locality, above or below or some special locality.

On the other hand, one may argue against it and say that locality necessarily implies place, for locality is either above or below, and these are without doubt place. To this, however, it may be said that above in the absolute sense is not a place, for the uppermost sphere is above absolutely, and it is clear that it is not in place, since there is no other body outside of it that can surround it. Therefore, we may attribute to Him location above, since it is not place. But this is based upon the opinion of Aristotle that place is the limit which bounds a body on the outside, and hence he says that the world as a whole is not in place because there is nothing outside of it to surround it.

But this opinion is clearly unsound, for according to him it would follow that the part has a different place from the whole. For the parts of fire have no other external surrounding limit except other parts of fire or air, whereas the natural place of the element fire is the concavity of the lunar sphere, which is different from the place of the parts of fire. The same thing applies to the other elements. Moreover, it would follow according to him that the elements remain in their places by force. For the natural place of the element fire is the concave surface of the lunar sphere, which is above. Hence all the parts of fire outside of those which are adjacent to the inner surface of the sphere remain where they are by force; and similarly in the case of the other elements. Again, if the place of the element earth is the surface of the element water which bounds it on the outside, the place of earth would not be below in the absolute sense, as he maintains, since below in the absolute sense is the center. Furthermore, it follows according to him that the place of the part is greater than the place of the whole. For if you remove part of the inside of a sphere, it will require a greater surface to bound it outside and inside than when it is solid. Besides, it would follow according to him that one and the same body will have many places differing in magnitude. For if you divide a body into parts, each of the latter will require a greater place than before the division, and the same is true if you divide the parts into other parts, and those again into parts. But this is contrary to the statement of Euclid in his book Concerning the Heavy and the Light, where he says that equal bodies occupy equal places. But according to the Aristotelian hypothesis this is not true. For of two equal bodies the one that is divided will require a greater place than the other.

All these difficulties follow from the opinion that place is an external bounding surface. But if place is defined as being the vacuum into which the body enters, none of the difficulties results. Aristotle objects to this definition on the ground that if there are such things as self-existent distances, and these distances are place, two absurdities will follow. One is that one and the same thing will have an infinite number of places all at once. The other is that places would be subject to motion, and that place, which is in the basin of water, would in turn require a place. This absurd result, however, follows only if the distances are subject to motion, but if we say that they are not subject to motion, and that it is the body and its parts that move from distances to other distances, no absurdity will follow at all. For the basin and the water have each special distance which they fill and which are not changed when they move. According to this opinion the uppermost sphere and the world as a whole are in place. And therefore, it is impossible to attribute to God locality any more than place.

And as to the fact that the Bible does attribute to God location above, in the expressions, "O Thou that art enthroned in the heavens," "He that sitteth in heaven laugheth," and others, it may be that because the divine power appears more clearly in the motion of the spheres by reason of the intensity and continuity of their motions, and because they are made of a nobler material than the other bodies, and because location above is superior, it says that the heavens are the dwelling-place of the spiritual beings. And it may be that the Bible attributes to God location as it attributes place and the other corporeal attributes, because, as the Rabbis say, "The Torah speaks in human language." We shall now conclude the discussion of the dogma of incorporeality. What we have said on this topic, may be used to throw light on analogous topics.

Chapter 18

The third dogma is that God is independent of time. This means that God existed before time and will exist after time ceases, therefore His power is infinite. For every one who is dependent upon time is necessarily limited in power, which ends with time. Since therefore God is not dependent upon time, His power is infinite. It must be understood therefore that when we say, God is prior, the expression is used figuratively and loosely. For the word prior is predicated of a thing in relation to something else, thus we say, Noah was prior to David, Enoch was prior to Eliyahu, because the one existed at a time which was prior to the time at which the other existed. But it is clear that the term prior as applied to God is not predicated in relation to anything else, as if to say that He existed a certain length of time before something else. If this were the case, time would limit His existence; and if so, time would necessarily be prior to Him, and He would exist at a certain time and not at another, and would be preceded by privation or non-existence. But whatever is preceded by non-existence is a possible and not a necessary existent, as we explained before. Moreover, the Bible, too, says, "Who hath preceded Me, that I should repay Him?" which means that He is prior to all existing things, and nothing is prior to Him. Therefore, the term priority which is predicated of God must be understood in a negative manner, in the sense that nothing was prior to Him, not even non-existence, but that He always existed in the same way without change.

Similarly, the term perpetual, applied to God, means that nothing is posterior to Him. For just as time can not be prior to Him, as we have explained, so nothing can come after Him, nor can time outlast Him in the direction of the end, as it can not be prior to Him in the direction of the beginning. For if time could outlast Him in the direction of the end, He would exist at one time and not at another, and would not be a necessary existent, as we explained in relation to the term prior. Therefore, the concepts of priority and perpetuity predicated of God are negative in meaning, they deny non-existence a parte ante as well as a parte post.

That time is not prior or posterior to God is true even if by time we mean unmeasured duration conceived only in thought, existing always, both before the creation of the world and after its cessation, but without the order apparent from the motion of the sphere, since the sphere was then neither in motion nor existent. Our Rabbis are of the opinion that time in the abstract is such a duration. Time measured or numbered through the motion of the sphere they call "order of times," not simply time. According to this there are two species of time, the one is numbered and measured by the motion of the sphere, to which are applicable the terms prior and posterior, equal and unequal. The other is not numbered or measured, but is a duration existing prior to the sphere, to which the words equal and unequal do not apply. This is what Maimonides calls imagination of time. This latter kind may be perpetual. The kind that has an origin is the "order of time," not time simply. In this way all the doubts and difficulties disappear, which are raised concerning the quiddity of time, namely whether time originates in time or not. The solution is that though time has no origin, the order of time originates in time.

We can also answer the other question in relation to the now. The now, it is said, divides the past from the future. There is therefore a time before the first now, and hence time and the sphere are eternal. The answer to this on the basis of our analysis is not difficult. Time in which there is motion has in it the elements prior and posterior, but time in which there is no motion has not the elements prior and posterior, and it is not subject to measure because measure can not apply to time without motion. The terms prior and posterior apply to it only figuratively and loosely. The same thing is illustrated in the saying that outside of the world there is neither a plenum nor a vacuum. To the objection that if there is an outside there must necessarily be a plenum or a vacuum, the answer is that the word outside is used figuratively and loosely. The same is true of the words prior and posterior as applying to the imaginary duration before the creation of the world.

The difficulty of understanding how the world can end with something which is neither a plenum nor a vacuum, or how there can be a duration before the creation of the world which has in it neither prior nor posterior, such as are contained in the order of time as it exists at present, accounts for the statement of the Rabbis that one must not ask what is above, what is below, what is before and what is behind. Above and below refer to what is outside of the world, before and behind refer to the duration which is prior to the creation of the world and posterior to its cessation, in reference to which the Rabbis say that one must not ask whether the words prior and posterior apply to it or not.

Sefer HaIkkarim BOOK [Maamar] TWO

One may object here on the basis of a statement of Rabbi Yehuda son of Rabbi Simon. From the expression in Genesis, "and there was evening and there was morning, one day," he infers that the order of time existed before creation. From this statement it would seem that his opinion was either that the sphere is eternal, as Aristotle thought, or that the unmeasured duration is called order of time. The answer is that this is not the meaning of Rabbi Yehuda. The purpose of his statement is to obviate the notion suggested at first sight that the order of day and night did not begin until the fourth day when the luminaries were suspended in the sky. Having this in view, he says that from the first day when the sphere was created it was in motion, resulting in the order of day and night before the fourth day. Thus the appearance of evening and morning mentioned at the beginning is true. The reason why the Bible mentions the suspension of the luminaries and the stars on the fourth day is to show that their different motions by which they serve "for signs and for seasons, and for days and years," are for the purpose of exerting an influence upon the lower world by the different position of their light in relation to the earth. This is explained in the statement, "And God set them in the firmament of the heaven to give light upon the earth." It is clear therefore from the words of Rabbi Yehuda son of Rabbi Simon that the time that is measured by the motion of the sphere is called order of time and not time simply, and that time simply is the duration which has no prior and posterior, nor order of time, since there is no motion in it.

If, however, time is not a conceptual duration but one that is measured by the motion of the sphere, according to Aristotle's view, the meaning of divine priority and perpetuity would be that God is prior to all existing things and to time which is numbered by the motion of the sphere. The essential meaning of priority and perpetuity, though they are different, would thus be the same, namely that God always exists in the same way before time and after time will cease.

Therefore, we make independence of time one dogma, in order to include priority and perpetuity, whether time is a conceptual duration, as the Rabbis maintain, or one that is numbered by the motion of the sphere, according to the opinion of Aristotle. Thus we find that wherever the Bible describes God as first it also characterizes Him as last, to indicate that He has one attribute, independence of time, which embraces both. Isaiah says, "Thus saith the Lord, the King of Israel, and his Redeemer, the Lord of hosts: I am the first, and I am the last, and beside Me there is no God." The meaning is, there is no existing thing outside of Me that can be characterized as first and last, for all other existing things have time before them or after them and therefore are possible existents, whereas I, being independent of time, am not a possible but a necessary existent. This is why Isaiah concludes, "And beside Me there is no God," i.e., among all existing things there is no necessary existent, i.e., one who is all-powerful, outside of Me, for there is no one to whom the names first and last apply outside of Me, and therefore it is clear that I alone am God, i.e., a necessary existent.

Chapter 19

From our discussion proving that God is not subject to time, it follows that every attribute applied to God, whether it be positive or negative, must be prior and perpetual like Him, i.e., must be infinite on both sides, a parte ante and a parte post. For it is impossible that any of His attributes should come into being, not having been before, else God would be composed of things having origin. But whatever is composed of things having origin, itself has origin and is not prior in the general sense of the term. Similarly, it is impossible that any attribute should be in Him at one time and not at another, for then God would be subject to change, which is impossible. For change is motion and the realization of the potential. Moreover, all motion takes place in time. God would therefore have need of time to change in, and if He is subject to change, He would be subject to genesis and would not be eternal, but we have already proved that He is absolutely eternal. It is clear therefore that no change can apply to Him.

The other existing things, however, are subject to time, therefore time causes them to change. Even the Separate Intelligences, which are not composed of opposites, and thus are not subject to qualitative or quantitative change which are due to the presence of opposites, may nevertheless be subject to change in time. Thus, the first effect, having come into being in time, was, let us say, two thousand years old in the time of Abraham, whereas now it is five thousand years old or more. Similarly, everything that was created is necessarily older to-day than it was in the time of David, and hence is subject to time. But we can not say of God that He is older to-day than He was in the time of David, or when He created the world, because He has always existed in the same way before the world was created, will continue the same after the world comes to an end, and time will not change Him.

This is the meaning of the statement of the Rabbis in their comment on the verse, "I have been young, and now am old ..." Who is the author of this observation? they ask. It can not be David, for he was not old enough to be warranted in making such a statement, in other words, the three-score and ten years that David lived are not sufficient to warrant a person in stating a universal proposition, such as, "Yet have I not seen the righteous forsaken." It can not be God who is responsible for the statement, for there is no old age in God. The author of the statement must, therefore, be the prince of the world. Here we see an explicit statement that God can not be described as old, while the Active Intellect, who is the prince of the world, is described as young and old. Being created, he is subject to time, and the terms youth and old age apply to him in respect to time, though not in respect to strength and weakness. For it necessarily follows that we can count the number of his days and years in so far as he is a created being, a fact which does not apply to God, for being prior to time, He is not changed by time. Therefore, there is no other being who can say about himself, "I, I am He," using the first personal pronoun twice, except God, who exists always in the same way. Therefore, the Bible says, "See now that I, even I, am He," "I, even I, am the Lord; and beside Me there is no saviour." The meaning of the latter expression is, I can save because I exist always in the same way without change, but no other being can save, because he is subject to change.

Chapter 20

The word **Kol** [all, every] denotes primarily the totality of a thing, as, "The Lord hath made all things for His own purpose"; "And God saw every thing that He had made, and behold, it was generally good." The last expression means that in all existing things, the good prevails and predominates.

The word is also applied to all the particulars that are included in the general, as, "And all the souls that came out of the loins of Yaakov were seventy souls," which without doubt applies to every one of the individuals. The same is true of the expression, "And Abraham took Ishmael his son, and all that were born in his house ... and circumcised ..."

Sometimes the word denotes the greater part of a thing, as, "That I may dwell in the house of the Lord all the days of my life," "And all the congregation lifted up their voice and cried," "But all the congregation bade stone them with stones." And similarly, in many other passages.

Sometimes again the word denotes a part of the whole, though not the greater part, provided it is a large part. Thus Isaiah says, "For the Lord hath indignation against all the nations, and fury against all their host," though he means only a small part of the nations, as he explains at the end, "For the Lord hath a sacrifice in Bozrah, and a great slaughter in the land of Edom," and it is in reference to Edom that he says, "From generation to generation it shall lie waste; None shall pass through it for ever and ever." Similarly, Jeremiah says, in reference to the destruction of Yerushalayim, "The whole land shall be desolate." Zephaniah also says, "But the whole earth shall be devoured by the fire of His jealousy; for He will make an end, yea, a terrible end, of all them that dwell in the earth," though he refers to the land of Israel alone. Similarly, Zechariah says, "And the Lord shall be King over all the earth." During the time of the first temple Israel worshipped idols and did not acknowledge God's kingdom through all the land of Israel. Therefore, the prophet says that during the time of the second temple, He will be King over all the earth, meaning that God's kingdom will be acknowledged over all the land of Israel, which will be under the rule of a prince descended from the seed of David, and will not any more be divided into two kingdoms. That this is the correct interpretation is shown from the sequel, which says, "All the land shall be turned as the Arabah, from Geba to Rimmon," which without doubt refers to Yerushalayim and a small part of the land of Yehuda, for he says, "From Geba to Rimmon south of Yerushalayim."

Sometimes the word **Kol** denotes a small part of the whole, and "all" means "some of all," as, "And all countries came into Egypt," which means, from some countries they came. Before this it says, "And there was famine in all lands," meaning that part of the world containing the lands near to the land of Egypt, to a small part of which lands he then refers in the words, "And all countries came into Egypt." In the same way should be interpreted, "And all the earth sought the presence of Solomon." It means, "and some of all the earth sought ..." Similarly, "All nations shall serve him," referring to Solomon, denotes a small part of the earth and of the nations. It is in the last sense of the word that we must understand such expressions, referring to God, as, "That I may tell of all Thy praise." It does not mean that a man is able to enumerate every one of God's praises, far from it! The meaning is that he will tell a small part of God's praises. The Bible frequently omits the partitive mem, as in the expression, "Thy throne, God, is for ever and ever," which

Sefer Halkkarim   BOOK [Maamar] TWO

means, "Thy throne given of God is forever and ever," alluding to David, concerning whose throne it was decreed by God that it shall be forever and ever, because "The sceptre of his kingdom was a sceptre of equity." Or it may allude to the Messiah. Similarly, "Having all goodly things of his master's in his hand," means, "of all goodly things of his master's in his hand." So the Bible says about Hazael when he went to meet Elisha, "And took a present with him, even every good thing of Damascus." Here too the meaning is, "of every good thing of Damascus."

We also find instances in which the word "all" does not mean "of all," and yet it denotes a small part of the whole, as in "I will pour out My spirit upon all flesh," in Joel. This refers to a small part of all Israel, not to all of them, and surely not to the Gentiles. The phrase, "upon all flesh," means upon any one at all of all flesh, even though he is not prepared for prophetic inspiration. There are many other such passages besides.

The various uses of this word must be carefully borne in mind, for they are very peculiar, and the distinction enables us in many cases to explain the character of certain prophecies, as to whether they are universal in meaning or not. Thus, we read, "For Joab and all Israel remained there six months, until he had cut off every male in Edom," whereas later we find a king of Edom in the time of the kings of Yehuda. In the same way we can find out as to certain prophecies whether they were fulfilled in the past or whether they are still awaiting fulfilment in the future.

Chapter 21

We will now explain the fourth dogma mentioned above, that God is free from defects. If we reflect very carefully and deeply upon the matter of attributes, we shall find that God must necessarily be characterized by many attributes, and not merely from the point of view of His acts alone and for the reason mentioned in chapter eight of this Book, but from the point of view of Himself.

The affirmative and the negative always divide between them the true and the false in all modes of predication, the necessary, the impossible and the possible. Taking the possible mode as an instance, it is clear that we can not escape the disjunction that God is either wise or not wise, possessing power or not possessing power, having a will or not having a will. But it can not be true that God is not wise, or does not possess power, for there can not be any defect in God. It follows therefore that the other part of the disjunction is true, namely that He is wise, possesses power, has a will, is kind, upright, reliable. The same thing holds of all perfections, viz. that He must have the perfection because He can not have the defect. This is a necessary conclusion without regard to the acts which emanate from God, as when we say He is living because life emanates from Him, or He is wise because wisdom emanates from Him, and so with the other attributes. No, He is living and wise because He can not be dead or ignorant. But since perfections are of different kinds, knowledge being different from power, power different from life, life different from will and from wisdom, it follows that He has many different attributes. Approaching the problem in this way, therefore, we come to the conclusion that God has many attributes, while from the discussion in the tenth chapter of this book we concluded that He has no attribute except Himself. The problem therefore is how God can have many attributes without introducing plurality in His essence.

Our solution is this: The attributes ascribed to God are of two kinds. There is one class of attributes which we ascribe to Him because He is a necessary existent and the cause of all existing things, neither of which He can be conceived to be unless He has the attributes in question. Such attributes are, one, eternal, perpetual, wise, having will, possessing power, and others besides, which God must have in order to be the author of all existing things. There is another class of attributes which we ascribe to Him because we imagine that they constitute perfection. Thus, we ascribe to Him riches because we imagine that riches constitute perfection in God as they constitute perfection in us, the opposite being a defect. We also ascribe hearing and seeing to God, because they are perfections in us, though we can exercise those powers only by means of corporeal organs.

Now every attribute ascribed to any subject has in it two aspects. One aspect is that of the perfection inherent in the attribute. The other is the defect which supervenes as a result of the attribute. Accordingly, the attribute is, so to speak, composed mentally of two elements, one being a perfection, the other a defect. Thus, if we attribute wisdom to a subject, the attribute is in itself a mark of perfection in the subject. But on the other hand, from the fact that it is acquired by the subject and accidental in him, there results a defect in the subject, because the attribute is not essential in him, and thus induces plurality.

Now when we attribute wisdom to God, we do so only with a view to the perfection that is involved and not the defect. The defect involved in the perfection exists only if we view wisdom in relation to ourselves who acquire it gradually through one conclusion after another as each is derived from its premises. It is therefore something that originates in us from a state of not being, and is an attribute added to our essence. But when we attribute knowledge to God we do not think of it as derived from premises or as coming into being in Him as it comes into being in us. We rather think of it as inherent in God Himself, in the same way as the axioms exist in man, requiring neither learning nor teaching, except that knowledge is in God in a more perfect manner. When we attribute wisdom to God, therefore, our purpose is to indicate that He has this perfection without any defect, though the only way we can conceive of attaining wisdom is that in which man acquires it. Similarly, we say concerning power, will and the other attributes, that they are ascribed to God with a view to the perfection attaching to the attribute in question and not with a view to the defect.

In this way we can ascribe to Him attributes of the second class also, which involve corporeal perceptions. Thus, we attribute to Him the sense of smell, which is a sensuous perception, as we read, "And the Lord smelled the sweet savour." But we do not attribute it to God as being a corporeal perception, but with a view to the perfection which it involves, namely that God accepts favorably the offering of a person who brings it with a worthy purpose; we do not think of God as deriving pleasure from the offering, which would be a defect.

This is what the prophet means when he says, "For I spoke not unto your fathers, nor commanded them in the day that I brought them out of the land of Egypt concerning burnt-offerings or sacrifices; but this thing I commanded them, saying: 'Hearken unto My voice.'" Here we are told that the purpose of the institution of sacrifices was that the heart of the sinner may be humbled so that he may return to God and hearken to His voice, but not to give God sensuous satisfaction, Heaven forbid! The following passage makes it clear, "Do I eat the flesh of bulls, or drink the blood of goats? Offer unto God the sacrifice of thanksgiving ... and call upon Me in the day of trouble ..." All this shows that the purpose of the institution of sacrifices was to direct the heart of the sinner to the worship of God, and nothing else.

For this reason, we do not attribute to Him the sense of taste and the sense of touch, because though they constitute a perfection in us, as corporeal animals, in that they enable us to pursue what is beneficial and to avoid that which is injurious, there is no spiritual perfection involved in them which we can attribute to God. Hearing is attributed to God, in the expression, "Let Thine ears be attentive ...," and so is sight, "Behold, the eye of the Lord is toward them that fear Him," "The eyes of the Lord, that run to and for through the whole earth," because people imagine there is spiritual perfection in these senses. Therefore, they are attributed to God, though taste and touch are not. This shows that the attributes are ascribed to God by reason of the perfection that is in them, and not by reason of the defect. Therefore, we say that the attributes ascribed to God must be conceived as unified in Him, though in us they are separate and distinct. We conceive of them as separate because we acquire them one after the other. Similarly, we think of them as adventitious because we acquire them, not having had them before. But in the case of God, we must conceive them as unified and not as acquired, else they would induce plurality in His essence, which is a defect.

We have thus made it clear that the attributes are ascribed to God with a view to the perfection they involve and not the defect, for God is free from defects. Our fourth dogma, therefore, that God is free from defects, signifies that all attributes of imperfection, such as ignorance, poverty, sleep, fatigue, and so on, must be rejected, and also that all attributes of perfection which are ascribed to God are conceived as being in Him so far as they involve perfection, but not so far as they involve or are the source of a defect, such as plurality or change, which are defects in God, since He endures forever in the same manner and without any change.

This is the meaning of the Psalmist when he says, "O God, keep not Thou silence; hold not Thy peace, and be not still, O God." That is, since Thou art not silent either because of sleep or ignorance or fatigue, since there is no defect in Thee and Thou art not subject to change, then, "Wherefore lookest Thou, when they deal treacherously, and holdest Thy peace, when the wicked swalloweth up the man that is more righteous than he?" "Hold not Thy peace, and be not still, O God." According to our explanation those positive attributes which we can not but attribute to God, like living, wise, possessing will, having power, and so on, must be conceived in a manner not to necessitate a defect. This explanation deserves careful attention because it is the true and correct one, and has been adopted by ancient and modern theological authorities. It is worthy of acceptance and the reader is so urged.

Chapter 22

All the philosophers think that it is impossible to ascribe to God any attribute, essential or accidental, which expresses God Himself, but only those which are expressive of His acts, as we explained in chapter nine of this Book. The theological authorities who follow the view of the philosophers are of the same opinion. Thus, Maimonides says that he who maintains that God has essential attributes, which yet do not induce plurality in His essence, is unconsciously combining the affirmative and the negative. Maimonides, therefore, follows a view of his own, namely that no positive attribute can be ascribed to God, but only a negative; that all negative attributes can be truly predicated of Him, but no positive attribute, except those expressive of His acts. Accordingly he says that as God is called ground, cause, principle because he is the ground, cause and principle of all things, which are His effects; and as he is called fashioner, worker, creator, maker, renewer, because He brings all things into being with His simple will and without any compulsion, so He is called wise because He brings forth all existing things with great wisdom which is evident in their formation, and He is called merciful and gracious and kind because He guides all existing things and treats them graciously, mercifully and kindly, not by way of recompense, for, as the Bible says, "Who hath given Me anything beforehand, that I should repay him?" and He is called generous or a "doer of charity" because He bestows blessings and perfection upon all existing things without the expectation of any benefit or reward, just as a generous and noble person is in the habit of doing. For generosity involves two elements, one touching the recipient and the other concerning the giver.

With regard to the recipient, it is necessary that he be given something that is useful to him. There is no generosity in giving a sword to a boy, a book to a woman, or a spindle to a man, gifts which are of no benefit to them. The proper thing is to give the spindle to the woman, the sword to the man, and the book to the boy to study from. With regard to the giver, it is necessary that the act be not done in expectation of something in return which he desires. For if the giver finds it expedient to make the gift, he is not a generous person, but a business man, who gives away a certain thing in order to receive in return money or the equivalent of money or honor. It is not generosity even if he gives away twice the value of the thing desired in exchange. For this simply means that he estimates his need of the object at that price. He is still no more than a business man who buys a thing for more than its worth because he needs it. Another requisite is that the author of the act should not be in need of appreciation or praise for that act. For a person who does a thing that he may receive praise or congratulation or fame, or be saved from disgrace, is in want of that praise, which he gets as a kind of reward, though he is not in the same category as the first.

Now God bestowed upon all things those qualities that were appropriate and agreeable and beneficial to them, as the Rabbis say concerning the works of creation, that they were made with their consent, with their beauty and their stature. The meaning is that when God created those things, He granted to them the beauty and form and excellence which were good and appropriate for them. This is the meaning of the expression, "with their beauty and their stature." "With their consent," means that if, for example, they had been asked whether they desired to have the form, i.e., the beauty, the stature and the excellence which was given to them, they would have said, yes. It implies also that God did not make these things in order to receive reward or to be saved from disgrace. It is clear therefore that He is truly generous. And inasmuch as generosity without the expectation of reward is charity, God is called the "doer of charity," which is the noblest act of generosity. He is called so not merely because of what He did at the time of creation, but because of His continued activity in maintaining the existence of things and in sending forth an influence which keeps them in being, for continued goodness is true generosity.

Thus, the Bible says, "O give thanks unto the Lord; for He is good," and concludes that the essence of His goodness is that "His mercy endureth forever," i.e., it continues. For this reason, God is spoken of as "He who does charity at all times," as in the verse, "Happy are they that keep the justice of Him that doeth righteousness at all times." The word 'oseh, being singular, must refer to God, and the meaning is, Happy are they that keep the justice of God, who does righteousness at all times, and that imitate His conduct, as the Rabbis say, by way of comment on the text: "And walk in His ways," "As He is merciful, be thou merciful; as He is gracious, be thou gracious." So, God is called, "Long-suffering and abundant in goodness ... visiting the iniquity of the fathers upon the children ...," by reason of the acts which emanate from Him in the government of mankind. Such attributes and their like may be ascribed to Him, though there are contradictory ones among them, like "merciful" and "visiting the iniquity of the fathers upon the children."

This was the information given to Moshe in answer to his request, "Show me now Thy ways." Moshe' question was, how can a person ask God to do contradictory things, since God is an absolutely simple unity and free from corporeal affections? In reply God showed him that He governs His creatures by means of the thirteen attributes, and petitions should be made in accordance with them. So, the Rabbis say, commenting on the text, "And the Lord passed by before him ...," "Said Rabbi Yohanan - If it were not for the explicit statement in the text, we should not think of saying it. But from the text we infer that God wrapped Himself up in His prayer-garment like a precentor and gave Moshe an object lesson, saying to him, 'Whenever Israel sin, they should do as I am doing now and I will forgive them.' " The meaning of this statement is that God informed Moshe through prophetic inspiration that it is. proper to use the thirteen attributes in praying to Him, because they are derived from the modes of His activity in governing His creatures, and attributes of this sort, Maimonides says, may be used in praising God and in making supplication to Him.

But those attributes which denote God Himself must not be used in praise or in prayer. Thus the Rabbis say, commenting on the words, "The great God, the mighty, and the awful," that even though Moshe used these attributes, we should not have permitted ourselves to use them in our prayers - they thought that these attributes refer to God Himself and not to His acts - if it were not that the men of the Great Synagogue explained that these attributes also have reference to the modes of activity in which God governs His creatures, and hence may be used in praising Him. Concerning these men, the Rabbis say: They are called the men of the Great Synagogue because they restored the Crown to its original position. They said, God's strength is shown in being long-suffering as against those who transgress His will. His awfulness is obvious, for if not for that quality of His, a single nation like that of Israel could not exist among the other nations. In the same way they interpreted the rest of the attributes, pointing out that they are named after the modes of God's conduct toward His creatures. And therefore, it is proper to embody them in prayer, in the same way as Moshe used the thirteen attributes in praying to God, because they are derived from God's acts.

But even the attributes of this class [i.e., those taken from God's acts] must be taken in the sense involving perfection, not in the sense involving defect. Thus, although these attributes cause emotion in us and make us change from one of the contraries to the other, they do not necessitate any change or emotion in God, for His ways are not our ways, nor are His thoughts our thoughts.

Sefer HaIkkarim — BOOK [Maamar] TWO
Chapter 23

Those attributes which are ascribed to God and are not based upon His acts, like one, eternal, true, and so on, can not, according to the philosophic view, be ascribed to Him except in a negative way, as we have explained in relation to the attributes one and eternal. The same thing applies to the attribute true. The meaning of this attribute is, as we shall see, one whose existence does not depend upon anything not himself. But these attributes can not be applied to God in a positive sense, because those attributes which are predicated of God as He is in Himself, if taken in a positive sense, far from being appreciative are rather derogatory in relation to God, and are not of the class of attributes which are becoming to Him, as Maimonides says.

He cites in this connection the words of Rabbi Hanina who, hearing a person employ many attributes in his prayer, used the following comparison. A king who had thousands upon thousands of gold denars was praised for his wealth, which was estimated at thousands upon thousands of silver denars. This praise was surely, in the king's estimation, derogatory.

It will be noticed that he does not say that they estimated his wealth at a thousand gold denars. In that case the derogation would be due to the fact that the amount attributed to him was less than the actual amount. But he says that they attributed to the king silver denars, indicating that the difference between the praise and the reality was not one of degree but of kind, as silver, though valuable, does not belong to the same species as gold.

This is the reason why Maimonides says that all those attributes which are not derived from God's acts must be understood as negative and not positive, as we explained in chapter ten of this Book in relation to the attribute one. For this reason we must refrain from using attributes of our own invention, not employed by Moshe and the prophets. And even those that are used by them, we must understand, are merely metaphorical when used positively, in reality they can only have a negative sense.

Accordingly, the attributes applied to God are of two kinds. First, those which describe His own nature, which is absolutely unknown even to the wise. These can not be understood in a positive sense, not to speak of being expatiated upon. The other kind are those attributes which are derived from the acts of God. This meaning of the attributes is known to all, even to fools and ignoramuses, as the Psalmist says, "Consider, ye brutish among the people; and ye fools,

Sefer HaIkkarim — BOOK [Maamar] TWO

when will ye understand? He that planted the ear, shall He not hear? He that formed the eye, shall He not, see? ..." The same is true of the manner in which God governs His creatures. These aspects of God we may expatiate upon.

David, in the one hundred and third Psalm, alludes to both kinds of divine praise. He says twice, "Bless the Lord, O my soul," in allusion to the two kinds of praise that we mentioned. Referring to the praise which attaches to God as He is in Himself, the Psalmist says, "Bless the Lord, O my soul; and all that is within me, bless His holy name." The meaning is, my soul, bless the Lord with the brevity of praise that befits Him, in view of the excellence of His nature and of His holy name, i.e., Himself. As to this, one must not multiply words, nay, one must not even pronounce them with his lips unless he understands them in a negative sense. Hence the Psalmist expresses himself briefly and without any explanations. The expression, "All that is within me, bless His holy name," signifies the praise which is becoming to Him in view of the excellence of His holy name, which is ineffable.

In allusion to the second mode of praise, which is derived from His acts, from the goodness which emanates from Him, and from the manner in which He governs His creatures, he says a second time, "Bless the Lord, O my soul," ending up with the words, "And forget not all His benefits." Here he enumerates at length the kindnesses received from God, "Who forgiveth all thine iniquity, who redeemeth thy life from the pit," and so on. Among the divine benefits he mentions, "He made known His ways unto Moshe," in allusion to the attributes with which He governs His creatures. For the thirteen attributes which were revealed to Moshe are derived from the acts of God by which He governs His creatures, as was said in the preceding chapter. These are attributes of mercy.

Moshe also describes God with the two kinds of attributes that we mentioned, and praises Him in the manner we described. Alluding to the attributes which denote God as He is in Himself, he says that he hesitates to use them in God's praise. But he uses freely and at length those attributes which represent God's acts. This is why he says twice, "Who is like unto Thee among the mighty?" in allusion, namely, to the two modes of praise. Referring to the first, he says, "Fearful in praises"; in reference to the second, he says, "Doing wonders." Then he expatiates at length upon the second, "Thou stretchedst out Thy right hand ... Thou hast guided them in Thy strength ..."

To obviate the notion that those attributes which it is permitted to ascribe to God and with which He may be praised on the basis of His acts, are to be understood in the same way as when they are ascribed to man, he says in the beginning of the song, "I will sing unto the Lord," as if to say, all the praises which I shall mention are to be understood as an expression of the poetic style, which is an exercise of the imagination and does not describe reality. By way of poetic license, I will describe God with attributes to afford the senses a point of support. Therefore, he says, "A man of war"; "And in the greatness of Thine excellency"; "And with the blast of Thy nostrils"; "Thou sendest forth Thy wrath"; "Thy right hand, O Lord, dasheth in pieces the enemy."

In reality, however, it is impossible to ascribe any attribute to Him, even one that is based upon His acts, in the manner in which we ascribe it to a human being, "For He is highly exalted." The meaning is, I speak of Him in poetic style, but in reality, He is highly exalted above all kinds of praise. The most fitting praise, therefore, in the case of God is silence, as David says, "For Thee silence is praise." The Rabbis understand it in the same way, when they say, the most wholesome recipe of all is silence, as is said, "For Thee silence is praise," and therefore Moshe called Him, "Fearful in praises."

Chapter 24

We have seen that there are two kinds of attributes by which God is characterized, attributes which describe Himself and attributes which are derived from His activities. In each of these classes there are attributes in respect to which it is perfectly clear that they describe God in respect to His activities or that they describe Himself, as the case may be. Thus the attributes, "Merciful and gracious, long-suffering and abundant in goodness," are obviously drawn from God's activities, while such attributes as "one" and "eternal" clearly describe God Himself, and, as we have seen, must be understood in a negative sense and not as really characterizing God's essence.

But there are certain attributes as to which it is doubtful whether they describe God's essence or the activities which come from Him. We must therefore explain the manner of understanding these attributes. We will explain a few as an example of the rest.

When we say that God is good, the attribute must be understood in both of the ways mentioned above. God is good because of His actions, for all good things come from Him, and the good can only come from the good, as we read in the Psalms, "The Lord is good to all." But when the same attribute is applied to God to describe His essence, it must be understood in a negative sense. God is called good because His essence is free from defect, since there is no potentiality in Him, as we explained before. Therefore, no change or privation attaches to Him, for all privation is evil.

We find that the Bible too has these two modes of characterizing God as good: "Thou art good, and doest good; Teach me Thy statutes." "Thou art good" is intended as a description of God's essence, while "doest good" has reference to the good things which come from God.

Similarly, when we say that God is wise, the attribute may be understood as referring to God's acts. Since God is the author of existence, which is perfect and wonderful in its order and arrangement, it follows that He is wise and understands all the things of which He is the author, as is said in the Bible, "He that planted the ear, shall He not hear? ... He that instructeth nations, shall not He correct, even He that teacheth man knowledge?" Here we see the Psalmist Inferring God's understanding and knowledge from the fact that all understanding and knowledge come from God. But when the attribute wise is applied to God to describe His essence, it must be understood in a negative sense, meaning that nothing is concealed from Him. For since God is pure intellect and separate from matter, as we proved before, nothing can be hidden from Him. It is matter that obstructs and prevents us from apprehending the sensible and intelligible things. Thus, water flowing from the eye or other diseases of the eye prevent it from seeing what it desires to see. The same is true of diseases of the nose and the ear. In general, it is true that matter prevents us from apprehending sensible things as they really are. In the same way the vapors rising from the stomach confuse the powers of the brain, preventing them from apprehending their objects, as is the case with persons who are drunk. Similarly excessive moisture hinders one from apprehending intelligible things, as we see in young people. During the period of growth, when the moisture is abundant, they do not attain the degree of comprehension which their intellect is able to attain. It is clear therefore that one who is pure intellect is called wise because nothing is hidden from Him, and He is not ignorant of anything which it is in His nature to understand, because there are no causes in Him which obstruct understanding.

When we say that God has will, the statement may have reference to God's activities. Then the meaning is that all things which exist in heaven and earth were made by His simple will, as we read,

Sefer HaIkkarim — BOOK [Maamar] TWO

"Whatever the Lord pleased, that hath He done, in heaven and in earth." This expression is constantly used in relation to God. When we see a certain act coming from God, being realized and completed like the act of a voluntary agent, we say that the agent no doubt willed the act, else it would not have been realized. So, we read, "Be pleased, O Lord, to deliver me"; "For the Lord taketh pleasure in His people; He adorneth the humble with salvation." The coming of salvation indicates will, as the prophet says, "That he understandeth, and knoweth Me, that I am the Lord who exercise mercy, justice and righteousness, in the earth; for these things I desire, saith the Lord." Here we see that the prophet infers God's desire from His doings, for in a person of intellect and reason the doing of a thing is an indication of the will and desire to do it.

It is clear therefore that since we see acts emanating from God which are similar to those acts which emanate from a voluntary agent, we speak of God as desiring and willing; though we can not understand how will and desire reside in God without causing change and affection. This is unknown to us, as the nature of His knowledge is unknown to us. We ascribe knowledge to Him because it is a perfection which it is inconceivable that God should be without. The same is true of will, as we explained in chapter three of this Book.

If we wish to explain this attribute in a negative sense, the meaning is that God does not reject or abandon or forget to bestow goodness and perfection, as we read in the Bible, "Lord, thou hast shown good will unto Thy land, thou hast turned the captivity of Yaakov." "Good will" in this case means that God did not reject or abandon them, and did not forget to show them mercy, unlike the sentiment expressed in the passage, "Then My anger shall be kindled against them in that day, and I will forsake them, and I will hide My face from them, and they shall be devoured." Hence the Psalmist adds, "Thou hast withdrawn all Thy wrath; Thou hast turned from the fierceness of Thine anger."

When we say that God is powerful or strong, we may likewise have reference to God's acts, in which case the meaning is that He can carry out His wish in relation to all existing things without any hindrance, as a strong man does whatever he desires. And if we use the word to describe God's essence, we must understand it in a negative sense as indicating that God is not infirm and unable to do what He desires. It follows therefore that He has infinite power. For if His power were finite, there would be some infirmity. But the meaning of the attribute powerful is that He has no infirmity.

The attribute living if applied to God with reference to His acts, means that life flows from Him. He must therefore necessarily be living; else life could not issue from Him. If applied to describe God's essence, it must be understood in a negative sense. In this sense our meaning is that the influences which emanate from Him do not come in the manner of light from a lamp or heat from fire, both of which flow from their sources without any knowledge or will on the part of the latter. Not so with God, for He exerts His influence in the best manner possible, namely with knowledge and will, like a living being. He knows what He bestows, He has the power to bestow, and He desires to bestow, else the object would not receive His influence. The meaning is that the influence which comes from God is accompanied by knowledge, will and power, like the influence which comes from a living being.

The matter is very subtle and difficult to expatiate upon. The important thing is to understand what is meant, namely that God has infinite power, i.e., is not unable to bestow, and is willing to bestow, viz. does not reject or abandon or forget the idea of bestowing. And He knows what He bestows, i.e., He is not ignorant and not unaware of the content of His bestowal or of the object which receives favors from Him. This is why we say that He is living, for a living being understands what it does and wills it, i.e., it does not act by nature like the radiation of heat from fire.

Thus, the four attributes, living, wise, willing, powerful, all come to one negative idea, as we have explained. All the attributes applied to describe God's essence must be understood in this way, namely in a negative sense, no matter how many there are, for all negative attributes can be truly predicated of God. And there is no harm if one enumerates more than those we mentioned, or if one says that there is an infinite number of them, as long as they are understood in a negative sense, so that no defect is implied in the nature of God. This is the reason why we lay down, as a fourth derivative principle, that God is free from defects, following the opinion of Maimonides, that positive attributes can not be ascribed to the nature of God, and must be excluded because they would imply a defect.

Chapter 25

There are certain corollaries which follow from the fourth derivative dogma, freedom from defects, whether we understand it in the philosophical or in the theological sense mentioned in the second chapter of this Book. One of these corollaries is that if we ascribe to God one of the applicable attributes, whether it be negative or positive, the attribute in question must be understood as being infinite in two respects, in time and in worth. For example, since we have shown that God is eternal and perpetual, i.e., that He exists in infinite time a parte ante as well as a parte post, it follows that any attribute characterizing Him must be eternal and perpetual like God Himself. For as God has existed and will exist an infinite time, so the attributes exist in God an infinite time, for they can not have arisen in Him at a given moment or be limited in their existence to a given time, as we explained before.

When I say an infinite time, I am using an inaccurate and loose expression. For we cannot say of God that He exists an infinite time, since He is prior to time, unless duration is time. But the meaning is that He has no limit either in the past or in the future. Hence every attribute of His is infinite in time.

Similarly, every attribute is infinite in worth. When we say that God is wise, there is no doubt that we mean to say that His wisdom is infinite in perfection. For since His essence is infinite in perfection, He must know His essence. But the infinitely perfect can only be known by infinitely perfect knowledge, for the finite can not embrace the infinite. Similarly, if we say that God is powerful, we must understand that His power is infinite. For if it were finite, we can imagine a greater power, and He would then be infirm, as not having the greater power imagined. So, when we say that God is good, we must understand that He is infinitely good. For if His goodness were limited, there might be a greater good than He, and He would not be absolutely good.

In the same way every attribute that is applied to God must be understood as being infinite in worth, without any defect. Thus the attribute existence, which is ascribed to God, must be understood as being in God by virtue of Himself and not acquired from another. But when we ascribe existence to something other than God, it can not be infinite in worth, for the existence is acquired from another. There is no other being, every one of whose attributes is infinite in worth, except God. Every one of His attributes is infinite in time, as we have explained, and also infinite in worth and goodness. This is the meaning of the biblical expression, "In Thy right hand bliss for evermore," as will be explained in the thirtieth chapter of this Book. We must also understand that the perfections existing in God are infinite in number. For since God must have all the kinds of perfection that can be conceived, and must be free from all kinds of defect, and since we can conceive of His having an in finite number of perfections, He must really have them, else He would not be absolutely perfect, if there are more perfections than He possesses. It is clear therefore that He must have an infinite number of perfections, such as we cannot conceive.

This is the reason why the name **Zebaot** [hosts] is one of those divine names that it is forbidden to erase. It is an allusion to this kind of perfection. It is also this kind of perfection to which the pious Rabbi Hanina alluded when he remarked to one who enumerated a great many attributes in his prayer, "Have you completed all the praises of your Lord?" The meaning is that since they are infinite it is not proper to use a definite number, indicating as it were that there is a number which completes them, for this would be a defect in God, whereas He is free from defects.

David alludes to these three kinds of infinity in the Psalm beginning, "O Lord, thou hast searched me, and known me." In this Psalm he undertakes to praise God's knowledge, pointing out its infinite character embracing as it does every one of His movements and acts, many and scattered as they are. "O Lord, thou hast searched me and known me," indicates that God's knowledge is not like man's knowledge. Man searches without attaining his quest, but God searches the heart, tries the veins, and finds and knows our thoughts. Hence the words, "Thou understandest my thought [re'i] afar off." Re'i is derived from ra'ayon. He then proceeds to explain this at length, using creation to illustrate his point. "For Thou hast made my reins Thou hast knit me together in my mother's womb." And he ends up the same way in the words, "Thine eyes did see my unformed substance, etc." He means to say that God knew him not only after he was formed, but when he was still a crude mass of stuff without form, God's knowledge already embraced him. And not merely dost Thou know my unformed substance, who am a king and equal in worth to all the people put together, but "in Thy book they were all written," all the unformed substances, small and great, and Thou knowest the days when the forms will come down and give shape to the substances, before any one of them has been in existence. This is the meaning of the expression, "Even the days that were fashioned, when as yet there was none of them," reading lo with an aleph according to the ketib, as a negative. If we follow the masorah, where lo is written with a vav and is not a negative, the meaning is that the plurality of the objects of knowledge does not make the knowledge itself plural, but God's knowledge of them is one. Then he says, "How weighty also are Thy thoughts unto me, O God! How great is the sum of them!" The meaning is, "Thou understandest my thought afar off," but I can not understand Thy

Sefer Halkkarim   BOOK [Maamar] TWO

thoughts, i.e., Thy knowledge and Thy ideas, for they are very precious to me, and I can not comprehend them by reason of their superior excellence.

Besides, they are infinite in time. This is expressed in the words, "How great is the sum of them!"

Moreover, they are infinite in number, "If I would count them, they are more in number than the sand." And with all that they form in Thee a perfect unity, as the Psalmist says, "and He has one in them," and they are not something added to Thy essence, for when I awaken from my contemplation of this matter, I find that I am still with Thee, and that they are not something distinct from Thee.

It is also possible to say that the word re'eka refers to the attributes of perfection which are in God. He calls them re'eka [friends] to indicate that as God is infinite in worth and in time, so every one of the attributes is infinite in worth and in time.

Then he says, "If I would count them, they are more in number than the sand," to point out that the attributes of perfection in God are infinite. Thereby he intends to explain that we need not wonder how it is that the multiplicity of the objects of knowledge does not multiply the knowledge. For we find likewise that the attributes of God are infinite in the three respects mentioned, and yet God's essence is not multiplied thereby at all.

He calls the essential attributes re'eka [friends] to point to what we said in the beginning of the chapter, that the attributes of God are necessarily eternal like Him. "How weighty" alludes to the fact that every one of them is infinite in quality and worth. "How mighty are their heads" alludes to the fact that the attributes existing in God were there an infinite time before the world existed and will be there after the world has come to an end, referring to the two heads which time has, one in the direction of the beginning, and the other in the direction of the end. Hence the expression, "their heads," i.e., the two heads or ends which time has.

Then he praises the multiplicity of the attributes, the fact, namely, that God's perfections are infinite and can not be bounded by any number, "If I would count them, they are more in number than the sand." And to prevent the thought that there is plurality in God by reason of the plurality of attributes, he says, "When I awaken, I am still with Thee." The meaning is, when I reflect on the attributes and find that they are necessarily many, because they denote perfections different from one another - for knowledge denotes something different from power and from will; and all these attributes denote something other than the quiddity - and this reflection suggests that the attributes necessitate a kind of plurality in Thee, "I awaken and am still with Thee." The meaning is, when I awaken from my reflection upon the plurality of attributes, I see that all these attributes are merely intellectual conceptions indicating that those perfections are found in Thy essence, but in reality they are not anything outside of Thee. "I am still with Thee," means that the attributes are not something other than Thou and do not necessitate plurality in Thy essence. For just as the attribute unity is not something added to the quiddity, but is an intellectual conception denoting the absence of plurality, so wisdom and knowledge are not anything other than the quiddity, but are intellectual conceptions denoting the absence of ignorance.

Similarly concerning all the infinite number of attributes existing in God, we can say that they are intellectual conceptions denoting that God is free from defects, and denoting nothing else. When the Cabalists call God the endless [En Sof], it is precisely this that they mean to indicate, namely that the perfections existing in Him are infinite in the three respects mentioned.

Chapter 26

The word baruk, blessed, is a homonymous term. It is applied to one who receives benefits and favors from another, as in the expressions, "Thou shalt not curse the people; for they are blessed"; "Blessed shalt thou be in the city, and blessed shalt thou be in the field"; and in many other cases. It is also applied to one who bestows favors and benefits upon another, as in the expressions, "Blessed be the Lord my Rock, who traineth my hands for war"; "Blessed be the Lord, For He hath shown me His wondrous lovingkindness in an entrenched city"; "Blessed art Thou, O Lord; Teach me Thy statutes"; "Blessed be the Lord, who hath delivered you."

Blessing is a term applied to addition and increase of benefit and favor. Hence when the word baruk is applied to the recipient, it is a passive participle. We find the infinitive absolute of the Kal of the root barak in the expression, "Therefore he even blessed [barok] you." Hence the other forms of the Kal are based upon it, and baruk is a passive participle, meaning receiving abundance of benefits. When the word is applied to the giver, it is an adjective, like merciful and gracious, which are adjectives applied to God, indicating that the act which emanates from Him is a blessing, i.e., an increase of influence and of goodness. Just as curse means lack of goodness, as all commentators agree, so blessing means an increase of goodness.

Sefer HaIkkarim   BOOK [Maamar] TWO

The word baruk, therefore, is an attribute descriptive of the one who bestows an abundance of goodness.

The term blessing [berakah] is applied to abundance of various kinds of prosperity and success. We find it used to denote wealth of various kinds. Thus, "And the blessing of the Lord was upon all that he had, in the house and in the field"; while Solomon says, "The blessing of the Lord, it maketh rich, and He doth not add sorrow thereto." Ordinarily manifold wealth is a cause of great sorrow and trouble, as we are told, "He who increases property, increases sorrow." Hence Solomon says that wealth which comes with the blessing of God, even if it be manifold in its sources, is not accompanied with an increase of sorrow, as is usually the case.

The word blessing is also applied to good fortune in respect to children, as in the expressions, "Blessed shall be the fruit of thy body"; "And God appeared unto Yaakov again, when he came from Paddan-Aram, and blessed him." It is also applied to good health - "And He will bless thy bread and thy water; and I will take sickness away from the midst of thee." For when the Lord's blessing is upon the food, a person is not afflicted even with those diseases to which one is naturally liable. This is the meaning of the expression, "And I will take sickness away from the midst of thee." Much more is it true that he will not suffer from unnatural diseases, hence he says, "None shall miscarry, nor be barren in thy land," and no one will die prematurely, hence he says, "The number of thy days I will fulfil."

The word blessing is also applied to honor. Thus, David says, "Now, therefore, let it please Thee to bless the house of Thy servant, that it may continue forever before Thee." It is also applied to wisdom, "Blessed art Thou, O Lord, Teach me Thy statutes."

Now all increase of benefits and abundance of goodness causing various kinds of good fortune, can not come to a man except through an agent who is living, possessed of will, wise and powerful. An agency which acts by nature, like fire emanating from a lamp, or heat radiating from a fire, can not, while remaining the same, increase its light at one time and diminish it at another time, but it is always the same, as due to the agent. It is not the same with a voluntary agent, who can increase or diminish the act at will. Now every voluntary agent is necessarily living, for we can not conceive of will except as coming from a living being. A voluntary agent also knows what he bestows, and has the power to bestow. He therefore who bestows blessings and an abundance of good things is necessarily living, wise, possessed of will and powerful. The reason therefore why the expression "blessed" has been chosen with which

Sefer HaIkkarim   BOOK [Maamar] TWO

to praise God is because it is a word denoting all kinds of good fortune, and indicates that it can come only from one who is an agent, living, wise, having will, and powerful. Thus, the word blessed is, as it were, a term inclusive of all perfections. For this reason, it alludes to the fourth dogma, God's freedom from defects, since the expression blessing is the opposite of curse, which denotes absence of goodness, as we have seen. The word blessing is also applied to praise and laudation generally. Thus, we read, "I will bless the Lord at all times," where bless means the same as praise, hence the verse concludes, "His praise shall continually be in my mouth."

This is the reason why the men of the Great Synagogue ordained that the expression of blessing shall be used in praising God for the manifold benefits which man receives from God, benefits of body of all kinds and benefits of soul. The benediction of grace after meals is an example of praise for physical blessings, while praise for spiritual blessings is illustrated in the blessings over the Torah, the blessings introductory to the performance of certain commandments, and other blessings besides, like those which praise God, indicating that He is the source of all blessings, and that all benefits and good fortune of every kind come from Him.

This is why the Rabbis say, "Four classes of persons are obliged to give thanks, etc." To prevent the thought that God is the author of good only, and that there is another power which is the author of evil, the Rabbis say that one is obliged to bless God for evil as well as for good, in order to show that everything comes from God. And as the word baruk embraces praise for all kinds of benefits and good fortune which are included in the term blessing, as we said before, David says, "And let all flesh bless His holy name for ever and ever." "All flesh" means every recipient of any kind of blessing whatsoever. For the word baruk denotes thanksgiving for all of them, i.e., for all kinds of perfection. For this reason, he begins with the words, "I will extol Thee, my God, O King." Then he explains that extolling God means, "And I will bless Thy name for ever and ever," which is the same as praise. Therefore, in the next verse, which begins, "Every day will I bless Thee," he concludes with the words, "And I will praise Thy name for ever and ever," using the word praise instead of bless, as in the first verse. Summing it all up, he says, "Great is the Lord, and superior to all praise." He is referring here to God's own being, for He cannot be praised except for His deeds. Therefore, he adds immediately, "One generation shall laud Thy works to another."

Sefer Halkkarim — BOOK [Maamar] TWO

We can not praise God in respect of His own essence, this being impossible for three reasons. First, because man's life is finite, and it is impossible in a finite time to give adequate praise which ought to last an infinite time. Secondly, because God's praiseworthy qualities are infinite in number, as we explained in the preceding chapter. And thirdly, because every one of the qualities is infinite in worth and intensity. This is why he begins with the words, "I will extol Thee, my God, O King; and I will bless Thy name for ever and ever." He does not mean to say that man can praise God for ever and ever, which is an infinite time, for this is impossible for human nature to do. What he means to say is that even if human life were infinite, and I were to extol Thy name for ever and ever, and the praise continued every day without any cessation in time and in praise [This is the meaning of the repetition: "Every day will I bless Thee; and I will praise Thy name for ever and ever"], even then, he says, he could not praise Him, because of the other two hindrances:

1. by reason of the infinite number of perfections in God - "The Lord is great, and superior to all praise" that any man could give by enumerating His qualities and excellences. And the other reason why this can not be done is

2. because every perfection of God is infinite in worth - "And His greatness" [i.e., any single quality] "is unsearchable," i.e., it is infinite in worth and therefore can not be bounded or embraced in a finite word. Therefore, to praise Thee as Thou art in Thyself is impossible for the three reasons we mentioned.

The proper way to praise Thee is with reference to the deeds and activities which emanate from Thee. They show that Thou art wise, possessed of will and powerful, as the Psalmist says, "One generation shall laud Thy works to another." The order of the acts and their perfection show that they emanate from a wise agent. Then he says, "And men shall speak of the might of Thy tremendous acts," which is an allusion to God's power. He continues, "They shall utter the fame of Thy great goodness," which is a reference to God's will, as we said before, for abundance of goodness indicates will.

The entire eulogy in the Psalm proceeds after the manner indicated. Then comes the verse, "All Thy works shall praise Thee, O Lord; and Thy saints shall bless Thee." Not everybody knows to discern God's excellence and perfection, but only the wise and the pious, who have some slight knowledge of God's excellence. Therefore, he says, 'All Thy works shall praise Thee, O Lord," i.e., praise Thee in a general way. But "Thy saints," i.e., the wise believers [for wisdom leads to saintliness], who know something of Thy greatness,

Sefer HaIkkarim — BOOK [Maamar] TWO

- they will not merely praise Thee in a general way, but will "bless Thee," which is more adequate praise, for the word "bless," as we have explained, indicates that God embraces all kinds of perfection, which He bestows upon the world, and that He is free from defects.

Chapter 27

"True" is a term used to indicate that that which is expressed is in agreement with that which is in the mind and with that which exists in reality outside of the mind. But if the expression is in disagreement with the thing as it exists in reality outside of the mind, though it agrees with the thing as it is in the mind, we call it untrue. Take an instance. Reuben saw Levi commit a homicide. Thinking that Levi was Simeon, he testified that Simeon committed homicide. His testimony is untrue, though there is no difference between his expression and his thought, the two being in agreement. On the other hand if he were to testify that Levi committed homicide, thinking that Simeon was the guilty party, he would not be saying an untruth, since the fact is as he stated it, nevertheless he would be guilty of lying, since his expression and his thought are not in agreement and his words belie his thoughts. In short, a **Kazab** [lie] is an expression used in relation to the speaker. A lie exists when the expression and the thought are not in agreement. **Sheker** [Untruth] is an expression used in relation to the thing itself. An untruth exists when the expression is in disagreement with the thing as it is in reality outside of the mind. If the expression is in disagreement alike with the thought and with the thing as it is in reality outside of the mind, we call it a lie and an untruth. And when all the three agree, we call it true.

It is clear therefore that the word **Nimza** [existent] can not truly be predicated of any existing thing except God. For existing things other than God can not have the term existent truly applicable to them at all times, but only at the time when they exist, not after and not before. But God, being in existence all the time in the same way, has a true existence, and the meaning of the word existent in the mind, as applied to Him, is in agreement with the reality outside the mind and with the expression. Therefore, the word existent applies to Him more truly than to any other existing thing.

Also, the word existent applies truly to one whose existence is not dependent upon any other, but upon his own essence. For since his existence depends upon his own essence only, he has no potentiality in him. If we say, for example, that the heavens are in continuous motion, the statement is true as long as the mover is in existence who causes them to move. But when the mover ceases to exist, the statement is no longer true. In the same way, if we say the Separate Intelligences are existent, the statement is true as long as the author of their existence, who maintains them in being, is there. Per se their existence is not absolute, since they are dependent upon another, and their existence is determined for them by their cause. Hence there is none among existing things to which the word existent applies truly except God, whose existence depends upon His own essence and not upon another, hence His existence is true.

This is what the Rabbis meant when they said, "The seal of the Holy One, blessed be He, is truth." The meaning is that there is none among existing things to whom the term existent applies at all times and from all aspects, i.e., whether we view it with reference to itself or with reference to another, except God.

This is the conception that was conveyed to Moshe at the burning bush in answer to his question, "And they shall say to me: What is His name? what shall I say unto them?" Moshe thought that the being who appeared to him might perhaps be one of the Separate Intelligences, whose existence depends upon another. He was therefore afraid that he might not obtain his request. For since the existence and the power of this being are dependent upon another, if this other chose to nullify the will of the former, it would no doubt become null and void, and the object of his desire would not be realized. Therefore God answered that His name is "I am that I am," i.e., the Existent whose existence depends upon His own essence and not upon another. Moshe might therefore feel assured that he can realize whatever he desires. The expression "that I am" is in the first person, as if to say I am because I am, and not because another than I is. My existence and power are not dependent upon another at all, as is the case in the other existents. None of the other existents could say of himself "I am that [because] I am." They would have to say, "I am that [because] He is," the expression "He is," referring not to the first person, but to a third person, who is the cause of the first. He would say then, "I am that [because] He is," i.e., I am in existence because another than I is in existence, namely the First Cause, upon whose existence that of all other beings depends. But God's existence depends upon Himself and not upon another cause. Therefore, to Him alone of all existing things is applicable the name "I am that I am," i.e., I am in existence because I am in existence, and not because another is in existence. And therefore, His existence is true because He has no need of another. And the word true applies to Him more than to any other existing thing.

We can say therefore that among all attributes there is none which is applicable to Him in all respects except the attribute true, because it adds nothing to the essence, and is merely an explanation of the expression necessary existence. Just as in the proposition, man is rational animal, animal and rational are explanatory of man and not something other than man, so "true" is the explanation of necessary existence and nothing else. The expression necessary existent means nothing else except a being whose existence is absolutely true, in whom there is neither potentiality nor dependence upon another. For this reason, this attribute is preferable to all the other attributes and names.

And the prophet, too, characterizes God as true in a manner different from his characterization of Him by means of other names and attributes. He says, "But the Lord God is the true God, He is the living God, and the everlasting King." In this expression he indicates the difference between describing God as true and describing Him as living or King or by any other attribute.

It is explained in the fourth book of the Metaphysics that whenever we say, "the same who," there may be imagined a kind of plurality or otherness, as in the expressions, "This is Ahasuerus who reigned from India even unto Ethiopia;" "These are that same Dathan and Abiram, the elect of the congregation, who strove ..."; "These are that same Aaron and Moshe ... These are the same that spoke to Pharaoh king of Egypt." In all these cases one might suppose [but for the description] that the persons named are other than those which are described later. The same thing is true of the expression, "He is the Lord our God; His judgments are in all the earth." For one might possibly suppose that the God of Israel has a specific kingdom like the other celestial rulers, who are assigned to rule the various nations. For this reason, the Bible explains that it is not so, but that the judgments of the Lord who is our God extend over all the earth, i.e., His rule is universal over the whole earth. So in all cases where the word "same" is used, it is for the purpose of making clear that the reference is not to another, as one might have supposed. In the word **true**, however, no other reference is possible, therefore the prophet is careful in his mode of expression. When he describes God as true, he does not use the word "same," but says simply, "But the Lord God is truth." But when he ascribes to Him the attributes life and royalty, he uses the expression, "The same is the living God, and the everlasting King." The meaning is that while one might suppose a distinction between God and the attributes life and royalty [though, as we said before, this supposition is not true], no such thing is possible in connection with the word truth. Hence he does not say, "But the Lord God, the same is truth." And by reason of the otherness which might be supposed in connection with the other attributes, we said above that all the attributes must be understood in a negative sense, so as not to necessitate any multiplicity in God's essence.

And because the understanding of this attribute is a more profound matter than the understanding of any of the others, Daniel said in his prayer, "Yet have we not entreated the favour of the Lord our God, that we might turn from our iniquities, and have discernment in Thy truth." Discernment in God's truth is nothing else than the understanding of His necessary existence. And inasmuch as the word "truth" points more clearly to a necessary existent than any other attribute, one of the ancient lawgivers said that truth is God.

Moreover, it is fitting that the word truth should be specially applicable to God as distinct from other beings, because it contains the first and last letter of the alphabet, and the mem too, which is the middle, indicating that God is first, last and middle, continually bearing all things by His power. The reason that we did not mention truth as a derivative dogma coming from the principle of the existence of God, as we mentioned unity, is because, as we have shown, truth is nothing more than an explanation of the expression necessary existent. To count it as a dogma would therefore be tautology. For to say God is true is the same thing as saying that God's is a true existence, and this is nothing else than an explanation of the term necessary existent.

Chapter 28

The name of God expressed in the letters, yod, he, vav, he, is called the Shem ha-Meforash, which means the separate name. The root parash is often used by the Rabbis to denote something that is separate and different from another. Thus, they speak of "flesh that is separated [ha-poresh] from a living animal"; "He who separates himself [ha-poresh] from the foreskin." Men who are different from others and superior in virtue and saintliness are called Perushim. This is the explanation given in Sifre.

In the Talmud, treatise Sotah, we find the following discussion: "The Bible says, 'On this wise ye shall bless'; 'on this wise,' denotes the use of the Shem ha-Meforash. We can not suppose that another appellation is permitted, for it says, 'So shall they put My name upon the children of Israel,' 'My name,' means the name that is peculiar to Me." We thus see in this explanation that the meaning of the expression Shem ha-Meforash is the name that is separate from the other appellations and is peculiar to God alone. For the other names are applied to God by reason of His activities, or by reason of some other aspect of His being, other than his necessary existence. Thus, the word Elohim denotes power, and therefore can be applied to others also, as for example to angels and judges. Similarly, Adonai, which denotes lordship, is applied to others besides God. Also, in the case of other names the same is true. They are applicable to God and to other beings either as pure homonyms or on the basis of some analogy. But the tetragrammaton can not be applied at all to any being other than God, because it denotes God as the necessary existent, as Maimonides says in chapter sixty-one of Part One of the Guide of the Perplexed. But this is a matter in which no other being shares. Hence the name is called Shem ha-Meforash [distinct and separate name].

And yet we sometimes find this name applied metaphorically to other beings, as in the biblical verse, "And the Lord [God] went before them by day in a pillar of cloud, to lead them the way …," while in a subsequent verse we read, "And the angel of God, who went before the camp of Israel, removed and went behind them; and the pillar of cloud removed from before them, and stood behind them." The explanation of this usage is that names are metaphorically applied to things other than that which they properly designate, for two reasons. One is because there is some similarity, though a remote one, between the two things. The other is because the name points in a distant manner to the thing in question, as an instrument points to the owner of the instrument. Thus, the Bible, in speaking of the Messiah, says, "But they shall serve the Lord their God, and David their king, whom I will raise up unto them." The reason for this is because the Messiah resembles David in his kingship, or princehood. The expression, "And My servant David shall be king over them," has reference to the Messiah's being descended from the seed of David, and points to the permanence of David's kingdom, as is specified in another passage, "And David, my servant, shall be their prince forever," which is no doubt a reference to David himself. For since the rule of his descendants is permanent, he is a prince forever. Similarly, the Bible calls the ark by the name of God, though it is a vessel artificially made, because it points to God, the giver of the Torah, which was in the ark. Thus, we read, "And it came to pass, when the ark set forward, that Moshe

Sefer HaIkkarim — BOOK [Maamar] TWO

said: 'Rise up, O Lord' ... And when it rested, he said: 'Return, O Lord, unto the ten thousands of the families of Israel.' " Also, Yehoshua said concerning the ark, "Behold the ark of the covenant, the Lord of all the earth, passeth on before you over the Jordan." The ark is not the Lord of all the earth, but he calls it so, because it owes its existence to the Lord of all the earth. So, he calls it by the name of the Lord of all the earth, because it is the usage of language to call a thing by the name of the master of the thing, or the one from whom the thing emanates, or to ascribe the act of the master of the thing to the thing because by means of it the act is realized, as in human language the act of an agent is attributed to the instrument by means of which the act is done. Thus, we say, the eye sees, the ear hears, though sight and hearing are functions of the soul, and the eye and the ear are merely instruments or organs by means of which the act is accomplished.

For both of these reasons at once Moshe called the name of the altar, **Adonai-Nissi** [Lord my miracle], because the altar is an instrument by means of which miracles are performed, and also because it points to God, who performs the miracles. In the same way the Bible calls the name of the Messiah, "The Lord our righteousness," because he is the medium through whom we obtain justice from God. For this reason, he is called by the name of God. Similarly, Yerushalayim is called, "The Lord is there," because it is a place where the glory of the Lord was revealed more constantly than anywhere else. And this is also what the Rabbis meant when they said, "Do not read, Adonai Shammah [the Lord is there], but Adonai Shemah [the Lord is her name], i.e., the name of Yerushalayim is the Lord, for the reason mentioned above. So, we find that Abraham called the name of the place, **Adonai-Jireh** [the Lord seeth], because there was seen an act which pointed to God, who sees and provides.

In the same way the Bible calls the Shekinah or the glory which was seen or apprehended in a prophetic vision, "the Lord," as in the expressions, "And when the Lord saw that he turned aside to see, ... and the Lord said, I have surely seen the affliction of My people that are in Egypt"; "I saw the Lord sitting upon a throne high and lifted up." It is also called the God of Israel, as in the expression, "And they saw the God of Israel." Also, God, "And they beheld God." Thus, we see that the Bible calls the Shekinah or the visible glory, "Lord," "God," and "God of Israel," though no creature can see God, as is said, "For man shall not see Me and live." The Bible also calls an angel God. Thus, concerning the angel who appeared to Gideon, the Bible says, "And the Lord turned towards him, and said: 'Go in this thy might' ... And the Lord said unto him, 'Surely I will be with thee ...' " Throughout the entire narrative the Bible calls the angel by the name of the Lord.

The Bible also applies the term **Glory** to various things. It is sometimes applied to the face of God Himself, who can not be seen. Thus, when Moshe asks of God and says, "Show me, I pray Thee, thy glory," God replies, "Thou canst not see My face." Here glory is applied to the face of God. The Bible also applies the term to something that is visible to the senses, "And the glory of the Lord appeared unto all the people"; "And the appearance of the glory of the Lord was like devouring fire in the top of the mount"; "And in the morning, then ye shall see the glory of the Lord." The reason for this is because the object which is visible to the senses symbolizes something that is hidden and not visible, which is called the face of the Lord, and the glory of the Lord. This is why the prophets took the liberty to refer to a thing that was visible to them by the name of a hidden thing that was not visible, namely God, with the result that they spoke with an angel or the glory that was visible to them as if they were speaking with God. Thus, Eliyahu addressed the angel who appeared to him or who spoke to him, in the second person, as though he were God, "For the children of Israel have forsaken Thy covenant, thrown down Thine altars, and slain Thy prophets with the sword." The reply was, "Go forth, and stand upon the mount before the Lord ... but the Lord was not in the wind ... but the Lord was not in the earthquake ..." Then he heard a voice speaking to him out of the stillness and saying, "What doest thou here, Eliyahu?" and was then commanded by God what he should do. Now there is no doubt that Eliyahu was not guilty of the error of thinking that the one who spoke to him first was God, for he said to him, "Go forth and stand upon the mount before the Lord," and yet he addressed him as though he were speaking to God Himself, when he said, "For the children of Israel have forsaken Thy covenant."

In relation to the expression, "Come up to the Lord," the Rabbis raise the question that the expression should have been "Come up to Me." Such a question is not raised in connection with the expression above quoted in relation to Eliyahu, "And stand upon the mount before the Lord." No question is here raised why it does not say, "And stand before Me," because they felt nothing strange in the case of Eliyahu that he should have been addressed by an intermediate being. In the case of Moshe, it was different. After the revelation on Sinai, Moshe attained the high privilege of speaking to God face to

Sefer HaIkkarim   BOOK [Maamar] TWO

face. Hence the Rabbis think it unusual that Moshe should be told, "Come up to the Lord," from which it would seem that he was speaking to an intermediate being, and not to God Himself. Their explanation is that the intermediate being was Metatron, whose name is the same as that of his Master, and who is the Prince of the Presence, but not such a subordinate being as in the case of the other prophets who were addressed by other angels and intermediate beings. And yet the prophets took the liberty to address them as though they were speaking to God, because they were the media through whom divine prophecy came to them. This is the meaning of the statement of the Rabbis, "Great is the power of the prophets, who compare the creature to the Creator." The meaning is, Great is the power of the prophets, who take the liberty to do an important thing like this. The reason for their doing this is because an angel is a medium of prophecy or an instrument through whom a sign or a miracle is performed, which indicates God's will and purpose being realized upon the beings of the world. And it is customary among mankind to speak of an order which comes from a messenger or official or general of the king as being the command of the king, and the representative is addressed with respect as if he were the king himself This is why the Bible calls him by the name of God, and the prophets speak of him as if he were God.

Angels are immaterial beings and not subject to those accidents to which material beings are liable, like envy, hatred, strife. They are free from all evil. They have no pride, nor desire to do evil or sin. They always choose what is good and right in the eyes of God. For this reason, when they are sent to mankind, they are given permission to speak in the name of the One who sent them. We see this clearly in many instances when the visible speaker is an angel and yet he speaks in the name of the One who sent him. Thus, the angel said to Hagar, "I will greatly multiply thy seed." To Abraham he said, "I will certainly return unto thee when the season cometh round." "Will return unto thee," is conditional upon God's sending him, as Rashi explains, for we do not find that the angel ever returned to Abraham. Yaakov also says, "And the angel of God said unto me in the dream: Yaakov; and I said: Here am I"; while at the end of the dream it is said to him, "I am the God of Beth-el, where thou didst anoint a pillar, where thou didst vow a vow unto Me." But Yaakov did not make his vow to the angel, but to God. Similarly, an angel said to Abraham, "For now I know that thou art a God-fearing man, seeing that thou hast not withheld thy son, thine only son, from Me." But Abraham offered Yitzhak to God alone. In the case of

Gideon, also, the angel said to him, "I will be with Thee." Also, in the case of Moshe, in the beginning of the vision of the burning bush, the Bible says, "And the angel of the Lord appeared unto him"; while when he begins to speak to him, he says, "I am the God of thy father, ... I have surely seen the affliction of My people that are in Egypt ..." This proves that an angel speaks in the name of the One who sent him. This matter deserves notice.

The reason for all this is because the angel can not disobey the command of God and alter the message or speak on his own responsibility. For the reason he is called angel is not because he is a separate intellect, but because he comes with a mission from God. If he changed the message, he would no longer be an angel. Moreover, he is not allowed during his mission to say or do anything which he was not commanded by God to say or do. This is the reason why an angel sent with a divine mission refuses to reveal his own personal name, or his special power, apart from the mission with which he is entrusted. Thus, when Yaakov says to the angel, "Tell me, I pray thee, thy name," the latter replies, "Wherefore is it that thou dost ask after my name?" Similarly, the angel said to Manoah, "Wherefore askest thou after my name, seeing it is hidden?" He also said, "Though thou detain me, I will not eat of thy bread, and if thou wilt make a burnt-offering, thou must offer it unto the Lord." The meaning is, if you offer me a burnt-offering, I will not accept it, and it will do you no good, for I do not appear to you in my personal capacity, as representing my own individual power. Hence it will be of no benefit to you to know my name and my personal power, for this might lead you into error, and you might imagine that I have some personal and independent power in this mission, which is not true. Therefore, "if thou wilt make a burnt-offering, thou must offer it unto the Lord," for the power and the mission come from Him.

For this reason, too, a person who worships an angel in his personal and individual capacity is guilty of "cutting the plants" and of idolatry, which is forbidden in the commandment, "Thou shalt have no other gods before Me," as our Rabbis explain in the Mekilta, and as will be made clear in the eighteenth chapter of the Third Book. But if one worships an angel in his capacity as a messenger of God, there is no offence. In the same way when one does obeisance to an official of the king in his individual capacity and power, accepting him as a master, and not as one who has power delegated to him from the king, he is guilty of treason to the king. But if he does obeisance to the official as a representative of the king, he does honor to the king. For this reason, it was permissible for Yehoshua

Sefer HaIkkarim   BOOK [Maamar] TWO

to bow down to the angel when he appeared to him in Jericho and said, "I am captain of the host of the Lord; I am now come. And Yehoshua fell on his face to the earth, and bowed down ..." For though genuflection is one of the four modes of worship which, like sacrifice, incense and libation, are forbidden to be practised even in honor of angels, nevertheless since the genuflection in that case was in honor of God, and the angel was His messenger, it was permissible. But if one prays to an angel or bows down to him in his personal capacity, as possessing independent power which is signified in his name, he is liable under the prohibition, "Thou shalt have no other gods before Me." This is also the opinion of Nahmanides.

This shows the error of those who mention the names of the angels in their prayer. For they use the names of the angels for the power which they exert in their personal capacity. But this is precisely what is forbidden in the commandment, "Thou shalt have no other gods before Me," as we said before. The origin of the error is because there are certain prayers of ancient authorship containing certain special names of angels. Hence, they thought that it is permissible to include all the names in the prayer. But it is not so. No name may be mentioned in prayer except those which are peculiar to God, but no other. This is why the science treating of these things is called **Cabala** [tradition], because tradition must be followed in the study and the practice of it, else one is liable to commit an error and to worship as God some one other than the Lord.

To make the matter clearer, I will give an illustration. We find in ancient prayers the name **Mzpz**, and one might think it is the name of one of the angels. But this is not true. It is merely another form of the tetragrammaton, which is derived by a substitution of letters according to the correspondence known as at bash. Similarly, **Kvzv Bmvksz** is a transformation of **God Elohenu** [the Lord our God], by changing every letter in **God Elohenu** for the letter which follows it in the alphabet. Thus, yod becomes kaf, he becomes vav, and so on. This is the reason why no one is permitted to make use of any of the statements of the Cabalists on his own responsibility, unless he has that particular matter by direct oral tradition from a Cabalist. Opinions in that science are forbidden except to one who has received the tradition from a wise man. The written word alone can not be used as authority. This is why it is called Cabala, as the name signifies.

I was obliged to make this observation because I have seen men fall into error by reading the Zohar and other cabalistic books without

Sefer Haikkarim   BOOK [Maamar] TWO

having any oral tradition. They presume upon their own opinion, exhibiting their great wisdom, and transgress the permitted boundary, reflecting upon things upon which reflection is forbidden. The greatest of the modern Cabalists, Nahmanides, has said by way of admonition that the words of the Cabalists can not be understood or known by any kind of reason or intelligence, but only through oral communication by a wise Cabalist to an intelligent person. Independent opinion in the matter is folly and the cause of great harm. This is what Nahmanides says in his commentary on the Pentateuch. To sum up, take heed unto thyself and be very careful lest thou be caught and fall into their snare, for they forsake the paths of uprightness and walk in ways of darkness. For those who make a study of the Cabala independently, without having an oral tradition from a learned Cabalist, know and understand nothing and walk in darkness.

Chapter 29

The word or [light] is applied first to light which is perceived by the senses, as in the expressions, "Who giveth the sun for a light by day"; "As soon as the morning was light." And inasmuch as light shows a person the way, the name is applied also, metaphorically, to denote guidance and leading, as in the verse, "And nations shall walk at thy light," which means, shall live by the guidance which they receive from thee. It is also used to denote divine guidance, as in the expression, "Come ye, and let us walk in the light of the Lord." For this reason, the Torah is called light, "For the commandment is a lamp, and the **Torah** [teaching] is light," because it guides and leads one to eternal happiness.

Inasmuch as light causes pleasure to the soul, as we read, "And the light is sweet," the name light is also applied figuratively to corporeal pleasure, "The Jews had light," as well as to spiritual pleasure, "Light is sown for the righteous, and gladness for the upright in heart." It is also applied metaphorically to denote good will, "In the light of the king's countenance is life"; "And the light of Thy countenance, because Thou wast favorable unto them"; "And cause Thy face to shine, and we shall be saved." It is also applied to the soul, "The light of the righteous rejoiceth; but the lamp, of the wicked shall be put out." It is applied also to understanding of wisdom, "A man's wisdom maketh his face to shine." Hence folly is called darkness, "But the fool walketh in darkness." It is also applied to things which are free from matter, "And the earth did shine with His glory." It is applied to God Himself, "And the light of Israel shall be for a fire, and his Holy One for a flame."

The reason for this is as follows. The existence of light can not be denied. Light is not a corporeal thing. It causes the faculty of sight and the visible colors to pass from potentiality to actuality. It delights the soul. One who has never seen a luminous body in his life can not conceive colors, nor the agreeableness and delightfulness of light. And even he who has seen luminous objects can not endure to gaze upon an intense light, and if he insists on gazing at it beyond his power of endurance, his eyes become dim, so that he can not see thereafter even what is normally visible. Similarly God's existence can not be denied. God is incorporeal. He causes things to pass from potentiality to actuality. There is wonderful delight in apprehending of God as much as one can. One upon whom the light of reason has never shone can not conceive the delight just mentioned. And even wise men who pry into the matter more deeply than is proper become blind and confused, as the Rabbis say, "Ben Azzai looked, and was stricken." This is the reason why the Bible speaks of God as light, to indicate that though God's existence is something that can not be denied, like light, nevertheless, since the human mind resides in matter, it is impossible for it to perceive of God's essence, by means of the Separate Intelligences, except a little bit. In this apprehension there is a wonderful, spiritual delight that man can not conceive. And the amount that is perceived is similar to the amount which the bat perceives of the light of the sun. By reason of the intensity of the sun's light the eyes of the bat are dimmed, so that it can not look at the sun, nor enjoy its light as the other animals do; though it has some idea of the matter, since it enjoys the weaker light of the moon, or a lamp, or the light which remains in the clouds after the sun sets. It can move about only in the darkness of night, and avoids the light of the sun. This shows that it takes pleasure in a little light, but can not endure and is pained by a bright light, and hence avoids it; unlike the eagle which, by reason of its intense power of vision, takes pleasure in light and flies high by reason of its desire to get near to it. All these qualities of light bear a greater similarity to the things which are free from matter than to anything else to which the things may be compared. Hence the Bible compares them to light so as to make the matter intelligible.

But in order to prevent the error that intellectual light is something emanating from a corporeal object like sensible light, Habakkuk, describing the conception of divine revelation when the Law was given, says: "God cometh from Teman, and the Holy One from Paran. Selah. His glory covereth the heavens ... and a brightness appeareth as the light." The meaning is that the brightness which appeared then was like light, but was not actually light, such as that which is perceptible to the senses. For sensible light emanates from a corporeal object, while that brightness did not come from a corporeal object. This is why he says "as the light" and not "light." In further explanation of the conception, he says in the sequel that the brightness which was perceived at the time when the Law was given did not come from the power of some intermediate being, who derived the sparks of light and the influence from some one else, but it came from God Himself. Hence, he says, "Rays hath He at His side," meaning that those sparks of spiritual light come to Him from Himself and not from any one else. This shows that it was not something caused, for the light and brightness and splendor of caused things is acquired by them from elsewhere, namely from God who is the cause of all. But the brightness and splendor and majesty, i.e., the attributes and perfections, of God come to Him from Himself and not from another, for He acquires no perfection from another. And inasmuch as it is very difficult to understand how He can have all the attributes of perfection imaginable without having plurality in His essence, and how every one of them can be infinite in excellence, he says, "And there is the hiding of His power." The meaning is that the attributes, which are comparable to rays emanating from His side, are the secret and hiding of His power. For since His strength and power are infinite, they are, so to speak, hidden, i.e., they can not be understood. For a finite being can understand of an infinite being merely the general nature, that He is an infinite being, but not the specific elements as specific; just as we say that a person conceives the general nature of all human beings, past and future, in a general way, but he can not conceive the specific nature of every individual.

It is clear therefore that the infinite perfections of God can not be comprehended except by God alone, who is infinite in every respect. Hence the Bible uses the expression, "And there is the hiding of His power." It is clear also that when God is compared with light, it is merely a linguistic metaphor in order to bring the matter nearer to the understanding, but nothing else. In the same way Ezekiel, describing the glory which appeared to him like brightness, said, "As the appearance of the bow that is in the cloud in the day of rain, so was the appearance of the brightness round about. This was the appearance of the likeness of the glory of the Lord." He compares it

Sefer HaIkkarim — BOOK [Maamar] TWO

with the appearance of the bow, not because it is similar to it in appearance, but because the colors seen in the bow are not really such as they appear, the appearance being due to the mixture of different vapors. This is proved by the fact that the moisture in the eyes sometimes produces the appearance of a circle in the air with the colors of the rainbow, though of course there are no such colors in reality.

Ibn Sina says, "I understand certain elements in the phenomenon of the rainbow, and certain elements I do not understand, but I do not understand the nature or the cause of the colors, and am not satisfied with the current opinions on the subject, which are untrue and foolish." From these words it appears that there is no explanation for the existence of the apparent colors, and that they are merely appearances, and do not really exist. This is why the Rabbis say, "If one looks upon the rainbow, his eyes become dim." The meaning is that if one looks carefully at the colors which appear in the rainbow, he will find that his eyes are dim, because they see what does not exist. This is the reason why the prophet compares the appearance of the brightness of the glory which he saw to those colors, to indicate that the attributes under which God appeared to the prophets do not exist in reality, as the appearance of the rainbow is not in reality such as it seems. This is why he says, "I fell upon my face." When he understood that the light and the brightness which appeared to him were not objective realities, he said, "This is the appearance of the likeness of the glory of the Lord." He does not say, "This is the appearance of the glory of the Lord," but adds the word "likeness," because a thing which is free from matter can not be perceived by the senses. For the senses can perceive only the accidents of things, but a separate intellect has no accidents. Having said therefore that he had seen colors like those of the rainbow, he was obliged to say that it was the color of the likeness of the glory of the Lord, and not the color of the glory itself, which has no color. Therefore he fell upon his face and refused to look at those colors, so that he might not come to think that those colors were such in reality, and that God is a corporeal substance and the subject of accidents.

Moshe did precisely the same thing during his vision of the burning bush. At first, when he thought that the thing, he saw was a corporeal object, he said, "I will turn aside now, and see this great sight." Then, when he was told, "I am the God of thy father," and knew that it was not a corporeal object, it became clear to him that those colors which appeared in the flame of fire in the bush were not in reality such as they seemed. Therefore, he hid his face, for he was afraid to look. His fear was due to the fact that the senses far from helping us to conceive a spiritual nature, hinder us from comprehending the truth, because they can perceive only the accident of a thing, like colors, length, width, and so on. This may lead one to think that an immaterial thing has accidents. Therefore, Moshe hid his face to show that the senses have no part in this conception at all, because there are no accidents in it. Hence the Rabbis praise him for hiding his face, "As a reward for hiding his face, he was given a shining countenance." And because, as we said, a spiritual object is compared with light, the Bible applies the term light to the world of the Separate Intelligences, as the Rabbis understand it.

In **Bereshit Rabbah** we find the following comment on the verse, "And God saw the light that it was good, and God divided…" Said - Rabbi Yehuda, son of Rabbi Simon, God set apart the light for Himself, for He said, no creature can use it except Myself. That is why it is written, i "And the light dwelleth with Him." Said Rabbi Abin, the Levite, God took the light and wrapped Himself up with it as with a garment, and caused His world to flash forth from its splendor, as is written, "Who covereth Thyself with light as with a garment." The Rabbis said, He hid it away for the righteous for the future world; like a king who sees a beautiful portion and says, this shall be for my son, as is written, "Light is sown for the righteous." We thus see that all these sages agree that it is not sensible light that is meant, but that the reference is to spiritual light, which is the world of the Separate Intelligences. Rabbi Yehuda, son of Rabbi Simon says that the human intellect can not apprehend them, and that they were created only that they might know the greatness of God and sing praises before Him. Rabbi Abin the Levite says that this light is causally prior to the other existing things, and that the spiritual substances were created to serve as God's instruments, as the philosopher said that God looked upon the world of Separate Intelligences and caused existence to emanate from them; while the Rabbis say that though the human intellect can not comprehend the Separate Intelligences perfectly, the righteous may achieve immortality as a result of such limited understanding as they may acquire of them. This is the meaning of the expression, "He hid it for the righteous for the future world."

Chapter 30

As men and animals differ in the appreciation of light, some, on

Sefer HaIkkarim — BOOK [Maamar] TWO

account of weak sight, taking pleasure in dim light and being annoyed by a strong light, like the bat, while others who have strong sight take pleasure in strong light, like the eagle, so do the righteous differ in the degree in which they attain spiritual delight, which the Rabbis speak of as light, as we said before. This difference in degree on the part of the righteous, wise and perfect in the enjoyment of spiritual delight depends upon the degree in which they apprehend the attributes of divine perfection, as the difference in degree of the angels also depends upon such understanding, as we explained in the twelfth chapter of this Book.

Now if the attributes are to be understood as we explained in the twenty-first chapter of this Book, we can see that there may be an infinite number of degrees in wise men, depending upon each one's apprehension of a given part of the infinite attributes of God's perfection. But if the attributes of divine perfection can be understood only in a negative manner, according to the opinion of Maimonides, as we explained in the twenty-second chapter of this Book, then the question arises, what difference can there be among wise men and philosophers? For if one knows that no positive attribute applies to God at all, and that negative attributes do, as we said there, he knows all that can be known of God. What difference would there be, then, according to this, between a beginner and Solomon, concerning whom it is said, "He was wiser than all men?" But it is absurd to suppose that they are both alike, and that there is no difference between one prophet and another, or between Moshe and Yehoshua, his attendant. The Bible says, "That I may know Thee, to the end that I may find grace in Thy sight." This request Moshe made after he had seen all that he had when he received the Law. It appears therefore that the more one knows of God the more favor one finds. Moreover, the Rabbis say, "The face of Moshe is like that of the sun, the face of Yehoshua is like that of the moon," which means that there is a difference in the degree of apprehension of spiritual light, as there is between the light of the sun and the light of the moon. The Rabbis say, also, "We can learn from this that every righteous man has a separate dwelling, and that every one is scorched by the canopy of the other …" All this shows that there is a difference in degree between one righteous man and another. The matter needs explanation. Maimonides treats of this subject at length in the fifty-ninth chapter of the first part of the Guide, but his explanation is not satisfactory. For we can say, by way of criticism, that one who believes that all negative attributes are applicable to God, has already differentiated God from all other existing things.

Sefer Halkkarim BOOK [Maamar] TWO

What superiority is there then in the wise man who knows specifically that God is not mineral or plant, and so on through the specific negations?

The proper way to understand this matter is as follows: Two contraries, like living and dead, wise and ignorant, can not be negated of God in the same way. For if He is neither dead nor alive, He is non-existent. The truth is this: When we say He is not dead, we deny death absolutely, because the opposite, which is life, does belong to Him. Similarly, when we say, He is not ignorant, we deny ignorance in a true manner, because the opposite, which is wisdom, exists in God, while death and ignorance are defects. But when we say, He is not living, He is not wise, which is the negation of the other contrary, we do not understand the negation as before - He is not living, but dead - He is not wise, but ignorant - for by living and wise we mean perfections. What we mean is that He is not living in the same way as man is living, that His life is not like that which we understand by life. So, when we say, He is not wise, we mean that the attribute of wisdom in Him is not, as in man, an accidental attribute, added to His essence, but that His wisdom is essential and not something added to His essence. Similarly in the other attributes which we deny of God, we must differentiate between the manner of negating the one contrary and the manner of negating the other. Herein is the superiority of one wise man over another, in the knowledge of the mode of negation, since not all attributes are negated in the same manner. For although it is true that all negations are predicable of God, still no wise man can negate any attribute unless he knows how the positive attribute applies to the thing characterized by it, and understands the aspect of perfection as well as of defect which the attribute contains. If the attribute denotes a defect, it is negated in one way, if it denotes a perfection, it is negated in another way, namely in respect to its defective element. To deny everything of God without reason or understanding would not indicate God's perfection.

All those attributes which we regard as defects, like dead, weak, ignorant, poor, bad, and so on, we negate absolutely, meaning that such attributes, which are defects, are not found in God, but that the opposite, which is a perfection, is found in Him. But when we negate the other opposite, which denotes a perfection in our estimation, like living, powerful, wise, rich, good, the meaning is not that this attribute does not exist in Him but the opposite, which is a defect, does. Such negation, far from ascribing perfection to God, is insult and blasphemy. What we do mean in the latter case is that the

Sefer Halkkarim BOOK [Maamar] TWO

perfections which we understand by the terms living, powerful, wise, and so on, are not found in God as they are found in us but in a manner more honorable and more excellent, so much so that there, is no relation between the perfection in us or as we understand it and the perfection when ascribed to God. The perfection or perfections in question are applied to man and to God as homonyms, considering the enormous difference that there is between them.

When we say that they are applied homonymously we do not mean that the attribute means one thing when ascribed to man, and the opposite when ascribed to God. We do not mean that when wisdom is ascribed to man it denotes a perfection, and when ascribed to God it denotes ignorance, a defect, which is the opposite of wisdom. This can not be. For if this were the case, then when we deny ignorance of God, we should be denying the word merely and not the signification of the word. But there can be no doubt that when we deny ignorance of God we mean to deny the signification of the word, and not merely the word. Therefore, when we deny wisdom, we mean to deny it in so far as it is a defect, not so far as it is a perfection. But in order that we may not suppose for a moment that the attributes of perfection are predicated of God in the same way as they are predicated of us, we do not permit their predication of God, except by way of negation.

The truth of what we are saying may be made clear from the concept of existence, which is attributed to God. It is true, indeed, that the term existence is applied homonymously to God and to all other existing things, because all of them acquire their existence from Him, and their existence is distinct from their quiddity, whereas in God His existence and His quiddity are identical, and as His quiddity is absolutely unknowable, so is His existence, while the existence of all other things is dependent upon His existence, for they all acquire their existence from Him. Nevertheless, it is certain that the word existence as applied to God does not denote the opposite of the same word's denotation when applied to all other existing things. In that case existence as applied to God would denote non-existence, the opposite of existence as we use it ordinarily. For we always necessarily understand by the word existence the opposite of non-existence. But in order to distinguish between the two kinds of existence and indicate that the one is true existence, and the other is not true and is similar to non-existence, we say that the word existence when applied both to Him and to us is used as a homonym, in order to differentiate between the two kinds of existence and to indicate that God's existence is absolutely unknown, as His essence is absolutely unknown; and that the existence which is ascribed to all other things denotes, as it were, non-existence in comparison with the existence which is ascribed to God.

It is clear from this that we can not characterize God with even negative attributes, unless we know in what way an object is characterized by a positive attribute, and can distinguish between the aspect of perfection and that of defect in the attribute. Only then can we permit ourselves to negate them in relation to God. For only in this way do we understand the meaning of the negation, since, as we said before, not all negations are predicated of God in the same way. Herein lies the difference between one wise man or philosopher and another. Their degrees differ according to the difference in their conception of the manner in which the attributes of perfection are ascribed to God.

Thus, we read in Vayikra Rabbah: "Rabbi Eleazar son of Rabbi Menahem said: The Psalmist says, 'And Thou makest them drink of the river of Thy Edens.' 'Edens' is used in the plural. This signifies that every righteous man has a separate Eden to himself." This is an allusion to the conception which each one has of the attributes of perfection in God, as we explained in the fifteenth chapter of this Book. It is called "Eden" because true sweetness, joy and delight are found in conception only. All the other agreeable things come to an end, and necessarily their enjoyment ends likewise. Moreover, an excess of those good things gives rise to harm. A person takes pleasure in food and drink. But if he eats and drinks to excess, he feels pain and nausea. The same thing applies to all the other corporeal pleasures. The only permanent delight and joy there is consists in the apprehension of spiritual things, especially if the thing is infinite. For the greater the understanding the greater the joy and the greater the delight, which never ceases. Now since the attributes of perfection in God are infinite, there are infinite conceptions, which are accompanied with infinite joy. This is the meaning of the biblical expression, "In Thy presence is fulness of joy." The meaning is, a great number of joys, corresponding to the number of conceptions of Thee. And inasmuch as all the conceptions of God are infinite in excellence and sweetness, and are eternal, as we explained in chapter twenty-five of this Book, the Psalmist concludes, "In Thy right-hand bliss for evermore." And since a human being can not embrace the infinite in his knowledge, his perfection must consist in a partial conception of God, hence the Psalmist says: "Thou makest me to know the path of life." He does not say **Derek** [way], but **Orah** [path], meaning one narrow path, to indicate that even one conception of the attributes of perfection contains a path and a way to eternal life, and as a person's understanding of the attributes of perfection in God increases, his delight in eternal life increases likewise, and so does his joy and enjoyment.

From this we may get an idea of the great joy and delight which God has in the apprehension of His own essence, for He has an infinite number of perfections, and each one is infinite in worth. Therefore, no other being can apprehend His essence, as the wise man said when they asked him if he knew the quiddity of God. His answer was, if I knew Him, I would be He. The meaning is, there is no one who apprehends His essence except God, though His existence is evident most plainly to all from His acts. Praise be to Him who surpasses us with His perfection; who is hidden from us despite His intense visibility, as the light of the sun and his agreeableness are hidden from those of weak sight. Their defective understanding does not prove His non-existence. The most that we can understand about God is that we can not understand Him, as the wise man said: The sum total of what we know of Thee is that we do not know Thee.

Chapter 31

If we reflect upon nature as a whole, we find that it consists of three parts, which can not be denied. First, the lower world, the world of the elements and of genesis and decay. Second, the world of the spheres. Third, the world of angels.

These three parts are absolutely different from each other. In the lower world, which is the world of genesis and destruction, we find that there is no individual permanence, but all the individuals come to an end. In the world of spheres, all the individuals are permanent as such and are not subject to decay, but they are corporeal and are affected with corporeal accidents. They have form and shape, they occupy space, they come under the category of quantity and are composed of parts.

These two divisions, though different, act and react upon each other. The motions of the spheres and their change of position produce motions and changes in the elements. Sometimes they cause the wet element to predominate, and sometimes the opposite, the dry; sometimes the cold, and sometimes the hot. This brings about a mixture of the elements, from which mixture are produced the various kinds of minerals. This mixture rises to a higher level, and a new and superior combination arises, assuming the forms of the various species of plants. The mixture rises still higher and is purified gradually until it is ready to receive the form of animal. These qualities emanate from the spheres not as dead bodies, but by reason of a certain power which they have to give life to composite things when the latter are prepared for it by the motions of the spheres. This power which gives life is called the soul of the sphere. And inasmuch as we see that the spheres move continually in a circle, and yet every sphere has a different motion from every other - one moves east, one moves west; one moves rapidly, one moves slowly - we infer necessarily that every one of them has a cause outside of it other than its soul, which gives it its peculiar motion. This individual cause of each sphere is responsible for its individual motion. Those who give the spheres their individual motions are their movers, and these movers are called Separate Intelligences, because they are free from matter, as is explained in the science of physics. In the Bible they are called angels.

It follows therefore that there must be a third division, which is called the world of angels. This division, though absolutely different from the other two mentioned before, acts upon the world of the spheres, as we said before, by giving them a great variety of movements, one moving to the east, one to the west, one inclining to the north, one inclining to the south, and those which have the same general direction differing in the specific character of their motions. These different motions bring about the union and combination of the different parts of nature, and maintain order continually in the world of spheres and the world of genesis and decay. The necessary inference is that these three parts have one controlling power which combines and unites them together.

A comparison with animal life will make the matter clear. We find in animals three distinct powers, the nutritive soul in the liver, the vital soul in the heart and the sensitive soul in the brain. All these powers or souls are different from one another in their functions. The nutritive soul in the liver is similar to the world of genesis and decay, because there the food loses its original form and changes into the form of blood. It is different, however, from the vital soul in the heart. The vital soul in the heart is similar to the world of the spheres. For as the motions of the spheres cause life to flow to the whole lower world, the world of change and genesis and decay, and if the sphere were to cease its motion for one moment, the world would by natural law come to an end, so the motions of the heart cause life to flow to the entire body, and if the heart were to cease

Sefer Halkkarim   BOOK [Maamar] TWO

moving for a moment the animal would die. The sensitive soul in the brain is similar to the world of angels, for from it come the five senses and the other psychic powers, like the forming power, the power of imagination, and the incorporeal powers which can not be perceived by the senses, but can be apprehended only through the acts or functions which come from them, as the Separate Intelligences can be apprehended only through the acts which come from them.

Now just as these three powers in the body of the animal have one unifying power, called the power which controls the body, a power which binds all the parts and powers of the body together, and is called by physicians' nature, so in the world as a whole there is one power which binds all the parts and powers of creation together and controls them.

I am not now intending to speak of the rational power which is in man alone, and by virtue of which man is called a microcosm, because he has an intellectual power which thinks and realizes the things in his intellect from their potential state by means of his will, as the world has an intellectual principle, which brings all things into existence by its great power and simple will, unlike the lower animals, which have no power acting with volition, which can do opposite things, but have only a natural power, as is explained in the De Anima. I am referring here to the power which controls the body of the animal in a general way only. Such a power exists in every animal, though some of them have more of it than others. Nevertheless, we can prove from this power, as Maimonides says, the existence of a being which controls and binds together all the individual existences and their parts. From the rational power in man, we infer that that being is an intellectual substance, acting with will, as there is in man an intellectual substance acting with will, else he would not have been given commands by God.

The only difference in this comparison between the powers of the body and those of nature as a whole is, that in the former every power act upon the other power and is in turn acted upon by the latter. Thus, the heart gives the power of life to the liver and the other organs, and the liver in turn gives the nutritive power to the heart, while the brain gives sensation and motion to the heart and the liver, and takes from them life and nutrition. But in the world as a whole it is not so. The substance which exerts influence does not receive any influence from that upon which it acts. For the influence which is bestowed upon the lower beings by the higher is exerted by way of generosity and kindness and not because of any benefit to

Sefer HaIkkarim BOOK [Maamar] TWO

the giver.

All this matter, discussed in this chapter, of the division of existence into these three parts and the existence of a being who contrılls all things, though absolutely distinct from them, was shown to Eliyahu in a nobler and more perfect way in the vision which he saw on Mount Horeb, when he was asked, "What doest thou here, Eliyahu?", when he ran away from Jezebel and was grieved because she persecuted him. His answer was, "I have been very jealous for the Lord, the God of hosts; for the children of Israel have forsaken Thy covenant ... and they seek my life to take it away." Then he was told, "Go forth, and stand upon the mount before the Lord. And, behold, the Lord passed by, and a great and strong wind rent the mountains, and broke in pieces the rocks before the Lord; but the Lord was not in the wind." This alludes to the power which controls the world of genesis and decay, which rends mountains and breaks in pieces rocks. The Bible says, "Before the Lord," because God sees to it that the power does His will, for it is like an axe in the hands of the one who hews with it. The expression, "But God was not in the wind," alludes to the fact that nature, which is the wind that rends mountains and breaks rocks, is not the power that controls the world of genesis and decay.

Then it continues, "And after the wind an earthquake; but the Lord was not in the earthquake." This is an allusion to the world of the spheres, concerning which it is said, "And the **Ofannim** and the holy **Hayyot** raise themselves with great noise," the spheres being called "holy Hayyot," as Maimonides says in the third chapter of Part Three of the Guide. "But the Lord was not in the earthquake," indicates that God is not the soul of the sphere, as the ancients thought.

He continues, "And after the earthquake a fire." This alludes to the world of angels, which are called in the Bible fire, "The flaming fire Thy ministers." The appellation fire is an allusion to the fact that as a man can not perceive the element fire with the sense of sight because the eye has no power over elemental fire, and yet we are aware of it through its functions or acts, so the angels are known through their acts, though the eye can not see them. For the very same reason the Bible compares God to fire, "For the Lord thy God is a devouring fire." The meaning is, He is known from His acts, though He can not be perceived by the senses. This is why the Bible calls the world of angels in this vision fire.

Our Rabbis also call the angel's fire. In the treatise Hagigah they say: "What is the meaning of hashmal? It stands for hayyot esh

Sefer HaIkkarim   BOOK [Maamar] TWO

Memalelot [fiery hayyot speaking]." "Fiery hayyot" means, not perceptible by the senses, like fire. The "holy hayyot," on the other hand, namely the spheres, which are perceptible by the senses, are not called "fiery hayyot." The angels alone are called fiery hayyot. "Speaking" has reference to the fact that they are known from their acts, which is their speech. And to prevent the error of supposing that "fiery hayyot" refers to the spheres, and that the expression "speaking" is to be understood in the same way as, "The heavens declare the glory of God," the author of the Talmud quotes a baraita, which explains the meaning of the word hashmal in another way, showing clearly that it alludes to the angels, as Rabbi Yehuda said. The difference is only in the interpretation.

The baraita says, "At times they are silent, and at times they speak. When speech comes from the mouth of God, they are silent, and when there is no speech coming from the mouth of God, they speak." The baraita means to explain a very subtle philosophical idea. The effect understands in a manner its cause and it also understands its own essence. As a result of the conception, it has of its cause, which is the more noble of the two, an angel emanates from it, i.e., a Separate Intelligence. As a result of the conception, it has of itself, a sphere emanates from it, as was explained in the eleventh chapter of this Book. This is the meaning of the expression in the baraita, "When speech comes from the mouth of God, they are silent." This refers to the fact that the conception which the first effect, let us say, forms of God results in the emanation of a Separate Intelligence which is not perceptible by the senses. This is the meaning of the expression, "they are silent." "And when speech does not come from the mouth of God, they speak." This refers to the fact that the conception which the effect forms of its own essence, causes the emanation of a sphere which is perceptible to the senses. "They speak," means the same thing as, "The heavens declare the glory of God." It is clear therefore that the Rabbis call the Intelligences, "fiery hayyot." In many passages the Rabbis call them, "fiery seraphim."

The meaning of the expression, "The Lord was not in the fire," is that God's existence is different from that of the angels. The angels are effects and possible existents, whereas God is a cause and a necessary existent. And to indicate that God's quiddity is absolutely unknown, and absolutely simple, in a manner inconceivable, the text says in the sequel, "And after the fire a still small voice," pointing to the impossibility of understanding God's quiddity, so much so that the only way to speak of Him or of the attributes of His

Sefer HaIkkarim — BOOK [Maamar] TWO

perfection is by way of negation, which is the still, small voice. The literal meaning of the biblical expression is, "a voice of fine silence," fine silence being an allusion to the subtle distinction to be observed in the understanding of the various negative attributes predicated of God, as we explained in the preceding chapter.

In the same vision Eliyahu was told, "Go, return on thy way to the wilderness of Damascus; and when thou comest, thou shalt anoint Hazael to be king over Aram; and Jehu the son of Nimshi shalt thou anoint to be king over Israel; and Elisha the son of Shaphat of **Abel-Meholah** shalt thou anoint to be prophet in thy room." In these words, it was made clear to him that the three worlds mentioned before are governed by God. In the world of genesis and decay, where it is the nature of one animal to overpower another animal or human being and put him to death, like Hazael, who prevailed over the king of Aram and slew him, this is not an accident, but the result of God's providence, rewarding and punishing individuals and groups and exercising judgment through them over those who transgress His will, as is said, "And it shall come to pass, that him that escapeth from the sword of Hazael shall Jehu slay."

The expression, "And Jehu the son of Nimshi shalt thou anoint to be king over Israel," indicates that divine providence stands above the prognostication of the constellations, and nullifies their influence in favor of God's will and purpose. The constellations sometimes indicate prosperity to the wicked and misfortune to the righteous. But Jehu killed all the wicked men who worshipped Baal and saved all the righteous men who worshipped God, indicating that the judgment in this case was due to divine providence and not to the influence of the stars. Then the text says, "And Elisha the son of Shaphat of Abel-Meholah shalt thou anoint to be prophet in thy room." This indicates that the prophetic inspiration which the prophets get from the world of angels, comes only through the will and command of God.

To sum up, then, we say that in this great vision Eliyahu was informed of the division of existence into the three worlds, the world of genesis and decay, the world of spheres and the world of angels. Also, that there is one Being over them who binds together all the parts of nature, and controls them, and watches over their effects in the lower world, realizing His purpose and will. This is God, who is absolutely different from them. His quiddity is absolutely unknown, and He can be described only in negative attributes, which are called a still, small voice, for the reason we gave before. This is the purpose of this chapter.

Sefer Halkkarim BOOK [Maamar] TWO

And so, we close the Second Book, which deals with the first principle, the existence of God, and the derivative dogmas derived from it. Praise be to God, who is One without a second, He is first and He is last, and beside Him there is no God.

Sefer HaIkkarim
ספר העיקרים

BOOK OF PRINCIPLES

BOOK [Maamar] THREE

Introduction

Treating of the second principle, which is revelation of the Torah. Inasmuch as the derivative dogmas depending upon this principle are, as we said in the First Book, the knowledge of God, prophecy, and the genuineness of the messenger, and since God's knowledge of the existing things of the lower world necessarily comes before all other dogmas, for if God does not know the existing things of the lower world, neither prophecy nor message can come from Him, would be appropriate to speak first of the knowledge of God. But inasmuch as God's knowledge of the lower existences must be compatible with the nature of the contingent, which depends upon freedom of choice, we found it proper to postpone treatment of God's knowledge until the Fourth Book, when we shall discuss the problem of freedom. We will therefore first speak of the principle of revelation of the Torah, and then we will explain the dogmas depending upon it, prophecy and the genuineness of the messenger.

Chapter 1

Man, being equable in temperament and more capable of thought and reflection than the other animals, is a nobler and more perfect object of creation than they. The equableness of his temperament is evident from the fact that he is equally affected by the contrary qualities, while his ability to think and reflect is shown in his invention of the arts and sciences.

We must not say that the animal species are more perfect in their organization than man because they require no shade or shelter from the heat and the storm, nor preparation of the food they need, which nature provides ready for their use. Moreover, they have certain instincts, like the beasts and birds of prey, which they use in hunting their prey to sustain life. Among the ancients there was one who maintained this very thing. He said that man is an inferior creation in comparison with the other animals. For the latter do not need other animals to ride on in order to go from place to place, being swifter of movement than man. Similarly, they do not have to prepare weapons with which to fight against their enemies, for they are provided with natural weapons, the ox has horns, the boar has tusks, the porcupine has quills, the turtle has a shell, and so on. Nor do they need to make themselves any garments, for their garments too are given them by nature, and they do not have to prepare their food, for they use it as found in nature; whereas man is devoid of all these things. For he requires garments to cover his body, and buildings to serve as shelter and protection against the wind and rain. His food must be subjected to many processes of preparation before it is fit for his nourishment, and many other things of this sort, as is found in the fourteenth book of the treatise On Animals.

But on reflection we shall find this idea quite erroneous. If we consider the various forms as they exist in their matters in the genesis of the lower forms of existing things, we find that they form an ascending series in regard to quality. The later form is superior to the prior one, as though the matter in receiving forms proceeds from imperfection to perfection, first receiving a lower form and then a higher form, and thus gradually ascending from an inferior grade of existence to a more perfect one. Thus, matter first receives the forms of the elements, then it rises to the stage of minerals, to which the elements stand in the relation of matter. Then it attains to the grade of plants to which minerals bear the relation of matter. Then it ascends to the degree of animals, to which plants are related as matter, and then it rises to the grade of man, animals being in the position of matter. Here the process comes to an end. As in a given motion, every part of the motion is for the sake of the part which comes after, so it seems, in the genetic process of the lower forms of existence, that every part is for the sake of the part that comes after. And as a given motion ends up with a result which is the final cause of all the partial motions, so the genetic process rises gradually until it attains finally to the human form, where it stops, because this is the end of all the lower genetic processes.

That matter always moves from a less perfect to a more perfect form of existence, as the character of the composition rises in quality, is proved by the coral, which is intermediate, so to speak, between mineral and plant; by the marine sponge, which has only the sense of touch, and is intermediate as it were between plant and animal;

Sefer Halkkarim   BOOK [Maamar] THRE

and by the ape, which stands midway between the animal species and man, where the process stops. It follows necessarily, therefore, that man, who is the end of all the lower creatures, is nobler and more perfect than all, since in him are combined all the earlier forms, which stand to him in the relation of matter. Therefore, he is greater than all the others, and subdues all the animals and rules them, because he has the power of comprehending the general, whereas the lower animals perceive only the particular, having no power to comprehend the universal. Therefore, they have particular organs and particular instincts corresponding to their perception of the particular. Thus, they have particular organs to fight with in a specific way, the boar with his tusks, the ox with his horns, the porcupine with his quills, the turtle using his shell as a protection. But man who is the end of all the lower existences, and in whom are combined all the particular perfections of the other animals, is endowed with general comprehension and intelligence. He comprehends all that the other animals do, and besides understands the general and not merely a particular thing. Therefore, his organs are general, like the hands which are potentially every kind of weapon to fight against all kinds of animals in all possible ways and to subdue them. The spear takes the place of horns, the sword represents the tusks of the boar, the shield or the coat of mail protects him as the shell protects the turtle. All these weapons and arms are not born with the human being as is the case with the animals, so that he might not have to carry a heavy burden with him all the time. Therefore, the Creator in forming man used His wisdom in giving him organs general in their utility, which are potentially all kinds of weapons, and an intellect capable of comprehending generalities rather than particulars, that he may be able to understand all that the animals perceive in the way of particulars, and utilize the weapons above mentioned in different ways when he needs them and lay them aside when he does not need them, so that they may not be a burden to him. Similarly, man's garments are not attached to his body, so that he may use such clothes as he needs in winter and take them off in summer that they may not be a burden, as their wool is to lambs, who have to be sheared. Intelligence and understanding is given to man to build strong buildings where he can fortify himself against the violence of wrong-doers instead of holes of the earth and of the rocks used by the animals.

By means of his general intellect he can comprehend all the particular instincts of the animals and their particular perceptions and characteristics, as is said in Job, "Who teacheth us through the beasts of the earth, and maketh us wise through the fowls of heaven." The meaning is not that the beasts and the fowls are wiser and more intelligent than the human species, and that the latter must learn from them, for experience belies this, seeing that man rules and manages them. The meaning is that man with his general intelligence and instruments learns from all the animals all their particular instincts and perceptions, combines them all and makes them general. So we find in the Talmud: "Said Rabbi Hiyya, The verse, 'He teacheth us through the beasts of the earth,' refers to the mule which urinates kneeling, while the verse, 'And maketh us wise through the fowls of heaven,' alludes to the cock, who pets his consort before copulation. Said Rabbi Yohanan, If the Torah had not been given to Israel, we should learn modesty from the cat, prohibition of robbery from the ant, and the wrongfulness of incest from the dove." This can be explained in the way expressed above, namely that the particular characteristics of the animal's man should learn with his intellect, which combines them and makes them general. In the same way, as, on account of his intellect and organs he is just as capable as though he were provided by nature with all instruments of war and with garments corresponding to the wool of sheep, and is able to prepare his food by combining articles of diet in a way that is appropriate and agreeable and wholesome for his nature and temperament, so he should learn all the particular good characteristics of the various animals and combine them, and thus invent the arts and the sciences.

This is the meaning of "Perek Shirah," concerning which the Rabbis say, "Whoever says Perek Shirah every day is assured of a share in the hereafter." "To say," means not merely to repeat by rote, but to understand with the mind, as in the expression, "I said in my heart." The meaning is that one should consider the fact that every visible creature has something to teach us, a good quality, or a moral lesson, or some wise inference. To quote an example from Perek Shirah, "What do the heavens say? 'The heavens declare the glory of God, etc.' " The word "say" that is used throughout Perek Shirah has the same meaning as "signify," like the Talmudic expression, "This says," meaning, this signifies. The meaning is that from the motion of the heavens we may infer that there is a Being who moves them without being Himself in motion, and that He is omnipotent, seeing that He moves such tremendous bodies, that is, He is God. This is a philosophic inference, as is explained in the proper place.

We also read there, "What do the dogs say? 'Come, let us bow down and bend the knee; Let us kneel before the Lord our Maker.' " The meaning is that from the dog, who knows his master or any one who treats him well, and is obedient, loyal and grateful to him as far as lies in his power, we may learn the moral lesson of thanking God for the good He has done us in providing us with food; of submission and obedience as far as lies in our power, even as He does good also to those who are guilty; and we should not be ungrateful.

Another example is, "What does the ant say? 'Who giveth food to all flesh, for His mercy endureth forever.' " The meaning is that if one reflects upon the ant, which is a tiny creature and yet prepares her food in the summer and gathers it in the harvest, he will learn the quality of industry, and will understand that God gives food to all flesh and prepares sustenance for all the creatures that He has created in that He has endowed each one with the instinct of seeking its food at the proper time and from the proper source. Man, therefore, who is endowed with knowledge and understanding, must make efforts to obtain food and not to be idle. For the blessing of God makes rich those who prepare themselves to receive it, as the Rabbis say in commenting on the biblical expression, "In order that the Lord, thy God may bless thee." To prevent the inference that God's blessing comes to the idle, the sequel reads, "In all the work of thy hand which thou doest."

But a man might say: inasmuch as the matter depends upon my own efforts, I will steal and rob and plunder as I find opportunity. To counter this they say, we learn the wrongfulness of robbery from the ant, which never steals or robs or takes anything that belongs to another. The experiment has often been tried to take a grain of wheat from one of them and put it in front of the others. When they approach it they know by the smell that it belongs to another ant and pass it by, refusing to take what does not belong to them. This is what Solomon meant when he said: "Go to the ant, thou sluggard: Consider her ways, and be wise; which having no chief, overseer, or ruler, ..." i.e., none to prohibit robbery, yet keeps away from it and takes pain to prepare her food in summer without robbery.

We read in the same place, "What does the dove say? 'O my dove, that art in the clefts of the rock ...' " The meaning is that Israel is compared to a dove, so that they may learn her ways, as we read in Midrash Hazit: The dove is modest, and so is Israel. The dove never changes her mate after she knows him, and similarly Israel never changed their God from the time that they knew Him. This is similar to the passage mentioned before, where it is said that we can learn to reject incest from the dove. In Midrash Hazit there are many similarities expressed between Israel and the dove.

We also find in Perek Shirah, "What does the apple say? 'As an apple-tree among the trees of the wood so is my beloved among the sons. Under its shadow I delighted to sit, and its fruit was sweet to my taste.' " The meaning is that God is compared to the apple-tree, as is said in Midrash Hazit. An apple-tree does not give as much shade as other trees, and yet one desires to sit in that small shade, because of the expectation of the fruit, which is so good and sweet smelling and agreeable to the taste. In the same way though a person who serves God may meet with trouble and suffering and find no prosperity in this world as long as he "dwells in the covert of the Most High and abides in the shadow of the Almighty," nevertheless he should not abandon his innocence, because of the expectation of future reward, which is so sweet and agreeable to those that know it. We also find in Midrash Hazit, "As all run away from the apple-tree in the hot season because it has no shade, so the gentile nations refused to dwell in God's shadow at the time when the Torah was revealed. Was Israel guilty of the same act? No! 'Under its shadow I delighted to sit.' " In this way should the entire Perek Shirah be interpreted. The teaching of the whole composition is that man can learn a lesson from all existing things which he perceives with his senses, a lesson concerning conduct. For the human intellect is general and must combine in it all the particulars observable in nature. It is clear therefore that he is more noble and more perfect than the other animals because he combines all particulars in a way no other animal does, and because he rules over them by his wisdom and subjects them to himself, as the Bible says, "Thou hast made him to have dominion over the works of Thy hands; Thou hast put all things under his feet."

Chapter 2

Every natural existent has in its specific form a certain property and purpose which distinguish it from other species. This purpose which exists in every species is the cause which determines its existence in that specific form. Man is also a natural existent, being the noblest and most perfect of them, as we have explained. He must therefore also have a proper purpose which is related to his specific form. It can not reside in the faculties of nutrition and sensation, for in that case the perfection and purpose of the ass and the pig would be the same as that of man. It is clear therefore that the perfection of man must consist in something which he has over and above the other animals.

Sefer HaIkkarim — BOOK [Maamar] THREE

Now we see that man has a potentiality and capacity of apprehending concepts, discovering sciences and bringing them from potentiality to actuality, more than all the other animals. Therefore, human perfection must depend upon this intellectual power. And this power being divided into theoretical and practical, human perfection must depend upon the theoretical part rather than upon the practical, for the former bears closer relation to man's nature.

We can not say that the purpose of the human intellect is exclusively practical, to enable man to invent arts and trades. For it is made clear in the Treatise on Animals, composed by the brethren of Purity, that as a general rule the lower animals are more adept in practical skill than man. Moreover, if this were the case, then since the purpose is more important than that which comes before the purpose, the practical arts would be more noble than the speculative, and those speculative arts which lead to no practical result at all would be vain and of no value whatever. But this is contradicted by our nature and universal opinion. For all agree that the theoretical arts are superior to the practical. Again, the joy we feel in a thing relates to the purpose, and to that which is near to the purpose more so than to that which is far from it. But we find that the satisfaction and joy derived from a little theoretical knowledge are infinitely greater than all the satisfaction derived from practice. This proves that the real purpose of man depends upon the theoretical part of the intellectual power.

This is why we find that man has a stronger desire for the sensibilia of sight and hearing than for those of smell and taste. Nature has put in us a stronger desire for the former because we are more apt through them to acquire theoretical knowledge, upon which human perfection depends. The other sensibilia, on the other hand, bear a closer relation to the corporeal sensations and desires, which are far away from the specific perfection of man. Man has them only for the maintenance of his body, like the other animals. Now as every existent has a greater desire for that which has a bearing on his specific form and proper purpose, he has also a strong desire for the powers and instruments which lead to that purpose. Therefore, man has a greater desire for these two sensibilia than for the others, because they play a greater part in leading man to his purpose than the others.

And this is the reason why the Bible ascribes to God the formation of these two senses, rather than the others. Solomon says, "The hearing ear, and the seeing eye, The Lord hath made even both of them." And since instruction which is imparted by a teacher is more permanent than that which is not so acquired, the author of Proverbs explains in another verse that hearing is superior to sight, "The ear that hearkeneth to the reproof of life abideth among the wise." In allusion to the superiority of these two senses over the others because they are instrumental in man's acquisition of perfection, Solomon says in the Song of Songs, "O my dove, that art in the clefts of the rock, in the covert of the cliff, let me see thy countenance, let me hear thy voice; For sweet is thy voice, and thy countenance is comely." In poetic figure he speaks to his own soul, which he pictures as a dove, and speaks of her as being in the clefts of the rock, in the coverts of the cliff, alluding to the fact that the soul is hidden in the body, its seat not being known. The word countenance in the above passage is expressed in the Hebrew by the plural to indicate two things, letters in a book, and the sensibilia, both of which are necessary means of acquiring knowledge, and both of them are comely. Then he says, "Let me hear thy voice," meaning to say that though the voice of the dove is not sweet, the voice of this one is sweet, meaning the voice through which the soul learns concepts from the teacher; that voice, he says, is very sweet. Therefore, he says, let me hear thy voice, that which thou hast received from thy teacher, for thy voice is sweet, and thy countenance is comely. For through these two senses man's capacities are realized in actu, and he attains his perfection if he uses them properly.

But if he directs them to the world's vanities, he is as though he were deaf and blind. Thus, the prophet calls those who occupy themselves with the vanities of the world, deaf and blind, "Hear, ye deaf, and look, ye blind, that ye may see." The reason is, because they do not employ their senses properly, i.e., to actualize their potential perfections, which is the only way by which man can realize his purpose.

In explanation of this we must say that there are two kinds of perfection, a first and a last. The first is that perfection which a thing has as soon as it comes into existence, the perfection of existence. The other is the perfection which a thing has not solely by existing. It is only potential in the existing thing, which attains that perfection when its potentialities are actualized. This is called the perfection of purpose. This is the perfection that is intended for man. Take a chair, for example. Its first perfection is attained as soon as it comes into existence, as soon as its manufacture is completed. The last perfection of the chair, the perfection of purpose, is not attained until it is sat on. In the lower animals the only perfection that is expected of them is the perfection of existence. Hence in speaking of their formation, the Bible says, "And God saw that it was good," to indicate that as soon as they come into existence, the good of which they are capable is attained and completed, and no other good is expected of them. But in the account of the formation of man there is no statement "that it is good," which seems strange. For it would seem that the formation of man should be characterized as good just like the formation of animals. The reason for the omission is in order to indicate that the good that is intended in the creation of man is not the perfection of existence merely, as in the other animals, but another nobler perfection, which can be attained only when he has actualized his potentialities. But as long as his intellect does not actualize its potentialities, the perfection intended, namely the perfection of purpose, is not attained.

This is the meaning of Solomon's statement, "A good name is better than precious oil; and the day of death than the day of one's birth." The meaning is, a good name acquired by good qualities is better than good oil, for a good name is heard much farther away than extends the odor of good oil. But a good name is not an essential and ultimate good of the soul. Therefore, the day of death, when a man has attained his complete knowledge, is better than the day of his birth; for on the day of death he has already actualized the potentialities of his intellect, which is not the case on the day of his birth, for then the perfection of the soul has only potential existence, though the perfection of the body is actual.

The difference between man and animals in the purpose of their creation is alluded to also in variation of expression. Thus in the account of the formation of animals, we find the expressions, "after its kind," "after their kind," "And God made the beast of the earth after its kind, and the cattle after their kind, and every thing that creepeth upon the ground after its kind," to indicate that in animals there is no difference between the purpose of one species and that of another. Nor is there a difference between the creation of the male and that of the female. There is one general purpose including them all, and that is the perpetuation of the species, which is the perfection of existence. This is the same for all species and for male and female, for the male has no superiority in this matter over the female. But in the case of man, since the purpose of his creation is not merely the perpetuation of the species, but also the perpetuation of the individual, the expression "after his kind" is not mentioned, and the female was not created at the same time as the male, to indicate the great difference between the two kinds of creation [man and animal].

Sefer Halkkarim   BOOK [Maamar] THRE

The purpose in the latter is perpetuation of the species, wherein male and female are equal. The purpose of the former is perpetuation of the individual, in which the female is not equal to the male, but was created to help him that he might attain the intended perfection, which was there potentially, at the time of creation, and must be brought into actuality.

As this perfection is in man potentially, and potential existence stands midway, as it were, between existence and non-existence, the Bible calls it nothing. Thus, Solomon says, "The pre-eminence of man above the beast is nothing; for all is vanity." The meaning is, the pre-eminence of man above the beast is something whose existence is weak. If the passage read: "There is no pre-eminence of man over the beast," it would have the meaning of a purely negative proposition. But since he says: "The pre-eminence of man above the beast is nothing," the judgment is affirmative, equivalent to the statement that man has pre-eminence over the beast, but this pre-eminence is nothing, i.e., something whose existence is weak, because it is mere potentiality. The student of logic will understand that this judgment has the value of an affirmative proposition rather than a negative. In reference to this power Job said, "But wisdom shall arise from nothing." The meaning is that wisdom comes from a potentiality residing in man, which is called "nothing" [ayin]. Man's final perfection is attained when it becomes actual, not before. And the manner in which this power can attain wisdom is by answering the question, "What is it?" in defining things. Hence, he says in the sequel, "And 'what' is the place of understanding."

Chapter 3

Everything that is potential must pass from potentiality to actuality. And if it does not, then its potential existence is vain, and as though it were not at all. It is clear, therefore, that if man's ultimate perfection and purpose which, as we said, is potential were not realized, the existence of the human species would be vain, for man would have no pre-eminence over the other animal species. We must therefore explain what this purpose is, that man may endeavor to attain it.

According to the opinion of the philosophers the ultimate purpose is the attainment of intellectual knowledge [lit. intelligibles]. They say also that the intellect that is acquired by means of it [lit. them] survives after death. This takes place when the intellect, the cognizing subject, and the intelligible object are consolidated into one substance and are identified with the intelligibles in the Active Intellect. This, they say, is the ultimate purpose of man and the happiness of his soul. They also maintain that except in this way we can not conceive of any survival of the soul, and therefore the existence of the human species would be vain, the human species would have no pre-eminence over the animal, and the perfection of the species of which we spoke in the preceding chapter would be vain. This is the opinion of the philosophers concerning human perfection. It is also the opinion of many Jewish theologians, as stated in their works. They adopted this opinion because they thought that it is the opinion of the Bible. For Moshe says, "That I may know Thee in order that I may find favour in Thine eyes." From this, they say, it seems that only he who knows finds favor in God's sight, and no one else. But this is not necessarily implied in the text, which only signifies that he who knows stands on a higher plane than the one who does not know, but nothing else. For the expression, "that I may know Thee," refers to God, and no one can know God outside of Himself. We must therefore examine this question briefly, enough to give the believer an idea, as is our purpose in this work.

If we examine this opinion, we shall find that it is absurd in itself and in disagreement with the divine Torah. For the philosophers can not by any means avoid the conclusion that the existence of man is vain, thus meeting with the same difficulty which they are endeavoring to escape. The purpose is either one that can be attained or one that can not be attained. If it can not be attained, then the existence of the human species is vain and man has no pre-eminence over the ass and the pig. And if it can be attained, it is clear that neither all nor the majority of mankind can attain it, but only one in a thousand, or one in a generation, like Socrates or Plato. But the other persons who have not as much knowledge as they, and have not reached their high plane, will be, in their opinion, in the position of the ass and the pig, since, according to their opinion, they have not attained the human purpose. The existence of all would therefore be vain except the one man in his generation. And if it happens that there is a generation without a man like Socrates, for example, the existence of the whole species at that time would be vain. Thus, we see that they are subject to the same objection which they endeavor to avoid. For according to this theory, it would follow that all God's work at certain times and the greater part of His work at all times never attains or can, by any possibility, attain its purpose. This is something that can not be charged to any perfect agent, how much less to the Cause of Causes, who is far above any such limitation.

Moreover, even according to their opinion, those ideas which the wise man or the unique one in his generation apprehends, may not lead him to his human purpose and perfection. For knowledge concerning the elements and objects of nature does not confer essential perfection upon the soul even according to the opinion of the philosophers. Certainly, this is true of mathematical knowledge. For what perfection can the soul attain by knowing that the angles of a triangle are equal to two right angles, or that the external angle of a triangle is equal to the sum of the two opposite internal angles, or that when you add the side of an inscribed decagon to the side of an inscribed hexagon, the resulting line is divided into a mean proportional and two extremes? This knowledge gives perfection to the soul only so far as it is an introduction and a means to the understanding of the heavenly objects and the causes upon which the natural objects depend, but it does not of itself give perfection to the soul. Therefore, the soul can not acquire eternity from such knowledge.

David calls attention to this fact in the nineteenth Psalm. The statement is there made that human speculation can make inferences from the motions of the spheres because we see that the heavens move continuously. As every moving thing requires a mover, we infer the existence of God who moves them. And being enormous bodies, they point to the mighty force of their mover, thus indicating His glory and power. This is the meaning of the expression, "the glory of **El** [God]," the word **El** indicating power in Hebrew, as in the expression, "Yesh le-el yadi," which denotes power. Similarly, the firmament, i.e., that part of the atmosphere in which rain and snow and hail and thunder and lightning originate, also points to the great power of God. It is possible also that the word firmament alludes to the diurnal sphere, which Ezekiel also calls firmament, as in the statement, "And over the heads of the living creatures there was the likeness of a firmament like the color of the terrible ice, stretched forth over their heads above." The Psalm continues to describe how the heavens and the firmament declare the glory of God and the work of His hands, by saying, "Day unto day uttereth speech, etc." The meaning is that they declare the glory of God through the diurnal motions which are visible every day and the changes by which one day differs from another. And similarly, "Night unto night revealeth knowledge". For in reality there is no 'speech,' that is a proposition or judgment, such as, "the world had an origin in time," nor 'words,' such as the component words of the proposition mentioned, viz. "world," "origin," etc. Nor is there even the 'voice' or sound of a single letter, for "their voice is not heard." The heavens have not any of these, but "Their line is gone out through all the earth, and their words to the end of the world", through their visible motions, through the sun for whom "He hath set a tent" in the heavens, and through whom are known day and night, and through the other celestial motions which cause the genesis of existing things in the lower world, thus pointing to God's handiwork. Further in the same Psalm we read, "which is as a bridegroom coming out of his chamber," the meaning of which is that the sun is forced in its diurnal motion by the diurnal sphere like a bridegroom who does not desire to leave his chamber but is forced to, as the prophet says, "Let the bridegroom go forth from his chamber, and the bride out of her pavilion." And despite this fact the sun "rejoiceth as a strong man to run his course," in order to do the will of his Maker. In explanation of the statement that the sun is forced in his diurnal motion, he refers to the other motion of the sun which is proper to him, "His going forth is from the end of the heaven, and his circuit unto the ends of it," i.e., to the north and to the south. For the sun does not rise to-day in the same place where he rose yesterday, and in this way he warms now the south now the north, "And there is nothing hid from the heat thereof." This is the knowledge that may be derived from the heavens and their motions. But it is not this that gives perfection to the soul, enabling it to cleave to the higher beings and return to the place of its origin. "The Law of the Lord," alone, "is perfect," and adequate to bring the soul back to its original home, "The law of the Lord is perfect, restoring the soul." In the sequel the Psalm describes the pre-eminence of the divine law over other laws, as was explained in the eighth chapter of the First Book.

From all this it is clear that knowledge of the motions of the spheres and of the natural phenomena that take place in the firmament of heaven does not confer perfection upon the soul. But if the soul is to attain perfection, it can come only from a knowledge of divine things. But this can not be unless the knowledge is true, i.e., unless what is in the soul is in agreement with that which is outside of the soul. Then only can the soul unite with the Active Intellect. But this union can take place only if there is a complete agreement. But this is impossible, for it is inconceivable that there be one so wise that his ideas should agree in every way with the ideas in the Active Intellect. This is the reason why some philosophers deny the immortality of the soul altogether, because that which man knows of divine things can not be absolutely true and in complete agreement with the ideas of the Active Intellect. For the soul's knowledge of things abstracted from their matter is mere surmise and conjecture, and it may be that the reality is quite different from the idea.

To give an illustration, there is a difference of opinion between the ancient philosophers and the modern, whether the first mover is an effect of the First Cause or not. Ibn Sina, Alfarabi and Rabbi Moshe ha-Lavi are of the opinion that the first mover is an effect of the First Cause, whereas Ibn Roshd maintains that the First Cause is the immediate mover of the sphere, and attributes this opinion to Aristotle. Now if Ibn Sina is correct, then Aristotle did not have the true opinion concerning this question, which is the most important of questions concerning divine things, but entertained a theory which is different from the truth. If so, then the entire existence of man from the time of Aristotle to that of Ibn Sina was in vain, since their opinion concerning the most important question was different from the truth. Clearly, then, the philosophers are subject to the objection which they endeavored to avoid.

Moreover, even if we grant that the perfection of man is dependent upon a knowledge of ideas, and that this knowledge may be acquired by the whole human race or the greater part of it, it can not be denied that there is a difference between one person and another, for it is a matter of experience. This being the case, I should like to know what would happen when Reuben has certain ideas, and Simeon has one idea more than Reuben. What difference would there be between them when they are both identified with the Active Intellect? And if it is maintained that no one can be identified with the Active Intellect unless he has all the ideas of the latter and the two become one, no man has ever attained this stage. And therefore, this kind of immortality becomes null and void, a species of immortality invented by men wise in their own eyes and following the desires of their evil heart, who dive in deep waters and bring up a potsherd.

David alluded to this when he said, "I hate them that are of a double mind; but Thy law do I love." The meaning is, I hate philosophical ideas, but I love Thy law, for through its man attains perfection of soul, embracing the entire species or the greater part of it. For the purpose of a given species must be realized in the whole species or in the greater part thereof. For example, the power of scammonia to pass red gall or the power of rhubarb to purify the bad mixture in the liver must apply to every individual in the species, whether he be strong or weak. It is impossible that it should not apply to the whole species or to the greater part thereof, for in that case the respective definitions would not be applicable to scammonia and rhubarb. It is clear, therefore, that all individuals to whom the definition of man applies or a majority of them should be able to realize the purpose of man, unless it be hindered through their own evil choice. If not at all times, this should be possible most of the time, else the existence of the human species is in vain. But it is absurd to suppose that there exists a species with a specific form which does not realize the function and purpose which it ought to realize. Hence Aristotle says that there must come a time when all men will pursue the truth and endeavor to know God as far as it is possible for man. He says this because he thought that otherwise the existence of the human species would be in vain. Now since the acquisition of knowledge in the manner explained is impossible for all men, we must explain what is the method by which human perfection, embracing the whole or a greater part of the species, may be obtained by the whole species or by the greater part thereof.

Chapter 4

Every existing thing, in accordance with its natural capacity, can easily acquire its appropriate quality and perfection, no matter to what species the thing belongs. This observation is clear if we examine the various kinds of perfection peculiar to the human species.
We observe that individuals properly formed and of strong constitution acquire good health without effort or work. Health is always theirs. There are others who have good health as an intimate quality, but they must do something, engage in exercise or take walks, to maintain their health. There are others again of whose constitution health is not so intimate a quality, and who must take great pains and make special efforts to maintain their health, but if they try hard, they achieve perfect health. There are others again whose constitution is so poor that they may try ever so hard and yet can not acquire perfect health, but with slight effort they acquire something like health, i.e., they prevent their illness from increasing. The same thing applies to wisdom or wealth. Some acquire wisdom or wealth with little effort, some only after great toil, some can not acquire it with all the labor in the world, but only a certain degree of wisdom or wealth.

The same thing holds of every thing in relation to its appropriate perfection. The First Cause, being sufficient in itself for maintaining in actu its own proper perfection, needs no act of its own or of another to acquire any perfection. The Separate Intelligences, being free from matter, always have the perfection which is proper to them, and need no act of their own to acquire their perfection, except the act of causing others to move, viz. the spheres. The spheres, on the other hand, though they have intelligent souls, as all wise men agree, yet since they have matter, can not acquire the perfection appropriate to their nature except by doing something in their own person, namely move. The act of motion confers upon their intellectual soul its perfection. For as the soul resides in a body it requires a corporeal act to attain the perfection appropriate to its nature. And yet the spheres differ from one another in this act. The noblest and most perfect of the spheres, the diurnal sphere, needs only one simple act to attain the perfection appropriate to its nature, namely the diurnal motion, which is one simple motion. The sphere of the fixed stars, being further away from nobility and perfection than the diurnal sphere, must have two motions, the diurnal motion and its own proper motion. Of the other spheres, every one needs more acts to attain its proper perfection according as it is farther from nobility. This is why the spheres have different motions, one having more motions than another according as it is farther from the attainment of its perfection. Thus, we find that some of the planets and especially the moon have many different motions. For by reason of the moon's distance from nobility it needs more acts than the other spheres, so that through the many motions the moon may acquire the perfection appropriate to its nature. The Philosopher agrees with this view in the third Summa of the second book of the treatise. De Caelo et Mundo.

This shows that no material being can attain the perfection appropriate to its nature except by doing corporeal acts which are completed by the body. Therefore, the spheres must move in order that they may attain the perfection which is appropriate to their souls, since they are powers residing in bodies. It follows also that man who is a material being and whose matter is thicker and coarser than the matter of the spheres, must necessarily have more activities than the spheres, in order that by the multiplicity of acts he may attain the perfection appropriate to his nature, viz. the perfection of his intellectual soul. For if it were possible for man to attain this through intellectual contemplation alone without any practical activity, the spheres could accomplish this even more easily and would not have to move and do corporeal acts to acquire perfection. The fact is, however, that no material being can acquire any perfection without a corporeal act.

As for the irrational animals, they are far removed from the degree of the beings endowed with souls, and can not, by reason of their nature, attain individual immortality because they are devoid of reason. They were given, therefore, a mode of immortality which bears some similarity to the immortality of the other beings who have souls, namely immortality of the species. This immortality can be attained through one act or a few, because this perfection is far from the perfection of the other beings, who are endowed with souls, viz. individual immortality. But in the case of man, since he has the capacity of individual immortality by reason of his rational soul, like the spheres, but is far removed from the degree of the latter, he was given a great variety of acts, through which he may correct his deficiencies and attain the same kind of degree which the spheres attain with one or a few acts.

It is clear that not all acts give perfection to the soul, but only those which are proper. Moreover, those acts do not give perfection to the soul in so far as they are purely corporeal. For in that case all corporeal beings endowed with an animal soul would attain that perfection. On the other hand, man, being a material being, can not attain human perfection through intellectual contemplation alone without practical activity, as we explained in reference to the spheres that, being possessed of matter, they must have a corporeal form of activity, such as motion, through which activity they may attain the spiritual perfection appropriate to their nature.

It follows therefore that the thing which gives perfection to a being having matter as well as an intellectual soul, must be something composed of a corporeal activity and an intellectual contemplation. The practical activity does not give perfection by virtue of its being corporeal merely, but by reason of the intellectual comprehension which is involved in the act, as we have explained. The act which is done in such a way, namely that it is a composite of a corporeal act and an intellectual conception, is the one that gives perfection to the soul. These are the activities we mentioned before, which follow man's rational form and issue from it, not the mere understanding of intellectual conceptions, as those who follow the Philosopher think.

Chapter 5

We spoke of intellectual conception as giving perfection to the soul when combined with practical activity. This intellectual conception does not mean the understanding of intellectual concepts, but the intention to serve God as the purpose of doing the physical act. In other words, he must do whatever he does with the intention of pleasing God and not for his own pleasure or any other purpose.

We can take an example concerning this from the spheres. They have bodies and rational souls like man, and attain their perfection by continuous motion in order to carry out the will of God who commanded them to move in order to maintain the natural universe. The Psalmist makes this clear when he speaks of the duty of the creatures to praise God for the kindness, He has bestowed upon them. He begins with the soul of man, "Bless the Lord, O my soul, and forget not all His benefits." Then, speaking of the stars and the constellations, he says, "Bless the Lord, all ye His hosts, Ye ministers of His, that do His pleasure." The meaning is that the sole purpose of their motions is to do God's will, and nothing else. This is the most perfect service any creature can give to God. For even in reference to the Separate Intelligences the Bible makes it clear that in moving the spheres their only purpose is to carry out God's decree, who commanded them to cause those motions, and nothing else, as we read, "Bless the Lord, ye angels of His, ye mighty in strength, that fulfil His word, Hearkening unto the voice of His word." He calls the angels, who are the Separate Intelligences, "mighty in strength," because they move the spheres continually with great force. Then he adds that in causing this motion they have no other purpose except to do God's bidding, who commanded them to cause the motions. This is signified by the expression, "hearkening unto the voice of His word" - they move the spheres because they are obedient to God's word, the greatest object they can achieve, and not in order to receive reward or for any other purpose. I have seen an explanation given of the expression, "hearkening unto the voice of His word," that they move the spheres in order that they may hear better the word of God, i.e., in order to attain a greater perfection than they otherwise would, for they think that in this way they will get more influence and reach a higher degree.

But this is impossible. For the verse in question deals with the angels causing the motions and not with the spheres. But the perfection of the angels is always in actu, there being no potentiality in them, and their perfection consists in continuous comprehension. And with all this the Bible explains that their perfection is not due merely to their conception of ideas, but to the act of causing motion in the spheres

Sefer Haikkarim   BOOK [Maamar] THRE

together with the intention to obey God who ordered them to move the spheres. In the same way the perfection of the spheres and the stars is due to the motions which they undergo in order to do the will of God, as we have said. The philosophers are wrong when they say that the sphere moves continually because of the desire to acquire perfect understanding by change of position and by making a potential position actual. This is surely erroneous. For according to this opinion, the motion of the sphere would be foolish and insane, like a crazy person who turns round a pillar all the time, thinking to acquire perfection by changing place, facing now the east, now the west, or the north or the south, and by making the potential places actual. This is clearly absurd, for since they admit that the spheres are rational animals, having intelligent souls, how can they move in this way? The true explanation is as we have written, that the purpose and intention of the Separate Intelligences in causing the spheres to move and the purpose of the spheres in moving, is none other than to do the will of God and to carry out His command that they should move. This is their only desire and perfection, and nothing else.

This may be illustrated by supposing the case of a person who was fond of a certain king, and on coming to visit him was accepted in the king's service. It is clear that his greatest happiness and glory are to be an acceptable servant to the king and that he does his work with great enthusiasm for no other purpose than to do the will of the king. This is also the consensus of opinion of the genuine ancient philosophers, as Ibn Roshd says in the third Question of the Destructio Destructionis. His language is as follows: "The opinion of the ancients is that there are immaterial beings [principles], which move the heavenly bodies, and the latter move from loyalty and love and obedience, in order, by means of motion, to carry out the command of the former and to acquire an understanding of them, for the heavenly bodies were created for the sake of their motions. Now since it is accepted that the principles which cause the heavenly bodies to move are free from matter and are not bodies, there is no other way in which they can move the heavenly bodies except in the sense that the moving body is commanded to move. Hence they inferred that the heavenly bodies are rational beings, who understand themselves and understand the principles which move them by way of command."

The men of the Great Synagogue also agree that the motion of the spheres is in order to do the will of God. We can see this in the Blessing of the Moon, which reads, "Who by His word created the heavens, and by the breath of His mouth all their hosts ... they are glad and rejoice to do the will of their Maker." All this shows that a corporeal act done with an intelligent purpose to carry out the will and command of God gives perfection to those beings who have an intellectual soul. This is also proved by the prophetic promise of reward to those who honor the Sabbath, "If thou turn away thy foot because of the sabbath ... and call the sabbath a delight.... Then shalt thou delight thyself in the Lord." The Rabbis also expatiate upon the great reward which comes to him who has pleasure on the Sabbath and the holidays, though pleasure is a corporeal matter and a physical act which man enjoys as a member of the genus animal and not by virtue of his being human in species. If the pleasure were something enjoyed without any purpose it would no doubt be the act of an animal. But if it is indulged with the purpose of serving God and obeying His command, it is without doubt an intellectual act like the motion of the spheres, and it is by this kind of an act only that the purpose is attained, as we have said.

Thus, the Rabbis say: This may be compared to the case of two persons who roasted their paschal lambs. The one ate it in the name of the paschal offering, while the other ate it merely to gratify his appetite. To the first we may apply the biblical text, "For the ways of the Lord are right, and the just do walk in them." To the second applies the sequel, "But transgressors do stumble therein." And it is properly so, for in this way human perfection may be attained by the whole species or the greater part thereof, though he who has knowledge stands higher than he who has no knowledge. But if attainment of human perfection depended upon intellectual conception alone, it would be impossible of attainment by the whole species or the greater part thereof.

There is an allusion to this also in the book of Ecclesiastes, where Solomon inquires into the purpose of man, "And I applied my heart to know wisdom ... Come now, I will try thee with mirth ... I searched in my heart now to pamper my flesh with wine ... till I might see which it was best for the sons of men that they should do under the heaven the few days of their life." The question in his mind is whether the purpose is conception of ideas, or great wealth, or high honor, or corporeal pleasure. Then at the end, after he has considered each one separately and discussed the reasons pro and con, he sums up, "The end of the matter, all having been heard: fear God, and keep His commandments; for this is the whole man." The meaning is, we have heard all the arguments, and considered the profit of great wealth or great wisdom or the other goods, and found that there is no good among them which embraces the whole race or the greater part thereof, except doing God's commandments from the fear of God. Therefore, "Fear God and keep His commandments," for this good is superior to all other goods, "for this is the whole man," i.e., this perfection embraces the entire human race; therefore, it stands to reason that of all perfections this is the true one.

That this is the true way of attaining perfection is also proved from that passage in which God is represented as finding fault with those who think that the perfection which they possess is the real one, and pointing out that none of them is possessed of human perfection unless he does the right thing with the proper motive: "Thus saith the Lord: Let not the wise man glory in his wisdom, neither let the mighty man glory in his might, Let not the rich man glory in his riches." Praise is due only with a view to the purpose. A horse is praised as a fast runner because the purpose is to use the horse in running. And if we praise his color or form, it is because they are indications of his speed as a runner, which is the purpose. Similarly a physician is praised for his knowledge of medicine, not for his knowledge of geometry or astronomy. This is the reason why the prophet names here three types of excellence which, one might suppose, determine human perfection, viz. wisdom, strength, wealth. And he says that the wise man must not insist on his wisdom, thinking that in this way he has attained human perfection, nor should the strong man boast of his strength, nor the rich man of his riches, for a thing is praiseworthy only if it leads to the purpose, whereas no man can attain the human purpose with any of these unless he associates conduct with every one of them, i.e., unless he benefits others with the excellence which he has. This is the meaning of the text, "Let not the wise man glory in his wisdom, neither let the mighty man glory in his might, let not the rich man glory in his riches," i.e., he has no reason to boast if the wisdom is confined to himself, and similarly the wealth and the strength, but only if he bestows the benefits thereof upon others, and that too not with the hope of reward, but in order that the other may have the benefit, as God does when He bestows good things in this manner. This is the meaning of the prophet's words, "That he understandeth and knoweth Me, that I am the Lord who exercise mercy, justice and righteousness in the earth," i.e., that he should understand and know that since I do mercy by reason of My wisdom, justice because of My power, and righteousness by reason of My riches, though I am not obliged to do so, it shows that these things are agreeable to Me, and that you too should endeavor to do the things which I desire, and should understand that "in these things I delight, saith the Lord." Man must have this end in view in his acts, namely to do the will of God and nothing else. He must not act with the expectation of reward, for God does good and shows mercy to others without expectation of reward, but because acts of this kind are acceptable to Him. Though the function of wisdom is primarily self-perfection, nevertheless it is proper as a matter of mercy that the wise man should benefit others too with his wisdom. This is why the prophet associates the benefits coming from the wise man with mercy. Similarly, though strength is given to the strong primarily to oppose an enemy and protect himself, still the superior strength which a person has is not intended solely for self-protection, but in order to help others and save them from violence. Therefore, the protection of others which proceeds from the strong man is given the name of justice. Finally, riches, which are given to a man primarily to supply his own wants and secondarily to do good to others, are intermediate between mercy and justice, and are therefore called righteousness.

In short, the idea of the prophet is that the acts which a person does, whether they be acts of mercy or of justice or of righteousness, must be done because they are acts which God desires to be done. Hence the prophet ends up his advice with the words, "For in these things I delight, saith the Lord." From this it is clear that God desires certain acts when accompanied with the intention of doing that which God desires, as is said, "That he understandeth and knoweth Me, that I am the Lord who exercise mercy, for in these things I delight, saith the Lord." Knowledge alone without the act is not sufficient. It is called knowledge when it is accompanied by the act, not before. Jeremiah says, "Did not thy father eat and drink, and do justice and righteousness ... He judged the cause of the poor and needy; then it was well. Is not this to know Me? saith the Lord." Thus, he says expressly that there is no virtue in the power of the king except when he does justice, and that this is what knowing God means.

And it is clear that there is no end more noble to enable man to attain human perfection than to know God. An act done in the manner described is called knowledge to indicate that by doing acts in this manner, namely with the intention of pleasing God, does man attain his purpose, namely immortality of the soul in the world to come. Similarly we find that the angel in the name of God promises Yehoshua the son of Jehozadak, the high priest, immortality of the soul in the future world, as a reward for keeping the commandments

Sefer Halkkarim BOOK [Maamar] THRE

and acting with the intention of serving God: "Thus saith the Lord of hosts: if thou wilt walk in My ways, and if thou wilt keep My charge, and wilt also judge My house, and wilt also keep My courts, then I will give thee free access among these that stand by." Jonathan ben Uziel translates the last phrase, "among these Seraphim." We see therefore that he promises him immortality of the soul, and access to the angels who stand continually before God, as a reward for judging His house and keeping His courts. This is what we desired to make clear.

Chapter 6

There are three possibilities as to the tendencies of human acts. Either all of them lead to the end and perfection of man, or none of them leads to the perfection of man, or some do and some do not. It can not be that all acts lead man to his perfection, for violence and robbery and the like are condemned by all men. Indulgence in sexual appetite and in gluttony are characteristic of the irrational animals. Neither of these can lead man to his end, for then the perfection of the swine and the ass would be the same as the perfection of man. Nor can it be that no human act leads to his end, for we have made clear that the perfection of man is necessarily dependent upon human acts since the latter embrace the entire species or the greater part thereof. It remains then that some acts bring man to the human end and some do not, but keep him away from it.

To know and to define the acts which bring man to the human end, namely the perfection of the soul, is very difficult. For if we do not know the essence of a thing, we can not know what things are beneficial to it and what things are injurious. If, for example, we do not know the nature of man's physical disposition, we can not know what things to give him so as to maintain his temperamental equilibrium, or to restore it to him when lost. We must first have a true idea, as far as possible, of man's nature, and then we can know what things are good for him and what things are not. Hence as we can not, by human investigation, know the true nature of the soul except that it is something emanating from an intellectual and immaterial principle, we can not know by investigation what things are injurious or beneficial to it. Hence a certain philosopher has said, "If thou knowest thyself, thou wilt know thy Creator." It becomes a difficult problem, therefore, to determine, by human investigation, what acts are beneficial to the soul, enabling it to attain its perfection. There is no doubt that the test must be found in the essential nature of man. If we should follow the consensus of the majority of mankind, we should have to say that we must keep away from the acts of prophets and pious men, for the majority of mankind act differently from them. On the other hand, there is no doubt that since the first man was created alone, there must be something in man's essential nature by which he can distinguish between good acts conducive to the perfection of his soul and those which are not good.

We find there are certain acts concerning which all agree that they are good, as for example to refrain from wrong doing, to do right, and so on. There are also acts concerning which all men agree that they are bad, for example, wrong doing, violence, etc. We find also that the soul finds pleasure in doing good, and feels pain and sorrow in doing evil. Everything finds pleasure in the like and pain in the unlike. Hence it would seem that the soul, being divine, would find pleasure in good deeds, which resemble its own nature, for all divine acts are good, and would feel pain in evil deeds, because they are different from and opposed to its nature. From this point of view we may say therefore that we can infer the character of an act as good or bad from the pleasure or pain which the soul feels in doing it. Those acts in which the soul always takes pleasure, before doing them as well as after, are good, and those acts which cause the soul pain and sorrow after they are done, are bad.

Even the wicked man who is eager to do evil, as Solomon says: "The soul of the wicked desireth evil," has the desire only before the act by reason of his strong passion which inspires him to do the act, but after the act is done and the intensity of the passion relaxes, the soul is aroused and feels grief and sorrow for the evil deed that he has done. For example, in sexual sin, before the act the desire is so intense that the person is unable to tell whether the act is good or bad. But after the act is done, and the passion has cooled down, the soul realizes the nature of the act, sees the evil of it, and suffers pain and sorrow.

The prophet Jeremiah uses this test of evil deeds, as he addresses Israel in the name of God and says to them that they must realize that the deeds they do are evil because the soul suffers pain and sorrow in the doing of them: "Thine own wickedness shall correct thee, and thy backslidings shall reprove thee: know therefore and see that it is an evil and a bitter thing that thou hast forsaken the Lord thy God, and not My fear that is in thee." The meaning is: It is proper that the evil deed which thou doest should correct thee and that the backsliding itself should reprove thee, because they impress upon the soul sorrow and grief after they are done. From this thou shouldst know that it is an evil and bitter thing that thou hast forsaken the Lord thy God, and not by reason of My fear in thee, i.e., I do not say this to thee because of the fear of My punishment and because of My dread which is upon thee, but because of the nature of the wrong deeds themselves which leave behind them in the soul a feeling of pain and sorrow. From this thou canst realize that they are bad and that it is an evil and a bitter thing that thou hast forsaken the Lord thy God, and not from thy fear of Me. And conversely, from the gladness and joy which a good deed impresses upon the soul it can be known that it is good. Similarly, the Psalmist says: "I considered my ways and turned my feet unto Thy testimonies." The meaning is, When I consider my ways in order to know which is good and which is evil, I turn my feet to Thy testimonies, which is the good way. And he also gives the reason, because he found intense pleasure in them, "I have rejoiced in the way of Thy testimonies, as much as in all riches," i.e., he found infinite joy like a person who has obtained all wealth, meaning an infinite amount of wealth. Thus a person may distinguish between good and bad acts by the pain or the pleasure which the soul feels after doing them.

Chapter 7

The test which we mentioned for distinguishing between good and bad acts is not sufficient to enable us to know all the good acts which are appropriate to the nature of the soul. For as men differ in their temperaments and dispositions, they necessarily have different qualities. A person whose temperament is hot will admire courage and take pleasure in it; while a person of opposite temperament will admire and take pleasure in quiet. The only way to determine what is becoming and what is unbecoming in the manner above mentioned is by referring to the standard of a person of equable temperament, who does not exist. And even if such a person did exist, we should find enormous difficulty in determining what is a good quality in a particular case, a difficulty that is due to the acts themselves. For an admirable act and a good quality represent the mean between the two extremes of excess and defect. Thus generosity is a mean between niggardliness and extravagance; courage is a mean between rashness and cowardice. But the mean between two extremes can not be determined, because it is only a point. Thus, it is impossible to determine the truly lukewarm, which is a mean between the hot and the cold, nor is it possible to determine the true mean between black and white so that it may be perceived with the eye. In the same way it is impossible to know or define actually the actions which are intermediate between the two extremes. It is clear therefore that it is very difficult to determine acts by intellectual investigation.

Moreover, even if it were possible by rational investigation to determine good acts in reference to human nature, it would still be impossible to know what things are acceptable to God. But we made it clear in the fifth chapter of this Book that human perfection depends upon doing those things which are acceptable to God. But we can not by investigation know what things are acceptable to God, because if we do not know the qualities of a ruler and his method and habits, or his perfection and the nature of his government and his station, we do not know what things please him and what things arouse his displeasure. Now as God is absolutely unknown to us, we can not know which of all the possible acts of man are pleasing to Him, and which are not. We can only have a general knowledge, for example that evil is displeasing to God, as the Bible says, "Thou that art of eyes too pure to behold evil, and that canst not look on mischief," and that good is acceptable to Him. But we do not know what particular good deeds are pleasing to Him.

Now inasmuch as it behooves every wise agent to devise a method by which to ensure the realization of the purpose of his acts, else his work would be in vain, God in His wisdom devised a method by which we may know what things are acceptable to God and what things are not, in order that by means of this method man may be able to attain the human end and perfection, since he can not determine this matter by intellectual investigation. This method is to bestow the spirit of prophecy upon a chosen individual of the human race through whom mankind may know what things are pleasing to God and what things are not. This is why the Rabbis say that in the beginning of creation the first man was given seven commandments, as is explained in the treatise Sanhedrin, chapter "Arba' Mitot," connecting the statement with the verse, "And the Lord God commanded the man saying: 'of every tree of the garden thou mayest freely eat;' " intimating that without the divine command it would be impossible to know what things are agreeable to God and what things are not; and that Cain was punished for killing Abel because he transgressed the command of God. Also that the generation of the flood were punished for their wrong doing, the men of Sodom for their sins, Pharaoh on account of Sarai the wife of Abraham, because all of them transgressed the command given to the first man. Otherwise, it seems from their words, they would not have been punished. This is the opinion of the rabbinical sages. The question, however, still arises, according to this point of view, why did not God have respect unto Cain and his offering, seeing that Cain had not violated any of the seven commandments given to Adam? Unless we say that he sinned in intention in a manner which bordered upon idolatry, an interpretation which is not suggested in the expression of the text.

The proper answer is this. There are two kinds of actions which ought to exist by nature in the human mind. One is suppression of wrong doing and continuous pursuit of right among men, so that the human race may be perpetuated. This is why Cain was punished for killing Abel, the generation of the flood was destroyed for violence, and Pharaoh and Abimelech were punished. This kind of acts makes the transgressor liable to punishment but does not confer any perfection upon the soul of the observer, for if a man were to live alone in a desert without participating in social and political life, he would not need this kind of perfection.

The second kind of acts is also natural to man and gives perfection to his soul. Examples are: submission to God, and doing those things in general which the human reason declares are acceptable to God. These things are known to man by nature, as the prophet says, reproving Israel for ignoring the ways and judgments of God: "Surely these are poor, they are foolish, for they know not the way of the Lord, nor the ordinance of their God." In another place he says, "Yea, the stork in the heaven knoweth her appointed times; and the turtle and the swallow and the crane observe the time of their coming; but My people know not the ordinance of the Lord." These observations do not refer to the ways and ordinances of the Torah, for these are not known to man by nature as the stork knows her appointed times, or as the turtle and the swallow and the crane observe the time of their coming. They refer to the knowledge of God which is known by nature to all, such as the fact that He supports the world and mercifully supplies food to all creatures and maintains them continually, and that He should be thanked because all things come from Him. This is the meaning of the expression, "way of the Lord." "The ordinance of their God," denotes the knowledge of the relation of the Creator to His creatures - the duty of constant submission to Him, as a slave submits to his master, and to refrain from showing disrespect to Him by equal treatment of the honorable with the inferior - all of them things which the nature of human reason dictates without any study or teaching.

Sefer Halkkarim BOOK [Maamar] THRE

The reason God did not have respect unto Cain and his offering, was because his service was not done with the proper intention, as the nature of the reason demands. Reason dictates that we should be thankful to a benefactor in accordance with the benefits we receive from him, and that one should not bring to the master a cheap present of an inferior quality if one can bring one of good quality, for this signifies an offence to the honor of the master. Therefore, Cain should not have brought of the fruits of the earth, like flax seed, beans, vegetables, and so on, but he should have brought of the fruit of the tree, like figs and grapes and pomegranates, which belong to a better species. Not doing so, he sinned, and deserved punishment, though he had not received any command concerning the matter.

But although the general principles of these two kinds of acts are known by the human mind, nevertheless, inasmuch as the human reason is not adequate to give a knowledge of particulars and of all the things which are agreeable to God, there must be a divine inspiration by which one may acquire true and complete knowledge and belief concerning the particular acts acceptable to God, by which the human purpose may be realized. It can not be that divine providence should fail in a matter of this sort which is almost indispensable for man for the attainment of human perfection, as we find that Providence has not failed to supply the lower animals with many things which are not indispensable for their existence, as for example the double sense organs, and other instances of provisions found in different animal species to improve their condition, which are not absolutely necessary, as we explained in the sixth chapter of the First Book.

Chapter 8

The divine inspiration which we said was necessary in order that we may know through it what things are acceptable to God and what things are not, man can not acquire by himself without divine consent. For it is not natural that the spirit of an intellect devoid of matter should rest upon a material thing. For this reason, all the ancients thought it impossible that the divine spirit should rest upon man, and that the latter should prophesy by means of a supernatural power and foretell the future. And therefore, the ancient peoples used to make images and burn incense and offer prayers to the stars to bring down the spiritual influence of some star upon one of their images, in order that through it the spirit of the star residing in the body of the star should rest upon man, who is a corporeal being, so that the latter might foretell the future through the spirit of the star exerting an influence upon the person. This is the meaning of divination.

And inasmuch as men are eager to know all the things that are going to happen to them from day to day, the ancients used to follow the diviners and pursued the study of astrology. Some nations practised magic and served evil spirits, depending upon their intellectual status. Some served the demons of fire and caused their sons and daughters to pass through the fire, others served the demons of the air. [Rabbi Hai writes in a responsum that there are demons composed of the element fire, and demons of the element air.] They did all these things in order that an unclean spirit of the demons should rest upon them and enable them to foretell their future. Others again smoked and burned incense, so as to have communion with the dead, and slept in cemeteries, in order than an unclean spirit of the dead should rest upon them. They went so far as to bury their dead in their idolatrous temples, where men and women gathered together and prayed over the graves. As a result, the unclean spirit of the dead rested upon them or upon their priests, and told them what was about to happen to them. Nahmanides, in one of his discourses, on the authority of those who are familiar with sorcery, describes the process as follows: a man and a woman stand by the grave, one at the head and the other at the foot, holding a little bell between them, pronouncing formulas of adjuration and sounding the bell. The woman watches, and the man inquires, and information is given to them of what will happen to them in the near future, as Saul inquired of the woman who had a familiar spirit. He says, too, that those who inquired of the demons relied much upon this method of inquiry. He says also that this is the origin of the Christian custom of burying their dead in their churches, where the men and women pray together and sound a bell while burying their dead, remarking that when the pagans adopted Christianity, they retained their ancestral customs. They also retained a custom of the fire worshippers, which consists in lighting fires on a given night in every year when the sun enters the sign of Cancer of the true zodiacal signs, and dancing and skipping around the fire.

All these practices are forbidden in the Torah because they are unclean and done in the service of evil spirits: "There shall not be found among you any one that maketh his son or his daughter to pass through the fire, one that useth divination, a soothsayer, or an inchanter, or a sorcerer, or a charmer, or one that consulteth a ghost or a familiar spirit, or a necromancer." And the reason given is, "For

Sefer Halkkarim   BOOK [Maamar] THRE

whosoever doeth these things is an abomination unto the Lord ..." The meaning is that God is holy and His ministers are holy and pure, therefore you must keep away from all these things which are impure. This is the reason, also, why the Torah legislates concerning uncleanness, and provides the penalty of being 'cut off' for one who enters the temple while unclean. The reason is that the spirit of uncleanness may cause the holy spirit to depart from the temple.

Then the Torah makes it clear that the other nations indulged in those practices in order to obtain a knowledge of the future, thinking that it can not be obtained in any other way, and that the holy spirit of God never rests upon a human being: "For these nations, that thou art to dispossess, hearken unto soothsayers, and unto diviners ...," because they think that there is no one else that one can hearken to, "But as for thee, the Lord thy God hath not suffered thee so to do;" i.e., it is not as they think, but, "A prophet will the Lord thy God raise up unto thee, from the midst of thee, of thy brethren, like unto me." one upon whom the holy spirit of God will rest, and from him you will learn the future. You must not grieve in thinking that you have no way of knowing the future, as the other nations have, and that you are without this privilege. It is not so, for you will be complete and perfect with the Lord your God. The meaning is that you will not merely have the ordinary human privileges, but also this one. This is the reason for doubling the letter mem [tamim], as if to say, you will want for nothing in association with Him, for He will reveal to you the future also through His prophets, and you need not follow the diviners or the service of evil spirits or inquire of ghosts and familiar spirits in order to obtain knowledge of the future. For though these agencies do impart knowledge of the future, nevertheless as they are connected with the spirit of uncleanness, they keep man away from his perfection, and man cannot on their account have human perfection and soundness, because it is impossible to know from them what things are acceptable to God and what things are not. This is the meaning of the expression, "Thou shalt be perfect with the Lord thy God," indicating that the idolatrous nations are not possessed of human perfection, but thou shalt be perfect with the Lord thy God, having both perfections through the prophet who prophesies by the holy spirit and by the will of God, for through him you will know what things are acceptable to God. The expression, "with the Lord thy God," denotes that the prophetic spirit is given to the prophets for the sole purpose of admonishing mankind to observe the Torah, to worship God and to do the things which are acceptable to Him in order that

Sefer Halkkarim   BOOK [Maamar] THRE

man may be whole-hearted with God, and not for the purpose of foretelling the future, as will be explained in the twelfth chapter of this Book.

The prophets had indeed also this power of foretelling the future as a secondary consideration, as a testimony to the truth of their prophetic teaching, in order that men may believe them. Accordingly, we find that all the prophets admonish us constantly to observe the Torah and carry out the commandments. The main purpose of God in inspiring the prophets was that through them man may attain to his perfection by doing those things which are acceptable to God and not in order to give mankind a knowledge of the future, as is the case with the diviners. These foretell the future by certain practices which strengthen the power of imagination in a natural way, and not through the spirit of God, as the prophets do; unless, indeed, we say that prophecy is also a function of the imagination, as is the opinion of some of our wise men who follow the Philosopher. They hold that prophecy is a natural phenomenon, pertaining solely to the power of imagination, like dreams. They go so far as to say that it is an unusual thing if a man does not prophesy being wise and prepared thereto, i.e., if his imagination is prepared for prophecy.

This is, however, contradicted both by our senses and our reason. The argument from the senses is that we never find the gift of prophecy in any one of the philosophers, though they were wise men in theoretical speculation; whereas we do find prophecy among the Jewish people. This shows that it is not a natural phenomenon associated with theoretical speculation. For if it were so, why should this gift have been kept from the other nations, so that their wise men despite their perfection of intellect and imagination are devoid of the prophetic inspiration? There is no doubt, therefore, that prophecy is a divine inspiration which comes by the will of God upon the rational power, either through the medium of the imagination or without it, as will be explained.

The argument from reason is that the diviners, the image worshippers, those who consult ghosts and familiar spirits, and those who indulge in other practices in order to strengthen the power of imagination so as to know the future, can not determine the things which are acceptable to God, because they have no means of knowing this, seeing that it is above nature and the spirit of uncleanness and the powers of the spheres, from which they obtain all their information. And for this reason, they are not always correct in their prognostications. And this for two reasons, first, because the power of imagination is necessarily deceptive from its nature, for not everything that is imaginable is possible, as is known to those who are familiar with the nature of that faculty. And secondly, because God can destroy the power of the constellations and bring about the opposite of that which they determine. Therefore, astrologers are necessarily liable to deception, as the Bible says: "Let now the astrologers, the star-gazers, the monthly prognosticators, stand up and save thee from the things that shall come upon thee." The Rabbis comment upon the expression "from the things," as meaning that they can save from some of the things, but not from all the things. They can not foretell truly all that has been determined for they are necessarily liable to error for the two reasons mentioned, either by reason of the nature of the imaginative faculty, or because God can nullify by His will that which is determined by the stars.

The prophet is the opposite of all this. His inspiration comes from God and is due to the will of God, and not to the powers of the spheres. Moreover, it descends primarily and essentially upon the rational power. Hence there can not be any error in it. The Bible testifies to this effect concerning Samuel, "And did let none of his words fall to the ground. And all Israel from Dan even to Beer-Sheba knew that Samuel was established to be a prophet of the Lord." The meaning is that the true character of his prophecy was known from the fact that none of his words fell to the ground, unlike the diviners and magicians. So Balaam says to Balak, "For there is no enchantment with Yaakov, neither is there any divination with Israel; Now is it said of Yaakov and of Israel: 'what hath God wrought!' " The meaning is, do not think that the good which is promised to Israel can be nullified in any way, as those things are nullified which are determined by the stars. No, it can not be, for they know what is determined, not by means of divination and enchantment, but through prophecy do they know "what God hath wrought," i.e., what God has decreed that He would do. Therefore it can not be nullified in any way. For God has power to destroy the constellation and the work of the diviners and the magicians as well as the results of their science, for He is "God who brought them forth out of Egypt, though they have lofty horns like those of the wild-ox." The word lo [lit. to him] refers to the people of Egypt, though it is in the singular, as in the expression, "Egypt said, 'let me flee from the face of Israel;' " "Shall Egypt be like women." The meaning is that though the people of Egypt had knowledge through diviners and magic, and great strength like the horns of the wild-ox through the constellations, nevertheless God took Israel out of their power and punished their gods.

From all this it is clear that it is impossible to know all the things that are acceptable to God in any way except through the will of God, i.e., through the medium of a special inspiration coming from Him for this purpose. Accordingly, the definition of prophecy from this point of view is that it is an inspiration coming from God to the rational power in man, either through the medium of the power of imagination or without it, by virtue of which information comes to him through an angel or otherwise concerning matters which a man cannot know naturally by himself. The purpose is to lead him or others to happiness, so that mankind may attain the human purpose. In defining prophecy as coming through the medium of the imagination or without it, our purpose is to embrace all degrees of prophecy. For there are prophets to whom, in the beginning of their career, prophecy comes through the medium of the power of the imagination. For this reason, they see extraordinary images in their prophetic visions by reason of their inferior status as prophets. Thus, some see forms of women, as Zechariah said, "And, behold, there came forth two women, and the wind was in their wings; for they had wings like the wings of a stork ..." Others see angels with great and fearful bodies, as Daniel said, "His body also was like the beryl, and his face as the appearance of lightning, and his eyes as torches of fire ..." And there are other instances of images named by the prophets when the inspiration of the rational power came through the medium of the imagination.

Some prophets remain in that stage, while others ascend to a higher stage, some reaching so high that their prophecy comes to them without a medium. That is, the inspiration of the rational power is not associated with the activity of the imagination at all. This was the status of Moshe at all times after the first revelation, when an angel of God appeared to him in a flame of fire out of the midst of the burning bush. Thereafter the Bible says, "With him do I speak mouth to mouth," i.e., without a medium. For this reason we do not find any figures of speech or allegories in his words, but his words are all plain. This was also the status of all Israel when the Torah was given, as the Bible says, "The Lord spoke with you face to face in the mount out of the midst of the fire." God desired to give through Moshe a law that should be free from all doubt, and hence He desired that Moshe' power should be of so high a character that the power of the imagination should have no part in it, so as to avoid suspicion and doubt. And for the same reason Israel who received the law also attained to the grade of being spoken to by God face to face at the time of the Sinaitic revelation.

Chapter 9

A question may arise as follows: Since the prophetic inspiration comes from God, who is One, and the purpose of the prophetic message is always the same, namely to lead mankind to happiness, how is it that the prophets differ in their expressions when they treat of the same topics, and why are their visions different, one prophet seeing God under one form, another under another?

The answer is that the differences of vision and expression do not prove difference in origin, nor do they necessarily indicate a change in the nature of the author of the prophetic inspiration or in the purpose. Different effects may come from the same agent, depending upon the nature of the recipients. Thus fire, being one and the same thing, causes wax to melt and salt to harden. Similarly, though the soul, according to the consensus of philosophers, is one in essence and indivisible, nevertheless it is the cause of different activities in the body, depending upon the different parts of the body in which its activity is visible. In the brain the soul exhibits one kind of activity, in the liver another kind, in the heart still another, though all the activities are for one purpose, namely to conserve the body. In the flesh again the soul has sensation, in the bones she has no sensation, and in different members the soul shows different powers. This shows that the same agent may exhibit his power in different ways in different places, causing different activities for one and the same purpose. The difference is due either to the media through which he shows his power or to the localities in which his power appears.

In the same way prophetic visions are different either by reason of the means through which the prophetic revelation comes or by reason of the recipients. This is clearly implied in the statement which God made to Aaron and Miriam, who were prophets, "If there be a prophet among you, I the Lord do make Myself known unto him in a vision, I do speak with him in a dream. My servant Moshe is not so; he is trusted in all My house; with him do I speak mouth to mouth, even manifestly, and not in dark speeches …" Here we are clearly told that it is God Himself who appears in a vision and who speaks in a dream, as is indicated in the expressions, "make Myself known," "speak." And it is also He who speaks in dark speeches and parables, but who speaks to Moshe "mouth to mouth,

Sefer HaIkkarim   BOOK [Maamar] THRE

even manifestly, and not in dark speeches." The purpose of this verse is to show that prophetic inspiration of whatever degree emanates from God, as we said when we gave a definition of prophecy, and yet it changes according to the preparation of those who receive it, and according to the means by which the inspiration comes to them. Therefore, we should not be surprised if one prophet says that he saw God "sitting upon a throne, high and lifted up," while another says that he saw Him as an old man, whose "raiment was as white snow, and the hair of his head like pure wool," and still another saw him like "a man of war," while a fourth likens him to a precentor wrapped up in his praying garment. Similarly, as regards the media, i.e., the angels, who are sent to the prophets, one prophet says that he saw the angel whose "body was like the beryl, and his face as the appearance of lightning," another saw him like "a man clothed in linen," while a third saw in a chariot "red, sorrel and white" horse. These differences are due to the two causes which we mentioned, the recipient and the medium.

The Rabbis explain this subject in Bereshit Rabbah: "A Cuthean asked Rabbi Meir, is it possible that God, of whom it is written, 'Do not I fill heaven and earth?' should have spoken to Moshe from between the staves of the ark? Said Rabbi Meir, bring me large mirrors. When he brought them, Rabbi Meir said to him, look at your reflection. He looked, and he saw they were large. Then he said, bring me small mirrors. When he brought them, Rabbi Meir said, look at your reflection. He looked, and he saw they were small. Then Rabbi Meir said, if you, a man of flesh and blood, can change yourself into many shapes at your pleasure, surely God who created the world can do so."

The purpose of the Cuthean was to deny that prophetic inspiration emanates from God. He thought that it was the work of the power of imagination, as the philosophers hold and those who follow after them. Their reasons are twofold. First, God being one cannot appear to the prophet under many different forms, for this would argue multiplicity or change in the agent. The second reason is that an abstract intellect can not appear to a material being.

These arguments Rabbi Meir refuted by means of the mirrors. The first argument is answered as follows: As in the mirrors a thing appears different in form, large or small, straight or crooked, bright or obscure, according to the nature of the mirrors through which the thing is seen, i.e., according as the mirrors are large or small, straight or crooked, clear or obscure, though the thing itself does not change, so God appears to the prophets under many and various forms

Sefer HaIkkarim — BOOK [Maamar] THREE

according to the brightness and purity of the media, though God Himself does not multiply or change. The change and the multiplicity come from the media, as in the illustration of the mirrors. A thing seen also varies according to the difference in the person who sees. Thus, if the person who sees a thing through a mirror has sharp and clear vision, he will see the thing in one form, whereas if his vision is weak or dimmed, he will see the thing in another form, though the thing seen and the mirror are the very same which appeared to the man of clear vision.

The second argument is answered as follows: As the person or the thing seen through a mirror is different from the mirror through which he or it is seen, nor does his existence depend upon that of the mirror; and yet the likeness of the person appears in the mirror, though there is no likeness in the mirror in reality, it only appears so to the eye, so though God is separate and abstract and can not be comprehended, He nevertheless appears to the prophet in a given form, which the prophet sees speaking to him, though in reality there is no such form in existence, the voice alone which the prophet hears being the real purpose of the vision, and nothing else.

And if the question is asked, how is it possible that one should see what does not exist and yet acquire truth by means of it? The answer is, when a person sees in a true dream a man speaking to him, the things are not real, though the dreamer imagines that they are, and he hears a voice speaking to him, which does not really exist, and yet the information which the person gets through that dream is correct. In the same way, from the analogy of the dream or the mirror, in which a person sees the form or hears a sound of words, the prophet understands the meaning of the prophetic inspiration which comes to him. As in the mirror in which one sees his likeness, there really is no such likeness as he sees, so the prophet understands that there is no such form in reality as he sees, though he sees it, and that the purpose of the form which appears to him is that he should hear the voice or get the meaning of the vision, in which the truth resides. In the mirror, too, the likeness seen in it does not really exist, but the significance of the visible likeness is real and points to the thing seen through the likeness, which is real. So in the prophetic vision the idea signified in the vision is true, though the form itself which appears is not real. It may be that the expression, "I make myself known to him in a vision [מראה]," is an allusion to the nature of the mirror [מראה], as we have explained.

And similarly, the expression, "I speak with him in a dream," has reference to our previous explanation. There is a great difference,

Sefer HaIkkarim   BOOK [Maamar] THRE

indeed, between a dream and a prophetic vision. There is no dream without foolish elements, whereas a prophetic vision is entirely correct and true. Nevertheless, since we can not imagine a voice speaking without corporeal organs except by thinking of a dream, the Bible uses the expression, "I speak with him in a dream," to indicate that as in a dream one hears a voice speaking and sees a person speaking, though in reality no such things exist, so in a prophetic vision, the truth in it is the information which the prophet obtains. This is God's purpose in sending the vision, but the voice that is heard expressing itself by means of corporeal organs is not really there. This is what the Rabbis meant when they said, "A dream is one sixtieth part of prophecy."

The illustration which Rabbi Meir employed of the mirrors has shown, therefore, that the variety and multiplicity of likenesses which appear to prophets are no indication of multiplicity and change in God, as the multiplicity and change of the mirrors or the multiplicity and change of the spectators imply no change or multiplicity in the thing seen in the mirror. It follows also from this that the variety of expression of the different prophets does not indicate change in God or in His purpose. For though the speakers use different expressions, the idea is the same necessarily since it comes from one author, and hence the purpose is the same. This is the meaning of the Rabbis when they say, "Many prophets have one idea, though no two prophets use the same expression." This is what we intended to make clear in this chapter.

Chapter 10

We must now explain the existence of prophecy and its various grades, so that believers may find it easier to understand the existence of prophecy and the different degrees thereof. At the moment of birth, the individual is devoid of all understanding. The first things that are formed in him are the five external senses, touch, taste, smell, hearing, sight. The individual does not get these all at once, but one at a time. At the moment of his appearance in the outer world he perceives only with the coarsest of the senses, that of touch. The objects of his perception at this stage are heat and cold, moisture and dryness, softness and hardness, roughness and smoothness and the like. After a further interval of time after birth, he perceives a finer and more 'important class of objects, namely tastes, like sweet, bitter, sour, astringent, sharp, and so on. Later on, he perceives another class of things still finer, namely the odors, the agreeable and the disagreeable, etc. Later still he perceives with the sense of hearing a class of objects that is still finer than those of the sense of smell, and that may be perceived at a greater distance, such as sounds and tones, and their various kinds, etc. Still later he perceives with the sense of sight another class of existents finer than all the rest, which can be perceived at a greater distance than the others, such as colors and forms according to their various kinds, and so on. One of these five senses can not perceive the objects of the others. Thus, the sense of sight can not perceive sounds, or tones or odors; nor can the senses of smell and taste perceive colors and sounds.

After he has advanced a considerable time and has become habituated to the five senses, he rises to a higher degree than that of perceiving the objects of the various senses. He now has the power of recognizing a thing when it is no longer actually perceived. He recognizes what he has once perceived when he sees it again, and though the thing has disappeared he remembers the knowledge which is impressed on his imagination and recognizes the object. This power of apprehension he acquires through the medium of the first faculty.

As he grows older still, he attains to a higher degree by means of the first powers, a new gate opens before him, and he acquires the power of intellectual apprehension. He strips the sensible object of its particular qualities and apprehends the general essence. For example, he takes animality and rationality in a human being and judges that these are common to the whole species and are different from those particular qualities which differ in different individuals.

As he advances further in years and acquires information, another gate opens before him which he has not entered hitherto. He now makes a distinction between substance and accident, and between the necessary, the possible and the impossible. He combines rational principles not based upon sense perception with each other, and acquires all the sciences, which he could not have acquired by means of the powers mentioned before. These four stages form the limit of the human intellect, beyond which it can not go. Some individuals do not reach the highest stage, but stop with the second or the third. These then are the powers which the generality of men have.

But it is possible that in addition to these powers, still another gate may open to a person and still another degree may be attainable by him of which he has no idea. For just as, if a person who has never seen them were told about lights and colors, he would not be able to imagine them and would not understand the different colors, as a eunuch can not imagine the pleasure of sexual intercourse, so it is

Sefer HaIkkarim   BOOK [Maamar] THRE

possible that though by the custom of nature man does not attain a greater degree than the four mentioned, nevertheless the mind may conceive of a higher degree. And experience testifies to this. For we see that beyond the four degrees above mentioned, a new gate opens before a given person which his own nature never imagined, and he speaks words of wisdom or words of song and praise to God in pure and fluent style such as he was incapable of hitherto. Everyone who hears him wonders at his knowledge and the manner of his expression, while he himself does not know whence this power came to him, as a child learns to speak without knowing whence the power came. But everybody recognizes his superiority in this respect. This degree is called the holy spirit.

Now just as the human intellect stops at the four degrees above mentioned and does not pass beyond, so there are persons who stop at the degree of the holy spirit and do not pass beyond it. There are persons whose imagination is strong by nature or who do certain things to strengthen it, like the practices of the diviners or the woman with the familiar spirit. As a result of this they have imaginative visions. There are others who have true dreams, like Pharaoh, Nebuchadnezzar, the chief butler and the chief baker. By reason of these powers some of them think they are prophets. They are the persons of whom the prophet in Scripture says that they "prophesy out of their own heart." For though they sometimes speak the truth, they are bound sometimes to speak falsehood. Thus, Ezekiel says, "Woe unto the vile prophets, that follow their own spirit, … They have seen vanity and lying divination, that say: The Lord saith; and the Lord hath not sent them, yet they hope that the word would be confirmed." The intimation is that it is impossible, for though their words may be partly true, they can not but be partly false, for such is the nature of the power of imagination, the source of dreams. Our Rabbis say: As there is no wheat without straw, so there is no dream without foolishness.

When, however, the rational power prevails over the imagination, then the person sees true dreams without foolishness. The explanation is given by the Rabbis: "Raba asked the question, How reconcile the statement, 'And the dreams speak falsely,' with the expression, 'I do speak with him in a dream?' His answer is, the two passages are not incompatible. The one passage refers to dreams that come through the medium of an angel, the other to those that come through the medium of a demon." Angel stands for the rational power, demon for the power of imagination. If the rational power prevails over the power of imagination, the person sees true dreams or visions which communicate to him information he never had before. In the measure in which the rational power prevails over the imagination is the person better or less well prepared for prophetic inspiration.

There are persons whose rational power is stronger than the imagination, but the superiority is not great, and hence the power of imagination maintains its strength. And therefore though the rational power is prepared to receive the prophetic inspiration, yet on account of the strength of the imagination and its opposition to the rational power, the person receives the inspiration in trembling and pain. His limbs shake, his sinews tend to dissolve, and a great trembling comes over him, that his soul almost leaves him. And after all that pain the prophetic inspiration comes to the rational power in a dream or vision of the night, and the person dreams prophetic dreams and learns things he has never known before - ideas about the separate substances, or particular notions, or universal ideas of existence, and the like. This is the first degree of prophetic inspiration.

There are others who do not stop here. They enter still another gate that opens before them and attain to a higher degree, which sometimes comes before the first degree and sometimes after. When the two powers are equally strong, the person receives the prophetic inspiration without trembling and without toil, while sleeping on his couch, or in a deep sleep which comes upon him during the day. This degree is called vision [מחזה, מראה]. In this stage he sees, by means of the power of imagination, forms which are not real, like the women and the horses seen by Zechariah, or the basket of summer fruit seen by Amos, and the like, which did not really exist. But by reason of the fact that the rational power is stronger than the imagination, it makes the ideas indicated by the forms true, though the forms are not real. This is the second degree of prophetic inspiration.

There are others who do not stop at this degree, but enter another door that opens before them and attain a still higher degree. This happens when the rational power prevails so completely over the imagination that it subdues it and does not allow it to imagine unreal forms. The visions that such a person sees in the prophetic state are real, like the visions of Ezekiel, which were all real, representing mysteries of nature and of the divine being as represented in the mysteries of the chariot. He may also see or hear an angel speaking to him and communicating to him some particular matter for his own benefit or for the benefit of others, or he communicates to him

Sefer Halkkarim   BOOK [Maamar] THRE

something of a universal nature, and gives him information concerning human events that are to come in the future, particular events that are to happen to an individual, or something general that is to happen to a nation or nations or to humanity as a whole. This is the third degree of prophecy. This degree sometimes comes after the earlier ones, and sometimes it comes first, depending upon the equipment of the recipient. Samuel is a good example. At the beginning of his prophetic career, he heard a voice speaking to him, and was free from trembling or toil, nor did he see any form. However, this did not take place while he was absolutely awake, but during a waking vision. A vision or appearance which one has while awake is called, "hand of the Lord," as Maimonides explains in the forty-first chapter of the second part of the Guide of the Perplexed. Thus we are told, "And the lamp of God was not yet gone out, and Samuel was laid down to sleep in the temple of the Lord, where the ark of God was." The verse should be construed as follows: "The lamp of God was not yet gone out in the temple of the Lord, and Samuel was laid down to sleep," i.e., in his upper chamber in the court. And "the Lord called Samuel", i.e., in a vision. This is as far as all prophets attain. In every case, even if the individual has the preparation, he does not get the prophetic inspiration except by the grace of God. And it happens sometimes that after having had a prophetic experience, a prophet ceases from prophesying for a long time. And sometimes he must undertake a certain preparatory practice to receive a prophetic inspiration, as in the case of Elisha, who said, "But now bring me a minstrel. And it came to pass, when the minstrel played, that the hand of the Lord came upon him."

There are others still who do not stop at these degrees, but rise to a higher degree where the power of imagination has no say at all. The person does not see or imagine any form, he does not see any angel or likeness before him, but hears a voice speaking to him and communicating to him general ideas for the benefit of a nation or nations, or a rule or rules of conduct for the human race or for a part of it, such as lead to human perfection. This inspiration comes to him without any apparition or vision, but in the daytime while he is awake. And whenever he concentrates his thoughts in reflection and considers a question, the answer comes at once while he is awake; and this happens not at great intervals, but whenever he desires. An individual who attains such a degree as this should no longer be called a human being, but an angel. There is no one among us who has reached this stage except Moshe our teacher, peace be upon him, whose prophecy is distinguished from that of all the other prophets in four respects, as enumerated by Maimonides in his commentary on chapter "Helek."

These four points of difference are the four degrees of prophecy which we named, and which are referred to in the Bible, "And the Lord spoke to Moshe face to face as a man speaks to his neighbour." "Face to face," means that the inspiration did not come through an angel or intermediary, as is the case in the third degree. "As a man speaks," indicates that the message did not come in visions of the night or in a deep sleep that fell upon him, as in the second degree, but Moshe was awake and heard the voice speaking to him, without feeling any trembling or pain, as is the case in the first degree, but "as a man speaks to his neighbour," i.e., without any pain. Whenever he desired to go into the tent of meeting, he heard the voice speaking to him, as we are told, "And when Moshe went into the tent of meeting ... then he heard the voice speaking unto him from above the ark-cover ... from between the two cherubim." We also have the testimony of Scripture in the passage, "Stay ye, that I may hear what the Lord will command concerning you." And immediately the answer came to him: "If any man of you ... shall be unclean by reason of a dead body ..." Similarly in the case of the daughters of Zelophehad we read, "And Moshe brought their cause before the Lord." And then came the answer, "The daughters of Zelophehad speak right."

No person can attain to any degree of prophetic inspiration at all unless he has the first four natural qualities which we mentioned. Our Rabbis say, "The prophetic spirit does not rest upon a person unless he is wise, strong, rich and tall." Unless he has the quality of wisdom and the other natural qualities, the prophetic inspiration can not come to him at all. This is why they say that Yaakov's ladder had four steps. The meaning is that Yaakov's prophetic experience was not preceded by the degree of the "holy spirit," which sometimes comes before prophecy, but that the preparatory quality in Yaakov was wisdom, which he learned in the school of Eber," where he concealed himself for fourteen years. Without wisdom the prophetic inspiration would not have come to him even in a dream, which is the first degree of prophecy.

The prophets and the righteous and the pious differed from each other in the degree of their association with God. There are some whose souls cleaved so intimately to the celestial beings that the powers of heaven were obedient to them and exerted their influence on the matters of this world at their bidding, for their own benefit or for the benefit of others. They could cause rain to come down by

Sefer HaIkkarim — BOOK [Maamar] THREE

their prayer, heal the sick, cause barren women to bear children, cause fire to come down from heaven, revive the dead, as in the case of Eliyahu and Elisha. We find that when a person thinks about a palatable article of food or sees another eating sour grapes, the salivary power is aroused and his mouth waters of its own accord; and similarly, when he is thinking about sexual intercourse, the seminal power is aroused and the organ stretches. In the same way the natural powers of the physical universe are obedient to the pure soul of the prophet, and dew or rain or a storm comes at his bidding. For just as the powers of the body were created to serve the powers of the soul, and therefore as soon as the psychic power determines upon anything, the corporeal powers and the limbs are impelled to carry it out, so the physical forces in the world of nature are subservient to the pure souls - the whole universe being as one individual - and obey them. Accordingly, when such a pure soul conceives the coming of dew or rain or a great and mighty wind, or an earthquake or the opening of the earth, and the like, immediately the power which controls the world of genesis and decay is impelled to carry out the conception.

Sometimes the degree of the prophet or pious man goes beyond this measure, so that the celestial powers too are obedient to him and do his will, bringing down fire from heaven, reviving the dead, and the like, since all things are subject and subservient to him, whether he be a prophet or not. This power varies among righteous men, pious men and prophets according to the degree in which their souls cleave to the higher beings. In this way the prophet or the pious man rules over nature and produces signs and wonders in the world according to the measure of his communion with the higher beings.

This explains the differences among pious men. There are some who reach such a degree of communion that they can produce signs and wonders in nature, like Honi ha-Me'aggel, Rabbi Phinehas ben Yair, Rabbi Hanina ben Dosa, and others, though they did not attain to the degree of prophecy. On the other hand, there are prophets who never performed any sign or miracle, like Jeremiah, Haggai, Zechariah and Malachi. Others have only one sign to their credit, like Samuel, who caused rain to come down in the season of wheat harvest by praying for it. Others again have two or three miracles recorded of them, like Isaiah, who brought about the destruction of Sennacherib, the cure of Hezekiah and the going back of the shadow a number of degrees. Some have still more miracles to their credit, like Eliyahu and Elisha.

All these miracles, however, performed by the prophets, have this in common that they did not last a long time, and were not performed in the presence of all or of a great concourse of people; whereas all the signs and wonders performed by Moshe were not merely more numerous than all those of all the other prophets, but they were superior to them in that they were performed in public and lasted a long time, for example, the manna lasted forty years, also the pillar of cloud by day and the pillar of fire by night.

For this reason, these differences between the miracles of Moshe and those of the others are mentioned at the end of the Torah. First the text refers to the differences between the prophetic inspiration of Moshe and that of the others in the expression, "And there hath not arisen a prophet since in Israel like unto Moshe, whom the Lord knew face to face," as we explained the passage above. Then the text proceeds to explain the differences between the miracles of Moshe and those of the others, "In all the signs and the wonders which the Lord sent him to do." This indicates their great number. Then it says, "In the land of Egypt, to Pharaoh, and to all his servants, and to all his land," alluding to the publicity of the miracles in the presence of his opponents. Then, referring to their duration, Scripture says, "And in all the great terror, which Moshe wrought in the light of all Israel." This refers, as we said, to the pillar of cloud by day and the pillar of fire by night, which lasted all the forty years that the Israelites were in the wilderness, as we read, "For the cloud of the Lord was upon the Tabernacle by day, and there was fire therein by night, in the sight of all the house of Israel, throughout all their journeys." This is the way to understand the conception of prophecy and its various degrees as shown logically and in the difference between the prophecy and miracles of Moshe and those of the other prophets. This is what we intended to show.

Chapter 11

What we said above concerning the manner in which the various degrees of prophetic inspiration come upon a person holds good when there is no prophet who may serve as a medium or instrument through whom inspiration may come to those who are not prepared. But when there is such a prophet, inspiration may come to those unprepared without reference to the degrees mentioned. This possibility was realized, at the time of the revelation on Sinai, when all Israel, the foolish as well as the wise, attained to the prophetic quality: "These words the Lord spoke unto all your assembly in the mount out of the midst of the fire." And not merely did they attain to prophetic inspiration, but they reached the degree called "face to face", which is the highest that any one can attain and which requires the grace of God, viz. the degree attained by Moshe. For we read concerning Moshe, "And the Lord spoke to Moshe face to face," and similarly in reference to the degree reached by all Israel at the time of the Sinaitic revelation, we read likewise, "The Lord spoke with you face to face in the mount out of the midst of the fire."

Now it is clear that the six hundred thousand men who came out of Egypt on foot and had been accustomed to hard work in clay and in bricks were not worthy of so high a degree, and yet they attained it through the instrumentality of Moshe. God said to him, "Go, I come unto thee in a thick cloud, that the people may hear when I speak with thee." The meaning of this verse is, I wish to come to you and to reveal Myself to you in the highest degree, face to face, though you are clothed in the thickness and obscurity of matter, symbolized by "thick cloud," and are not worthy of it, - all this I do in order that the people may hear when I speak with you. This is the highest degree possible, namely that a person in the waking state should hear a voice speaking to him, without seeing any form, "Ye heard the voice of words, but ye saw no form."

This degree the people attained through the grace of God and the instrumentality of Moshe, in order that they might give up the doubt which they entertained concerning the possibility of a human being receiving prophetic inspiration. They expressed their wonder after the revelation, saying, "For who is there of all flesh, that hath heard the voice of the living God …" This shows that the Israelites doubted the possibility of prophetic inspiration until that day. But Moshe did not wonder at the prophetic inspiration of an individual, but at the attainment thereto by the whole people. Hence, he said, "Did ever a people hear the voice of God …" After the revelation they all acknowledged the possibility, as we read, "We have seen this day that God doth speak with man, and he liveth." This proves that the experience at that time removed the doubt from their mind. In the same way the prophetic power was communicated by Eliyahu to Elisha without the preparatory degrees. For there was not a single one of the sons of the prophets who did not serve Eliyahu and learn from him before Elisha came to serve Eliyahu, for only when God wanted to take Eliyahu away did he say to him in Horeb, "And Elisha the son of Shaphat of Abel-Meholah shalt thou anoint to be prophet in thy room." Through the instrumentality of Eliyahu he attained to a higher degree than any of them.

Sefer HaIkkarim BOOK [Maamar] THREE

Also, Yehoshua owed the degree which he attained to the instrumentality of Moshe. And hence the Rabbis in discussing this matter say, "The face of Moshe was like that of the sun, the face of Yehoshua was like that of the moon. The elders of that generation used to say, 'Oh, the shame and disgrace!' " The meaning is, Yehoshua himself was not worthy to attain the degree which he did. It was due to the instrumentality of Moshe. Therefore, Moshe was like the sun, who gives of his light to the moon, while Yehoshua was like the moon, which receives her light from the sun, having none of her own. Hence, they said, "Oh, the shame and disgrace" that Yehoshua himself should not have been worthy of prophecy and should get it through Moshe only!

Similarly, the seventy elders owed their prophetic gift to the instrumentality of Moshe, not having been worthy of it in their own right: "And I will come down and speak with thee there; and I will take of the spirit which is upon thee, and will put it upon them." The meaning is, though they are not worthy of it on their own account. Hence when Yehoshua said to Moshe, "Eldad and Medad are prophesying in the camp," Moshe replied, "Art thou jealous for my sake?" He meant to say, you should not be jealous on my account, for the prophetic spirit comes upon them through my spirit and instrumentality, "Would that all the Lord's people were prophets" on their account, worthy in their own right without my influence, "that the Lord would put His spirit upon them," not through my instrumentality, but that they should themselves be worthy of the prophetic spirit without any intermediary.

The need of a medium may be explained as follows. When a spark of sunlight strikes a bright body, like a polished mirror, it is reflected upon a dark place, which is then illuminated by the reflection, not having been illuminated before. Similarly, when the divine influence descends upon a perfect prophet, it is reflected from him upon one who is not worthy, thus inspiring with the prophetic spirit one who is not perfect and not prepared, and causing him to prophesy. Still, even in case of reflection, the one who is prepared gets a greater portion than he who is not prepared.

My opinion is that this is the reason why prophecy existed among the people of Israel in the land of Palestine and not among other nations in other lands. The Shekinah rested upon the ark and the tables of stone, and from these it was reflected like a ray of sunlight, and the prophetic spirit then rested upon a person who had in him a certain preparation analogous to the contents of the ark, that is a person who really had the ideas of the Torah, which are written upon

Sefer HaIkkarim   BOOK [Maamar] THRE

the tables of the covenant. We find this illustrated in the prophecy of Samuel. He lay in his chamber and the prophetic voice came to him from above the ark-cover which was upon the ark that was then in Shilo. Samuel himself did not know who called him, for he did not think that he was worthy of the prophetic gift, that he should hear a voice in the waking state in a prophetic vision. Therefore, he rose from his bed and went to Eli, until Eli understood, as we read, "And Eli perceived that the Lord was calling the child."

An inspiration of this kind, which comes in this way without the mediation of a prophet, requires preparation in the recipient, that is the recipient must be himself prepared to a certain extent. Divine inspiration of this nature comes only when the recipient has a certain degree of preparation, and upon this is dependent the degree of inspiration which comes to him. The prophetic inspiration, however, which comes through the mediation of a prophet, comes also to a person who is not worthy of prophecy, as it came to all Israel at the time of the Sinaitic revelation; or it comes to one who is not prepared for it, as it came to Aaron and Miriam through the mediation of Moshe, though they were not prepared for it at that time. This is the reason why the Lord called Moshe with Aaron and Miriam, so that the prophetic spirit should come upon them through the mediation of Moshe. For though they were worthy of the prophetic gift, they were not prepared for it at that time. This matter requires attention, for many learned men have wondered why God called Moshe with Aaron and Miriam.

It is worth noting that when the prophetic spirit comes through the mediation of a prophet upon a person who is not worthy or who is not prepared, the recipient is able to pass it to another only when the nation has in its midst the ark and the tables. Moreover, after the ark disappeared, the unprepared could not get prophetic inspiration even through a prophet. This is why Baruch son of Neriyah did not receive the prophetic gift through Jeremiah, because he was not prepared for it, and the ark had been hidden. Prophetic inspiration did come to Haggai, Zechariah and Malachi, because they saw Jeremiah and Ezekiel and were more prepared for it than Baruch. But it did not reach others through them, because the ark was not there and the inspiration, they received was not sufficient to pass from them to others, since there was no ark. The proof of this is that there was no prophecy during the second temple, though there were at that time pious men and men of good works more worthy of prophetic inspiration than the men of the first temple. The reason was because they did not have the ark. Ezekiel could receive his inspiration outside of Palestine because he had already received it in Palestine, as our Rabbis explain the verse in Ezekiel, "The word of the Lord came expressly unto Ezekiel the priest, the son of Buzi, in the land of the Chaldeans by the river Chebar." They construe the verb [היה היה] as meaning: 'it came' because 'it had come' before.

Chapter 12

The principal purpose of the prophetic institution existing in the human race is not to foretell the future or to regulate particular matters that interest individuals, such as are communicated by diviners and star-gazers, but to enable a whole nation or the entire human race to attain to human perfection.

The Rabbis make this clear in the treatise Berakot: Commenting upon the biblical verse, "And the Lord spoke unto Moshe, Go, get thee down; for thy people ... have dealt corruptly", they say, God said to Moshe, get thee down from thy greatness. I gave it thee only for the sake of Israel. Now that Israel has sinned, why do I want thee? This clearly shows that the prophetic gift of Moshe was given to him solely for the sake of Israel, that they might receive the Torah and fulfil it. We find the same idea in **Torat Kohanim**. Commenting on the verse, "These are the commandments, which the Lord commanded Moshe for the children of Israel", they say it was the merit of Israel that was responsible for Moshe' receiving divine inspiration.

Hence some learned men say that the beginning of Moshe' prophetic experience did not take place in the gradual manner we described in chapter ten, but that it was a miraculous phenomenon and came upon him suddenly by the will of God, though he was neither prepared nor worthy of that high degree, the purpose being that the human race or the Jewish nation as a whole should attain to the destined end of man. This is why God said to him, now that Israel has sinned, why do I need you? That is if I can not realize My purpose, there is no need of the prophet's inspiration. This is the reason why when the Rabbis say, in the treatise Nedarim: "Prophecy rests only upon a person who is wise, strong, rich and tall," they derive these requisite qualities from Moshe. Since the prophetic gift is bestowed for the sake of the nation's perfection, the prophet must have the qualities of Moshe, whose prophetic gift was given to him for the same purpose. Therefore, one of these attributes is tall stature, so that he should be admired and respected by the people. But if a prophet has not these qualities which are for the people's benefit,

Sefer HaIkkarim — BOOK [Maamar] THRE

there is no purpose in giving him the prophetic gift. This will also explain why we made revelation of the Torah a fundamental principle, while we considered prophecy as a derivative principle dependent upon the former, though one might suppose that the reverse is true, namely that prophecy is the fundamental thing and revelation of the Torah the derivative.

The truth is this. If the purpose of the prophetic institution among men were that people may know the particular events of the world or that by means of it signs and wonders may be produced for a particular purpose, as might seem at first sight, then the objection would be well taken. But since we have made clear that the necessity of prophecy is that men may be guided toward eternal happiness, that they may know through it what is agreeable to God and what is not, and that they may attain to the destiny intended for mankind by doing those things which are agreeable to God, the above objection does not hold. For since the purpose of prophecy is that the human race may be guided by God, which means revelation of the Torah, the latter must be a fundamental principle, because it is that which makes prophecy necessary. For this reason, we consider prophecy a derivative principal dependent on revelation. For the same reason also, we considered Providence a subordinate principle derived from reward and punishment, though it might appear that the reverse is true. One might say that since providence precedes reward and punishment, the latter is derived from it.

The answer is as follows: If God's providence of human individuals were of the same nature as in the other animals, namely the preservation of their species, reward and punishment would be derivative from providence. But it is not so. The providence which we consider as a principle is not the kind which provides for the lower animals by maintaining the species merely, but the kind that rewards a man according to his deeds both in this world and the next, as the divine wisdom decrees. Hence, we considered reward and punishment a fundamental principle and providence a subordinate principle derived from the former, because the providence which is concerned with reward and punishment is not the same as that which has to do with the lower animals, preserving merely their species.

In the same way must be understood all the relations of the subordinate principles to the fundamental ones, where the former are prior to the latter. Thus, prophecy is prior by nature to revelation of the Torah, and prior in time also, for the prophetic inspiration of the patriarchs came before the revelation of the Torah through Moshe; and yet we considered prophecy subordinate to revelation of the Torah. The reason is because all the instances of prophecy that occurred before the revelation of the Torah were for the purpose of the Torah, and similarly all the prophetic teachings of the prophets who came after the Torah were for the purpose of the fulfilment of the Torah. Inasmuch as in the mind of an agent the purpose or final cause is necessarily prior to the other causes, our Rabbis say that the Torah came two thousand years before the world. The Torah is the purpose for the sake of which the human race was created, which is the highest form of existence in the world of genesis and decay. All other things exist for the sake of man, and man exists for the sake of the Torah. This principle may be applied to all the other dogmas which we considered as derived from the fundamental principles.

Chapter 13

We now desire to investigate whether it is possible that a given divine law of a given people should change in time, or whether it can not change but must be eternal.

It would seem that a divine law can not change, for reasons based upon a consideration of the giver, of the recipient, and of the law itself. Considering the giver, it would seem inconceivable that God who is the giver should desire one thing at one time and then change His will and desire its opposite at another time. It can not be that God should desire right at one time and wrong at another. Why then should God change His law for another?

Considering the recipient, we can not see why, since the nation is the same, the law should change in the course of time. We can not use the analogy of the individual and say that just as the rules of health for a child are different from those of a young man and those of a young man are different from those of an old man, as the time changes from childhood to youth and from youth to old age, so the rules of divine law must change with the times. For while it may be true in the case of an individual that his behavior is bound to change as the period of his life changes, the rule does not apply to a political group in which there is no such change from childhood to youth and to old age, for the convention of law is that all the times are the same. Hence, we can not see that divine law should change by reason of the recipient.

Now if we consider the law itself, it would seem that since the purpose of the divine Torah is to teach men intellectual conceptions and true opinions, there can be no reason for its changing at any time. For true opinions can never change. Monotheism can not be true at one time and dualism or trinitarianism at another, any more than it is possible that a thing that has already been should change and not have been. It seems clear therefore that there can be no change in a divine law, whether we consider the law itself, the giver, or the recipient.

Nevertheless, if we consider the matter carefully, we shall find that it does not necessarily follow that a divine law can not be changed for one and the same people. For though the ideas themselves do not change, nor the giver, a change may occur on the part of the recipient. A perfect agent does his work in a manner corresponding to the preparation of the recipient. As those changes, the work of the agent changes, no doubt. Nor does this imply any change in the agent. A physician prescribes a certain regimen to his patient for a term known to himself, which he does not reveal to the patient. When that time passes and the patient gets better, the physician changes his regimen, allows what he prohibited before and forbid what he formerly permitted. The patient has no reason to wonder at this, for it does not imply any change in the physician's original intention or imperfection in the physician because he did not in the first place prescribe a regimen good for all time. When the physician prescribed the first regimen, he knew the length of time that the patient would have to conform to it. And though he did not say anything to the patient, he knew when that regimen would have to change, estimating as he did, from the condition of the patient, the time required to pass from disease to health. When he prescribed the first regimen, his purpose was to improve the condition of the patient so that he might be ready and prepared to follow the second regimen, which was to come after its work had been done by the first. And when the time came, he changed the first regimen for another which he had in mind in the first place.

In the same way it argues no defect in God if He did not give at the beginning a law and a regimen that would suffice for all times. For when He gave the Torah, He knew that that law would suffice for the time which in His wisdom He estimated would be required to prepare the recipients and improve their condition so as to fit them to receive the second regimen, though He did not reveal this purpose of His to any one. When the time comes, He gives the second regimen, which may contain rules different from and opposed to the first, but it was in His mind from the beginning. On the contrary, as it would show a defect in the physician if he prescribed solid and substantial food, like bread and meat and wine, for convalescents

Sefer Halkkarim — BOOK [Maamar] THREE

and children and infants before they grow up or are strong enough to stand such food, so it would argue a defect in the giver of the Torah if He gave the same law for all time to novices and to habituates. The proper thing is to change it according to the change in the capacity of the recipients. As soon as they are accustomed to an easy regimen, He can advance them to a more difficult one, suitable to their nature, like bread and meat and wine and other substantial foods which, though unsuitable for children, are fit and proper for adults. And children, as they grow up and become accustomed to solid foods, change their mode of sustenance. A teacher treats his pupil in a similar manner. First, he trains him in matters easy to understand until he gets accustomed to study little by little. Then he advances him to a more difficult and more profound plane for which he was not fit at the beginning before he became accustomed to study.

And if one object that it is not fitting to suppose that God's power is so limited that He can not prescribe a rule of conduct that will embrace all men, young and old, for all time, his objection would be analogous to the question that is asked, why did not God create all men righteous and eager to worship Him so that there be not one that is crooked? assuming that this would show perfection. The fact is not so, as Maimonides has shown, touching this and similar matters, in the thirty-second chapter of the third part of the Guide of the Perplexed. We do not say that perfection would require that God should have created all animals with reason to praise Him, because it is contrary to nature. Similarly, we do not say that it would be a credit to God if all things happened by way of miracle and not in accordance with natural law. For all theologians are agreed that nature is precious to God and He does not change it except when it is absolutely necessary. We are here discussing this subject as reason demands and as a study of the Torah suggests. Any one who chooses may disagree and insist that God constantly creates miracles in opposition to nature. When the Rabbis say that the Torah is a panacea and a drug that gives life to all, they mean for all the organs of the body. Similarly they say that "the words of the Torah are a salve for the eye, an emollient for the heart, and a medicine for the bowels ... as is said, 'and health to all their flesh,' " but they do not say that it is the same for all men, women and children, and for all time. The truth of our statement will be made clear in the following chapter.

Sefer HaIkkarim BOOK [Maamar] THRE
Chapter 14

If we investigate the divine laws of the world, we find that they changed from time to time, forbidding what was originally permitted, and then again permitting what had been forbidden. Thus in the beginning Adam was given a few commandments which, according to the tradition of our Rabbis, mankind followed till the time of Noah. Noah was permitted to eat animal food, which was forbidden to Adam. Originally animal food was forbidden to Adam, plants alone being permitted, "Behold, I have given you every herb yielding seed, which is upon the face of all the earth, and every tree, in which is the fruit of a tree yielding seed - to you it shall be for food." Later, Noah was given permission to eat animal food, "Every moving thing that liveth shall be for food for you; as the green herb have, I given you all." An additional commandment was given to him, forbidding him to eat a limb cut from the living animal. Abraham was given the additional commandment of circumcision. Moshe received many other commandments. Also, God prohibited certain marriages of relations which were permitted to the Noahites and permitted certain matters which were forbidden to the Noahites. Thus, an Israelite may eat an animal after it is slaughtered even though it is still struggling, whereas a Noahite would deserve the penalty of death if he ate the animal before it died, for it would come under the prohibition of eating the limb of a living animal. Similarly, a Noahite is punishable with death if he is guilty of robbery, even to the extent of less than a perutah, not so an Israelite. Also, a Noahite seeing another committing a robbery without preventing him is guilty of a capital crime. This is why all the inhabitants of Shechem deserved the punishment of death, because they saw Shechem committing a robbery and did not prosecute him, as Maimonides says in **Sefer Shofetim**. Also, a Noahite who marries a half sister on the father's side goes unpunished, whereas an Israelite guilty of such an act is punishable with death.

We find even a more remarkable statement than this in "Sifre," by way of comment on the verse, "Neither shalt thou set thee up a pillar, which the Lord thy God hateth." "Though it was dear to God in the days of the patriarchs," is the comment there made. And this includes the time of Moshe also, for at the time of the Sinaitic revelation he built an altar at the foot of the mountain, and set up twelve pillars for the twelve tribes of Israel. The prohibition came in the plains of Moab in the fortieth year. God said to Yaakov, "I am the God of Bethel, where thou didst anoint a pillar." It is clear, therefore, that a thing which the worshippers of God were in the habit of doing in God's honor and which was absolutely permitted in the time of Moshe at the Sinaitic revelation, was forbidden in the plains of Moab, according to the opinion of the Rabbis. So far as certain marriages of affinities are concerned, which were permitted to the Noahites, we see them expressly forbidden in the Bible. All this shows that the divine law did change, now permitting, now forbidding, in accordance with the times. This was the situation in the times of Adam, Noah and Abraham, until Moshe came. There has been no change since his day.

The opinion of Maimonides is that the Torah will never change in whole or in part. Hence one of his principal dogmas is the immutability of the Torah. Now inasmuch as we have found that the divine laws which existed before Moshe did undergo changes in the matter of permission and prohibition, immutability would be a principal peculiar to the Mosaic law. Maimonides bases this dogma upon the scriptural passage, "Thou shalt not add thereto, nor diminish from it." The reason he gives, in the Guide of the Perplexed, is because a thing which is harmonious and perfect can not have anything added to it or taken away from it, as the harmony and perfection would be destroyed. But the Torah is perfect, as Scripture testifies, "The law of the Lord is perfect, restoring the soul," therefore it can never be changed. This is the gist of Maimonides' opinion in this matter, as expressed in a number of places.

But his ideas on this point require careful consideration in respect to their source. The dogma is surely of great importance, nevertheless we must know whether Maimonides derives it from tradition or from his own ratiocination. If the former, we must gracefully accept it, but if it is the latter, we have something to say about it. The prohibition against adding to or subtracting from the commandments has no reference to the number of the commandments, but to the manner of performing them. The meaning of the prohibition is that we should not invent of our own mind or borrow from the idolaters some addition or diminution in the manner of performing the commandments, because we may think it does greater honor to God. The context proves that this is the meaning. In section **Reëh** the Bible warns against idolatry: "When the Lord thy God shall cut off the nations from before thee, whither thou goest in to dispossess them ... take heed to thyself that thou be not ensnared to follow them, after that they are destroyed from before thee; and that thou inquire not after their gods, saying:

'How used these nations to serve their gods? even so will I do likewise.' Thou shalt not do so unto the Lord thy God; for every abomination to the Lord, which He hateth, have they done unto their gods; for even their sons and their daughters do they burn in the fire to their gods. All this word which I command you, that shall ye observe to do; thou shalt not add thereto, nor diminish from it." Now there is something strange in the sequence of thought in the above passage, "Take heed to thyself that thou be not ensnared to follow them, after that they are destroyed from before thee." Would a person be likely to be ensnared to follow them after he has seen them destroyed? Why then does the text connect the idea of inquiring after their gods with their destruction?

The explanation of the text is this. The Bible is concerned that one should not be enticed in any manner after idolatrous practices. Therefore, it says, a person might make a mistake and suppose that the reason God commanded the destruction of the idolaters is because they offered to the idols the honorable service that is becoming to God. Hence the text says, after destroying the idolaters you might inquire after the manner in which they worshipped their idols, thinking to do likewise and to serve God in the manner in which they served their idols, believing that it would be doing God a great honor. Hence the Bible says, "And that thou inquire not after their gods, saying: 'How used these nations to serve their gods? even so will I do likewise,' " i.e., to God. "Thou shalt not do so unto the Lord thy God." Then comes the reason, "For every abomination to the Lord, which He hateth, have they done unto their gods." The meaning is, you must not suppose that the reason God forbid those practices is because He is jealous on account of their being performed for others, but because they are despicable and an abomination in His eyes, and the proof of it is that "even their sons and their daughters do they burn in the fire to their gods." They think this is doing honor to God, but it is an abomination to Him, for God does not desire the destruction of the world, nor does He command the killing of human beings. So the Rabbis comment, in the treatise Ta'anit, on the statement of Jeremiah, "And they have built the high places of Topheth ... to burn their sons and their daughters in the fire; which I commanded not nor spoke it, neither came it into My mind." "I commanded not," say the Rabbis, refers to the son of Mesha, the king of Moab, concerning whom it is said, "Then he took his eldest son that should have reigned in his stead, and offered him for a burnt-offering upon the wall." "Nor spoke it," refers to the

Sefer HaIkkarim — BOOK [Maamar] THREE

daughter of Jephthah the Gileadite. "Neither came it into My mind," refers to Yitzhak, the son of Abraham.

Mesha the king of Moab was never commanded to offer sacrifices as Israel was, therefore he is referred to by the expression, "I commanded not." Jephthah was an Israelite and was commanded to offer sacrifices, but God never spoke to him that he should make a burnt-offering of his daughter, hence, "nor spoke it." And as for Abraham, God did command him to offer sacrifices, and also spoke to him, telling him to offer Yitzhak his son as a burnt-offering, but his intention was not that he should actually sacrifice him, hence the expression, "neither came it into My mind," is referred to Yitzhak, the son of Abraham.

The Rabbis thus make clear that God does not desire sacrifices. The meaning of the Bible therefore is, do not think to honor God by performing for Him those services which the idolaters did for their gods. For far from being agreeable to Him, they are an abomination to Him, "for every abomination to the Lord, which He hateth, have they done unto their gods; for even their sons and their daughters do they burn in the fire to their gods." Then the Bible sums up the matter and explains how God should be worshipped, "All this word which I command you, that shall ye observe to do; thou shalt not add thereto, nor diminish from it." The meaning is, you must not merely not do anything that was not commanded, but you must not make any additions in the manner of the service.

This is also the explanation given by Nahmanides in his commentary on section "Reëh." And we find the same idea in Sifre: "Hence they said that if the blood that requires one sprinkling is mixed with other blood that requires one sprinkling, there shall be only one sprinkling." From this verse, Sifre makes an inference applying to all the commandments of the Torah: "How do we know that it is not allowed to add to the **Lulab** and the **Zizit**? Answer: 'Thou shalt not add thereto.' How do we know that it is not allowed to take away? Answer: 'Nor diminish from it.' How do we know that if he began to pronounce the priestly benediction he must not say, since I began the benediction, I may as well add the words, 'The Lord, the God of your fathers add unto you?' Answer: The text says, 'this word,' meaning, you must not add even a word." Thus, we find express support for our view. Rashi, in his commentary on section **Vaëthanan**, says, in explaining the words, "Ye shall not add unto the word which I command you," for example, to have five compartments in the phylacteries; and similar is the meaning of the

Sefer HaIkkarim   BOOK [Maamar] THRE

expression, "Neither shall ye diminish from it." There is therefore no proof in these verses of Maimonides' opinion.

Moreover, if the meaning of the text were too forbid adding to or taking away from the number of the commandments, how could the Rabbis say that the court may decide to suspend a biblical commandment, where the suspension involves merely non-feasance? Is the court allowed to violate the command not to diminish from it? Similarly, Solomon, who introduced the 'erub and the washing of hands, was guilty of violating the commandment not to add thereto. In short, I do not see any evidence in the passages cited by Maimonides that immutability is a dogma of the Mosaic law at all, as Maimonides thinks.

Moreover, assuming that the biblical expressions have the meanings he gives to them, that does not prove that the Torah will never be repealed or changed. The Bible merely warns us not to add to or take away from the commandments on our own account. But what can there be to prevent God Himself from adding or diminishing as His wisdom decrees? As for the argument that the equal and the mean can never be added to or taken away from, that applies to the true and absolute mean, whereas the relative mean may very well change with the nature of the recipients. Thus food that is fitting for a child is milk, while for an adult the proper food is bread and meat and wine.

Similarly divine commandments change with the times. Thus flesh was forbidden to Adam and permitted to Noah and his descendants by reason of the degeneration of Cain and his descendants, as we shall explain later. Some have written that the reason Adam was forbidden to eat meat is because the world was new, and if Adam had been allowed to eat meat, many animal species might have been exterminated. But this can not be the reason, for in that case permission should not have been given to Noah and his children either, for in their time also the number of animals was small, while Noah and his three sons and their wives were more than Adam and Eve, who were the only persons in existence when they were forbidden to eat meat. Moreover, if the explanation be as these men say, then there was no reason for again forbidding Israel the meat of certain animals. At any rate it is thus proved that though divine laws are not completely repealed, they may change in their permissions and prohibitions, as the character of the recipients' changes.

Sefer HaIkkarim
Chapter 15

We must now explain the reason for the change that we have found, namely that that which was forbidden to Adam was permitted to Noah, and that a part of that which was permitted to Noah was forbidden to Israel. In order to explain this properly, we must first inquire what was Cain's sin when he brought an offering to God from the fruit of the ground, as a result of which God refused to have respect unto him or his present. Was it that he did not bring of the best of the sheep and rams of Nebayoth, as Abel did? Surely this is no sin. If his occupation was the tilling of the ground and he prospered therein and brought of its fruit a present to God to thank Him for His benefits, why did the Lord refuse to have respect unto him or his offering? It stands to reason that when a person receives a benefit from another, having been treated with food and drink, he should return thanks to his benefactor corresponding to the kindness which he received. He is not obliged to thank him for having clothed and enriched him if he has done nothing of the sort. But the thanksgiving must correspond to the benefit received. If it is not greater, that is no cause for criticism and surely does not involve guilt.

And if we say that Cain's sin consisted in the fact that he did not bring of the fruit of the tree but only of the fruit of the ground, as we said before, this did not deserve such severe punishment as is expressed in the verse, "If thou doest well, shall it not be lifted up? and if thou doest not well, sin coucheth at the door ..." The question also suggests itself, since God favored Abel as well as his present, how is it that he was killed? Why did not an angel of God protect the God-fearing man and save him from death? Another question is, why is it that we read about Seth, "And begot a son in his own likeness, after his image," while there is no such expression in reference to Abel, though God favored his present?

The explanation of all this is, I think, as follows: In the killing of animals there is cruelty, rage, and the accustoming oneself to the bad habit of shedding innocent blood, but the eating of the flesh of some animals produces besides, coarseness, ugliness and stupidity, as is stated in the Bible. After prohibiting the food of certain animals to Israel, the text ends up, "Ye shall not make yourselves detestable ... neither shall ye make yourselves unclean with them, that ye should be defiled thereby." The word translated "defiled" [ונטמתם] is written without an aleph, thus indicating that the forbidden food produces mental coarseness and obtuseness. The Rabbis also say, in reference to the verse in question, "Transgression of a law stupefies the person, as is said, 'that ye should be defiled thereby.' Read not **defiled** [ונטמאתם], but **stupefied** [ונטמתם]." This is the reason why, though the flesh of certain animals is good food and suitable for man, God chose to deprive him of the slight good of eating the meat, in order to prevent the much greater evil which might result therefrom. This is why he forbade Adam the eating of animal food. He made up for this loss of good food by assigning to Adam vegetable food which was very good and nourishing, like wheat, barley, and the other seed-bearing plants that can be sown, also all those trees which bear fruit having seed in them. To other animals he gave for food all green grass that has no seed that may be planted. The purpose of this was to show the superiority of the human species to the other animals.

When Cain and Abel were born and saw their father Adam laboring in the tillage of the ground and planting wheat and barley and other grains, and nourishing himself by eating the plants, each one of them chose his own way, indicating his purpose and ideas in his practice. Cain took to tilling the ground because he thought that the only superiority of man to the animals consisted in his ability to till the ground and live on the choice plants. Seeing that Adam lived on plants like the animals, he thought that the spirit is the same in all and that all die alike. Therefore, he brought an offering of the fruit of the ground, to thank God for the superiority He gave him over plants. He did not bring an animal offering, because he did not think that his superiority to them in the ability to till the ground was important enough to warrant bringing an offering. Part of his sin consisted, as we said before, in the fact that instead of bringing fruit of the tree, which is the best of plant life, he brought of the fruit of the ground, i.e., green vegetables. But his main offence was that he did not think that man's superiority to the animals amounted to anything. Also, he thought that he was forbidden to kill the animals because they were like him and were subject to death like him. He thought too that the main purpose of man is to eat and drink, since he fed on plants like the animals.

Abel, on the other hand, thought that man was superior to the animals, but that the superiority lay in the fact that he has control over them and can subdue them and make them do his work. But he did not think that man was authorized to kill the animals. So far human superiority did not reach, according to his opinion. Hence, we read, "And Abel, he also brought of the firstlings of his flock." The meaning is, he, too, thought like Cain that man is not allowed to kill animals except for God as an offering to show that God is superior to both man and animal, for He remains forever, while they perish. Man is superior only, he thought, in that he pastures them, governs countries, and so on. This is why Abel was killed, because his opinion was close to that of Cain, and more calculated to mislead men.

Nevertheless, Abel held that man has superiority over the animals and controls them, and is allowed to kill them for God - an opinion which is likely to lead to a recognition of the general superiority of man over the animals. Also, he recognized the greatness of the Lord and brought of the first-born of his flock and of their fat ones. Hence God had respect unto Abel and his offering, because it was nearer the truth than the opinion of Cain, but He did not have respect unto Cain and his offering, because he was very far from the truth, since he thought man had no superiority over the animals and failed to appreciate the greatness of God in that he brought of the fruit of the ground instead of the fruit of the tree, as we said before. Therefore, God said to him, "Why art thou wroth? and why is thy countenance fallen? If thou doest well, shall it not be lifted up?" The meaning is, you are right, man is born a wild ass, and has no superiority over the animal in actuality when he comes into the world, but he has superiority potentially if he practises goodness and realizes his potentialities and recognizes the greatness of the Lord. If he does well, he will be lifted up above the animals. This is the meaning of the expression, "If thou doest well, shall it not be lifted up?" For this reason, envy took hold of Cain and he killed Abel. For he still held the opinion that man is not superior to the animal. Therefore, he said to himself, Since God favors Abel and his present, it is clear that it is permitted to kill animals, and hence it is just as lawful to kill Abel as any other animal. On the other hand, since Abel's opinion was not altogether correct, he was not protected by God from violence.

Then when God revealed Himself to Cain and announced his punishment for the crime, Cain did not yet understand that to shed the blood of a human being is a more serious matter than to shed the blood of an animal, but he thought that as he was punished for shedding human blood, so he would be punished for shedding animal blood, since Adam was not permitted to kill animals; for the spirit of man and the spirit of the beast are alike, as the one dies so does the other. This erroneous opinion remained among the descendants of Cain until Seth was born, who knew the superiority of man over the animals, as his father Adam did. Therefore it says in reference to him, "And he [Adam] begot in his own likeness, after his image." For he alone was in the image of God like Adam, whereas those before him did not understand the dignity of the human form in them, which is in the image of God.

According to these three opinions of Cain, Abel and Seth, respectively, all mankind are divided into three classes. One class follow the opinion of Cain, and think that the most important human occupation is agriculture. They feel hostility toward political rulers and desire to kill them, as Cain killed Abel. A second class follow the opinion of Abel, thinking that politics is the most important pursuit, and risk their life for political activity like Abel, because they think that it leads to human perfection, as we are told concerning certain Roman rulers. So kings risk their lives for the sake of power, which is natural to them as it was to Abel, who was the first shepherd and ruler and lost his life on that account. The third class follow the opinion of Seth, thinking that the important thing is to worship God, and despise power and the other pleasures. As the opinion of Seth is not easily grasped at first sight, he was followed by only a few rare individuals. But the opinion of Cain was widely prevalent among his descendants, and hence the earth was filled with violence on their account, their belief being that man has no superiority over the animal, and might is right. Therefore they were corrupt and lived like animals. For this reason it was decreed that their name should be wiped out from the earth in the flood.

When they were all destroyed and only Noah and those with him in the ark remained, God wanted to eradicate this opinion. Hence when Noah, after leaving the ark, brought an animal offering to God because he knew that man is superior by virtue of his reason and can know his Creator and serve Him better than the animals and can be thankful to God for this privilege, his offering was accepted with favor, as is said, "And the Lord smelled the sweet savour." But He feared that unless this opinion was made firm, the Noahites might deviate in the direction of Abel's idea and assume that God accepted their father's offering as he accepted Abel's offering, thus going back to the former errors and wrongdoing. Hence immediately after the offering, He hastened to permit the killing of animals and the eating of their flesh, "As the green herb have, I given you all." The meaning is that as even Cain admitted that man is superior to the plants, since they are created for man, so all the animals are also for the sake of man, who is superior to them, and there is not the same spirit in all. For this reason, He prohibited the shedding of human blood, giving as a reason that the spirit of man is not like the spirit of the animal, for in the image of God made He man, i.e., man has a rational form which is nobler than the spirit of the animal. For this reason, it was necessary to permit all animals without distinction, which He did, in order to eradicate the former opinion and wipe off its memory.

But when the Torah was given to Israel, and the opinion in question had been wiped out, God prohibited certain animals which produce coarseness and ugliness of soul. Nay, even the animals that were permitted were merely a concession to human lust and desire, in the same way as the Israelites were permitted women taken in war. Thus, the Rabbis say, commenting on the verse, "because thy soul desireth to eat flesh," There is a moral lesson in this expression, namely that one should not eat flesh unless he has an appetite for it. This shows clearly that the eating of flesh was permitted only because of necessity. For this reason, it was forbidden at the time of creation, though it is good for food, for the reason we mentioned at the beginning of the chapter. The same is true of wine. It is good food and is permitted, and yet the Bible calls the Nazirite, who abstains from it, holy. At any rate all this shows that a given thing may be forbidden and then permitted, and vice versa. We may say, therefore, that there are matters in the divine law which are forbidden for a certain length of time, as God's wisdom decrees, and later are permitted in accordance with the same divine wisdom. There is no evidence in the Bible to the contrary. As to the kind of things that may be abolished or repealed, this will be explained later on in this Book.

Chapter 16

Some have thought to prove the eternity of the Mosaic law from the expressions which are used in connection with some of the commandments, such as, "a statute forever," "throughout your generations," "a sign it is for ever." Thus, in connection with the day of atonement and the prohibition of new fruit we find, "It is a statute for ever throughout your generations in all your dwellings." In connection with the Sabbath, we read, "It is a sign between Me and the children of Israel forever." In the commandment concerning Passover, we find, "For an ordinance to thee and to thy sons forever;" and so there are other commandments besides in which we find the expressions, "a statute for ever," or "throughout your generations," or "in all your dwellings."

This, however, is no proof, for the opponent may say, this rather proves that the other commandments will be abolished, since these

Sefer HaIkkarim   BOOK [Maamar] THRE

alone are so qualified. Besides, we are expressly told in the treatise Kiddushin: Why do we find the expression, "in all your dwellings," in connection with the prohibition of fat and blood? Answer: If the expression were not there, we might argue that since the prohibition is found in connection with the sacrifices, it holds only of the time when sacrifices are offered, but not when there are no more sacrifices. In the same place they explain why the expression, "a statute forever," occurs in the commandments concerning the day of atonement and the prohibition of new fruit, and not in other commandments. And it appears from their answers that if the expressions were not there one might suppose that the commandments in question might become obsolete even while the others are still in force. But the expressions in question do not denote the eternity of the law, for it is possible that when the other commandments are abolished, these will be abolished also.

Nor can any evidence be found in the expression's **Eternity** [עולם], **Unto eternity** [צר עולם], **A statute for eternity** [חקת עולם], or - **To eternity** [לעולם]. For these expressions and their like are also applied to a limited and not an infinite time. Thus, we read, "Remove not the ancient [צולם] landmark, which thy fathers have set." The word צולם [eternity] is here used to denote a time limited and dating from the fathers. Other passages are: "For of old time [מעולם] I have broken thy yoke;" "Then shall the offering of Yehuda and Yerushalayim be pleasant unto the Lord, as in the days of old [עולם]." The Plural צולמים is also used to denote a finite time, as, "I will dwell in Thy Tent for ever [צולמים];" "O Israel, that art saved by the Lord with an everlasting [צולמים] salvation." This refers to the salvation from Sennacherib. Similarly in the expression, "It hath been already, in the ages [לצולמים] which were before us." The word denotes here, "a long time." The word לצולם is also applied to a finite short time, as, "And he shall serve him forever [לצולם]," which means, until the year of the jubilee. The expression צד צולם has a similar use. Thus, Hannah said, "I will bring him, that he may appear before the Lord, and there abide for ever [צד צולם]." The expression here means fifty years, which is the term of a Levite, as we find, "And from the age of fifty years they shall return from the service of the work, and shall serve no more." The expression צד צולם is also applied to a finite short time not known to man but to God alone. Thus, Isaiah says: "For the palace shall be forsaken; the city with its stir shall be deserted; the mound and the tower shall be for dens for ever [צולם צד]." And later it says, "Until the spirit be poured upon us from on high." Similarly, the expression, **All the days of eternity**

Sefer HaIkkarim BOOK [Maamar] THREE

[עולם כל ימי] is applied to a finite short time. Isaiah says: "And He bore them, and carried them all the days of old [כל ימי עולם]," while in the sequel it says, "But they rebelled and grieved His holy spirit; therefore, He was turned to be their enemy, Himself fought against them."

In short, none of these expressions or those like them necessarily denotes eternity or infinite time, but each one must be explained from its context. The very word לנצח, which signifies perpetuity, is applied to a finite brief time. Thus, in reference to the dwelling of the divine glory on Mount Sinai, we read, "The mountain which God hath desired for His abode, yea, the Lord will dwell therein forever [לנצח]." But the divine glory did not dwell on Mount Sinai forever, for when the tent of meeting was built, the glory departed from Mount Sinai and dwelt in the tent of meeting. Similarly, the expression, "a statute forever [חקת עולם]," does not necessarily signify that the thing will last an infinite time. For in the commandment concerning the candelabrum we find the expression, "a statute forever, throughout your generations," and yet it has been interrupted from the time of the destruction of the second temple to this day. Similarly, the expression, "a statute forever," is used in relation to the feasts of Passover and Tabernacles, and yet our Rabbis say in **Vayyikra Rabbah** that all festivals will be abolished except Purim and the Day of Atonement. It would seem then that their interpretation of the expression, "a statute forever," is that we may not abolish them on our own account, but that there is a possibility of their being abolished by God's command.

We find also that in the time of Ezra they ceased counting the months from Nisan, though this is the method of counting prescribed in the Torah, as we read, "This month shall be unto you the beginning of months; it shall be the first month of the year to you,' this being the first commandment given to Israel. Although Tishri is the beginning of the year when we count the years of the world, as we read, "And the feast of ingathering, at the turn of the year;" "And the feast of ingathering, at the end of the year;" and when we compute the sabbatical and the jubilee years, yet the Torah commanded us to count the months from Nisan whenever we count them, because in this month Israel came out of Egypt and the nation first came into existence. The Torah itself computes all its calculations from Nisan. Thus, "And it came to pass in the second year, in the second month, on the twentieth day of the month;" "In the third month, etc.;" "And in the seventh month on the first day of the month;" "And on the tenth day of this seventh month is the day

Sefer HaIkkarim   BOOK [Maamar] THRE

of atonement." According to the usage of the Torah the months have no names, but must be called second, third, fourth, fifth, sixth, seventh, beginning with Nisan, in memory of the Exodus from Egypt. This is the meaning of the verse, "It shall be the first month of the year to you." That is to say, when you count months, begin with Nisan, though when you count years, you must count from Tishri, as we said before.

But when they returned from Babylon, they desired to commemorate the second deliverance, which they did in two ways. The first was that they discontinued the Hebrew script and adopted the Assyrian in memory of the redemption from the Assyrian exile. Thus, our Rabbis say, in the Tosefta of the treatise Sanhedrin, "Why is it called Asshurit? Because it came with them from Assyria [Asshur]. Rabbi says, The Torah was given to Israel in these characters ... And the reason it is called Asshurit [אשורית] is because it is the most excellent [משורית] of writings." According to the sense of the Talmud in the beginning of chapter "Kol Kitbe," it seems that the characters we now use and in which our books are written, are not Hebrew. If so, we may say that Rabbi's difference of opinion consists merely in saying that since the Tables of Stone were written in these characters, the name Asshurit was not given to them because they came from Assyria; but he admits that the Hebrew characters used by the people anciently were changed. But even if we grant that he does not agree that there was a change, it matters not, because his opinion, that of a single person, does not count as against the opinion of the majority of the wise men.

Moreover, in Talmud Sanhedrin Chapter - **Kohen Gadol**, the Amoraim explain the words of the wise men. The passage is as follows; "Rab Hisda says in the name of Mar Ukba: Originally the Torah was given to Israel in Hebrew characters and in the holy tongue. When the exiles came back in the days of Ezra, they chose Assyrian characters and the holy tongue, leaving the Hebrew characters to the common people, i.e., the Cutheans, who lived in Palestine before the exiles came. These used the Hebrew characters and the Aramaic language." The Amoraim, therefore, agree that the characters now in use are not Hebrew.

Nahmanides also testifies that when he was in Palestine he found in 'Akko an ancient silver coin with the jar of manna and the rod of Aaron engraved upon it, and with characters all around that he could not read. When they showed it to the Cutheans, who retained the ancient Hebrew characters, they read it [שקל השקלים]. These are the words which he adds as a note at the end of his commentary which

Sefer HaIkkarim   BOOK [Maamar] THRE

he sent from Palestine, from which it is clear that the characters now in use are not Hebrew.

As for the statement of the Rabbis that the mem and the samek maintained themselves on the Tables of Stone by a miracle, it may be that this statement is made according to the opinion of Rabbi that the Tables of Stone were written in Asshurit or square characters, or else they also held the opinion that the Tables of Stone were written in the square characters, though the people at that time used the Hebrew characters. Or it may be that they were not referring to the mem and samek which we now use; and that in the Hebrew characters in which the Tables were written, the mem and the samek were closed letters, or there were other letters similar to the mem and samek of the square characters now in use. For Rab Hisda himself who said that the mem and the samek in the Tables maintained themselves by a miracle holds that the characters were changed. It is possible that the expression, "They chose the square characters," refers not to the whole alphabet but only to a part. They selected some of the square characters and left the rest. Thus, the mem and samek were retained in their closed form, as they were in the Tables, though some of the square characters were adopted in memory of the second deliverance. This is, however, not likely.

At any rate it is clear from all that went before that they changed the whole or part of their writing in memory of the second deliverance. And they also did another thing in memory of the second deliverance, namely they ceased counting the months from Nisan, as they had been accustomed to do in memory of the Exodus from Egypt, and adopted another method of counting. This is what our Rabbis mean when they say, "The names of the months came with them from Assyria." That is to say, they counted the months by name, Tishri, Marheshvan, Kislev, as they did in Assyria, in memory of the second deliverance, and not second, third, fourth, as they did before. This is also the explanation of Nahmanides in his commentary on section "Bo."

It seems from this, then, that they understood the pentateuchal commandment concerning the numbering of the months to be temporary, i.e., as long as that deliverance lasted. But after they were exiled a second time and were delivered again, and were told by Jeremiah, "They shall no more say: 'As the Lord liveth, that brought up the children of Israel out of the land of Egypt;' but: 'As the Lord liveth, that brought up and that led the seed of the house of Israel out of the north country' ....," they thought that it was proper to give up the first mode of counting which was in memory of the Exodus from

Sefer HaIkkarim — BOOK [Maamar] THREE

Egypt, and adopted a different one, beginning with Tishri, when they counted the years of the world. And they also retained the names of the months which they brought with them from Assyria, in memory of the second deliverance, for they understood that the commandment in the Pentateuch to count the months from Nisan was temporary and not perpetual, though there is no mention of time. There is nothing therefore to prevent us from supposing that the divine law may in the future permit some things which are forbidden now, like fat or blood or the slaughter of animals outside of the temple. These things were originally forbidden when the Israelites left Egypt because they were addicted to the worship of evil spirits, and ate the flesh with the blood and also ate fat and blood, as we read in relation to the killing of animals outside of the temple, "And they shall no more sacrifice their sacrifices unto the satyrs, after whom they go astray." But when this form of worship has been forgotten, and all people shall worship God, and the reason of the prohibition will cease, it may be that God will again permit it. And some of our Rabbis have the same opinion. In **Yelammedenu** they say, commenting on the biblical expression, "The Lord looseth the prisoners" [מתיר אסורים], "He permits the forbidden" [מתיר איסורין]. To sum up, I see no evidence, nor any necessity, from Maimonides' arguments, that the immutability or irrepealability of the law should be a fundamental principle of a divine law generally or of the law of Moshe in particular. This is also the opinion of my teacher Rabbi Hasdai, namely that it is not a principle or dogma of the law of Moshe. But he says that it is a doctrine which every one professing the Mosaic law should believe. The reason he gives is that if we examine all the parts of the Mosaic law, we find that they embrace all those moral qualities and theoretical ideas which are calculated to give perfection to the soul in some manner. This reason is similar to that which we quoted above from Maimonides' Guide. We will come back to the subject and inquire from a different point of view whether the Mosaic law is liable to change as are other divine laws or not. This requires some preliminary considerations.

Chapter 17

All the words of the prophets are true without doubt. Nevertheless, there is a difference in degree. The greater the dignity of the prophet and the higher the degree of his prophetic inspiration, the greater the truth value of his words. Some prophets, by reason of their weakness of comprehension, do not apprehend things with sufficient clearness. Prophetic apprehension has certain similarities to sensible apprehension. If a sense faculty or organ is healthy and strong, it apprehends the objects clearly; whereas if it is weak, it does not apprehend them clearly. It may apprehend the species to which the object belongs or it may apprehend the genus only without being able to tell to what species it belongs. Thus, a person who has powerful vision apprehends color correctly, as, for example, red or green. But he also apprehends the degree of redness or greenness. On the other hand, a person with weak vision will apprehend the genus only, i.e., he will know it is a color, and no more. Or he may know the species too; that it is red or green, but will not know what degree of redness or greenness it is. The same thing is true in hearing and the other sensibilia.

The same thing applies to the prophetic apprehension. The prophet who has a strong power of apprehension perceives the thing as it is without imagination and his words come out clear and not obscure; hence they may be understood in their literal meaning. On the other hand, a prophet who is inferior in degree to the one mentioned, will express himself in obscure language, in riddles and parables which are not clear. Hence the truth is not in the literal meaning, but in the allusion. If his words are taken literally, one gets an idea different from the one intended. Thus Ezekiel, prophesying after the exile, speaks in parables and riddles, which can not be understood literally; so much so that he complains about this to God, "They say of me: Is he not a maker of parables?" Similarly, Zechariah, coming toward the end of the prophetic period, experienced his prophetic inspiration in visions, the truth of which lay not in the vision itself as it appeared, but in the ideas which it suggested. Thus, when he says that he saw horses and women and a golden candelabrum and two olives upon it, the candelabrum and the olives are not to be taken as real things, but only as alluding to a certain idea.

Jeremiah, on the other hand, who lived before the destruction of the temple, spoke always plainly and clearly. God Himself made clear the difference between Moshe' prophecy and that of the others. In relation to the prophecy of Moshe He says, "With him do I speak mouth to mouth, even manifestly and not in dark speeches," From this we infer that the other prophets spoke in dark speeches which were not clear, and saw visions which were not real. For this reason, their prophetic messages must be interpreted so as to agree with the words of Moshe. In general, the words of an inferior prophet must be interpreted so as to agree and not be in conflict with the words of a superior prophet. For example, Isaiah says, "I saw the Lord sitting

Sefer HaIkkarim   BOOK [Maamar] THRE

upon a throne high and lifted up;" whereas Moshe said, "for man shall not see Me and live." Now if we did not know the relative greatness of these two, we should suppose that Isaiah's words are true and should say that by reason of his greatness as a prophet he apprehended as much as can be apprehended of God, and hence he said, "I saw the Lord;" while Moshe, being inferior to Isaiah, and having apprehended of God only very little, said, "Man shall not see Me and live." But since we know that Moshe was the master of the prophets, concerning whom the Bible says, "And the Lord spoke unto Moshe face to face, as a man speaketh unto his friend;" "If there be a prophet among you, I the Lord do make Myself known unto him in a vision, I do speak with him in a dream. My servant Moshe is not so; ... with him do I speak mouth to mouth, even manifestly and not in dark speeches;" we know that the words of Moshe are true as they are in their literal meaning; while the words of Isaiah, who was inferior to Moshe, are not correct. It is because of his inferiority that he said, "I saw the Lord," because he thought he had seen God, but he had not really seen him, except in imagination. Moshe, on the other hand, in whose prophetic inspiration the imagination played no part at all, but the reason only, as separated from all corporeal powers, said, "For man shall not see Me and live," which is the truth.

Isaiah, on the other hand, made use also of the power of imagination, called by the Rabbis, a non-transparent glass, and hence was misled by it into thinking that he saw God. He was not unaware that his perception was an error due to the imagination, and said so, explaining that his matter was not as pure as that of Moshe, "Because I am a man of unclean lips;" and that his moral qualities were not all that they should be, "And I dwell in the midst of a people of unclean lips;" for association with men of bad morals corrupts the morals of a good man. This is why he complained, "Woe is me! for I am affected by imagination." The meaning is, I am affected by the power of imagination and my prophetic inspiration is not through a luminous glass like that of Moshe, who heard a voice speaking to him, without seeing any image before his eyes. But as my prophecy is through a non-luminous glass, through the medium of the power of the imagination, I am not able to apprehend speech without seeing a form in the act of speaking. And this is due to the fact that I am a man of unclean lips and that I dwell in the midst of a people of unclean lips. Therefore, I complain and say, "Woe is me! for I am influenced by imagination ... For mine eyes have seen the King, the Lord of hosts," and I know that it is the work of the imagination, for

Sefer HaIkkarim BOOK [Maamar] THRE

God can not have any attribute or likeness ascribed to Him, even in a prophetic vision, if one prophesies through a luminous glass.

This is the meaning of the statement of the Rabbis: Menasseh killed Isaiah. Then they say, he first tried him and then killed him. He said to him, your teacher Moshe said, "Man shall not see Me and live," whereas you say, "I saw the Lord." Then they remark that Isaiah could have answered Menasseh but did not, because he knew that he would not accept his answer. The answer he could have made is that even concerning the contemporaries of Moshe it is said, "And they saw the God of Israel," because their apprehension was not through a luminous glass.

From all this it is clear that an inferior prophet must not oppose the words of a prophet who is superior to him, but that his words must be so interpreted that they should not conflict with the words of the superior. Now since it is clearly stated in the Torah that the prophecy of Moshe stands on a higher plane than that of any other prophet, it follows that we can not accept the words of any other prophet in opposition to and refutation of the words of Moshe. Whether, however, any prophet may interpret the words of Moshe and say that though they are stated without qualification, they are conditional in their meaning, or that a time limitation should be attached to them, though no such limitation is explicitly stated, this will be discussed in the sequel with the help of God.

Chapter 18

There is a great difference between a thing which a prophet learns from God, and a thing which is told him by another prophet. A thing which a prophet hears from God can not be abolished unless he subsequently hears from God a statement opposed to the first. Thus, Abraham was told, "Take now thy son, thine only son, whom thou lovest, even Yitzhak, and get thee into the land of Moriah, and offer him there for a burnt-offering." Later he was told, "Lay not thy hand upon the lad, neither do thou anything unto him." Iddo, the prophet, was devoured by a lion, as a punishment because he listened to the old prophet in Bethel and went back to Bethel and ate bread there, contrary to the order he had received directly from God. But any command that comes to one through a prophet may be opposed by a contrary command from another prophet. For this reason, God desired that all Israel should hear from Him directly the ten commandments, so that no prophet may have the power to abolish them in whole or in part. This is stated explicitly in Scripture: "These

Sefer HaIkkarim   BOOK [Maamar] THRE

words the Lord spoke unto all your assembly in the mount … And He wrote them upon two tables of stone, and gave them unto me."

But there is some difficulty in connection with the statement of the Rabbis at the end of the treatise Makkot, that the first two commandments were heard directly from the mouth of Omnipotence [lit. strength]. This is strange. For the Bible says, "And the Lord delivered unto me the two tables of stone written with the finger of God; and on them was written according to all the words, which the Lord spoke with you in the mount out of the midst of the fire in the day of the assembly." And again, "And He wrote on the tables, according to the first writing, the ten words, which the Lord spoke unto you in the mount out of the midst of the fire in the day of the assembly; and the Lord gave them unto me." From all this it appears clearly that all the ten commandments which were written on the tables were spoken to all Israel. How then can the Rabbis say that they heard from God the first two commandments only and not the rest?

Maimonides, in the Guide of the Perplexed, says that the expression of the Rabbis, "They heard them from the mouth of strength," means they heard them through the force of rational demonstration. For his idea is that the first commandment teaches the existence of God, and the second, the unity of God, both being principles which can be proved by reason. He is also of the opinion that a thing that can be known by reason is equally known to the prophet and the layman. Hence although they heard them from God, these two should not be counted among the commandments. But the other commandments belong to the class of things known by tradition or generally accepted. Hence it was necessary that they should be heard from God, and the Rabbis do not speak of them as having been heard from the mouth of strength. So far Maimonides.

Now since he agrees that Israel heard all the ten commandments from God, his words require examination. If it is true that the first two commandments teach the existence and unity of God, why was it necessary to reveal these two commandments through prophetic inspiration? Human reason is sufficient to prove them, and any one denying them can be compelled by rational arguments to acknowledge the truth. There was more need to reveal through prophetic inspiration those things which the human mind alone can not discover. And there are still greater objections to Maimonides' opinion. He says in the book **Madda**: The heathen argued as follows: God created stars and spheres to control the world. He placed them in heaven and showed them honor. They are His servants and serve Him continually. Hence, they deserve praise and glorification and honor. It is God's desire that we should show honor and respect to any one whom He honors and to whom He gives greatness, as a king desires that honor be shown to his servants who stand before him. For this reason, the heathen offered sacrifices to the heavenly bodies and praised and glorified them and bowed down to them in order to obtain the favor of God. Such was their erroneous opinion. In the second chapter of the same treatise he says, It is not proper to serve them [the stars] as mediators between man and his Creator. According to Maimonides' opinion, therefore, since reason might seem to favor the worship of the stars, the spheres and the constellations on the two grounds just mentioned, the first commandment should have warned against it, instead of concerning itself with God's existence and unity, which not even the heathen denied, according to his opinion.

My opinion is that the heathen were led to their wrong worship by different reasons. The error of some was due to the fact that they denied the existence and unity of God, believing that God is a corporeal power and that He is the soul of the sphere, which is the belief of the Epicureans. These require no prophetic refutation, for reason can convince them with conclusive proofs. Others were led into the error of worshipping the spheral powers for the two reasons we mentioned above in the name of Maimonides. Examples of this are Ahab and other kings of Israel and Yehuda. Solomon too seems to have fallen into this error, as appears from the literal meaning of the scriptural text. All these men believed in the existence and unity of God, in prophecy and revelation of the Torah, and yet they fell into this error either because they thought in this way to honor God, or because they thought of making mediators between themselves and God, as Maimonides says.

There is still another sect of men who erroneously incline to idolatrous worship for a deeper reason. They hold with some of the philosophers that "God hath forsaken the land." Believing in the existence, unity and incorporeality of God, they hold that God has no care of the lower world at all, thinking it a sign of greatness in God that He pays no attention to the human species because man is inferior and despised by Him. They think it a virtue and a sign of nobility in God to refuse attention to that which is inferior, saying that in respect to inferior things ignorance is better than knowledge. Job inclined to this opinion when he said, "What is man that Thou shouldest magnify him, and that Thou shouldest set Thy heart upon him?" Therefore, he thought that the lower world is controlled by the spheres. Referring to such persons David said, "Who exalt Thee with wicked thought." That is to say, they exalt and lift Thee up, but this exaltation is with a wicked thought, in that they say that Thou dost not pay attention to particulars, because they think that it would be a defect in the nature of God if He took account of particulars, since this would necessitate His being favorably disposed at one time and angry at another, and so with other qualities which indicate change in us, and therefore would argue a defect in His nature also if He changed from favor to anger. Their opinion therefore is that the lower world is governed by the spheres and that God has no knowledge of it.

They also say that since God created stars and constellations and angels to rule over the lower world, and assigned to them dominion over the nations, as we read, "Which the Lord thy God hath allotted unto all the peoples under the whole heaven," and influence comes through them, we must prepare ourselves to receive this influence from them, and must worship them since they control us and exert an influence upon us. This was the opinion of the accursed women who said to Jeremiah, "But since we left off to offer to the queen of heaven and pour out drink-offerings unto her, we have wanted all things ..." They say also that every one of the seven metals is peculiarly related to one of the seven planets, gold corresponds to the sun, silver to the moon, lead to Jupiter, and so on. And when a figure is made of a certain metal at a certain hour, when the corresponding star is in a certain position in relation to the other stars, the spiritual power of the star will come down upon the figure, and by worshipping the figure one will obtain the influence of the star in question. Hence comes the worship of figures by the heathen. They also say that if a drop of human seed enters the uterus at the moment of a certain position of the stars, the person born of that seed will come under the influence of a certain star, and will be a diviner or a prognosticator by virtue of the spiritual influence of the star, and may even obtain so high a degree that he may be worshipped himself like the figures which the ancients made. This was the error of Pharaoh and of Hiram, king of Tyre, who made themselves gods, and of Nebuchadnezzar, who made of Daniel an object of worship, as we read, "And worshipped Daniel, and commanded that they should offer an offering and sweet odour unto him." All this error is due to the fact that they do not believe that God takes care of the human race.

Inasmuch as this opinion sounds very plausible so far as reason goes and was very prevalent at the time when the Torah was given, God was concerned about it, and wanted to eradicate it completely. It could not be eradicated through a prophet, for one who denied providence and revelation would deny the divine origin of prophecy in which the religionist believes. God therefore wanted to show as firmly as possible the refutation of this idea, as well as of the idea that absence of providence is a sign of greatness, and of the idea of making the heavenly bodies mediators between man and God. This end He accomplished by showing to them that there is such a thing as prophecy and revelation of a law to guide men in the right path. But this can not be unless God does provide for man.

This was made clear to them when they received from Him through prophetic inspiration, face to face, the two first commandments. The first commandment teaches that God provides for us and guides us. This is the meaning of the expression, "thy God," i.e., the one who guides thee. The commandment ends with the words, "Who brought thee out of the land of Egypt." i.e., I am the one who took care of thee and took thee out of the land of Egypt. "Out of the house of bondage," points to providence, for the constellations indicated that you were to be a slave, but I took you out of there with great strength, hence the expression, "out of the house of bondage." What you saw with your own eyes at the time of the Exodus proves the existence of Providence, and what you hear me now speaking to you proves that there is such a thing as prophecy. Thus, this commandment refuted the philosophical opinion which we mentioned.

But there still remained the possibility of retaining the other ideas, namely that the angels or the stars or the constellations are mediators between God and man, or that it is proper for man to worship them on the ground that one thus exalts God and performs His will, seeing that God has shown them honor, therefore He added the second commandment, "Thou shalt have no other gods before Me." This is a prohibition of worshipping the Separate Intelligences, i.e., the angels. For, as our Rabbis say in Mekilta [so Nahmanides says in his commentary on section Jethro], the angels are everywhere called, "other gods." "Before Me," means, even if you do believe in My providence, you must have no other gods to bring in as mediators between you and Me, nor must you think that you will exalt Me by worshipping them, not to speak of expecting to receive any influence from them without My knowledge. Then He says, "Thou shalt not make unto thee a graven image, nor any manner of likeness …," as a warning against those figures which are made to receive through them astral influence, figures which are everywhere in Scripture called, "molten gods." The commandment ends up, "For I the Lord thy God am a jealous God." That is to say, do not think to exalt Me by worshipping them, for it will have the opposite effect, as I shall be jealous of them.

Thus, all possible opinions are refuted which might lead to the worship of idols or any god but the Lord. But God was not concerned to refute the opinion of Epicurus, who denied the existence and unity of God and thought that God is the soul of the celestial sphere, for he can be convinced by conclusive, rational arguments; whereas the other opinions needed refutation, as we have explained.

That our explanation of the purpose of the first two commandments [namely, to refute the opinions of the philosophers] is correct, is proved by the fact that immediately after the Sinaitic revelation Moshe was told, "Thus thou shalt say unto the children of Israel: Ye yourselves have seen that I have talked with you from heaven. Ye shall not make with Me gods of silver, or gods of gold …" It seems very strange that immediately after the ten commandments we have again a prohibition of idolatry, which has already been forbidden in the second commandment. But the meaning is this. He explains once more that the erroneous idea of the philosophers, namely that God being exalted and dwelling in heaven is too dignified to have anything to do with corporeal things, and that He does not provide for the human race because man is inferior and despised and unworthy of such dignity; or the idea that there is need of figures or other mediators between Him and us through whom God's spiritual power may descend, - these were the cause of Israel's mistake in making the calf. Therefore, He says, "Ye yourselves have seen that I have talked with you from heaven." That is to say, you have seen that though I am exalted in heaven, I lowered My dignity, and did not refrain from speaking to you, though all of you except Moshe were unprepared for such a dignity. This shall be an indication to you that I provide for man though he is inferior and despised and unworthy of My providence. Therefore, "Ye shall not make with Me gods of silver, or gods of gold," so as to cause My spirit to descend; for My influence can be obtained with something less valuable - "An altar of earth thou shalt make unto Me;" "I dwell in the high and holy place, with him also that is of a contrite and humble spirit;" or even with something less substantial than this, namely with prayer - "In every place where I cause My name to be mentioned I will come unto thee and bless thee;" i.e., I will cause My blessing to emanate upon you. In this way were refuted those opinions which led to error and idolatry, so prevalent in those days.

It might seem, however, that the first two commandments would be sufficient. But one might say that the first two commandments do not necessarily show that there is special providence in human affairs. For they deal only with God Himself, and prohibit substitution of other worship for the worship of God. This proves only general providence of the species as a whole, but not special and individual providence, since the first two commandments say nothing about the conduct of men in their relations to one another, which would indicate special providence. For this reason, it was necessary to give them on the same occasion other commandments, necessary to teach revelation and providence, as will be explained later with the help of God.

The difference between the first two commandments and the rest is that the first two Israel heard from God without the mediation of Moshe. Therefore, they are expressed in the first person, "I am the Lord thy God," "Thou shalt have no other gods before Me," "For I the Lord thy God am a jealous God," "Of them that love Me and keep My commandments." But beginning with the third commandment, all is in the third person, because Moshe was speaking to them in the name of God - "Thou shalt not take the name of the Lord thy God in vain, for the Lord will not hold him guiltless that taketh His name in vain," instead of, "I will not hold guiltless," or "taketh My name." Similarly, we read, "For in six days the Lord made," "And rested on the seventh day, wherefore the Lord blessed the sabbath day," instead of "I made," "I blessed," "I sanctified," and so on. This shows the difference between the first two commandments and the rest. The first two they heard directly from God without the mediation of Moshe, whereas in the others they heard the voice speaking to Moshe, and Moshe then explained the words to the people. Hence, they are in the third person, as we explained.

This is what the Rabbis mean when they say, "They heard the first two commandments from the mouth of the Almighty [strength]." The meaning is that since God spoke these two commandments to Israel Himself, face to face, without the mediation of Moshe, no prophet has the power to say anything against them, or to weaken them in any way, even as a temporary measure. This is why they use the expression, "from the mouth of the Almighty," and not "from the mouth of God," to indicate that anything which is told through a prophet another prophet has the power to abolish, either as a temporary measure, or as circumstances determine, as for instance Jeremiah abolished the counting of the months from Nisan. But that which is told to a person by God without the mediation of a prophet, no prophet has the power to abolish even temporarily. Hence the statement of the Rabbis, "If a prophet tells the people to worship idols, even temporarily, he must not be obeyed; but if he says that we should violate the Sabbath or transgress some one of the commandments as a temporary measure, or even permanently, provided he does not subvert the foundations of the religion, we must listen to him, because it says, "Unto him ye shall hearken." And if he says, God commanded me that you shall pray to a certain star or a certain angel that he should be a mediator between Him and you, we must not pay any attention to him, because it is in opposition to the first two commandments, which we heard from God, and no prophet may listen to another prophet trying to abolish something which he himself heard from God, as we explained in the beginning of this chapter.

Chapter 19

From what we have said it is clear that a divine law can not change in respect to the three general principles which we mentioned. For when they heard the first two commandments from God, they were convinced of the reality of revelation and the existence of God who gave the commandments, also that He takes notice of, and punishes those who transgress His will, while He rewards those who fear Him, freeing them from bondage, as they saw how He punished the Egyptians and delivered the Israelites. The expression, "Who brought thee out of the land of Egypt, out of the house of bondage," shows the extent of divine providence, from which we conclude that we must not worship any one else even as a mediator. All this is contained in the expression, "Thou shalt have no other gods before Me," as we have seen. It is clear, therefore, as we have written in the twenty-fifth chapter of the First Book, that the difference between divine laws does not lie in their general principles. What still remains to be explained is whether the other commandments in the law of Moshe may be changed by a prophet or not.

Now as there is a difference between the first two commandments and the others in that the former were spoken by God without the mediation of Moshe, while the latter, though heard from God, were explained by Moshe, so we can say that there is a difference between the ten commandments and the other precepts in that the ten commandments were heard from God, whereas the others were commanded by Moshe. And as we have found that the last eight commandments of the decalogue may be changed by a prophet temporarily, so we may say that the other precepts of the Mosaic law can be changed by a prophet even permanently. And it is for this reason that they could abolish counting the months from Nisan in the time of the second temple by the command of Jeremiah, as we have seen.

But if it were true that any prophet or any one who professes to be a prophet is authorized to change any commandment of the divine law except those of the decalogue, or to say that the time has come to change it, the entire law would fall and it would have no permanence at all. On the other hand, if we say that no prophet has the right to change the commandments of the divine law given by another prophet, it would cause grave difficulty, for if this were the case, then why did Israel believe Moshe when he changed the **Noachian law** which they had received by a continuous tradition from their ancestors, who were prophets?

The changes, moreover, which Moshe introduced did not concern merely the details of conventional and positive rules, or matters which are relative to the recipients, or those things in which nations may differ and which differentiate one divine law from another, as we explained in the First Book, but they concerned also those matters in which human convention plays no part, like the laws concerning the red heifer, or the sowing of mixed seeds, or the permission to eat an animal as soon as slaughtered, though it is not yet dead, and the other things permitted to Israel, which had been forbidden to the Noahites, as we find in chapter "Arba' Mitot," for example the law that a heathen who observes the Sabbath is guilty of death, and so on. All this would indicate that a thing which is commanded by a prophet in a divine law may be changed by another prophet. How then can we tell what things may be changed or abolished by a prophet and what things may not?

Our opinion therefore is, as the matter appears from an investigation of the Torah, that one is not permitted to budge from his traditional belief which came down to him by a continuous chain of communication, going back to the teaching of a prophet, provided he is convinced that the principles, fundamental and derivative, of the belief in question are true, as we explained in the First Book of this treatise, unless he is absolutely certain that God desires to abolish the words of the first prophet from whom the traditional belief came down to him.

The manner in which one can have this latter certainty is by having an absolute verification of the genuine character of the second divine messenger. This proof can not consist in the performance of miracles, since we see many other persons who are not prophets performing miracles either by creating an illusion or by magic, like the Egyptian magicians, or through some other art. Moreover, we find that those prophets who are not sent to announce a law also perform miracles, hence we can not tell whether the miracle performed by the person in question shows that he has been sent to promulgate a law, or whether it merely indicates that he is a prophet. It is clear therefore that a miracle is no proof that the messenger is genuine, as was explained in the eighteenth chapter of the First Book, but the proof must be derived from the law of Moshe for the reason given in the eleventh chapter of the First Book. Accordingly, if his mission is proved in the same manner as was that of Moshe, it is proper to listen to the second prophet even if he desires to abolish the precepts of the first.

This is the reason why the Israelites believed the words of Moshe, even though some of his precepts were opposed to the **Noachian law**, as we said before, which they knew by tradition as divine. But they were absolutely convinced that God desired to promulgate a law through Moshe; else they would not have had the right to budge from their tradition, from the law which came down to them by an unbroken tradition from their ancestors, going back ultimately to Adam and Noah. This conviction was reached in two ways. They felt certain that the last prophet, who was introducing changes, was greater than the first; and they verified the genuineness of the last prophet's mission as firmly as that of the first. Both of these kinds of proof applied absolutely in Moshe case.

He was a greater prophet than those who lived before him, for he performed wonderful miracles, such as had never been performed before. The Bible makes this clear when it says, "And I appeared unto Abraham, unto Yitzhak, and unto Yaakov, as God Almighty, but by My name God, I made Me not known to them." The meaning is that God revealed Himself to Moshe with His great name, by means of which he was able to perform miracles openly and publicly, changing the laws of nature, such as had never been done for the earlier prophets, who could only perform invisible miracles, to deliver them from death in time of famine, and from the sword in time of war. The mission of Moshe was verified, because all Israel heard the voice speaking to Moshe, as the Bible says, "That the people may hear when I speak with thee;" for I desire to promulgate a law through thee, and this will make them believe what thou sayest. For this reason, Israel was obliged to believe his words, even

Sefer HaIkkarim — BOOK [Maamar] THRE

though he were to abolish all that was said by the prophets before him, since his mission was verified, as we explained in the eighteenth chapter of the First Book, and his prophetic grade was superior to all the rest, as we explained in chapter ten of this Book. Whether in the future there may come another prophet who will abolish the words of Moshe and whom we shall be obliged to believe - this can happen only, as we have said, in one of two ways. Either the new prophet will be proved to be greater than Moshe, or his mission will be verified as was that of Moshe. Now the Bible says that there can not be a prophet greater than Moshe, "If there be a prophet among you, I the Lord do make Myself known unto him in a vision, ... My servant Moshe is not so; he is trusted in all My house; with him do I speak mouth to mouth." It seems then that Moshe' prophecy is superior to any other. And at the end of the Torah we read that there will never arise another prophet like Moshe whom God knew face to face. This is the degree which Moshe asked for and it was granted to him, as we read at the end of the Torah, "And there hath not arisen a prophet since in Israel like unto Moshe, whom the Lord knew face to face."

Therefore if any prophet or any one professing to be a prophet should come and say that he has attained a higher grade than Moshe, which is impossible, and should say that we should listen to him and abolish any of the commands of Moshe, not as a temporary measure merely, we will refuse to listen to him, but will tell him that he must prove his superiority to Moshe and all the prophets who came after him and who were his disciples, by performing miracles greater and more wonderful than those performed by Moshe and all the other prophets; by humiliating all those who dispute with him, as Moshe did to Korah and his assembly; by triumphing over and overcoming all the wise men of his age and all his opponents, as Moshe did to Pharaoh and to all the magicians and wise men of Egypt; by performing miracles in public and in the presence of all the people, as Moshe did in the presence of Pharaoh and of all Israel; and by maintaining the miracles a long time, as Moshe caused to go before the people a pillar of cloud by day and a pillar of fire by night, and caused the manna to come down for forty years without ceasing, except on the Sabbath day, when it did not come down, in order to show the sanctity of the Sabbath and the truth of his words; and by fulfilling many other conditions of this kind, without which he can not make good his claim.

The reason the Israelites obeyed Jeremiah and abolished counting the months from Nisan, as we have seen, is perhaps because they

Sefer HaIkkarim — BOOK [Maamar] THRE

based their action upon the interpretation of a biblical verse, as we find in the Tosafot on the first chapter of the treatise Megillah, that the reason Ezra changed the written characters when he returned from the exile was because of his interpretation of a biblical verse. "He shall write him a copy of this law [התורה משנה]," he interpreted to mean, a writing that is destined to change [mishne, משנה, from the rabbinic shanah, שנה, to change]. Or it may be that they obeyed Jeremiah because his precept did not concern any of the ten commandments, or because there was no intention to abolish any of the Mosaic commandments, but to commemorate the second redemption as they commemorated the first. For they had a tradition that it should be commemorated, provided that the exodus from Egypt should not be ignored, as the Rabbis say, "Not that the exodus from Egypt should be entirely removed."

But if a prophet or one professing to be a prophet should come and say that he has been sent by God to promulgate a law, abolishing permanently the words of Moshe, he must not be believed so far as concerns the ten commandments, since they were heard from God. But neither must he be believed in respect to the other commandments outside of the decalogue, unless he can verify his mission as Moshe verified his, when all Israel heard the voice saying to Moshe, "Go say to them: Return ye to your tents. But as for thee, stand thou here by Me, and I will speak unto thee all the commandment, and the statutes, and the ordinances, which thou shalt teach them."

This is the reason why God revealed Himself to all Israel and spoke to them face to face, in order that Moshe' mission should be absolutely verified. Therefore, God said to Moshe, "Lo, I come unto thee in a thick cloud, that the people may hear when I speak with thee, and may also believe thee forever." The meaning is: God said to Moshe that He desired to reveal Himself to him face to face despite the fact that he [Moshe] was in a thick cloud, i.e., wrapped in the coarseness and obscurity of matter and unworthy of such a dignity, for the sake of two advantages to follow: one was with reference to the immediate present, namely, "that the people may hear when I speak with thee," and obey all his commandments even if they are opposed to the **Noachian law**. The other concerned the future: that they should believe in Moshe forever as the messenger of God.

Hence, they will not listen to any prophet who may come to abolish the words of Moshe, unless they hear from God that he was sent for that purpose. For to obey a prophet and permanently violate a

Sefer HaIkkarim — BOOK [Maamar] THREE

Mosaic command, is like obeying a prophet and violating that which one has heard from God Himself. In such a case one must not obey a prophet. It is for a thing of this kind that the prophet Iddo was punished by being devoured by a lion, because he obeyed another prophet and violated that which he himself heard from God. It is clear therefore that we must believe no one, whether he be a prophet or one professing to be a prophet, if he says that he was sent by God to abolish the words of Moshe, or if he says that they are temporary and that the time has come for their abolition, unless his mission can be proved as publicly as the mission of Moshe was proved in the presence of six hundred thousand people.

As to the question whether there will ever be in the future such a great publicity as the first, when all Israel will hear the voice of the Lord God speaking to them out of the midst of the fire, the opinion of our Rabbis is that there will be such an event. Thus, we read in **Midrash Hazit**, on the biblical verse, "Let him kiss me with the kisses of his mouth," "Said Rabbi Yehuda, when the Israelites heard the first two commandments, the Torah was impressed upon their minds and they learned without forgetting. Then they came to Moshe and said, Moshe our teacher, you be the messenger between us, as is said, 'Speak thou with us and we will hear.' Thereupon they learned and later forgot. They said then, as Moshe who is made of flesh and blood is temporary, so is his teaching temporary, i.e., it is forgotten. Hence, they went back to Moshe and said: we should wish that God would reveal Himself to us again, 'Let Him kiss me with the kisses of His mouth.' Said Moshe in reply, not now, but in the future He will, as is written, 'I will put My law in their inward parts.' " It is clear from this that the Rabbis are of the opinion that in the future all Israel will experience a second revelation like the first, which will come directly from God without any mediation.

My own opinion is that since this does not necessarily follow from an interpretation of the biblical verses, it is more proper to say that this matter depends upon the will of God. According to the Torah it belongs neither to the category of the necessary nor to that of the impossible. Our position at present is that of a prophet who heard something from God. He must not listen to any other prophet who advises him to act contrary to the command he himself received from God, unless he himself hears to the same effect from God. And even if we can verify the mission of a new prophet as the mission of Moshe was verified, we will refuse to listen to him if he bids us abolish any one of the ten commandments which we ourselves heard from God.

Sefer HaIkkarim   BOOK [Maamar] THRE

In this way we can reply to our opponents, who argue from the verse in the Torah: "I will raise them up a prophet from among their brethren, like unto thee; and I will put My words in his mouth, and he shall speak unto them all that I shall command him." This verse signifies, they say, that a law will be given through the new prophet as it was given through Moshe; also, that "from among their brethren," means from the brethren of Israel and not from Israel itself. Our reply to these men is that granting that, according to the verse quoted, a prophet will come to give a law, as Moshe did before, the expression, "I will raise them up a prophet ... like unto thee," signifies that his "raising up" and the verification of his prophetic mission, which is a fundamental dogma of divine law, as we have seen, must be of the same kind as the verification of Moshe' prophetic mission, which took place in the presence of six hundred thousand people, so that there was no doubt and no suspicion of any kind.

Chapter 20

An opponent might say that the passage in the Torah, "If there be a prophet among you, I the Lord do make Myself known unto him in a vision, I do speak with him in a dream. My servant Moshe is not so ...," has reference merely to Aaron and Miriam, but there may be in the future a prophet like Moshe or even greater. Similarly, the expression, "And there hath not arisen a prophet since in Israel like unto Moshe," does not signify that there will never be another like him or even greater than he. For we find similar expressions where we know that another like the persons so characterized will arise in the future. Thus, we find in reference to Hezekiah, "After him was none like him among all the kings of Yehuda, nor among them that were before him." Similarly in reference to Josiah we find, "And like unto him was there no king before him, that turned to the Lord ... neither after him arose there any like him." And yet it is not possible that there shall never arise another like him or even greater than he, for the Messianic king will be equal to him or greater. The expression, "there has not arisen like him," does not mean that there will never arise a person like him, but that in some specific attribute there will be none like him, or the meaning is that there was no one like him in the entire period of the kings until the exile when the kingdom was cut off from the seed of David, but not that there will never be another like him. There is no reason therefore why we should not say the same here. "There hath not arisen a prophet since in Israel like unto Moshe," means that there was none like him in the entire period of the prophets until the prophetic institution ceased; but there will be another in the future like him or even a greater than he. As for the word "since" [עוד], which is used in reference to Moshe and not in the other cases cited, the word "since" [עוד] denotes a short time, as, "Let him drink, and forget his poverty, and remember his misery no more [עוד]". עוד denotes here the time during which the effect of the wine is still present. Similarly, "Neither shall they learn war any more [עוד]," means in that generation. Also, "The vile person shall be no more [עוד] called liberal," is to be explained in the same way.

The answer to such an argument is that our conviction concerning the superiority of Moshe as a prophet does not rest merely upon the verses quoted, else the opponent might say that the passage reads, "hath not arisen in Israel," but he might have arisen among other nations. The real basis of our opinion is that Moshe asked of God that Israel and himself should be raised above all other nations in respect to prophetic inspiration. This is what he asked for when he said, "So that we are distinguished, I and Thy people, from all the people that are upon the face of the earth." He asked of God two things, first, that no nation should be equal to Israel, i.e., that the Shekinah should not rest upon the idolatrous nations and give them prophetic inspiration. So, our Rabbis say, "Moshe asked that the Shekinah should not rest upon the idolatrous nations, and his request was granted." Second, he asked that no man should be equal to him in prophetic power, hence he said, "I and Thy people." Just as he asked that no nation should be equal to Israel in having the Shekinah rest upon them, as our Rabbis say, so it seems that in the word "I" he asked that no one should be equal to him as a prophet.

In reply to this he was told, "I will do this thing also that thou hast spoken, for thou hast found grace in My sight, and I know thee by name." God therefore granted the elevation which he sought. This is the reason why the Torah testifies about him at the end that a prophet will never arise again like Moshe; even in Israel, which has the prerogative of the prophetic institution, there will never arise another like him, as he was promised; not to speak of the other nations, who are not worthy of the prophetic spirit. The Rabbis indeed say, commenting on the passage, "And there hath not arisen a prophet since in Israel like Moshe," there hath not arisen in Israel, but there hath arisen among the heathen, namely Balaam. By this they mean to say that just as Moshe' prophetic power was given to him for the sake of Israel, as we explained in chapter twelve of this

Sefer HaIkkarim   BOOK [Maamar] THRE

Book, so Balaam owed the degree of prophetic power which he attained, though only a diviner, solely to Israel, namely in order that he should bless them. They can not mean that Balaam's prophetic power was equal to that of Moshe, Heaven forbid! God had promised him, "I will do this thing also that thou hast spoken, for thou hast found grace in My sight, and I know thee by name." In other words, God granted his request that no prophet should be equal to him in prophetic power, and that the gift of prophecy should not be given to the Gentiles.

Moshe, seeing that God granted his request, inferred from these two things: First, that prophecy does not come to a man by nature, but by the will of God. Hence God granted Moshe' request that the prophetic gift should not be given to the heathen. For if prophetic inspiration came by nature, God would not deprive mankind of their natural good by refusing prophecy to the heathen. Second: he inferred that his own prophetic gift would be something miraculous, transcending the power of the human mind, which the latter could not grasp by means of prophetic inspiration even through the Torah, and even though he was prepared for it. For if his power had been such as the human mind was itself capable of attaining, God would not have promised as he did, "I know thee by name," and that no prophet would arise in Israel like Moshe. God does not deprive any one of his natural benefits, so as to refuse the gift of prophecy to a member of the people of Israel, the nation that is chosen as a seat of the prophetic gift, if he is prepared for it. But if Moshe' prophetic power was a miraculous thing, and a result of extraordinary divine grace, such as human nature alone can not attain, God could have promised that He would not lend such grace to any one else.

Now Moshe, having perceived that the moment was propitious for obtaining grace, added another request, namely, "Show me, I pray Thee, Thy glory." Moshe thought that since God consented to give him special grace, such as no man can attain, He would also consent by special grace to let him see or apprehend the divine glory, though it is not in the nature of man to have such apprehension. The reply to this was, "Thou canst not see My face, for man can not see Me and live." Our Rabbis explain this to mean, not even the angels, who are ever-living. The meaning of the reply is, then, this: Do not think that the reason I withhold this power from you is because it is not in the nature of man to have it, but because it is not even in the nature of the ever-living angels to have such power. Therefore, you can not attain such a degree, for it is enough if you attain to the power of apprehension of angels, more than that you cannot have. For this reason, he did not withhold from him the apprehension of the "back," i.e., a knowledge of the manner in which existing things result from God's causality. He withheld from him only an apprehension of His "face", i.e., a knowledge of God's essence, which no one but God Himself can have.

It follows, then, as a result of what we have said, that since God granted Moshe' request, as He said, "I know thee by name," we must understand the verse, "And there hath not arisen a prophet since in Israel like Moshe," to signify a permanent miracle showing the superiority of Moshe as a prophet to all the prophets who came after him. Therefore, no prophet has the authority to oppose Moshe' words.

Now it would seem according to this that the superiority of Moshe as a prophet should be counted as a special and separate dogma of the Mosaic law, because it signifies the perpetuity of the latter. But an opponent may object to our interpretation. He may say, it is true that no prophet like Moshe or greater than he will arise in Israel, but he may arise among the other nations, as our Rabbis say by way of comment on the verse, "He shall be exalted and lifted up, and shall be very high:" He shall be exalted above Abraham, and shall be higher than Moshe, from which it seems that there may arise one greater than Moshe. For this reason, we regard this point as a derivative dogma under the principle of the genuineness of the messenger, and not as an independent dogma. Our idea is this. Granting that their interpretation is correct and there may arise in the future another prophet as great as Moshe, we can not believe such a prophet or one professing to be a prophet in opposition to Moshe unless we are clearly convinced of the genuineness of his mission. This means that his mission as the promulgator of a law must be verified in the presence of six hundred thousand people, as the mission of Moshe was verified.

Whether such a thing will ever happen in the future, that all the people at once will hear the voice of God speaking out of the midst of the fire, as was the case with Moshe - this is something that is hidden from us and can not concern us, as it depends solely upon the wisdom of God. But as long as a prophet's mission is not verified in this manner, we will pay no attention to any one who comes to abolish permanently the commands of Moshe.

There is something strange, however, in Maimonides' procedure. After having laid down the superiority of Moshe' prophetic power as a principal dogma, and explained the differences between Moshe as a prophet and the others, saying that all the prophets who came before Moshe, as well as those who came after him, were inferior to him, he adds as another dogma, the irrepealability and immutability of the law. From this it would seem that he thought that if not for the latter dogma, we might have to obey a prophet who desired to abolish the laws of Moshe. But how can that be? How can we listen to an inferior prophet and abolish the laws of Moshe, the greatest of all the prophets, as he himself says? Unless we say that his interpretation of the verse, "And there hath not arisen a prophet since in Israel like Moshe," is that it refers to the period of the prophets, but that in the future there may arise a prophet equal to Moshe. Therefore, there is the need of an additional dogma, the irrepealability of the Law. But we have made it clear that there can not arise at any time another prophet greater than Moshe or equal to him; and that it is not proper to listen to an inferior prophet at any time who desires to abolish the laws of his superior. But inasmuch as the opponent may obstinately insist that there may arise in the future among the other nations a prophet equal to Moshe or greater than he, we did not lay down the superiority of Moshe as a basic dogma, but only as a derivative dogma depending upon the dogma of the genuineness of the prophet's mission. The result is that we can not permanently abolish the laws of Moshe at any time unless we can verify the prophet's mission in the way in which the mission of Moshe was verified. Hence, we do not have to regard the irrepealability of the Law as a main principle or dogma, as Maimonides did. For we have made clear that there is no evidence of it in the Torah. It is not therefore an independent principle, but a true belief, which depends upon the genuineness of the prophet's mission, as we explained. The same idea seems to be contained in the words of our Rabbis in **Torat Kohanim**. Commenting on the verse in Leviticus, they say: "These are the commandments" - this shows that hereafter no prophet is authorized to make changes; "Which the Lord commanded Moshe" - the messenger is worthy of the one who sent him. We see here that the Rabbis attach the perpetuity of the Law and the commandments to the mission of the prophet. This is what we desired to explain.

Chapter 21

The Torah is called "testimony" [עדות], as we read, "And in the ark thou shalt put the testimony;" "If thy children keep My covenant and My testimony that I shall teach them." This is to signify that the Torah must be understood literally like the testimony of witnesses.

Sefer HaIkkarim — BOOK [Maamar] THRE

When witnesses testify, we do not say let us change the time or interpret the testimony so that the witnesses shall not be guilty of perjury. For example, if they testified that Reuben killed Simeon on the first day of the week, and their testimony is proved false, we do not say let us interpret their testimony so that they shall not be false witnesses, viz. that "on the first day of the 'week' " means on the first of the seven years ending with the sabbatical year; or that "killed" means did not give him alms to support him, or did not teach him Torah, which would give him life in the world to come. We do not say all this because testimony must be understood literally, and if witnesses are shown to have given false testimony, they must be put to death, and we do not interpret their words so as to save them from death. In the same way the law of God is called testimony because the commandments must be understood literally. We must not give them figurative interpretations and read into them conditions or time limitations which are not there.

Therefore, David said, "The testimony of the Lord is sure," i.e., it is true as written. And the burden of proof is upon him who gives figurative interpretations, saying for example that the prohibition of swine's flesh was temporary, or that 'swine' means the evil instinct, and so on, or that the important thing in the Torah is belief and not performance of the commandments. He can not abolish the literal meaning of the commandments by imposing a condition or time limitation which is not mentioned. This is what the Psalmist meant when he said, "The proud have digged pits for me, which is not according to Thy law." Then he explains that the pits are their statement that, "All Thy commandments are only a matter of belief [אמונה]", and that their time has already passed and there is no need of performing the commandments at all. And with this "falsehood they pursue me." Therefore, "Help Thou me," for I need Thy help, else, "They had almost consumed me upon the earth." But with all that, "I forsook not Thy precepts." He ends up, "Quicken me after Thy loving kindness, and I will observe the testimony of Thy mouth." The meaning is: they had almost consumed me, but Thou with Thy loving kindness quicken me, and I will keep the commandments according to their literal meaning, for they are the testimony of Thy mouth, i.e., they are like testimony, which must be understood literally. No man has the power to abolish the literal meaning of the commandments by interpretation.

Though there are many passages in the Torah concerning which all the wise men agree that they bear allusion to noble, sublime and intellectual things, like the story of the Garden of Eden, and the four rivers, and so on, nevertheless they do not deny the reality of the literal meaning. Their opinion is that while those things do exist in reality, they at the same time bear allusion to more noble and celestial things. Thus, the account of the Tabernacle refers to real things, and at the same time bears allusion to sublime and celestial things. In the same way the human organism has by nature a tongue, teeth and lips for eating, the same as in the lower animals, but at the same time they exist in man for a nobler purpose also, namely as organs of speech and expression to laud God and speak His praises, which is a nobler purpose than that which they serve in animals. So, in the world of nature, we find four rivers and so on, which at the same time allude to more noble things. In this way the Rabbis say, Yerushalayim on earth is representative of Yerushalayim in heaven. In saying this they do not mean to deny that Yerushalayim does exist on earth and serves an important purpose, namely as the dwelling place of the Shekinah. Nor do we deny the existence of Ezekiel for an important purpose in himself like any other righteous man, because the Bible says, "Thus shall Ezekiel be unto you as a sign." In the same way we must understand that there are in the Torah expressions which allude to other nobler and more sublime things, and yet are also true in their literal meaning. This is especially true of the commandments. They do allude to noble and sublime things, but at the same time there is an important purpose in themselves and in their performance. This is the reason why the Torah is called testimony, as we have explained, namely to signify that the words are true in their literal meaning, and that they must not be interpreted figuratively so as to abolish the literal meaning.

Chapter 22

The Torah which we have to-day and which has been handed down to us by unbroken tradition from father to son is the same that was given to Moshe on Sinai, without any change. It could not have received change in the time of the first temple when the priests and teachers were in the temple and the Torah was well known to everybody. And though there were among them kings who worshipped idols, they also had prophets during the entire period until the time of the destruction, who admonished the people to observe the Torah. And as for the great alarm which Josiah felt when the priest Hilkiah found a book of the Torah in the house of the Lord, this does not signify that they had no copy of the Torah, for Jeremiah was alive then. But the reason was this. Amon and Menasseh were

Sefer HaIkkarim — BOOK [Maamar] THREE

worshippers of idols and offended God, so much so that our Rabbis say, Menasseh cut the names of God out of the Torah and substituted names of idols in their place. Accordingly, one of the priests who feared that the king might do the same with the original copy of the Torah which Moshe wrote, if it got into his hands, hid it in the walls of the building. Later, in the days of Josiah, who returned to the Lord with all his heart, with all his soul and with all his might in accordance with the law of Moshe, they looked for this book and could not find it. And when they repaired the temple, Hilkiah found it in the wall and was very much elated over it, as if he had found a great treasure. He then sent a message to the king, saying, I have found the book of the Law, the well-known book which Moshe wrote; he did not say I found a book of the law. Now the reason that king Josiah was so alarmed at the find and rent his garments when he heard the words of the book, is as our Rabbis explain in the Yerushalayim Talmud. The Torah which Moshe wrote was rolled up so that it opened on the beginning of Genesis, whereas the manuscript which they found opened on the verse in Deuteronomy: "The Lord will bring thee, and thy king whom thou shalt set over thee, unto a nation that thou hast not known." This is the reason why the king was alarmed, and not because the people had forgotten the Torah, God forbid!

Nor could the Torah have undergone change when the Israelites were exiled to Babylon. For in the beginning of the exile under Jehoiachin, before the destruction of the temple, the craftsmen and the smiths and the leaders of the wise men of Israel were exiled, Daniel was among them and also the prophet Ezekiel, as we read, "One that had escaped out of Yerushalayim came unto me, saying: 'The city is smitten'." And all the Jewish exiles who were scattered through all the land of Assyria had in their possession a copy of the Law, for even the Cutheans, whom the king of Assyria settled in the cities of Samaria, had a copy of the Torah. When the temple was destroyed, the Torah had already spread through all Babylonia and could not have undergone any change by reason of the destruction of the temple.

When Ezra returned from Babylon, only a few went with him, while the leaders of Israel and the wise men and those of noble lineage, all remained in Babylon. Thus, our Rabbis say, Ezra did not leave Babylon until he made it like fine flour; that is to say, he left those of pure descent and took with him those who were not pure, because he knew that in Palestine, he would be able to prevent the Israelites from mixing with them. Thus, none of the tribe of Levi returned with him, as we read: "And I viewed the people and the priests, and found there none of the sons of Levi." He, therefore, sent to Babylon, and they sent him eighteen persons of the sons of **Mahli**. Since, therefore, all the great men who were conversant with the Torah remained in Babylon, Ezra would not have dared to make any changes in the Torah, for then his Torah would not have agreed with that of all those who remained in Babylon, and who lived in the cities of Samaria and in the land of Assyria and in other places, who refused to return with him.

It is true that he changed the mode of writing, as we said before, in commemoration of the second deliverance, but he was not authorized to make any changes in the content of the Torah. Changing the count of the months from Tishri instead of from Nisan was not regarded as a real change, because in the Torah also Tishri was the first month when they computed the sabbatical and the jubilee years. It is possible that they were told by Jeremiah, who in turn had a tradition going back through the prophets to Moshe, that they should commemorate the second deliverance so long as they retained the Passover, which was in memory of the exodus from Egypt, in its original place. But he did not change anything of the contents of the Torah. The differences in word and expression which are found in the Torah among the other nations are due to errors of translation into the other languages by unskilled persons. The Jews were very careful about the letters of the Torah, the plene and defective writings. They prided themselves on knowing the number of letters and verses, which they recorded in the margins of their copies, calling it Masorah - a practice which the other nations did not follow. "Why were they [sc. the Scribes] called - **Soferim** [counters]? Because they counted all the letters of the Torah." This shows that they kept it in the form in which it was given to Moshe without any change. A proof of this is that the Torah is exactly the same to-day without any change among all Israel who are scattered all over the world from the extreme east to the farthest west.

The Rabbis speak of certain words in the Torah as being corrections of the Scribes, for example in reference to the verse, "But Abraham stood yet before the Lord," they say that the reading ought to be, "The Lord stood yet before Abraham," but the expression was changed by the Scribes. Also, "Let me not look upon my wretchedness," they say, is a correction of the Scribes for "Let me not look upon Thy wretchedness," and they say the same thing about other expressions. But this does not mean that anybody changed any words in the Torah, God forbid! No one who falsifies a book would

Sefer HaIkkarim — BOOK [Maamar] THREE

admit that he falsified it or made changes in it. How then could the Rabbis say that the **Soferim** [Scribes] made changes? The meaning is that from the context it would seem that Moshe should have said, "Let me not look upon Thy wretchedness." The reason for the changed reading, "my wretchedness," is like a correction which a scribe makes out of respect to God. Moshe was not speaking in reference to himself, but in reference to God, but he changed the expression by divine order, as a scribe changes an expression by way of euphemism. The other instances must be explained in the same way. Similarly, we must explain the dots which we find in the Torah over the word ואהרן [and Aaron] in the verse, "Whom Moshe and Aaron numbered;" over the words ולבנינו לנו [unto us and to our children], and in other passages. The word in question remains in the text, and the dot indicates something intermediate between retaining the word and deleting it. The meaning is that though the text reads, "Whom Moshe and Aaron numbered," the one who did the numbering was Moshe, while Aaron was merely with him, and his name is mentioned out of respect, for Moshe was the important person in the act and not Aaron. Similarly, the dots on ולבנינו לנו are intended to show that though children may be obligated by the parents, the obligation is not of the same degree as when the parents obligate themselves. The other cases must be explained in a similar manner.

Chapter 23

A thing is perfect if we can not conceive it to receive addition or diminution. Now since David characterizes the Torah as perfect, it follows that it can not in any respect be deficient in the realization of its purpose. Now every written document of whatever nature it be, can be understood in two different ways, one of which corresponds to the intention of the writer and the other is very far from it. Thus, Maimonides says in his epistle on resurrection that the expression, "Hear O Israel, the Lord our God, the Lord is One," is understood by the Jews to mean absolute unity, whereas the Christians interpret it to teach the Trinity. For this reason, it was necessary, in order that the divine Torah should be perfect and should be understood in the correct way, that when God gave the Torah to Moshe in writing, He should explain it to him in the proper manner. Similarly, Moshe explained it to Yehoshua, Yehoshua to the elders, the elders to the prophets, and so from generation to generation, so that there should be no doubt in the correct meaning

Sefer HaIkkarim BOOK [Maamar] THRE

of the written document.

This interpretation of the written law which Moshe transmitted to Yehoshua and Yehoshua to his successors, is called the oral law, because this interpretation can not be in writing, else the same uncertainty of which we spoke would attach to this writing as to the first, and we should require an interpretation of the interpretation, and so on without end. Thus, the Mishnah, which is an interpretation of the written Torah, gave rise to doubt and confusion and required another interpretation, namely the Talmud, which Rab Ashi composed to explain the Mishnah. The Talmud, in turn, which is an interpretation of the Mishnah, required another interpretation, and so there is a multiplicity of commentaries on the Talmud and a variety of opinions, and the same is true of the commentaries. It is clear, therefore, that the written Torah can not be perfect unless it is accompanied by this oral interpretation, which is called the oral law. This is why the Rabbis say, God made a covenant with Israel only for the sake of the oral law. This is because the written law can not be understood except with the oral law, and also because the law of God can not be perfect so as to be adequate for all times, because the ever-new details of human relations, their customs and their acts, are too numerous to be embraced in a book. Therefore, Moshe was given orally certain general principles, only briefly alluded to in the Torah, by means of which the wise men in every generation may work out the details as they appear.

These principles are mentioned in **Torat Kohanim**, in the beginning, in the baraita which begins, "Rabbi Ishmael said, thirteen rules are applied in the interpretation of the Torah, the inference from minor to major, similarity in expression ..." By means of these principles, or of any one of them, we may know something that is not explicit in the Torah. But if a thing is expressed in the Torah, or is handed down by tradition, the principles mentioned have no force to abolish the text or the tradition. Thus, we find often in the Talmud the question asked, "How do you know?" and the answer is, "It is a **Halakah** which dates from Moshe and Sinai." We also find the expression used by an opponent, "If it is a matter of tradition, we will accept it, but if it is a question of inference, we can argue against it."

A point which is not handed down by tradition, but is the result of applying one of the thirteen principles or some other mode of inference, is liable to be the subject of difference of opinion among the learned men of Israel. Hence in order to remove dispute as much as possible and make the Torah perfect, divine wisdom decreed that the decision in every generation should belong to the majority of the learned, as we read, "To incline after the many;" also, "Thou shalt not turn aside from the sentence which they shall declare unto thee, to the right hand, nor to the left." The Rabbis comment on this: Even if they tell thee the right is left and the left is right. The meaning is this: Every person thinks he has more understanding, judgment and common sense than the other, and thus even fools and women and ignorant persons speak disrespectfully of the learned and think they have more understanding than the latter. Hence the text says that even if it appears to one that the learned call the right left and the left right, he must not deviate from their decision, and the power of deciding must always be given to the majority of the learned. And though it is possible that a single individual may be wiser than every one of them, and his view more in agreement with the truth than that of all the rest, nevertheless the rule is as the majority decide, and an individual has no authority to oppose them in a practical decision.

This was the point of the dispute between Rabbi Yehoshua and Rabbi Eliezer in the Talmud **Baba Mezi'a**. For though Rabbi Eliezer was more learned than all the rest, and a voice from heaven said, "Why do you dispute with Rabbi Eliezer? He is right every time," nevertheless Rabbi Yehoshua stood his ground and said, "The law is not in heaven," i.e., though the truth may be in the opinion of Rabbi Eliezer, we must not ignore the opinion of the majority and follow an individual, for the Torah was given to us on Mount Sinai, and therein is written, "Incline after the many." If we abandon the majority and follow an individual in one matter, there will be a serious division in Israel in every generation. For every individual will claim that he is right and that the law shall be as he decides. This would destroy the Torah entirely. We must not therefore abandon the general rule, which is to follow the majority and ignore the individual or the minority, provided, however, that the majority consists of learned men and not ignoramuses, for the masses and the ignorant people are easily persuaded of a thing that is not so, and strenuously insist that it is.

Solomon admonishes us against following the masses, for they agree on many things which are not true. The masses "do not despise a thief, if he steals to satisfy his soul when he is hungry." They are agreed on this and do not condemn it, but they are wrong; "But if he be found he must restore sevenfold, He must give all the substance of his house," according to the laws of the Torah, which says, "If he have nothing, then he shall be sold for his theft." Similarly, the masses are of the opinion that an adulterer does not deserve punishment, for they say, "He that committeth adultery with a woman lacketh understanding," and should be pitied, for he does harm to himself and destroys his own soul. He does the wrong and the evil to himself, but no sensible person does injury to himself, therefore the common people say that he lacketh understanding and should not be punished. But they are wrong, for "Wounds and dishonor shall he get ... For jealousy is the rage of a man, and he will not spare in the day of vengeance. He will not regard any ransom; neither will he rest content, though thou givest many gifts." Therefore, the agreement of the masses is no argument, as they are often agreed in opposition to the truth. In the days of Ahab and Menasseh and their like, all agreed on the worship of idols except the prophets and their disciples. Therefore, the decision belongs to the majority of the learned men only, for wisdom is a gift of God, "For the Lord giveth wisdom, Out of His mouth cometh knowledge and discernment." In this way will the Torah of the Lord be perfect in every generation, and free from any deficiency.

Chapter 24

This divine Torah of Moshe embraces in general three parts, representing three different elements, namely, wisdom, will, power. The first part embraces true ideas, and is called "words," as we read: "These words the Lord spoke unto all your assembly ...;" also, "And he wrote upon the tables the words of the covenant, the ten words," because of the theoretical ideas it contains, such as concerning the existence of God, divine revelation of the Torah, Providence, the incorporeality of God, the creation of the world, and so on. This part comes from the influence of God's wisdom, i.e., it comes from God as wise.

The second part embraces those things which are desired by God. These come from His will and show that God has will. They go by the name of "statutes," and embrace all those commandments whose reason is not known, such as the prohibition of swine's flesh, or of wearing garments of wool and flax mixed, or of sowing diver's seeds, or the commandment concerning the red heifer, and so on, which are royal fiats, things which God willed after He commanded them. Thus, our Rabbis say: What difference can it make to God whether one slaughters an animal by cutting its throat or by breaking its neck? God simply takes pleasure in having His will carried out. Similarly in relation to the offerings, they comment on the expression, "A fire offering and a sweet smell," saying, it is a pleasure to Me to have My will carried out.

The third part embraces the doing of right and the removing of evil in human relations. These are called "judgments," and emanate from God's power.

Now it is clear that a conventional law can not include the first part, namely true ideas, for, as we said in this Book, the important principles upon which these ideas depend are still the subject of dispute. Nor can it include the second part, namely the statutes, or those things which God desires, for the human mind has no way of knowing in detail the things which God desires, except by means of prophetic inspiration, as we explained above. It is therefore concerned mainly with the third part, namely, judgments, endeavoring as it does to remove wrong from among men and to establish right, and establishing law and justice in human relations, so as to make society perfect.

But when we consider the matter carefully, we shall find that even in matters of the third part it can not judge correctly, because it can not determine accurately what is right or just in every case. For what human knowledge can determine how much a thief shall pay, whether double or treble or four times or seven times? Some legislators provide that a thief be put to death, whether he stole much or little. But this is against human reason, for why should a man be put to death for stealing money, even if he has done it repeatedly? For this reason, the divine Torah undertook to fix different penalties for the stealing of money. Thus, one who refuses to return a deposit, and the like, which is a light kind of theft, must pay double. He who steals a sheep, must pay four sheep for one. If he steals an ox, he must pay five oxen, because the damage he caused to the owner in the loss of the ox's work, makes the crime greater than that of stealing a sheep. The reason he has to pay four-fold when he steals a sheep is because there is more damage caused to the owner than in stealing other chattels, the loss of the milk, the wool and the young. And in all these cases, "If he has nothing, then he shall be sold for his theft." This is just law and true equality, viz., that a person who causes loss to his neighbor must make compensation, and if he has no money to give, he should be sold for his theft, so that compensation should be made from his body if necessary. But that a person should be put to death for the theft of property is not true justice, except when he steals a human being. Thus, "If a man be found stealing any of his brethren of the children of Israel ... then that thief shall die," but no one else. A conventional law therefore is not able to determine what is justice and true equality in the greater part of the matters with which it deals. It was necessary, therefore, that the divine Torah in addition to the first two parts should also embrace the "judgments," in order to show that no man is able to determine true justice and decide a case correctly, except God alone. Accordingly, the Torah is divided into these three parts, in order to show God's wisdom, will and power, as we said before.

This is expressed by the Psalmist, who praises God because He bestows certain things, which show that He is wise, possessed of will and powerful, adding that God is gracious and gives of His own accord to Israel these three parts, words, statutes and judgments, which also show that He is wise, possessed of will and powerful. Hence, he says, "For it is good to sing praises unto our God; for it is pleasant and praise is comely," i.e., it is pleasant and good and becoming to exalt and praise Him about all the things which come from His wisdom and His will and His power, and which show His providence. He begins therefore with, "The Lord doth build up Yerushalayim, He gathereth together the dispersed of Israel." This shows that He has will, like a king who builds a country according to his will and admits into it any people he likes, seeing that no one can prevent him, since he is greater than all those over whom he rules, and hence can do as he pleases. Then he says, "Who healeth the broken in heart, and bindeth up their wounds." This indicates God's power. If the heart is broken, that is, if its parts are severed, there is no natural cure for it, as we are told by medical writers. Any other members if broken can be cured. Therefore, the Psalmist attributes to the Lord the cure of a broken heart, in which the parts are severed, though it can not be cured in the ord nary way. This shows His great power in delivering the oppressed from his oppressor, as David says, "The Lord is nigh unto them that are of a broken heart, and saveth such as are of a contrite spirit." The meaning is that just as God cures the broken hearted, who could not recover if left to nature, so He saves those of a crushed spirit, who can not be saved in a natural way, as Solomon says: "The spirit of a man will sustain his infirmity; but a broken spirit who can bear?" The meaning is, if a man is sick and the animal spirit is strong, he can sustain the infirmity, but if the spirit is sick and broken, who can bear it? That is, who can sustain it? For by nature, it can not get well. Then he says: "He counteth the number of the stars; He giveth them all their names." This shows God's wisdom. Then he adds: "Great is our Lord, and mighty in power; His understanding is infinite," alluding to all three attributes. "Great is our Lord," refers to will, meaning that God is great enough to do what He wills, without any one preventing Him, corresponding to "The Lord doth build up Yerushalayim." "Mighty in power," refers to His ability to heal the broken hearted, corresponding to "Who healeth the broken in heart." "His understanding is infinite," alludes to His wisdom, in that He knows the number of the stars, and the powers of each, as well as the composition of their powers with one another, corresponding to "He counteth the number of the stars." The meaning is, since His wisdom is infinite, He can embrace the infinite, much more so the number of the stars, which is necessarily finite, as there can not be an infinite number of bodies. But by reason of the immense quantity of their powers when they are combined together, he attributes the knowledge of their number and of the immense quantity of their powers when combined to infinite wisdom.

The statement of naturalists that the number of the stars is known and that it amounts to eleven hundred and twenty-two, has reference to the visible stars only. The stars which are not visible to us are very, very many, as we find in the Bible, "Behold, ye are this day as the stars of heaven for multitude," and in other passages besides. We see only a few of them because of the feebleness of our vision, but we must not say that what we can not see does not exist. The bat does not see the light of the sun, but that is no proof that it does not exist. The Psalmist proves God's wisdom from the fact that He counts the number of the stars, in order to indicate how immensely great is the result when their powers are combined, and yet they are subject to Him, and He can annul their prognostications, as His wisdom decrees. "He giveth them all their names," like a master who calls his servant to do his will.

The sequel of the Psalm contains the same idea, alluding to God's wisdom, will and power. "The Lord upholdeth the humble ...," refers to His power. "Who covereth the heaven with clouds," denotes God's wisdom. Thus, Elihu cited the wonders of the rain as proof of God's wisdom. "He delighteth not in the strength of the horse," alludes to His will, and the meaning is that His will is not in favor of horsemen or of men of stature and strong arm. But "The Lord taketh pleasure in them that fear Him, in those that wait for His mercy;" for God saves not with valor and strength. "Glorify the Lord, O Yerushalayim," corresponds to "The Lord doth build up Yerushalayim," denoting His will. The same idea is expressed in the sequel where he speaks of the rain and the other things in the world which emanate from God, to indicate that all things come from Him and point to His wisdom, will and power. Hence, he says at the end of the Psalm: "He declareth His word unto Yaakov, His statutes and His judgments unto Israel," to indicate that these three parts which the Torah embraces, namely, words, statutes and judgments, also show that He is wise, has will and has power, as we said before, and that He should be praised because He bestowed these three parts upon the entire people. This is why he calls them His words, His statutes, and His judgments. "He hath not dealt so with any nation," makes plain the great kindness which God showed to Israel in that He gave them words, statutes and judgments, by which they should guide themselves in order to acquire their human perfection - a thing which He has not done to any other nation. And even the judgments, with which conventional law is concerned and which it determines, the other nations "have not known them." For their knowledge was not sufficient to determine true justice and equality, as we explained before, hence he says: "And as for His ordinances, they have not known them." He ends up with the word "Hallelujah" [praise ye the Lord], to indicate that it is fitting to praise the Lord for the extraordinary kindness He showed Israel by providing for them in so wonderful a manner, and bestowing upon them words and statutes and judgments emanating from His wisdom, His will and His power, so as to realize the purpose of man.

Chapter 25

In a discussion I had with a Christian scholar he said to me: A thing must be tested by reference to its causes, the material, the formal, the efficient and the final. If we test the Torah of Moshe in this way, we find that it is defective in all four respects. It is defective in respect to its matter, for it contains stories and other matters which are not Torah, i.e., teaching and guidance; whereas the teaching of Jesus has nothing but instruction. It is defective in respect to the efficient cause, because it expresses the divine mysteries alluding to the Trinity in a very obscure manner, so that it is not possible to understand from it the perfection of the Maker and His attributes; while it is very clear in the teaching of Jesus the Nazarene that God is father, son and holy ghost, and that they are all one. It is defective in respect to the final cause, for it says nothing about spiritual happiness, which is the purpose of man, but speaks only of material happiness. The teaching of Jesus, on the other hand, promises spiritual happiness and not material prosperity. It is defective in respect to the formal cause, for a law should embrace three things:

Sefer HaIkkarim — BOOK [Maamar] THREE

1. The relations between man and God, i.e., commandments relating to divine worship, called ceremoniales in their language, "cere" in Greek meaning God.

2. Relations between man and man; these are judgments, called judiciales, i.e., rules and principles having their origin in the business transactions of a man with his fellow. These are necessary for the maintenance of the social group.

3. Relations between a man and himself, called morales. These are precepts which a man follows in order to acquire a good character, such as virtuous living, humility, and so on, which develop character.

Now his opinion was that if we examine the Law of Moshe in respect to these three kinds of precepts, we find that it is defective in all of them. It is defective in the duties of man to God, i.e., in the ceremonial part, which prescribes the manner of divine worship. For it commands the slaughter of animals, the burning of the flesh and the fat, the sprinkling of the blood, all of which are unclean forms of worship; whereas the manner of worship prescribed in the law of Jesus is clean, consisting of bread and wine. It is defective also in the social and judicial precepts, which concern human relations, for it permits interest, saying: "Unto a foreigner thou mayest lend upon interest;" whereas interest is destructive of social life. Also, it prescribes that an unintentional homicide should live in exile until the death of the high priest. But this is an unequal punishment, for sometimes the period is long and sometimes it is short. Moreover, an unintentional homicide is not deserving of death, and yet the law of Moshe exposes his life to the avenger of the blood, who may kill him with impunity; the result is that the intentional homicide goes free, while the unintentional loses his life. This is not so in the law of Jesus, where all depends upon the opinion of the judges. It is defective in the matter of a man's duty to himself, for the law of Moshe commands only right action, and says nothing about purity of heart; whereas the law of Jesus commands purity of heart, and thus saves man from the judgment of gehenna. This is the gist of the views of the Christian scholar.

My answer was as follows: All these statements are untrue, and are due to a lack of understanding or insight or knowledge of the ideas of the Torah. Before answering his arguments, however, I will make an introductory statement which no man of intelligence can doubt, namely that anything that is the subject of belief must be conceivable by the mind, though it may be impossible so far as nature is concerned, as was explained in the twenty-second chapter of the

Sefer HaIkkarim   BOOK [Maamar] THREE

First Book. Such natural impossibilities as the dividing of the Red Sea, the turning of the rod into a serpent, and the other miracles mentioned in the Torah or in the Prophets can be conceived by the mind, hence we can believe that God has power to produce them. But a thing which the mind can not conceive, for example that a thing should be and not be at the same time, or that a body should be in two places at the same time, or that one and the same number should be both odd and even, and so on, can not be the subject of belief, and God can not be conceived as being able to do it, as God can not be conceived able to create another like Him in every respect, or to make a square whose diagonal is equal to its side, or to make now what has happened not to have happened. For since the mind can not conceive it, God can not do it, as it is inherently impossible. Therefore, it can not be the subject of belief, for belief in impossible things does not give perfection to the soul, else reason would have been given to man to no purpose, and man would have no superiority to animals, since the mind does not affect belief.

Having made this preface, I will say that the opponent's statement that the law of Moshe is defective in respect of its matter shows his ignorance of the law of Moshe. For there is not a word and not a narrative in the law of Moshe which is not essential either to inculcate an idea or moral, or to explain one of the commandments. Even the verse, "And Timna was concubine to Eliphaz, Esau's son," serves a necessary purpose, namely to differentiate between Amalek, whose destruction is commanded in the Torah, and the other sons of Esau, concerning whom it is said: "Thou shalt not abhor an Edomite, for he is thy brother." So are all other narratives understood by the initiated, and the commentators of our Torah have explained them at length.

As for the law of Jesus, we do not find that Jesus gave a law. He commanded his followers to keep the law of Moshe. The Gospels are not a law, but an account of the life of Jesus; and the miracles which they say he performed are similar to those which we find were performed by the prophets, who did not give any law. The moral instruction in the Gospels and the teaching of right conduct are expressed altogether in the form of parables and dark sayings, which is not appropriate for a law. For it is hard to get at the meaning of anything expressed in the form of parable and metaphor. Hence the Torah says plainly in reference to the prophecy of Moshe that it was not in the form of dark sayings. For since the Torah was given through him, it was not proper that he should speak in dark sayings, like the prophets of an inferior grade. A statement expressed in the form of a parable or allegory, like the prophecies of Zechariah, has not the perfection it ought to have, for it needs explanation, and may bear many different meanings. This is why Ezekiel complained because his prophetic messages took the form of parables: "Ah Lord God! they say of me: Is he not a maker of parables;" indicating that this was a defect. And God then spoke to him in plain words. Now it is clear that a law must represent the very highest degree of prophetic message, and for this reason the Bible praises the prophecy of Moshe: "With him do I speak mouth to mouth, even manifestly, and not in dark speeches." From this it is clear that any legislative matter expressed in obscure language is defective in respect to its matter, and we come to an opposite conclusion from that of the Christian.

He also said that the Torah is defective in respect of the efficient cause, because it does not describe the attributes of God. But the very opposite is the case. The Torah expressly emphasizes the dogma of the unity and incorporeality, and makes clear that God can not be apprehended, "For man shall not see Me and live." It also declares that the conception we have of God comes from the qualities shown in His government of His creatures, as He explained to Moshe. Moshe said to God, "Show me now Thy ways, that I may know Thee, to the end that I may find grace in Thy sight." And God replied that the thirteen attributes with which He governs His creatures are His ways, which man may know more or less, depending upon the ability of the person, but his essential attributes can not be known.

The law of Moshe says nothing about trinity because it is not true from the point of view of reason, and the Torah does not inculcate an idea which is not true, such as that one is three and three are one, while remaining separate and distinct, as they say. The statement of the philosophers that God is intellect, intelligent and intelligible, and at the same time one, is a different thing. For they do not believe that there are in Him three different things self-existing, Heaven forbid! They merely say that the one Being may be called by those three names from three different aspects. God Himself is a simple intellect without any composition. But since He is intellect, He must necessarily comprehend, therefore He is intelligent. But He comprehends nothing except Himself, for His perfection can not depend upon another, so that the other should cause Him to pass from potentiality to actuality. Hence, from this point of view, He is always intelligible, and yet His unity is not in any way changed to plurality. But that there should be in Him three distinct things, each one existing by itself, distintos an persona as they say, and that they should nevertheless be one, this is impossible, unless two contradictories can be true at the same time, which is opposed to the primary axioms and inconceivable by the mind. For the same reason the Torah rejects corporeality and admonishes us not to believe in it: "Take ye therefore good heed unto yourselves - for ye saw no manner of form ... lest ye deal corruptly and make you a graven image, even the form of any figure ..."

As for his statement that the Torah is defective in respect of its purpose because it does not speak of spiritual happiness, it is not true. There is an allusion which the wise understand, as we shall explain in the Fourth Book with the help of God. The reason this point is not clearly stated and at length is because the Torah was not given to the wise and intelligent only, but to all people, great and small, wise and foolish. It must therefore contain such things as are understandable of all and calculated to inspire belief.

Now those things which can be perceived by every one with his senses, inspire strong belief, whereas those things which are apprehended by the intellect and can not be perceived by the senses, being understood by the wise only, do not inspire belief at all. The people say that that which can not be perceived by the senses is improbable and untrue. For this reason, the Torah of Moshe promised explicitly corporeal rewards, which every one can see and perceive with his senses, whereas intellectual things, which the intelligent alone understand, are contained by way of allusion. The purpose is that every one may understand, according to his ability, that through the Torah is obtained all corporeal and spiritual happiness, so long as sin does not prevent. Nay, the corporeal rewards which can not be obtained in the ordinary way of nature are evidence of spiritual rewards.

Balaam also, who was a great sage and a prophet, though not a member of the Israelitish nation, testifies to this. He said: "Let me die the death of the righteous, and let mine end be like his." It seems that through his wisdom or prophetic inspiration he understood that Israel had an end and a hope after death, hence he expressed the desire to have after his death such an end and hope as Israel had. He understood that providence in this world proves happiness in the world to come. And especially when extraordinary miracles take place constantly in the life of a nation, it is proof of their spiritual happiness in the next world. During the whole period of the first temple prophecy existed in Israel continually, and even in the time of the second temple, when there was no prophecy, the people often had their questions answered by a voice from heaven [בת קול], and there were other miracles taking place constantly, for example, every sixth year the land produced enough for three years, as we read: "I will command My blessing upon you in the sixth year, and it shall bring forth produce for the three years." Also, in accordance with the verse, "Assemble the people, the men, and the women, and the little ones, and thy stranger that is within thy gates ...," all Israel went up during the feast of Tabernacles of the sabbatical year to Yerushalayim to hear the Torah, and the Bible says: "Neither shall any man covet thy land, when thou goest up to appear ..." And there were many other miracles constantly in the temple, such as are enumerated in the treatise Abot. In Yoma we are told that a thread of red wool turned white every year on the day of atonement. And there are other miracles told there which took place continually. The Christians have no continuous miracle to prove the truth of their belief.

The proof they bring from the prosperity of those who believe in their faith is no proof at all. For more than two thousand years before the law of Moshe was given, all the nations worshipped idols, except a few rare persons, like the patriarchs and the like, and yet every one of the nations prospered in its own government and lived in quiet and tranquillity. And after the law was given, too, all the nations worshipped idols except Israel, and yet they were all prosperous in their own states. Surely the fact that Sennacherib and Nebuchadnezzar and Alexander were successful in ruling over Israel is no sign that their faith was better than that of Israel. Even now the Christians maintain that the law of the Mohammedans is positive and conventional, not divine, and yet they are successful and rule over a great part of the world. It seems clear therefore that the prosperity of a nation is no proof of the truth of its faith. The real proof of the truth of a faith is the continuity of miracles, such as we find in Israel when they lived on their own land. We do not find any such condition among the believers in Christianity or Mohammedanism. As for their claim about the happiness of the soul in the world to come, this is precisely the point of dispute, whether it is so or not, and what proof have they?

His statement that the Torah is defective in respect to its form is absolutely untrue. For it is absolutely perfect in all the three parts which he says the Torah embraces. Take the part which contains the commandments dealing with man's relation to God, i.e., the ceremonial commandments which concern themselves with the service of God. It is perfect, for it commands prayer, as the Rabbis

Sefer HaIkkarim   BOOK [Maamar] THRE

say in commenting on the verse, "And you shall serve the Lord your God, and He will bless thy bread, and thy water." The service mentioned here, they say, is prayer, as we shall also explain in the Fourth Book, with the help of God. The law also tells us to love God and to fear Him: "And thou shalt love the Lord thy God;" "But thou shalt fear thy God;" "Thou shalt fear the Lord thy God; and Him shalt thou serve."

He says that the offering of the sacrifices is unclean, because it consists of the burning of the flesh and the fat and the blood. In answer to this we may say that if we agree with Maimonides that the institution of sacrifices was not intended for its own sake but only as a means to keep the people away from sacrificing to idols, the objection is removed; for the purpose of the sacrifices was merely to purify their intentions and keep them away from offering sacrifices to idols. Thus, Jeremiah says, "For I spoke not unto your fathers, nor commanded them in the day that I brought them out of the land of Egypt, concerning burnt-offerings or sacrifices; but this I commanded them, saying: Hearken unto My voice ..."

But even if we say that some part of the institution of sacrifices was intended for its own sake, namely to call the attention of the sinner or of man generally that just as the sheep or other animal which he offers as a sacrifice was a living thing that sustained itself with food like himself, and now it is burned and destroyed, nothing being left of it except in so far as God has pleasure therein, so man will be destroyed in the same way, without anything being left except the works that he does which are pleasing to God in having His will fulfilled, this being the superiority of man to the animals. [This has the purpose of causing man to devote himself to doing good and that which is right in the eyes of God in order to acquire immortality, which is the real perfection of man.] Or if we say that the purpose of the sacrifices is to bring together and unite the upper powers with the lower, as the Cabalists think - in any case we can not say that the mode of worship is an improper one, since the senses testified that those things were pleasing to God. For the fire came down from heaven and consumed upon the altar the burnt-offering and the fat. Fire came down for Moshe in the tent of meeting, for Solomon in the temple, for David in the threshing floor of Aravna the Jebusite, for Eliyahu on Mount Carmel. The Shekinah or holy spirit rested upon Israel through the offerings, and the priest foretold the future through the Urim and Thummim, as the senses testified. Nothing like this can be cited in all the offerings of the Christians. They can not show a single continuous and public sign, well known to all, as

Sefer HaIkkarim — BOOK [Maamar] THREE

in the sacrifices. Their statement that their offerings benefit the soul, is one which is not testified to by the senses nor proved by the intellect. The Rabbis say in reference to such a situation, if one desires to lie let him cite witnesses which are far away.

Moreover, the sacrament of the bread and wine of which they speak is not an offering at all. The bread and the wine is not an offering to their God, but, as they say, it is the body of their God. For they say that the body of Jesus, which is in heaven and is of very great extension and magnitude, comes to the altar and clothes itself in the bread and the wine as soon as the priest has pronounced the words - no matter who the priest is, a good man or a bad - and the whole becomes one with the body of the Messiah, who comes down from heaven instantaneously. And after the bread and the wine have been consumed, he goes up to heaven again where he was before. This takes place at every altar. Such is their idea concerning this offering. Now this belief the human mind utterly rejects, and can not accept or conceive, for it is in conflict with first principles and with the evidence of the senses.

In the first place it demands belief in instantaneous motion from the highest heavens and the throne of glory to the earth. Secondly, it requires belief in the simultaneous presence of one body in two or more different places; for the body of the Messiah is present on different altars at the same time. Thirdly, it involves the belief that the body of the Messiah goes up and down without breaking through the body of heaven, since the heavens can not be broken through. Moreover, they say that the flesh and the blood which comes into being at the particular moment from the substance of the bread and the wine, which is finite and limited, is the very body of the Messiah, who existed from eternity, and does not thereby increase or diminish in quantity. This leads to belief in the interpenetration of bodies.

All these things not merely deny first principles but they are in conflict with the evidence of the senses. For they say that the bread and the wine which appear to the eye are not food and do not nourish the animal or the man who eats it. But we believe that if the bread and the wine were a large quantity, they would nourish the person who consumed them and help to form his limbs or organs like any other bread and wine. Again, they say that the substance of the bread and the wine changes into the body of the Messiah, while the accidents [properties] remain just as they were without any subject. The taste and the color and the odor and the feeling and the heaviness and the lightness and the softness and the hardness which we perceive in the bread are not in the bread at all, for the matter has

Sefer HaIkkarim — BOOK [Maamar] THRE

disappeared and become the body of the Messiah. These are things which the reason can not conceive, the mouth can not utter, and the ear can not hear. How then can one believe things like these, which the mind rejects and the senses contradict? Therefore, a Jew who is used to true opinions, which are not in conflict with the evidence of the senses and do not contradict first principles, opinions found in the law of Moshe, which all acknowledge to be divine, since it was revealed with great publicity in the presence of six hundred thousand people, can hardly force his mind to believe things which the mind can not understand. For how can a man believe what he can not understand or even conceive?

It is especially difficult for him to believe in the things stated in the law of Jesus when he considers that the fact which they lay down as the basis of their belief, namely, that Jesus was Messiah the son of David, is uncertain. For chapter one of the Gospel of Matthew traces the ancestry of Joseph, the husband of Miriam, or as they say, her betrothed, to Solomon and David, and says that he was of royal descent, whereas in the third chapter of the Gospel of Luke it is said that he was not of royal descent and was descended from Nathan the son of David. Both of these genealogies concern Joseph alone. For they say that Joseph never knew Miriam either before the birth of Jesus or after. This despite the fact that in the Gospel of Matthew, the statement is made that Joseph did not know Miriam until Jesus was born, which would indicate that afterwards he did. We also find in the same Gospel that Jesus had brothers, which would lead to the same result. They explain, however, that brothers mean relatives. The statement, too, that Joseph did not know Miriam until she gave birth to Jesus they explain like the verse, "For I will not leave thee, until I have done that which I have spoken to thee of," and as we explain the passage, "The scepter shall not depart from Yehuda, nor the ruler's staff from between his feet, until he comes to Shiloh and unto him shall the obedience of the peoples be," the meaning of which is that afterwards too the scepter shall not depart. If this is so, Joseph's descent does not benefit Jesus at all, and how do we know the genealogy of Miriam?

Moreover, how can a Jew who is familiar with the Bible and sees that the biblical passages cited in the Gospels and in their other books as evidence do not prove the thing intended at all - how can such a person bring himself to believe in their ideas? Thus, it says in Matthew that Jesus was born of a virgin to fulfil the words of the Bible, "Behold the young woman [עלמה] shall conceive." But every one who can read knows - even a child in school is aware - that this verse was said to Ahaz about six hundred years before the birth of Jesus as a sign that the kingdoms of Syria and Israel would be destroyed, and that the kingdom of Yehuda would remain under the kings of the house of David. How could Jesus' birth of a virgin be a sign to Ahaz?

In the second chapter of Matthew, it says that Herod killed all the young males, whom it calls innocent, to fulfil the verse of the Bible, "Rachel weeping for her children." But it is obvious from the context that the expression refers to the exile at the time of the first temple, for we read in the same place, "And they shall come back from the land of the enemy;" "And thy children shall return to their own border;" "I have surely heard Ephraim bemoaning himself ... turn thou me, and I shall be turned." There are other verses quoted in the Gospels and interpreted erroneously. All this prevents one believing that the law of Jesus is divine. One is rather inclined to believe that it is a conventional law laid down by persons who were not familiar with the Bible, and did not understand the meaning of the text. Nor did they take the trouble to understand the manner of worship in the law of Moshe, or to note that divine influence was bestowed upon Israel through the offerings at the time of the temple, and that the perfect worship of God at all times and places is to carry out the commandments.

In that part of the commandments which pertains to the relations between man and man and which are called judiciales, the law of Moshe is more perfect than any other law. It enjoins upon us the love of mankind, "And thou shalt love thy neighbour as thyself." It forbid hatred, "Thou shalt not hate thy brother in thy heart." In respect to the stranger it says, "And ye shall love the stranger," and it admonishes us not to vex him, "He shall dwell with thee, in the midst of thee, in the place which he shall choose within one of thy gates, where it liketh him best; thou shalt not wrong him." And this applies not merely to a proselyte, but also to one who is not converted to Judaism, provided he does not worship idols. The Torah also commands to be kind to him, "Thou mayest give it to the stranger that is within thy gates, that he may eat it." This refers to a foreigner living in Israel, who is permitted to eat the flesh of an animal that dies of itself. Interest is permitted to be taken only from a foreigner who worships idols, as the Bible says: "Unto a foreigner thou mayest lend upon interest." One who worships idols, and refuses to carry out the seven Noachian commandments, which the stranger observes, may have his life taken, too, according to the consensus of all religions. Even the philosophers permit to take his

Sefer HaIkkarim   BOOK [Maamar] THRE

life. "Kill the one who has no religion," they say. And so, the Torah also admonishes us in relation to idolaters, "Thou shalt save alive nothing that breatheth." Now if it is permitted to take his life, surely one may take his property. The idolater should be killed and deserves no pity.

In the other rules the Torah is more perfect than other laws. For it measures the proper punishment according to the magnitude of the wrong, as we explained in the preceding chapter in connection with the punishment for stealing property. As to the rules relating to the unintentional homicide, we must bear in mind that an unintentional homicide is often very close to an intentional one. Therefore the Torah permits the avenger of the blood to take his life, in order that a person may be very careful in this matter. That this explanation is correct is proven by the fact that if the homicide could not avoid the result, he does not have to go into exile and the avenger of the blood is guilty of a capital offence if he puts him to death. For example, if he threw a stone and the other put out his head and was struck.

The reason for making his return from exile depend on the death of the high priest is explained by the Rabbis as follows: This matter is made dependent on the life of the high priest, they say, in order that he may be careful to pray for mercy in behalf of his contemporaries that no wrong may occur on account of them. Besides, it is generally the case that the righteous bear punishment and suffering for the sake of the common people who are sinful. Thus, Ezekiel was told by God to lie on his side and endure suffering, so that he might bear the iniquity of the house of Israel. It is not to be wondered at, then, that the priest is punished for the iniquity of the people.

The real and extraordinary wonder is that any one should say that the laws of the Torah of Moshe, which is divine, are defective, and are completed by the law of Jesus. The law of Jesus has no civil laws governing human relations. The Christians follow in their civil life the rules of their learned men by order of the emperor or of the Pope. How is it possible that rules which are laid down by learned men on the basis of human opinion, should supply the defect of the rules in the law of Moshe, which is divine? And even if the rules were laid down by the Apostles, they could not improve upon the rules of the law of Moshe, since this is not a matter that depends upon belief.

A still more important consideration is that a person should correct only that which he knows. But the Apostles, as it seems, were not familiar with the law of Moshe. For we find in the seventh chapter of the Acts of the Apostles that according to Stephen, Joseph brought his father Yaakov to Egypt with seventy-five souls. Then

Sefer HaIkkarim — BOOK [Maamar] THREE

Yaakov and his ancestors died and were buried in Shechem in the cave which Abraham bought with silver from the sons of Hamor, son of Shechem, all of which is different from the explicit account of the Torah. In the book of Genesis, section **Vayyiggash**, all the persons are enumerated by name who came to Egypt with Yaakov. And together with Joseph and his sons, there are not more than seventy. And we have an explicit statement, "Thy fathers went down into Egypt with threescore and ten persons." The cave which Abraham bought was in Hebron and not in Shechem. And he did not buy it from the sons of Hamor, son of Shechem, but from Ephron the Hittite, as is explicitly stated. Moreover, in the thirteenth chapter, Paul says that the Israelites asked Samuel for a king and he gave them the son of Kish, a Benjaminite, who reigned forty years. This contradicts the text, according to which he reigned only three or four years. They can not answer these criticisms by saying that the Jews falsified the text, for the point does not affect religious belief. It seems therefore that they were not familiar with the words of the Torah and the Prophets.

But even if we suppose that, as they say, the Apostles had the authority to change the civil laws, who gave authority to the Pope to change the commandment of the Sabbath, which is not one of the civil laws? The descent of the manna is a valid proof that the Sabbath day is essentially holy through the power of God and not merely for the sake of rest, as would be the case in a conventional rule laid down by man. Therefore, the Bible says, "See that the Lord hath given you the Sabbath …" The meaning is that as the manna came down on the six days of the weeks and not on Sabbath, and on the sixth day it came down in double the amount, this was a sign of the essential holiness of the Sabbath day, and of its divine origin. No man can abolish it, especially since it is one of the ten commandments. Jesus and all his disciples observed the Sabbath, and it was only about five hundred years after Jesus that the Pope changed it and substituted Sunday for the Sabbath. This despite the fact that the manna was a clear sign of the essential holiness of the Sabbath day, a sign without any defect, and that the Sabbath is one of the ten commandments, which they admit to be free from defect. But it seems that their purpose was to destroy the law of Moshe on their own account without any reason or argument, for neither Jesus nor his disciples gave any such command. It is clear therefore that the charge of imperfection which he makes against the true laws of the Torah of Moshe, is not at all sufficient to abolish them.

The charge of imperfection which he brings against the third part of the Torah, namely the moral precepts, on the ground that the Law of Moshe prescribes only correct action, but not a pure heart, is the opposite of the truth. For do we not read, "Circumcise therefore the foreskin of your heart;" "And thou shalt love the Lord thy God with all thy heart …;" "And thou shalt love thy neighbour as thyself;" "But thou shalt fear thy God;" "Thou shalt not take vengeance, nor bear any grudge against the children of thy people"? The reason it commands right action is because purity of heart is of no account unless practice is in agreement with it. The important thing, however, is intention. David says, "Create me a clean heart, O God." And there are many other passages of the same kind, more than we can enumerate here.

It is clear therefore that the law of Moshe is perfect in all manner of perfection and not imperfect, as the Christian thought. David made allusion to this briefly, praising the law in respect to its four causes. "The law of the Lord is perfect, restoring the soul." The word law refers to the material cause; and in calling it Torah [teaching, law] he indicates that all the narratives in it like those of the drunkenness of Noah and Lot, and so on, were put there to give rules and regulation and guidance, and for no other purpose. The expression, the law of the Lord, indicates that it is perfect in respect to the efficient cause. For since the efficient cause is God, it can not have any of the defects which may exist in a human law. The word perfect denotes perfection in form; while the expression, restoring the soul, refers to perfection of purpose, namely, the happiness of the soul. "Restoring the soul," is similar to the statement of Solomon, "And the spirit returneth unto God who gave it."

Here the Christian translator Jerome erred in his translation of the word תמימה [perfect], which he renders, "without blemish." He did this so as not to ascribe perfection to the Torah, in order that he might say that it is defective and that the law of Jesus completed it. But this is a mistake. The word תמימה means perfect, without any doubt. In the section dealing with the red heifer, the word תמימה occurs, and yet the text finds it necessary to add, "wherein is no blemish," which shows that תמימה means one thing and "no blemish" means another. Our Rabbis explain that תמימה means perfect in redness. This shows that תמימה always denotes ultimate perfection in a given line. Since, therefore, the Torah has been described as perfect in form - תמימה; in purpose - "restoring the soul;" in respect to its efficient cause, who is God, and therefore perfect; and in matter, which is Torah, i.e., guidance and rule, it is clear that it is free from all defects and perfect in all manner of perfection. This concludes what we intended to explain in this chapter.

Chapter 26

Inasmuch as the divine law is a rule and a guide for the human race, emanating from God, it necessarily points to a bond and a union between God, who is the author of the commands, and man, who is the subject of them. Hence it is clear from this aspect that hearing a command from God necessarily proves that there is such a thing as prophetic inspiration, divine revelation, and that there is a God who is the author of the law and who exercises providence. This is especially true when one hears the first two commandments of the decalogue, for they denote essentially these three dogmas, as we explained before. Nevertheless, God desired to let Israel hear from His mouth the ten commandments so as to indicate all those duties which a man becomes liable to by reason of this bond between God and him, both from the point of view of the master who is the author of the command, and from the point of view of the servant, who is the subject. For this reason, they were expressed in two separate tables, to indicate that these two aspects are different from each other. Those five which have reference to God, the Master, are in one table, while the five which concern specially man, who is the servant, are in the other table, to show that both are necessary for the attainment of human perfection.

The ten commandments are general rules embracing the two classes of commandments, as follows: The first table contains the first five commandments, which a person is obliged to follow by reason of his acceptance of the divine being. Take the following instance: A king builds a city, then frees a body of slaves and settles them in the city, and then comes to speak to them in order to induce them to accept his lordship. Clearly the first thing he has to tell them is that he is the master who cared for them and liberated them from bondage. This is the meaning of the first commandment in the decalogue, "I am the Lord thy God ..." It behooves you to accept My lordship because I made you free. Then he commands them that they shall not give the power to any one else, "Thou shalt have no other gods before Me." Similarly, he commands them not to rebel and set another king over them, "Thou shalt not make unto thee a graven image, nor any manner of likeness." Then it is proper to command them that they should show him honor, and not treat him with disrespect, as by swearing falsely in his name, "Thou shalt not take the name of the Lord thy God in vain." Then it is necessary that

Sefer HaIkkarim   BOOK [Maamar] THRE

he should fix a mode of commemorating the building of the city. For in this way they will remember that they have a lord who built the city, and that they had been freed from slavery and settled therein. For this reason, He commanded them to keep the Sabbath, which bears allusion to the creation of the world and the deliverance from Egyptian bondage.

The Rabbis say, "Remember" and "Keep" were pronounced in one statement. The meaning is this The Sabbath is not intended merely to signify the existence of an agent who created the world, as is indicated in the commandment beginning with the word, "remember." The phiosopher, too, believes in the existence of such a being, and no one denies it except the sect of Epicurus. The main reason for the Sabbath is to show that there is a being who acts with will continually, even after the creation of the world. This is alluded to in the commandment beginning with the word, "keep," mentioning as it does the deliverance from Egypt, from which it became known that God acts with will and desire. And not only at the time of the creation of the world, but even after the world has come into being, He exercises providence and changes nature, compelling it to perform His will and desire at all times, as He did in delivering Israel from Egypt, to refute the notion of those who say there is nothing new under the sun. Hence the Rabbis say that the commandment beginning, "remember," which calls attention to the existence of a divine agent, and the commandment beginning, "keep," which calls attention to the existence of a divine agent who acts continuously with will and exercises providence, both were said in one word or command, i.e., in the word which commands the Sabbath. For the purpose of the Sabbath is to call attention to the existence of a divine agent continually acting with will and exercising providence, and not merely to teach the existence of a divine agent.

Consider this carefully, for it is a wonderful interpretation of the rabbinic passage, which I have not seen adequately explained by any of the commentators. Some say that the word "remember" denotes a mandatory commandment, while the word "keep" signifies a prohibitive or negative commandment, as the Rabbis say: " [take heed, lit. keep thyself], [lest] and [do not ...] are indications of prohibitive commandments." Accordingly, the meaning of the passage in question is that the precept of the Sabbath necessarily embraces both a positive and a negative commandment, a positive commandment alluding to the creation of the world, and a negative commandment, viz., cessation from work, as a memorial of Israel's

Sefer HaIkkarim — BOOK [Maamar] THREE

deliverance from bondage. For as a slave can not cease from work, cessation from work is a memorial of the deliverance from Egypt. But according to this explanation, the version of the commandment beginning with the word "remember" should not contain the prohibition to do work. And since it does contain that prohibition, what need is there of saying that "remember" and "keep" were pronounced in one commandment?

Another explanation is this: rest in general would be a commemoration of the deliverance from Egypt, for a slave can not rest. If the prescribed rest were to take place one day in ten, it would still be a memorial of the deliverance from Egypt. But since the command is to rest one day in seven, it is a memorial of the creation of the world, "For in six days the Lord made heaven and earth, and on the seventh day He ceased from work and rested." Hence the Rabbis say that the two versions of the Sabbath commandment were pronounced in one statement. This explanation, however, is not satisfactory. Why not say that the whole is a commemoration of the creation? And if the idea intended in that statement is that there are various reasons for the commandment of the Sabbath, that is no reason for saying that the two versions were pronounced "in one statement." There are many commandments which have more than one reason, and yet the Rabbis did not say that they were pronounced in one statement.

According to my explanation, however, the two versions had to be pronounced in one statement; the one to indicate that there is a divine agent who brought things into being, and the other to show that He is a voluntary agent, that He acts continually and that He exercises providence. The one is not sufficient without the other. The Sabbath day, therefore, points to both these ideas because they are both necessary for a proper conception of God.

According to the Rabbis, there is still a third idea contained in the commandment of the Sabbath. "All agree," they say in the treatise Shabbat, "that the Torah was given to Israel on a Sabbath." If this is true, then the commandment of the Sabbath embraces three principles of religion, existence of a divine agent, providence, and revelation. And at the same time the Sabbath commemorates the day when the King revealed Himself to them in the city and they acknowledged His lordship. Inasmuch, however, as this latter idea is acknowledged only once a year, it was not mentioned explicitly in the Torah. We thus see that the Sabbath is obligatory and necessary for a true conception of God, in the three aspects mentioned.

Sefer Halkkarim   BOOK [Maamar] THRE

Then comes the commandment, "Honour thy father and thy mother." For it is well known that the king who built the city does not reveal himself every day to the men of the city. And while the men of that generation, who saw the king come into the city, remember that he built that city and freed them from bondage, and that they accepted his sovereignty, those who come after them, having never been slaves, and not having seen the king enter the city, may rebel, thinking that the city has always been theirs, and that they have no overlord. There is no way of escaping such folly except by submitting to parents and receiving instruction from them. For the parents will inform their children that they were slaves and that a certain lord freed them from bondage, that it was he who built the city and settled them therein. Hence it was necessary, in order that the rule of the king throughout the city and the benefit he conferred upon them in freeing them from slavery might not be forgotten, that children of every generation should obey their parents and accept their instruction. Hence the fifth commandment, "Honour thy father and thy mother," teaches respect for tradition, viz., that a person should follow the tradition of the fathers, which is a fundamental dogma of all religions. Their existence can not be conceived unless a person is obedient to the tradition of the fathers and the wise men of that religion.

We did not count it among the primary or derivative principles because it is a particular command. Obedience to parents is expressed in the words, "Honour thy father and thy mother;" obedience to the learned and the wise is taught in the expression, "Thou shalt not turn aside from the sentence which they shall declare unto thee, to the right hand, nor to the left." This commandment completes all those things which concern the relation of man to God, i.e., the things which the servant must do in relation to the master.

Then the Bible inculcates those general principles which men must have as social and political beings in order that the political group may be perfect. The first commandment is to preserve his fellowman's body, "Thou shalt not murder." Then comes the command to preserve his neighbor's property, "Thou shalt not steal," which is to be understood literally. Then comes the commandment to preserve that which is intermediate, as it were, between a man's body and his property, namely his wife. For the wife is in a sense the man's body, as it were, and in a sense, as it were, his property - "Thou shalt not commit adultery." Then he adds that it is not sufficient if one refrain from injuring his neghbor in his body or his property or his wife, but that he must take care not to injure him even by a word, "Thou shalt not bear false witness against thy neighbour;" nor even by a thought, "Thou shalt not covet thy neighbour's wife, nor his field nor his man-servant, nor his maid-servant, nor his ox, nor his ass, nor anything that is thy neighbour's." This completes the general rules which are necessary for man as a being that must associate with others, as we said in the First Book.

Hence the ten commandments were placed on two tables, to show that though these two classes of commandments are distinct, they are necessary for human perfection, the one for the perfection of man as an individual, and the other for his perfection as being part of the state. The first five were all on the same table to show that they also represent one special class. All commandments are included in these two classes, as is seen on examination. The Rabbis say in **Torat Kohanim**: "Thou shalt love thy neighbour as thyself:" says Rabbi Akiba, this is a very important principle of the Torah. Ben Azzai said: "This is the book of the generations of Adam," is a more important principle, as we explained in the twenty-fourth chapter of the First Book.

Chapter 27

An important principle to bear in mind in connection with the performance of the commandments is that all depends upon intention, as the Rabbis say, "God requires the heart." One may, therefore, perform many commandments without any benefit at all, or at least without enough benefit to realize human perfection or an appreciable part thereof. On the other hand, one may observe one commandment and succeed, according to his intention in the performance thereof, in acquiring a great part of perfection, more than the performer of many commandments. Since, therefore, intention is the important thing, it follows that all the commandments of the Torah, whether positive or negative, are a means to the attainment of human perfection, or a certain degree thereof, if they are done with the proper intention. A man attains to eternal life not only by doing good deeds. The soul's perfection is attained also by abstaining from evil deeds through fear of God.

This is proved as follows: The Torah says explicitly, "And walk in His ways." From this we see that walking in God's ways is the essence of man's service of God. Now we find that the Psalmist explains that he who refrains from doing evil for fear of God is called one who walks in the ways of God, "Happy are they that are upright in the way, who walk in the law of the Lord." The meaning

Sefer HaIkkarim — BOOK [Maamar] THRE

is, happy are the mass of believers who are described as, "upright in the way," i.e., they do not seek to be too clever in their relation to God, but follow the law of God with simplicity. Then he explains that those who walk in the law of the Lord are those who keep His commandments with the intention of the heart, "Happy are they that keep His testimonies, that seek Him with the whole heart." And to obviate the idea that only he is described as walking in the ways of the Lord and keeping His testimonies, who keeps the positive commandments, and that a negative commandment can not be conceived as bestowing perfection upon the soul, he adds in the sequel, "Yea, they do no unrighteousness; they walk in His ways." The meaning is, a person who intentionally refrains from doing evil is also a man walking in the ways of God; as the text says, "They walk in His ways." The Rabbis also say, if one refrains from committing a transgression, he is rewarded as if he had performed a positive commandment.

It may seem strange that a person should be able to acquire any perfection by sitting idle and doing nothing. The Rabbis seem to be opposed to it. For in commenting on the verse, "Who is the man that desireth life ... keep thy tongue from evil ... depart from evil, and do good," they say, if you think that you can win life by indulging in sleep, the text emphasizes, "And do good." From this it seems that good deeds are necessary if one is to merit eternal life and the good which is reserved for those who fear God, as is expressed in the verse, "Oh how abundant is Thy goodness, which Thou hast laid up for them that fear Thee ..." It is this goodness which is referred to in the verse, "Who is the man that desireth life, and loveth days, that he may see good therein."

The answer to this is that, to be sure, if a person sits idle, he can not in this way acquire any perfection. But if the temptation to commit a transgression comes to him and he refrains from committing it for fear of God, he merits thereby eternal life as if he had done a good deed. In this way all the prohibitive commandments in the Torah give perfection to the soul. Thus, if a person does not eat swine's flesh because he has other things to eat or because he does not like swine's flesh, he does not deserve any reward. But if he has a desire to eat swine's flesh, or if he has nothing to eat and swine's flesh is given to him and he refrains from eating it for fear of God and in order to fulfil God's command not to eat it, though he is hungry and eager to eat it - such a person is surely deserving of reward. This is the meaning of the verse, "Thou shalt not eat it [the blood]; that it may go well with thee, and with thy children after thee, when thou

Sefer HaIkkarim — BOOK [Maamar] THREE

shalt do that which is right in the eyes of the Lord;" concerning which the Rabbis say, "A person must not say, I do not want to eat swine's flesh, I do not want to wear garments of wool and flax mixed; but he must say, I want to do these things, but what can I do, seeing that my Father in heaven has forbidden them!" This shows clearly that a person deserves merit for refraining from transgressing a commandment only if the opportunity is present and he refrains through the love and fear of God and not for any other cause.

This may seem easy to attain, but it is not. It is very difficult. David himself, who said, "Keep my soul, for I am godly," was unable, in the incident of Bathsheba, when there was no other preventive except the fear of God, to conquer the temptation through the love of God. But to refrain from doing a wrong act for the fear and love of God is equivalent to the doing of a good deed in the proper manner and with the proper intention. In this manner negative precepts give perfection to the soul by not being performed, as positive precepts give perfection to the soul by being performed.

The Rabbis explain this in the Talmud **Makkot**: Rabbi Simlai held the following discourse: "Six hundred and thirteen commandments were given to Moshe on Sinai, three hundred and sixty-five corresponding to the days of the solar year, and two hundred and forty-eight corresponding to the number of organs [limbs] in the human body ..." This passage endeavors to explain that the Torah in prescribing the particular number of precepts, intended to show how it is possible to acquire perfection by means of negative precepts as well as by means of positive precepts, though they are opposites, for positive and negative precepts are without doubt opposites.

The number two hundred and forty-eight of the positive commandments, corresponding to the number of members in the body, indicates that as the members of the body by their actual existence give man the perfection nature intended for him as an animal being, so the positive commandments give man the perfection intended for him as a human being, if they are actually carried out in practice, not if they are merely the subject of knowledge and belief. The number three hundred and sixty-five of the negative commandments, corresponding to the days of the solar year, indicates that these commandments give perfection to the soul though they are not actual existents. Time is not an actual existent, for the past is no longer here, the future is not yet, and the present is merely the now which binds the past to the future. The now itself is not real time, since it is not divisible, whereas time is divisible, pertaining as it does to continuous quantity. The now is related to time as the point is related to the line. Time is therefore not an actual existent, and yet it gives perfection of existence to all things existing in time. In the same way the negative commandments, though they are not actual existents, give perfection to the human soul as non-existents. Hence their number is three hundred and sixty-five, to indicate that as time is non-existent, so these commandments must be actually non-existent. And by being actually non-existent they give perfection to the soul, provided the forbearance from doing them is caused by the proper motive, like time which, being non-existent, gives perfection to existing things.

Chapter 28

From our explanations in the preceding chapter, it follows that human perfection can be attained only by means of the positive and the negative precepts. Just as no human perfection can be acquired except by means of the actually existing limbs and the non-existing time, so the perfection of the soul can be attained only by the positive and the negative commandments. For this reason, every one of the three parts into which the Torah is divided, namely ideas, statutes and judgments, as we explained in the twenty-fourth chapter of this Book, includes positive and negative commandments, in order that every part should contain the means for acquiring perfection, or a part of that perfection which man attains by means of the positive and the negative commandments.

In theoretical ideas, positive commandments are, for example, belief in the existence, the unity and the incorporeality of God; while examples of negative precepts are, not to entertain the notion that there is another god, not to incline after idolatry, and so on. In the statutes, the wearing of **zizit** [fringes] is an example of a positive commandment, while prohibited foods illustrate the negative precepts. In the judgments the positive precepts are illustrated in the following passages: "In righteousness shalt thou judge thy neighbour;" "In the same day thou shalt give him his hire;" "Thou shalt furnish him liberally." The negative commandments are exemplified in the following passages: "And ye shall not wrong one another;" "Ye shall not steal; neither shall ye deal falsely, nor lie one to another," and many other passages besides.

Now it is clear that perfection may be acquired through the theoretical part of the Torah, its negative as well as its positive side. Similarly, perfection may be acquired through the part containing the statutes, i.e., the rules concerning those things which are pleasing to God and those which are displeasing to Him, as we said before. The thing that requires explanation, however, is, how can perfection of the soul be acquired through the third part, which embraces judgments? It is hard to conceive how any of its parts, whether the positive commandments or the negative, can give perfection to the soul. Those positive commandments which deal with injuries caused by an ox or an open pit or a fire, and negative commandments like, "Ye shall not steal," "Thou shalt not oppress thy neighbour, nor rob him," and so on, are no doubt right rules for the preservation of social life, but by what merit does the soul of a mortal man acquire perfection by means of them? And if their virtue consists in the fact that they are a guide to right morals, which alone enable one to acquire human perfection, then it would follow that the intensive occupation with the Talmud on the part of the Jewish sages and their study of Talmudical questions, is of no benefit in acquiring perfection, and their labor is in vain! Besides it is not likely that so large a part of the Torah bestows perfection only because it leads to right morals and for no other reason.

The solution of the question is as follows: The performance of a precept must be considered from two points of view. One is the doing of the commandment and its complete performance. The other is the intention of the doer. Now the perfection which is acquired through the commandment does not come from the act of performance, for the Rabbis say, "The transgression of a commandment for a good purpose is better than the performance of a commandment without such purpose." In the same place they say: The matter may be illustrated by the case of two persons, each of whom roasted his paschal lamb. One ate the lamb to celebrate the Passover, and the other to satisfy his craving for food. To the first we apply the verse of Scripture, "And the just do walk in them," to the second we apply the expression, "But transgressors do stumble therein." They thus make plain that an act without the proper intention is not credited to one as the performance of a divine command.

On the other hand, mere intention without the act is of no value at all. For if that were the case, then the knowledge of a commandment and its deep study would take the place of the performance. But the fact is not so. To read the sections of the Pentateuch which are inclosed in the phylacteries can not take the place of laying the phylacteries on the head and arm. Moreover, we find an explicit statement in the treatise Kiddushin, in connection with the

Sefer HaIkkarim   BOOK [Maamar] THRE

discussion as to which is more important, study or practice. It was decided by a vote taken that study is more important. But the reason given is because study leads to practice. It is clear therefore that since the importance of study is due to its being an incentive to practice, the essential thing is the end, which is practice.

Whenever two arts are so related that the one is prior by nature to the other, like bridle-making in relation to horsemanship, or the art of weaving in relation to tailoring, the prior art is inferior in worth to the other. For the prior art serves the other, so to speak. Thus the art of quarrying stones is inferior in degree to the art of building, being subordinate to it, although the building art can not be realized without the art of quarrying. In the same way though practice is impossible without study, for "An ignoramus can not be a pious man," nevertheless since study is only for the sake of practice, practice is the important thing.

But since we have shown that the act alone is not the essential thing, nor intention alone, it follows that the essential thing in the performance of the commandments is a combination of the two, as is the case in the relation of theory to practice, as we have explained in this Book. Accordingly, in the performance of the commandments, an act accompanied by the proper intention constitutes a perfect performance, such as gives perfection to the soul, for intention gives completeness to an act, as we explained in the fifth chapter of this Book. My opinion is therefore that the part of the Torah which contains judgments is more calculated to give perfection to the soul than the corresponding part of a conventional law.

When a person living under a conventional law does a right or just act, no matter what his intention, and realizes the purpose intended, viz., improvement of social life, he has exhausted the situation. There is no other perfection or end to be realized. The judgments of the Torah are different. Social welfare is realized through their performance as in the others. But when their performance is joined with the proper intention, there is realized another perfection, more noble than the first. As the teeth and the tongue and the lips are found in animals for the intaking of food, and at the same time they have in man a more honorable purpose, as organs of speech and expression to laud God and declare His praises, so the judgments of the Torah have a more honorable purpose than the improvement of social life, though it may not seem so at first sight. This purpose is that in performing these judgments one should have in mind that God commanded them. This intention, joined to the act, gives perfection to the soul of the agent, since he does the act not merely to preserve social life, but for the love of God, i.e., in order to fulfil the commandments which God gave. It follows, therefore, according to this, that if one does a given act, such as giving alms, or lending to a poor man in need, or refraining from oppressing one's neighbor or from stealing his property, - if one does any of these in obedience to the conventional law, because they are good acts leading to social welfare, he will get no special perfection from this except that which follows from the improvement of social life. But if one does these things in obedience to the Torah, because God commanded them, and in order to submit to Him and do His will and carry out the commandments which He gave, he will realize another special end, more honorable and more worthy than the other, namely the service of God. This intention, joined to the act, gives one perfection of soul, as we explained in the fifth chapter of this Book.

This is what the Bible means when it says: "And the work of righteousness shall be peace; and the effect of righteousness, quietness and confidence forever." That is, the doing of righteousness will bring peace in the social community and the poor man will not rob the rich. But the intention of charity, if it is in order to obey the command of God, being then called, "the effect of righteousness," gives "quietness and confidence forever," which means the immortality of the soul. In relation to this the Rabbis say, "Greater is he who does what he has been commanded to do than he who does a thing without having been commanded." The reason is because one who does an act which he has been commanded to do, accomplishes two things, first, he does a good and just act; and second, he performs the will of his Father in heaven. Whereas one who does a good deed without having been commanded, does it only because it is right. In this way we can understand how a person can acquire perfection and future life through the judgments of the Torah, positive as well as negative, if he performs them for the love and fear of God, and in order to carry out God's commands.

It is clear from this that the mere act of performance by itself is not calculated to bestow perfection, and that the latter comes from the evidence that is implied in the performance of submission to God, obeying His will and loving Him. It is like one lighting a lamp. The purpose is not the act itself and the immediate and inherent effect, namely the consumption of the oil and the burning of the wick, which is the immediate result of the act of lighting. The real purpose of lighting the lamp is the light which results from the act. So the purpose of the Torah is to guide man in the service of God, to illumine before him the way in which he should go in doing God's service, and to show him what he must do to obtain God's love.

This is why the Bible compares a commandment to a lamp, "For the commandment is a lamp," and the Torah to light, "and the Torah is light." The meaning is that the Torah, like light, is the end itself, intended for its own sake, whereas the commandment is not intended for its own sake. The act involved is like the lamp, which is not intended as an end in itself, but for the sake of the light which comes from it. So, the purpose of performing the commandment is the meaning implied in the performance, namely the service of God, which is the light coming from Him. This is called Torah [teaching], "The teaching [Torah] is light." Hence when the intention is lacking in the performance of a command, the agent is like one walking in deep darkness, who is bound to stumble. For this reason, our Rabbis call a person who performs a commandment without the proper intention a transgressor, saying that a person who observes the commandments of the Passover in the wrong manner, i.e., not with the proper intention, comes under the biblical expression, "Transgressors do stumble therein." Solomon says, "The way of the wicked is as darkness; they know not at what they stumble." On the other hand, in relation to intention joined to the proper act, they say: "For the ways of the Lord are right, and the just do walk in them;" and Solomon says, "But the path of the righteous is as the light of dawn, that shineth more and more unto the perfect day," i.e., it never goes out.

Chapter 29

We must consider now a very important question, namely, whether this divine law bestows perfection if observed in its entirety or also if observed in part. This is a matter of dispute between Rabbi Simeon, the son of Lakish, and Rabbi Yohanan in chapter "Helek." Commenting on the biblical text, "Therefore the nether-world hath enlarged her desire, and opened her mouth without measure," said Rabbi Simeon, son of Lakish, the nether-world opens her mouth for the one who neglects even one statute of the Torah. Said Rabbi Yohanan, The Lord is not pleased with this that you say about them [Israel]. The meaning of the expression is, the nether-world opens her mouth for him who has not performed even a single statute of the Torah.

Now it would seem that in order to attain perfection the Law must be fulfilled in its entirety, as Rabbi Simeon, son of Lakish, says. For if a part is sufficient for the attainment of human perfection, why should God have burdened us with a multiplicity of commands and admonitions? For it seems that if a given end can be attained with one act it is useless to do many acts to attain it. Thus, if one can cure a certain disease with a simple and easily obtainable drug, it would be idle work to make a compound of many drugs, hard to obtain, as the wise man says, "It is vain to accomplish with many acts what can be realized with one." It would seem, then, that all the commandments and admonitions found in the Torah are essential to the attainment of human perfection, else God would not have commanded them.

But such a proposition is very strange and hard. For if this were the case, no man would be able to acquire the perfection in question, "For there is not a righteous man upon the earth, that doeth good, and sinneth not." If he lacked one commandment, according to this opinion, he could not attain to human perfection, and the Torah which was given to Israel as an act of grace, so as to bring them all to eternal life, would be the very thing which would prevent them from attaining this happy privilege. This is the contrary of God's intention. Not merely would the result be that not all Israelites could attain to perfection, but not even one person in a generation can embrace all the ideas of the Torah, or perform all the statutes and fulfil all the judgments which are found therein. All Israel would then go down to the pit, "Far be it from God, that He should do wickedness; and from the Almighty, that He should commit iniquity." Besides, our national tradition is opposed to this idea, for we find in the Mishnah, "All Israel have a share in the world to come." This is a very important question and must be solved.

We find many things in nature which are not absolutely necessary, but are there to make things better than they would be without them. For example, the duplication of the sense organs is not absolutely necessary, for animals could exist and maintain themselves without this duplication. But they exist in animals to make their condition better than it would be otherwise. So, God, in His desire to lead man to his perfection, seeing that there are so many hindrances which prevent him from attaining this end, devised a means to make the attainment possible. He multiplied ways and means, not all of them necessary for the attainment of perfection, but making it easier, so that human perfection or a part of it may be obtained by means of any one of the ways, the purpose being that not a single human being in general or Israelite in particular, should fail to attain that perfection if he tries to obtain it in any one of the ways.

This is the meaning of the Rabbis' statement at the end of the treatise Makkot, Rabbi Hanania, son of Akashia, said: God desired to favor Israel, therefore He gave them many laws and commandments, as is said: "The Lord was pleased, for His righteousness' sake, to make the teaching great and glorious." They thus make clear that the reason Israel were given so many commandments is to bestow upon them righteousness and merit. Now it is clear that if all were necessary for the attainment of perfection, the effect would be not merit, but guilt. This is why Rabbi Yohanan said, "The Lord is not pleased with this that you say about them, the verse means that the nether-world opens her mouth for him who has not observed even one commandment of the Torah."

Maimonides is of the same opinion in his commentary on that Mishnah. It is a fundamental belief of the Torah, he says, that if a person fulfils one of the six hundred and thirteen commandments in the proper manner without any selfish or material motive, but performs it for its own sake and for the love of God, as I explained, he merits thereby eternal life. This is the meaning of Rabbi Hanania, that if there are many commandments, it is not possible that one should not sometime in his life do at least one of them in the proper manner, so that his soul merit eternal life. This belief is proved in the Talmud, where Rabbi Hanina, son of Teradyon, asks Rabbi Jose, son of Kisma, what are my chances for eternal life? The answer is, have you any good deed to your credit? i.e., have you performed any act in the proper manner? Rabbi Hanina replied that he had performed an act of charity in as perfect a manner as possible. Thereby he merited eternal life. So far Maimonides.

It is clear, therefore, as we said, that one commandment alone is sufficient to give perfection to man. And the reason there are so many commandments in the Torah is not because they are necessary, but to make things better, so that no Israelite should fail to merit eternal life by means of some one of them, whichever it be. We have support for this opinion in no less a man than Maimonides, who says that the opinion of our Rabbis is that the reason for the multiplicity of commandments was not to load us with a heavy burden which we could not bear, but that it was an act of divine grace, to enable Israel to acquire merit and righteousness. He increased the Torah and multiplied the commandments, in order that they may have many different ways of acquiring human perfection, though they do not understand this. They think that because they are "a people robbed and spoiled," the multiplicity of commandments is for the purpose of loading them with a heavy burden. This is why in Isaiah, the verse, "The Lord was pleased for His righteousness' sake, etc." is followed by, "But this is a people robbed and spoiled, etc." They think that because the performance of a single commandment is not sufficient to connect divine providence with all their activities in detail so as to deliver them from their troubles, it is for that reason not sufficient to give any perfection to the soul. But it is not so. Even one commandment done properly, as we explained before, is sufficient to enable one to acquire eternal life. Hence the Rabbis say, "All Israel have a share in the world to come," for it can not be that a single one of them should fail to do some one of the commandments of the Torah by means of which he would attain to some degree of future life. To be sure, the more commandments he performs, the greater is his degree in the future life. This is why Moshe was eager to enter the land of Israel, because by performing those commandments which can not be performed outside, he would no doubt attain to a higher degree in the world to come.

Sometimes a single person performs so many commandments that Providence takes care of him in every detail of his life here below, like Rabbi Hanina, son of Dosa, and other pious men. It may also happen that the many commandments or the whole of them are performed by a number of persons collectively. In that case the group of persons is more cared for by Providence than a single person. In other words, the group is in the position of a single person who performs a great many commandments. This is why a group is always better cared for by Providence than an individual, because in the group a great many commandments are performed or the whole of them, which is less likely to be the case in an individual. Therefore, a group are always more promptly answered when they pray and are more directly under God's providence, being protected from harm, than the individual.

This is true in reference to the fortunes of this world, but in the world to come every one stands on the basis of his own actions and the number of commandments which he has performed. The Rabbis go even farther than this in their statements in many places that even if a person does an act which is neither commanded nor forbidden, provided he does it for God's sake, to honor Him or His law, he thereby merits future life, i.e., he attains to some degree of future existence. They tell in the Talmud **Ketubot** concerning a fuller who lived in the neighborhood of Rabbi and died by throwing himself from the roof, that a voice from heaven said, this fuller is destined

Sefer HaIkkarim — BOOK [Maamar] THREE

to enjoy the future life. From this it appears that a person who is grieved because he did not show honor to a wise man at the time of his death, and commits suicide because of his grief, merits the future life, since his grief as well as his death was for the sake of God.

There is also a story in the Talmud **Abodah Zarah** about an official who was charged with the duty of executing Rabbi Hanina ben Teradyon. Because he hastened the execution so that Rabbi Hanina might not suffer more than was necessary, we are told that he was entitled to future life. Similarly in Talmud Ta'anit, in the second of the two chapters entitled, "Seder Ta'aniyyot," we are told of a number of persons concerning whom Eliyahu said that they would enjoy life in the world to come, though the acts which they had to their credit were not commandments, positive or negative, but just good deeds, as for example the act of the keeper of the prison, who separated the men from the women so that they might not be led into temptation and do wrong, and other instances besides.

The Rabbis give a general principle explaining the good deeds which cause a man to attain the future life, outside of the specific commandments of the Torah. Commenting on the verse, "And thou shalt walk in His ways," they say, Be thou gracious, as He is gracious; be thou merciful, as He is merciful; be thou benevolent, as He is benevolent; bury the dead, even as He buries the dead, and so on. The principle is that any act which a man does for the sake of God helps him to attain to the future life, even if it seems to be a bad act. "In all thy ways acknowledge Him," says the author of Proverbs, and the Rabbis comment, - even if thou art doing a bad act. Again, they say, better is a transgression committed for the sake of God than the performance of a commandment which is not for God's sake. This principle should be understood and borne in mind, for it is essential to the Law of Moshe. If not for this principle the mass of Israelites would not enjoy the future life through the Torah, but only one person in a city or generation. And then the great love which God showed to Israel in giving them the Torah, as we find, "Beloved is Israel, because God gave them a precious article …," would be converted into a means of vengeance, for they could not perform all of it and would be punished for it.

The truth is as we have explained. It is a special principle of the Mosaic law, alluded to in the rabbinic expression, "All Israel have a share in the world to come," that all Israelites attain to some degree of life in the future world. There are, indeed, certain scholars who deny this and hold that one must have a majority of the commandments to his credit in order to merit the future life. But it is not so. The greater the number of commandments that one performs, the higher is his degree in the future world, as we said before, but one may attain to some degree of future life with one commandment alone. In the Talmud **Makkot** we read "Rabbi Simlai in a discourse said, six hundred and thirteen commandments were given to Moshe on Sinai ... David came and reduced them to eleven ... Isaiah reduced them to six ..." From this it might seem that one must perform all the commandments in order to acquire perfection, but that David reduced them to eleven, Isaiah to six and so with the rest. But this is not the case, and we shall explain the meaning of the passage in the following chapter, with the help of God.

Chapter 30

The degrees which are attained by means of the commandments are different for many reasons. They differ - first, according to the different commandments. The degree attained through one commandment is greater than the degree attained through another commandment, though the motive be equally sincere in both. This we learn from the rabbinical statement: "Be as careful about an unimportant commandment as about an important one, for you do not know the reward that attends the various commandments." This shows that there is a difference in the rewards of the different commandments. We also learn from this that we were right in our statement in the preceding chapter that the attainment of perfection does not depend upon a performance of all the commandments. For if this were the case, there would be no meaning in the admonition to be as careful in the observance of an unimportant commandment as in that of an important one on the ground of our ignorance of the rewards attending the various commandments. Even if we knew what the reward was in each case, it would still be necessary to observe them all in order to get any reward. This statement therefore proves that there is a degree of reward attaching to each commandment separately, that the rewards are not equal and that it is not necessary to do all the commandments in order to receive the future reward that is promised.

The degrees of reward differ, secondly, according to the differences of motive in the performance of the commandments. For there is no doubt that the same number of commandments or even the same commandment would be attended by a different degree of reward according to the difference of motive in its performance. Our Rabbis are of the same opinion. "Consider," they say, "the case of two

Sefer HaIkkarim   BOOK [Maamar] THREE

persons who roast their respective paschal lambs. The one eats it for the sake of the Passover, and the order to satisfy his craving for meat. The one who ate it for the sake of the Passover comes under the designation of the scriptural verse: 'For the ways of the Lord are right, and the just do walk in them;' while the other one who ate it to satisfy his appetite is referred to in the sequel, 'But transgressors do stumble therein,' " as we explained above.

Thirdly, assuming equal sincerity in motive and equality of the number of commandments performed, the degrees of reward attained will be different according to the greater or less frequency of performance of a given act. For there is no doubt that the repeated performance of a given act will be followed by a greater degree of reward than a single performance. Take the following case as an example. Two persons equal in wisdom, in wealth and in everything else, donate to charity. The one gives one thousand **Zuz** all at once with the proper motive, while the other gives a thousand times, one **zuz** each time. There is no doubt that the merit of the second is superior to that of the first, though the amount of the donation is the same. The reason is because the performance of many commands of the same act and the repetition of the motive in every one of the acts is more meritorious than a single performance with a sincere motive. Similarly, one who honors his father by giving him a thousand **zuz** at one time attains a different degree from the one who gives him one **zuz** a thousand times, since in the latter case there is a multiplicity of performances of the same commandment.

Fourthly, the degrees differ according to the difference in the number of commandments performed. The performance of many commandments gives rise to a higher degree without any doubt, because we have a combination of many commandments and many acts. As a result of this variety of degrees it may happen that one person may have more commandments to his credit than another, and yet attain only a very low degree of future reward because he did not perform the commandments with the proper motive. He may not be able to attain any degree of future life at all. In such a case, since God does not withhold the reward of any creature, He pays him in this world for the commandment or commandments which he performed without the proper motive. It may happen on the other hand that a person may be a transgressor all his life, and then at the last moment he performs one commandment or does one good deed with the proper motive and dies under the influence of that motive. This one motive may be sufficient to give him a certain degree of reward in the future life, as we have seen in the last chapter in the

Sefer HaIkkarim — BOOK [Maamar] THREE

case of the official who hastened the execution of Rabbi Hanina ben Teradyon. Then there are cases in which the degree that a person attains by the doing of many commandments with the right motives is such that he is the subject of divine providence in this world and is delivered from all accidents, like many of the pious men of Israel, who were able to change the laws of nature by their will, as for example, Rabbi Hanina ben Dosa, Nahum of Gamzo, Rabbi Phinehas ben Yair, and others. There are cases, too, where a person, through the performance of many commandments with the right motives and the attainment of a knowledge of God, may reach in this world the degree of Isaiah, Elisha or the others. This is the highest degree there is, being that of the greatest prophets who lived after Moshe.

We are now ready to interpret the statement of our Rabbis at the end of the Talmud **Makkot**: "Rabbi Simlai expounded: Six hundred and thirteen commandments were given to Moshe on Sinai. David came and reduced them to eleven, as we read: 'Lord, who shall sojourn in Thy Tabernacle? He that walketh uprightly, and worketh righteousness.' Then came Isaiah and reduced them to six, as we read: 'He that walketh righteously and speaketh uprightly …' Then came Micah and reduced them to three: 'And what the Lord doth require of thee: Only to do justly, and to love mercy, and to walk humbly with thy God.' Then came Habakkuk and reduced them to one: 'But the righteous shall live by his faith.' " The meaning is not that by the doing of eleven or of three commandments one can acquire as much of human perfection as by doing all the commandments of the Torah. Nor does it mean that only by performing those eleven or three can one acquire any degree of perfection and not by less. It means merely that every one of the prophets wanted to lay down general principles embracing many commandments of the Torah and many good qualities, such as men show in their conduct, through which one may attain a high degree of perfection. Inasmuch as it is difficult for a person to carry all the six hundred and thirteen commandments, and it is similarly difficult to perform a commandment properly in every respect, as we explained before, the prophets desired to establish general rules by which a high degree of perfection may be attained, similar to that which is attained through all the commandments, though it can not be equal to it.

David enumerated eleven things which embrace good qualities, rather than ideas or commandments. For the expressions, "Speaketh truth in his heart … Nor taketh up a reproach against his neighbour;

in whose eyes a vile person is despised," are not identical with any commandment in the Torah. But the intention of David was to lay down general rules, embracing many commandments and good qualities, by which a person may acquire a high degree of human perfection. Thus, the expressions, "Walketh uprightly, and worketh righteousness, and speaketh truth in his heart, that hath no slander upon his tongue, nor doeth evil to his fellow," admonish us not to sin in thought or speech or action, and to improve our character by means of the good qualities which follow from these general rules; in thought - "speaketh truth in his heart;" in speech - "hath no slander upon his tongue;" in deed - "nor doeth evil to his fellow, nor taketh up a reproach against his neighbour;" i.e., who is as zealous about the good name of his neighbor as he is about himself. These admonitions lead to perfection though they are not identical with any commandment in the Torah, but teach merely the improvement of moral qualities. He also mentions certain specific commandments against which the people of his time offended, or such as a person is apt to neglect, thinking they are not wrong, for example: "Nor taketh a bribe in behalf of the innocent," which means that he did not even take a gift to acquit the innocent, an act regarded as harmless, and so with the rest.

This interpretation of ours is confirmed by David himself. In the twenty-fourth Psalm, he asks, "Who shall ascend into the mountain of the Lord? And who shall stand in His holy place?" For an answer he names only three requirements, "He that hath clean hands, and a pure heart; who hath not taken my name in vain." Why does he not name the eleven qualities mentioned in the fifteenth Psalm? The answer is that in the twenty-fourth Psalm he embraces all the commandments and good qualities under three heads only, act, thought and speech; act - "clean hands;" thought - "pure heart;" speech - "who hath not taken my name [soul] in vain," i.e., who did not take a false oath even by the life of David, who did not know the hidden things. This is the meaning of the expression "my soul," which refers to David, as the Masorah has it. Or we may read, "His soul," as the ketib has it; in which case it refers to God, as we find: "There are six things which the Lord hateth, Yea, seven which are an abomination unto His soul." Or the pronoun "his" may refer to the person concerning whom he asks, "Who shall ascend into the mountain of the Lord?" The meaning would then be that the intellectual power which he has was not given to him in vain, he did not "take it in vain," but perfected his soul as far as it is in man's power to do so; "And hath not sworn deceitfully," for it is possible that one may swear not falsely but the truth, as in the story of Raba's staff. Nevertheless, he says that it is not right to do so, since it is a deceitful oath.

In these three general concepts are included all the commandments which he names in the fifteenth Psalm; except that in the latter place he specifies a number of things which are not included in Psalm twenty-four, such as have to do with certain moral qualities against which the men of his time were in the habit of offending, or which a person is apt to neglect, thinking there is no harm in them, as, for example, despising the learned. Therefore, he adds, "But he honoureth them that fear the Lord," also, "Nor taketh up a reproach against his neighbour."

They have the same idea in mind when they say that Isaiah reduced them to six. The meaning is that Isaiah laid down six general principles of the commandments, as follows:

1. That one should not sin in act, but should do good deeds - "Walketh righteously;"

2. That one should not sin in speech - "Speaketh uprightly;"

3. That one should not sin in thought - "Despiseth the gain of oppressions." For to despise is the opposite of desire, which is in the heart [mind].

4. Then he says that it is not sufficient that one does not sin in any of the ways mentioned, but that one must refrain from upholding the hands of transgressors - "Shaketh his hands from holding of bribes," which means that he does not merely refrain from taking a bribe, but he shakes his hands from supporting the hand of him who takes a bribe.

5. And he not merely refrains from supporting those who do wrong, but he keeps away from the sight or the hearing of evil - "Stoppeth his ears from hearing of blood, and shutteth his eyes from looking upon evil."

6. Then he says: "He shall dwell on high; his place of defence shall be the munitions of rocks." The meaning is that a man of this sort may be trusted to guard the fortress of faith, for "his bread shall be given, his waters shall be sure," he will not be afraid of any evil thing, for in famine the Lord will deliver him from death, and in war from the hand of the sword. Or it may be that the words, "He shall dwell on high," refer to the reward of the soul in the higher world.

The same idea is expressed in the statement that Micah reduced them to three, as is said: "And what the Lord doth require of thee; only to do justly, and to love mercy, and to walk humbly with thy God."

Sefer Haikkarim   BOOK [Maamar] THRE

These three embraces all the commandments of the Torah or a majority of them. "To do justly," embraces all rules governing the relations of a man to his fellow. "To love mercy," includes all kinds of benevolence; while "to walk humbly with thy God," embraces all those matters which concern the relations between a man and God, namely true ideas and beliefs. The expression, "humbly," is used in connection with these to suggest, as we said in the Second Book of this treatise, that the divine attributes are negative, attributes to be stated humbly and modestly, so to speak, for a person must not give free rein to his tongue and ascribe to God any positive attribute that occurs to his mind. Our Rabbis say in this connection: "The best remedy of all is silence, as is said: 'To Thee, praise is silence'." This is the meaning of the expression, "To walk humbly with thy God."

The same idea is expressed in the statement that Habakkuk reduced the commandments to one, as is said, "But the righteous shall live by his faith." Habakkuk, having been complaining of the prosperity of the wicked and the sufferings of the righteous, lays down at the end the following principle, that if the righteous man will persevere in his faith, believing in the words of the prophets and in the promises which God made to punish the wicked and reward the righteous, he will live without concerning himself about the vicissitudes of fortune, will bear everything with good grace, and thus merit life in the future world.

Similarly, the sages of the Talmud were in the habit of laying down general principles of the commandments of the Torah. A story is told about one of the later sages, to whom an armed bandit who had committed many sins came one day and said: I want to repent and observe the commandments of God, but I can not assume the responsibility of observing the great number of commandments in the Torah, for it is too much. The wise man said, are you willing to assume the responsibility of observing one thing properly? Yes, said the bandit. Very well, said the sage. Take upon yourself the duty of telling the truth. The bandit promised and went on his way. Sometime later the bandit was on his way to rob a certain person and to put him to death, when he was met by a person who asked him where he was going. The bandit recalled the promise he had made to tell the truth and told the inquirer where he was going. He was then met by another person who asked him the same question and he gave him the same answer. Then the bandit reflected that those two persons might testify against him and have him put to death. The same thing happened to him again and again whenever he was about to do something wrong, with the result that he refrained from evil deeds: This shows that by keeping one or two general principles a person may come to observe the greater part of the commandments of the Torah, or at least a considerable part, and thus attain to future life or to an important degree thereof.

Chapter 31

The aim which the soul is capable of attaining while in the body by performing the commandments of the Torah, is nothing else than the permanent acquisition of a disposition to fear God. And when it acquires this attribute of fearing God, the soul is elevated and is prepared to attain eternal life, which is the good reserved for the righteous, and is the happiness of the soul, as we read: "Oh how abundant is Thy goodness, which Thou hast laid up for them that fear Thee." This is made clear from the fact that the Bible announces severe punishment upon Israel and their descendants if their souls do not acquire the character of the fear of God by performing the commandments of the Torah: "If thou wilt not observe to do all the words of this law that are written in this book, that thou mayest fear this glorious and awful Name, the Lord thy God; then the Lord will make thy plagues wonderful, and the plagues of thy seed ..."

The question may be asked, how can the fear of God lead a person to so great a privilege, namely, the attainment of eternal life? Intellectual knowledge would seem to be a more likely cause to lead to such an effect. The answer is, Solomon has stated clearly in the book of Ecclesiastes that fear is the cause of immortality, and nothing else. God's wisdom has decreed that it should be so, and we must not seek for any reasons. Solomon begins by inquiring whether there is anything that confers immortality: "What profit hath he that worketh in that he laboureth?" Then he says: "I have seen the task which God hath given to the sons of men to be exercised therewith." This means: I have seen the works which God gave to the sons of men to concern themselves with, viz. arts and trades, and they are all "beautiful in their time," i.e., for the moment, so that the arts and the sciences should not perish. "Also, He hath set the world in their heart, yet so that man cannot find out the work that God hath done from the beginning even to the end." The meaning is, God also set in their hearts the desire to know the world, i.e., the science of nature. And though it is a thing that can not be attained, because man cannot comprehend the work that God hath done from the beginning even to the end, nevertheless the desire which He gave to them is also beautiful in its time, in that it prevents that art or science from perishing, but not because it may lead to eternal life, as people think; for sometimes what one learns in this way is not the truth, as we explained in the third chapter of this Book. Therefore, he says later: "I know that there is no good in them except to rejoice, and to get pleasure as long as they live." The meaning is, all these human endeavors, including knowledge, have no other good than the joy which they afford. Every one finds pleasure in any work that he does voluntarily and by which he thinks he attains his purpose. The work also helps to do good to him in his life, for philosophy instructs a person to do that which is good and beneficial in human conduct during one's life, but it is not good for anything else. Therefore, we may say, "But also that every man should eat and drink, and enjoy pleasure for all his labour, is the gift of God," like the task which God hath given to the sons of men to be exercised therewith. But there is nothing in all this that leads to immortality.

Then he says: "I know that, whatsoever God doeth, it shall be forever; nothing can be added to it, nor anything taken from it; and God hath so made it, that men should fear before Him." The meaning is that all that which God makes without the mediation of nature which belongs to the sphere of generation and dissolution, as for example the heavens and all their hosts, will be forever, for we see that they are individually permanent, as David says: "He hath also established them forever and ever," But in order that the intellectual soul in man, which is God's work, as is said: "And breathed into his nostrils the breath of life," may have immortality, God hath so made it that men should fear before Him. It is clear from this that fear of God is, as it were, the true mean, to which nothing should be added and from which nothing should be taken away. For this is the definition of the true mean, that it admits not of addition or diminution, for the latter remove the mean and destroy it. God made "fear" before Him, i.e., the Torah and the commandments, which are the true mean, and which produce fear of God, conferring immortality upon the soul. Hence it necessarily follows that the Torah will exist forever, for whatsoever God doeth, it shall be forever. Or we may interpret the passage thus. God hath so ordered that they should have fear before Him. Hence this fear is, as it were, the true mean, which admits not of more and less and can not be destroyed. Therefore, it is a fitting means for the attainment of the human end.

Now, since His wisdom has so decreed, it is not proper to pretend wisdom and say, how is it possible for fear to lead man to human perfection? Fear is like the true mean, which admits not of addition or subtraction for the attainment of the end, namely permanence and immortality. Hence the expression in the Torah: "Thou shalt fear the Lord thy God," though a specific command, is a general principle, embracing all the commandments of the Torah, or a great many of them. For fear is that disposition which is acquired through the commandments of the Torah, and is the noblest disposition for a man to acquire, nor can it be acquired except after great pains and effort. The patriarch Abraham was not called "God-fearing," until after he had gone through his trials. Then it is said about him, "For now I know that thou art a God-fearing man," i.e., that thou hast attained the noblest character that a man can attain in this world in order to merit life in the world to come. For this reason, the Torah calls attention in many places to this disposition: "And thou shalt fear thy God, I am the Lord;" "Thou shalt fear the Lord thy God;" because it is extremely difficult to attain this quality, and yet it can be attained by observing the commandments of the Torah.

For the same reason the Bible says: "And now, Israel, what doth the Lord thy God require of thee, but to fear the Lord thy God, to walk in all His ways, and to love Him, and to serve the Lord thy God with all thy heart and with all thy soul; to keep for thy good the commandments of the Lord." The interpretation of the passage is as follows. Moshe is explaining to the people the extraordinary kindness of God. By right, in order to attain the perfection of one's soul, a person should fear God, walk in His ways, love Him, and serve Him with all his heart and soul. But it is very difficult for a person to attain the required degree of fear, love and service with all heart and soul. Hence God made it easier for man. He commanded him instead to observe merely God's statutes and commandments, and thereby he may attain that disposition which he would get from service with heart and soul. The meaning of the above passage is therefore this: Now, Israel, consider the wonderful kindness of God. What does He ask of you? Instead of the fear of God, instead of walking in His ways and loving Him, instead of serving Him with all your heart and soul, all of which you are obliged to do - He asks you merely to keep the commandments of God and His statutes which I command you this day, for your good, i.e., all this is for your good, because by keeping the commandments of the Torah one may attain the human purpose which we should attain by great labor and enormous effort through fear and love and God's service with all one's heart and soul.

This interpretation of the passage is worth careful attention, for it is very remarkable, and solves the difficulty raised by the Rabbis. They say, "Is fear so small a thing?" And the answer is given, "Yes, for Moshe it is indeed a small thing." The answer is not satisfactory. For the opponent may say, it is not fair for a man of great wealth to say to a poor man, who has nothing, I ask of you only a thousand gold pieces. A thousand gold pieces for a poor man are a great matter and hard to get. The rich man is not fair in speaking thus. But according to our interpretation there is no difficulty. God does not ask anything that is hard to acquire. He asks merely the performance of the commandments of the Torah, because the quality of fear through which one may attain human perfection follows from the performance of the commandments of the Torah.

David also says: "The fear of the Lord is the beginning of wisdom." The meaning is, the best and essential part of wisdom is to attain to the fear of God. The word, "beginning" [התחלה], has the same meaning here as in the expression, "And anoint themselves with the chief [ראש] ointments." Commenting on the sequel, "A good understanding have all they that do them [sc. His commandments]," the Rabbis say, "that do them," not "that study them." This is to indicate that the performance of the commandments leads to the aim realized by understanding, that aim which all acknowledge to be the ultimate end of man. Also, in Job we read, "Behold, the fear of the Lord, that is wisdom." The meaning is, the aim of wisdom is to attain the fear of the Lord. And inasmuch as this quality is the aim of all the other qualities which are attainable from the Torah through the performance of the commandments, we must treat of it at length in the following chapter.

Chapter 32

Fear in every case is the receding of the soul and the gathering of all her powers into herself, when she imagines some fear-inspiring thing. The latter may be of two kinds. The soul may imagine a harmful thing, which she fears by reason of the injury which she thinks may come from it. Or the soul may imagine something very great, exalted, elevated and high, which she fears when she considers her own poverty and lowliness in comparison with that great thing, though she has no fear of any harm coming to her from the thing.

Now when a person performs the commandments from fear of the first kind, fear of punishment or love of reward, he is called, in the rabbinic terminology, an insincere server. In the Talmud **Sotah**, chapter **Notel**, we read: There are seven kinds of **Pharisees**" ... i.e., such as pretend to virtues they have not. Among these are named, the Pharisee from fear and the Pharisee from love. Thereupon they say to the Tanna, you must not include the Pharisee from love and the Pharisee from fear, for Rabbi Yehuda said in the name of Rab, one should always occupy himself with the Torah and the commandments, even if it is not for their own sake, for from such occupation he will come to do them for their own sake. Rashi explains the expressions, "from love," and "from fear," as meaning from love of reward and from fear of punishment. It is clear therefore that he who concerns himself with the Torah and the commandments from love of reward or fear of punishment, is spoken of as one who does it not for its own sake.

The person, however, who performs the commandments from the fear and love of God and because he is submissive to His commandments, is called by the Rabbis a person who occupies himself with the Torah for its own sake. That is, he does not perform the commandments from fear of punishment and love of reward, but because he imagines the sublimity and dignity of God, and therefore he submits to do His will. This is fear of the second kind explained above. It is the true fear, with which Abraham was praised, when God said to him, "Now I know that thou art a God-fearing man." And it is the final quality which one attains by means of the commandments of the Torah. For if a man reflects and considers that God sees his open as well as hidden acts, and compares his imperfection and poverty of understanding with the sublimity and dignity of God, he will stand in great awe before Him and will be ashamed to transgress His commandments and not to do His will, as a person is ashamed to do an unbecoming thing in the presence of an honorable prince, a respected and wise old man, who has a reputation for learning, character and dignity. Though he may not contemplate that any harm will come to him from a violation of his command, nevertheless he will without doubt feel ashamed and abashed and hesitate very much to offend his honor in his presence. This kind of noble fear, the intellect by nature has a desire for, because everything has a desire for that which is of the same nature as, and similar to itself. And just as every person desires to carry out the wishes of a perfect and pious man, and to serve him with sincerity and eagerness, without the hope of reward or the fear of punishment, so the mind desires to fulfil the will of God, because it is natural for it to do so. For this reason, the wise man used to say, "Master of the universe, it is well known to Thee that it is our will to do Thy will, but the leaven in the dough prevents …" The meaning is, it is in conformity with the nature of the reason, which decrees that the inferior should be subordinate to the superior, as the animals submit to man. But matter and the evil inclination - the leaven in the dough - are opposed to this, and are always thinking of doing evil and rebelling and offending the honor of the great. Therefore, the Torah lays down punishments in order to compel matter and the material forces to serve God from fear of punishment. But it is not necessary to compel the reason, for it is natural to the reason to serve God and to submit to Him without the fear of punishment or the love of reward. Both of these kinds of fear are therefore necessary for man that he may attain his perfection, the one from the side of matter, the other from the side of reason.

Job boasts of both the kinds of fear, saying that he refrained from doing wrong for fear of punishment, and that he did those things which were pleasing to God, submitting to Him on account of His sublimity, exaltation and dignity: "For calamity from God was a terror to me, and by reason of His majesty I could do nothing." The first part of the verse refers to the fear of punishment, the second refers to the fear of infinite sublimity and exaltation. When I consider His exalted character, says Job, I can not transgress His words and neglect to do His will, for I am ashamed to do that which displeases Him, apart from any fear of punishment, to which reference is made in the first part of the verse.

Similarly, when Job reproved his companions and charged them with insincerity, and with flattering God with false words, he said, "Will ye speak unrighteously for God, and talk deceitfully for Him? Will ye show Him favour? Will ye contend for God? Would it be good that He should search you out? Or as one mocketh a man, will ye mock Him? He will surely reprove you, if ye do secretly show favour. Shall not His majesty terrify you, and His dread fall upon you?" "Shall not His majesty terrify you," denotes the fear which one feels because of God's exaltation and sublimity and because He sees all that a man does openly as well as secretly. This deters a man from speaking unrighteously or deceitfully. The second part of the verse, "And His dread fall upon you," denotes the fear and the dread which comes upon a person from fear of punishment, which represents the side of matter. Therefore, he adds, "Your memorials shall be like unto ashes, your eminences to eminences of clay." The meaning is, when you remember that you are similar to ashes and that you are made of clay, you must fear God for the two reasons mentioned. This is the conception of fear which one must have before God and which entitles one to be called God-fearing.

Sefer Halkkarim
Chapter 33

That which gives completeness to a commandment so that the purpose intended by it may be attained, is joy. For joy gives completeness and perfection to anything done. One and the same act if done joyfully and cheerfully is called a virtue, while if done in ill humor is called a vice. This is explained in the second book of the Ethics of Aristotle, namely that when a person performs an act of generosity cheerfully, his act is a virtue; while if he does it with ill humor, it is called a vice. The Bible also promises reward for practising charity joyfully: "Thou shalt surely give him, and thy heart shall not be grieved when thou givest unto him; because that for this thing the Lord thy God will bless thee." The blessing is made to depend on "Thy heart shall not be grieved," and not on "Thou shalt surely give him."

This may be explained more fully in the following way. There is no doubt that the noblest and most worthy deed should be rewarded by God, and that punishment should be given for its violation, according to the idea of the Torah. But there is no deed that is more noble and more worthy and more deserving of reward, according to the truth and the consensus of mankind, than the service of God. And we find that the Bible announces severe punishment for not serving God joyfully: "Because thou didst not serve the Lord thy God with joyfulness, and with gladness of heart, by reason of the abundance of all things; therefore, shalt thou serve thy enemy...." The punishment is here made to depend on not serving God with joyfulness, not on not serving Him at all.

That this is the interpretation can be seen as follows: The meaning can not be that punishment will come because he did not serve God when he was in good humor, for it would follow from this that one is not obliged to serve God when he is not enjoying gladness and abundance. We have proved therefore that performance of a commandment joyfully gives completion and perfection to the commandment. Therefore, the Psalmist urges that the service of God shall be with gladness: "Serve the Lord with gladness; come before His presence with singing." We must inquire, therefore, if the service of God can not be performed perfectly unless it is done with gladness and good humor, how can this be reconciled with our explanation in the preceding chapter that the service of God must be with fear, which makes the heart tremble and grieve? For one can not serve God with grief and gladness at the same time, since they are opposites.

Sefer Haikkarim   BOOK [Maamar] THRE

The solution of the question is as follows: The proper performance of a function is an indication of the soundness of the power or faculty in question, while the improper performance of a function is an indication of a defect in the power or of its want of soundness. Now as it is a sign of perfection in a person if he does not fear that which should not be feared, so it is a sign of perfection if he fears that which should be feared. Not to fear that which should be feared would be a defect. If one is not afraid to put his hand into the fire, it shows either an aberration of mind or insensibility of the hand, as Hippocrates says in the second book of his Aphorisms: "If any part of the body is diseased and the person does not feel pain because of absorption in his affairs, it shows an aberration of mind." The same thing applies to the soul. If she is afraid and stands in awe of that which she should be afraid and stand in awe of, that is an indication of health and perfection of intellect. And as the virtue of the soul and the excellence of the intellect increase, she appreciates more the sublimity and exalted character of God, and stands in greater awe of Him and fears to transgress His commandments.

Now when a person finds in himself this degree of fear, he should rejoice in this fear, for it shows health of soul and perfection of intellect. To prove that this is the correct idea, David, in another passage, makes clear that the expression, "Serve the Lord with gladness," does not mean that the service should be conducted in a light, frivolous and vulgar fashion, but that it should be inspired with fear, "Serve the Lord with fear, and rejoice with trembling." The meaning is that the fundamental spirit of the service should be one of fear and trembling. When the soul considers the sublimity of God and His exalted character, she will be afraid of Him, as she compares her own lowliness with His greatness and worth. At the same time she will be glad and rejoice at the fear and trembling she feels, because she will realize that she fears that which is deserving of fear - an indication of intellectual perfection and health on her part. This joy, therefore, makes the service perfect and complete - "And rejoice with trembling" - i.e., joy gives completeness and perfection to the service.

Similarly, joy gives perfection and permanence to the word or command. Thus, David says: "Thy testimonies have I taken as a heritage forever; For they are the rejoicing of my heart." The Torah is divided into three parts - judgments, testimonies and statutes. Concerning the judgments, he has said, "I have sworn, and have confirmed it; to observe Thy righteous judgments." Here the words, "and have confirmed it" [and have carried out in practice], allude to

Sefer HaIkkarim — BOOK [Maamar] THREE

the fact that the perfection of the judgments consists in their being actually in existence. Therefore, he says now that the testimonies, i.e., the ideas, in the Torah are in agreement with sense and reason because the mind accepts them with gladness, and gladness causes them to remain permanently in the soul. Therefore, he says: "Thy testimonies have I taken as a heritage forever."

As for the statutes, they are those commandments of the Torah which the mind does not accept, because no reason is known for the prohibitions they enjoin, such as swine's flesh or wearing a garment of wool and flax mixed. The reason therefore does not accept them with gladness and must be subdued so as to consent to perform them with gladness. Therefore, the Psalmist says: "I have inclined my heart to perform Thy statutes, forever. Their reward is eternal." The meaning is, I compelled my intellect against its will to perform them. And this was because of the hope of eternal reward which is promised for their performance: "Their reward is eternal." The reward causes rejoicing and the joy makes the soul take them in permanently. This is what David was priding himself upon when he said, "I rejoice at Thy word, as one that findeth great spoil." This refers to the statutes, the joy in which is not due for their own sake, but only because they are the word of God. In performing these, says the Psalmist, I rejoice as one that findeth great spoil.

In order however, to make a distinction between the joy felt in the statutes, which is due merely to the expected reward, and the joy which one feels in the testimonies, i.e., those commandments to which the reason assents, he says elsewhere, "I have rejoiced in the way of Thy testimonies, as much as in all riches," i.e., joy without end. "All riches," includes all the money in the world, more than which can not be imagined.

All this proves that joy causes a thing to remain permanently in the soul, and gives completeness and perfection to an act, no matter what it be. Even the doer of a bad act, in order to attain his purpose completely, must perform it with gladness, as the Bible says when it warns Israel of the punishment which will come to them if they transgress the words of the Torah: "And it shall come to pass, that as the Lord rejoiced over you to do you good, and to multiply you; so the Lord will cause you to rejoice in order to cause you to perish, and to destroy you." The meaning is that God will bring it about that the evil doer will rejoice in his evil deed so that he should perform it completely. The verb ישיש is in the hiphil, which is causative, to indicate that not God, the absolutely good, will rejoice in doing evil, but that He will cause the evil doer to rejoice. Far be it from God that He should rejoice in doing evil! Solomon warns us against it, when he says: "Rejoice not when thy enemy falleth." And the prophet says: "Neither shouldst thou have rejoiced over the children of Yehuda in the day of their destruction." All this shows that it is wrong to rejoice in an evil deed.

But when it comes to doing good, the joy is attributed to God Himself, and the intransitive form of the verb is used: "For the Lord will again rejoice over thee for good, as He rejoiced over thy fathers." The verb is used in the kal form, which is intransitive. To indicate that joy gives perfection to an act, Solomon says: "To do justly is joy to the righteous, but ruin to the workers of iniquity." The meaning is that the righteous, who rejoices in doing justly, produces a result that is perfect in its nature; whereas the wrong doers, who when they do right do it unwillingly and without pleasure, because it is their ruin, necessarily produce a justice which is all crooked, since they take no pleasure in doing it.

Chapter 34

The essence of divine service in performing a commandment is, as we have seen, the fear of God. We have also found that divine service must be inspired with joy if it is to be complete. But it is hard to reconcile fear with joy. We must therefore treat of this matter more at length so that we may have a complete and practical understanding how one inspired with fear can at the same time be glad and rejoice, seeing that fear and trembling depress the heart and make it grieve.

Every person understands that in order to attain some high degree or honor, he must undergo great toil and trouble for a certain time. Now although while enduring that toil and trouble he undoubtedly suffers pain and grief, nevertheless when he considers in his mind the great honor or high degree which he expects to attain through that trouble, the latter is reduced to nothing in comparison with the expected good. The same thing applies to the fear of God that we have been speaking of. When one considers the high degree which he may attain through fear, - the fear which results from reflecting upon the divine sublimity and worth, - he ignores all the trouble and the grief and the trembling which come upon him by reason of the fear.

Solomon has a very apt analogy which is in agreement with what we have said: "If thou seek her as silver, and search for her as for hid treasures; then shalt thou understand the fear of the Lord." The meaning is that although there is great trouble involved in mining the silver, which comes out mixed with water; and similarly in digging for a hidden treasure on one's premises there is great trouble and toil and effort, and one may injure a finger or a foot or a thigh and feel great pain, nevertheless one searches after these things with eagerness, and even though he feels pain and suffering when he is hurt, still when he considers the purpose, namely the treasure or the silver, he rejoices and bears all the pain and trouble gladly and in good humor. In the same way we must think of the toil and fear and trembling which one suffers when he is inspired with the fear of God. He must nevertheless feel great joy when he reflects on the great value of the purpose to be attained, namely submission to God and His service, which is the purpose of fear. This is the meaning of the passage quoted above: "If thou seek her as silver, and search for her as for hid treasures; then shalt thou understand the fear of the Lord." That is, if you bear all the trouble in good humor like one who digs for a hidden treasure, or who mines silver, then you will understand the fear of the Lord. For in the very same way, you should be glad and rejoice despite the pain and trouble and toil which come to you through the service of God.

Not every one can attain this degree, hence the person who does is called, "one who serves from love," and not merely "God-fearing." Abraham was told at the end of his trials, "Now I know that thou art a God-fearing man." But he is also called "friend," Israel being spoken of as "The seed of Abraham My friend." Our Rabbis say: Those who act from love of God and take pleasure in their sufferings come under the biblical designation: "But they that love Him shall be as the sun when he goeth forth in his might." For he who loves God, pays no attention to all the trouble and toil and pains which come to him through the service of God. When God first revealed Himself to Abraham, He told him to leave his land and his birthplace, in order to try him and to accustom him to bear for His sake the trouble and toil which have to be borne in travel. Then when Abraham stood his test joyfully and with good humor, the Bible called him friend. All this shows that the cheerful endurance of toil and trouble in the service of God gives perfection to the service and the fear of God.

The fear of God is not like the fear of a human being. If one is in fear of a human being or a king or a prince, he is in constant terror and dread, which shorten his life; whereas the fear of God, far from shortening a man's life, increases it: "The fear of the Lord prolongeth days." The wicked, on the other hand, who do not fear

God, not merely do not live longer than the others, but their lives are shortened.

Similarly, although it is natural that a timid and fearful person should have children as timid as he, and that he should never become rich or maintain his wealth because, being always afraid, he does not attend to his affairs properly, nevertheless David says: "Happy is the man that feareth the Lord, that delighteth greatly in His commandments. His seed shall be mighty upon earth …" The meaning is, happy is he who fears God, for this fear does not lead to timidity but to might, so that his seed shall be mighty upon earth. Also, he who delighteth in His commandments, though this involves expense, will not lose his wealth for, "Wealth and riches are in his house; and his merit endureth forever." This is to show that the fear of God does not shorten or diminish either wealth or life, and does not bring about misfortunes like the fear of man. Solomon says: "The fear of the Lord tendeth to life; and he that hath it shall abide satisfied; he shall not be visited with evil." That is, the fear of God does not cause death, but leads to life. The man who fears God will want for nothing, but will abide satisfied. And he will not be afraid of misfortune, for he shall not be visited with evil.

Chapter 35

The love of God is a degree than which there is none higher, and a person can not attain it unless he has reached the highest degree of fear, as we have explained. Abraham did not get the title "My friend," until the end of his life and after the incident of Yitzhak's sacrifice, when he was told: "Now I know that thou art a God-fearing man." We must therefore explain the meaning of love and the various species thereof.

Love is of three kinds: The love of the good, the love of the useful, and the love of the agreeable. To love the good is to love a thing solely because it is good, without the element of the usefulness or pleasure of the object entering into the feeling. To love the useful is to love a thing solely because of the utility one may derive from it. To love the agreeable is to love a thing because of the pleasure one derives from it, not because it is good or useful, but only because it is agreeable. The love of the useful and the love of the agreeable admit of degrees of more and less according to the degree of the utility or pleasure, and they may cease altogether. The love of the good for the sake of the good itself can not change or be destroyed, for the lover does not love the loved one because he is good to him,

Sefer HaIkkarim — BOOK [Maamar] THREE

i.e., in relation to the lover, but because he has found that the loved one is good in himself and the loved one is known to the lover and he alone is engraved in his heart, so that the concept of love applies to both. For love is the union and complete intellectual identification of the lover and the loved; whereas in the case of the useful and the agreeable what the lover knows is not the loved one, but the benefit which he derives from him or the pleasure which he gets. Therefore, the lover and the loved can not be united. And for this reason, the love changes with the change in the utility or pleasure, or it may cease entirely. But the love of the good can not change, for the lover receives no benefit from the loved, but the knowledge of him alone. For this reason, the love of the good because it is good is the best of the kinds of love.

Now since God is the absolute good in whom there is no evil at all, since there is in Him neither privation nor potentiality, the love of God is the love of the good because it is good. And it increases as the knowledge of God increases, since we said that the love of the good is dependent upon knowledge alone. Since, however, God is the creator of all things, and the gracious author of the existence of all existing things, and the giver of life to all those things that have life, He is also useful and is deserving of love also because of His benefits. Further, if we reflect upon the manner in which He provides food for all the things He created and observe that He did not merely create those things which are necessary for animal and man for bare existence, but that He also provided luxuries, which are not necessary for bare existence - thus, man may exist on bread alone, yet God created figs and grapes and pomegranates and other fruits which give pleasure, though they are not necessary for the preservation of existence - we realize from this aspect that He deserves to be loved also because of the pleasure He gives, i.e., because He created pleasant and agreeable things. Hence, although He is an absolute unity, all the species of love are appropriate to Him, love of the good, love of the useful, love of the agreeable. It follows therefore that He should be loved as much as possible with all the kinds of love, because it is not conceivable that there can be any other being that is better, or more useful, or more agreeable than He.

For this reason, when Moshe commanded Israel to love God with all the kinds of love, as we shall see, by saying, "And thou shalt love the Lord thy God with all thy heart, and with all thy soul and with all thy might," he prefaced his commandment with the expression, "Hear O Israel, the Lord our God the Lord is one." The meaning is,

Sefer Halkkarim BOOK [Maamar] THRE

though He is one, nevertheless all the kinds of love are appropriate to Him, love of the good, love of the useful and love of the agreeable, because He is the absolutely good, and bestows benefits and confers pleasure, and you must not love any one else no matter what the nature of the love be, because in Him are contained all the causes of love. He must therefore be loved, "with all thy heart and with all thy soul and with all thy might," for there is nothing to prevent the love of Him from being as perfect as possible.

A person can not love two things or two persons with a perfect love, for if he loves them both, neither love is perfect since it is divided between two. It is impossible for the lover to be completely united with the loved, as the idea of love requires, unless the loved is one. Therefore, he says: "The Lord is one," to indicate that since God is one, the love is not divided, and your love may be perfect, since it is not divided into two parts. Nor is there any objection from the fact that there are different kinds of love, namely of the good, of the useful and of the agreeable. For since God is one and has in Him all the different causes of love, you should love God perfectly with all your heart and with all your soul and with all your might.

Nor does the change in a person's age cause any hindrance to his love. For we find that a man's life may be divided into three parts, the years of growth, the stationary years, and the years of decline. The changes in his love during these periods follow the three species of love, the good, the useful and the agreeable. In the years of growth, until the age of thirty or thereabouts, a person loves the agreeable and follows it. Such love is found in young men, in women and in those who are on the same plane as youths. For example, a person who indulges in sexual intercourse because it is pleasant, without considering the injury which results therefrom for body and soul, is like a boy who indulges the appetite for food, without considering the injury resulting from overeating, and cares for nothing else except food and other agreeable delights. During the stationary years, from thirty to fifty or thereabouts, the love of the useful predominates, so much so that there are persons who neglect food and drink and other pleasures by reason of their passion for gambling, because of the great winnings that may be made in a short time. Others again risk their lives in ships on the ocean with expectation of gain, caring for no other pleasure. During the years of decline, from fifty on, a person cares no longer for the useful or the pleasant, but only for the good as such. This is why we find that old people are more diligent in serving God and abstain more from the appetites than others. When they see that the love of the pleasant and the useful are not permanent, they care only for the love of the good as such, which is permanent and unchangeable, as soon as this love finds its object in God, as we explained above. This love gives salvation to the soul.

A young man, by reason of the heat of his blood and his indulgence in the appetites, does not appreciate the soul's reward and salvation. Being absorbed in the things of sense, he thinks that they will remain permanently, but he does not believe in the salvation and immortality of the soul, which is something that can not be perceived with the senses. This is why the Bible says in reference to the person who trusts in God, "Through long life will I satisfy him, and make him to behold My salvation." The meaning is, Through length of days, i.e., through reaching old age, when the desires grow weak, he will be able to appreciate the salvation and immortality of the soul, and will come to understand that these privileges are attained through the love of God. And hence he will have a tendency to serve God and to love Him, for it is characteristic of old people that they are more addicted to the service of God than others. This is the general rule as applicable to the generality of men. But there are old people who follow after pleasure like young boys, or after utility and power like a man of forty; and on the other hand there are young men who are in love with the good like old men. Persons differ also in this respect according to their temperaments and habits, and according to the customs in which they have been brought up. Still, in general, the life of a person is divided into the three kinds of love, as we explained above.

It seems that the difference in the character of the love at these three different ages is due to the difference in the influence exerted by the powers of the soul upon the individual. During the time of youth and the years of growth, the influence of the appetitive soul predominates, and hence the person follows pleasure. At the age of young manhood and during the stationary years, the animal soul predominates, to which belongs the spirited faculty and other similar powers, and hence the person pursues power, authority, wealth and utility as he sees it. In old age, when the desires and the other powers become weak, so that he no longer pursues power and authority, the rational faculty comes to the fore, and he comes to realize that all the other things are evanescent, and that there is nothing that is permanent and can give him permanence except the service of God and those things which it is characteristic of reason to follow. Accordingly, he will reject the desires and pursue those things which his intellectual soul dictates, such as the love and fear of God, and

Sefer HaIkkarim BOOK [Maamar] THRE

in general the love of the good, i.e., God, as such, and not because He is useful or pleasant.

This rational power, it seems, is called in our language, lebab [heart]. The word leb is applied to the animal organ in which the power of life resides; whereas the word lebab applies only to the rational power. Thus, we find: "But I have understanding [lebab] as well as you;" "But an empty man will get understanding [yilabeb]." The word nefesh [soul] is used in a general as well as in a special sense. It is applied to the psychic powers collectively. This is the most frequent use. It is also applied specially to the powers of the animal soul. Thus, we read in Job: "In whose hand is the soul [nefesh] of every living thing, and the breath of all mankind." The words, "the soul of every living thing," denote the animal soul as a whole, while the expression, "and the breath of all mankind," denotes the rational power in man.

Since the appetitive soul is always eager to attain its desires and acquire money, the Bible calls it "wealth" [meod]. Accordingly, Moshe, wishing to allude to the love of God exercised by these three powers during the three ages of man, as we explained, said: "And thou shalt love the Lord thy God, with all thy heart [lebabeka], and with all thy soul [nafsheka] and with all thy wealth [meodeka]." "Thy heart," refers to the love of the rational power. "With all thy heart," signifies that all the ideas of the intellect must be concentrated upon this matter. "Thy soul," refers to the love of the animal power, while "thy wealth," refers to the love of the appetitive power.

It may be explained as follows: He wishes to teach man that he should love God as much as he can, with all the powers of his body, at all times. First, because the object of his love is good. Such love is dictated by reason, hence, "with all thy heart." Second, because He is useful, for God it is who breathes the breath of life into man's nostrils and maintains him, hence, "with all thy soul," for the word nafsheka [thy soul] refers to the animal power. The word **all** refers to all the animal powers, as the Rabbis say: "with all thy soul," means even if He takes away thy soul. Third, because He is agreeable, hence, "with all thy wealth," which refers to the appetitive power and the love which emanates from it, embracing a variety of kinds, like love of money, of property and of pleasure. All this is intended to show that God is the absolute good, that He is beneficent, seeing that He made man and is gracious to him in that He breathed into his nostrils the breath of life, and that He is also the giver of wealth and property and pleasure to man as long as he lives.

Therefore, it is proper to love Him with all the kinds of love and at all times.

And inasmuch as the love of God must consist in serving Him and observing His commandments as far as possible and at all times, in thought, in word and in deed, he adds, "And these words which I command thee this day, shall be upon thy heart [lebabeka]," indicating thought; "and thou shalt teach them diligently unto thy children, and shalt talk of them" - referring to speech; and this must be all the time, "when thou sittest in thy house, and when thou walkest by the way, and when thou liest down, and when thou risest up." But this service must also be performed in practice, hence, "And thou shalt bind them for a sign upon thy hand." Man's act, however, is of a double nature, such as continues only as long as the individual is alive, and such as survives the individual. Hence, He commands both kinds of act. "Thou shalt bind them for a sign," refers to the temporary act; "and thou shalt write them, etc.," refers to that kind of act which remains after the death of the individual. All this is to indicate that God must be loved with all the kinds of love, and with all the powers of the person; that this love will result in doing God's service as far as possible, in thought, in speech and in action, and at all times.

Chapter 36

Love of God gives joy and delight to the soul. Ordinarily love of a thing that can not be obtained or that is difficult of attainment causes trouble and confusion to the soul, which casts about for means to obtain the object of its love. And for this reason, lovers are always in pain and sorrow until they obtain the object of their love. But the love of God does not cause trouble or confusion to the soul, although God is not a thing that can be obtained. The reason is because the little of Him that man can attain gives wonderful joy and pleasure and delight to the soul. This is the way of the lover: the little that he obtains of the object of his love is much pleasanter to him than a great deal of something else.

This is why Solomon praises this kind of love above all others: "How fair and how pleasant art thou, O love, for delights!" The meaning is, how superior is the beauty and the pleasure of the love of God to those of any other love, for this love is one of delights - man has wonderful delights in it, and there are as many kinds of delights in it as there are different kinds of understanding. The other kinds of love give a person great pain before he obtains the object

Sefer Haikkarim   BOOK [Maamar] THRE

of his love. And when he obtains a little thereof, he finds pleasure therein, but the pain increases until he obtains the whole of it, since it is possible of attainment. And when he has obtained the whole of it, his love ceases, and his desire subsides. But the love of God is different. Man rejoices in the little that he obtains, when he considers how great is the worth of the object to be attained. He takes delight in that which he obtains, without any addition of pain because he knows that God can not be attained. Therefore, he takes wonderful delight in the little that he attains, and the more he attains, the greater is the love and the delight.

Moreover, this love can not cease because the object is infinite. As one attains a certain degree, he finds delight therein and is eager to get more, and so on without end. Therefore, it can not stop, but the person's joy continues with the little that he attains, as we explained in the fifteenth chapter of the Second Book. The greater the worth of the thing desired, the greater the joy and delight in as much as is attained. Therefore, even if the search for this love and attainment cause a man great trouble, he will not on that account desist from the pursuit when he considers the great end that is sought. Particularly the person who serves from love has no reason to regard any utility or damage that may accrue to him from his service, because his purpose is merely to do the will of the beloved. Hence, he ignores any benefit or injury which may come provided the beloved is benefited. Thus Jonathan, because of his love for David, cared not about the fact that he would lose the kingdom as long as David was alive, as Saul said to him: "For as long as the son of Jesse liveth upon the earth, thou shalt not be established, nor thy kingdom." His purpose was to benefit David, whom he loved, even if he did injury to himself.

This is the way of true love, which considers only the interest of the beloved, whereas the love which considers the interest of the lover is like the love which man has for animals, because of the benefit he receives from them. And the love which is due to protection from injury is like the love of a man for a dog. A man loves dogs because they protect him from injury. True love is that which a man has for the beloved for the sake of the beloved alone, having no other purpose than to do the will of the beloved, because he does not love the beloved for any cause other than the beloved himself. Love which is due to an extraneous cause is sure to change and cease, as our Rabbis say: "All love which is dependent upon something extraneous ceases with the cessation of that thing." But the love which is for the sake of the beloved solely, and for no other cause, will last as long as the beloved endures. Now since God endures forever, love for Him never ceases.

Such love as this, which considers only the interest of the beloved, can exist only in men of intelligence and understanding. For the love of another for his own sake can be due only to the intellect of the beloved. Therefore, if the beloved loses his mind or dies, love ceases, because the beloved object is not there any more, since the soul leaves the dead body. Now inasmuch as this is the best of all kinds of love and is found only in persons of intellect and understanding, a person is praised or blamed for it. Hence there must be no admixture of compulsion therein, for a person is not praised or blamed for that which he is compelled to do, but only for a thing that is altogether dependent on his choice. This is why the patriarch Abraham was praised for this kind of love more than others; and the Bible calls him, "Abraham, my friend," because he had no other purpose in mind than to do the will of God whom he loved. Nor was there any other cause compelling him to do this, for there was no element of compulsion in the incident of Yitzhak's sacrifice. Not even the command of God was a compulsion, as our Rabbis explain, in connection with the verse in Genesis: "Abraham said to God, Lord of the universe, it is known to Thee that when Thou didst say to me, 'Take, now, thy son, thine only son, whom thou lovest, even Yitzhak ... and offer him to Me as a burnt-offering,' I could have said in reply, Hast not Thou said to me, 'For in Yitzhak shall seed be called to thee?' but I did not say so, I suppressed my compassion and did not criticize Thy conduct." It seems clear from this that even though God commanded him, Abraham was not compelled to obey, seeing that he could have excused himself on good grounds if he had desired. But he did not do so. He suppressed a father's compassion for a son for the sake of his love for God.

This is why the credit in the incident of the sacrifice is given to Abraham and not to Yitzhak, though the latter was thirty-seven years old, as our Rabbis say. Abraham could have avoided the act of sacrificing his son, but Yitzhak had no excuse for refusing to offer himself when he was commanded to do so. This is the reason also why in our prayers we always mention the sacrifice of Yitzhak by Abraham and do not mention the sacrifice of all the pious and holy men who offered their lives to sanctify the name of God, like Rabbi Akiba and his associates and all the holy men in every generation. The reason is because all the others offered their lives in fulfilment of the commandment, "And ye shall not profane My holy name; but I will be hallowed among the children of Israel;" whereas Abraham was not compelled by God's command. Moreover, he knew very well what he was doing, for more than three days elapsed between the time when he was commanded to take his son and the time of the sacrifice, as we read: "On the third day Abraham lifted up his eyes, and saw the place afar off."

An absolutely free act is one the opposite of which the person at the time of doing the act knew how to do and was able to do without any prevention or hindrance, and yet chose to do what he did and not something else. But if the person did not know or understand how to do the opposite, and did what he did without distinguishing between the thing and its opposite, merely by accident or by habit or custom, or because he could not do the opposite, his is not a free act for which he deserves praise if it is good or blame if it is bad. Even an offering, which is a good act, if a person brings it without distinguishing between good and evil, merely as a result of habit and custom, is worth nothing.

This is the meaning of the verse in Ecclesiastes: "Guard thy foot when thou goest to the house of God," i.e., take care that you're going there should be the result of discrimination and not of habit and custom. The same idea is expressed in the words in the sequel: "And be ready to hearken: it is better than when fools give sacrifice; for they know not that they do evil." The meaning is, to be ready to listen to the words of the wise is better than the offering which fools bring, for by listening to the words of the wise a person learns to distinguish between good and evil, and does good as a result of perfect discrimination because the thing is good, and keeps away from evil because he knows that it is evil. This is not the case in the actions of fools. Even the offering which they bring is not accounted to them as service; because, since they are not ready to listen to the words of the wise, they do not understand the difference between good and evil and do not know how to do evil freely. Hence even the offering, which is a good act, is not credited to them, because they do not do it from choice between good and evil. They do not know how to do evil and they bring the offering, not because they choose it in preference to its opposite, which is evil, but as a result of habit and custom. Therefore, they do not deserve to be praised for it, for a person deserves praise for a good act only if he knows how to do evil and has the ability to do it, and yet chooses to do good. Accordingly, the person who serves from love deserves praise only if his service is prompted by true love in which there is no mixture of compulsion or of protection from injury or of utility. This love gives delight and is deserving of eternal and infinite reward.

Solomon refers to it in the Song of Songs: "If a man would give all the substance of his house for love, he would utterly be contemned." The infinite can not be exchanged for the finite, viz. "all the substance of his house."

Chapter 37

We must now explain whether it is possible that there should be love between God and man as there is between man and God. A person may say, it is indeed right that man should love God, first, because of the love of the good as such; second, because of the benefits he receives from Him, and third, because He is pleasant. But it is inconceivable that God should love man, who has not one of these qualities. Love can exist between two persons when it is mutual, though different in degree. But if they are at the opposite poles, it does not seem that there can be love between them, because they are like opposites. For opposites are at the extreme distance from each other. But the opposite flees the opposite, and love can be, it would seem, only between things which are like. This is why persons are eager to be honored and loved by wise men and men of worth, in order that it may seem that they have something in common with them. And for the same reason love between persons is more complete if they are alike in a certain virtue or accomplishment. On the other hand, if the difference between them is great, the love is slight, so much so that some persons do not wish their friends prosperity for fear that if they rise high in the world the equality between them will change and friendship will cease or diminish. The exception is when the friend is so closely attached to the other as a father is to a child, where the two personalities are almost one. Then he wishes all the good things to his friend as he wishes them to himself, because he recognizes no difference between himself and his friend. But those friends who do recognize a distinction can not have a perfect love for each other.

This can be shown in experience. There can be no friendship or attachment at all between the extremely good and the extremely bad, and neither expects it. Similarly, men in a very lowly station do not expect to be, nor does it occur to them that they might be, loved by kings, because the distance between them is very great. What shall we say then of the distance between man and God, which is infinite? It is clear therefore that though man may feel love for God because of the benefits which he receives from Him, or the pleasure he feels in that which he attains of Him, or for love of the good as such, God can have no kind of love for man, either as the good or as the beneficial or as the pleasant. How, then, can there be love between God and man, as we are promised in the divine Torah: "And it shall come to pass, because ye hearken to these ordinances, and keep, and do them, that the Lord thy God shall keep with thee the covenant ... and He will love thee and bless thee and multiply thee ...?" The prophet also says: "I have loved you, saith the Lord;" "The Lord loveth the righteous."

The answer to the question is that there are three kinds of love between friends.

First, there is the love of equality or similarity, the kind that obtains between friends who are equal in a certain respect in a virtue, in an accomplishment, or in beneficence, i.e., if each derives a benefit from the other or finds pleasure in the other, or they are both equal in goodness. That one of the two who receives more benefit than he gives must love his friend more than his friend loves him because of the greater benefit or pleasure he receives from the other or because of his friend's superior goodness. If they are equal in beneficence, pleasure or goodness, their love is without doubt more complete. This kind of love admits of quantitative equality.

The second kind is natural love, and has two subdivisions, the love which a parent has for his child because it is a part of him, and the love which an artificer feels for the art which he invented by his pains and efforts. This is why mothers love their children more than fathers, because they combine both these elements, more so than the fathers. The greater part of the child comes from the mother, who contributes the material part, and the mother takes more trouble in bringing up the child.

The third kind is proportional love, which has three subdivisions.

First, love between the king and the people, or between the governor and the governed. Love between the king and the people is not equal in quantity on the two sides, but only in ratio and proportion. It is proper that the king should be loved by his people more than they are loved by him. Moreover, the purpose intended in the king's love for the people is not the same as the purpose intended in the people's love for the king. What is expected from the king is that he should benefit the people by maintaining justice among them, protecting their possessions as far as possible and maintaining their welfare; whereas what is expected from the people is that they should honor the king and exalt him, and recognize his rule and superiority and beneficence and their dependence upon him. In this way the king's love prompts him to benefit the people, and the people's love induces them to honor and exalt him.

Second, the love between a father and a son. In addition to the natural love between the parent and the child, there is also another love between them, a proportional love, similar to the love between a king and his people. The son expects from the father that he should treat him as a father by being good to him as far as is in his power. The father expects that the son should honor him.

The third subdivision is love between husband and wife. In addition to the natural love between them, the love of male and female for the perpetuation of the race, there is also another kind of love between them, a proportional love, similar to the love between the governor and the governed. For the husband is expected to supply the wants of the wife, to honor her, and to provide for her in as honorable a manner as possible. The wife, on the other hand, is expected to attend upon the husband, to honor him, and to take care of his property, and not to love another. In the third kind, namely in proportional love, the love of the inferior for the superior must be greater than the love of the superior for the inferior. The equality in this kind of love is therefore not arithmetical but proportional.

Now it is clear that the love of God for man can not belong to the first kind, which is the love of equals. But one might suppose that it is of the second kind, natural love. And Moshe alludes to the two subdivisions of this kind. "Is not He thy father that hath gotten thee?" - this refers to the first subdivision, the love of a parent for his child. "Hath He not made thee and established thee?" - this refers to the second subdivision, the love of an artificer for his art. The prophet, too, in his prayer alludes to these two subdivisions: "But now, O Lord, thou art our father; we are the clay, and Thou, our potter." The meaning is, and therefore Thou oughtest to provide for us and have mercy on us as a father has mercy on his children. But Thou shouldst love us also with the second species of natural love, for "we all are the work of Thy hand". Thou didst even create the matter before Thou didst put the intellectual form upon it. Hence, thou oughtest to provide for us as every agent provides for the work of his hands whether it is worthy or not.

However, if we examine the matter carefully, we shall find that all these expressions are figurative. Neither the form nor the matter is a part of God, as the son is a part of the father. Moreover, since God produces by verbal command, we can not say that He should endeavor to take care of His work. All other agents endeavor to take care of the work of their hands because they have taken trouble in

Sefer Halkkarim BOOK [Maamar] THRE

producing it, as the poet loves his poems, but one who takes neither trouble nor pains can not have a love of this kind. It is clear therefore that the love of God for man can only be of the third kind, proportional love.

This is why the Bible describes God as King, Father and Lord. As King: "For God is the King of all the earth;" "Thus saith the Lord, the King of Israel, and his Redeemer;" "The Lord is out King; He will save us." As Father: "For Thou art our Father; for Abraham knoweth us not;" "Is He not thy Father that hath gotten thee?" and many other passages. As the king and the father supply the wants of the people and the son respectively, and all that is expected of the latter is that they should honor their benefactors, as we said before, so God supplies the wants of mankind, and all that He expects from them is to do honor to His name, as we read in the Bible: "Every one that is called by My name, and whom I have created for My glory." This is why we find that God blames the Israelites for not giving Him honor as a son is expected to give to his father, and for not fearing Him, as a servant fears his master: "A son honoureth his father, and a servant his master: if then I be a father, where is My honour? And if I be a master, where is my fear?" Not that the Lord needs the honor of any one, for He is the King of all honor, as we explained in the fourteenth chapter of the Second Book. Nevertheless, He blamed Israel because they did not conduct themselves properly in order that they should be prepared to receive the divine influence and His providence, which would protect them from the accidents due to the heavenly bodies. Such influence does not come except to the one who prepares himself for it by honoring God as a son honors his father, and by fearing Him as a servant fears his master. Thus, the prophet says: "If ye will not hearken, and if ye will not lay it to heart, to give glory unto My name … Then will I send the curse upon you, and I will curse your blessings …;" "Give glory to the Lord your God …"

The Bible also compares God's love of Israel to the proportional love between husband and wife: "For thy Maker is thy husband;" "And I will betroth thee unto Me in faithfulness;" "Thou shalt call Me Husband;" "Plead with your mother, plead; for she is not My wife, neither am I her husband." The meaning is, She did not behave as a wife should to her husband. As a husband is obliged to supply all the needs of the wife whom he married and singled out of all other women, so God should supply all the needs of Israel, the people which He chose as His possession out of all the peoples which are upon the earth. Therefore, Israel must love and honor and

Sefer Halkkarim   BOOK [Maamar] THRE

fear Him, and observe His commandments and statutes, and not love any one else, as a wife is obliged to honor, love and fear her husband, and not love another.

To show that God's love of Israel in preference to every other nation and tongue is not like the love of equals, nor like natural love, but a free love, due to the will of the lover alone and without any reason, the Bible calls God's love of Israel by the name heshek [desire]: "The Lord ... set His love [hashak] upon you ... [and] choose you." The word heshek is applied to extraordinary love without a reason. Thus, the love of a man for a particular woman in preference to another more beautiful is called heshek because it is without a reason. Thus, we read: "The soul of my son Shechem longeth [hashekah] for your daughter," i.e., even though he can find one more beautiful. So, God's love of Israel is like that love [heshek] which is without a reason. The entire book of Canticles is based upon this analogy between the love of God for Israel and the love of a man for his sweetheart, which is without a reason.

This is why the Bible calls this love "peculiar" [segulah]: "For thou art a holy people unto the Lord thy God: The Lord thy God hath chosen thee to be His own peculiar people [segulah] out of all peoples that are upon the face of the earth. The Lord did not set His love upon you, nor choose you because ye were more in number than any people ..." The meaning is that just as a property [segulah] pertains to a species and is inseparable from it, and yet is not to be explained either by the quantity or the quality of the thing, so this love is in the nature of a property attaching to the people not because of their quantity: "The Lord did not set His love upon you ... because ye were more in number ..." Nor is it because of their quality: "Not for thy righteousness, or for the uprightness of thy heart ... for thou art a stiff-necked people." This love is like the love [heshek] which has no reason, but is due solely to the will of the lover. And it is this love which was promised to the people at the time of the Sinaitic revelation, as a reward for accepting the Torah: "Now therefore, if ye will hearken unto My voice indeed, and keep My covenant, then ye shall be Mine own peculiar property [segulah] from among all peoples ..."

As it is the character of a lover that a little which he obtains of his beloved is more appreciated and enjoyed than a great deal of another, so God appreciates more a small service coming from Israel than a great deal coming from another nation or from all the nations, hence the expression, "from among all peoples; for all the earth is Mine." Or it may be that the words, "For all the earth is Mine," are

Sefer HaIkkarim   BOOK [Maamar] THRE

connected with the sequel, "And ye shall be unto Me a kingdom of priests ..." That is, since all the earth is Mine and all the governments come from Me, I can promise you that I will make you greater than all the peoples that are under the heaven, for My rule includes all, and there is no God outside of Me, who can give power to a people other than you, even though it be greater than you. For this is the nature of a property [segulah], love attaching without any reason like that called heshek.

The prophet also explains the same thing: "I have loved you, saith the Lord. Yet ye say: 'Wherein hast Thou loved us?' " The meaning is, love in word alone is not worth anything unless it is followed by acts which show love. Hence, He says in the sequel, "Was not Esau Yaakov's brother? Saith the Lord; yet I loved Yaakov; but Esau I hated ..." That is, although as a father I should have chosen Esau, the first born, yet I did not do so, but I hated him, "And made his mountains a desolation."

We find also that the Bible emphasizes God's love of Israel on the analogy of a father's love for his son, in every way in which such love can exist: As a father usually loves his eldest son because he is the first born, the Bible says: "For I am become a father to Israel, and Ephraim is My first-born;" "Israel is My son, My first-born." Also, inasmuch as sometimes one loves his son because he attends him like a boy [i.e., servant], the Bible says: "For Israel is a boy, therefore I love him." Sometimes also a father loves his son for his worth, because he is a darling child, or because he is small and his father dandles him. Hence the Bible says: "Is Ephraim a darling son unto Me? Is he a child that is dandled?" That is, is my soul so attached to him in love as that of a father to his darling son or to the child that he dandles, that "as often as I speak of him I do earnestly remember him still?", as a lover always finds delight in thinking of his friend and hence thinks of him again and again when he speaks of him. Also, by reason of his great worth in My eyes and My love for him, "My heart yearneth for him," and My sympathies are aroused, like a person who is moved to pity on account of the pain of his beloved son. Therefore, I must have pity upon him as a father has pity upon the child which he dandles, or his darling son. Hence the conclusion of the verse, "I will surely have compassion upon him, saith the Lord."

As no one has more compassion upon another than a father upon the son, we always say in our prayers, "Our Father, our King, may Thy compassion be moved for us." "Our Father," is intended t6 show that we pray the kind of compassion which a father has upon the son.

Sefer HaIkkarim   BOOK [Maamar] THREE

"Our King," means that He has power to help us as a king helps his subjects.

All this makes clear that God's love for Israel belongs to proportional love, like that of a king for his subjects, of a father for his children, of a husband for his wife. And in order to indicate that this love is an intellectual thing, and that it is permanent and unchanging, the Bible says: "I have loved thee with an everlasting love." It is also clear that man's love of God, though it belongs to this third kind, viz. proportional love, may nevertheless embrace all three aspects, the good, the useful and the agreeable. Therefore, man is obliged to love God to his utmost ability. The love of God is the purpose of the whole Torah, because it brings the love of God to man, as we have explained. So much for the subject of love.

Here ends Book Three, which explains the second principle, divine revelation of the Torah. Praise be to God who has helped us till now. He is blessed and exalted and uplifted above all blessing and praise. Amen, Selah.

Sefer HaIkkarim
ספר העיקרים

BOOK OF PRINCIPLES

BOOK [Maamar] FOUR

Introduction

Herein is explained the fourth principle, which is reward and punishment - the purpose of the Torah as a whole - as well as the derivative principles implied in it and other matters dependent upon it and the derivative principles.

We said in the First Book that Freedom and Purpose are not principles of a divine law as such. Freedom is a principle of all human activity; hence we did not include it among the dogmas which are peculiar to divine law. As to Purpose, though that too is a principle of all conventional laws, still inasmuch as the purpose of divine law is different from the purpose of conventional laws, we did make the purpose of reward and punishment a fundamental principle of divine law. Inasmuch, however, as it is impossible to explain this purpose, namely reward and punishment, without knowing first about freedom, we must first speak about the latter. But we can not explain freedom without first discussing God's knowledge of existing things. Accordingly, we shall first treat of God's knowledge, then of freedom, then of Providence, and finally of reward and punishment and the other matters depending upon it. It is clear that we must follow this order if we want to treat of reward and punishment. For if God has no knowledge of the things existing in the sublunar world, there is no meaning in reward and punishment for conduct. And even granting that God does know the things of this world, if man is not free to choose his conduct, he should not receive either punishment or reward for it. And finally, even assuming that God knows the things of this world and man is free to determine his conduct, if God knows those things in a generic way only, as he knows the lower animals, if he exercises no provision over the particulars of their conduct, punishing them for disobedience and rewarding them for their good deeds, there can be neither reward nor punishment. It is clear, therefore, that these three, namely, God's knowledge, freedom and providence are necessarily prior to the principle of reward and punishment and are implied in it. We must therefore consider them first and the things which depend upon them and issue from them, and then we shall speak of reward and punishment and of the things which are dependent upon it, such as repentance, resurrection and the Messiah. All this we shall discuss very briefly so as not to burden the reader, but just enough to give the believer a conception of the matter.

Chapter 1

We laid it down as a principle, in the Second Book, that God must be free from defects. But there is no defect greater than ignorance. Hence it is clear that God must know all the things that happen in the world, and that nothing can happen in the world of which He is ignorant and which He does not know. From this it necessarily follows that God knows all human acts, which is the subject of our discussion. But the question whether His knowledge determines one of the two alternatives or not, is one that requires careful investigation. The problem is this: If God's knowledge does determine the act, then a person is under compulsion in his conduct, and should not receive reward or punishment for the things he does, since he does them under necessity, for a person deserves praise or blame only when the initiative of his acts is his own and there is no compulsion. On the other hand, if God's knowledge does not determine the act, then the act may be realized contrary to God's knowledge, His knowledge would then be in disagreement with the facts, and it would not be knowledge, but ignorance and error and falsehood.

Moreover, it is clear that the category of the possible does exist. This appears both from reason and from the Torah. By reason, as follows: If the possible did not exist, all effort would be in vain. The one who makes an effort to obtain a thing and the one who makes an effort to the contrary would be in the same position, and there would be an end to all the trades and the arts and the professions. There would be no purpose in learning and training, no advantage in pursuing the useful and avoiding the injurious, and no place for the will at all. But this is opposed to the evidence of our senses and to the purpose for which we were created.

From the Torah we draw the same conclusion, both from its general statements and from the specific commandments. If the possible did

Sefer HaIkkarim — BOOK [Maamar] FOUR

not exist, the revelation of the Torah to guide mankind in the right path would be in vain, and the admonitions in the Torah that we should serve God and love Him and do righteousness and justice would be without any purpose. And yet the Torah exclaims: "Oh that they had such a heart as this always, to fear Me, and keep all My commandments …" As for specific commands, the Torah says, "Thou shalt make a parapet for thy roof;" "Let him go and return to his house;" "Thou shalt not commit murder;" "Thou shalt not oppress thy neighbour nor rob him," and there are many other specific commands, which show that the category of the possible exists. Moreover, if the possible did not exist, reward and punishment would be absolutely wrong, whether divine or human, since every one, on this supposition, would be acting from necessity. It is clear therefore that the possible must exist. Now if the possible must exist and it can not be that God does not know particular things, for it would be a defect in His nature, the question arises, How can God's knowledge be in agreement with the truth and at the same time fail to determine one of the two possible alternatives? How can these two propositions be compatible, being seemingly contradictory at first sight?

Saadia Gaon in his book, "Emunot ve-Deot," says that God's foreknowledge of the possible things is not the cause of their existence, just as His knowledge of that which has already come into existence is not the cause of its having come into existence. The thing retains its own nature. Similarly, His knowledge of possible things is not the cause of their existence, and hence they retain their character as possible things. For if His knowledge were the cause of their existence, they would always exist, like the natural species. But since we see new individuals appearing every day, it follows that their existence is not determined by His knowledge. And therefore they retain their character as possible things. These are the words of the Gaon, and the author of the Cusari in the fifth book of that treatise adopts the same view. But this is not satisfactory, for it is very much like saying that God does not know possible things. For if He knows them, and yet their existence is not determined by His knowledge, it might turn out that His knowledge would be different from the actual result, and this would not be knowledge but ignorance.

Some one of the moderns solved this difficulty by saying that a thing may be necessary if we consider it in relation to its causes, and possible if we consider it by itself. Take, for example, the question of rain to-morrow. Considered by itself, it is possible; considered in relation to its causes, namely the rise of the vapors, the great quantity of moisture and similar things already in existence, it is necessary. God, therefore, knows that it will rain to-morrow, because, considered in relation to its causes, it is necessary, though considered by itself it is possible. The author in question expatiates at length in making his solution appear plausible.

But if we examine this view carefully, we shall find that unlike the first opinion this one is very close to the view that all things are determined and that the possible does not exist. For since the things are necessary considered in relation to their causes, if God knows the causes, they are actually necessary. What good is there then in saying that they are possible considered by themselves, as long as they are determined and necessary from that side which brings them into existence, namely the causes? For they can not come into existence in any other way. They are possible in the theoretical sense that the causes might have been different and then the effect would have been different. But in reality, the effect is necessary when the causes are there and God knows them. It would follow then according to this opinion that there is no thing that may equally be or not be when considered in relation to its causes. For if the causes determining the two opposite alternatives are equal, the question arises again, what is it that determined one of the alternatives in preference to the other? If it is the knowledge of God that determines, the category of the possible is done away with; and if we retain the possible, God's knowledge is taken away, unless indeed we say that the possible exists only logically and conceptually, but not actually. But this is contrary to hypothesis. Much has been said in the solution of this question. But if we examine it all we find that it is of the nature described above, namely some of it approximates to the first opinion, and some of it approximates to the second opinion. Therefore, I do not think it necessary to quote it here, so as not to prolong our discussion needlessly. My own opinion will be explained after I have made an introductory observation in the following chapter.

Chapter 2

The speculative sciences are not always in agreement on a given subject, but differ from one another in their fundamental and other principles. Every exponent of a given science believes and maintains that the principles of his science are absolutely true and clear, and that only a fool or an ignoramus refuses to accept them. The

Sefer Halkkarim — BOOK [Maamar] FOUR

exponent of another science denies those principles and maintains his own, which are in disagreement with the others. This may be illustrated in the relation of the astronomer to the physicist. The astronomer lays down two principles upon which he bases all the proofs of his science, namely eccentric and epicycle. The physicist on the other hand assumes three kinds of motion, from the center, to the center and around the center. This is the most important principle which he has. He also maintains that circular motion can take place only around a body that is permanently at rest. The astronomer denies all this. For if we assume an epicycle, we have a motion that is neither to the center, nor from the center, nor around the center, unless we say that in the center of the epicycle there is a body permanently at rest, an earth as it were around which the epicycle revolves, as the diurnal sphere revolves around the earth, which is the central body and permanently at rest. It would follow according to this that within the epicycles which the planets are supposed to have there are other earths around which they revolve. There would then be other worlds in heaven. On the assumption of an eccentric it also follows that circular motion may exist around a body not permanently at rest. For the eccentric revolves around a point which is in constant motion. For, as is explained in the Treatise on Distances, the centers of the planetary eccentrics are some of them above the elements, in the lunar sphere, some above the lunar sphere, and some above the solar sphere, as Maimonides says in the Guide of the Perplexed, Part II, ch. 24.

All these strange and impossible ideas assumed by the astronomer he proves from lunar and solar eclipses which are perceived by the senses, and from the observations of conjunctions [in the aspects] of the stars, which favor his assumptions. Accordingly, he bases all his proofs upon them and pays no attention to the assumptions and principles of the physicist. The physicist on the other hand denies the principles and assumptions of the astronomer, on the strength of physical theory, though the senses favor the ideas of the astronomer. The physicist does not deny the data of the senses, but maintains that they have nothing to do with the principles and assumptions laid down by the astronomer, which are inherently impossible, and he holds that the phenomena are to be explained on some other principles which are not known.

Another illustration of the disagreement of the sciences is the relation of the astrologer and the philosopher. The philosopher denies God's knowledge and maintains the reality of the contingent. The astrologer, on the other hand, holds to the reality of God's

Sefer Halkkarim — BOOK [Maamar] FOUR

knowledge, saying that God knows that which the constellations determine, and which can not be otherwise. Therefore he denies the reality of the contingent. The theologian agrees with both, maintaining the reality of the contingent with the philosopher, which he proves from the evidence of the senses, as we explained in the preceding chapter, and believing likewise in the reality of God's knowledge in agreement with the astrologer. This he proves by reason, which holds that we must not ascribe ignorance to God, for it is a defect in Him if His knowledge does not embrace all that happens in the world. He also holds that God's knowledge is not incompatible with the category of the contingent, for we see with our senses the reality of divine providence when rain comes down in the summer in the absence of moisture and clouds, through the prayers of the righteous and the pious.

Now since the senses testify to his ideas, we pay no attention to those who deny them, any more than we pay attention to the naturalist's disagreement with the astronomer, as long as the senses confirm the ideas of the astronomer. In the same way we pay no regard to the physicist who says that a point at rest can not exist except in a body at rest, seeing that the mathematician can show, in a revolving spherical body, two points, called poles, which are not in motion, but at rest, while the sphere as a whole is in motion. Similarly everything to which the senses testify we must admit to be true, though we do not know the cause, as the physicist admits the truth of the ideas of the astronomer, which are testified to by the senses, while denying the causes alleged by the astronomer to explain the phenomena, and holding that they are not the true causes, but that there are other causes which we do not know.

Chapter 3

Having shown that the exponents of the different sciences differ from one another in their assumptions, we must find for everything a basis in sense perception, and pay no regard to anybody's ideas, except where they are in agreement with sense data.

Now the senses testify, in agreement with the theologian, that the contingent exists; also, that God communicates through the prophets knowledge concerning particular and individual things; also we know that God provides specially for particular individuals, witness the patriarchs in all their relations, according to the continuous tradition which has come down to us, the exodus from Egypt, and other special individuals mentioned in the books of the Prophets.

Sefer Halkkarim BOOK [Maamar] FOUR

Hence, we pay no regard to those who deny these things. For we do not deny what we see with our senses despite the speculations of philosopher, as we do not deny that a sphere revolves about two stationary poles, though the physicist according to his theory denies it. We must use the senses as a basis in everything, even though the reason is not able to know the cause thereof.

For the reason is imperfect in two respects. First, there are many things which the intellect can not comprehend as they really are. And second, it can not know the causes of all things, even of those things which are perceived by the senses. Thus, we can not deny the reality of the diurnal motion, since we see it with our senses. And yet the human mind can not understand its nature in any way. If we say that the cause of this motion is a ninth body, as many scientists agree, calling it the diurnal sphere, because it determines the appearance of evening and morning which are called one day, we can not understand how this body can move all the spheres. If the motion is caused by contact, for a body can not move another body except by contact, how can we suppose that the contact between the sphere of Mars and the sphere of the sun imparts to the latter the diurnal motion which came to Mars per accidens through contact with the sphere of Jupiter [which in turn received it through contact with the sphere of Saturn, which in turn received it from the sphere of the fixed stars, which received the diurnal motion per accidens through contact with the ninth sphere, i.e., the diurnal sphere] and yet the sphere of the sun does not receive through its contact with Mars the proper motion of the latter, which is its motion per se? Similarly, how is it that the sphere of the moon receives the diurnal motion through indirect contact with the ninth sphere, and does not receive the proper and essential motion of the sphere of Mercury, with which it comes into immediate contact?

This may be the reason why Rabbi Abraham Ibn Ezra says in the name of a great Spanish scientist that it is clearly proved that there is no body above the sphere of the fixed stars. This means that the diurnal motion can not be due to a ninth body. Nor can we say that the diurnal motion is caused by the sphere of the fixed stars, as I have seen some one actually maintains, because the sphere of the fixed stars has also a retrograde motion, and one and the same sphere can not have two different per se motions, but the one must be per se and by itself while the other is per accidens and due to an external agent. But it seems that Ibn Ezra means to say that the cause of the diurnal motion is not a body but a Separate Intelligence. But I am not satisfied with this explanation either, which is inadequate. For a

Sefer Halkkarim — BOOK [Maamar] FOUR

Separate Intelligence can not move a body unless the latter has a soul. The motion is then caused by means of a concept, as is explained in the proper place, and as Maimonides explains the matter in the Guide of the Perplexed. But a body endowed with a soul can not at the same time have two different motions due to two different concepts, just as a man can not move to the east and to the west at the same time in obedience to the commands of two kings, one of whom commands him to move toward the east, and the other orders him to move toward the west. Furthermore, the elements are inanimate bodies and yet we see that the comets which become visible through the element of fire, have the diurnal motion, as is stated in Aristotle's Meteorologics. This motion is perceptible by the senses, and it can have no other cause except contact with the sphere of the moon. But if so, why does this comet which becomes visible in the element fire have the diurnal motion only and not also the specific motion of the lunar sphere with which it is in contact? For we see the chain-stars following the diurnal motion of the sun for a month or two, but having no connection with the motion of the moon. This is a serious difficulty which stands in the way of the theory that their diurnal motion is due to contact.

Nor can the motion be due to a concept, because the elements are dead bodies and do not move by way of representation at all. Hence when Samuel said, "The paths of the heavens are as clear to me as the paths of Nehardea," he was asked, "Do you know the comet?" That is, do you know why the tailed or chain-star has the diurnal motion and not the motion of the moon? His answer was that he did not know. For the explanation is really unknown, unless we suppose that the diurnal sphere is below the lunar sphere. We should then have to assume that every planet has a diurnal mover below it which imparts to it the diurnal motion, as was the opinion of the ancients before Ptolemy. The human mind is not adequate to know this, any more than it is able to explain the cause of the heavenly motions without doing violence to the theories of physics. The human mind is not even able to explain the causes of natural things upon the earth, for example the magnet's attraction of iron. Therefore we must not ignore and deny that which we perceive with our senses merely because we do not know its cause. In the same way we must not deny the category of the contingent, which we perceive with our senses, and God's knowledge, which follows from reason, because we do not understand the causes.

But if you ask, how is it possible to maintain both of these opinions, viz. to maintain the reality of the contingent and at the same time to hold that God's knowledge embraces it? Our answer is the same as that of Maimonides, who says. that since God's knowledge is essential in Him and not something added to His essence, the investigation of the character of His knowledge is tantamount to an investigation of His essence. But His essence is absolutely unknown, hence the character of His knowledge is also absolutely unknown. As there is no comparison or similarity between His existence and the existence of other things, so there is no comparison between His knowledge and the knowledge of others. Hence though if we picture His knowledge on the analogy of our own, a great many objections follow, such as that we must either deny the reality of the contingent or assume that His knowledge embraces that which we can not conceive as knowable, for He would have to know the infinite, or His knowledge would change with the change of the objects, and other difficulties of this sort - this would follow only if we conceive of His knowledge on the analogy of our own, but since His knowledge is not of the same kind as ours, these difficulties do not follow. God's knowledge is infinite, and infinite knowledge is not liable to these difficulties.

Isaiah uses this argument when he reproves those who deny God's knowledge: "Why sayest thou O Yaakov, and speakest, O Israel: 'My way is hid from the Lord, and my right is passed over from my God?' Hast thou not known? Hast thou not heard …" "Hast thou not known," refers to investigation; "Hast thou not heard," refers to tradition. "That the Lord is the everlasting God," i.e., it can be proved apodictically that there is a being who is a necessary existent, and He is the everlasting God, i.e., the cause of all existing things; and He is the Lord, i.e., He is a separate Intelligence, neither a body nor a corporeal force. Hence, we infer that He is one and eternal in both directions, as well as all the other things which follow necessarily from the principle of the existence of God as proved by investigation. And though He is a Separate Intelligence, He is nevertheless "the Creator of the ends of the earth," i.e., He is the cause of all corporeal existences. And despite His infinity He is the cause of the corporeal world, which is finite, the "Creator of the ends of the earth." This is not due to weariness and lack of strength, for "He fainteth not;" nor is it due to change, for He is not "weary."

We challenge therefore the one who believes in the eternity of the world and denies God's knowledge to tell us how a corporeal thing can come from a separate and unchangeable Intelligence. He will have to admit that for a material thing to come from a Separate Intelligence is such a change as the coming of something out of nothing, of which the human intellect can give no explanation. We also challenge him to explain how a finite world can come from a being whose power is infinite. We must therefore admit that this matter rests in God's knowledge in so far as it is infinite, and that He knows the explanation of all this, though we with our knowledge are unable to conceive it. Similarly, we must say that the error of those who deny God's knowledge and say, "My way is hid from the Lord," is due to the fact that they compare God's knowledge with human knowledge. Human knowledge being finite, all the difficulties that we mentioned present themselves, namely that the knowledge changes with the change of the objects, and that it can not embrace the unembraceable, namely the infinite, so far as we can conceive with our knowledge. But as God's knowledge is infinite, it can embrace the infinite and the non-existent, without necessitating a change in God. Hence, he concludes the verse, "His discernment is past searching out." Likewise, when you say, "and my judgment is passed over from my God," which means that your choice of and determination upon one of the two possible alternatives can not be known by God, or else the contingent would cease to exist - your statement is not true. For such an inference may apply to finite knowledge, but the discernment of God is past searching out, and since His knowledge is infinite, the category of the contingent is not destroyed thereby, though we do not know the nature of His knowledge any more than we know the character of His essence.

This is Maimonides' conception of God's knowledge. He says, as we can not compare His essence with our essence, so we can not compare His knowledge with our knowledge, for the term knowledge is applied to God and to us as a pure homonym. Maimonides does not mean that the term as applied to us means knowledge and as applied to God means ignorance, or vice versa, as absolute homonymity would signify. By no means. What he means is this. The term existence is applied to God and to ourselves in an absolutely homonymous manner. Yet there is no doubt that though God's existence is absolutely different from the existence of anything else, nevertheless the term does not denote existence in the one case and non-existence in the other. So far as the negative signification is concerned, i.e., the denial of non-existence, the term has the same meaning in both cases, as is explained in Book Two, chapter 30. The term existence denotes the negation of non-existence, whether applied to us or to God. The absolute homonymity of the term applies to its positive signification, because

Sefer Halkkarim   BOOK [Maamar] FOUR

there is no comparison at all between God's existence and the existence of anything else. Similarly, the term knowledge, both as applied to God and as applied to us, means negation of ignorance. In this respect, i.e., in respect of its negative signification, the relation of the two applications, i.e., to God and to us, is one of priority and posteriority, and not of absolute homonymity. In respect of the positive signification, on the other hand, the term knowledge is applied to God and to us as a pure homonym, and God's knowledge is absolutely unknown as His essence is absolutely unknown.

If we understand the words of Maimonides concerning God's knowledge in this manner, all the objections adduced by later writers will disappear. The result of all this is that God's knowledge, being infinite, embraces everything that happens in the world without necessitating change in God, and without destroying the category of the contingent. It also embraces the infinite. I have selected this view as the best in this matter. Our Rabbis also adopt it, expressing the idea anonymously and without naming any opponent thereof: "All is foreseen, yet permission is given." "All is foreseen," signifies that God's knowledge embraces everything that happens in the world, and that nothing happens by accident without being known in advance. "Yet permission is given," signifies that the category of the contingent is real and God's knowledge does not destroy it. This is the truth in reference to this matter, though our knowledge is not sufficient to understand the possibility of this thing. This much will suffice as a brief discussion of God's knowledge.

Chapter 4

We must now discuss the signification of the constellations. Among the ancients we find that there were two opinions concerning the signification of the constellations. One is the view of the Philosopher, who says that the heavenly bodies and the stars exert an influence upon the lower world by means of their various motions, by which they cause the elements to move, and combine them and prepare them in various ways to receive the natural forms, so that some persons are prepared to acquire wisdom and others are not; some are prepared to receive the divine prophetic influence, and others are not. This form of signification or of control which the stars have over the lower world can not be denied, for we see that the sun warms the air, and the moon moistens and cools it, and increases the force of water. Hence, we can not but admit that by their motions they sometimes increase moisture or dryness, sometimes cold or heat, and in this way prepare matter to receive various forms. As for any other signification the stars may have in relation to other things which have no connection with their elemental qualities, as for example in the determination of poverty or wealth, or whether a given person will marry one wife or more than one, or whether he will be virtuous or vicious - this school denies any such power. It is false, they say, and extremely unlikely that the stars should give indications of things which have nothing to do with them, like poverty, wealth, love, hate, etc.

The second view is that of the astrologers and star-gazers. They say that all things that happen to a man, do so by the decree of the stars. And they prove it by actual verification. The astrologer tells a person what will happen to him in all particulars, whether he will live long, whether he will be poor or rich, in what occupation he will make a better success, how many wives he will have and how many children he will beget, and so on. This shows that all things that happen to a man are due to the decree of the stars, which it is impossible to escape. In this way, they say, we can maintain God's knowledge without any change. Some of the Rabbis hold this view - "The constellation makes rich; the constellation makes wise - Israel is governed by the constellation."

Both of these views are open to criticism. We may object to the first view as follows: Wherever anything causes another to pass from potentiality to actuality, the efficient cause must have actually that which the thing acted upon has potentially, as is explained in the Metaphysics. But the stars have no qualities. How, then, can the sun heat the air and the moon moisten it? We must therefore say that the proposition just mentioned, viz. that the efficient cause must have actually what the thing acted upon has potentially, applies only to a physical agent, and not to an intellectual agent. And as the spheres are living beings, endowed with intelligent souls, they may act upon the lower existences and produce in them what they themselves have not. Hence, they give predominance now to the element fire, now to the element water, now to the element air, and now to the element earth. For as we see that the spark of the sun, though incorporeal, moves the element of fire, causing it to predominate, and the moon acts in the same way upon the element of water, so it may be that the sparks of the other planets move the other elements and cause them to predominate sometimes, in a mysterious manner which we do not understand. In the same way, therefore, we may say of the other indications, that they indicate poverty or wealth or wisdom or ignorance, or other things, though they have no such qualities in themselves, and that they do this by virtue of some condition or relation which is unknown to us, provided the recipient has in him the capacity to receive the effect. So a teacher produces knowledge in the pupil, which gives more benefit to the one who is prepared than to the one who is not prepared to receive the instruction. Moreover, since our senses testify to the realization of those things which the astrologers foretell to individuals, we can not deny the data of our senses.

The second view also, namely that of the astrologers and star-gazers, is open to manifold objection. In the first place they remove the category of the contingent, the reality of which is proved by experience and by our discussion in the first chapter of this Book. Secondly, their principles are open to objection. They say that in the sphere of the fixed stars there are the forms of lamb, ox, twins, and so on, which indicate so and so. They draw imaginary lines from star to star so as to produce the figure in question, making in this way forty-eight figures. Why do they not draw other lines in another way and produce other forms? Thus, they say that the sixth of the southern forms has the shape of a small dog, saying at the same time that there are only two stars in it. Now, how can such a figure be made out of two stars? They say that the ancients, who were more perfect creatures than we, saw those forms, though we do not see them. But this is foolishness. How can any one imagines that the human person of to-day is inferior in his powers of sense perception to the ancients? On the contrary, the smaller the intellect, the stronger the sense perception. Thus, the lower animals, who have no intellect, have much stronger senses than man. They say there are forty-eight figures which the ancients saw. How did they see them? And how did they know that in a given constellation there was a given figure? Thus, they say that in the third aspect of the sign of the ox there is a man, all of whose thoughts are evil. In the first aspect of cancer there is the form of a pig of iron, whose head is of copper. In the third aspect of it, there is a man about to enter a ship for an ocean voyage, to bring back gold and silver in order to make a ring. In the first aspect of Virgo, there is the form of a virgin, holding a lamp in her hand and walking among the myrtles, desiring to go to her father's house. How can they know all such things, when they can not be seen?

And if you say that they know this by means of divination, then the principles of this science are built on the ideas of the imagination, upon which the entire science of divination is based. And the astrologer is like a person who gives free rein to an insane fantasy and thinks that whatever is conceivable in the imagination is possible. Or he is like a dreamer. But how can the truth of such things be known by the human intellect? They also speak of the positions of the stars, their aspects and relations to one another, for example the aspect of opposition is, according to them, an aspect of absolute hatred. The reason they give is that at that time the two stars are the extreme distance apart, namely 180°, as it is usually the case that enemies are as far apart from each other as possible. For the same reason they say that a quarter aspect [distance of 90°] denotes half hatred. But according to this why do they say that a third aspect [distance of 120°] denotes perfect love, seeing that the distance here is greater than in the quarter aspect? Their explanation is that those stars which face each other at a third aspect, i.e., at a distance of 120°, have more inclination for each other than those which face each other at a quarter aspect, which is 90°. But all this is prophecy and assumption and hypothesis, which the opponent will not admit. If they say that the matter is verified by experience, the same claim is made by those who are given to geomancy or other means of prognostication that are prevalent among mankind. Without any rhyme or reason some persons decide everything that happens by means of these arts, although the figures in themselves bear no relation whatsoever to the idea expressed, and yet they say that the truth of the art is verified by experience. Thus the one who is an adept in geomancy says that when a figure with lifted head comes out first, it denotes prosperity or happiness, while a figure with head lowered signifies the opposite. And yet there is no difference between these two figures except in the position of one point, which is located above in the one figure, and below in the other. The same thing applies to the other figures. The whole thing has no real meaning in itself and is purely arbitrary, like the method of prognostication by means of the shoulder blade. There are indeed some persons who have a special knack in such things, like Ahithophel, who had the peculiar knack of giving correct advice, so that David found it necessary to pray to God to mislead him into giving wrong advice.

And even if we grant all their principles and assumptions, they must admit that the assumptions are not necessary determinants. For when a plague or a famine or war happens in a certain city, people die before their proper time. Now why should the individual horoscopes be nullified, which were determined by the constellations at the time of the birth of the various individuals, and which indicated different

Sefer HaIkkarim — BOOK [Maamar] FOUR

terms of life to the different individuals, according to the time of their birth? Their explanation is that a general indication annuls a special indication, and therefore the indication of famine or plague which is decreed upon the country, nullifies the indication concerning the various individuals. It is clear therefore, on their own showing, that the indication of a special horoscope is not a necessary determinant, since it may be nullified in various ways.

Another objection to their views is the following. We may grant the propriety of the general nullifying the particular in respect to those things which happen in the course of nature, like famine, plague, and the like, but what explanation can they give in the matter of those things which happen as a result of human choice, whether it be the choice of a group, like a war, or the choice of an individual, as when a person builds a ship of his own accord and the ship sinks with a hundred or more passengers on board, every one of whom, no doubt, had a different horoscope? Why should the lives of those men be shortened because the stars decreed that that individual's ship should sink? Why should the horoscopes of all the passengers be annulled rather than that of the owner of the ship?

The truth of the matter is that this proves that the indications of the stars are not necessary causes; and though we see some of them being verified, like the prognostications of astrologers, nevertheless they may be nullified for various reasons, through the freedom of the will, or by reason of some merit or good deed, as the Rabbis say - "The constellations play no part in the destinies of Israel." Rashi's comment on the passage is that charity, prayer, or some meritorious deed can change the horoscope from evil to good; not to speak of the will of God, which is the highest principle of all and nullifies all other indications, no matter what their origin, the reason being known to God alone. This was the purpose for which the Torah was given, namely that by performing the commandments man may be saved from the decrees of the stars, as the prophet says: "And be not dismayed at the signs of heaven; for the nations are dismayed at them."

So, Rabbi Abraham Ibn Ezra in his **Sefer ha-Moladot** [Book on Nativities], names the general causes which annul particular horoscopes. Speaking of the eighth cause, he says that the freedom of the rational soul may annul a particular indication. He also says in the same place that if a man trusts in God, by whom all actions are controlled, the Lord will contrive means to deliver him from any evil which is indicated in his horoscope. This is true, as we have said, and agrees with the opinion of the Rabbis. They say that change of name, change of act, charity and prayer nullify the destiny indicated for man. Also, "Abram had no children, Abraham did." Some of them also say that Yitzhak was born under the sign of Mars, which was an indication that he would be killed. Hence God ordered that he be offered as a burnt-offering and then substituted a ram as ransom in order that he might be delivered from his fate. In the same way God contrives means to deliver those who observe the Torah and its commandments from the fate decreed for them by the stars. Hence, we see that the prophets admonished the people to turn away from their evil ways. Jeremiah says: "Amend your ways and your doings, and I will cause you to dwell in this place." They knew that observance of the commandments and obedience to God have the power of nullifying the indications of the stars, which are nullified also by other causes, according to the astrologers, as we explained in our examples of war, plague and the ship. So much for the decrees of the stars.

Chapter 5

It is appropriate now to discuss freedom of the will. Human acts are either all absolutely necessary, or all absolutely free, or all composed of necessity and freedom, or some of them are necessary, some are free and some are composed of necessity and freedom.

The first, namely that they are all necessary, as the astrologers say, is impossible, because this opinion does away with the category of the contingent, which is proved by experience, and upsets all the principles of the Torah, in general and in particular, as we have already explained. Moreover, the reason for their adoption of this view is because they think that in this way, they can maintain God's knowledge without any change. For if God knows what has been decreed concerning a person by the stars, and the decree is bound to be realized, then God's knowledge is true. On the other hand, if it were possible that the opposite of the decree of the stars might happen, God's knowledge would have to change, and it would not be uniformly true. But this opinion does not protect them from change. For the knowledge of a thing before it comes into being is not the same as the knowledge of the thing after it has come into being. If, therefore, we assume that His knowledge is similar to ours, there would still be a change in His knowledge in this respect as there would be in ours. The truth of the matter is that we can not institute any comparison between God's knowledge and ours, as we said above. His knowledge does not undergo any change, because it

Sefer Haikkarim   BOOK [Maamar] FOUR

is infinite. It is clear, therefore, that this opinion can not be maintained.

The second view that all human acts are absolutely free, and that effort is of value in all cases, as is implied in the nature of the contingent and as is the opinion of the Philosopher, is also impossible. For we see with our senses many instances in which a person endeavors to attain something, making all the possible preparations for the attainment of the end, and yet he not merely fails to attain his end, but the very preparations which he has made produce the opposite effect. We see an illustration of this in the Joseph story. The brothers of Joseph endeavored to nullify the dreams which he had dreamed by doing the opposite of that which was indicated in the dreams. They sold him as a slave so that it should not be possible for him to rule over them at all. But those very efforts which they made to nullify the decree brought about its realization, namely Joseph's rule over them. Similarly, Adonijah endeavored to obtain the kingdom by making the princes and servants of the king love and obey him. But these very efforts brought about his failure. For David became angry when he heard of it, and made Solomon king in his lifetime. There are also many cases in which good comes to a man without any effort at all. Thus, Saul obtained the kingdom without any previous effort. All this shows that not all human acts are absolutely free.

The third opinion that all human acts are composite and made up of necessity and freedom, is also impossible. For if this were true, there would be no acts for which a person deserved praise or blame, for the acts involving praise and blame are those in which there is no necessity at all. If all acts are composed of necessity and freedom, a person would not deserve praise if they are good, nor blame if they are evil, he would have an excuse every time and would never deserve either praise or blame. Now since not all acts are necessary, nor all free, nor all composed of freedom and necessity, it remains that some are free, some necessary, and some made up of necessity and freedom. And we must now explain every one of these three kinds of human acts.

Absolutely free acts are those which have the character of contingency, which may be affected by diligence and effort and for which a person deserves praise or blame. Command and prohibition apply to such acts, and reward and punishment attach to them, because the initiative resides in the agent himself, and there is no compulsion or hindrance.

Absolutely necessary acts are those which are determined either by

Sefer Halkkarim — BOOK [Maamar] FOUR

the stars or by the providence of God, as we shall see. Human choice has no control over these acts, and effort therein is to no purpose, because they do not depend upon a man's choice, whether they be good or evil. Free will has indeed the power to nullify a decree of fate, but it sometimes happens that by reason of the prior disobedience of a person or of his ancestors, he loses a good which his effort and diligence would normally have obtained for him, or that by reason of a prior meritorious act of his own or of his ancestors, he obtains a good without any effort at all. It happens also that a good or an evil comes to one from the stars if there is no sin to prevent the good from coming or merit to counteract the evil decreed by the stars. In such a case the good may come to a person without his expecting it. Thus, a person may desire to go on a certain journey, and is prevented from doing so by accidentally injuring his foot on a stone. Or a person may intend to board a ship and is prevented from doing so by suddenly becoming ill. Later those who took the journey are attacked by robbers and put to death, or the ship sinks. It is clear in these cases that the failure of his efforts to go on the journey or to board the ship was a good, which saved him from the misfortune of being killed by the robbers or drowned in the shipwreck, by reason of some prior merit of his.

In this connection our Rabbis, commenting upon the verse, "I will give thanks unto Thee, O Lord; for Thou wast angry with me," say: "The text has reference to the case of two persons who intended to go on a journey for business, and one of them met with an accident by injuring his foot with a thorn and was unable to go. He was much annoyed and began grumbling and cursing his fate. Later on, he heard that the ship in which he was to sail was wrecked on the sea, and he began to thank God for his escape. This is the meaning of the sequel to the verse quoted above: 'Thine anger is turned away, and Thou comfortest me.' Hence the statement of Rabbi Eleazar: 'The Psalmist says: "Who only doeth wondrous things." ' The meaning is that even the person in whose behalf a miracle is performed, is not aware of his good fortune." In the same way evil may befall a person unexpectedly, without his having done anything deserving such punishment. Such good or evil, it is clear, comes by the decree of fate without any choice.

Acts which are mixed and composed of necessity, i.e., decree of fate, and freedom, may be illustrated as follows: A person digs a foundation and finds a treasure, or he plants grain and prospers. It is clear that if he had not taken the trouble to dig the foundation or plant the grain, he would not have found the treasure, nor had

Sefer Halkkarim   BOOK [Maamar] FOUR

success in his crop. These are, therefore, cases in which necessity and freedom are combined. Sometimes a person obtains a given good through his efforts, and thereby misses a greater good. For example, he is trying to buy wheat, which would give him a great profit in a short time. But not being worthy of such great profit, he encounters, by divine contrivance, on his way to buy the wheat, beautiful garments, which he buys with the money intended for the purchase of the wheat, and makes no profit at all or very little. Or the opposite thing may happen. The wheat would not have brought him much profit, therefore the Lord puts the garments in his way, from which he makes a great profit, by reason of the meritorious deeds which he has to his credit, or because of a decree [of fate] that he should make profit or lose. The greater number of human acts which come by way of reward and punishment through divine providence are of this nature, i.e., they are made up of divine decree, i.e., necessity, and freedom.

Confusion and perplexity in respect to human affairs is due to the fact that people are ignorant of this matter and do not know that some acts are purely necessary, some are absolutely free, and some are mixed, combining necessity and freedom. But some people think that all the evils befalling them are determined and necessary, owing nothing to free choice; and they find in this way an excuse for their evil deeds, because they think that everything is determined. Others again think that all acts are free and deserve praise and blame. This confusion is prevalent not only among the generality of men, but also among men of thought. Among the latter, too, some maintain that all the good and evil fortunes of men are determined and necessary, some say that everything is due to man's free choice, and some say that all acts are made up of necessity and freedom.

It appears that Job maintained that all the good and evil fortunes of man are determined by the heavenly bodies. Therefore, he cursed his day. Eliphaz opposed him in his first reply, and said that if all good and evil fortune were due to the determination of fate, then the righteous and the wicked would owe their respective characters also to fate, but it is impossible that God should determine that a given person should be a righteous man. Hence, he said to him: "Shall mortal man be just through God? Shall a man be pure through his Maker?" The meaning is, is it possible that a man is righteous through God's decree, or pure through the decree of his Maker? This can not be, for, "Behold, He putteth no firmness in His servants ..." He does not determine the stability of their character, that they should not change, "How much more them that dwell in houses of clay," who are constantly changing by reason of the elements of which they are composed. Surely there is no determination in their respect, making it necessary that a given person should be righteous or wicked, without being able by his free will to change. But since righteousness and wickedness depend upon a person's choice, it follows that good and bad fortune also follow man's free choice, and Job is wrong in thinking that all is determined. This is why Eliphaz adds, "For anger killeth the foolish man, and envy slayeth the silly one," to show that there are evils which come upon a man through his free choice, like those which are the result of anger or envy. And since there are free acts and evils which are their effects, it follows that those evils which come upon a man not of his own free will, are in the nature of punishment. Hence, he says at the end of his speech: "Behold, happy is the man whom God correcteth ... For He maketh sore, and bindeth up ..."

The true and pious philosophers hold this opinion that all the evil and good fortune which befalls a man is by way of reward and punishment, as Eliphaz said, in opposition to the opinion of Job. Hence the Rabbis always say that every evil which befalls a man is in the nature of punishment. Thus, they relate: "Four hundred barrels of wine of Rab Huna became sour ... Said the Rabbis to him, Look into your conduct. Said he to them: Am I suspect in your eyes? Said they, Is the Holy One, blessed be He, suspect of doing injustice? They made an investigation and found that he had not given to the gardener the portion of the grapes due to him by law." Here Rab Huna thought that the wine became sour because of his bad luck or as a natural thing. His pupils, however, and the members of his school said that it must be a punishment, and that a man of his character should examine carefully all his acts. Rab Huna replied that they should not suspect him of being a sinner, and therefore the occurrence was an accident. But they replied, from their point of view that everything comes from God by way of reward and punishment, that they would rather suspect him than cast aspersion upon God's ways. Finally, it was discovered that the incident was a punishment for a sin he had committed in connection with the wine. And when the sin was removed the punishment was removed too. Similarly, we find in many places that the Rabbis attribute all things that happen to man as being in the nature of punishments.

The truth of the matter is as we have said, namely that there are things which should be attributed to punishment, other things should be attributed to man's choice, and still others are made up of necessity and choice, and inferences should not be applied from one class of things to another. Thinkers have not been aware of this situation and made inferences from one class of acts to another, and hence they got hopelessly perplexed without the possibility of a solution. Some of them maintain fate and necessity and deny the contingent, others maintain absolute freedom and deny God's knowledge. But the truth is as we have said, that there are three kinds of human acts, but man can not distinguish between them, and hence mistakes the one for the other and grumbles and finds fault with God's ways and doings.

Chapter 6

Diligence and effort are useful and necessary in all human acts. This is clearly true of those acts which are contingent. For since they are wholly the result of free choice, without compulsion or hindrance, there is no doubt that effort therein brings about realization. It is also clear that effort is necessary to bring about the realization of those acts which are made up of necessity and freedom. For whenever anything is an effect of two causes, both being requisite for the existence of the thing in question, like wheat which is produced by the work of the farmer and the rain, there is no doubt that the work of the husbandman and his efforts are as necessary a condition of the growth of the wheat as the rain, and without them the wheat would not grow. Similarly, ink can not be made without gall-nuts and vitriol, for both are requisite for the existence of ink. This is clear.

As to the necessary acts which are determined, viz. the decrees of fate, as we said before, it might seem that effort has no place in these. But if we consider the matter carefully, we shall find that here too effort is proper and necessary. For we have said that the failure to realize a good which comes from effort is due to punishment for an evil deed, or it may be that fate has decreed otherwise and the person's merit is not sufficient to nullify fate's decree. Hence when a person sees that he tries very diligently to obtain some good or some end and is not able to attain it, he may be sure that such is the decree of God as a punishment for his sins, or that the stars have so decreed and he has not enough merit to nullify the decree of the stars. This will lead him to examine his conduct and he will return to God and receive compassion. For when a man sees that he labors in vain, and that his work does not succeed, and he is not able to realize the purpose which he strives to attain, he may be sure that this is due to punishment which has been decreed for his sin. He will know then that there is something wrong with his conduct and will try to correct it as soon as possible. The Rabbis say: "If a man sees that misfortune comes upon him, he should examine his deeds, as is said: 'Let us search and try our ways.' If after the search he has found the cause, he should do penance, as is said: 'And return to the Lord.'"

But if a man sees that by dint of work and effort, he obtains what he expects, and that his work is not in vain, he knows that he is not guilty of any great sin which might prevent him from obtaining his livelihood through his efforts and will not cease from doing all that is in his power to obtain what he desires, since he knows that there is no decree against him, and he will be glad of it. Hence the Bible says: "When thou eatest the labour of thy hands, happy shalt thou be, and it shall be well with thee." The meaning is, if the labor of your hands and your toil enables you to obtain your livelihood, and your strength is not spent in vain, "happy shalt thou be, and it shall be well with thee." The Rabbis, commenting on this expression, say: " 'Happy shalt thou be,' in this world, 'and it shall be well with thee,' in the world to come." "Happy shalt thou be in this world," because you will be sure that you are not guilty of any sin serious enough to interfere with your obtaining what you desire through your efforts. "And it shall be well with thee in the world to come," for your good fortune is an indication that your conduct is good and upright and acceptable to God, since you have attained the degree of the righteous, concerning whom the Bible says: "They shall not labour in vain, nor bring forth terror ..."

It is clear, therefore, from all this that effort and diligence are desirable in all cases. Hence Solomon praises diligence: "The hand of the diligent maketh rich," and blames idleness in order to urge man to make all the efforts in his power to obtain his desires. The Rabbis also say: "In order that the Lord thy God may bless thee" - Will He do so even if a man sits in idleness? No, "In all the work of thy hand which thou doest," thus explaining that God's blessing comes with effort. The Psalmist also says: "Except the Lord keep the city, the watchman waketh but in vain." The inference is that if God does keep the city, the watchman does well to wake, for divine help comes with human watching and effort but not otherwise. Therefore, a man should endeavor as far as he can to exert himself in all those matters which can be obtained by human effort, for we know that effort is useful everywhere and, in all actions, as we have explained. We must not assume that because there is a particular event which seems destined [as the Rabbis say, commenting on the verse, "If any man falls from thence:" It was destined that he should fall], all things are determined. But we should exert our efforts in all things as though they were dependent on our free choice, and God will do as He thinks fit. So much will suffice as a brief discussion on freedom of will.

Chapter 7

We must now treat of the various kinds of Providence. Every one who professes a divine religion is obliged to believe that God provides for the individuals of the human race, that He takes notice of their particular acts, and rewards and punishes individuals and classes. This is a fundamental belief of all divine religions.

Whether according to rational speculation also this is possible, requires examination. If the opinion of the Philosopher is correct, who says that God's knowledge does not embrace particulars, it follows a fortiori that He takes no notice of individuals to punish them for disobedience. But we have decided, as a result of proofs conclusive to every intelligent man, that God knows all existing things and all individual acts. The point that requires investigation is this: Granting that God knows individuals and their acts, does He take notice of them and pay each one according to his conduct, or does He know them as He knows the individual animals? Since His knowledge embraces everything that exists and happens in the world, and nothing great or small is hidden from Him, He necessarily knows the animals, but He takes no notice of them individually to reward or punish them for their deeds, He provides for the individuals as part of the species which He preserves, and no more.

The motive which has led men who admit God's knowledge to deny providence is the unjust distribution in the world, according to them, of the world's goods and evils, for we find good men faring as if they acted like wicked men, and vice versa. This difficulty led Job to think that God pays no attention to the individual man, and that there is no difference between the good and the bad in the human race, as there is none in the animal species: "It is all one - therefore I say: He destroyeth the innocent and the wicked. If the scourge slays suddenly, He will mock at the calamity of the guiltless. The earth is given into the hand of the wicked; He covereth the faces of the judges thereof; if it be not so, who then is it?" Job says there is one reason which leads him to think that God's providence does not attach to the individuals of the human species, and that He destroys both the innocent and the guilty and makes no distinction between the righteous and the wicked, and that reason is that he sees the scourge and misfortune befalling those who are innocent of sin, and putting them to death suddenly and mocking them and making trial of them. The wicked men, on the other hand, prosper, so that the earth is given into the hand of the wicked, and he, as it were, covers the faces of the judges, and makes them not to see, since they are not permitted to exercise justice upon him. This shows that there is no one in the world who takes notice of the individual. Hence Job finishes with the words, "If it be not so, who then is it?" i.e., if it is not so, then who is the leader who does such wrong or allows its being done?

The prophets too, who believe in Providence and preach it to the world, and the wise men believing in the Torah complain of these two situations, the prosperity of the wicked and the adversity of the righteous. The two cases are not indeed of the same gravity. The complaint of the prosperity of the wicked is very real and serious, for all people see with their eyes the wickedness of the bad man, his idolatry, licentiousness, bloodshed, open violence and injustice without the fear of God, and yet he prospers. This leads all men to doubt Providence, and they say, "Wherefore doth the way of the wicked prosper?" The complaint about the adversity of the righteous is not so serious, because wrongdoing is not visible to everybody, and all people know "that there is not a righteous man upon the earth, that doeth good, and sinneth not," whether little or much. If then the righteous man meets with misfortune, they are not surprised, for they say, may be he has sinned secretly when no one saw him but God - "If a man profanes the name of God secretly, he is punished openly" - or may be he sinned in thought. In this connection the Rabbis say: "If one says to a woman, thou art married to me, provided I am a wicked man, she is married to him even if he is as righteous as Rabbi Akiba, for it is possible that he thought of idolatry in imagination." It is clear from this that not everybody can judge whether a given person is a righteous man or not, for man judges by appearance and thinks the man is righteous, but God sees into the heart and knows that he is not righteous, but wicked.

From the expression of the Tanna in the treatise "Abot" it is also clear that the problem of the adversity of the righteous is not as serious as that of the prosperity of the wicked. For he says: "We do not know anything about the tranquillity of the wicked," i.e., we do not know the reason of the prosperity of the wicked. And then he says, "And neither do we know of the misfortunes of the righteous,"

Sefer Halkkarim   BOOK [Maamar] FOUR

i.e., one might suppose that we do know the reason for the sufferings of the righteous, but that is not so. We infer this interpretation from the expression, "and neither," when he might have said, "nor." This indicates that the complaint about the adversity of the righteous is not so serious, for the world does not know who is a really righteous person. The only one who can properly make the complaint, is the one who knows in himself that he is a truly righteous man. Thus, Jeremiah says: "But Thou, O Lord, knowest me, thou seest me, and triest my heart toward Thee" ... Job, too, complained of God's judgment because he felt that he was a righteous man.

The fault of Job's companions was that they ascribed evil to Job, because they knew of no explanation why evil should befall a righteous man, except that he is really wicked, though they were able to explain good coming to a wicked man. Job, who knew his own righteousness, was not satisfied with their explanation. This is why Elihu became angry, as we read: "Also against his three friends was his wrath kindled, because they had found no answer, and had condemned Job." The meaning is, they knew no explanation why evil should befall a righteous man, unless God was unjust, and therefore they condemned Job and accused him of wickedness. This is why God said to Eliphaz: "My wrath is kindled against thee, and against thy two friends; for ye have not spoken of Me the thing that is right, as My servant Job hath." The meaning is, Job believed that evil may befall a truly righteous man, and in this he was right. His error consisted in the fact that, not knowing the explanation of this, he accused God of injustice if He had notice of the individual man, or he denied Providence, for he did not know how it was possible that misfortune should befall the righteous with God's knowledge, unless God was unjust. Then when Elihu showed him that there must be Providence, and charged him with sin because he had accused God of wrong, he changed his mind and believed that evil may befall a righteous man with the knowledge of God, and yet without any injustice on God's part. For God may test the righteous man to find whether he served God for love and would think nothing of bearing pain and trouble, no matter how great, for the love of God, and would not grumble against God's treatment of him. Job's sin was that he did grumble against God and accused Him of wrong.

Thus, were verified the words of Satan, who said: "Doth Job fear God for nought?" The test of the righteous, whether he serves God for love, is not when he is prosperous, but when he endures misfortune for love of God. When Job found this out from God, who said to him: "Wilt thou even make void My judgment? Wilt thou condemn Me that thou mayest be justified?" and the rest of that answer, in which God showed Job that he was guilty of sin in charging God with weakness or limitation or injustice, he admitted his error and said: "I know that Thou canst do everything, and that no purpose can be withholden from Thee." The meaning is, I know that it is impossible to charge Thee with weakness or inability, for Thou canst do everything, and canst realize Thy will. Nor can one charge Thee with wrongdoing because of want of knowledge, for no purpose can be withholden from Thee and Thy knowledge embraces all things. Hence wrong can not come from Thee, since Thou canst do everything and art wise in everything. He ends up by saying: "Wherefore I abhor my words, and am comforted ...," i.e., Job despised all the desires of the world and its goods, and was comforted for the suffering which he had endured, sitting in dust and ashes, because he knew that it was for his good.

The purpose of the book of Job is to answer these two questions. And since the solution of these questions is essential to a divine law, the chief of the prophets saw fit to compose this book, namely the book of Job, in dialogue form, representing wise men endeavoring to solve these two questions in various ways, the most important arguments of whom I shall mention briefly. But since these two problems can not be solved without first proving the existence of Providence, I will first speak briefly of the arguments for Providence found in this book, i.e., Job, and elsewhere. There are three kinds of proof in favor of Providence. One kind consists of arguments derived from the providence which exists over the general things. The second takes its arguments from the providence which exists over particular things; while the third kind uses arguments derived from the intellect. I will speak of each of these in a separate chapter.

Chapter 8

A. Arguments derived from general things:

    1. The first argument is derived from the visibility of the dry land. He who denies Providence maintains that the world has always been going on in accordance with the laws of nature which we observe to-day, holding that there is no one who can by his will force things to behave against their nature. As against a person of this class we can use the visibility of dry land as an argument to show that the world was created by a voluntary agent.

According to the nature of the elements the earth should be covered with the element water, and there would then be neither plants nor

Sefer Halkkarim   BOOK [Maamar] FOUR

animals. The visibility of the dry land is therefore a proof of the existence of a voluntary agent who compels nature to do His will. This is the first argument which God mentioned to Job when He began to speak to him: "Where wast thou when I laid the foundations of the earth? Declare, if thou hast the understanding." The meaning is this: He who believes in the eternity of the world holds to this opinion because he applies what he observes to-day in the particular objects of nature to the whole of creation. But this is not correct. For if the world were eternal and had always been going on according to the laws of nature observable today, without any interference of a voluntary agent, we would necessarily expect that that which nature requires should at some time exist actually. Now nature requires that the earth should be covered with water. If then the world is governed by nature, why does it never happen that the whole earth should be covered with water? We must say, therefore, that the element water is always forcibly kept away from its natural place. But this can not be due to nature, for by nature the element should realize at some time its natural tendency, and at that time there would be neither man nor animal nor plant. And if this condition was realized at some time in the past, the question arises, who compelled the element water to depart from its own nature in order that the existing plants and animals might come into being for the sake of man? This is proof positive that the world is the work of a voluntary agent and has not always been going on naturally as it does to-day, but that it came into existence through a voluntary agent.

This is what God meant when He said to Job: "Where wast thou when I laid the foundations of the earth?" That is, Thou Job who thinkest that the world was not made by a voluntary agent, but has always been going on according to nature, "Declare, if thou hast the understanding," where wast thou, or the human race, when the element earth was the base of all the elements, i.e., was covered by water and surrounded by all the elements, as its nature demands that it should be the foundation of everything? Thou must necessarily admit that the earth became visible through a voluntary agent. And when the land became visible, "Who determined the measures thereof, if thou knowest? Or who stretched the line upon it?" That is, who determined that just so much of the element earth should appear, no more and no less? And again, "Whereupon were the foundations thereof fastened?" That is, what natural law made it necessary that earth should stand above water? "Or who laid the cornerstone thereof?" It is customary in the creation of great edifices to have the cornerstone laid by a king or prince to the accompaniment of bells and cymbals and stringed instruments and the timbrel and the harp, so that the building may stand permanently. Hence, he says in rhetorical fashion, who was the prince who laid the earth's cornerstone, when the stars were the musicians and the singers and all the sons of God shouted aloud, i.e., the earth became an element in this manner, "when the morning stars sang together"? Then he adds, "Or who shut up the sea with doors?" That is, who is the prince who shut up the sea with doors that it should not return and cover the earth, as I have done? And he adds by way of explanation, "And broke for it My decree," i.e., I changed for it the decree of nature, "And set bars and doors, and said: Thus far shalt thou come, but no further...." The meaning of the entire passage is that the appearance of the dry land and its remaining permanently in that condition are a proof that there is a voluntary agent who maintains the world with His will and not merely in accordance with impersonal nature.

Jeremiah also, reproving his generation because they had no fear of God and thought that there was no personal being who provided for the world and acted with will, but that the world was ruled by natural necessity, spoke to them in the same strain: "Hear now this, O foolish people, and without understanding, that have eyes and see not, that have ears, and hear not: Fear ye not Me? Saith the Lord; Will ye not tremble at My presence? Who have placed the sand for the bound of the sea, an everlasting ordinance, which it can not pass ..." The prophet means that the mind is compelled to acknowledge that the appearance of the dry land shows that the world was made by a voluntary agent and is not simply the work of impersonal nature. Our Rabbis also say in "Bereshit Rabbah:" "When God said, 'Let the waters be gathered together,' the Prince of the Sea rose up before God, and said: 'Lord of the universe, I fill the whole world.' At once the Lord struck him and put him to death, as is said: 'He stirreth up the sea with His power.' " The Rabbis use the expression, "Prince of the Sea," to denote the substance of water. He fills the universe, i.e., the natural tendency of water is to cover the earth, but the latter appears above the water by the will of God. Hence they say further that in the future God will restore them to their places, thus indicating that the appearance of dry land is not due to nature, but to the will of a being who made the world and maintains it. Since that which is natural must be realized at some time, they say that in the future God will restore them to their proper places. This is proof conclusive that the universe is maintained by the will of God and

Sefer Halkkarim   BOOK [Maamar] FOUR

not by nature. God provides for it and governs it with righteousness and justice.

The Psalmist also argues in the same way: "He loveth righteousness and justice; the earth is full of the loving-kindness of the Lord." The meaning is, although God loves righteousness and justice, i.e., those things which follow the necessity of nature, nevertheless the earth is full of the loving-kindness of the Lord, i.e., it can not be denied that the world is maintained by kindness and will. And the proof is again derived from the appearance of the dry land: "He gathereth the waters of the sea together as a heap." Then he adds: "Let all the earth fear the Lord ... For He spoke, and it was." That is, since the world came into being and continues in being by the order and command of a voluntary agent and not by nature, there is in this an important argument for Providence, upon which the whole Psalm is built. "The Lord looketh from heaven; He beholdeth all the sons of men. From the place of His habitation, He looketh intently ... That considereth all their doings." The meaning is, since the appearance of the dry land so as to produce plants and animals for man's need is due to the will of a personal being, we can infer from this that God provides for man more than He does for the lower animals. The latter are provided for as species, while man is provided for as an individual, by the will of God and not merely by nature. For, "A king is not saved by the multitude of a host; a mighty man is not delivered by great strength," as is the case among the lower animals, and as nature requires. This being so, it is clear that though all the lower animals are provided for as species, man is looked after as an individual.

     2. The second argument derived from general phenomena is the one taken from the phenomenon of rain. At first sight it does not seem to be a real argument in favor of individual Providence of the human race. But since we find that Eliphaz mentions it in his first speech and Elihu in his fourth, and God confirms it in His first answer, we must explain the nature of the argument derived from rain.

It is clear that sublunar nature can not exist without rain. Rain is required to make plants grow so as to supply food for animals. It is also required to supply moisture to the bodies of animals that they should not dry up and become black from the great heat of the sun. Eliphaz speaks of both these utilities: "But as for me, I would seek unto God ... Who giveth rain upon the earth, So that He setteth up on high those that are low, and those that are black are exalted to safety." The meaning is, there are two benefits in rain. One is that the rain makes the low plants grow high above the earth, and the other is that He "Sendeth waters upon the fields," in the inhabited parts of the earth. This is in order that the bodies of those who become black from the heat of the sun should become moist and be able to maintain themselves - "Those that are black are exalted to safety." Elihu also alludes to this when he says: "Which the skies pour down and drop upon the multitudes of men," and in the sequel describes more fully the wondrous phenomenon of rain.

Rain is indeed necessary for the existence of all animals in general, but since all animals exist for the sake of man, the rain too is for the sake of man. Now the existence of rain can not be ascribed to nature, because it is not a thing which occurs every year at the same time in the same way, like the other natural phenomena. Rain comes at different times, in different ways, in a wonderful manner, not uniformly and naturally. For when there has been no rain for a long time and the drought is very great, we would not expect the air to become moist again and send up vapors. This shows that the coming of rain at different times is not the work of nature, but is due to the will of a personal being. God in speaking to Job alludes to this argument. Job having said: "When He made a decree for the rain," from which it would seem that he thought the rain was governed by natural law, God replied: "Hath the rain a father? Or who hath begotten the drops of dew?" The meaning is, has the rain a natural law, as you say, which is like a father begetting it to make plants grow in a determinate manner in order to supply all animals with food? Or what is that nature which must always beget drops of dew when there is no rain in order to moisten the bodies of animals in the inhabited parts of the earth? For you can not deny that this is not a purely natural phenomenon.

Nor can its origin be ascribed to chance, for chance phenomena do not happen regularly to maintain the existence of the world in so perfect a way as we observe in experience. But since it is not due to nature or to chance, it remains that it is due to the will of a personal being, God, who provides for the human species and maintains plants and animals for the need of man. This Providence takes care of the species. Nevertheless when we see that rain is brought down sometimes through the instrumentality of perfect men like Eliyahu and Honi ha-Me'aggel, there is no doubt that it shows special providence so far as that individual is concerned, and is not simply a natural phenomenon. Hence the Rabbis say: Three keys have not been handed over to intermediaries, the keys of fertility [childbirth], of rain, and of the resurrection of the dead. The meaning is that these three matters are not controlled by purely natural laws. [Fertility denotes bearing of children by a barren woman.]

The prophets also cite rain as a sign of Providence. Jeremiah says: "But this people hath a revolting and a rebellious heart; they are revolted, and gone. Neither say they in their heart: 'Let us now fear the Lord our God, that giveth the former rain, and the latter in due season; that keepeth for us the appointed weeks of the harvest.'" The Psalmist says: "Who covereth the heaven with clouds, who prepareth rain for the earth." For rain can not come unless the wind blows, covering the heaven with clouds and carrying them from place to place, whithersoever God wills to take them. Amos, reproving the people because they denied Providence, says: "And I also have withholden the rain from you, when there were yet three months to the harvest; and I caused it to rain upon one city and caused it not to rain upon another city," intimating that this is proof that rain is due to God's will. The Rabbis say: "Greater is the day of rain than the day of the resurrection of the dead. For the resurrection is for the righteous only, whereas the wondrous phenomenon of rain benefits the righteous as well as the wicked." They mean to say that as the resurrection is not a natural phenomenon, neither is the rain purely a phenomenon of nature, but is dependent upon the will of a personal being, and gives indication of Providence which is renewed every year according to the will of God.

One might say, however, that this does not point to individual providence but to providence for the species, as they say that rain comes alike to the righteous and the wicked, hence the prophet says: "Ask ye of the Lord rain the time of the latter rain," for the rain which comes as a result of prayer is a sure indication of Providence. For the same reason Elihu cites the rain which comes in answer to public prayer: "Which the skies pour down and drop for the sake of the multitudes of men." This shows that the rain comes not as a natural thing but providentially, in answer to the prayers of the many. In the same way Providence can be proved with certainty from the rain which comes in answer to the righteous and pious men of every generation and from examples of divine providence which attaches to each man according to his perfection or to the many according to their perfection. David also says: "In the day that I called, thou didst answer me; Thou didst encourage me in my soul with strength." That is, because it is a sure sign of Providence. Moshe also cites the acceptance of public prayer as a proof of Providence: "For what great nation is there, that hath God so nigh unto them, as the Lord our God is whensoever we call upon Him?"

Sefer HaIkkarim — BOOK [Maamar] FOUR
Chapter 9

B. The proofs which are derived from special and particular events in human life are three in number.

1. Many clever and shrewd persons endeavor with appropriate means to realize their purposes in doing harm to a given person, but fail; the very means they employ for harm often prove to be causes for good, as in the case of the brothers of Joseph. The very means they employed to do harm to Joseph brought about his success. Similarly the very means that Saul used to ruin David were the cause of his success: "For Saul said: 'Let not my hand be upon him, but let the hand of the Philistines be upon him.' " This very thing spread his fame among all Israel as a strong man, a fighting man who was successful in his battles. Such instances prove without a doubt the reality of Providence, particularly in the case of those who are weak and without help, as the Psalmist says: "Who executeth justice for the oppressed."

The Rabbis say: "A certain heretic asked Rabbi Yehoshua son of Hanania, 'How can a lamb maintain itself in the midst of seventy wolves?' Rabbi Yehoshua replied: 'Great is the Shepherd who protects it.' " The heretic expressed his astonishment at the fact that all the nations aim to do harm to Israel, as wolves aim to harm the lamb, and yet their purpose is not realized. The reply was that it is the Shepherd who protects them, namely the divine Providence which looks out for them. This shows that the evil which comes to men also comes through divine providence, since we see many wicked people trying to do harm to the simple without success. This is a proof that the simpletons are preserved by Providence and not by their own wisdom, as David says: "The Lord preserveth the simple." Eliphaz also mentions this proof: "He frustrateth the devices of the crafty, so that their hands can perform nothing substantial. He taketh the wise in their own craftiness; and the counsel of the wily is carried headlong. They meet with darkness in the daytime, and grope at noonday as in the night. But He saveth from the sword of their mouth, even the needy from the hand of the mighty. So, the poor hath hope." God confirmed this statement in His first answer: "But from the wicked their light is withholden ..." The meaning is, it is withholden from the wicked to realize their purposes, which he calls their light. If there were no Providence, we would expect the wicked to realize their purposes, since they employ the appropriate means to the end. In the arts we see that the purposes are realized because the artisan employs the appropriate means. If the purposes of the wicked are not realized, there is proof therein of Providence.

    2. The second proof is derived from the special punishments which come upon the wicked corresponding to their offences. This proves that there is a being who takes notice and judges justly. For instance, if a person injures another financially, he is himself injured financially. If he injures him physically, for example, cuts off his hand, or blinds his eye, his own hand is cut off, or his eye is blinded. And if one kills another, he is killed. So, we observe in all punishments that they fit the crime. Thus, the Egyptians wronged Israel by throwing them into the water: "Every son that is born ye shall cast into the river." For a punishment they were drowned in the Red Sea. Similarly, when the dogs licked the blood of Naboth, it was said to Ahab: "In the place where dogs licked the blood of Naboth shall dogs lick thy blood, even thine." For David's wrong of lying with Bathsheba, he was told: "And he shall lie with thy wives." Similarly, the Tanna says: "Thou wast drowned because thou didst drown others." This shows that God punishes a man in a manner corresponding to his deeds. Jeremiah says: "Great in counsel, and mighty in work." "Great in counsel," because He contrives means and makes far-flung combinations in order to punish the sinner according to the measure of his sin and after the manner thereof, "according to his ways." The expression, "according to his ways," has also another meaning: A person follows an evil way, and makes special effort to harm his neighbor. He is punished even if he does not succeed in doing the harm intended. For since the failure of his effort to do harm is not due to him but to God's providence who preserves the simple, He punishes him because he followed an evil way, though his intention was not realized. "According to the fruit of his doings," means that God punishes a man for the consequences of his deeds as affecting his neighbor, even though there was no deliberate effort on his part, but merely a word, "as a madman who casteth firebrands, arrows, and death …" He is punished for the harmful result which comes to his neighbor, whether by his deliberate effort or not. This proves beyond a doubt that God looks after and judges the wicked, since He punishes them according to their ways.

This is the meaning of the Psalmist's words: "The Lord hath made Himself known, He hath executed judgment …" The meaning is, We, know that God does justice when the wicked man is punished for the evil which he does and the harm which he causes to others: "In the net which they hid is their own foot taken." This matter is

Sefer HaIkkarim — BOOK [Maamar] FOUR

explained in many passages in the book of Psalms: "The wicked have drawn out the sword ... Their sword shall enter into their own heart." And the Rabbis expatiate upon the matter at length. Thus, they say, commenting on the verse: "And God seeketh that which is pursued:" God always seeketh him who is pursued, even if the righteous pursues the wicked. The prophet also testifies to this: "For three transgressions of Moab, yea, for four, I will not reverse it: because he burned the bones of the king of Edom into lime." This is not because of the goodness of the king of Edom, but solely because he was the persecuted. We also find frequently in the prophetic books warning of punishment of the wicked, corresponding to their crimes. Isaiah says: "But ye said: 'No, for we will flee upon horses,' therefore shall ye flee; and: 'we will ride upon the swift;' therefore shall they that pursue you be swift." Joel says: "And they have cast lots for My people; and have given a boy for a harlot, and sold a girl for wine and have drunk ... behold, I will stir them up from the place whither ye have sold them ... and I will sell your sons and your daughters into the hands of the children of Yehuda, and they shall sell them to the men of Sheba ..." Our Rabbis also say: "In the measure which one employs for others is it measured out to him." This is a conclusive proof of Providence that should make a great impression upon those of little faith.

  3. The third proof is found in the words of Elihu, and is taken from the information which comes to man concerning particular matters in a dream: "In a dream, in a vision of the night ... Then He openeth the ears of men ..." Then he explains the reason: "That men may put away their purpose, and that He may hide the body from man." The meaning is, in order to keep man away from the evil deed in which he is entangled, by concealing from him the corporeal things and the shameful attributes, so as to separate him from them. Then he explains the benefit which follows from this in this world and the next: "That He may keep back his soul from the pit" - i.e., in the next world; "And his life from perishing by the sword" - in this world. Or it may be that both expressions refer to this world, and "keep back his soul from the pit," refers to natural death, while "his life from perishing by the sword," has reference to accidental death. Now this information which comes to a man in a vision of the night is conclusive proof of individual Providence over the human race. It is not general providence, since it concerns particular individual things, and the other species have not got it. If it were due to general providence, it would have to exist also in other species beside the human and would not concern itself with particular things.

Chapter 10

C. The arguments derived from the intellect are of two kinds. The one is derived from a consideration of the recipient, and the other from a consideration of the giver.

1. The first is as follows: The intellectual power in man can not have been intended merely for the preservation of the species, for we see that the other species are preserved without it. Since therefore we see that man has this superiority to the lower animals, it is unlikely that he would be abandoned to himself and no notice be taken of his particular affairs, as is the case with the lower animals, since he is superior to them in knowledge.

To this argument God alludes in His first answer to Job, where He first enumerates the benefits, He bestows upon the various animal species in providing for each one specially, as distinct from the other species, by preserving it or by giving it a peculiar perfection different from that of other species: "Who provideth for the raven his prey ... Who hath sent out the wild ass free? Knowest thou the time when the wild goats of the rock bring forth? Or canst thou mark when the hinds do calve? ... Hast, thou given the horse his strength?" Then he describes the benefit He bestows upon man in implanting in his nature a peculiar perfection, namely the power to apprehend intelligible concepts: "Who hath given understanding to the mind?" The Hebrew word sekvi denotes the intellectual power in man, as I explained in the First Book. First, he says: "Who hath implanted secure wisdom?" alluding to the "prima intelligibilia" or axioms, which were placed in man at the basis of his created nature. These first intelligibilia are the real causes which make demonstration possible, preventing an infinite regress. [The bet, the first letter of the Hebrew word battuhot, is part of the root, as was explained in the First Book.] He says this in order to explain that this gift that was given to man was without doubt intended for a more noble purpose than is realized in the lower animals. This superiority of man indicates that he is taken more notice of by God than any other animal species. This being so, it follows that divine providence should attach to him in a greater degree in accordance with the superiority of his intellect to that of the lower animals. Maimonides has the same idea, namely that the degree of divine providence one enjoys depends upon the degree of intellectual power he possesses. It follows that he who perfects his intellect as far as lies in his power will enjoy a greater degree of divine providence than one who has not done so. On the other hand, he who does not perfect his soul at all and wastes his intellectual energies is reduced to the degree of the lower animals, and loses divine providence altogether. This is a conclusive proof that the measure of divine providence attaching to a rational individual depends upon the perfection of his reason, just as in the beginning, when the human species was created, Providence took more notice of man than of the other animal species in giving him that ability.

David also uses the intellectual faculty in man as a proof that divine providence takes care of the sublunar world: "O Lord, our Lord, what glory is there in Thy name in all the earth!" The word mah [how, what] is derogatory, as in the expression: "and what [mah] are we …" The Psalmist expresses his wonder and says, what worth and glory can there be for Thy name upon all the earth, seeing that "Thou hast put Thy majesty above the heavens," which are as "strong as a molten mirror," and permanent and bright without any doubt? I do not see that among the creatures of the earth there is any one through whose creation one may have an idea of Thy dignity and the glory of Thy name. But when I consider the matter carefully, I find that, "Out of the mouth of babes and sucklings hast Thou founded strength," i.e., valid propositions or principles, which are innate in man and not derived from experience and habit. These are the "prima intelligibilia," which are in the mouth of babes and sucklings, or the "sensibilia," all of which are strong foundations of knowledge and proofs of the reality of Providence; "because of Thine adversaries," those who say: "The Lord hath forsaken the land," and, "that Thou mightest still the enemy and the avenger," who afflicts the poor and the needy, and follows his own desires, since he denies Providence.

Then he explains at length the same topic, which he has stated briefly: "When I behold Thy heavens, the work of Thy fingers … What is man, that Thou art mindful of him?" That is, when I behold the heavens and their noble beauty and the structure of the moon and the stars, which Thou hast established, I say in my heart, What is man …? For man is nothing in comparison with their nobility, and he is not worthy of divine providence, since he is a lowly creature made of waste matter and a putrid drop. Then again he contradicts this idea, and says: "Yet Thou hast made him but little lower than the angels" … That is, when I consider the creation of man and see the perfection thereof, namely that he possesses an intellectual faculty by which he comes near to the angels [being only a little below them, they being active intelligences, while he is a potential intelligence] - "Thou hast made him but little lower than the angels" - through the glory and the honor and the beautiful divine crown with which Thou didst crown him, and by means of this power "Thou hast made him to have dominion over the works of Thy hands;" for without it he could not have subdued, and would not have been worthy of subduing, all the animals, which are stronger and mightier than he, and of putting them all under his feet; nor could he have made a way in the sea and a path in the mighty waters; all of which shows that the divine power mingles with him through his intellect and he has some of the knowledge of his Maker, - this being so, I say that from the creations of the earth proof may be derived of the glory of Thy name and Thy worth, since Thou didst bestow a rational faculty upon so coarse a matter. Therein can be seen Thy noble perfection, for the worth of an artisan can be seen when he bestows perfection upon an inferior material which is far from perfection, as I explained in the first chapter of the Second Book. Hence, he concludes, "O Lord, our Lord, how glorious is Thy name in all the earth!" The word mah [how, what] in this passage is intended to magnify the attribute, as in the expression: "How [mah] manifold are Thy works, O Lord!" "How [mah] great are Thy works, O Lord!" The meaning is this: Although the heavens are made of a much nobler material than the sublunar creatures, nevertheless, from the rational faculty in man, who is but little lower than the angels, we can infer that Thy name is glorious in all the earth and that Thy providence takes care of the human race in the sublunar world.

2. The second proof is taken from a consideration of the giver, and has two forms. One is based upon God's wisdom and power and the other upon the consideration that man is the work of His hands.

A. The first, based upon God's wisdom and power, is as follows: It is an axiomatic proposition that all kinds of perfection should be ascribed to God, and all kinds of defects should be denied of Him. Now it is a sign of perfection in man if he takes care of the work of his hands so that it may completely realize its purpose. It is also a sign of perfection in a master if he takes care of those who are governed by him, whom he guides with righteousness and justice. And if they fail to do this, it is a sign of a defect in the man and the master respectively. A human being may have such defect for lack of knowledge or of power. A master who has the necessary ability may owe his defect to the fact that he is wicked, unjust or indifferent. But God is "Wise in heart and mighty in strength," as Job himself says. Hence, He has absolute power, and there can be no failure of providence on account of weakness and inability to satisfy the needs of those governed by Him. And since He is wise there can be no failure of Providence on account of ignorance. Nor can there be a failure to take care of those under His guidance by reason of wickedness or injustice, as Job argued when he said that God, being one without any one to oppose Him, does wrong, if He so desires, to those dependent upon His rule: "But He is at one with Himself and who can turn Him?" also: "There is no arbiter betwixt us, that might lay his hand upon us both." For Elihu answered this argument when he said: "Far be it from God, that He should do wickedness, and from the Almighty that He should commit iniquity." "Far be it from God," refers to His absolute power, for the word El [God] denotes power. And since He has absolute power, He does no wrong or iniquity by failing to punish evil-doers. Nor can He fail to take care of the work of His hands and reward the righteous because He can not supply their needs, for He is Shaddai [lit. having enough], Almighty, who has enough in His being to bestow upon everything its final perfection. Having enough therefore to supply every one his need, if He did not do so, it would be iniquity. Hence, he says: "And [far be it] from the Almighty that He should commit iniquity."

Then he says: "For the work of man will He requite unto him," alluding to reward; "And cause every man to find according to his ways," an allusion to the punishment which comes upon the wicked. Then he emphasizes his argument from power and says: "Yea, of a surety, God will not do wickedly, neither will the Almighty pervert justice." That is to say, God has absolute power, as we have seen and as the word El [God] signifies. Also, He can supply every existing thing with the perfection of which it is capable, as is indicated in the word Shaddai [Almighty]. But this can not be unless He takes care of the particular acts of man and recompenses every one according to his work, and causes every man to find according to his ways. For if He does not pay the wicked according to his wickedness, it would be wickedness in God, and God does not do wickedness. Also, if He does not reward the righteous according to his ways, it is perversion of justice, and the Almighty does not pervert justice. We must therefore say that God does take notice of human acts, and requites every one according to his ways.

He then proves that God has absolute power: "Who gave Him a charge over the earth?" i.e., Who is in charge of Him, who commanded Him to make the earth, and has more power than He? "Or who hath disposed the whole world?" and is more generous than

Sefer Haikkarim   BOOK [Maamar] FOUR

He? "If He set His heart upon man, If He gather unto Himself his spirit and his breath; all flesh would perish together ..." The meaning is, who is the one in charge, who has more power than He, so that if he set his heart upon the world of nature, all flesh would perish together, and man would return unto dust? There is no other being who can do all this except Him, hence it is clear that He has absolute power. And since this is clear, He can not do this, for it would be wickedness or iniquity, and He would be a hater of justice. Therefore, he says: "If now thou hast understanding, hear this; Hearken to the voice of my words. Shall even one that hateth right govern? And wilt thou condemn Him that is just and mighty - Is it fit to say to a king: 'Thou art base?' Or to nobles: 'Ye are wicked?' That respecteth not the persons of princes, nor regardeth the rich more than the poor? For they all are the work of His hands." The meaning is, since we have shown that He has power and is king of all, we can not say that a lord who hates justice can govern. Nor can we condemn the one who is absolutely righteous. We can not say to a king who has absolute power that he is base and does iniquity and chooses to be called a wrongdoer. Nor is it proper to call a generous person who can give as much as he pleases, wicked. For he would not choose to be called wicked or iniquitous by withholding the good that is due to the deserving and failing to reward him according to his righteousness. Nor can we say that He does this because He is obliged to respect the great ones of the land, for God respects no persons, as we read, "That respecteth not the persons of princes ... For they are all the work of His hands," and should therefore be judged all of them in an equal manner, since He has the power to do so and there is no one who can prevent Him; "For in a moment they die, even at midnight; the people are shaken and pass away," through His messengers, "and they [the messengers] take away the mighty and the strong without touching them with the hand." This proves that "His eyes are upon the ways of a man, and He seeth all his goings. There is no darkness, nor shadow of death, where the workers of iniquity may hide themselves." This is the style of the whole second reply in which Elihu argues to prove the existence of Providence on the basis of God's power.

B. The second form of the proof, which is based upon the fact that man is the work of God's hands, is given by Elihu in his fourth speech, as follows: The strongest argument which Job advanced against the idea of Providence is based upon man's inferiority, "What is man, that Thou shouldest magnify him, and that Thou shouldest set Thy heart upon him, and that Thou shouldest

Sefer Halkkarim — BOOK [Maamar] FOUR

remember him every morning, and try him every moment?" Job thought that because man was despicable and contemptible in the sight of God, He does not pay any attention to his various deeds any more than He takes notice of the acts of the pig, for the same reason. At the same time Job held this to be unjust on the part of God, and an improper withholding from man of that which is his due, since man is the work of God's hands and is endowed with a rational faculty. For this reason, he calls man God's "handiwork," because his origin is not due to nature alone, like the lower animals, but to nature and the divine power, i.e., the intellectual power with which man is endowed, as we are told, "Let us make man in our image, etc." Accordingly, Job said that it was injustice in God to deprive man of God's care on the ground of man's great inferiority to God; for it is not proper for a perfect being to despise the work of His hands and to reject it because it is inferior. Hence, he said: "Is it good unto Thee that Thou shouldest oppress, that Thou shouldest despise the work of Thy hands, and shine upon the counsel of the wicked?" The meaning is, Dost Thou think it is right, because Thou art absolutely perfect and man is lowly and despicable in comparison with Thy greatness, that Thou shouldest deprive him of his due and prevent him from attaining that perfection of which he is capable through the rational power which Thou gavest him, and abandon him by reason of his worthlessness, thus despising the work of Thy hands? By so acting Thou art, as it were, confirming the words of the wicked, who say that right doing is of no benefit.

Accordingly, Elihu in his fourth reply undertakes to answer the argument based upon man's inferiority: "Behold, God is mighty and despiseth not him who is mighty in strength of understanding." The meaning is, it is impossible that God should ignore the human species by reason of their inferiority. For it is not the nature of a wise agent to abandon the work of his hands because of its inferiority, seeing that he can improve it. "God is mighty," i.e., He is all-powerful and all-wise in actuality, being able to cause man to attain the measure of perfection of which he is capable, by reason of His great power. Hence it is not possible that He should despise man, who has a strong intellectual potentiality, and is capable of intelligence. Since man has intellect potentially, it stands to reason that God will help him to bring it to actuality and would not rob mankind of the perfection which it is capable of attaining, for this would be a defect in God, since He has the power. As Job said at the end of his argument: "Thou shinest upon the counsel of the wicked," Elihu says here that it is not so, but the converse is true: "He preserveth not the life of the wicked; but giveth to the poor their right. He withdraweth not His eyes from the righteous; But with kings upon the throne, He setteth them forever, and they are exalted. And if they be bound in fetters, and be holden in cords of affliction; then He declareth unto them their work, and their transgressions, that they have behaved themselves proudly. He openeth also their ear to discipline, and commandeth that they return from iniquity." In this way he shows that all evil that comes to the righteous is due to divine providence.

At the end of this reply, following this argument, he concludes by calling attention to the wonderful phenomenon of rain, which indicates wisdom and Providence, and the marvels of the thunder, which is evidence of power, wisdom and power being very strong arguments, which God Himself emphasizes in His two replies. In one answer He proves His wisdom and providence from the wisdom that is evident in the formation of the animals and the providence which is similarly evident in the way in which the various species of animals are provided with their appropriate protection and endowed with their specific form of perfection. This denotes wisdom, which it is the purpose of that reply to prove. In the second reply He proves power: "Wilt thou even make void My judgment? Wilt thou condemn Me, that thou mayest be justified?" The meaning is, Wilt thou deny My providence and say that I do not deal justly with existing things, as if I were not able to do so? "Or hast thou an arm like God? And canst thou thunder with a voice like Him? Deck thyself with majesty and excellency, ... And look upon every one that is proud, and abase him. Look on every one that is proud, and bring him low; and tread down the wicked in their place."

The whole answer proceeds in this style to point out the great power of God to create huge creatures which man is afraid to look at, and at the sight of which he falls full length upon the ground. Hence, He says: "Shall not one be cast down even at the sight of him?" All this is to show that since God has absolute power, it is impossible to attribute to Him any inability in any respect. Nor can we attribute to Him lack of knowledge after seeing the extraordinary wisdom contained in all the things which He created. As a result of this Job was reconciled and admitted the two arguments. He acknowledged the argument proving God's power when he said: "I know that Thou canst do everything," and the argument proving God's knowledge in the expression: "And that no purpose can be withholden from Thee."

Sefer HaIkkarim — BOOK [Maamar] FOUR
Chapter 11

As we find that God provides in various ways for the several species of animals in order that the species may reach the most perfect form that is possible for it, so it is reasonable to suppose that He similarly provides for every individual human being according to his degree and worth, in order that he may reach his proper perfection.

In the lower animals we see that God has provided for every one of the animal species in a wonderful manner in giving them all the perfection of which they are capable. This is evident in every one of the animal species. God gave them members and organs and faculties calculated to preserve the species so that it may have permanent existence in a perfect manner. Take as an example the horned animals that eat grass. The material intended for the teeth was used up in the formation of the horns and nature was not able to make teeth for them in the upper jaw, as a consequence of which they can not masticate their food properly. Hence nature gave them the power to chew the cud in order that they might complete in the second mastication what was left undone in the first. Again, those animals that can find food readily digest their food quickly, as for example fish and fowl, as the Rabbis say: In the case of fowl and fish, their food is digested in the time it takes them to be consumed when thrown into the fire. The dog on the other hand, who can not find food readily, digests his food slowly, as the Rabbis say, commenting on the verse, "The righteous taketh knowledge of the cause of the poor:" God knows that the dog can not find food in sufficiency, therefore He makes his food stay in his bowels three days. Beasts and birds of prey, which do not feed on plants, are provided by nature with organs which enable them to feed on what they catch, and with a poison in their claws, which they inject into the flesh of the animal they kill, and which cooks the food and grinds it. The virus of the poison and its heat takes the place of fire and prepares the flesh for food. From the nature of the ant, which is a tiny creature and yet is so active, we can form an idea of God's wisdom and providence, taking care of all existing things and of every part of them. The camel is provided with a long neck, proportional to the length of his thighs, so that he may be able to pick up his food easily.

All these examples are, indeed, instances of divine providence touching the genus or the species. Nevertheless, we can infer from them the existence of divine providence in relation to the individuals of the human species. For we find that the mode of provision varies

Sefer HaIkkarim   BOOK [Maamar] FOUR

in the different species in accordance with that which every species requires to attain its perfection. According to its temperament and nature it is provided with organs for its protection and the procuring of food, in order that it may attain the means of perfection intended for it. Those animals which require especial care, like the young raven, are provided with food, and we never see young ravens die of hunger. The roe is protected and provided for at the time of its birth, not one of them being without this protection at that time, as the Rabbis say: "The roe has a narrow uterus, therefore God sends her a snake at the time she has to give birth, which bites her." And we find similar instances of providence in the various animal species. This proves conclusively that there is one who provides for existing things and gives to each one what it needs for its perfection, as its nature requires and according to its capacity, and not one thing is deprived of that which it needs and is capable of receiving.

But human individuals differ more widely among themselves in respect to the degree of their rational power than one animal species differs from another. One individual is almost on a level with the irrational animals, while another approaches the degree of the angels. Hence it follows that divine providence must vary with the individual in the human species as it varies with the species in the animal kingdom. And it follows from this that the difference between one individual and another in the matter of providence depends upon the difference in their perfection and worth. Hence a person may have such a high degree of perfection that providence takes care of him and God communicates with the person himself in a prophetic revelation or in a dream.

Prophetic revelation is illustrated in the case of Abraham, to whom God said: "Get thee out of thy country ... and I will make of thee a great nation ..." Communication in a dream is illustrated in the case of Abimelech, who was told in a dream of the night: "Behold thou shalt die, because of the woman whom thou hast taken." Pharaoh, who was a wicked man, received the divine communication in the shape of plagues, as the Bible says: "And the Lord plagued Pharaoh and his house with great plagues ..."

Sometimes the divine communication comes to a person through the message of a prophet, as it came to Barak, the son of Abinoam, through Deborah, or to Eli and Saul through Samuel. Sometimes again a person occupies a lower grade, and the divine communication comes to him neither in a prophetic revelation nor through the message of a prophet, but through a divine impulsion, such as Yehuda experienced when he turned aside to visit his

Sefer HaIkkarim — BOOK [Maamar] FOUR

daughter-in-law Tamar, the divine purpose being that Perez and Zerach should be his descendants, or the impulse which came to Abigail to go out to meet David, who knew that it was divine in its origin. Therefore, he said: "Blessed be the Lord the God of Israel, who sent thee this day to meet me." Or the impulse which came to some of the judges to go out to fight and save Israel. Sometimes also such divine impulsion comes to a person so that God may punish him for a previous sin, like the impulse which came to Ahab to go out to fight, the purpose being that he should be killed, as a punishment for the death of Naboth. There are many illustrations of this.

Sometimes persons are afflicted with suffering in the shape of sickness, imprisonment, and the like, either as a warning that they should abandon the evil in which they are enmeshed and return to God, or in order to wipe out the few sins which they have committed. Sufferings of the last kind are used to test those who serve God. If the motive of their service is love, they will accept the suffering gracefully for the love of God. But if the motive of their service is fear of punishment and love of reward, they will grumble against God's treatment of them and say improper things about Him, as Job did. Job was a God-fearing man, but he served God from love of reward and fear of punishment. Therefore, when he was afflicted with suffering he grumbled against God's judgment. Elihu in his first speech explained to him this type of divine communication: "In a dream, in a vision of the night, when deep sleep falleth upon men … Then He openeth the ears of men, and by their chastisement sealeth the decree, that men may put away their purpose, and that He may hide the body from man." The meaning is, that sometimes divine communication may come to a person in a dream in order to turn him aside from the evil deed in which he is entangled and to conceal from him the corporeal interests, so as to withhold his soul from the pit. He goes on to say that sometimes the divine communication may be made through illness: "He is chastened also with pain upon his bed, and all his bones grow stiff," i.e., he is punished with great pain. He describes at length the pain that he suffers through the sickness, and then says: "He prayeth unto God, and He is favourable unto him, so that he seeth His face with joy; and He restoreth unto man his righteousness." The meaning is, that when he prays unto God, He shows him favor and restores his righteousness unto him, i.e., He credits him with the knowledge that his illness was the effect of his sins, and therefore he returns to God and acknowledges before Him in a great assembly and in the seat of

Sefer Halkkarim — BOOK [Maamar] FOUR

the elders that his sins were the cause of his illness: "He cometh before men and saith: 'I have sinned, and perverted that which was right.' " And this is accounted to his credit.

Similarly in his last speech Elihu says that sometimes sufferings of a different kind come upon a man, like imprisonment, etc., in order to rouse him up that he may turn away from the sins in which he is caught: "And if they be bound in fetters, and be holden in cords of affliction; then He declareth unto them their work and their transgressions, that they have behaved themselves proudly. He openeth also their ear to discipline, and commandeth that they return from iniquity." Then he concludes the subject: "If they hearken and serve Him, they shall spend their days in prosperity ... But if they hearken not, they shall perish by the sword ... But they that are insincere in heart lay up anger; they cry not for help when He bindeth them." The meaning is, that when sufferings, such as imprisonment and the like, come upon a person, it is a divine communication to a man that he should turn away from his sins and also a way of finding out whether he accepts his sufferings gracefully, as a punishment for his sins. If he returns to God and serves Him, God will reward him: "If they hearken and serve Him, they shall spend their days in prosperity ... But if they hearken not, they shall perish by the sword ...," i.e., if one does not accept his sufferings gracefully and does not believe in the admonition to return to God, he is doomed to the sword and will expire without knowledge: "But they that are insincere in heart lay up anger; They cry not for help when He bindeth them." The meaning is, that those who serve God insincerely - "the insincere in heart" - alluding to Job, are exceedingly angry with God for having inflicted suffering upon them, as Job was angry, and do not return to God, "They cry not for help when He bindeth them." Hence, "Their soul perisheth in youth, and their life as that of the depraved."

But the afflicted man is delivered from these sufferings through his affliction, i.e., since he has endured the suffering of affliction, "He delivereth the afflicted by His affliction, and openeth their ear by tribulation." That is, through the tribulation which he suffered on account of the affliction, He opens their ear that they should return to God, and there is no need of imprisonment or other sufferings. But if one does not return to God despite his sufferings and regards them as matters of chance and accident and not as a punishment for his sins, then the Bible tells us what the punishment for that is: "If ... ye ... will walk with Me as though your sufferings were an accident, then will I also walk with you in the same manner," i.e., until you understand that it is not accident.

Chapter 12

An answer to the complaint about the prosperity of the wicked.

The wicked man is well treated for four reasons, assuming that the person we think wicked is really wicked and the person we think righteous is really righteous.

1. Good things may come to the wicked as a result of general providence, as for example by reason of the fact that it has been decreed that the nation as a whole shall dwell in quiet and tranquillity and its members shall be prosperous. This corresponds to the providence governing the species that is ordered by the heavenly bodies, against which it is unreasonable to grumble. Just as there is no sense in complaining against God that He gave the wicked man hands to do evil with, and perfect organs and good health and strength to be able to indulge in illicit sexual relations, and so on, so it is unreasonable to complain that God does not change the constellations or the decree concerning the nation, in order that the wicked man may not receive benefits through the nation as a whole or the country in which he lives, concerning which it has been decreed that its members shall enjoy tranquillity. Benefits may also come to the wicked in this manner by reason of his own specific horoscope, if he is not so wicked that the astral decree is overruled and is changed from good to evil. This mode is similar to general providence, for the benefit which comes in this way is due to the general law which determines that one born under a given star shall be prosperous.

2. Benefits may come to a wicked man as a result of individual providence. The purpose may be to reward him for some merit of his or for some good deed that he has done. For God is just and upright and does not withhold the reward of any creature. Hence it is proper that He should recompense the wicked man for the good deeds he has done so as to exclude him from spiritual reward and spiritual happiness. This is the meaning of the biblical expression: "And repayeth them that hate Him to their face, to destroy them." Onkelos translates the above verse: "And repays His enemies for the good deeds which they performed before Him in their life time, in order to destroy them [in the future life]." The Rabbis also say: "If a wicked man is prosperous, it is an indication that he is not absolutely wicked." Also, "If a person's sins predominate over his

Sefer HaIkkarim   BOOK [Maamar] FOUR

good deeds, he is well treated, as if he had fulfilled the entire Torah." Another statement is as follows: "The two tears which Esau shed were accounted to his credit, and hence he became the ancestor of the Aluphim …"

This idea is also clearly expressed in the words of the Psalmist: "A brutish man knoweth not, neither doth a man understand this. When the wicked spring up as the grass, and when all the workers of iniquity do flourish." It is, as he explains in the sequel, in order that they may be punished eternally: "It is that they may be destroyed forever." Then at the end he explains the reason for their prosperity. It is, "To declare that the Lord is upright," and does not withhold its reward from any creature. Ahab was an idolater, and we read concerning him: "But there was none like unto Ahab, who did give himself over to do that which was evil in the sight of the Lord." And yet because he covered himself with sackcloth and humbled himself before God, the reward for that act of submission was not withheld from him, and the decree was kept in abeyance during his life time, and was realized in the time of his son. God said to Eliyahu: "Seest thou how Ahab humbled himself before Me?… I will not bring the evil in his days …" Our Rabbis infer from the benefits which come to the wicked in this manner that the righteous will be rewarded in the next world: "If those who transgress His will are treated thus, how much better will be the treatment of those who carry out His will." They say also: "As the wicked are rewarded in this world for any slight merit which they have, so the righteous are paid in the world to come."

     3. Benefits may come to the wicked for the sake of others whom Providence is protecting, good men or wicked as the case may be. Examples of a wicked man well treated for the sake of a good man are: Laban, who prospered for the sake of Yaakov; the house of the Egyptian, which was blessed for the sake of Joseph; Lot, who was saved through the merit of Abraham. And not merely Lot, but the inhabitants of Zoar were saved for the sake of Lot, who in turn was saved for the sake of Abraham, as the angel said: "See, I have accepted thee concerning this thing also, that I will not overthrow the city …" In this way, sons may be prosperous, though they are wicked, through the merit of their fathers, as Moshe said: "Remember Abraham, Yitzhak and Israel, Thy servants." Similarly fathers may prosper for the sake of their children: "He may prepare it, but the just shall put it on;" "And the wealth of the sinner is laid up for the righteous." Sometimes a wicked man succeeds in accumulating great wealth and achieving prosperity, so that he may

Sefer HaIkkarim — BOOK [Maamar] FOUR

die before his son. On the other hand, the wicked man may live long in order that he may beget a righteous son, as the Rabbis say that God prolonged the life of Ahaz in order that Hezekiah should be descended from him, and there are many instances of this kind.

A wicked man may receive benefits for the sake of a bad man whom God desires to punish through the instrumentality of the former as, for example, God gave prosperity to the wicked Nebuchadnezzar, to Sennacherib and Titus, in order that they might be instrumental in punishing the wicked men of Israel and other nations. In reference to Sennacherib the Bible says: "O Asshur, the rod of Mine anger, in whose hand as a staff is My indignation! I do send him against an ungodly nation, and against the people of My wrath do I give him a charge, to take the spoil, and to take the prey, and to tread them down like the mire of the streets." In reference to Nebuchadnezzar, it is said: "Thou art My maul and weapons of war, and with thee will I shatter the nations."

4. Benefits may come to the wicked for their own sake or for the sake of the righteous. For their own sake they are well treated sometimes so as to harden their hearts that they may not repent after having rebelled against and grieved His holy name and committed great wrong. This is what the Rabbis mean when they say that God withholds the ways of repentance from the wicked, or the opposite, namely that God is kind and prolongs their days in order that they may repent.

A wicked man may also be prosperous for the sake of the righteous in order to increase the reward of his righteous contemporaries who, despite the example of the wicked man's prosperity, continue in their innocence and integrity. For if the wicked man were punished as soon as he commits a wrong act, the righteous men who serve God from love would not receive their due credit, for one might suspect that their worship of God was due not to love, but to the fear of punishment which they see coming upon the wicked. But when one sees that the wicked are not punished as soon as they do evil, he thinks that they will never be punished, and hence every one does as he pleases.

Solomon calls attention to this in Ecclesiastes: "Because sentence against an evil work is not executed speedily, therefore the heart of the sons of men is fully set in them to do evil." In these words Solomon expresses the problem. Why is it, he says, that the wicked man is not punished as soon as he does an evil deed? This surely leads to men's hearts being fully set in them to do evil. Then he answers the question by saying that there are two reasons, as we

Sefer HaIkkarim   BOOK [Maamar] FOUR

said, for this situation: "Because a sinner doeth evil a hundred times, He prolongeth his days." What he means to say is that the reason God prolongs the wicked man's life is either in order that he may repent, or in order that he may not, as we said before. Then he says that there is another reason: "Though yet I know that it shall be well with them that fear God, that they may fear before Him," i.e., the reason for prolonging their life is also in order to benefit those who fear God, that they may fear Him and serve Him from love and not from fear of punishment.

These are the reasons why prosperity comes to the wicked. This is on the assumption that we admit both the predicate and the subject, namely that the supposedly wicked is really wicked, and that the supposed benefit is a real benefit. But it is possible to deny the subject. We may say that the person we think wicked is not really wicked. He who knows a man's inner thoughts may know that he is a righteous man, as the Rabbis say: "If a man says to a woman, 'You are sanctified unto me as my wife, provided I am a righteous man,' she becomes his wife, even if he is an absolutely bad man. For it may be that he has repented in his heart."

We may also deny the predicate, and say that the apparent good is not a good at all, as Solomon says: "Riches kept by the owner thereof to his hurt;" or as Eliphaz says: "The wicked man travaileth with pain all his days," i.e., it may be that those strokes of fortune which come to him are evils, because he is always in pain and sorrow and worry, as the Rabbis say: "Increase of possessions leads to increase of worry;" or as David says: "Many are the sorrows of the wicked." Even that which clearly appears to be a good, may not be a good. For example, the hidden treasure under the wall which was about to fall. If the wall fell, the owner would have found the treasure. By divine providence, however, the wall became straight and everybody wondered at the extraordinary good fortune that happened to the wicked man by divine providence, whereas in fact the incident happened to the wicked man's hurt, to prevent him from finding the treasure. Examples may be multiplied indefinitely.

Chapter 13

An answer to the complaint of the adversity of the righteous.
Sometimes men know that their sins are the causes of their sufferings, and yet they complain and grumble against the ways of God. It is like a man whose eye-sight is injured as a result of excessive sexual indulgence, or a sick man who knows that his bad

habits are responsible for his illness, and yet he is irritated and complains because of his illness. Solomon had such cases in mind when he said: "The foolishness of man perverteth his way; and his heart fretteth against the Lord." Joseph's brothers are a case in point: "What is this that God hath done unto us?" they exclaimed, though in the same breath they said: "We are verily guilty concerning our brother." There is no need of expatiating on this class of cases.

Sometimes God in His mercy waits a long time for the sinner to repent, until the sinner forgets his sin. And then when God brings misfortune upon him for his sin in order to rouse him to repentance, he complains. He has forgotten his sin and thinks that God has forgotten it also, hence he complains that the misfortune came upon him without cause. Men who do not know or remember their sins, wrongly misjudge God. It is like the case of a man who lends his neighbor one thousand zuz. The creditor is kind to the debtor and extends the time of the loan. A long time passes and the debtor forgets the debt. When finally the creditor demands his debt from the debtor, the latter denies it and complains that the creditor is pressing him without cause. The other people, who do not know of the debt, exculpate the debtor, saying that if the debtor owed the money, why did not the creditor demand it before this. The debtor, on the other hand, when he recalls the debt still complains, desiring further extension as before. But this is foolishness, for then God would never collect His debt at all.

The Rabbis had this in mind when they said: "If any one says that God yeilds easily, may there be a yielding of his bowels. God is long-suffering, but He exacts His penalty in the end." The prophet thought of this when he said: "Behold, it is written before Me; I will not keep silence, except I have requited." The meaning is, you must not think that because you have forgotten your sins, I have forgotten them also. No, they are written before Me, and I will not keep silence, but will requite the iniquities of the sinners. We are not concerned either with those who forget their sins or with those who are well aware of them and nevertheless complain by reason of their simplicity and folly. Eliphaz says: "For anger killeth the foolish man."

There are also many people who complain and find fault with God and His ways without any rhyme or reason, though they are supplied with sufficiency for a livelihood. They complain because they have not a great abundance of wealth to enable them to fill their bellies and get drunk with strong wine, and because they have not enough health and strength to be able to indulge freely in eating and drinking and sexual intercourse without discomfort, and live the life of a pig and an ass, complaining that others have more money than they.

Maimonides has already answered these people at length in the twelfth chapter of the third Part of the Guide of the Perplexed. It is clear that complaints of this sort have no justification at all. The general answer to all of them is denial of the subject or the predicate. The person they think to be righteous is not righteous. A fool and a simpleton who forgets himself, or a glutton and a drunkard, or a greedy person who is never satisfied with the money that he has, can not be called a righteous man. For the reality is not as man sees it. Man sees the surface, but God sees into the heart. We can also deny the predicate. What is thought to be evil is not evil. Sometimes a small evil comes to a man so as to save him from a great one, as the Rabbis say, by way of comment on the verse: "I will give thanks unto Thee, O Lord; for Thou wast angry with me ...", which we mentioned above. Elihu says the same thing: "He delivereth the afflicted by His affliction." We also find often people complaining of a small evil which leads to a great good. This the prophet had in mind when he said: "Though I have trained and strengthened their arms, yet do they devise evil against Me." In short all such cases can be answered by denying the predicate or the subject.

But even if we assume that the man is really righteous and the evil that befalls him is real evil, there still are instances of evil befalling the righteous, and the reasons are four, similar to the four which we mentioned in discussing the prosperity of the wicked.

1. One reason is general nature, the nature of generation and destruction. Thus, the rain floods the righteous as well as the wicked, unless the righteous man stands so high that Providence delivers him from such evil. Or general nature as shown by the stars, if the man is not so meritorious that the prognosis of the stars is overruled. Or it may be that a person is of weak constitution and is always sick. Or he is a member of a low race, or an inhabitant of a country concerning which a certain decree has been declared and the righteous man is involved in the decree and suffers accordingly. For the general decrees of fate which concern a nation come upon the individuals not per se, but by virtue of their being part of the nation in question. And therefore, the evils come upon them whether they deserve them or not, as Daniel and his companions were exiled in the captivity of king Jehoiachin, and Jeremiah went into exile in the captivity of Zedekiah. They did not deserve to be exiled personally, but were involved in the decree which was made concerning Yerushalayim or the nation.

Sefer HaIkkarim   BOOK [Maamar] FOUR

Sometimes also a righteous man is afflicted with misfortune on account of the nation as a whole, as a punishment for his sin of omission in not asking for mercy for his fellow men, as the Rabbis say that Elimelech, Mahlon and Chilion, the greatest men in their generation, were punished because they did not carry out their duty of praying for mercy for their contemporaries. The reason is because the righteous man ought to follow in the ways of God and desire the continuance of the world as God desires its continuance: "For I have no pleasure in the death of him that dieth, saith the Lord God, but rather that he should return from his ways and live." And if the righteous man does not act in accordance with such desire he is punished.

Sometimes again misfortune comes upon the righteous on account of the nation as a whole, not, however, by way of punishment, but in order to atone for the nation as a whole. God desires the world to continue, and He knows at the same time that the righteous man will accept his sufferings gracefully without grumbling against God's methods. Therefore, God inflicts sufferings upon the righteous as ransom and atonement for the calamity which was destined to come upon the whole nation. Hence the Rabbis say that the death of the righteous is an atonement. We find this idea clearly expressed in the Bible also. God said to Ezekiel: "Moreover lie thou upon thy left side, and lay the iniquity of the house of Israel upon it; according to the number of the days that thou shalt lie upon it, thou shalt bear their iniquity ... and again, when thou hast accomplished these, thou shalt lie on thy right side, and shalt bear the iniquity of the house of Yehuda ..." The same idea is expressed in the fifty-second chapter of Isaiah, in which Israel is called "My servant:" "Behold, My servant shall prosper;" "Fear not, O Yaakov, My servant;" "But thou, Israel, My servant;" "Surely our diseases he did bear, and our pains he carried; whereas we did esteem him stricken, smitten of God and afflicted." The meaning is that if we see misfortune coming upon the righteous, we think that they are due to some guilt of their own, and we wonder; whereas it is not so, the sufferings are not due to their own sins, but are inflicted upon them as an atonement for the whole world or nation or country.

    2. Sometimes misfortunes come to the righteous through individual Providence. There is no man in the world so righteous that he does good and never sins. Hence it is possible that he committed certain wrongful acts, with intention at the beginning or the end of the act, and did not think of repenting, or there was no real regret. God now desires to wipe out those transgressions of his

Sefer Halkkarim   BOOK [Maamar] FOUR

with a little suffering in his lifetime, so that he may be free from all sin and may merit the future life. Just as God recompenses the wicked man for his good deeds in this world in order to punish him with eternal destruction, so the righteous man is punished here for the few transgressions of which he is guilty in order that he may enjoy eternal delight. So, our Rabbis say: If one has many merits and few demerits, he pays for the few light transgressions in this world, so that he may get his reward in full in the next world.

Sometimes also sufferings come to the righteous through individual Providence in order to protect him from a sin in which he is about to be entangled or which he is ready to commit on account of prosperity: "Jeshurun waxed fat, and kicked," Our Rabbis say in this connection: "Poverty is as becoming to Israel as a red strap to a white horse." If they have it too good, they may kick, as the prophet says: "And multiplied unto her silver and gold, which they used for Baal."

3. Sometimes the righteous suffer on account of the wicked, as the wicked are sometimes well treated for the sake of the righteous, as we have seen, and this in a variety of ways. Their ancestors may have been wicked and punishment was decreed upon them and their descendants. The punishment must therefore necessarily come upon their descendants whether the latter be wicked or righteous, as all the seed of Eli were punished for the sin of their ancestors, and the result was the death of Ahimelekh and the priests of Nob. The punishment for the sin of Adam continues to be inflicted upon all his descendants, whether they be righteous or wicked, as our Rabbis say: "Four persons died through the instigation of the serpent." This means that they were not personally guilty of any sin for which they deserved death, outside of the original sin which Adam committed on the advice of the serpent.

Or it may be that the punishment was decreed for the fathers only, and yet it befalls the children also per accidens, even if they are righteous. The father may have been a rich man who lost his wealth by reason of his sins. The result is that the children are poor, though righteous, by reason of the sin of the father. Or it may be the fathers were exiled for their sins, and the children remain in exile because of their fathers' sin. This is the meaning of the biblical expression: "Our fathers have sinned, and are not; and we have borne their iniquities." If the fathers had not sinned, they would not have lost their money, or would not have gone into exile. Their sons would then have remained in their own land, or they would have inherited their fathers' wealth, provided the sons themselves were not wicked

Sefer HaIkkarim   BOOK [Maamar] FOUR

men deserving exile or loss of possessions. They might not have been so righteous as to merit restoration to their own land or acquisition of wealth on their own account, nevertheless if they had been in their own land in the first place they would not have been exiled, and if they had inherited their fathers' wealth, they would not have lost it. We see, therefore, that the exile or poverty which comes to the fathers for their sins is borne by the children, not that the son suffers for the iniquity of the father, for this would be injustice in God. Ezekiel made this clear when he said: "The soul that sinneth, it shall die; the son shall not bear the iniquity of the father with him, neither shall the father bear the iniquity of the son with him," unless the sin involves the profanation of the holy name, and is such as might influence for evil the masses who witness it. In that case the punishment follows the children also, as in the case of Eli.

    4. Sometimes the righteous man is afflicted with misfortune for his own good. These are called sufferings for love; they are also called trials. They may be of three kinds.

A. First are those sufferings which come upon an absolutely righteous man, who serves God from pure love. To such a man God in His love for him brings suffering to wipe out some impurity or sinful stain in his soul. For a person can not help committing a light sin sometimes, such as does not oblige him to bring an offering, or neglecting the performance of some duty. And even the really righteous man may not think of doing penitence in these cases. Now though these things are not so serious as to require an offering or to deserve punishment, nevertheless they put a stain of impurity upon the soul and lower its degree in the future world. This is the reason why the violation of a law, without intention either at the beginning or at the end, requires atonement, though it does not deserve punishment, as is mentioned in the first chapter of the treatise Shebu'ot. In such a case God in His love for the righteous man inflicts suffering upon him to wipe out the stain of impurity in the soul in order that she may attain the degree which she deserves through her good deeds, without being hindered by anything.

These sufferings are in reality for the purpose of wiping out sins, nevertheless, since no one knows why they come when they do come, they are called trials and also sufferings of love. This is in accordance with the opinion of Nahmanides in his treatise on Reward and Punishment. Quoting the words of Rabbi Ammi, who said, "There is no death without sin, and no suffering without iniquity," he agrees with him in part and holds that the refutation of Rabbi Ammi's view applies only to the first part, that there is no

Sefer HaIkkarim   BOOK [Maamar] FOUR

death without sin, but not to the second. Hence, he holds that sufferings never befall any person unless he is guilty of sin. But when they are such as I have described, they are called sufferings of love; because they are due to God's love of the person, for He desires that no stain of any slight and unconscious sin should prevent his soul from attaining the degree which it deserves in accordance with its conduct.

B. The second species of punishment under cause number four is explained according to an old opinion well known among us, the opinion held by the Geonim, who say that a person may suffer for no sin at all. Such sufferings are called sufferings of love, because they are not due to sin, and they are also called trial. For God sometimes brings sufferings upon a righteous person to try him in order to see whether he serves God from pure love, as we find in the Bible: "For the Lord your God putteth you to proof, to know whether ye do love the Lord your God ...," or whether he serves God from love of reward and fear of punishment.

Not every man who is sincere and serves God out of pure love in times of tranquillity and prosperity has enough strength of character and will to endure hardship and trouble for the love of God and to serve God in poverty and affliction as he served Him in quiet and tranquillity, without complaining and finding fault with God when trouble comes upon him. Therefore, God brings sufferings upon the righteous to find out whether his good deeds coincide with his good intentions. Thus, Job was "whole-hearted and upright and one that feared God and shunned evil." His thoughts and intentions were good, and yet he could not bear actual hardship and trouble for the love of God. When sufferings came upon him, he found fault with God, and thus verified the words of Satan who said: "Doth Job fear God for nought? Hast not Thou made a hedge about him, and about his house, and about all that he hath?" It thus became known that his service of God was motivated by love of reward and fear of punishment, and not by perfect love. Hence when God brings sufferings of this kind upon a righteous man, they are called sufferings of love, because in this way those persons who say that the righteous men who are prosperous do not serve God from love will be convinced when they see that those righteous men serve God in time of suffering as they did in times of tranquillity.

This is what the Rabbis have in mind when they say: "If a person sees suffering coming upon him, he should search his conduct, as is said: 'Let us search and try our ways.' If after searching he finds something wrong, he should repent, as it says, 'and return.' If, however, he has not found any wrong in his conduct, he should charge his suffering to neglect of the study of the Torah, as is said: 'Happy is the man whom Thou instructest, O Lord, and teachest out of Thy law.' If he can not find that he is guilty of neglect of the study of the Law, then it is certain that they are sufferings of love, as is said: 'For whom the Lord loveth, He correcteth.' And what is his reward if he accepts his sufferings with love? 'He will see his seed, prolong his days.' And not only this, but he will retain all that he has learned, as is said: 'And the purpose of the Lord will prosper by his hand'."

In this passage the Rabbis included all kinds of sufferings which come to a person. They say, "If one sees that sufferings come upon him," i.e., upon him specially, that is if he sees that they are not determined by general nature, as discussed under the first head, but that he is singled out specially and not as coming under the general rule, then he should search his conduct, to see if they belong to the species discussed under the second head, namely punishment for intentional transgression. He must therefore examine his conduct, and if he finds anything, he must repent and return to God, who will have mercy upon him. If after searching he does not find, i.e., he does not find that the suffering can come under the second head, he must charge it to neglect of the Torah, i.e., to ignorance and unintentional wrong. He may have failed to recognize his sin because he was not sufficiently familiar with the Torah and its commandments, as the Rabbis say, "An ignoramus can not be a pious man." Or he can not understand in what way suffering may come upon him, though he is not guilty of sin. This comes under the third head in our discussion. "But if he can not charge it to this either, then they must be sufferings of love, as is said: 'Whom the Lord loveth, He correcteth,'" The meaning is, If he is a wise and absolutely righteous person, and can not charge his sufferings either to the second or to the third cause, i.e., to lack of knowledge as to certain sins, then his sufferings must surely be those of love. That is, they come under the fourth head which we are now considering. It may be the first class under this head, viz. that they are due to God's love, whose purpose is to wipe out any light sin which requires atonement, so as to cleanse the stain and uncleanness of the soul, in order that it may attain to the degree it deserves, as a father chastises the son whom he loves, not in order to have the satisfaction of punishing him, but in order to purify him of his impurity for his own good, so that he may attain a high station, as we read: "Even as a father the son in whom he delighteth." Or it may be the second class, to try him, so as to see whether he can endure hardship and trouble for the love of God without finding fault with His treatment. Hence the statement of the Rabbis, "And what is his reward if he accepts them with love, etc.?" For if a person accepts suffering with good grace, his reward is increased. For all people realize through his example how far the love of God can go, and are thus inspired to serve God from pure love.

C. The third kind of suffering is called suffering of love in the true sense. These are sufferings which come upon a person not to wipe out any sin he has committed, for he is not guilty of any sin, having had his stain wiped out; nor in order to put him to the proof, for he has already been put to the proof. But God in His loving kindness brings suffering upon him, not merely such as everybody can see, but also such as nobody knows, like the sacrifice of Yitzhak, which took place on one of the mountains, where nobody saw but God. This is in order to increase his reward, that he may deserve the reward for good deeds and not merely for good intentions.

One may object against the second and third kinds by saying that since God knows whether the person will stand the test or not and, in the third case, that he serves God from pure love with all his heart and soul and might, as is shown by the test, why the need of suffering? The answer is that the reward of him who actually endured pain and trouble for the love of God can not be the same as that of him who has not actually endured. This is what the king had in mind when he said: "Let not him that girdeth on his armour boast himself as he that putteth it off." The meaning is, let not him who has not actually shown bravery, though he is armed and ready to show it, boast himself as much as he who has actually shown it and is now taking off his armor.

For this reason, God often brings punishment upon a righteous man to habituate him to combine good intentions with good deeds, so that he may earn greater reward, for practice will strengthen his heart in the love of God. For an act makes a greater impression upon the soul than intention without act, and hence the person earns the reward for deed and intention instead of the reward of intention alone.

Habituation in God's service is called trial, as Maimonides writes. The biblical expression, "That He might afflict thee, to prove thee," Maimonides interprets: "To habituate thee to endure actually hardship and trouble for the love of God." He interprets in the same way the verse in Exodus: "For God is come to prove you." God, he says, came with awful thunders and fearful lightnings for two reasons. One is to habituate you to endure actually hardship and trouble and pain for the love of God, for practice makes a strong impress on the soul, inspiring it with the love of God. And when your good intention and good word - "We will do and obey" - are realized in act, you will have the reward due to the one who is habituated to do good deeds, and not merely the reward of good intention. The second reason is to call your attention to the greatness of the punishment which is inflicted upon him who transgresses the words of God, hence the words, "And that His fear may be before you."

Similarly the verse, "For the Lord your God putteth you to proof," is explained by him to mean that God habituates you in the ways of His service in order that love of God may be firmly implanted in your hearts, and that you may also be rewarded for good deeds, when it becomes clearly known that you serve God from love and are not led astray by the words of a certain prophet or dreamer of dreams because of the imaginary advantage which you see in the worship of other gods, and the prosperity and wealth and honor derived from it - considerations which induce people to worship idols. Moshe says: "For ye know how we dwelt in the land of Egypt ... and ye have seen their detestable things ... lest there should be among you man, or woman, ... whose heart turneth away ... from the Lord our God, to go to serve the gods of those nations." The meaning is, though you saw that their detestable things and idols are wood and stone, you at the same time saw the great quantities of silver and gold which those idolatrous nations had. Therefore, I fear lest some of you may be enticed to follow them because of your desire for that prosperity. Hence the expression, "Lest there should be among you ..." The same idea is expressed in the words, "For the Lord your God putteth you to proof." The meaning is that if you will not be induced to follow after the prosperity in question, you will habituate yourselves to the quality of love, and your reward will be greater because of the hardship you will actually endure for love of Him, and it will be known that your service is motivated by pure love and not by the desire of reward and the fear of punishment. This is sufficient as an explanation of the sufferings which are inflicted for the second reason.

The meaning of the word trial, which is mentioned in the sacrifice of Yitzhak, belongs under the third division. God desired that the good intention in the mind of Abraham should be realized in actuality, so that he might be rewarded for good deed and good intention and not merely for good intention alone. Now inasmuch as the knowledge of a thing after it is realized is necessarily different

Sefer HaIkkarim — BOOK [Maamar] FOUR

from the knowledge of the thing before it is realized, the Bible says: "For now I know that thou art a God-fearing man," though there was no new knowledge in God which He had not before. A similar expression is: "Behold now, I know that thou art a fair woman to look upon." The knowledge was not new, but the actual circumstance was new, which called attention to the truth of what was known before. So, in the case of Yitzhak, God said, the circumstance has actually come to pass which shows that you are a God-fearing man, and that you serve Him from pure love.

As to such knowledge, we have explained in the third chapter of this Book that though it necessitates change in us it does not imply change in God. The Torah uses the expression, "I know," a human form of speech, because it was not given to angels, and therefore has to use expressions which we can understand. This is the meaning of the word trial wherever it occurs in the Bible. The expression, "Now I know," is used because it was then that the actual incident occurred which showed what He knew already, namely that Abraham was God-fearing and served God from love and not from the fear of punishment. For there can not be a greater punishment than to kill one's only son, after he has reached the age of thirty-seven. Nevertheless, Abraham did not hesitate to do this for the love of God. This is a conclusive proof that he served God from pure love. Hence the Bible describes him as a friend, "The seed of Abraham My friend."

These are the real sufferings of love, of which the Geonim speak, i.e., such as God in His love brings upon a righteous man to increase his reward. In other words, the suffering is inflicted in order that the person may actually endure trouble and hardship for the love of God, and be rewarded for good deeds and not merely for good intentions. These are not the kind of sufferings which were inflicted upon Job, nor is it the same kind of trial as came to Hezekiah, concerning whom it is said: "Howbeit in the business of the ambassadors of the princes of Babylon, who sent unto him to inquire of the wonder that was done in the land, God left him, to try him, that He might know all that was in his heart." For Hezekiah failed to stand the test, as the Bible testifies: "But Hezekiah rendered not according to the benefit done unto him; for his heart was lifted up …" These sufferings and trials belong to the second class only. But those sufferings which belong to the third class come only to absolutely righteous men, as our Rabbis say in Bereshit Rabbah. Commenting on the verse in the Psalms: "The Lord trieth the righteous," they say, "When a potter examines his kiln, he does not use the weak jars which break as soon as he knocks on them; he uses the good jars, which do not break no matter how many times he knocks on them, hence we read: 'God proved Abraham.' "

When such sufferings come upon the righteous, like Rabbi Akiba and his associates, they do not constitute injustice in God, on the contrary, they indicate mercy and kindness, because He desires to reward those who serve Him from love for good deeds and not merely for good intentions, for a person does not reach the degree of pure love until he actually endures trouble and hardship for the love of God.

This, then, is the answer to the objection which is raised against this third form of suffering, namely that since God knows that the righteous person in question is a devotee of long standing and will endure the test, why does He try him? The answer is as we have said. The reward destined for one who serves God in deed is not the same as the reward of him who serves in thought only. The objector might as well say, why did God command us to perform the commandments actually, is it not sufficient that we have the intention of performing them? The answer here is obvious, the reward for a good deed is given for doing it and not merely for thinking it. The Torah mentions it frequently: "And ye shall do them;" "Hear, therefore, O Israel, and observe to do it." The same thing applies to the matter of trial. God desires that the person should have the actual experience and not merely the good intention.

Consider carefully what we have said under this fourth head concerning sufferings of love and trial, for our point of view is correct and nearer the truth than anything we have seen elsewhere.

To return to the subject of this chapter, we will say in a general way that the evils which the righteous suffer come upon them rightly and justly, though we may not know to which one of the four causes which we mentioned the sufferings are due.

Chapter 14

Having explained the justice of God's ways, and having made clear that we have no complaint to make either on account of the adversity of the righteous or the prosperity of the wicked, we must now give a reason why the prophets and the sages were so much exercised about these two phenomena. For according to the Rabbis, even Moshe had this perplexing question in mind when he said to God: "Show me now Thy ways, that I may know Thee." And Job, too, complained of this, as we have seen. Asaph also said: "But as for

Sefer Halkkarim — BOOK [Maamar] FOUR

me, my feet were almost gone; ... For I was envious at the arrogant, when I saw the prosperity of the wicked." This is the problem of the prosperity of the wicked. In the sequel he says: "Surely in vain have I cleansed my heart, and washed my hands in innocency; For all the day have I been plagued, and my chastisement came every morning." This deals with the problem of the adversity of the righteous. Jeremiah also says: "Wherefore doth the way of the wicked prosper?" Habakkuk says: "Wherefore lookest Thou, when they deal treacherously, and holdest Thy peace, when the wicked swalloweth up the man that is more righteous than he;" again, "For the wicked doth beset the righteous; Therefore, right goeth forth perverted." Malachi says: "Ye have wearied the Lord with your words. Yet ye say: 'Wherein have we wearied Him?' In that ye say: 'Every one that doeth evil is good in the sight of the Lord ...;' " also: "Yea, they that work wickedness are built up; Yea, they try God, and are delivered." Ecclesiastes says: "There is a vanity which is done upon the earth: that there are righteous men, unto whom it happeneth according to the work of the wicked; again, there are wicked men, to whom it happeneth according to the work of the righteous;" and there are many other passages in the Prophets besides. This matter surely requires explanation.

Asaph, it seems to me, set down the difficulties in the seventy-third Psalm in order to state their solution. His solution of the two questions, the adversity of the righteous and the prosperity of the wicked, is like that which we discussed under the second head. He begins: "Surely God is good to Israel," meaning to emphasize the fact that every evil which comes to the righteous is for a good purpose. This is why he says, "surely," meaning that though at first sight it does not seem that the evil which comes to Israel, who are righteous, is a good, nevertheless it is nothing else than a good. However, the knowledge that it is a good is not given to every one, but only "to such as are pure in heart." All other people are ready to believe erroneously that the evil which comes to Israel is not for a good purpose. This is why he says: "As for me, my feet were almost gone ..." The reason is because "I was envious at the arrogant" and their prosperity. I saw the continual peace of the wicked and their tranquillity, which endures as long as they live. They die without pain or suffering, "For there are no pangs at their death." Their health is good at the time of their death; and even in their life time: "In the trouble of man they are not ... Therefore, pride is as a chain about their neck ..."

And so, he goes on describing their prosperity: "Their eyes stand forth from fatness," i.e., they are handsome in form and appearance, their color is whiter than fat; or the meaning is, they are so fat that their eyes protrude from the abundance of fat. And lest one think that the fat disfigures them and makes them ugly in form and figure, he says: "They are gone beyond the imaginations of the heart;" i.e., they are more handsome than any picture one can imagine in one's heart. Moreover, they are unpleasant to their fellowmen, "They scoff, and in wickedness utter oppression." They are also wicked in relation to God. "They speak as if there were none on high. They have set their mouth against the heavens, and their tongue walketh through the earth."

Then he explains the evil which follows from the prosperity of these men: "Therefore His people return crushed ..." The meaning is that when the people of Israel see the prosperity of the wicked in this way, they return beaten down and crushed to their homes, "And waters of fulness are drained out by them," i.e., they imbibe a spirit of unbelief from these bad waters, from the man who is full. They are led to deny Providence and to say: "How doth God know? And is there knowledge in the Highest?" Behold, such are the wicked, and they are always at ease and increasing their riches, therefore it is vain to serve God, and in vain have I cleansed my heart, and washed my hands in innocency from sin. For with all that I have been plagued the whole day, I endure suffering every day, and my chastisement comes every morning.

Then the Psalmist proceeds: If I should express such doubts as these, I would be excluded from the company of righteous men and be "faithless to the generation of Thy children." And if I should try to know the reason of all this, it would be "wearisome in mine eyes, until I entered into the sanctuaries of God" - a place where every man is destined to come at the end of his life, that his soul may unite with other souls. He calls it, "the sanctuaries of God," because it is under the Throne of Glory and is divided into different parts for the various degrees of soul. "And considered their end," i.e., the end of these wicked men, to see whether they can cleave and unite to that holy place. But I see that they can not cleave to it, because everything cleaves to its like and turns away from its opposite. There is no doubt, therefore, that the wicked can not cleave to that place, because it is contrary to their nature. They will rather slip away from it and fall into the nether part of Sheol. This is the meaning of the verse: "Surely thou settest them in slippery places," and as a result, "Thou hurlest them down to utter ruin." Or we may say that the verse in question is an allusion to the fact that in giving prosperity to the wicked in this world, God merely humors them, so that they may not repent, to the end that they may enjoy the few merits which they have in this world and be hurled down to everlasting ruin in the world to come. And then they will "become a desolation in a moment." And as a dream which one dreams while sleeping during waking time, namely during the day, is very short and insignificant, so wilt Thou despise their image [zelem], i.e., their soul, as Maimonides interprets the word "image" [zelem]. This is the solution of the problem of the prosperity of the wicked, as we discussed it under the second head.

Then he undertakes to solve the problem of the adversity of the righteous in a different way. The evil which comes to the righteous, he says, is not evil if we consider the eternal good which is destined for him. "For my heart is in a ferment …," i.e., although I have assigned a reason for the prosperity of the wicked, the problem of the adversity of the righteous still remains, and my heart is in a ferment about it, "and I am pricked in my veins." And with all this, "I am brutish and ignorant," knowing not the reason of the adversity of the righteous. But I see and feel in myself that when "I am continually with Thee," and my thought cleaves to Thee, "Thou holdest my right hand," to help me and deliver me from the accidents that would come to me by the laws of the natural world, as the Psalmist says in another passage: "My soul cleaveth unto Thee; Thy right hand holdeth me fast." The meaning is, when my soul cleaves to Thee, and I follow after Thee and serve Thee with a pure heart, I am immediately upheld by Thy right hand, i.e., divine providence, which helps me as though Thou didst hold my right hand and guardedst me from injury. I see that during this corporeal life, "Thou guidest me with Thy counsel," i.e., with divine inspirations, as we said in the eleventh chapter of this Book, thou guidest and leadest me, so that I am saved from the hand of the evil one. And after this life, "Thou wilt receive me with glory." On this great glory and distinction which are destined for me I ponder and say: "Whom have I in heaven but Thee?" namely Thy glory which hovers over me and takes care of me from heaven. "And beside Thee," whom I have in heaven, "I desire nothing upon earth." For I know that when the body and its powers - "My flesh and my heart" - those psychic powers which are dependent upon the body, are destroyed, I am not destroyed. There will still remain something permanent in me - "the rock of my heart" - i.e., the rational power, which is as permanent as a strong rock, and my portion in existence is that I shall cleave to God forever, because He is eternal, and I shall not fear destruction, since I cleave to an eternal being. "But they that go far from Thee shall perish," without doubt, "Thou wilt destroy all them that go astray from Thee," i.e., those who depart from Thee and cleave to something else. "But as for me, the nearness of God is my good," i.e., all my good is that I may cleave to God, and that I shall "make the Lord God my refuge, that I may tell of all Thy works," viz. the missions of the prophets and the wonders performed by them.

This is the method in which Asaph solved these problems. It is correct and in agreement with the truth.

Chapter 15

The next question is, since Asaph stated these problems and solved them, as we have seen, why did the prophets who came after concern themselves again with the same problems, and what new ideas did they contribute to the problems or their solutions?

We might say that the matter was no longer a problem to the prophets since Asaph had given the solution; but that they mentioned these two points because it gave them great pain when they saw with their own eyes wicked men prosper and righteous men suffer. For actual seeing of a thing causes more pain than mere knowing about it. A person is moved more by that which he perceives with the senses than by that which he merely knows, though he has no doubt whatever of its reality. For example, Moshe was told by God on the mountain, "Go, get thee down; for thy people ... have made them a molten calf ..." And since God had told him this, he had no doubt it was true. And yet that did not prevent him from taking the tables down with him. He did not want to leave them on the mountain. But when he came near to the camp and saw the calf with his own eyes, he became angry and cast away the tables and broke them at the foot of the mount. We see thus that he was more affected by that which he saw with his eyes, being moved by pain and anger, than by what he heard, though he knew that that which God had told him was absolutely true. In the same way it is possible to say that when the prophets saw with their own eyes righteous men suffer and wicked men prosper, they were grieved and complained, as a sick man complains of his sickness, even if he knew the cause of his sickness in advance and knew that he must get sick, nevertheless this does not keep him from complaining when he is sick. This is clear from the statement of Jeremiah: "Right wouldest Thou be, O Lord, were I to contend with Thee." He means, I know that Thou art right and that Thy judgments are correct when I

Sefer HaIkkarim   BOOK [Maamar] FOUR

contend with Thee, i.e., when I complain of this matter, and yet I can not forget the sorrow I feel: "Wherefore doth the way of the wicked prosper?" We might say therefore that all the prophets were in the same position. But this is altogether unsatisfactory, and is not in agreement with the biblical texts.

It seems to me that the prophets were not troubled by the same aspect of the problem that troubled Asaph. Their complaint is expressed in the words of David: "Let me fall now into the hand of the Lord, for very great are His mercies; and let me not fall into the hand of man." God's judgments are right, and a righteous man may suffer for various reasons, as we have seen. But it does not seem just that this suffering should be inflicted upon the righteous by the wicked man himself. This leads people to find fault with God's judgments and the Torah loses its hold upon them. This is indicated in the expression of Habakkuk's complaint: "For the wicked doth beset the righteous; therefore, right goeth forth perverted." He knew that Israel had sinned and deserved punishment, but he complained because the punishment was inflicted upon them through the wicked Nebuchadnezzar. The proper thing would have been that their punishment should come from God, as a plague or a famine, or sickness, such as afflicted Job, or that Yerushalayim should be overthrown instantaneously like Sodom, and not that the wicked should beset the righteous.

To show that this is the meaning of his complaint, he says: "Wherefore lookest Thou, when they deal treacherously, and holdest Thy peace, when the wicked swalloweth up the man that is more righteous than he?" He does not say, "Swalloweth up the righteous," simply, but, "The man that is more righteous than he." His meaning is, The Israelites are not, indeed, absolutely righteous men, but they are more righteous than the wicked Nebuchadnezzar, who swallowed them up. This was his complaint, why does God arrange the world so that the wicked should inflict evil upon a person more righteous than he, though he be not absolutely righteous?

Jeremiah's complaint was of the same kind. He complained of the men of Anathoth, who were wicked men and pursued him, seeking his life, and desiring to make him drink poison without his knowledge: "But I was like a docile lamb that is led to the slaughter; and I knew not that they had devised devices against me: 'Let us destroy the tree with the fruit thereof, and let us cut him off from the land of the living, That his name may be no more remembered.' " If not for divine providence, he would have fallen into their hands, as he says: "And the Lord gave me knowledge of it, and I knew it; Then

Sefer HaIkkarim   BOOK [Maamar] FOUR

Thou showedst me their doings." The point of the complaint is not that it is not just that God should use the wicked man as an instrument to avenge himself on the wicked, as I explained in the discussion of the prosperity of the wicked under the third head. The point of the criticism is that it leads men to suspect God's justice.

This is why Habakkuk says: "Therefore the law is slacked, and right doth never go forth." Solomon had the same thing in mind when he said: "As a troubled fountain, and a corrupted spring, so is a righteous man that giveth way before the wicked." The meaning is this: Just as the harm and the injury of a troubled fountain and a corrupted spring do not affect the fountain or the spring, but those who look at it and use it, who are grieved at seeing their fountain troubled and their spring corrupted, so when a righteous man gives way before the wicked, there is no harm done to the righteous, for he knows that the sufferings which are inflicted upon him are for his good, in order to wipe out the few iniquities which he has. He knows also that God has many ways of punishing those who transgress His will, and it makes no difference to him whether his sin is atoned for through a serpent or a lion or some other animal, or through a wicked man. But the harm that is done is to the spectators who will throw suspicion upon God's judgments and say: "So and so is an absolutely wicked man, and he did harm to so and so, who is more righteous than he, though he is not an absolutely righteous man." And it will seem to them that the thing is unjust, not that it is really unjust, for Habakkuk himself explains it when he says: "O Lord, thou hast ordained them for judgment, and Thou, O Rock, hast established them for correction." The meaning is, the wicked man is nothing more than an instrument with which God exercises judgment upon the wicked, and He also corrects the righteous through it, causing them pain and grief, in order to wipe out the few iniquities which they have, so that they may merit life in the world to come, and that the wicked man may perish instantaneously and forever, as all the seed of Nebuchadnezzar perished, while Israel returned from the Babylonian exile and prospered.

The upshot of it all is that all the sufferings of the righteous are for a good purpose, and the prosperity of the wicked is for a bad purpose. But the character of a thing as good or bad is determined by the purpose. This is the way we must understand all the prophets and the sages. Some of them speak from the point of view of Asaph and Job, and some from the point of view of Habakkuk and Jeremiah. This will suffice as a discussion of Providence.

Sefer Halkkarim — BOOK [Maamar] FOUR
Chapter 16

Having treated of Providence, it is proper to follow it up with a discussion of prayer. For though prayer is not a fundamental principle of the Torah, nevertheless it is a branch growing out of Providence. The acceptance of prayer necessarily indicates Providence, as we said before. And on the other hand, every one who believes in Providence must believe that prayer will help him and save him from misfortune. If one does not pray in a time of trouble, it is either because he does not believe in Providence, or because, though he does believe in Providence, he doubts God's ability to save him - both of which are forms of unbelief - or because, though he believes in Providence and doubts not God's ability to save him, for God is all powerful, he doubts whether he is worthy of the privilege of having his prayer heard.

Now it is true that a man must never be righteous in his own eyes, nevertheless this should not prevent him from praying to God to satisfy his needs. For to refrain from prayer on this account indicates a belief that the good which comes to man from God is a reward for his good deeds and not due to God's mercy and kindness. But this opinion is incorrect, as we read in the Bible: "We do not present our supplications before Thee because of our righteousness, but because of Thy great compassions." The kindness of God and the mercy He bestows upon all His creatures are based upon pure loving kindness, and are not in the nature of compensation, as God said to Job: "Who hath given Me anything beforehand, that I should repay him?" The Rabbis say: If a man makes a mezuzah have, I not given him the house? And if he attaches **zizit** [fringes] to his garment, have I not given him the garment?

The proper belief, then, is that all benefits which come from God are due purely to His loving kindness, and are not compensation for one's good deeds. This being so, benefits may come from God whether the recipient deserves to receive them or not. For prayer confers a capacity upon a person who is not by nature fit to receive a given benefit. No one else except God can do anything like this unless the recipient has a capacity, natural or artificial; because all the superlunar powers are finite and can act only upon that which is prepared to receive their influence. As fire has the power to make warm, and water to make cold, so Mars has the power, for example, to destroy, to kill and to ruin. But it can not bestow the opposite of that which the recipient is prepared to receive or vary its activity, as the fire has no power to make cool. Similarly, Jupiter has the power

Sefer HaIkkarim BOOK [Maamar] FOUR

to make prosperous and rich, but he can not change that indication and give the recipient the opposite, as water has not the power to make warm, except per accidens. The same thing applies to the other superlunar powers.

The Rabbis explain this matter in the Talmud: "When the wicked Nebuchadnezzar cast Hananiah, Mishael and Azariah into the fiery furnace, Yurkemi, the spirit of hail, came before God and said, Lord of the world, let me go down and cool the furnace, and save the righteous men. Thereupon Gabriel rose before God, and said: This is not in consonance with the dignity of God, but let me, the spirit of fire, go and heat the furnace on the outside and cool it within so that there may be a miracle within a miracle." It is clear from this that Yurkemi only had the power to cool and Gabriel had the power only to heat, except when God desired otherwise. The superlunar powers, therefore, can not act upon the recipients unless the latter have the capacity, whether the influence comes upon the recipient through a visible property or an invisible. For example, drugs act upon those who take them, either through their natural qualities or through their properties, which are invisible qualities, according as the recipients are prepared to receive the quality or property in question.

Now when the recipient prepares himself to receive the influence which comes from the visible nature of a given star, as for example, to receive moisture from the moon or heat from the sun, there is no likelihood of an erroneous opinion that the effect is due to the favor of the star. But if the recipient prepares himself to receive the influence of the star through one of those acts whose causes are unknown, like the acts of drugs which come from their properties, people are led into the erroneous opinion that the effect is due to the favor of the star. But it is not true. The fact is this, that just as the influence of the teacher affects the pupil who is prepared more than the one who is not prepared, though the teacher is not directing his instruction to the one more than the other, so the influence of the star reaches the one who is prepared more than the one who is unprepared, without any intention or will on the part of the star.

The error of the idolaters was just this, namely, that they thought that the influence which comes from the star is due to the favor of the star gained by doing those things which are of particular interest to the particular star, not knowing that the real reason is because those activities prepare the recipient. The error was due to the fact that the causes are unknown. For this reason, they bowed down before the star and prayed to it, offered sacrifices, burned incense

Sefer HaIkkarim — BOOK [Maamar] FOUR

and poured out libations to it, thinking to obtain its favor through these rites.

The error here is clear, for the force of the higher powers is limited, and no one of them can do anything else than that which its nature determines. And its activity depends upon the preparation of the recipient and is not in the nature of a voluntary act. Baal Peor, for example, had the power to act as a purgative for those who performed the act of defecation before him. The Rabbis say that the priests fed the person with beets and gave him beer of hizme to drink. The purpose was to prepare the recipient for the effect, which followed in the person who defecated before it, whether he needed it or not, thus benefiting the one who needed it, and injuring and killing the one who needed it not, for the effect was not voluntary. This is why the Bible calls that service, "sacrifices of the dead:" "They joined themselves also unto Baal of Peor, and ate the sacrifices of the dead." The point of the analogy is that just as the dead have not the power to will or not to will, so the stars have not the power to will or not to will. As the fire has not the power to refrain from burning the garment of the righteous man if he comes near it, nor the power to burn the garment of the wicked when he is far away, or if the object is such that it is not subject to being burned, so the star has no power to do good or evil except as its nature dictates and as the recipient is prepared for the effect. Therefore, it is not proper to pray to it since it can not act voluntarily. God alone is the one to pray to, because His activities are voluntary. He can will or not, can do a thing as well as its opposite, can do a kindness gratis, i.e., whether the recipient is deserving or not, provided he prepares himself by prayer alone.

This is stated clearly in the Bible in many places, and especially in relation to Menasseh, son of Hezekiah, king of Yehuda, who was a thoroughly wicked man, and never had his like before or after in disobedience and wrongdoing. And yet we read: "And when he was in distress, he besought the Lord his God ... and he prayed unto Him; and He was entreated of him, and heard his supplication, and brought him back to Yerushalayim into his kingdom." We learn from these two things, one is that even though a person is thoroughly wicked like Menasseh, he may become fit to receive divine grace through prayer. The second is that prayer is heard even though it is forced by distress, as the text testifies: "And when he was in distress"

This shows how wonderfully great is God's kindness to His creatures. For a human being under similar circumstances would say, "Why are ye come unto me now when ye are in distress?" But God delights in loving-kindness, and his right hand is extended to receive penitents at all times. Thus, the Psalmist says: "Then they cried unto the Lord in their trouble, and He delivered them ..." Jonah says: "I called out of mine affliction unto the Lord, and He answered me." He means, although I did not deserve to have my prayer in distress accepted, after I ran away from Him, nevertheless He did not forbear to answer me.

Chapter 17

All kinds of loving-kindness emanate and derive from God, and there is no other being who can bestow a kindness on any one. The reason is because one can not expect an absolute kindness from any one unless the latter has the following four attributes.

1. He must be unchangeable; for if he is subject to change, the kindness coming from him can not be absolute because it will not be permanent. But God is the only unchangeable being, as I explained in Book II, chapter 2.

2. He must not require the aid of any other being in bestowing the kindness or benefit in question. For if he requires the aid of another, the recipient can not be sure of the continuance of that kindness unless the aid continues. The superlunar powers are a case in point. They indicate a certain event if a certain other condition or cause is there to assist them, for example, if the rising star is in its elevation, or faces a favorable star, and the like. But there is no other being who requires no assistance except God, as the Bible says: "I am the Lord that maketh all things; That stretcheth forth the heavens alone; That spread abroad the earth by Myself."

3. He must be equally able to do either of two opposed things, else the recipient would not be able to obtain his desire at all times. For a person sometimes needs one thing and sometimes its opposite, for example sometimes he has to make war, and sometimes he has need of peace. Now it is well known in relation to the superlunar powers that the star which indicates war does not indicate peace, and the star which indicates destruction does not indicate building up, and the star which indicates war has no power to change its indication into one of peace. Similarly the star which indicates disease does not indicate health. Hence the recipient of a kindness can never be sure that he will always have the kindness that he needs, unless the giver has equal ability to give either of two opposite things. But there is no one else who has this power except

Sefer Haikkarim   BOOK [Maamar] FOUR

God, as we read: "I form the light, and create darkness; I make peace and create evil; I am the Lord that doeth all these things."

4. The giver must be so situated that there is no other being who can prevent him from doing his will. For if there is one who can prevent him, then the recipient of the kindness can never be sure of obtaining the favor which he desires of the giver, for the latter may be prevented from doing it. Now it is clear that every being except God can be prevented by God, but no one can prevent God from doing His will, as we read: "Behold, He snatcheth away, who can hinder Him? Who will say unto Him: 'What doest Thou?' "

When these conditions are combined in the giver, the recipient is assured that he will obtain his desire and that the kindness he receives will be permanent. Now since there is no one but God who combines in him these four conditions, it is clear that one should not desire or hope for any favor from any one else. The Bible makes this clear in the Song of Moshe: "See now that I, even I, am He, and there is no God with Me …" The meaning is as follows: The Gentiles, who oppress the Jews, think that God can not save them. "Where are their gods," they say, "The rock in whom they trusted; who did eat the fat of their sacrifices …?" These words indicate that they think the God of Israel is like the other superlunar powers, that He is subject to change, or that He needs the help of another god, or that He is not equally able to do all things and opposite things, or that there is another being who can prevent Him. Hence the text explains that the God of Israel is not like the other superlunar powers, as they think, but on the contrary that God is eternal and unchanging. This is the meaning of the expression: "See now that I, even I, am He," i.e., there is no other being in the world who can say about himself, "I, I am he," except God.

The prophet says: "To whom then will ye liken Me, that I should be equal? saith the Holy One," i.e., that should be equal to Me in deserving the name holy. For every other being except God changes from day to day, and is not to-day what he was yesterday, having changed since then. Hence, he can not use the expression, "I, I am he," for He is not always the same in attribute. God, on the other hand, who is not subject to change, can say of Himself: "I, I am He." Similarly, the prophet says: "I, even I, am the Lord." The repetition of the pronoun can apply only to God, who is to-day what He was yesterday without any change. This is a reference to the first attribute. Then Moshe says: "And there is no God with Me." This means, I do not need any one else to help Me in My work, and refers to the second attribute. Then he continues: "I kill, and I make alive."

This means, I can do equally either of two opposite things - an allusion to the third attribute. Then, alluding to the fourth attribute, he ends up: "And there is none that can deliver out of My hand." This means, there is no being who can prevent Me from doing what I desire. And since there is no other being who combines in himself these four requirements, no kindness can come from any one else but God. Hence the Psalmist says: "O Israel, hope in the Lord; For with the Lord there is mercy." The meaning is, hope in the Lord, because that which you desire is not a matter of compensation, but an act of loving-kindness, and there is no being but God who can do kindness, for He alone is the source of all favor and kindness: "For with the Lord there is mercy," and not with any one else.

Prayer should therefore be directed to Him alone and to no one else. For how can a man pray to one who can not grant his prayer or request? Reason dictates that one should pray only to one who is able to grant one's request. For the impulse to pray comes from reason. It is true that we read in the Bible: "Lord, Thou hast heard the desire of the humble," from which it may appear that the impulse to pray is due to the faculty of desire, but it is not so. As soon as the power of desire begins to act, the rational faculty is aroused and reflects and seeks for a way to realize the desire. And when it determines that it can not be attained except through God who can do all things, and bestows kindness even upon those who are not deserving, it comes at once to the conclusion that God is the one to pray to.

It is because the first beginning comes from the power of desire that the Bible connects the hearing of prayer with the power of desire. Hence the Bible says: "Lord, thou hast heard the desire of the humble," as if prayer came from the faculty of desire. But it is not so. Prayer is due to the power of reason, which prompts man to do good and to love God, whereas the power of desire has the opposite tendency. For this reason, the biblical verse ends up with the words: "Thou wilt direct their heart, thou wilt cause Thine ear to attend", to indicate that God does not hear the desire of the humble until the rational power is prepared for prayer and to cleave to God. First, "Thou wilt direct their heart," and then, "cause Thine ear to attend." Daniel also was told: "From the first day that thou didst set thy heart to understand, and to humble thyself before thy God, thy words were heard." In explanation of this our Rabbis say: "From this we learn that the intention to fast, even before the actual fasting, helps one in having his prayer received, by reason of the fact that his heart is prepared." This is the meaning of the biblical expression: "And it

Sefer Halkkarim   BOOK [Maamar] FOUR

shall come to pass that, before they call, I will answer." The meaning is, when the rational power prepares itself to pray or to submit to God and fast, even before the actual prayer and fasting take place, I will answer; and while they are talking about praying and fasting, I will hear them, even before they actually begin their prayer; provided, however, that the rational power has decided that the thing in question is a proper thing to pray for, and that it is possible of attainment, not merely so far as the giver is concerned - for God can do everything - but that the possibility is there also so far as the recipient is concerned, i.e., that he is properly prepared to receive the favor in question. For if the recipient is not capable of receiving so great a kindness, if it is something which it is not in his power to receive, it is wrong to pray for it. Thus, it is wrong to pray to God that He should make one king of the whole world like Alexander the Great, though it is possible so far as the giver is concerned, since God can do everything. The reason is because the recipient is not capable of receiving so great a favor, for not every one is fit to rule over all the inhabitants of the earth, as there may be among them some one who is better prepared for it than he, and God would not deprive the other one on account of this one. The kindness of God invoked by prayer shows itself to the recipient according to the power of the latter to receive. This is what the Psalmist had in mind when he said: "Commit thy way unto the Lord ..." The meaning is that it is the wisdom of God that determines what things are beneficial to man, and who is worthy to receive His benefits.

Chapter 18

The reason which leads men to doubt the efficacy of prayer is the same as that which leads them to deny God's knowledge. Their argument is as follows: Either God has determined that a given person shall receive a given benefit, or He has not so determined. If He has determined, there is no need of prayer; and if He has not determined, how can prayer avail to change God's will that He should now determine to benefit the person, when He had not so determined before? For God does not change from a state of willing to a state of not willing, or vice versa. For this reason they say that right conduct is of no avail for receiving a good from God. And similarly, they say that prayer does not avail to enable one to receive a benefit, or to be saved from an evil which has been decreed against him.

Job argues in this manner in the name of the wicked and inclines to

Sefer Halkkarim　　　　　　BOOK [Maamar] FOUR

it. Sceptically he asks, If God takes notice of human conduct, why does He not punish the wicked for believing in this manner? "Wherefore do the wicked live, become old, yea, wax mighty in power? Their seed is established in their sight with them, and their offspring before their eyes ... Yet they say unto God: 'Depart from us; for we desire not the knowledge of Thy ways. What is the Almighty, that we should serve Him? And what profit should we have, if we pray unto Him?' " This shows their opinion that right conduct is of no benefit: "What is the Almighty that we should serve Him?" and that prayer is of no avail: "And what profit should we have, if we pray unto Him?" The reason for this belief is their opinion that when a certain evil has been determined for any one, it can not be annulled in any way.

That Job was inclined to sympathize with this idea appears from the remark which follows: "Lo, their prosperity is not in their hand; the counsel of the wicked is far from me." The meaning is, I see that their prosperity is not in their hands, i.e., they can not increase their goods by right conduct, nor do their evil deeds injure them by taking away from them the benefits which they get. Hence, I say: "The counsel of the wicked is far from me." That is, the divine plan which decides that these wicked men should spend their lives in prosperity is far from my understanding. Therefore, I say that everything is pre-ordained, for if everything were not pre-ordained, and right conduct were of any benefit, the wicked should have misfortune for their deeds. But it is not so, for: "How oft is it that the lamp of the wicked is put out? That their calamity cometh upon them? That He distributeth pains in His anger?" That is, how often does it happen that they are punished for their evil deeds, and that God sends misfortunes upon them in His anger on account of their wrong doing? From this it seems that Job inclined to the opinion of the wicked men who said that everything is pre-ordained, and that neither right conduct nor prayer can avail to annul the pre-determined event.

But this opinion is not true, for the influences from above come down upon the recipient when he is in a certain degree and state of preparation to receive them. And if a person does not prepare himself, he withholds the good from himself. For example, if it has been determined from on high that a given person's crops shall prosper in a given year, and he neglects to plow or sow his land that year, then God may bring the most abundant rain upon the land, but his crops will not prosper, seeing that he has not plowed or sowed.

Sefer HaIkkarim — BOOK [Maamar] FOUR

He withheld the good from himself because he did not prepare himself to receive it.

Our idea therefore is that when a benefit is determined in favor of any one, it is conditional upon a certain degree of right conduct. This must be taken to be a general principle as regards the promises in the Bible. In the same way when a certain evil is determined upon some one, it is also conditional upon his being wicked in a certain degree or of being predisposed to it. And if the degree of wickedness or predisposition thereto changes, the pre-determined event or fate changes also necessarily for the better or the worse.

The matter is similar to the hypothetical case of a king who made a decree that all the uncircumcised persons in a given country should be killed, or should receive a talent of gold. Now if one of the people has himself circumcised, there is no doubt that the decree is of no effect so far as he is concerned, whether for good or for evil, by reason of the new state into which the person has been brought. The effort, therefore, to do good is essential everywhere, for it serves as a preparation for the reception of the divine influence or for the annulment of a divine decree.

This is in agreement with the statement of our Rabbis: "Rabba came to Mamla, and saw that all the people had black hair. He inquired for the reason and was told that they were descendants of Eli, concerning whom it is said; 'And all the increase of thy house shall die young men.' Then he said to them: Go and study the Torah, concerning which it is written: 'For she is thy life and the length of thy days.' " From this it is clear that divine decrees are conditional upon the recipient being in a certain state and degree of preparation. And if that changes, the decree changes also. This is the reason why the Rabbis say that a change of name may avail to nullify a decree, as also change of conduct may have the same effect.

In this way repentance benefits a wicked man, for through repentance he becomes another person, as it were, concerning whom no such decree was made. Take the case of Ahab. The Bible says concerning him: "But there was none like unto Ahab, who did give himself over to do that which was evil in the sight of the Lord," and a divine decree was made against him. And then, because he fasted, and covered himself with sackcloth, and humbled himself before God, it was said to Eliyahu: "Because he humbleth himself before Me, I will not bring the evil in his days; but in his son's days will I bring the evil upon his house." This shows that when a decree is made upon a wicked person, it is conditional upon his maintaining his state of wickedness. But if he changes that state through repentance, he, as it were, changes into another person upon whom that decree was not made.

In this way it is clear that prayer and right conduct help to prepare the person to receive the good influence or to nullify the evil that has been decreed concerning him, because he changes from the evil state in which he was. Zophar alludes to this argument when he blames Job for not praying to God to deliver him from his misfortune, and for not preparing himself to nullify the decree: "If thou set thy heart aright, and stretch out thy hands toward Him - If iniquity be in thy hand, put it far away ... Surely then shalt thou lift up thy face without spot ..." That is, if you set your heart to pray and to improve your conduct, there is no doubt that through prayer and right conduct you will escape from these troubles. From this it is clear that prayer and right conduct are always helpful in nullifying a divine decree. Our Rabbis also say: "The cry [of prayer] is good for a man both before the divine decision and after."

As for the objection that the divine will can not be changed by prayer, the answer is that the divine will in the first place is that the decree should be realized if the person in question continues in the same state, and that the decree should be changed if the person's state changes.

The other problem, namely that God's knowledge would change as the man's state changes through prayer, is related to the problem of the relation of God's knowledge to the category of the contingent. Now just as we do not find it necessary that God's knowledge should change because the contingent is a real category, so we do not find it necessary that it should change because of prayer, but we believe that as God's knowledge does not change because of the existence of the contingent, so it does not change because of the efficacy of prayer. We believe that the contingent is real because experience testifies to it, and similarly we believe that prayer has the effect of nullifying a divine decree because experience testifies to it, as we shall see, and though we do not know how to reconcile God's changeless knowledge with the efficacy of prayer, as we do not know how to reconcile it with the contingent, we do not on this account deny what experience proves, namely that God listens to prayer and grants the person's request, whatever it be.

This is the answer which Eliphaz gave to Job when he saw that Job was inclined to accept the view of the wicked, who say: "What is the Almighty that we should serve him? And what profit should we have, if we pray unto Him?" In answer to this Eliphaz says: "And thou sayest: 'What doth God know? Can He judge through the dark cloud? Thick clouds are a covering to Him, that He seeth not …' " That is, since you incline to the opinion of the wicked, who say: "What profit should we have, if we pray unto Him?" thus denying the efficacy of prayer in order to save God's changeless knowledge, you must also in the same way deny God's knowledge of the contingent in order to save His changeless knowledge: "And thou sayest: 'What doth God know?' " Your opinion seems to be that the world is ruled by unchanging law, which Eliphaz calls "The way of the world," when he says to Job: "Wilt thou keep the way of the world which wicked men have trodden? … who said unto God: 'Depart from us;' and what could the Almighty do unto them?" He calls those men wicked who say that the world is ruled by unchanging law, because they deny the efficacy of right conduct and prayer. Hence he concludes: "If thou return to the Almighty, thou shalt be built up … thou shalt make thy prayer unto Him, and He will hear thee …" alluding, as it were, to the fact that his misfortunes came upon him because he believed that his prosperity had been due not to God, but to nature; and he entertained the same belief about the origin of his misfortune, and hence he did not pray to God concerning them. Eliphaz, therefore, says to him that if he returns to God and prays to Him and acknowledges that everything came to him from God, He will hear his prayer, will save him from his sufferings and will prosper his affairs. Hence he says: "Thou shalt make thy prayer unto Him, and He will hear thee … and the Almighty be thy treasure, and precious silver unto thee," i.e., through prayer your affairs will prosper. The Bible also testifies to the truth of this when it says: "And the Lord changed the fortune of Job, when he prayed for his friends." When he came to believe that prayer has efficacy, he prayed to God, and immediately God changed his fortune.

Chapter 19

The blessings conferred upon persons by the prophets, the righteous men and the pious are a subject that has caused perplexity to commentators, who have not been able to explain the matter properly. Their argument is as follows: These blessings are either in the nature of a prayer or of a prognostication of the future. If they are a prayer, why was Yitzhak so terrified when he found that he had blessed some one other than Esau, exclaiming as he did, "Who then is he that hath taken venison … yea, and he shall be blessed?" He could have prayed again for Esau as he had prayed before for

Yaakov. And there is no doubt that his second prayer for Esau, made voluntarily, would have been more likely to be heard than the one for Yaakov, which had been obtained through fraud. On the other hand, if the blessings are prognostications, why was Esau so indignant, exclaiming as he did, "He took away my birthright; and, behold, now he hath taken away my blessing?" Also how could Yitzhak say to him: "Behold, I have made him thy lord, and all his brethren have I given to him for servants?" Yitzhak had done nothing, he had merely foretold by prophetic inspiration the things that would happen to the person who received the blessing. Why then should Yitzhak or Esau have been indignant?

A great deal has been said on this matter. The best interpretation that has so far been agreed upon is that the blessing is a composite of both prognostication and prayer in the following way. The prophet sees through his prophetic inspiration what will happen to the recipient of the blessing, and prays for him to increase the good that is to come to him. For example, the prophet sees that the person in question will prosper as a tiller of the soil, and he blesses him to the effect that the produce of his field may be a hundred-fold. Or if he sees that the person in question will prosper as a breeder of cattle, he will bless him by praying that his cattle should multiply many folds, and should not drop their young prematurely; and so on, they say, with all other kinds of prosperity. Any difficulty which arises from the prayer aspect of the blessing is solved by bringing forward the aspect of prognostication, and a difficulty arising from the element of prognostication is answered by emphasizing the element of prayer. Adopting this interpretation, they have to make a distinction between the blessings conferred by a prophet and those pronounced by the righteous men and the pious who are not prophets.

Against the above interpretation are also all those blessings conferred upon Israel by the priests, in which there is no element of prognostication at all, unless we say that all these are in the nature of prayers, while the blessings of Yitzhak, who was a prophet, had the element of prognostication in them. This is the reason why Yitzhak was so much troubled. Esau was very dear to him, and therefore he was grieved when he saw the good fortune that was destined for Yaakov and the prosperity which he was destined to enjoy at the expense of Esau. But the difficulty remains, if prayer avails in blessings, why did not Yitzhak pray for Esau that he should be more prosperous than Yaakov, as the righteous men pray for those who receive a blessing at their hands? Also why did he not say

Sefer HaIkkarim   BOOK [Maamar] FOUR

to Esau that the blessings were prognostications of the future and that Esau had lost nothing by Yitzhak's blessing Yaakov? This would have been a very proper thing to do, so that Esau should not hate Yaakov for the blessing which he received from his father.

My opinion therefore is that the blessings are not declarations of the future at all. A blessing is a prayer plus the bestowal upon the recipient of the capacity to receive the divine influence. Celestial influences descend upon the recipients through a chain of intermediate agents and in varying degrees, provided, however, that the recipients are worthy, and occupy a certain definite relation and order, and are in addition prepared to receive the influence in question. And if the transmission is interrupted in any of the intermediate agents, or the relation or order is changed, or the recipient is not prepared, the influence or relation gets confused, and the divine influence does not rest upon the person if the order is changed. For this reason, there must be in the recipient the proper preparation to enable him to receive the influence in question.

But if the recipient is not himself prepared to receive the divine influence, he may be prepared by a prophet or a righteous or pious man, and thus the one who bestows the blessing becomes an intermediate agent in causing the influence in question to descend. This is the reason for the laying on of hands by those who gave the blessings upon those who received them. The purpose was to confer upon the recipient of the blessing the capacity or preparation to receive the influence or good in question. Thus the pious or righteous man who conferred the blessing was a sort of channel conducting the divine influence. We found similarly that the prophetic inspiration rested, through the mediation of a prophet, upon those who were not fit, provided they had some measure of preparation. Thus, God said to Moshe: "Take thee Yehoshua the son of Nun, a man in whom is spirit, and lay thy hand upon him." The degree of the influence received corresponds to the quality of the one who lays on his hands or who confers the blessing. For this reason, when Elisha, in answer to the question of Eliyahu: "Ask what I shall do for thee, before I am taken from thee," said: "I pray thee, let a double portion of thy spirit be upon me," Eliyahu replied: "Thou hast asked a hard thing." For a person can not give to another as a preparation more than he has himself. Therefore he said to him that if he saw him after he was taken away, his request would be granted. For Eliyahu would surely stand on a higher plane after being taken away than before, and would therefore be able to bestow upon Elisha twice as much as Eliyahu had before he was taken away, a thing that he could not have done before he was taken away.

The expression, "Thou hast asked a hard thing," shows that the words, "A double portion of thy spirit," have not the same meaning as the words, "Shall acknowledge the first-born ... by giving him a double portion ...," which are used in connection with the law of the first-born, as some commentators have said. For if this were the case, he would not have said, "Thou hast asked a hard thing." For Elisha was on his own account more fit to prophesy than the other sons of the prophets, although they waited upon Eliyahu before Elisha and prepared themselves for prophecy more than he did. This we learn from the fact that Eliyahu was told on Mount Carmel: "And Elisha the son of Shaphat of Abel-Meholah Shalt thou anoint to be prophet in thy room." since therefore Elisha was the "first-born," so to speak, among the sons of the prophets, it would not have been a hard thing to ask that he should receive a double portion of what the others received. The truth of the matter is that he asked for a double portion of the spirit of Eliyahu as it was before Eliyahu was taken away. And his request was granted, for Eliyahu is credited with eight miracles, while Elisha had sixteen miracles to his credit.

The Rabbis support this view in the first chapter of the treatise Hullin. It also appears from the text of the Bible that Eliyahu appeared to Elisha after he was taken away, as the Rabbis say that he appeared to some of the pious men of the Talmud. We read: "He took up also the mantle of Eliyahu that fell from him, and went back, and stood by the bank of the Jordan ... and said: where is the Lord, the God of Eliyahu? And when he also had smitten the waters, they were divided hither and thither; and Elisha went over." Since the Bible says, "And Elisha went over," and does not say simply, "And he went over," we infer that Elisha was not alone in smiting the waters, but that Eliyahu was with him, having appeared to him at that moment, and Eliyahu also is referred to in the words, "And when he also had smitten the waters."

I find a similar interpretation ascribed to the ancient commentators, namely that Eliyahu appeared to Elisha at that moment and that then the spirit of Eliyahu rested upon Elisha, and the latter's request was granted in that he obtained a double portion of Eliyahu's spirit, since he saw him after he had been taken away from him. We also find, after Eliyahu had been taken away, that: "There came a writing to him [Jehoram son of Jehoshaphat, king of Yehuda] from Eliyahu the prophet;" from which it seems that Eliyahu at that time appeared among men and corrected their conduct.

In reference to laying on of hands there is no doubt that it is more effective when the person upon whom the hands are laid has much preparation than when he has little. For this reason, Yaakov laid his right hand on the head of Ephraim, who had much more preparation than Menasseh. For he desired that through his instrumentality a generous blessing should rest upon Ephraim in accordance with his abundant preparation. On the other hand, since Menasseh had little preparation for receiving the divine influence, he thought it sufficient to lay his left hand upon him in order that through the blessing of Yaakov he might receive the influence which he was capable of receiving.

The same purpose is intended in the priestly benediction. The priests blessed the people in order that they [the priests] might be the intermediate agents to cause the divine influence to rest upon the recipients of the blessing in accordance with each one's preparation. The lifting of their hands at the time of the blessing was a sort of laying on of hands. The priests blessed all Israel, or the congregation, because the many collectively are more prepared to receive divine influence than an individual. For it is impossible that there should not be among them some one who has preparation for receiving some measure of divine influence through the mediation of the priests. Of similar nature are the blessings which the righteous or the pious confer upon their recipients. The purpose is that the divine influence may rest upon the recipient through their mediation, as we explained in connection with prophecy in the eleventh chapter of the Third Book of this treatise.

The question may be asked, how can the righteous or the pious man be an instrument through which a blessing may come upon a person when the pious man himself is poor and dependent upon the bounty of others. The answer is given by the Rabbis, who say that the merits of the righteous avail others, but do not avail the righteous man himself.

After the influence is transmitted to the recipient of the blessing through the instrumentality of the blesser and in accordance with the amount of preparation of the recipient, the blesser has no power to stop the influence and prevent it from descending upon the recipient. For it descends of its own accord, the blesser being merely an instrument for the blessing to reach the recipient. Therefore, though the instrument be removed, the blessing does not depart. It is the same as if a person drew [by means of an aqueduct] the water of a spring to a garden in order to promote the growth of the plants. The author of the conduit might cease to exist, but the stream made by the channel would not cease to water the garden. Similarly, a person makes windows in a dark house so that the light of the sun may enter. The artisan who made the windows may disappear, but the light of the sun will not cease to illuminate the dark house.

This is the meaning of the words Yitzhak used when he was troubled exceedingly: "And have blessed him, yea, and he will be blessed." The meaning is, he will be blessed whether I will or no since I blessed him. The words, "Yea, and he will be blessed," form part of the reason for Yitzhak's alarm, the meaning being, I can not put a stop to the influence which I was instrumental in drawing upon him. It is like the case of a person who orders a goldsmith to make beautiful vessels of gold with beautiful figures engraved upon them, for a friend of the goldsmith. The artist, thinking that the vessels are really for his friend, engraves them most beautifully, and works upon them with zest and joy. Then he finds out that the vessels are not intended for his friend at all. Undoubtedly the goldsmith is very much disappointed and troubled, but he can not prevent the beautiful engravings from being on those vessels, even though he knows that they are intended for his enemy. This is why Yitzhak said to Esau: "Behold, I have made him thy lord ..." i.e., through my instrumentality and through the means of his preparation all this influence has already come to him, and I have no power to stop it, since it has already been drawn, "And what then shall I do for thee, my son?" Then Esau replied: "Hast thou but one blessing, my father?" meaning that Yitzhak should give him another blessing that should not conflict with the previous one. And Yitzhak did so, but he included in Esau's blessing the words: "And thou shalt serve thy brother," for he could not dispense with them. So much concerning the subject of the blessings.

Chapter 20

Prayer is, indeed, one of the commandments of the Torah, as our Rabbis explain in Sifre. The words, "And to serve Him with all your heart," they say, refer to prayer. The Rabbis also say: "Be as careful about a light commandment as about a weighty one, for thou knowest not the reward of the commandments." This latter remark does not mean that all commandments are rewarded alike, and that there is no distinction of value and measure of reward between one commandment and another. The meaning is rather as one might say concerning medicinal drugs, be as careful about an unimportant drug as about an important one, for they are all of great value to the body. This would not mean that some drugs are not more valuable than

Sefer HaIkkarim — BOOK [Maamar] FOUR

others. It would mean simply that though rhubarb, for example, is very valuable and saranjun is not so valuable, still one should be careful of both, though they are not equally valuable, because each has a specific property which is beneficial to the human body as a whole. For just as rhubarb has the property of curing diseases of the liver, so saranjun has the property of curing diseases of the feet, the thighs and the knees, which is also beneficial to the human body. At the same time, however, each one of them has its own specific value in its place, and in this their values differ. Thus, rhubarb has the property of curing a vital organ, whereas saranjun, though it has its own specific property, can not cure a vital organ.

The same thing is true of the commandments. Although every one of them has a common property and benefit as being a divine commandment - a value common to all the commandments - and therefore we should be careful about a light commandment as well as a weighty one, nevertheless their values are not equal, for every one has its own peculiar property and its own peculiar benefit, as being the specific commandment that it is. And in this respect, some must be superior to others.

Therefore, I say that though prayer is one of the commandments of the Torah and is rewarded in a general way like any other, nevertheless it is much superior to all the others. For every commandment by itself has appertaining to it a specific reward. Thus, in connection with the commandment not to take the mother bird together with the young, we read, "That it may be well with thee, and that thou mayest prolong thy days." And in relation to charity, we read: "That the Lord thy God may bless thee in all thine increase and in all the work of thy hands." But the specific property of prayer is a general benefit which is available for all things. For we find that it avails in curing illness, as in the case of Hezekiah, where we read: "I have heard thy prayer ... behold, I will heal thee; on the third day thou shalt go up unto the house of the Lord." It is also effective to deliver from death. Thus, when Israel committed the sin of the golden calf, Moshe was told: "Let me alone, that I may destroy them," and Moshe saved them by his prayer. Similarly, Jonah was saved by his prayer from the bowels of the fish.

Prayer is also efficacious in causing barren women to bear children, as we find: "And Yitzhak entreated the Lord for his wife ... and the Lord let Himself be entreated of him, and Rebekah his wife conceived." Hannah also was remembered as a result of her prayer. Prayer avails also in time of famine, as we read: "And there was a famine in the days of David three years ... and David sought the

Sefer HaIkkarim — BOOK [Maamar] FOUR

face of the Lord." Prayer avails also in time of war. Thus, in the war of Sennacherib the Bible says: "And Hezekiah the king, and Isaiah the prophet the son of Amoz, prayed because of this, and cried to heaven. And the Lord sent an angel, who cut off all the mighty men of valour, and the leaders and captains, in the camp of the king of Assyria."

Prayer is thus a universal balm, good for all kinds of diseases and poisons, whether hot or cold, unlike the other kinds of theriaca, which are good only for particular diseases, some only for hot poison, some only for cold. Not one of them is good for both hot and cold poison and for contrary diseases, except the great theriaca only. Similarly, prayer is good for all things, even contrary things. Thus, Moshe said in his prayer: "Remember Abraham …" while Asaph said: "Remember not against us the iniquities of our forefathers." We see, therefore, that prayer is good for remembering as well as forgetting. There is no other commandment that is good for all things except prayer. This is the meaning of the statement of the Rabbis that the verse: "And ye shall serve the Lord your God …," refers not to service by means of sacrifices, which is confined to one place, but to service which is good everywhere. Nor can this service be compared to that which a servant does for his master, for God needs not anybody's service. Necessarily, therefore, this service consists in mentioning God's praises, acknowledging that all things come from Him, requesting God to supply our needs in supplicating Him and acknowledging that we have no other helper and support outside of Him. This is divine service.

As the Rabbis found in the verse above cited and the one following it four general things obtainable by prayer alone, and not by any other commandments or services, they say that the service mentioned here denotes prayer, or service of the heart. Thus, we read here in reference to this service: "And He will bless thy bread and thy water," and in the days of David we find that prayer was good for famine, as we said before. Similarly, we read here: "And I will take sickness away from the midst of thee," and in the case of Hezekiah we find that he was cured by prayer. Again, we read here: "None shall miscarry, nor be barren, in thy land," and we find that Hannah was helped by prayer. Further, we read here: "The number of thy days I will fulfil," and we find that Hezekiah and the Israelites after they made the golden calf were saved from death by prayer. We also read here: "I will send My terror before thee, and will discomfit all the people …," and we find in the days of Hezekiah that Sennacherib, the king of Assyria, and his camp were destroyed

Sefer HaIkkarim   BOOK [Maamar] FOUR

as a result of prayer. We find also that prayer is good for all troubles, as we learn from the prayer of Solomon: "If there be in the land famine, if there be pestilence, if there be blasting or mildew, locust or caterpillar ... whatsoever plague, whatsoever sickness there be ... what prayer and supplication soever be made ... hear Thou in heaven ..." Prayer is also good for salvation from distress and captivity. Thus, when Israel was in Egypt we read: "And they cried, and their cry came up unto God by reason of the bondage. And God heard their groaning ..." Moreover, through the prayers of Daniel and Ezra the Israelites returned from captivity.

We find, therefore, that prayer is like a universal balm, which cures all diseases, and is good for all bodies, and therefore for all kinds of people. Thus, Solomon says: "Moreover concerning the stranger that is not of Thy people Israel ... when he shall come and pray ..." Prayer is good even for absolutely wicked men, as was stated in the sixteenth chapter of this Book in connection with the prayer of Menasseh.

Chapter 21

There is a great difficulty in connection with the subject of prayer. There was no greater man than Moshe, the chief of all prophets, and yet though he prayed to God that he might be allowed to enter the land of Israel, he was not answered. Thus, we read: "And I besought the Lord ... Let me go over, I pray Thee ... and the Lord said unto me: 'Let it suffice thee ...' " This would seem to indicate that a thing decreed by God can not be changed by prayer. This being so, one may very well say that it is in vain to serve God and that there is no advantage in praying to Him, since that which has been decreed can not be annulled.

The solution of this problem is that prayer does avail, at any rate before the matter in question has been finally decreed, and it avails also after the decision if the latter is not accompanied by an oath. Our Rabbis also say: "Prayer is good for a man both before the decision and after," as we infer from the case of Hezekiah, who was told: "Set thy house in order; for thou shalt die and not live." And shortly after we read: "I have heard thy prayer ... behold, I will add unto thy days ..." This was a change after the decision, as our Rabbis say. In the case of Moshe, however, the decree was accompanied by an oath, for we read: "Therefore ye shall not bring ...", and our Rabbis say that the expression, "therefore" [laken], indicates an oath, inferring this from the words, "And therefore I have sworn

Sefer HaIkkarim — BOOK [Maamar] FOUR

unto the house of Eli ..." This is the reason why the prayer of Moshe was of no avail.

There is a difference, however, between an individual and a community. A decree announced concerning an individual can not be reversed if it was accompanied by an oath, whereas a decree concerning a community may be reversed by prayer. This will be seen to follow from the sequence of thought in the text.

Accordingly, in order to make the matter clear, I will explain the language used in the prayer of Moshe to make clear the connection of thought. In the beginning he says: "And I besought [vaëthanan] the Lord." Now the Rabbis say that the word hanan [to beseech] denotes asking a favor gratis [hinnam]; their reason being because the word hinnam [gratis] is derived from the root hanan. The idea is that one should not, in praying to God, support his claim by his good deeds or his own merit, for, as Eliphaz said: "What is man that he should be clean? And he that is born of a woman, that he should be righteous?" The talmudic sages find fault with Hezekiah who based his prayer on his own merit, and they say that because he based his request on his own merit, God granted his request for the merit of others, and he was told: "I will defend this city to save it, for Mine own sake, and for My servant David's sake." Moshe, accordingly, did not support his prayer on his own merit, but requested a favor gratuitously. Hence, he said: "O Lord God, thou hast begun ..." i.e., it has always been Thy way to show me kindness gratis. Thou hast in the beginning, of Thy own accord, at the burning bush, shed Thy prophetic influence upon me, though I was neither worthy nor prepared.

Our Rabbis in Sifre explain it in the same way: "Thou hast begun to show Thy servant wonders and strength," as it is said: "I will turn aside now, and see this great sight." It is clear, therefore, that the Rabbis refer the expression: "Thou hast begun," to the beginning of Moshe' prophetic call. Moshe said in effect, O Lord, thou needest not hesitate to show me a kindness even though I do not deserve it, or to do me a favor gratis, for it has been Thy way with me. Thou of Thy own accord, didst begin at the burning bush to show Thy servant, etc. Since, therefore, this has been Thy way with me, do me this kindness also which I ask: "Let me go over, I pray Thee, and see the good land ..." [This attitude is well expressed in the words: "Save us, O God of our salvation"]. What is there to keep Thee from doing this kindness to me? The decree of death that has been made concerning me can only be due to one of three causes. It is either in the nature of punishment from Thee for my sins, or it is my fate as determined by the stars, or my time has come to die. These are the three fixed causes determining a person's death. Thus, David said concerning Saul: "Nay, but the Lord shall smite him; or his day shall come to die; or he shall go down into battle, and be swept away," indicating that there are three kinds of death, penal, natural and accidental. "The Lord shall smite him," denotes penal death, death as a punishment for a sin. "Or his day shall come to die," denotes natural death, when the time has come for a man to die by reason of his temperament [mixture of humors]. "Or he shall go down into battle, and be swept away," denoted accidental death, which comes to a man prematurely and not for any sin, but through the indication of the stars, or by reason of a universal decree or law that every one going into a particular battle shall die. If he had not gone into the battle, he would not have died; if he does go, he will die by reason of this general indication, though he is not guilty of having committed any sin. He did not mention voluntary death, because no man prefers death to life. But he made a mistake, for Saul's death was voluntary, as we read: "Therefore Saul took his sword, and fell upon it." Moshe too did not mention voluntary death, for he did not prefer death to life. Therefore, he mentioned these three only.

His plea was then as follows: O Lord, if the death decreed upon me is a punishment for my sin, is my iniquity so great that it can not be forgiven? As Cain said: "Is my iniquity too great to bear?" which the Rabbis explain as follows: Cain said to God, O Lord, thou bearest heaven and earth, and canst not bear my sin! What they mean is this: Cain said to God: If my sin is so great that it can not be forgiven, then my power to sin is greater than God's power to forgive; but this is impossible, for God's power is infinite. This was the doubt he expresses in the words: "Is my iniquity too great to bear?" And Moshe expressed precisely the same idea when he said: "Thy greatness ..." What he meant to say was: I know that Thy greatness is infinite, and that my iniquity can not be so great that thy infinite greatness is not sufficient to forgive it. Then he said, "And Thy strong hand ...," meaning to say: If my death is due to the stars, thou hast shown me miracles and wonders which prove that Thy hand is strong enough to overcome the stars. Then he said: "For what god is there ...," referring to natural death, such as the righteous die of. Thus, the Rabbis say: "God counts the years of the righteous ..." The meaning is, God counts their years to see that they should not be shortened either by punishment or by accident, but that they should live as many years as they are capable of living in accordance with their nature, the composition of their humors, and the

Sefer HaIkkarim — BOOK [Maamar] FOUR

fundamental vigor which they possess from the time of their creation. This is the reason why the Bible, referring to Sarah, uses the expression: "The years of the life of Sarah," having just said: "And the life of Sarah was a hundred and seven and twenty years." The Bible desires to indicate that the hundred and twenty-seven years that she lived was the number of years of her life, i.e., the number of years which her nature and fundamental and original vigor determined that she should live. Her days were not shortened as were those of Abraham, who, as the Rabbis say, should have lived a hundred and eighty years, like Yitzhak, but lived only a hundred and seventy-five, his years having been shortened by five, so that he should not see the evil life of Esau. In order to indicate this the expression used in his case is: "And these are the days of the years of Abraham's life which he lived," i.e., these are the years which he actually lived, but not those which, according to the nature of his temperament and his original vigor, he should have lived, as was the case with Sarah.

Accordingly, Moshe said: If my death is natural, that is, if there is no power in the composition of my temperament to enable me to live longer, thou canst renew my youth like an eagle, and give me power to be restored like a green fir tree so as to be strong, for there is no other god in the world beside Thee who can do what Thou doest, namely who can create living things and endow them with new natural strength. If, therefore, thou shouldest give me new life and make me a new creature, there would be none to say Thee nay, for there is no one in the world who can do what Thou doest, or who has Thy strength. All this being so, and there being none to prevent Thee, "Let me go over, I pray Thee, and see ..."

But God replied: "Let it suffice thee ... But charge Yehoshua ... for he shall go over ..." To such an extent, continues Moshe, was the divine decree fixed against me, that when we reached the valley opposite Beth-peor, we dwelt there and He did not allow me to go further: "So we abode in the valley over against Beth-peor," i.e., we could not go on further, because I was to be buried there, as is written: "And he was buried in the valley in the land of Moab, over against Beth-peor."

To this statement Moshe adds the exhortation: "And now, O Israel, hearken unto the statutes ... that ye may live, and go in and possess the land ..." He says in effect: I took all this trouble in order to enter the land, but was not given the privilege. You are given the privilege to enter the land, therefore be strong in observing the commandment of God that you may be worthy to enter.

Sefer HaIkkarim BOOK [Maamar] FOUR

You might perhaps say: if my prayer was not heard, it is possible that to-day or to-morrow you may sin and your prayers will not be heard either; my answer is: "Your eyes have seen what the Lord did in Baal-peor ... But ye that did cleave unto the Lord ... For what great nation is there, that hath God so nigh unto them ..." The meaning is, do not think that an individual and a congregation are equal in this matter, for it is not so. With all my worth, my prayer in my own behalf was not accepted, because I am an individual; whereas though you worshipped idols and bowed down to Peor - and there is no one the Lord hates as much as the one who worships idols - my prayer in your behalf was accepted. When I prayed for you on the occasion of the golden calf and of Peor, my prayer was accepted, and God forgave you, though my own prayer for myself was not accepted.

It appears also from the language of the Rabbis in Sifre that the reason Moshe speaks of the sin of Baal-peor in this place is in order to indicate the difference between the prayer of an individual for an individual and his prayer for a congregation. Although the two prayers may be equal and of the same kind, yet the prayer for the congregation is more likely to be heard than the prayer for the individual. Therefore, he adds the words: "As the Lord our God is whensoever we call upon Him," the meaning being that no matter what the content of the prayer is, if it is for the congregation, it is accepted. Hence the Rabbis say: "God does not reject the prayers of the congregation, as is said: 'Behold, God despiseth not the many.'" They also say: "A person should always join a congregation," thus indicating that the prayer of a congregation is always accepted, while that of an individual is not accepted when it concerns a matter that has been decided under oath, as was the case with the prayer of Moshe to be allowed to enter the land of Israel. It was not accepted because the matter had already been decided under oath.

Chapter 22

We must, however, explain the reason why the decision concerning Moshe was accompanied by an oath, so that his prayer was not accepted. According to the Rabbis the essence of Moshe' sin at the waters of Meribah was the expression: "Hear now, ye rebels," used by Moshe, which was an insult to the honor of Israel. And they infer from this that he who insults the honor of a community is guilty of an offence equal to that of profaning the name of God. But it is very difficult to suppose that such a sin should not be capable of

Sefer HaIkkarim — BOOK [Maamar] FOUR

atonement. Besides we find in Deuteronomy that Moshe again says to Israel: "Ye have been rebellious against the Lord." If Moshe had been punished for saying to them: "Hear now, ye rebels," he would scarcely have used a similar expression again.

The explanation of the sin of the waters of Meribah has given the commentators a great deal of dufficulty, so much so that Maimonides gave a far-fetched explanation, saying that the sin of Moshe consisted in becoming angry with Israel for no sufficient reason, when God was not angry with them. For God was not angry with them when they asked for things that were necessities, like water or the manna. According to Maimonides, then, there was here a profanation of the Holy Name, for the people would think that God was angry with them because they asked for water, although they needed it. Else, they would say, Moshe would not have been angry with them for no reason. For anger is an unworthy quality, and it is not likely that the head of the prophets would give way to such a low impulse without reason, far be it! Hence the people would come to think ill of God, assuming that He was angry for no good reason. This is the gist of Maimonides' interpretation, but it is far fetched.

Nahmanides refuted this opinion in his commentary on the Torah. It appears, however, from his words that he, too, agrees with Maimonides that the sin did not consist in the fact that they did not speak to the rock; and for the following reasons: either because the rock is not a rational being to receive a command from God, or because, since Moshe was told: "Take the rod, and assemble the congregation, thou, and Aaron thy brother, and speak ye unto the rock …," it seems that he was expected to strike the rock, since he was told to take the rod, else why was it necessary to mention the rod? But this is no proof, for in Horeb he was told: "And thy rod, wherewith thou smotest the river …," and yet it was found necessary to state specifically in the sequel: "And thou shalt smite the rock." Here too therefore he should have been told to strike the rock if that was the intention, as he was told the first time. The taking of the rod is no proof that he would have to strike, for the rod does not cause the flow of the water by the force of striking, for it is not the natural property of a rod when it strikes a rock to split it and bring out water by the force of the blow. The phenomenon is a miracle, and the waters come out by decree of God when the rod is near the rock. In the beginning of his prophetic career Moshe was told: "And thou shalt take in thy hand thisrod, wherewith thou shalt do the signs." This shows plainly that the rod was endowed with the property of being the instrument in the performance of the signs, according to

Sefer HaIkkarim — BOOK [Maamar] FOUR

the decree of God as commanded through Moshe. The proof is as follows: In connection with the plague of hail Moshe was told: "Stretch forth thy hand toward heaven, that there may be hail …" and in the sequel it says: "And Moshe stretched forth his rod toward heaven; and the Lord sent thunder and hail, and fire ran down unto the earth." Now the hail was not produced by the rod's striking the air. But the miracle of the hail was produced in the air by the will of God when the rod in the hand of Moshe was in contact with the air. Here too, therefore, the taking of the rod is no proof that it had to be used to strike.

As for the first argument that God would give a command only to a rational being, and the rock was not a rational being to receive a command from God to give forth its waters [this is the opinion of Maimonides, as can be seen in "Pirke Moshe," ch. 25], it is not valid, for matter does not become affected by itself, but is acted upon by a mover which moves it and prepares it to receive the form. Now when God commands the matter to receive a form or undergo a certain change, as in the verse: "Let the earth bring forth the living creature …;" "Let the waters swarm with swarms of living creatures" …, and similar passages, the command is not given to the matter, but to the mover that he should prepare the matter to receive the form or to undergo the change which God has decreed. Now the command which is directed to the mover is given to a rational being undoubtedly.

My opinion is that the sin at the waters of Meribah was that they [Moshe and Aaron] did not speak to the rock, as the Bible literally says. The text proves it, which says: "Because ye rebelled against My word at the waters of Meribah." Such an expression cannot apply to the words: "Hear now, ye rebels," nor to Moshe' anger, but only to their violation of God's command. The essence of the sin, however, which caused God to take an oath, was that the act evinced a lack of faith, as we read: "Because ye believed not in Me … therefore ye shall not bring …"

The explanation is as follows: One great principle of the Torah and foundation of faith which is contained in the belief in God's Providence, is that God subjects' nature to the control of believers, as Moshe says in the Psalm following his prayer. In the name of God, he assures him who dwells "in the covert of the Highest," and abides "in the shadow of the Almighty," that God will deliver him from the snare of the fowler and from pestilence and from natural accidents, so that he shall tread "upon the lion and asp," and trample under feet "the young lion and the serpent."

Sefer HaIkkarim — BOOK [Maamar] FOUR

We find this verified in the lives of some of the pious men. For example, we are told about Rabbi Hanina ben Dosa that he set his foot on the hole of a lizard and was bitten; but the lizard died, a reversal of the natural course. Rabbi Hanina then said to his disciples: My children, it is not the lizard that kills, but sin it is that kills. We thus see that by the command of the righteous changes occur in nature. We are also told concerning Rabbi Hanina that he said: "He who said that oil should burn, will command vinegar to burn," and it was so, and we find other similar cases. Similarly, the Rabbis say concerning Rabbi Phinehas ben Yair that by his command he divided a river many times. A river is not a rational being, and yet it was divided for those who fulfil the divine commandments and those who associate with them. We are also told of a great many miracles that were performed by Nahum of Gamzo and other righteous men by a mere word without prophecy or divine speech or command. Similarly, Eliphaz said to Job: "Thou shalt also decree a thing, and it shall be established unto thee." From this it appears that the prophets and those who speak with the Holy Spirit, like Eliphaz, agree that nature changes by the command of the righteous according to their will, not to speak of the prophets, who performed miracles by their commands. Thus, Eliyahu said: "As the Lord, the God of Israel, liveth ... there shall not be dew nor rain these years, but according to my word." He also said: "If I be a man of God, let fire come down from heaven, and consume thee and thy fifty," and it was so. Elisha said: "To-morrow about this time shall a measure of fine flour be sold for a shekel ...," and it was so. Also, he "made the iron to swim," and performed other miracles without a previous prophetic message or divine commandment concerning the matter. The same is true of the other prophets. Moshe himself said: "If these men die the common death of all men ... But if the Lord make a new thing ... And it came to pass, as he made an end of speaking all these words, that the ground did cleave asunder that was under them. And the earth opened her mouth ..." But we are not told that God commanded him to do this. Isaiah also says: "That confirmeth the word of His servant, and performeth the counsel of His messengers."

He, therefore, who doubts that God performs the will of the prophet or the righteous or the pious man that is worthy, is virtually casting doubt upon the Torah and one of its principles. Particularly on an occasion for the sanctification of the divine name is it incumbent upon one to publish the fact that nature is subject to, and is compelled to do the will of those who observe the Torah and fulfil its commandments. A prophet therefore who is worthy to perform miracles and refuses to do so when he can save thereby a nation or a community, is surely responsible for casting a doubt upon the belief. For the bystander will think that there is no truth in the biblical statements, made in many places, that nature is subject to those who perform the commandments of the Torah, and this will lead to doubting the Torah.

This is especially the case when people see that the very same prophet through whom the Torah was given does not rely upon this belief to make a decree against nature so as to change its course or to perform a miracle, though the prophet in question is more worthy to perform miracles than any one else. This no doubt leads to profanation of the Holy Name and to the casting of doubt upon the faith. It looks as if the prophet himself were in doubt whether it is true that nature can be changed by his word, as the Torah promises. This is why it says: "Because ye believed not in Me." For if, when the Israelites asked for water, Moshe and Aaron had decreed that the rock should split and water should flow, God would without doubt have "confirmed the word of His servant and performed the counsel of His messengers," and He would thus have been sanctified in the eyes of all the people.

But Moshe and Aaron did not do so, instead they went to the door of the tent of meeting as though they were fleeing from the people, as Ibn Ezra explains, and as though they had no idea what to do. This was no doubt a profanation of the divine name, and was likely to cause lack of faith in God and His Torah on the part of those who witnessed the affair. Therefore, the Bible says: "Ye believed not in Me." For if you had believed you would have decreed a change in the course of nature, in order that My name might be sanctified through you, when all people would see that I "confirm the words of My servant and perform the counsel of My messengers."

And though Moshe and Aaron acted as they did by reason of their great humility, not wishing to take any credit unto themselves without the command of God, nevertheless it was accounted to them as an iniquity and a lack of faith because of the profanation of the divine name which resulted from it, as we have explained. Hence we find that when Yehoshua was in a similar predicament, he did not wait for divine permission or advice, but relied on God that He would do his will, and said: "Sun, stand thou still upon Gibeon ..." As the Bible testifies: "Then spoke Yehoshua to the Lord ...; and he said in the sight of Israel: 'Sun, stand thou still upon Gibeon ...' " God confirmed his word, and the Bible even says that such a great thing did not happen even in the days of Moshe, namely that Moshe should of his own accord have given so great a command and it should be fulfilled. The Bible says: "And there was no day like that before it or after it, that the Lord hearkened unto the voice of a man," i.e., that God should confirm such an important command given by a man of his own accord. This is an allusion to the lack of faith which the Bible imputes to Moshe and Aaron because they refused to act of their own accord without divine authority. Then again when they were told: "And ye shall speak unto the rock," and they did not speak, but struck it instead, they sinned again in that they transgressed the command of God. For if they had spoken, the name of God would have been sanctified and they would have made good part of their error. But not having spoken, they added to their sin.

The reason they committed the sin was that they thought that as in Horeb the waters came out by striking, they would in this case too come out only by striking. But God had intended otherwise. At the first time the Torah had not yet been given and nature was not as yet subject to Israel to such an extent. But now in the fortieth year they were worthy of having miracles done for them and of having nature submit to them by the mere word of Moshe. Therefore, there was rebellion in the fact that they did not speak to the rock as they had been commanded, and lack of faith and profanation of the Holy Name in that they did not, on their own responsibility and without divine command, decree that the rock should give forth its water. Similarly, we find when God said to Moshe: "Get thee up into this mountain of Abarim ... and be gathered unto thy people," that the Bible mentions two things: "Because ye trespassed against Me ..." and "Because ye sanctified Me not," alluding thereby to the two sins. Now since the sin involved lack of faith and profanation of the Holy Name, it was not subject to forgiveness, as we find in the treatise Yoma: "But if one is guilty of profanation of the Holy Name, repentance has no power to suspend punishment, nor can suffering wipe out the guilt, death alone erases the stain." Therefore, God made a decree with an oath, and for this reason neither Moshe' prayer nor his repentance availed him in this sin. Study this chapter very carefully that you may understand it, for it contains the best that has been said on this subject, and may God in His mercy deliver us from error, amen.

Chapter 23

Some words denote good solely and absolutely, and do not denote

Sefer Halkkarim   BOOK [Maamar] FOUR

evil at all. Some denote evil absolutely, and in no way denote good, while there are certain words that denote for the most part good, but in some aspect denote also evil, and vice versa.

Those which denote good only, like "upright," "faithful," "merciful," "gracious," and so on, may be applied to God and used in praying to Him. Those which denote absolute evil, like "wicked," "wrong doer," "robber," "doer of violence," and so on, may not be ascribed to God, much less be used in prayer. Those words which denote good for the most part may not be applied to God unless the prophets apply them to Him, like the word Hasid [pious, merciful], for example. For though it denotes good for the most part, nevertheless since we also find it used sometimes, though rarely, to signify shame, as: "Lest he that heareth it revile [yehasedeka] thee;" "It is a shameful [hesed] thing", we should not permit ourselves to apply it to God if we did not find in the Bible the expression: "For I am merciful [Hasid], saith the Lord, I will not bear grudge forever." But those words which denote for the most part something evil or shameful, we must not permit ourselves to apply to God in our prayer even though we find that the prophets apply them to Him, unless they apply them in prayer. For example, grief and sorrow are ascribed to God in the Bible: "And it grieved Him at His heart;" "And His soul was grieved for the misery of Israel." And yet we do not apply such phrases to God in prayer, as, "Grieve for me," or "May Thy soul grieve for me." Similarly, we do not permit ourselves to ascribe to God weeping, although the prophets do ascribe it to Him, according to the opinion of our Rabbis: "Said Rab Samuel's son of Unya in the name of Rab: There is a place where God weeps, and its name is Mistarim, as is said: 'But if ye will not hear it, my soul shall weep in Mistarim for your pride.' 'For your pride,' means the pride of Israel, which has been humbled. Is there weeping in the presence of God? Do we not read: 'Strength and gladness are in His place?' Answer: The two are not incompatible, the one has reference to the inner chambers, the other to the outer."

The Rabbis, as we see, take the verse to represent the words of God and not those of the prophet, because the section begins: "Hear ye, and give ear, be not proud; for the Lord hath spoken." This language shows that they are the words of God and not those of the prophet, as we read: "Hear, O heavens, and give ear, O earth, for the Lord hath spoken: Children I have reared, and brought up …" The passage reads: "Give glory to the Lord your God, before it grows dark … But if ye will not hear it, my soul shall weep in Mistarim for your pride." According to the Rabbis, the meaning is as follows: The

Sefer Halkkarim   BOOK [Maamar] FOUR

words: "Hear ye, and give ear, be not proud [tigbahu]," mean: Do not think you are eternal like those on high [gebohim], for it is not so. You belong to that part of nature which is subject to genesis and decay, and if you desire permanence, "Give glory to the Lord your God," i.e., give your soul, which is called glory, as in the verse: "Yea, let him lay my glory in the dust." Give it to God, and see to it that it should obtain spiritual perfection, which is also called glory, as in the verses: "And his resting-place shall be glorious;" "Let the saints exult in glory." This perfection is called glory, because it shows God's glory in that He created the human soul in such a way that though man belongs to that part of nature which is subject to genesis and decay, if the soul cleaves to Him, it can become permanent and eternal.

The prophet then says that they should endeavor to attain this perfection before the day of death, "before it grow dark," as Solomon says: "Remember then thy Creator in the days of thy youth ... Before the sun, and the moon, and the stars, are darkened," which refers to the day of death. Then the prophet continues: "But if ye will not hear it, my soul shall weep in Mistarim," i.e., if you will not hearken to My counsel to endeavor to attain this glory, namely the perfection of the soul, my soul will weep in Mistarim. The meaning of which is: Be assured that My wisdom and My will have decreed that you should be destined for evil and destruction. [Weeping, as is well known, is always done for something that has ceased to be.] He thus alludes to the fact that there is a place to which privation and evil attach, namely the sublunar world, which the Rabbis call the inner chambers, because the earth is in the center of the world, surrounded on all sides, while the heavens are called the outer chambers where gladness, i.e., permanence, reigns; or it may be that because privation attaches to "hyle" [matter], which can not be perceived by the senses, he calls it inner chambers, while the designation outer chambers applies to sensible existence. In this way they mean to indicate that the whole of existence is cared for and guided by God, even that portion to which privation attaches, which is called inner chambers. The existence of this part is due to the gladness which exists in that sensible nature which is called outer chambers. This is an allusion to the fact that since privation in existing things is due to matter [hyle], none of them can be eternal except through the soul. The words: "My soul shall weep," signify: The human soul, which is Mine, will be destroyed, for "weeping" alludes to destruction. Or the words may be used figuratively, as though the Maker is grieved when His work does not realize the final perfection which He intended. Therefore, the prophet says that the weeping is for the pride of Israel which is humbled. The virtue of Israel and their perfection which is intended for them through the Torah, is the perfection and permanent existence of the soul. Therefore, God is grieved if the soul does not maintain its permanence and ceases to be. This is the meaning of the expression that He weeps or that there is weeping before Him.

Now, as to this and similar expressions, though we find that, according to the Rabbis, the prophet applies them to God, we must not permit ourselves to apply them to God in our prayer and say: "Weep for me," or "Grieve for me," or, "Let Thy soul grieve for me." We may, however, say: "May Thy mercies yearn for us," because we find that the prophet also uses this expression in a prayer. Isaiah says: "The yearning of Thy heart and Thy compassions, now restrained toward me."

It is thus clear that not every one is free to express himself as he pleases in prayer, and especially is he not free to ascribe an attribute to God for which there is no authority. This is what Ecclesiastes had in mind when he said: "Be not rash with thy mouth, and let not thy heart be hasty to utter a word before God." Abraham Ibn Ezra goes into this matter at length in his commentary on Ecclesiastes on this verse. His ideas are right and need no corrections. To sum up, a prayer must satisfy three requirements in order to be acceptable:

1. It must be brief and have appropriate expressions indicating the suppliant's ideas. One must not be verbose, for verbosity is the quality of a fool, hence one must not bring oneself under the verse: "For a dream cometh through a multitude of business; and a fool's voice through a multitude of words." The words of the prayer must be pleasant to the hearer and not tiresome. For this reason, songs and piyyutim and supplications in verse have been chosen for the prayers because all the requirements mentioned are contained in them, and they correspond to musical rhythm besides, for the definition of a poem is that it is a composition in which the parts bear relation to and have connection with each other, and it expresses the idea of the composer in brief and pleasant words, metrically arranged in accordance with musical rhythm.

2. The intention of the mind must be in agreement with the words one expresses. The suppliant must not put himself under the designation: "But they beguiled Him with their mouth, and lied unto Him with their tongue. For their heart was not stedfast with Him." He must be of those whose speech agrees with their thoughts, as David said: "Let the words of my mouth and the meditation of my heart be acceptable before Thee." The meaning is, since the words of my mouth are in agreement with the meditation of my heart, let them be acceptable before Thee.

3. The voice must be low and indicative of submission, as of a person who beseeches his master, as the Psalmist says: "Hear my voice, O God, in my complaint;" "Hear the voice of my supplications, when I cry unto Thee." One must not lay oneself open to the charge: "She hath uttered her voice against Me; therefore have I hated her."

These three requirements are alluded to by David in the fifth Psalm. "Give ear to my words," alludes to the first requirement, which is that of brevity. "Consider my meditation," alludes to the second requirement, sincerity; "Hearken unto the voice of my cry," alludes to the third requirement, submissiveness as indicated in the voice. These are the indispensable conditions, without which prayer can not be accepted. But even though the three requirements are present, it does not follow that the prayer is bound, under all circumstances, to be accepted. It may be that the suppliant is so far from God that he must pray repeatedly and intensely before he can be heard, but after he has prayed repeatedly and devoutly, he may be heard. This is why Isaiah finds fault with Israel because they did not importune God with prayer: "And there is none that calleth upon Thy name, that stirreth up himself to take hold of Thee." From this it seems that if they had persisted in praying to God, they would have been heard. Similarly, we find in relation to the men of Nineveh: "Let them cry mightily unto God," and they were heard. Moshe, also, when he prayed concerning the matter of the calf, continued and persisted in his prayer many days until he was answered. The same is true of his prayer at the time of the spies, until he was told: "I have pardoned according to thy word."

And sometimes the suppliant is so far from God, or the thing that is requested is so great that prayer alone, though continuous and earnest, is not enough, and there is need of some act or acts indicating submission and repentance. Isaiah says: "Yea, when ye make many prayers, I will not hear," and later he says: "Wash you, make you clean ..." In relation to the men of Nineveh it says: "Let them be covered with sackcloth, both man and beast." The righteous men, too, performed acts indicative of submission. Daniel said: "I ate no pleasant bread, neither came flesh nor wine in my mouth, neither did I anoint myself at all." And the angel said to him: "From the first day that thou didst set thy heart to understand, and to humble thyself before thy God, thy words were heard."

There are certain persons for whom it is sufficient to pray in thought alone. David says: "The Lord is nigh unto them that are of a broken heart;" "The Lord is nigh unto all them that call upon Him." There are still others of so high a degree that they are granted even what they do not ask for. This is the position of the "God-fearing:" "He will fulfil the desire of them that fear Him." Nevertheless, they are obliged to pray actually, as the verse continues: "He also will hear their cry, and will save them." Finally, there are those who occupy the highest degree, the "lovers of God." They do not need to pray to God, who keeps them of His own accord, as the sequel has it: "The Lord preserveth all them that love Him." The Rabbis say, in commenting upon the verse: "Who alone doeth wondrous things," The one for whom the miracle is done does not realize that a miracle has been done for him. This was the position of Abraham.

Chapter 24

All the acts which a man does do not necessarily realize the purpose intended in doing them. It happens that a person does all that is necessary in the proper way and yet fails to realize the purpose intended. Thus, the physician in many cases does all that is necessary and in the best way in which it can be done, without any error on his or the patient's part, and yet the cure, which is intended, does not come about. Similarly, the farmer may do all that is proper, he may sow at the proper time and his field may be good and kept in good shape, and yet the seed may not prosper. The explanation of all this is clear. Neither the physician alone nor the physician plus the patient are the cause of the cure, but the physician and nature. Similarly in agriculture, the cause of the produce is not the husbandman alone, nor the field, but the husbandman and nature.
So, in the case of prayer. It often happens that a person prays in a proper way, at the proper time, and yet his prayer is not accepted, not because of any sin on his part, but because the will of God does not assent. In the same way a shipbuilder, in many cases, makes his ship properly, navigates it properly on the sea at the proper time, and yet fails to reach his desired destination, simply because the will of God does not desire it, either as a punishment, like the case of Jonah, or by way of providence, for a good end, as determined in the several ways discussed above. So prayer sometimes fails of acceptance, either as a punishment, as we explained in the case of Moshe, or because the recipient [of God's influence] is not prepared until he persists in offering many prayers, or performs certain acts indicative

Sefer HaIkkarim   BOOK [Maamar] FOUR

of submission, such as fasting or putting on sackcloth, like the men of Nineveh, and so on, as we explained; or there may be some other obstacle, as the Rabbis say, that David's prayer that he should not die on the Sabbath, was not accepted, because the time had come for Solomon his son to reign, and one reign can not encroach upon another even a hair's breadth. Or because God knows that the favor requested is not good for the suppliant, and hence his prayer is not accepted by way of providence, for his own good. For example, a person may pray for children, and his prayer is not accepted because God knows that his children will be hostile to him and will seek to kill him, as Absalom sought to kill David; or a person may pray for wealth, and God knows that his wealth will be the cause of his death, as Solomon says: "Riches kept by the owner thereof to his hurt;" or the cause of unbelief, as Solomon says: "Lest I be full and deny, and say: 'Who is the Lord?' " or for some other cause hidden from us and known to God.

The best kind of prayer is therefore that of the wise man, who said: "O Lord, do Thy will in heaven above, show kindness to those who fear Thee here below, and do what is good in Thine eyes." He meant that God should do His will in heaven, so that pleasure may be afforded below to those who fear the Lord, i.e., that He should overcome the stars and annul their decree against those who perform His will, so that they may have power to save themselves from their trouble. Then he says: "And do what is good in Thine eyes," that is, whatever it is that I pray to Thee for, attend not to my words or request, to do what my heart desires, or what I ask, for many times I ask and pray for something which is bad for me, thinking it is a good. But Thou knowest better than I whether the thing is good for me or bad. Therefore, decide Thou and not I; do what Thou knowest is good. Therefore, he says: "Good in Thine eyes," and not in my eyes. This is the meaning of the rabbinical statement: "One is obliged to bless God for evil, as well as for good." The reason is because God knows what is good, not man, and it is God who has to choose the way of good and of salvation for man, but man has nothing to do but to bless God always. This is what David meant when he said: "Salvation belongeth unto the Lord;" i.e., God alone knows how to choose the way of salvation, not man. Upon man it is incumbent always to bless the Lord for good as well as for evil, and to recognize that everything is for his good. Hence the Psalmist concludes: "Thy blessing be upon Thy people, Selah."

For this reason, the most fitting prayer is to ask the divine favor in general terms, and not in terms definite and specific. A person who prays to God in particular and specific terms is, as it were, desirous of forcing the divine will to his own ideas and preferences instead of bending his ideas to God's will; but this is tantamount to a contempt for God's knowledge and power, as though God knew no other way of granting his request except the one which he has chosen. Concerning such as he does the Psalmist say: "Only for God wait thou in stillness, my soul; For from Him cometh my hope," i.e., when thou prayest to a human being, thou must specify thy request and state the way in which thou desirest to attain thy purpose, for without this he would not know what is in thy mind, what thou requirest and what is good and advantageous for thee. But when thou prayest before God, thou must not specify thy request, but, "wait in silence for Him, my soul," and do not thou choose the way for thy salvation, for He knows what is good and beneficial for thee better than thou. This is the meaning of the words: "From Him cometh my salvation," or, "From Him cometh my hope," for He knows the way of salvation or the way to realize the hope better than I. For sometimes I think of a certain way of obtaining honor or some other good or salvation and the result is the opposite. Therefore, one must pray to Him in general terms and cast one's burden upon Him. This is the meaning of the Psalmist who, after saying: "So shalt thou delight thyself in the Lord," adds: "Commit thy way unto the Lord; trust also in Him, and He will bring it to pass." That is, he will bring to pass what is good and beneficial to thee, for He knows how to choose the way of good or honor or salvation better than thou. Hence the Psalmist also says: "Upon God resteth my salvation and my glory." That is, the reason I say, "Only for God wait thou in stillness, my soul," is because it is for Him to choose what is salvation for me or relief or deliverance or honor, for I am not able to tell, but I put my trust in Him that He will choose what is good and proper and beneficial for me. Hence, he concludes: "The rock of my strength, and my refuge, is in God." This will suffice concerning prayer.

Chapter 25

If we examine all the mandatory precepts in the Torah, we do not find any one precept through which alone one may attain the purpose intended by the Torah except repentance. The purpose intended by the Torah to be realized through the performance of its commandments, as we explained in the Third Book of this treatise, is the love of God, which leads man to the great reward destined for the soul. Now we find that this very purpose is stated in the Torah in relation to repentance. This proves the great importance of this commandment, and shows that it is a more comprehensive precept than prayer. For though prayer avails for particular purposes, it does not give the soul the comprehensive reward that is attained by repentance. Therefore, we must treat this subject after prayer, rather than the other precepts, and with due brevity, as required by the limits of our treatise.

If we examine carefully the section "Nizabim," we find that the words: "See, I have set before thee ... in that I command thee this day to love the Lord thy God ... to hearken to His voice, and to cleave unto Him ...," as the context and sequence of thought show, have reference to repentance. For it says first: "And shalt return unto the Lord thy God, and hearken to His voice ..." And it concludes with repentance, saying that it must be with perfect sincerity and that God will help one if it is; hence the concluding words: "If thou turn unto the Lord thy God with all thy heart, and with all thy soul." Then the Bible speaks of the great importance of repentance and the ease with which it may be performed: "For this commandment which I command thee this day, it is not too hard for thee, neither is it far off. It is not in heaven ... Neither is it beyond the sea.... But the word is very nigh unto thee ..." All this no doubt has reference to repentance, as is shown by the words: "In thy mouth, and in thy heart, that thou mayest do it." For the essence of repentance consists in confession as expressed in words, and regret as felt in the heart, as we shall explain. Nahmanides also says that the text in question deals with repentance. The text gives it exceeding high praise, when it says: it is not in heaven, nor beyond the sea.

The idea is: This thing [viz. repentance] is so valuable that you should undergo for its sake all the trouble in the world, even to go up to heaven, if possible, or beyond the sea, in order to obtain it, for it is something extremely valuable. For logically speaking, the sinner should not be forgiven under any circumstances, as the prophet says: "Wherewith shall I come before the Lord ... Will the Lord be pleased with thousands of rams?" That is, the price of being delivered from punishment for one's sins ought to be so great that he knows not how much he should give, or what would be sufficient, thousands of rams or ten thousand of rivers of oil; whether he should give his first-born for his transgression or the fruit of his body for the sin of his soul. All this shows that, logically speaking, no ransom should suffice to remove one's sin. How much less reason is there then that the sinner should be received and forgiven for mere verbal repentance, as the prophet says: "Take with you words, and return

Sefer Halkkarim   BOOK [Maamar] FOUR

unto the Lord," unless it be by divine grace? Therefore the Torah calls solemn attention to it: "See I have set before thee this day ... therefore choose life, that thou mayest live ..."

Having shown the facility of obtaining it: "But the word is very nigh unto thee ..." he says: "See I have set before thee ..." That is, you have no excuse in this case as you may have in respect to the other commandments, which, by reason of their great number and difficulty, you can not perform. It is not so here, for this commandment is very easy. And if you perform it you will obtain life and good, while if you indolently neglect it, death and misfortune will come upon you. Therefore, you must be careful not to slight it. It is like the case of a person who is suffering from a serious illness which is regarded as incurable. Then a physician comes and says to the patient: I will tell you of a drug which will cure you of your illness. The patient thinks that since it can cure what is regarded as an incurable disease, the drug must be very costly, and extremely difficult to obtain. But the physician says: Do not think that there is any difficulty in obtaining this drug, or that you have to go up to heaven for it, or to spend a great deal of money to cross the sea in a ship, as ought to be the case. No, it is very easy to get. This is the meaning of the concluding words: "But the word is very nigh ...," i.e., since it is nigh, you must not be indolent and neglect to obtain it, for it is life to your soul, and as you do not indolently neglect to seek life, so you must not neglect this. Hence he adds: "Therefore choose life ...," explaining that the life which is obtained through this commandment is the very purpose intended to be obtained through the Torah: "To love the Lord thy God, to hearken to His voice, and to cleave unto Him; for that is thy life and the length of thy days; that thou mayest dwell in the land ..." "For that is thy life," refers to the world of souls. "And the length of thy days," means this world, viz. to "dwell in the land." In other words 'through this love are obtained communion with God, eternal life and physical happiness.

This is all true if repentance is motived by love, but if the motive is fear, he will indeed receive his reward, but it is not that complete repentance which confers the great reward of which we have been speaking. Our Rabbis say: "Resh Lakish said: 'Great is the penitent, for his wilful sins are accounted to him as errors, as is said: "For thou hast stumbled in thy iniquity." "Iniquity," is a wrong done deliberately, and yet he calls it stumbling!' But did not Resh Lakish say: 'Great is the penitent, for his deliberate wrongs are changed into merits, as is said: "And when the wicked turneth from his wickedness, and doeth that which is lawful and right, he shall live thereby?" ' Answer: The two statements are not contradictory, the one has reference to a person who repents from love, the other refers to one who repents from fear."

This matter requires explanation. How does Resh Lakish infer that if a man repents from fear, his wilful deeds are converted into errors? Justice requires that if one repents from fear of punishment, his repentance should not avail him at all. For an act deserving praise or blame or reward or punishment is one that is done voluntarily, without any mixture of compulsion, whereas the act of repentance from fear is not completely voluntary, why then should one receive any reward at all?

The answer is that there are two kinds of repentance from fear. The first is that of the man who repents from fear of the punishment which is upon him, like a slave entreating his master while he is beating him, but as soon as his master removes the rod from him, he disobeys him as before, as was the case with Pharaoh. As long as the plague was upon him, he said: "The Lord is righteous," but as soon as he was relieved, he hardened his heart again as before. This showed clearly that the first repentance was forced by the terrors of death which had fallen upon him …, and was not a free act. Such an attitude should not be regarded as repentance at all.

The other is the case of the man who repents from fear of God and His punishment, who has the fear of the Lord before him even in time of respite. He is afraid of God's punishment because he believes that all things come from God as reward or punishment, and does not ascribe events to nature and chance, as Pharaoh did, who as soon as the plague departed went back to his original bad behavior. Even after the plague of the first born, the moment he thought the Israelites had lost their way, he ascribed all the signs and wonders which he had seen, to chance. Therefore, he took courage and pursued the Israelites, thereby proving clearly that his repentance in the first place was due to compulsion on account of the plagues, and was not voluntary.

In this way we must explain the statements in the Bible that God hardens the heart of the wicked, or makes them stiff-necked, and prevents them from repenting. The wicked man, when misfortune comes upon him, pretends to become pious, and returns to God from the fear of the punishment which is upon him, as Pharaoh said: "I have sinned this time; the Lord is righteous." Now, since this act is like one that is forced and not free, God hardens his heart, by suggesting to him other causes to which he can attribute the

Sefer HaIkkarim — BOOK [Maamar] FOUR

misfortune, accident, for example, rather than divine providence. This is done in order to remove from his heart the softening effect which came from the misfortune, so that he may return to his natural state, and act freely without compulsion. Then it may be found out whether his repentance was free or not. Now since, when the yoke of the plague was removed from Pharaoh, his choice was evil, God said: "I hardened his heart," i.e., I removed from his heart the softening effect which came from the plague and restored him to the natural state of freedom; while he, owing to his wicked attitude, when in a state of freedom, sought for various causes and excuses to which he might ascribe the plagues so that they might seem accidental.

This is the meaning of the words: "If you will walk with me **Keri** [קרי]," i.e., if you ascribe events to **Mikreh** [chance], "Then will I also walk with you with the wrath of Keri, etc." It is in this way that the gates of repentance are closed before the wicked. God does not prevent a person from making a good choice, Heaven forbid! As the Bible says: "For I have no pleasure in the death of the wicked, but rather that he should return from his ways and live." But God leaves him to his freedom without any external compulsion, and he chooses his own way. This was also the case with Sihon, concerning whom the Bible says: "For the Lord thy God hardened his spirit, and made his heart obstinate." Sihon was guilty before God for his wickedness, but he was afraid to come into conflict with Israel because he feared God's punishment, therefore God introduced various remote circumstances in order to remove from his heart the softening effect due to what he had heard of the miracles that were done for Israel, and to leave him solely to his freedom.

God commanded Moshe to send messengers to the king of Edom, saying to him: "Let us pass, I pray thee, through thy land." And when Edom refused and came out against Israel, "with much people, and with a strong hand," God commanded Israel to turn away from him. When Sihon saw this, he planned and plotted wickedly, saying to himself that Israel's success was not due to divine providence, seeing that they turned away from the king of Edom and from the king of Moab, as Jephthah explained, and hence he thought he was no whit inferior to these, took courage and went out against them to fight, but Israel smote him with the edge of the sword and took possession of his land. If Moshe had not sent messengers to the king of Edom, Sihon would not have had the courage to go out to fight against them, for fear of the Lord, and they would have required a long time to subdue all his land. This is the meaning of the hardening

Sefer HaIkkarim — BOOK [Maamar] FOUR

of heart of which the Bible speaks in such expressions as: "For the Lord thy God hardened his spirit ... that He might deliver him into thy hand ..."

In this way we can explain why the Torah mentions the incident of the mission to the king of Edom. For at first sight, it would seem to be obviously discreditable to Israel. When Israel said: "Thou shalt sell me food for money ...," the king of Edom thought that they were in want of bread and water, since they were willing to pay him for water, and therefore he asked to be paid also for allowing them to pass, so that Israel was obliged to say: "And if we drink of thy water, I and my cattle, then will I give the price thereof," explaining that it was not necessary for them to buy water, but if they drank it, they would pay. But, they said, we will not pay for the mere passage. Then the king of Edom said: "Thou shalt not pass through. And ... came out against him with much people, and with a strong hand." God, then, commanded Israel to turn away from him, and Moshe and all Israel were astonished at this. Later when God commanded them to send messengers to Sihon, king of Heshbon, against whom, when he came out against them, they fought and whom they defeated, they understood the deep thoughts of God. It was clear to them then that the command of God to send messengers to the king of Edom and the king of Moab and to turn away from them, was in order to strengthen the heart of Sihon, that he should go out to fight, so that Israel might defeat him and take quick possession of his land, in order to show his bad will.

Accordingly we say that one who repents from fear in the manner of Sihon and Pharaoh, is not credited with repentance at all, but he who repents from fear because he believes in Providence, and for this reason is afraid of the word of God and does not seek for pretexts and extraneous explanations for God's righteous judgments, but recognizes that all things that happen to a person are the result of providence and in the nature of punishment for his evil deeds, - a person of this sort deserves compensation for his repentance, though it is from fear, and concerning him Resh Lakish said that his wilful deeds are accounted as though they were unintentional, as he infers from the biblical expression: "For thou hast stumbled in thine iniquity." From the text it would seem as if it refers to one who has not repented at all, but Resh Lakish infers from the expression: "Return O Israel, unto ['ad] the Lord" [instead of to ['el]], that the text refers to one who has returned a little, but has not completely returned to God, from love. The first mode of repentance, namely from fear, still has remaining in it the obstacle of iniquity: "For thou

Sefer Halkkarim   BOOK [Maamar] FOUR

hast stumbled in thine iniquity."

We still have to explain, however, the statement that if a man repents from love, his wilful misdeeds are converted for him into merits. Justice dictates that it is sufficient that repentance wipes out a man's sins, so that they are as if they had never been, but how can such a person attain any degree meriting future life? If he has no merits, his status is zero and there is no distinction in this respect between the one who repents from fear and the one who repents from love.

The explanation of the difficulty is as follows: Strict justice has no room for repentance at all, as we explained in the beginning of the chapter. Repentance is a matter of divine grace and charity. Hence there is no reason for surprise if God's infinite kindness goes so far. Hosea explains this matter, when he says concerning the penitent: "I will heal their backsliding." His contemporaries expressed their doubts and said to him: How is it possible that repentance should avail the person to obtain reward or happiness, since it is quite sufficient if it wipes out his sins? The person remains, therefore, equally devoid of sins as well as merits, how then can he be entitled to divine pleasure or love, which are promised in the Bible to the penitent? To this the prophet answers in the name of God: "I will hear their backsliding, I will love them freely," i.e., It is true that the penitent does not deserve any degree of happiness by his own merit, the love of God which comes to him through repentance is due to divine grace and is in the nature of charity. This may be either because the precept of repentance stands higher than all the other precepts of the Torah, and through it alone one can attain the purpose intended by the Torah, viz. the love of God, or it means literally that the penitent gets his reward as a matter of pure grace and generosity, as we read: "I will love them freely," i.e., as their repentance came from love, so I will love them freely. David also, when he repented of the Bathsheba affair, said: "And let a willing spirit uphold me," i.e., a spirit of free gift and grace, not as the result of any merit, but as coming purely from God's love and from the kindness which flows from God and influences every man in the measure in which he prepares himself to receive the divine kindness. The Psalmist also says: "So shalt thou delight thyself in the Lord;" "Ask of Me, and I will give the nations for thine inheritance;" "Open thy mouth wide and I will fill it." We thus see that he makes the granting of the favor dependent upon the asking.

A person who repents from fear, does so because he is afraid that punishment will come upon him for the sins he has committed. God, as a reward for his repentance, gives him grace as he requests, protects him from punishment, converts his wilful misdeeds into errors, and he is not punished for them, but requires atonement as for a deed done in error. But he who repents from love, not from fear of the punishment that may come upon him for his sin, who is not afraid of punishment, his heart being "as an adamant harder than flint," in bearing punishment, who repents solely from a love of God, because he desires to do that which is pleasing to God solely because it is pleasing to God, as a lover does that which is pleasing to his friend, not because of the fear of any punishment, - such a person attains through such repentance the purpose intended by the Torah, viz. the love of God. Therefore, it is fitting that God should love him, as we read: "I love them that love me," which is not the case in the one who repents from fear. Therefore, it is not proper that they should stand on the same plane. Nevertheless, although the repentance is not at first due to love, as is proper, but to fear of punishment, God promises that He will help him who repents in the first place from fear to achieve complete repentance before God, viz. repentance from love. This we infer from the fact that in the beginning of the section dealing with repentance, it says: "In thy distress, when all these things are come upon thee …," showing that the original motive of repentance was the fear of punishment which has come upon him. Then it says: "And the Lord thy God will circumcise thy heart …," which indicates that though originally repentance was due to fear, God will circumcise the heart of the sinner and help him to repent from love, which is true repentance, as we explained.

Chapter 26

The elements of repentance by which a person may be cleansed of his iniquities and purified of his sin before God are correction of thought, speech and act. Correction of thought means that he should feel regret on account of his sins. Correction of speech signifies that he should confess his transgressions; while correction of act denotes that he should take it upon himself never again to return to his folly, but should do instead such acts as would indicate that the former were done in error and unintentionally.

It is clearly expressed in the Prophets that regret is essential to repentance. Jeremiah says: "No man repenteth him of his wickedness, saying: 'What have I done?'" Joel says: "Who knoweth whether He will not turn and repent, and leave a blessing behind Him." Confession is specifically mentioned in the Torah: "Then they shall confess their sin which they have done;" "And they shall confess their iniquity and the iniquity of their fathers;" "He shall confess that wherein he hath sinned." A promise not to repeat the sin is also mentioned by the prophet: "Neither will we call any more the work of our hands our gods;" and in the Psalms we read: "For He will speak peace unto His people, and to His saints; But let them not turn back to folly."

The things hindering and preventing repentance are three: ignorance of having committed a sin, excusing oneself, and the love of money and glory. It is clear that every one of these hinders repentance. If a man does not recognize or know that he has sinned, he will never regret doing the thing he does, nor repent, as a sick man can not be cured as long as he does not feel or know that he is sick, for he will never seek a cure. So, if one does not know that he has sinned, he will never repent. For this reason, God found fault with Israel for not recognizing their sins, for this was a reason why they did not repent: "I will go and return to My place, till they acknowledge their fault, and seek My face," i.e., until they regard themselves as transgressors and sinners, when they will repent and seek My face. David also said: "For I know my transgressions." God said: "Cry aloud," indicating that a knowledge of one's sin is essential to repentance.

It is also clear from the thing itself that self-excuse prevents repentance. For if a man thinks that excusing himself for his sin will avail him, he will never regret the doing of it, nor confess his sin. Such a one is called a man "who covers his transgressions," as Solomon says: "He that covereth his transgressions shall not prosper." Covering one's sin means to make something else responsible for one's sin, as Job says: "If after the manner of Adam, I covered my transgressions." The reference is to Adam, who excused himself for his sin by saying: "The woman whom Thou gavest to be with me, she gave me of the tree ..." But his excuse did not do him any good, for man was given reason so that he should always watch his conduct and not sin. This is why one who commits a misdeed through error is called a sinner and requires atonement. Similarly, one must be careful not to be misled by any one, and hence Adam was told: "Because thou hast hearkened unto the voice of thy wife ... cursed is the ground ...," although Adam had not been told not to listen to the voice of his wife. This shows that it does not avail one to excuse himself by saying, So and so made me sin, for nothing excuses a sin except absolute compulsion, concerning which the Rabbis say that heaven acquits a man in case of

Sefer Halkkarim   BOOK [Maamar] FOUR

compulsion. We shall treat of the subject of compulsion in the next chapter.

Love of money and of glory prevents repentance. For if a person repents in order to get some financial benefit or honor, his act is not repentance at all. One must undertake not to return again to folly for the love of God and not for any other motive. Thus, David said that his repentance should be accepted because there was no element in it to prevent its acceptance: "I acknowledged my sin unto Thee, and mine iniquity have I not hidden ..." The words: "I acknowledged my sin," allude to the necessity of knowing that one has sinned. "And mine iniquity have I not hid," indicates that he did not excuse himself for his sin. Then he says: "I said: 'I will make confession concerning my transgressions,' " to show that his repentance and confession were solely for the love of God and not for the sake of money or glory.

Saul's repentance when he sinned in reference to Amalek lacked these three requirements, and therefore even though he confessed his sin before Samuel twice, saying: "I have sinned," his repentance was not accepted. At first, he denied the sin, not knowing that he had committed one. When Samuel said to him: "Wherefore then didst thou not hearken to the voice of the Lord ...? he replied: "Yea, I have hearkened to the voice of the Lord, and have gone the way which the Lord sent me ..." And when Samuel said to him that this obstinacy was a greater sin than his disobedience in the first place, which was the sin proper: "For rebellion is as the sin of witchcraft, and stubbournness is as idolatry and teraphim," - i.e.: rebellion, which was the main sin of Saul, is like the sin of witchcraft, which is an ordinary negative commandment, whereas stubbornness, viz. his insisting that he had not sinned, is like idolatry and teraphim, which is more serious than witchcraft to which his main sin is compared - when Samuel said these things to him, Saul was led to admit that he had sinned, and said, "I have sinned," but he excused himself for his sin by words of falsehood, when he said: "Because I feared the people ..." Therefore, Samuel refused to return with him when he asked him: "And return with me, that I may worship the Lord," and replied: "I will not return with thee; for thou hast rejected the word of the Lord ... And as Samuel turned about to go away ..." This was because the acknowledgement of his sin was not genuine, since he excused himself with words of falsehood. Later on, when Saul admitted that he had sinned, and said simply, "I have sinned," Samuel consented to return with him. But since Saul showed that his repentance was for the sake of receiving honor, as he said: "Honour

Sefer Halkkarim — BOOK [Maamar] FOUR

me now, I pray thee ...," and not for the love of God, his repentance was not accepted, and Samuel was told at once to anoint David as king.

For this reason, the years of Saul's reign after this time are not counted as part of his reign. This we infer as follows: David was a fugitive from Saul two years or more, for the Bible says that he was a year and four months in the country of the Philistines, not to count the long time that he hid himself in Palestine in the wilderness of Ziph, in the fortress and in Carmel with the shepherds of Nabal. And yet the Bible tells us: "When Saul had reigned a year [Saul reigned two years over Israel], Saul chose three thousand men ..." The meaning is that one year after he was anointed king, he chose the three thousand men and began to wage wars, and after that, we are told, he reigned over Israel two years and no more. Now it is impossible that he should have waged all those wars which the Bible mentions: "And fought against all his enemies on every side, against Moab, and against the children of Ammon, and against Edom, and against the kings of Zobah, and against the Philistines ..." - all this in two years, while pursuing David at the same time. The only explanation is that the moment David was anointed king, Saul's reign was not counted, though he was still king in fact. In the same way we find that Ish-bosheth reigned over Israel all those years that David reigned in Hebron over Yehuda, namely seven years, and yet he is credited only with the two years that he was king without any wars, as we read: "Ish-bosheth, Saul's son, was forty years old when he began to reign over Israel, and he reigned two years." After his two years' reign, war broke out between the house of Saul and the house of David. The house of Saul was getting weaker and weaker, while the house of David was getting stronger. These years were not counted in Ish-bosheth's reign. In the same way Saul's years were no counted to his credit after David was anointed king.

There is a question, however, why was Saul punished for his sin by having the kingdom taken away from him, and not in some other way, as David was punished for the Bathsheba affair, without losing his kingdom? The reason, according to my opinion, is that David's sin did not regard a specific commandment which was given to him after he was king, or a specific command given in the Torah which concerned him as king. His sin concerned a commandment which he had in common with all men, for the prohibition of adultery or homicide is common to all men. Therefore, it was fitting that his punishment should be like that given to the generality of men. Saul, on the other hand, sinned in reference to a specific command given

Sefer HaIkkarim   BOOK [Maamar] FOUR

to him by Samuel after he was king, or given to him because he was king, for Samuel said to him: "Seven days shalt thou tarry, till I come unto thee." He also told him: "Now go and smite Amalek ... and spare them not ..." For this reason, he was punished by having the kingdom removed from his descendants and by dying prematurely. Hence, when he transgressed Samuel's command and offered a burnt-offering in Gilgal before Samuel came, he was told: "But now thy kingdom shall not continue," i.e., the kingdom would be cut off from his descendants, but he was not told that he would die before his time. But when he sinned in relation to Amalek, he was told: "Because thou hast rejected the word of the Lord, He hath also rejected thee from being king." This means that he would die prematurely and that henceforth the kingdom would not be credited to him, for a thing that has been rejected can not be maintained by man. Therefore, when Saul brought up Samuel with the aid of the witch, Samuel said to him: "Because thou didst not hearken to the voice of the Lord, and didst not execute His fierce wrath upon Amalek ...; and to-morrow shalt thou and thy sons be with me." In these words, he indicated to him that because the commandments in question were specifically given to him, he would die before his time, and his kingdom would be cut off from him.

An allusion to this reason is found in the promise God made to Jehu, that the kingdom would be established in the hand of his descendants unto the fourth generation, because he observed the specific command, he had been given to destroy the house of Ahab and the worshippers of Baal. Similarly, because Solomon transgressed the commandment against multiplying wives and other specific commandments given to him as king, the kingdom of the ten tribes was taken away from his descendants, and he had left only the tribes of Yehuda and Benjamin because of the oath God had sworn to David. This is my opinion in this matter.

Some have given another explanation of this matter, as follows: Saul committed a misdeed in relation to the kingly art, hence it was fitting that he should lose that art, whereas David did not sin in relation to the kingly art, his sin was different and had nothing to do with the kingly art, hence he was forgiven. It is like the case of two scribes of whom one is found guilty of forging a document and the other of an incestuous marriage. When the king administers to each of them the punishment that befits the crime, punishing with stripes the one guilty of incest, there is no reason why he should lose his position, and he therefore retains his position as before. The scribe, on the other hand, who forged a document, in addition to being punished for his crime, deserves to be removed from his position and not to be trusted with such an office. In the same way, since Saul committed a wrong pertaining to the kingly art, in that he spared Agag and did not execute proper vengeance on Amalek, he deserved to be removed from it.

This explanation, however, without further qualification, will not do, because he was told before the war with Amalek: "But now thy kingdom will not stand," as a punishment for bringing a burnt-offering in Gilgal before Samuel came. But it is possible to amend this explanation and reduce it to the first, as follows: viz. by explaining the qualities requisite in a king in such a way that the first sin will be included under one of them.

It seems, then, that there are six qualities a king, as such, must have. The purpose of appointing a king is to fight the enemy and to judge the people justly. When Israel demanded a king, they said: "That our king may judge us, and go out before us, and fight our battles." Hence, he must have the qualities necessary for this purpose. Now we know that judges must have four qualities: They must be men of valor, God-fearing, men of truth, and hating unlawful gain. If we add to these the qualities necessary in war, we shall have six.

One is that the king must be cruel to strangers, but merciful to his own people and willing to give his life to save them, as a shepherd ought to risk his life to remove harm and to fight with the lion and the bear in order to preserve the flock and show kindness to them: "Gathereth the lambs in his arm, and carrieth them in his bosom, and gently leadeth those that give suck." The second quality is to be good to those who are good to him, to his servants and those who fight his battles, for if he will not do this, who will risk his life for the king's glory and who will take his part against those who are treacherous? The third quality is that he should hate unlawful gain and not be covetous. A shepherd that is appointed to guard the sheep must not strip their skin and their flesh from their bones, for in that case the relation would be reversed, the flock would support the shepherd instead of the shepherd guarding the flock. For this reason, the Bible says: "Neither shall he greatly multiply to himself silver and gold," for if he takes pains to gather silver and gold, even though it be from the enemy, he will take from his own people if he can not find it among the enemy. The fourth quality is that he should be a man of valor, strong and mighty to "break the jaws of the unrighteous." He must not respect the faces of the poor, nor honor the faces of the great, nor fear to do justice. The fifth quality is that he should speak the truth, no wrong must be found upon his lips, and he should judge a righteous judgment, for the man who lies or speaks falsehoods, does so either from fear or because he can not obtain his desire without it, but the judge must not be afraid of any man, as we read in the Bible: "Ye shall not be afraid of the face of any man," not to speak of the king, for there is no one to prevent him from doing what he will. Hence, he must not speak falsely. Besides, no one will trust the words of the king if he speaks falsely. The sixth quality is that he should fear God and tremble at His words. He should be submissive to those who serve God, and observe those commandments which he was given in the capacity of king or after he became king. And in regard to the other commandments, too, he must not consider himself as superior to his brethren and think he is free from the commandments any more than they, as the Bible says: "That his heart be not lifted up above his brethren and that he turn not aside from the commandment, to the right hand, or to the left." A similar thought is expressed in the saying of the wise man: "The king and the law are faithful brothers." If, therefore, the people see the king disregarding the law and the teachers thereof, they will all come to ignore it, and the whole Torah will fall.

Now if we examine Saul's qualities, we find that he was lacking in all of them.

1. He spared Agag [The Rabbis say, commenting on the verse: "And he lay in wait in the valley" - "In the valley," means concerning the doings in the valley. Saul used a foolish a fortiori argument. If, said he, when one life is taken, the Torah says: Take a heifer and break its neck ...], and was cruel to his own people, in that he destroyed Nob, the city of the priests. David acted differently. He smote Moab and put them under saws and under harrows of iron, but when he saw the destroying angel, he said: "Lo, I have sinned, and I have done iniquitously; but these sheep, what have they done? Let Thy hand, I pray Thee, be against me, and against my father's house."

2. He did not treat David kindly, who risked his life when he slew Goliath. David, on the contrary, gave an order at the time of his death: "But show kindness unto the sons of Barzillai the Gileadite."

3. The Bible says concerning Saul: "But didst fly upon the spoil." David was different. He was generous and divided the spoil, saying: "Behold, a present for you of the spoil of the enemies of the Lord."

4. Saul said: "Because I feared the people, and hearkened to their voice," whereas David was not afraid to do justice, as the Bible

Sefer HaIkkarim   BOOK [Maamar] FOUR

says: "And David executed justice and righteousness unto all his people."

5. Saul lied to Samuel so as to cover his transgressions, while David confessed at once when Nathan the prophet came to him after he had gone in to Bathsheba.

6. He did not obey Samuel, but violated the specific commands which were given to him, whereas David obeyed all the commands of Nathan the prophet, Gad the seer, and Samuel. In this way it is clear that by reason of this sixth quality, the second explanation is reduced to the first.

When we examine the texts, we also find that David was perfect in all these qualities, while Saul lacked them all. This was why God saw to it that the kingdom did not remain with Saul and why Saul left no descendants worthy of the kingship. Even Abner, the chief of his army, died in order that the kingdom might be firmly established in the hand of David and his children, as a lesson and example to the kings who came after him, that they should not in their pride disobey God's will, for the kingdom is His. Hence a human king should not slight those who serve God and observe His Torah, for He alone is the King of Glory, as I explained before, and the Bible says: "He removeth kings and setteth up kings."

To return to the subject of the chapter, we say that just as the repentance of Saul was not accepted because it lacked the three requirements that we mentioned, so the repentance of David after the Bathsheba affair was accepted because it fulfilled the three requirements mentioned. This is clear from the expressions he uses on that occasion: "Be gracious unto me, O God, according to Thy mercy." These words indicate that repentance is accepted only as a matter of grace, as we said before. Then he says: "According to the multitude of Thy compassions blot out my transgressions," i.e., even though my transgressions are great and many, blot them out according to the multitude of Thy compassions, which are infinite, so that my power to sin may not be greater than Thy power to forgive. Then he adds: "For I know my transgressions," alluding to the first requirement, and stating that the sin was not unknown to him. "And my sin is ever before me," indicates that he offered no excuses for his sin, nor pretended that he had not sinned, but was always aware that he had sinned. "Against Thee, thee only, have I sinned," alludes to the third requirement. It shows that his repentance was not due to the desire for honor or money or the fear of human punishment, but to the love of God, for his transgressions were those which concerned the relations between God and man, i.e., private matters, which men did not know, but only God.

He repeats: "And done that which is evil in Thy sight," to indicate his confession of both kinds of sins, those concerning the relations between man and God, and those between man and his fellow. He alludes to the former in the words: "Against Thee, thee only, have I sinned." To the latter, such as, "You shall not steal," "You shall not oppress," and so on, he refers in the words: "And done that which is evil in Thy sight," the meaning being that though they are precepts which govern the relations between man and man, nevertheless since God is the author of those commandments, the man who violates His commandments is evil in the sight of God. "That Thou mayest be justified when Thou speakest, and be in the right when Thou judgest," - these words go back to the prayer: "Blot out my transgressions, wash me thoroughly from my iniquity, and cleanse me from my sin," and the meaning is: Blot out my transgressions in order that Thou mayest be justified in Thy statement that Thou receivest penitents and forgivest their sins. And in order that Thou mayest be right when Thou judgest a man for his sin, since he can repent and does not, cleanse me from my sin, since I do repent before Thee. Some say that the words in question allude to the statement made to Cain: "If thou doest well, shall it not be lifted up?" and to the judgment decreed upon him.

Since a sin may be committed in thought, in speech and in act, or in all the three combined, repentance must include the three. Regret corresponds to thought, confession to speech, and corresponding to act it is not sufficient that one discontinues the sin, but he must do acts of a nature opposed to the transgressions which he has committed.

For this reason, David prayed for all three. In relation to thought he said: "Create me a clean heart, O God …" In regard to speech, he said, "O Lord, open Thou, my lips; and my mouth shall declare Thy praise." With regard to action, he said: "I will teach transgressors Thy ways," i.e., he will do acts opposed to the transgressions in order that men may see and take instruction and learn to return to the Lord. The prophet also makes it clear that repentance requires the doing of acts opposed to the transgressions: "And God saw their works that they turned from their evil way." Our Rabbis explain this verse as follows: It does not say: "He saw their sackcloth and fasting," but, "He saw their works." This shows that if one of them, by force, took away a beam from his neighbor and inserted it into a palace he was building, he threw down the whole palace [in order to return the beam to its owner.] Isaiah also said: "Let the wicked forsake his way, and the man of iniquity his thoughts." The first part of the verse refers to a transgression carried out in deed, in which case the remedy is recommended of doing acts opposed to the transgression and choosing another mode of conduct. For example, if his sin consisted in eating forbidden food, he should fast and not eat enough even of those things which are permitted, as the Rabbis say: "Sanctify thyself in those things which are permitted to thee." And if his sin was that he did not give alms, he should give lavishly of his money to the poor. And if he taught men to neglect the commandments, he should teach them the proper way to be punctilious about the commandments and to return to God, for he who makes others sin can not do complete repentance. For how can he correct the wrong he has done in causing a man to sin? Hence David says: "Then will I teach transgressors Thy ways," and similarly in other cases of transgressions. If a man's sin is one of thought only, he should purify his thoughts before Him who knows man's thoughts: "And the man of iniquity [shall forsake] his thoughts."

"And let him return unto the Lord and He will have compassion upon him" - this alludes to the fact that repentance must be solely for the love of God and not for the pleasure of money or the love of glory. "And to our God [let him return] for He will abundantly pardon" - this is intended to encourage penitents, who must not despair of repentance because of their many sins, for God's forgiveness is more abundant than their iniquities. Hence a man must know that if he does not repent, he deserves severe punishment, since it lies in his power to repent and he does not; he should fear that God will punish him if he does not repent when he is able: "For with Thee there is forgiveness, that Thou mayest be feared." At first sight the expression just quoted seems strange, for how does it follow that because forgiveness is with God, He is to be feared? The contrary would seem to be the case, namely that if a man knows that God will forgive all his iniquities, he will not be afraid to sin. But the passage is to be explained as we suggested. A man is not afraid of a thing that is inevitable, for example death. If then punishment were inevitable when one has sinned and there were no hope of forgiveness, a person would not be afraid of God, as he would know that he can not escape punishment, since he can not help sinning. But since as a matter of fact he knows that God forgives sinners if they repent and he can escape punishment, he will necessarily be afraid that if he continues to sin and does not think of repenting, God will refuse to forgive him. Therefore, the sinner will be afraid of

God, since he knows that punishment is not inevitable for a sinner, and that if he repents before God with all his heart and with all his soul and with all his might, God will have pity upon him and abundantly forgive him, for forgiveness is His.

Chapter 27

There is a great difficulty in connection with repentance as we explained it, as follows: Since the transgression has been carried out in deed, how can repentance, in the form of regret and confession, avail? If a man takes a life or profanes the Sabbath, does the life of the murdered person return to him, or does the profaned Sabbath become observed through confession and regret? It is like a person throwing down a house and then rebuilding it with his mouth. Words without deeds can not rebuild the house. How then can such repentance avail to wipe out and cleanse a sin actually committed? This is a matter that requires an explanation, viz. in what way repentance benefits the penitent.

Human acts deserving praise or blame are those which are voluntary and done of one's own free will. This means that the person who does the act knows at the time of doing the act that he is doing it, and desires to do it in preference to something else. Hence drunkards excuse themselves for acts committed by them while they were in a state of intoxication, saying that they did not know what they were doing, though they did the act voluntarily and freely. Similarly, we do not blame a person for an act committed involuntarily, even though it was done knowingly and deliberately, i.e., that he knew what he was doing at the time and chose to do it rather than bear the punishment he would have received if he had not done it. As long as the act was not done voluntarily but under compulsion, the person is not blamed. It follows then that an act for which a person deserves praise if it is good and blame if it is bad, is such as he does knowingly when he does it and willingly, in preference to something else. Acts to which praise and blame do not apply at all are those of absolute compulsion, such namely as the person does not know of, does not desire, nor prefer to other acts, as for example, when a person throws a stone and another puts out his head, is struck and dies. Here the person who is the cause of the death did not know of the act when he did it, exercised no preference in regard to it, and did not desire it. This is an instance of absolute compulsion, to which praise and blame do not apply. Hence the Torah does not banish a compulsory homicide of this sort, but only an unintentional homicide in which there is a combination of compulsion and free will.

Those acts which combine compulsion and freedom and which stand midway between the two kinds mentioned before, are hard to classify. Shall they be assigned to the class of compulsory acts or to that of free acts, or shall we say that some of them should be classed with compulsory acts and others with free acts? Thus if a man does a bad thing from fear of violence at the hands of strong men, it would seem as if such an act belongs to the compulsory class and is done under necessity; except that if the act is such that one should endure any pain and trouble rather than do it, it should be classed in the voluntary group; while, on the other hand, if the act is such that it is not worth while suffering great pain and trouble on account of it, it should be classified among compulsory acts.

Now if we examine the matter carefully, we see that there must be certain acts rather than do which one should endure any pain in the world. Such acts, when done, must be classified as voluntary rather than compulsory; because any act which a person does and at the time of doing it chooses to do it in preference to something else, is to be classed as voluntary rather than compulsory. Hence a person deserves blame if he does not suffer great trouble or extraordinary pain rather than lift his hand to strike his father or rebel against his king or his God. On the other hand, there are acts for the sake of which it is not necessary to endure great pain or trouble.

It seems therefore that we should define a voluntary act as follows: Any act a person does which, at the time of doing it, he desires and prefers to something else, and which, after it is done, he desires to maintain, i.e., desires it to have been done, must be classified as voluntary, even though at the beginning there is some element of compulsion; as, for example, when travellers on the sea cast their cargo overboard when a great storm comes. Although no man throws his cargo overboard voluntarily, and the act seems compulsory, nevertheless, since he chooses this in preference to his own pain and danger, it should be classed as voluntary, because even after they land, they accept the deed that was done and desire it to have been done because they owe to it their survival. Such acts must therefore be classed as voluntary and not as compulsory. On the other hand, if after landing they are not satisfied and desire the opposite, the act should be classed as compulsory, since they do not desire to maintain the act. It seems, however, that since there is no man who would not always prefer to cast his merchandise into the sea in order to save his life, we must class such an act as voluntary

Sefer HaIkkarim — BOOK [Maamar] FOUR

without qualification, since a person in all cases desires to maintain it. From the above it follows that any act done voluntarily at the time which, after it is done, the author does not accept or ratify, but desires it not to have been done, should be classed as compulsory or as done by mistake even though in the beginning it was done voluntarily, or at least the will played a part in its doing. But if after the act is done, he desires and accepts it and is satisfied that it should have been done, it must be classed as voluntary, even though in the beginning there was some compulsion.

The same thing appears also from the statement of the Rabbis: "The rule is that a leading question is permitted for releasing a vow in case the person regrets it." In the Talmud it is explained that the person is asked, "Do you still desire to abide by the vow?" or, "Are you sorry?" This shows that everything depends upon the continuance of the will. If the will continues, the oath continues to bind him, and if the will does not continue, the oath is regarded as having been made by mistake and is annulled even though originally it was taken voluntarily. According to this if a penitent regrets his sin and determines in his mind that he wishes he had not done the transgression which he has done and that if he finds himself in the same position again, he will not do it, his regret shows that the act was done in the first place by mistake and without real understanding. This agrees with Aristotle, who says in his Ethics that an act of reason does not permit of retraction.

The Rabbis say: When is one a penitent? Answer: If a temptation comes to him more than once and he escapes it. Rab Yehuda says: Provided it happens at the same time and place and in relation to the same woman. The meaning is that if the temptation comes to him under the same circumstances as before and he subdues his desire for the love of God and does not yield, it is clear that he feels real regret and has determined in his mind that the act which he committed in the first place was done in error and without knowledge, since he regrets it. A man should not be punished for a transgression of this sort, as one should not be blamed for an act done in ignorance and through a mistake. Similarly, a person should not be praised for a good act unless it was done voluntarily in the first place and its continuance is desired after it is done, i.e., it is accepted and the person feels no regret. If he changes his mind, he loses his reward and the act is not credited to him.

The Rabbis explain this matter. Commenting on the biblical verse: "But when the righteous turneth away from his righteousness, and committeth iniquity ... for his trespass that he trespassed ... shall he die," they ask: Why should he not be treated as though he were half meritorious and half guilty? And the answer is, as Rab says, that the text refers to a person who regrets the good acts he has done formerly. Here we see that even a good act is not deserving of praise or reward unless the agent accepts it as done and does not regret it, but if he does regret it, it is as if it had not been done and he does not deserve any reward. According to this it is clear that if one duly regrets a transgression he has committed and does not desire its continuance, he shows thereby that the act was not absolutely voluntary and that if he had been left to his simple will in its present determination, he would not have done it. The proof of it is that the same temptation came to him another time and he escaped it knowingly, willingly and freely, because he thought that the thing is evil in the sight of God and a man must not do that which is evil in God's sight. This is complete repentance. This is the way in which repentance benefits the penitent. It renders the evil deed as though it had not been done and as though it had been done in error and ignorance. In this way one has his sins wiped out. By grace it is credited to him as a merit, and God loves him by an act of charity, as was explained above.

Chapter 28

The acceptance of repentance is, indeed, a matter of grace, as we have explained, nevertheless there is a certain necessity in the existence of this grace. Every agent always desires that his activity should realize the purpose intended. The purpose of the creation of man is the survival of the soul after death, as we explained in Book Three. Since man is the work of God, He desires that he should attain the purpose intended, namely the immortality of the soul.
Now the evil inclination of man importunes him every day and entices him to sin, as Solomon describes in Ecclesiastes. In speaking of the inveigling words of the evil inclination, he describes how he entices and persuades man with smooth words, little by little, until he finally makes a complete sinner of him. At first he says to him: "Go thy way, eat thy bread with joy." From the context it is clear that these are the words of the evil inclination, speaking to the penitent, who is always worried about his sins. So he says to him: "Go thy way, eat thy bread with joy ... For God hath already accepted thy works." Now there is no one, however pious he may be, who would not be persuaded by words like these, in which there seems to be nothing lurking of sin or evil. When the person lends a

willing ear to this, the evil inclination continues: "Let thy garments be always white," i.e., take care of thy personal appearance and make thyself handsome. Having persuaded him to this, too, in which there is no sin, he continues: "Enjoy life with the wife whom thou lovest ..." Having brought him to this stage, where he obeys him in all these things, which are legitimate, he does not rest until he brings him to deny the fundamental principles of the faith, saying: There is no judgment, there is no judge and there is no giving account for one's deeds: "Whatsoever thy hand attaineth to do by thy strength, that do; for there is no work, nor device, nor knowledge, nor wisdom, in the grave, whither thou goest." He goes on to prove his statement by saying: "I returned, and saw under the sun, that the race is not to the swift ... neither yet bread to the wise ... but time and chance happeneth to them all."

With these words and others like them he turns the man away from the right path and leads him in an evil way, pretending that he is interested in the person's good and concerned about his honor and welfare, as he behaved in the early time of the creation towards Eve, when he said to her: "**Af** [Yea], hath God said: Ye shall not eat of any tree of the garden?" The word af here, in my opinion, denotes "anger," and the meaning of the sentence is, I am very angry that God said to you you shall not eat of all the trees of the garden except certain ones, for the command was not given for your benefit, as the opposite would be more beneficial to you. In this way he persuaded her, so that she left the ways of right to walk in the ways of darkness. In the same way a man's evil inclination constantly devises means to hurt him and to seduce him, as God Himself testifies: "For the imagination of man's heart is evil from his youth." And the Rabbis say in this connection: Bad indeed is the dough which the baker himself admits to be bad.

Hence a person can not help sinning in act whether little or much, and if he sins, he can not help doubting in his mind some one of the principles of the faith; for whoever commits a sin deliberately, would never have permitted himself to commit it unless an evil thought had come into his mind, as our Rabbis say: A person does not commit a sin unless a spirit of madness enters into him. Either he denies in thought the existence of God, thinking there is no one who governs the world, and therefore he permits himself to commit the transgression, as the Bible says: "The fool hath said in his heart: 'There is no God;' they have dealt corruptly, they have done abominably; there is none that doeth good." We thus see that the reason for committing a sin is that he thinks there is no God. Or he

Sefer HaIkkarim — BOOK [Maamar] FOUR

admits that there is a God who brought the world into being, but thinks that He does not concern Himself with the individual and does not reward or punish him for his deeds. This too leads him to permit himself to sin, as we read: "Wherefore doth the wicked contemn God? Because he sayeth in his heart: 'Thou wilt not require.'" Or he admits that there is a God who governs the world and takes account of man's deeds, but he says to himself, may be God did not give this command or did not prohibit this act - for example, he thinks that God did not forbid the eating of fat or blood or intercourse with a menstruous woman, and therefore he permits himself to do these things. Such a person virtually denies revelation of the Torah. For our Rabbis say: He who says concerning a verse or even a single word of the Torah that Moshe said it of his own accord, comes within the designation of those who deny the divine revelation of the Torah.

Now it is clear that if he thinks in any one of the three ways we mentioned, he is denying one of the fundamental general principles of a divine law, principles which embrace all the rest, as we have explained. This is surely a more serious thing than the eating of fat or blood. This is the reason why the Rabbis say: Thoughts of sin are worse than sin itself. The reason is because the punishment for the commission of a sin is finite in duration, as we shall see, whereas the punishment for denying a principle is infinite in duration, as our Rabbis say: The judgment of the wicked in gehenna lasts twelve months, i.e., those wicked persons who transgress the words of the Torah without denying the fundamental principles. As for those who deny the fundamental principles, the Rabbis explained before that their punishment lasts forever: "But heretics [Minim] and traitors, those who deny the Torah, and those who deny the resurrection of the dead, go down to gehenna and are judged therein for generations and generations."

Now since those persons who escape denying one of the fundamental principles are, as we have seen, very few, and the majority would therefore deserve eternal punishment, God in His mercy and great kindness devised a mode of showing favor to the human race by opening to them the gates of repentance, in order that by means of it they may escape the snares of the evil spirit and the death of the soul. Our Rabbis say: A person's evil inclination opposes him constantly, as is said: "The wicked watcheth the righteous …," and if it were not for the help of God, he would not be able to overcome him, as is said: "The Lord will not leave him in his hand." This shows that through the help of God a person is delivered from the death which the evil spirit seeks to inflict upon him. Ezekiel explains that the death spoken of is that of the soul: "For I have no pleasure in the death of the dead, but rather that he should return from his ways and live." The expression, "in the death of the dead" [be-mot ha-met], indicates that he is speaking of one who is already dead, and the meaning is: I do not desire the soul's death of one who has died, but that he should return from his way during his lifetime so that his soul may live. It appears therefore that through repentance a man who has died does not die, but his soul lives and obtains life in the world to come. In this way man, who is the work of God, realizes his final purpose, his eternal life, even if he is guilty of a sin which is deserving of eternal punishment.

Isaiah has the same idea in mind, when he says concerning the penitent: "For I will not contend forever, neither will I be always wroth ..." The meaning is: Although by rights I should contend and be wroth for ever, inflicting upon the sinner eternal punishment, nevertheless I will not do it, "For the spirit [ruah] that enwrappeth itself is from Me, and the souls [neshamot] I have made." That is, although the animal spirit, which enwraps the body, is before Me, i.e., comes from the movers of the heavenly bodies who are before Me, the human souls I Myself made and must show them especial kindness since they are the work of My hands. [The word neshamah applies to the human soul, while ruah refers to the vital soul of animals: "He that giveth breath [neshamah] to the people upon it."] Since, therefore, the souls are the work of My hands, I must see to it that the human race should obtain the purpose intended in its creation. And therefore although "for the iniquity of his covetousness I was wroth and smote him," I did not smite him cruelly, but only to chastise him, in order that he may turn to Me in repentance. I did not smite him according to the punishment which he deserved for his sins, but, "I hid Me and was wroth," i.e., I hid My wrath from the punishment and was wroth only a little, in order to chastise him, because, "He went on frowardly in the way of his heart." But when "I saw his ways," i.e., his repentance, "I healed hini," i.e., I accepted his repentance even though he was near to his death; and therefore, "I will lead him" in the way of all the earth, and he will be gathered to his fathers, so that he may go to the world to come, with his sins forgiven, and I will thus "requite with comforts him and his mourners" - him, by giving him a share in the world to come; and his mourners, who will be comforted for his death when they know that his soul will not be cut off. The expression, "Comforts to his mourners," shows that he is speaking of a dead person. The expression, "I will heal him," is used because acceptance of repentance is a healing to the soul, which merits the life of the world to come.

We have thus explained that the existence of the Torah requires the existence of penitence, in order that the human race may obtain the purpose intended by its creation, which is the purpose of the whole sublunar world. This is what the Rabbis had in mind when they said that the Torah and repentance came before the creation of the world. This will suffice concerning repentance.

Chapter 29

We will now treat of reward and punishment, which is the third of the general principles of a divine law. It takes the place of the purpose intended by all laws. It is true that he who serves God from love does not concern himself at all about reward and punishment, having no other purpose except to fulfil the will of the object of his love, as the Rabbis say: "Be not like servants who serve their master in order to receive compensation …" But this does not mean that there is no reward and punishment, Heaven forbid! The above statement simply means that one who serves God from love must not be prompted in his service by love of reward and fear of punishment, though he believes that there is reward in store for those who believe and fear God and think on His name. All this reward is as nothing in his sight as compared with the purpose of fulfilling the will of the object of his love. Service of this sort leads to the ultimate reward and punishment that is intended in all laws.

Now inasmuch as the purpose of a divine law is different from those of conventional laws, as we said before, we laid it down as a general principle of divine law. We analyze the possibilities as follows: Either there is reward and punishment or there is not. If there is, it is either all corporeal and, in this world, or all spiritual and in the other world, or there is both corporeal reward in this world and spiritual reward in the next world.

Opinion, we find, is divided in the matter of reward and punishment into four classes according to the four possibilities of which the situation admits. Some believe there is no reward and punishment, either corporeal or spiritual. Some believe there is both corporeal and spiritual reward. Some believe there is corporeal reward but no spiritual, and some believe there is spiritual reward but no corporeal. This difference of opinion is based upon the division of opinion among men concerning the nature of the soul. Some say that the

Sefer HaIkkarim BOOK [Maamar] FOUR

human soul is not superior to the animal soul except that man has more shrewdness than the other animals in devising means and inventing arts necessary for arranging his life in a complete manner, as in the animal world some are superior to others in this respect. For this reason, those who hold this opinion think that there is no reward or punishment at all, either corporeal or spiritual. They hold that man is governed by accident like the other animals, concerning which the divine purpose is directed merely to the preservation of the species. This opinion has been given its death-blow by the philosophers, who say that the human soul can not be compared to the animal souls. The latter have only knowledge of particulars, while man has knowledge of universals. Moreover, man can perceive a thing when it is no longer present to the sense, while an animal can not. Man, moreover, distinguishes between substance and accident, and so on, all of which shows the great difference between the human soul and the animal soul. Hence there must be a special purpose that is peculiar to the human soul, as we explained before. Hence, though there is no spiritual perfection in animals, there must be such in man. The Jewish sages were also opposed to this opinion and maintained that there ought to be reward and punishment for man, either spiritual in the world to come, or corporeal in this world through divine providence, as we explained when we treated of Providence.

The second opinion is that there is reward and punishment, but that it is corporeal and in this world. Some believe that the human soul is superior to that of the animals because it has a rational power through which the divine spirit cleaves to man and provides for him according to the superiority of his intellect. But since this superiority is merely a capacity or preparation, it always requires, they say, a subject; and when the union between soul and body is sundered, the soul disappears. A certain school of philosophers erroneously adopt this view, saying that we can not conceive of any perfection of soul without the body. The Zadokites and the Boethusians adopted this view. They believed in the Torah of Moshe and in Providence, but maintained at the same time that reward and punishment are only corporeal and, in this world, as is mentioned in Abot de Rabbi Natan, and denied spiritual reward after death altogether. They adduced as proof of their opinion the fact that in the Law of Moshe there is no mention at all of spiritual reward, but only of physical prosperity. They adopted this erroneous opinion because they thought that the human soul is composed of various faculties, such as nutrition, growth, sensation, reason. And since we see that the other powers disappear when the union between soul and body is sundered, they said that the power of understanding which it has will also disappear along with the conceptions which it already has, and therefore the human soul will cease to exist like the souls of animals, and the one will die like the other.

The great philosophers, however, have refuted this opinion, saying that the variety of activities emanating from an agent does not necessarily prove multiplicity in the essence of the agent, as we explained above. Nor does the cessation of the life of the body necessarily prove the cessation of the rational soul, any more than the cessation of the power of growth after forty makes necessary the cessation of the soul. The body is an instrument through which some of the activities of the soul become visible. Hence when the instrument is destroyed, these functions alone disappear, like nutrition, growth, sensation. But it does not follow from this that the essence of the soul should disappear. For the existence of the reason is not dependent upon the body like the other corporeal powers. On the contrary, the reason grows stronger after the age of forty, when the corporeal powers grow weaker. Moreover, the reason is not like the corporeal powers, for it can perceive itself as well as its instruments, which is not the case in the corporeal powers. They adduce also other strong and irrefutable arguments to show that the human soul can not be compared with the soul of animals, but there is no need to expatiate upon this matter.

As an indication of the erroneous character of this opinion, Maimonides says in the Introduction to his commentary on Abot that the term soul in its application to the soul of man and that of animal is a homonym. And though we see that the functions emanating from the one are similar to those emanating from the other, it does not follow from this that the respective agents are similar in essence. The light of the sun and the light of a lamp are similar in that they illumine dark places, but this does not show that the agencies are alike. The light of the sun is permanent and does not go out, it illumines also where the sun does not shine; while a lamp goes out, is not permanent and illumines only where the ray strikes. It does not follow, therefore, that because the soul of the animal is destroyed, the human soul too is destroyed and ceases to be when it is separated from the body, since they admit that it is superior to the soul of the animal. As for the argument which the Zadokites and the Boethusians adduce in favor of their view from the fact that no mention is made in the Law of Moshe of spiritual reward, but only of corporeal, the facts are not as they say. Corporeal reward is mentioned only in those cases where there is no room for spiritual reward, and spiritual reward is mentioned by allusion, for a reason which we will explain later with the help of God.

The third opinion is the converse of the second, and is adopted by some of our Rabbis, who say: There is no reward for good deeds in this world. They adduce an argument from experience. A father says to his son, go up upon the tower and bring me some pigeons. The son goes up upon the tower, sends away the mother pigeon and takes the young, and on his return, he falls down and is killed. Where is his good and where is his length of days? The answer is that the scriptural promise, "That it may be well with thee," has reference to that world which is wholly good; and the promise, "That thou mayest prolong thy days," refers to that world which is altogether long [eternal]. The world that is wholly good and altogether long is none other than the world to come after death, and the promise has reference to spiritual reward.

This opinion is also adopted by a great school of philosophers, and some learned men of the Torah follow them. Their opinion is that man has no perfection qua man except after death, when the intellect is separated from matter and corporeal things. This follows from the fact that rational things are graded according to their degree of understanding, the one that understands more is superior to the one that understands less. Since, therefore, man's superiority to animals consists in his reason, his perfection must be a degree of excellence based upon intelligence alone. For if it consisted in a corporeal thing which is common to him and the animals, the perfection and rational superiority which were given to him above the animals would be a tantalizing punishment rather than a degree of perfection. For the animals, being devoid of reason and intelligence, are not troubled by the thought of misfortune which is fated to come upon them and are not grieved by the knowledge that they must die, as man does, nor do they anticipate in imagination the pain which is to come to them, and they worry about nothing; whereas man feels all this; he is worried and grieved on account of the evil that is destined to come upon him and lives in sorrow. Nay, the greater his power of understanding the more does he grieve for the evil that is destined to come upon him. For this reason, they say that it is not likely that the perfection to be attained by reason is something corporeal that is common to the lower animals, but that it must be something which distinguishes man from the animal, viz. intellect, and not a corporeal thing. This is the opinion of the Philosopher in this matter. Although he denies Providence, nevertheless he believes that the soul of man has a perfection after death, when it is separated from the body. And many of the sages of the Torah follow his opinion.

But there is a difficulty in this explanation. For though these arguments are a sound reply to the second opinion, still they do not prove that man's perfection is after death. For since perfection and permanence can pertain only to a rational thing, as they maintain, and the rational power in man is merely a preparation or capacity, how can we conceive of its surviving the body, since a capacity can not exist by itself? The statement in reply to this, namely that the acquired intellect becomes a substance through the concepts, so that the intellect and the concepts become identical, is unintelligible. For if the rational faculty in man is a hylic [material] power whose nature it is to cease to exist except through the activity of understanding, how can that activity exist by itself? And how can we conceive of its identifying itself with the Active Intellect? All this is very unlikely, as we explained before. Hence, some scholars say that the soul is a spiritual substance, having independent existence and the capacity of understanding. It can not therefore cease to exist, since it is an independent substance, and it feels pleasure according to its activity in cognition. But this is not correct, either. For, even though the soul be an independent substance, nevertheless, since it has the capacity of cognition, the perfection of this capacity would be in vain if the soul should not attain this cognition, and not one in a thousand would attain the perfection of the soul, and possibly no one at all, as we explained above; unless we say that the perfection of cognition consists in an understanding of the axioms. But if so, the righteous and the wicked would stand on the same plane, an idea which never occurred to any one before. It seems to us therefore that the proper and correct opinion of the Torah is that the soul is a spiritual substance, having the capacity to understand the service of God, and not mere understanding. Hence when a person attains any degree of understanding of God's service, by reason of attaining some idea or notion of God, be it great or small, he immediately attains a certain degree of life in the world to come. The Rabbis also say, commenting on the verse: "A seed shall serve Him," When do small children deserve the future life? Said they in the name of Rabbi Meir: As soon as they are able to say Amen, as is written: "Open ye the gates, That the righteous nation that keepeth faithfulness [emunim] may enter in." Read not: "That keepeth [shomer] faithfulness [emunim]," but: "That sayeth [she-omer] Amens [amenim]." The meaning of this is made clear from our explanation above, namely that the soul's perfection consists in

Sefer HaIkkarim — BOOK [Maamar] FOUR

understanding the service of God, whatever it be; so that when a child attains understanding of the least important service, viz. to say Amen to any benediction, he merits some degree of future life. This is in agreement with what we have written before, namely, that a man may attain a certain degree of future life by the fulfilment of one precept.

That the soul is an independent spiritual substance is also clear from the statement of the Rabbis that the world is maintained only by the breath of the mouth of the school children. Said Rab Papa to Abaye, What about your breath and mine? Said the latter: You can not compare breath that is without sin to breath that is with sin. Now if the soul is not an independent substance, how can school children, who have attained a very small degree of cognition, be superior to Abaye and Raba who attained a very high degree, without doubt? The truth is that a very small degree in God's service on the part of one who is not stained by sin, avails more than a high degree of one who is stained by sin; for the soul, being an independent spiritual substance, depends for its degree of worth upon the measure of its purity and its worship of God by fulfilling the commandments. This is the reason why Moshe was grieved because he could not enter the land and perform the commandments actually. He was not grieved about attaining ideas, for there is no doubt that Moshe had attained the degree where he could comprehend by means of understanding, but he was eager to carry out the commandments in practice, i.e., divine service with understanding, which gives perfection and permanence to the soul, as we explained before.

The Rabbis discuss the question whether the soul is in its essence a hylic [material] power or an independent substance. Two and a half years, we are told, the schools of Shammai and Hillel disputed the question whether it was worth while for man to have been created. The one said, It would have been better for man not to have been created than to have been created. The other said, It was better for man to have been created than not to have been created. They took a vote and decided that it would have been better if man had not been created, but now that he has been created, he must be careful about his conduct.

Now it seems to us that he who said it was better for man to have been created, held that man's soul is a hylic power, as the Philosopher thinks. Hence, he said that it was better for him to have been created, because existence is always better than non-existence, and one may rise to the degree of permanent existence by rational activity. On the other hand, the one who said that it would have been

Sefer HaIkkarim — BOOK [Maamar] FOUR

better for man not to have been created, believed that the soul is an independent spiritual substance. Now as a result of creation the soul may be destroyed or severely punished. Hence, he said, it would have been better if man had not been created, i.e., that the soul had not been put into the human body. Solomon also said: "But better than they both is he that hath not yet been." Now if the soul were a hylic [material] power, how could he say about a non-existent thing that it is better than both? How can non-existence be better than existence, since all existence is good, as the Bible testifies: "And God saw everything that He had made, and, behold, it was very good"? Without doubt, then, his opinion is that the soul is a spiritual substance and not a material power. And since this is the correct opinion and the one that is in agreement with the Torah, they voted and decided that it would have been better for man if he had not been created, and they added that he must be careful of his conduct, so that the soul may not be destroyed or punished.

From this the Cabalists derived the doctrine of transmigration. Since the true opinion is, according to the Torah, - so they argued - that the soul is not a material power but an independent substance, as we said before, then just as the spiritual substance entered the human body when it was created, it is possible that after having functioned in one human body, it may return and live in another. But this is not correct. The divine Wisdom did indeed decree that the spiritual substance, which by its nature is not a free agent, should dwell in the human body in order that it may become a free agent in the body, because this is no doubt a valuable quality in it. So much so that, as we are told by the Rabbis, the angels made a mistake and when God created man, they wanted to worship him … This was because he was a free agent and they were not. Nevertheless, why should a soul which has already functioned in a human body and has become a free agent, return to the body again? And why should the seminal drop have the capacity to receive a soul which has already functioned in a body rather than to receive a soul which has not functioned in a body and is not a free agent? A still less likely view is that of those who say that human souls are transmigrated into bodies of animals. God knows.

The fourth opinion is that some reward is corporeal in this world and some is spiritual in the next world, after death. This is the opinion of our sacred Torah, which makes specific material promises to the righteous, like the patriarchs and others, and also spiritual promises for the soul alone, punishment or reward, as we shall explain with the help of God. This is also the opinion of our Rabbis in many

Sefer HaIkkarim — BOOK [Maamar] FOUR

places, and particularly in Sifre, where, commenting on the verse in Deuteronomy, they say: "That your days may be multiplied" - in this world; "And the days of your children" - in the times of the Messiah; "As the days of the heavens above the earth" - in the world to come. It is clear from this that the Bible promises, for the fulfilment of the commandments, reward in this world and in the next. This is a general statement of human opinion concerning reward and punishment and the opinion of our Torah on the subject.

Chapter 30

Concerning the spiritual reward which comes to a man after death, the later Jewish scholars are divided into two schools. The one holds that while it is true that the perfectly righteous receive in this world reward for their deeds, as did the patriarchs, nevertheless, the main reward is spiritual, bestowed upon the soul alone in the world to come, i.e., the world which comes to a person after death as soon as the soul is separated from the body - a world in which there is no eating or drinking or any of the physical pleasures. As our Rabbis say: Rab was accustomed to say: In the next world there is neither eating nor drinking, nor hatred, nor envy, nor strife, but the righteous sit with their crowns on their heads and enjoy the splendor of the Shekinah. The meaning is: the crown of a good name resulting from their good deeds stands above their heads and confers upon them the privilege of enjoying the splendor of the Shekinah.

The men of this opinion also hold that while the main reward is purely spiritual, there is also another corporeal reward in this world at the time of the Messiah. This is the same as the time of the resurrection, when the perfectly righteous will come to life, either in order to publish God's miracles and truth, or in order that they may receive some corporeal pleasure corresponding to the pain they suffered during life, or more, according as the divine Wisdom shall decree, or in order that they may acquire a higher perfection than before, in case they were not able in their lifetime to attain the degree to which they were entitled, considering their upright character, on account of external hindrances and the yoke of the exile. Then they will die again and return to dust, and then the souls will, by reason of their attainments during the second life, be privileged to enjoy the future world in a higher degree than the one they enjoyed before resurrection. This is the view of Maimonides and the distinguished men who came after him and adopted his opinion. If we examine this view, we find that it is correct and inevitable logically, and in agreement with the Torah.

Since the works of God are absolutely perfect, it follows that everything that can exist should exist in all the divisions which a logical classification suggests. Now we find that some corporeal things are permanent as individuals, for example the spheres and the stars, as the senses testify and as the prophet, too, agrees: "Lift up your eyes on high, and see: who hath created these? ... Not one faileth." Some are permanent only as species, for example, those animals which are born of individuals of the same species, while some are permanent neither as individuals nor as species, as, for example, those animals which are generated of putrefaction. It follows, therefore, that the remaining class of the division should also exist, namely there must be beings which are permanent both as individuals and as species, though in different aspects. This is the human species, which, in respect of the body and its material powers, has specific permanence only and not individual, like the other animals, but in respect of the rational soul and its intellectual power, man has individual permanence like the angels.

These two kinds of permanance are alluded to in the book Yezirah in the words: "He made a covenant with him between the ten fingers of his hands and the ten toes of his feet by the circumcision of the tongue and the circumcision of his nakedness." Specific permanence is cearly indicated in the expression, "the circumcision of his nakedness," which needs no explanation, while individual permanence is indicated in the words, "circumcision of the tongue," i.e., the rational [speaking] soul. The reason for this is because an eternal being can not make a covenant with a thing that is subject to genesis and decay except in so far as it has some permanence.

The subject must be explained as follows: The powers existing in the composite beings in the sublunar world can not be perceived by the senses, nevertheless we infer their existence from their activities, which are perceived by the senses, for from the activities we know the powers. We see, for example, a plant moving in all directions, and we know that the natural power is not sufficient to cause such motion, for natural motion is either from the center to the circumference or from the circumference to the center or around the center, whereas the plant moves in all directions. Hence we infer that in the plant species there is another principle which causes this motion, and we call this principle the vegetative soul. In the same way we find that an animal besides having the principle of the vegetative soul has sensation and voluntary motion, activities which do not reside in a natural power or in the vegetative soul. Hence we infer that in this species there is another principle from which these activities follow, viz. those of growth and sensation, and we call it animal soul. Similarly, we see that man, in addition to this principle has the ability to understand universals, to know the essences of things, to distinguish between substance and accident, and so on, activities which can not be attributed to the vegetative or animal powers. Hence, we infer that he has a still higher power which we call human or rational soul.

Further, we find that this superior function which the human soul has, namely cognition, is different from the perceptions of the corporeal faculties. The corporeal faculties are destroyed by a strong perception [intense stimulus]. For example, an intense light destroys sight, so that thereafter the person can not even perceive a dim light, and the same thing is true of an intense sound. In the rational power the case is reversed. The more profound the subject of thought, the stronger the intellect becomes and the more brilliancy it acquires for further understanding. Also, the perceptions of the material powers are changeable because they are particular, whereas the cognitions of the intellect are not changeable but permanent because they are universal. Hence, we infer that he who gives this soul which has this power of cognition is superior to the one who gives the animal soul to animals. Therefore, the philosophers say that the animal soul comes from the power of the spheres, for the spheres through their motions prepare the matter to receive the forms, while their souls bestow the various forms of plant and animal, which exist in matter only, according to the latter's status of preparation. Hence the perceptions of animals are changeable and concern particulars according to the change and variety of the particular degrees of preparation [of the matters]. But the rational soul in man comes from a permanent rational principle separate from matter and unchangeable, a principal superior to that which bestows the animal soul. Hence its cognitions are universals and permanent.

We find that the prophet or the perfectly pious man can influence the matter of the sublunar world, as the Separate Intelligences do, because the principle of his soul comes from a Separate Intelligence. The Torah testifies to this, for we find in the account of creation that the Bible ascribes the animal soul to a material principle solely. Thus, in the creation of the animals, the text says: "Let the earth bring forth the living creature after its kind." But in the creation of man the Bible ascribes the soul to a rational principle: "Then the Lord God formed man of the dust of the ground, and breathed into

Sefer Halkkarim — BOOK [Maamar] FOUR

his nostrils the breath of life," concluding: "And man became a living soul," thus indicating that the vital power in man comes from the rational power which God breathed into his nostrils, and not from another principle, as in the lower animals.

Now since the vital soul in animals and the human soul which has intelligence come from two different principles, it does not follow because the vital powers in animals disappear as soon as the union between them and the body is sundered [because they come from the power of the sphere, which is a material thing, and from its soul, which is a material power], that the human soul ceases to exist, since it comes from another principle, a rational principle separate from matter, not having in it the possibility of dissolution at all, as a material thing has. Therefore, if we find that the powers of growth and nutrition and sensation in man and the other powers disappear in death, this is merely because the union has ceased between the soul and the body, which was the instrument through which the soul performed those functions. On the other hand, since we see the power of reason existing in angels without the other powers, and we also see the powers of growth and of life disappear by themselves in plants and animals, we infer that since man has in him both material powers and a rational power, even though the material powers cease to exist as soon as the instrument is removed, the rational power is not destroyed with the destruction of the vital power, any more than the vital power is destroyed with the destruction of the power of growth in animals, for the vital power is a preparation and background for the rational soul, as the power of growth is a preparation and background for the vital power.

And since we find that the intellect in angels exists by itself without matter, and the intellectual power in man similarly has a function peculiar to itself, viz. the apprehension of the separate substances and things abstracted from matter, we infer that since this intellect depends upon something permanent, it is not destroyed with the destruction of the body and the disappearance of the material powers. But when it is separated from the body it will, by reason of its obedience to God's will, unite with the permanent thing which it apprehended. It will thus attain the degree of the angels, whose perfection essentially consists in their obedience to God's will, as was explained above. This is the purpose of man, and the essence of the reward and punishment which the Torah promises to man after death when the soul parts from the body. This is the correct conception of this subject, as Maimonides and his followers understand it.

Sefer HaIkkarim — BOOK [Maamar] FOUR

The second opinion is that though the perfectly righteous get material reward in this world, yet since their number is small, and the great majority of righteous men do not get corporeal reward in this world, there should be in the next world corporeal as well as spiritual reward. This comes, they say, after the resurrection when the soul and the body will exist in conjunction, but without food and drink, as Moshe lived forty days and forty nights with body and soul without eating and drinking. This is what, according to them, the Rabbis call the world to come, when they say concerning the righteous that they are prepared for the life of the world to come. They believe at the same time that the human soul does not die when the body dies, but that there is a stage of existence called Gan Eden [Paradise] where, immediately after death, the souls of the righteous are kept until they rise in resurrection and obtain the life in the world to come after the resurrection. This is what the Rabbis mean when they relate concerning Rabban Simon ben Gamaliel that he said to Rabbi Ishmael, who was weeping when he was condemned to die: Master, why weepest thou? In a brief moment thou wilt be placed in Gan Eden in the community of the righteous. We are also told that Rabbah bar Rab Huna said concerning Rabbah bar Shela, who died a short time before him: He preceded me in Gan Eden by a brief hour. This is the opinion of Nahmanides, of Rabbi Meir Halevi, and a number of modern writers who follow them, may they all be blessed.

The argument in favor of this opinion is explained by one of the great disciples of Nahmanides in the following way. There are three degrees of rational creatures: 1. Pure intellect existing without body. This is the most perfect existence. 2. Intellect joined with a body existing forever. These are the spheres. 3. Intellect joined with a body that is subject to destruction. This is man, the lowest in rank of the intellectual creatures. Those that come after, namely the lower animals, which consist of body and soul, both subject to dissolution; and plants, consisting of body that is subject to dissolution and having no animal soul, all these are for the sake of man. Man was created last because of his perfection. The lower creatures were made for his sake, they reached their perfection in his creation, and are all embraced in him - the four elements, the power of growth, the animal power, and in addition to all he has reason. Therefore, he rules over all of them, and he came last to complete their activity and to rule over them, because he possesses reason, which has immortality. But it needs the body for its perfection, hence the expression that the souls of the righteous are "hidden" under the

Sefer HaIkkarim   BOOK [Maamar] FOUR

throne of glory or in Gan Eden. For the word, "hidden," denotes something incomplete, i.e., they need the body and are not complete without the body. But at the end he will be an honorable and permanent body. This is their idea of the human intellect, as Rabbi Aaron Halevi says.

And if the objection is raised that since the intellect can exist only with the body and the body is dissolved like the beast and returns to dust, how can the intellect survive to receive its reward, since according to them it can exist only with the body? Rabbi Aaron says that when the time of the resurrection comes, God will create a new body for every one of the righteous, under exactly the same constellation as their original bodies, and they will rise again and eat and drink and have children; every member of the body will perform its proper function, will receive all that belongs to it, will be nourished properly, will do what it should without any hindrance internal or external, - such will be the state of all those who will live at that time. Their bodies will enjoy the best of health that is attainable according to their temperament, and will obtain the highest perfection possible, each according to his degree. Then after a long time, as each one in turn has attained the highest perfection possible for him, he will consciously and deliberately rise to the status of Eliyahu. That is, the matter of their body, namely the matter of the four elements, will be changed and receive another form, and become a simple element, permanent, mobile, bright in color, like the whiteness of sapphire, and invisible like Eliyahu, prepared to receive the divine splendor and the light of the King's living countenance, like the moon, which is a light-receiving body. Hence, we say in the benediction of the moon: "A crown of glory to those who are laden with a body [i.e., the righteous], who will be renewed like her [the moon]," namely after the resurrection, when their body will be changed and will receive another structure.

There are examples of this in this world, where certain animals undergo a transformation and their body receives a different form. Some of them need certain things to eat, for example a certain kind of food. This is the meaning of the tree of life, whose fruit prepares the one who eats thereof to receive this form, and he lives forever, as is alluded to in the account of the creation. This is the meaning of the resurrection of the dead, for the divine intention is that man should live forever with his body. For man is not complete without a body, like the spheres to which he is compared, bright as the "brightness of the firmament," and as "the stars for ever and ever." If man were complete without body, he would be a separate intellect

Sefer HaIkkarim — BOOK [Maamar] FOUR

and more perfect than the spheres, who have bodies. But this is impossible, for in the series of creations the higher comes first and the lower come later, as we explained before. Since, therefore, man is not complete without body, he must attain this completeness in accordance with the original intention of his creation. This change of form and swift mobility is described in the expression that God makes wings for them. So far Rabbi Aaron Halevi.

It is obvious that there are many objections to this conception. 1. This opinion is close to that which holds that the soul is a material power and therefore always needs the body for its existence. 2. If the human soul can not exist without a body, how can it exist immediately after death, as soon as it is separated from the body? They say that its existence is incomplete in paradise, in which the soul has no complete delight and does not attain any degree at all. If you ask them, why is not the body purified right after death, changing from its perishable to a permanent nature, as they say happens later, they say that they must come to life again after they die in order that they may merit immortality. But it is very unlikely that immortality can not be attained except after resurrection. The Aramaic proverb is applicable here: Your surety requires a surety. For according to this a person must first experience a first resurrection and then immortality. But if at the time of the resurrection men eat and bear children, as they say, and are free agents, they may sin again. How can they be sure, then, of the higher degree?

According to that Rabbi who says that only the perfectly righteous are resurrected, it follows that none of all those men that have existed and that will exist until the time of the resurrection will be privileged to participate in immortality or in any degree of the future life except the perfectly righteous. And even among the perfectly righteous, who will merit resurrection, none will enjoy any degree of the other world until that time. And even in the case of those who will experience resurrection, how can their bodies, which are composed of the four elements and are perishable by nature, become permanent, and how can the nature of impermanence change to one of permanence? Moreover, if, according to them, it is possible that matter, by nature perishable, may change and assume the nature of permanence, like the matter of the spheres, why not assume that the human soul, though it is a material power, as they say, nevertheless, since it has the capacity to receive perfection of ideas, can change from imperfection to perfection, so that it may exist by itself like a Separate Intelligence?

Sefer HaIkkarim   BOOK [Maamar] FOUR

This is more plausible and appeals more to reason than that matter should change its nature and assume another. It would not then be necessary for them to say that real immortality does not come until after resurrection. Besides, their opinion contradicts that of the Rabbis, who say that souls exist before they come into the human body. And in Bereshit Rabbah we find the biblical verse: "There they dwelt occupied in the king's work," explained as follows: "With the King of kings, the Lord, blessed be He, the souls of the righteous sat, and were consulted by God when He created the world." The soul is not therefore a material power, but they were created on the first day, as we are told: " 'And the spirit of God hovered ...' - this is the spirit of Adam the first man." Nahmanides also writes in a responsum that souls were created together with the primitive light, according to the Rabbis. They are not therefore a material power.

Moreover, they prove their idea from Eliyahu, but it is well known that the case of Eliyahu was extraordinary and miraculous, no one else can stand in his position, and not even Moshe had the privilege of so great a miracle. Besides, Eliyahu, according to tradition, never tasted death, and did not require the miracle of resurrection; whereas, according to their opinion, a person can not attain to this degree unless he dies and comes to life again as before. Moreover, the resurrection that they speak of is altogether unintelligible: For how is it possible that in the course of the sphere's motion there should be a position such that at one and the same time the constellations of all the righteous men that lived at various times should be the same as their original ones. And assuming that this is possible, it is a new creation and not resurrection.

In short, the arguments which these people use to support their idea are very far-fetched. If it is a tradition from the prophets we must accept it, but if it is a question of argument, we can certainly refute it. Besides their opinion is close to that of the Christians who hold that the righteous were punished for the sin of Adam, that their souls attained but a small degree of perfection until the 'Messiah' came, as they say, and atoned for the sin. Then the patriarchs and the righteous men attained the degree of perfection which they deserved. From this dogma they derive other secondary principles which they lay down as fundamental to their faith - may the Lord deliver us from them!

Sefer HaIkkarim — BOOK [Maamar] FOUR
Chapter 31

The foundation upon which the advocates of this second opinion base their great idea that the world to come is a degree of reward to which a man can not attain until after the resurrection, is a passage in the Mishnah: "These have no share in the world to come - He who says that the resurrection of the dead is not referred to in the Torah …" The Talmud, commenting upon this statement, says: He denies the resurrection of the dead, therefore he will have no share therein. From this passage they inferred that the world to come, which is the main reward referred to in the statement of the Rabbis that all Israel have a share in the world to come, comes after the resurrection of the dead and only to those who deserve resurrection.

But the inference is invalid, for we may say that the expression, "resurrection," in this place denotes the reward of the soul and its life in the world of souls, which comes right after death. They call it resurrection of the dead in opposition to the Sadducees and the Samaritans, who denied the immortality of the soul and said that the soul dies with the body. This follows also from the language of the Talmud in that place: Rabbi Eliezer son of Rabbi Yose said: I showed the Cutheans that their books are corrupt. They say that the resurrection is not mentioned in the Torah. So, I said to them: You corrupted your Torah but accomplished nothing. You say that the resurrection is not mentioned in the Torah, but it says: "That soul shall utterly be cut off, his iniquity shall be upon him" - "Shall utterly be cut off" [hikkaret tikkaret], refers to this world; "His iniquity shall be upon him," refers to the next world. Said Rab Papa to Abaye, why could he not have inferred both worlds from the expression, "Shall utterly be cut off" [hikkaret tikkaret]? Answer: They would have replied that the Torah uses a current expression. From this it would seem that his intention was to prove to them from the Torah that the soul has an existence after death, and nothing else. But this can not be, for this would be in conflict with the accepted belief among our people concerning the resurrection of the dead, and any one who denies it is ascribing a defect to God's power. It is one of those beliefs which every adherent of the Mosaic Law must hold, as we explained above.

I say, therefore, that the expression in the Mishnah: "All Israel have a share in the world to come," refers to the reward of the soul after death, both that degree which man has after the resurrection and that which he has immediately after death. This is proved by the statement of the Rabbis that the pious men of other nations have a share in the world to come. Now if the world to come denoted only a stage which comes after the resurrection, how could they say that the pious men of other nations enjoy it, since that stage is reserved exclusively for the perfectly righteous, as they say: "The benefit of rain is for the righteous as well as for the wicked, the resurrection of the dead is for the perfectly righteous only?" The expression, "world to come," in this place must therefore mean that degree which a man attains after death, at the expiration of the twelve months during which the soul is purged of its material habits.

The stage which a man attains immediately after death, within the twelve months, is called in the language of the Rabbis, Gan Eden [Paradise]. And it is in reference to this that it is said that the whole nation enjoys it, entering this stage immediately at death. Thus we find: "Rab Yehuda said in the name of Samuel: When Moshe died and entered Gan Eden, he said to Yehoshua: 'Ask me all the things about which you are in doubt …' " It seems therefore that the reward or the degree of existence which Moshe enjoyed as soon as he died was Gan Eden. The Rabbis also say: Jose ben Joezer dozed off and saw the bed of Yorkis of Zereda flying in the air. He said then: "He has preceded me in Gan Eden by a brief hour." This stage is incomplete before the end of twelve months. After twelve months one rises to one of the stages of the 'world to come,' which is a degree of perfection and glory. Thus, we are told: The souls of the righteous are hidden beneath the Throne of Glory, as is said: "The soul of my Lord shall be bound in the bundle of life with the Lord thy God." Also, we find: "The inside thereof being inlaid with love from the daughters of Yerushalayim" - these are the souls of the righteous which are with Him in heaven. In the Midrash on Psalms, they say that this degree is attained right after death and before the resurrection. Commenting on the verse in the Psalms: "Let the saints exult in glory," they say: In what glory? Answer: In the glory which God confers upon the righteous when they depart this world. And they praise God, who bound them in the bundle of life, as is said: "The soul of my lord shall be bound in the bundle of life." Also in the treatise Hagigah: "Arabot is the place in which are righteousness and judgment, treasures of life and treasures of peace and treasures of blessing, and the souls of the righteous. There are the Ofannim and the Seraphim and the Holy Hayyot and the attending angels and the Throne of Glory, while the Living and Eternal King, high and exalted, dwells above them." Here it is stated clearly that the degree occupied by the souls of the righteous after they leave the body and before resurrection is the same as that of the attending angels. The literal meaning of the verse in Zechariah points to the same thing: "I will give thee free access among these that stand by." This degree is called in the Mishnah, "world to come," because it comes to a man after death. The statement: "All Israel have a share in the world to come," refers to it.

But there is another degree which is also called "world to come" without qualification. This is that which comes after resurrection. This is referred to in the Mishnah above mentioned, where the Talmud says that the one who denies resurrection will have no share in resurrection. For it appears from that passage that "the world to come" is a state of reward which comes after resurrection, a reward which is accepted traditionally among our people as conferred upon those whom God brings back to life at the resurrection. The same thing appears also from the statement of the Rabbis: "There are three classes on the day of judgment ... the perfectly righteous are immediately written down, and their destiny is sealed for life in the world to come." This shows that the world to come is a state which comes to a person after the great day of judgment, i.e., after the resurrection, as is traditionally accepted among our people. The same idea can also be found in the statement of the Rabbis: " 'The land of the living,' i.e., a land whose dead are the first to live again in the world to come. If so, how can those men who died outside of Palestine, like Moshe and Aaron, be resurrected and enter the world to come? Answer: At the time of the resurrection God will make for them pathways under ground ..." It is thus clear from this that Moshe and Aaron must first be resurrected before they can attain the world to come. This also shows that the degree of Gan Eden in which Moshe and Aaron have been from the time of their death until now, is not the same as the state of life in the world to come after resurrection. The latter is a much higher degree than Gan Eden and superior to all others. Only those perfectly righteous men have this privilege who merit the life of the resurrection, as the Rabbis say that resurrection is only for the perfectly righteous.

We must say, therefore, that the expression, "world to come," is used both in a broad and a narrow sense. In a broad sense it applies to any degree of reward which the soul gets after death. In a narrow and specific sense, it denotes the highest degree that the soul of the perfectly righteous man can attain, a degree which comes after resurrection. This degree is called "life in the world to come" par excellence. "All Israel have a share in the world to come," means that in the world of souls which is after death every Israelite will

Sefer HaIkkarim   BOOK [Maamar] FOUR

attain to some degree according to his conduct. The pious men of other nations also have a share in the world to come in this sense. But the highest and last degree - "life in the world to come" - no one can attain except the perfectly righteous, and that only after the resurrection. Those righteous men who, as God knows, were unable to fulfil the whole Torah, not because of evil will, but because of the yoke of the exile and external hindrances, or for some other cause, like Moshe and Aaron who were not able to fulfil the entire Law, namely those commandments which can be performed only in Palestine, because they did not enter the land of Palestine - these men will be resurrected, so that they may perform all those commandments which are rooted in Palestine as well as those other commandments which they were not able to perform in their first life, and then they will attain to the highest and last degree, viz. "life in the world to come."

I found a support to these ideas in the Midrash of Rabbi Nehunyah ben ha-Kanah: Rabbi Berechiah held forth, saying: We speak of the world to come [Olam Haba] and we do not know what we are saying. We translate the Hebrew expression **Olam Haba** [the world to come] by the Aramaic **Alma Deate** [world to come], but what is Alma Deate? Answer: Before the world was created God thought of creating light. So, he created a great light which no creature could control. Seeing that the creatures would not be able to endure it, He took a seventh part thereof and put it in its stead and the rest He hid away for the future, saying at the same time: If they are found worthy of this seventh part and take good care of it, I will give them this on the last day. Hence it is called **Ha'olam haba**, the world that has come, i.e., it came before the six days of creation. This is the meaning of the verse: "Oh how abundant is Thy goodness, which Thou hast laid up for them that fear Thee; which Thou hast wrought for them that take their refuge in Thee!" So far, the Midrash,

Nahmanides comments on this as follows: Olam Haba means the world that has already come. He mentions the Aramaic expression used by the Rabbis, Alma Deate, which means, the world that is about to come. Then he explains that this "world to come" is light, viz. the light which God intended to, and did, create before this world, to indicate that this is the last attainment to which a man can rise. So far Nahmanides. This explanation agrees with what we said, namely that the world to come is always in the act of coming, namely for every righteous man immediately after death, before resurrection. Hence it is called 'alma deate. Then there is an ultimate

Sefer HaIkkarim — BOOK [Maamar] FOUR

degree to which man rises, which is also called **Olam Haba**.
It appears therefore that there are four different periods of reward:

1. This world.
2. The world to come after death, either before resurrection or after resurrection.
3. The days of the Messiah.
4. Resurrection. These rewards are all different from each other. Some are fortunate enough to receive reward in all these periods, namely the perfectly righteous. Some are rewarded in this world only, viz. the wicked, who are paid for the few good deeds they have to their credit in this world, so that they may be punished in the next. Then there are good men who have not the privilege of receiving reward in this world. They enjoy life in the world to come right after death, but not resurrection. Then there are some who have the privilege of resurrection also, and some there are who merit the days of the Messiah also.

The four different expressions for reward which occur in the Yozer prayers for the Sabbath probably refer to the four different kinds of reward which we have mentioned. The expressions are: "There is none to compare with Thee," "There is none beside Thee," "No other, save Thee," "Who is like unto Thee?" And the explanation of these various expressions as referring to the four different periods and kinds of reward follows in the immediate sequel: "There is none to compare with Thee, O Lord our Lord, in this world, and there is none beside Thee, our King, in the life of the world to come." These are the two general periods of reward. Then he speaks of the best reward in this world, which was mentioned first: "There is no other save Thee, our Redeemer, in the days of the Messiah," and then comes the best reward in the world to come after death, at the time of resurrection: ["And there will be none like Thee, our Saviour, at the resurrection of the dead]." The "world to come" is mentioned right after this world because it comes right after death for every one, before the days of the Messiah and before resurrection. This is more in agreement with the words of Maimonides. For according to Nahmanides, Gan Eden should have been mentioned after this world, because that is the state which comes after this world and not life in the world to come, which is the last stage, according to him. Since Gan Eden is not mentioned at all, it seems that the term, "world to come," includes all the stages which come after death. But he speaks of "life in the world to come," because it is the best of all.

Sefer HaIkkarim — BOOK [Maamar] FOUR
Chapter 32

Every change from the customary, even though natural and for the person's good, causes him pain so long as he does not understand the good. Thus, when a child leaves his mother's womb, he passes from potentiality to actuality and to a form of existence superior to and more worthy than the first, being prepared to see the light, to perceive objects with his senses, and to apprehend concepts with his intellect. And yet he cries because he can not understand the good. Similarly, when he is weaned and his milk food is discontinued, he cries, although the change is for better and more substantial food and such as is more fitting and wholesome. Yet he feels pain because it is a change from that to which he has been accustomed. Similarly, if one is accustomed to sit in darkness a long time and he suddenly comes out into the light, the light is difficult for him and causes discomfort until he gets gradually accustomed to it. So in the day of death, although a person changes for a superior and worthier existence and for a perpetual brightness which the intellect can not know while it is sunk in matter, yet he is extremely grieved by death - not because he is removed from existence to non-existence, as those think who hold that the human intellect can not exist without the body, but because the change from that to which a person has been accustomed is hard and painful until he becomes gradually accustomed to the new. Hence the Rabbis say, concerning the souls of the righteous, that during the entire twelve months [following the person's death] the soul comes up and then comes down again, i.e., because it is hard for her to be taken away from the corporeal things to which she was accustomed.

And although after she is separated from the body, she does not need to pay any attention to it, nor does she require sensations in order to receive the spiritual influence which she was prepared to receive during life when the body and its powers hindered and prevented her from complete communion with the spiritual, whereas as soon as the hindrance of the body and the corporeal powers is removed in death the veil is removed, the obstacle is taken away and the communion is constant, - nevertheless the soul is grieved at the time of death, and after death it is hard for her to be separated from the body and the corporeal things of which she made use, because she was accustomed to them at first when she needed the sensations and the corporeal powers in order by means of them to acquire the sensible images, from which the soul removed the element of particularity, which is perishable, and retained the element of universality, which

Sefer Halkkarim   BOOK [Maamar] FOUR

is permanent. Thus, of Reuben and Simeon the soul retains only animality and rationality in general, but not the particular. Similarly in all things the soul removes the elements of particularity and retains the elements of universality. This universality, however, the soul can not comprehend except by means of the particular sensations which the corporeal powers receive.

A human being is like a house of five gates, through which there come into the house all the moneys and possessions and provisions which are needed by the master of the house. They are all gathered at first in one house, and later all the possessions and provisions are distributed from that house into the various rooms, each thing being placed in the appropriate room. After all the rooms have been filled with the moneys and possessions, each room according to its capacity, the open gates are no longer needed to bring anything into the house or to keep the valuable possessions. It is better for the house that the gates should be shut in order that the valuable contents should be safe in their rooms.

So, the human being has five senses by means of which all sensations are perceived. After being all taken into the common sense, the perceptions are distributed among the various compartments in a proper manner. The power of imagination takes from them that which is appropriate to it, while the rational power takes their universal element and essence, removing the elements of particularity, and separating the accidents from the substances. And after the universal elements of things enter the soul, she does not need any longer the senses and the sense perceptions, as the house no longer needs the open gates after the rooms are filled with all the valuable things. And as it is best to shut the gates in order to keep the valuable property, so it is better for the soul to abandon the corporeal powers. The sense perceptions, in relation to the soul, are like a net or like a ship or animal which bring a man to his destination. When he has arrived there, he has no longer any need of the ship or the animal and they become a great trouble and a heavy burden, though at first, he could not have reached his destination without them. Similarly, the sense perceptions and the corporeal powers, after the ideas have been apprehended, are no longer needed to keep the ideas in the soul; on the contrary, they hinder and prevent the soul from comprehending the idea completely and from being in constant communion with it, because the Active Intellect is abstract, pure and free from matter. Hence the soul can not properly unite with it as long as she is entangled in matter.

But despite all this it is hard for the soul to get away from the things to which she has been accustomed, and she feels pain in death, for every man feels pain in parting from that to which he has been accustomed. Our Rabbis say: " 'All the days of the poor are evil' - even their Sabbaths and holy days, as Samuel said: Change of habit is the beginning of intestinal disease." The meaning is, it is hard for a poor man to change his habits even if the change be to a state of greater pleasure. In the same way it is hard for the soul to give up corporeal things until she gets accustomed to it in the course of twelve months. Hence our Rabbis say: The entire twelve months the soul goes up and comes down, after twelve months the soul goes up but does not come down.

Therefore, the man of intelligence who understands the good which comes to a person after death will not grieve on account of death, but will be eager for it, because he knows that the body and its powers hinder the soul from obtaining that good and from the enjoyment of continual delight. He will understand that a man's grief at the time of death is like the child's pain when it leaves its mother's womb, which it feels because it does not know the good which it obtains in birth. The reason we find righteous men, like Moshe and others, being grieved on account of death, is because they knew that the degree which the soul attains in the world to come depends upon its service in this world. Hence, they wanted to acquire more perfection during life in this world in order that they might merit a greater degree of existence in the world to come, because they knew how great the reward and the pleasure in the other world are. Their grief was not because they thought that they were passing from existence to non-existence because the soul can not exist without the body, as the fools think, far be it!

Chapter 33

We will now explain the conception of future reward and punishment according to the two opinions mentioned above. Those who say that the main reward in the next world is conferred upon body and soul together, argue as follows: Since, as they believe, the soul lives and exists only in the body, and the body is an instrument of the soul, giving it existence so that it may perform the will of the Creator, it follows from the justice of God that He should compensate the body for the toil and trouble which it had in the service of God together with the soul. This reward consists in the entire person - body and soul - continuing to exist forever after the resurrection. This, they say, will happen when God will purify the

Sefer HaIkkarim — BOOK [Maamar] FOUR

matter of the body so that it becomes like the matter of the spheres or the stars. The body together with the soul will then exist forever as the stars exist, who are living and intelligent beings, having body and soul.

Now if this is the nature of the reward, as the advocates of this opinion say, it follows that punishment is also eternal and of the same nature. God will create in the body a strong attribute or property enabling it to endure the punishments of gehenna, as Job said in allusion to gehenna: "A land of thick darkness, as darkness itself; a land of the shadow of death, without any order, and where the light is as darkness." He says it is like the shadow of death, not like death itself, in order that the wicked may have sufficient power to receive punishment. If it were like death itself, they would be destroyed and would no longer feel punishment.

If, on the other hand, the reward is bestowed upon the soul alone and not upon the body at all, as Maimonides says, the question arises, how can we conceive punishment being inflicted upon the soul, which is immaterial? The solution depends upon a proper conception of reward. When the soul parts from the body after death, she longs eagerly for her natural activity which is connected with her understanding, namely to serve God, and at the same time she still has an inclination for the things to which she was accustomed while in the body. Therefore if the person in question was one whose deeds were all in the name of God and whose purpose was to serve the Creator by fulfilling His commandments and doing His will as far as is possible while he was alive, that same purpose will not part from the soul after death and will not leave her until she unites with the Separate Intelligences, who serve God with the same intention, which is so much higher in degree as to be scarcely comparable with the other, though they are of the same kind.

Solomon compares the relation of these two purposes to each other to the relation of the light of Venus before dawn to the light of the sun: "But the path of the righteous is as the light of Venus, That shineth more and more unto the perfect day." The meaning is this: As the planet Venus, when it occupies its greatest morning distance, rises before the morning, illumines the night and continues shining the whole morning until the light of the sun gets strong and it is veritable day, so the way and the purpose of the righteous in serving God during their lifetime is a perfect way which makes darkness before them as light [like the light of Venus which illumines the night] and continues to shine before them until the day of death, when they are placed in a great spiritual light, similar to the light called veritable day, which can not be compared at all with the first light although they are both of the same kind, as the light of Venus can not be compared with the light of the sun which causes the perfect day, although they both belong to the species light. Therefore if the soul was wise and understood immaterial things and divine matters truly, she will, on parting from the body, experience great delight when she sees that the ideas which she had agree with the divine things as they are.

The understanding which the soul has during life is like a dream. Hence just as a delightful dream disappoints and wearies a person when he finds that it does not agree with reality, so the ideas of the soul will cause him pain after death when he finds them in disagreement with reality. But if they do agree with reality, that is, if they are true ideas, the soul will experience great delight. It is like a hungry man who dreams that he is eating, or a thirsty man who dreams that he is drinking, and then he wakes up and feels empty. His pain is great. But if he wakes up and finds before him a spring in a garden, from which he proceeds to drink, or a table set with all kinds of palatable food, which he eats to his heart's content, he experiences great delight in the actual eating and drinking, a delight that can not be compared with that of eating and drinking in a dream, which is merely in imagination, whereas this is real. So, the soul will feel delight when she perceives in the spiritual world in reality those things which she perceived in this world, which is like a dream. Hence, we say, in order to explain the matter by analogy, that the relation of the mind's understanding in this world to the soul's understanding in the next world is like that of a dream to the waking state. Hence the Bible compares the conception of the restoration of Zion as understood by the prophets - though it is true and undoubted - to a dream: "When the Lord brings back those that will return to Zion, we were like unto them that dream:" i.e., we shall know and realize that in the conception of that event which we had from the prophets we were like those that dream, for there is no comparison between the conception we had from the prophets and the thing we shall see in reality, any more than there is between a dream and the waking state. Therefore, when we see the thing in reality, we shall rejoice exceedingly and, "Then will our mouth be filled with laughter." This shows that the relation of the conceptional understanding of a thing to the thing as it is in reality is like the relation of a dream to the waking state. Therefore, if the soul during life centered all her purpose upon the service of God and keeping His commandments and pursuing righteousness and loving-

Sefer HaIkkarim — BOOK [Maamar] FOUR

kindness, she will experience wonderful delight in the world of souls, when she sees that the permanence and perfection of the angels and the celestial forms are solely of this nature, i.e., that they consist in their obedience and submission to the will of God, as we explained before.

It is like the case of a person who was told that there is a great king in the cities on the sea, very awful, who loves righteousness and kindness, hates flattery, has any number of servants all standing very high and taking delight in recounting the praises of their king and doing his bidding in great awe, and that all men must finally stand before that king and give him an account of all the deeds which they did. Hearing this, the person made up his mind to follow the paths of right and to serve that king. He endeavored to find out what the king did and what was agreeable to him, and took pains to perform his will as far as lay in his power. Finally, when his time came to go to the king's palace and stand before him and greet him, he rejoiced greatly and experienced great delight when he saw the royal splendor of the king and his great glory, his servants standing before him, as he had been told. And the king rejoiced to see him when he knew that the man had served him from love on the basis of report only. This man surely deserved a much greater reward than he who knew the king before. Therefore, the king, being a lover of justice and kindness and divine rectitude, showed him favor, as we explained above.

This is the degree of those who believe on the basis of hearing and tradition, the righteous men who follow tradition, concerning whom the Rabbis say: "In the future world there is neither eating nor drinking, but the righteous sit with their crowns on their heads and enjoy the splendor of the Shekinah." They say the "righteous" and not the "wise," to indicate that they are speaking of believers, as we said before. The words, "enjoy the splendor of the Shekinah," allude to the fact that just as a person enjoys the rays of light coming from the sun, which make his sight pass from potentiality to actuality if he has good sight, so if he has pure thought and intentions he will enjoy in the spiritual world the rays of intellectual light, which will reach him in actual reality and which are called the splendor of the Shekinah. No corporeal being can conceive this delight. Not even the prophets were able to conceive it, as the Rabbis say: All the prophecies have reference to the days of the Messiah, but as to the world to come: "No eye hath seen it, O God, beside Thee." The meaning is that since the pleasures of the days of the Messiah are to be enjoyed by body and soul together, an image of their sweetness may be perceived with the eye, i.e., the senses. But the world to come being spiritual and abstract, no likeness of it can be perceived by means of the corporeal powers. All that the prophets knew of it was that it is a spiritual pleasure and delight, nothing more.

This is the reason why the Rabbis denominate it by the expression, "Wine kept in the grapes:" "What is the meaning of the words: 'No eye hath seen it, O God, beside Thee?' Said Rabbi Yehoshua ben Levi, this is the wine that has been kept in its grapes since the six days of creation." The meaning is as follows: A person who eats grapes and enjoys them but has never seen wine, can not imagine that there can come from the grape something that is sweeter, more delightful and more beneficial than the grape itself, and if he were told that by viniculture he can obtain more delight than by eating grapes, he would be very much surprised and would refuse to believe it, but if he were given wine to drink he would know that the wine which comes from the grapes is much better and sweeter and more wholesome than the grapes themselves, and he would wonder how such a wonderfully delightful thing can come from grapes. So, the soul can not imagine that by performing the commandments she will obtain spiritual delight, until she is separated from the body. Then she will understand how such delight can come from performing the commandments as wine is obtained by cultivating a vineyard, and will realize that this delight is contained in the attribute or character which results from performing the commandments, as wine is contained in the grapes which are obtained by cultivating a vineyard. Hence it is called, "Wine that is kept in the grapes," to indicate that just as there is no comparison between the taste of grapes and the taste of wine, so there is no comparison between the delights of this world and the delights of the world to come. It is also called "celestial paradise," to indicate that the soul can not conceive the pleasure of the spiritual which is celestial, as long as she is in the sublunar world.

As for the nature of the soul's pain and punishment, that is to be explained as follows: If a person in his lifetime pursued his desires and physical pleasures, and his soul departed from doing the will of God and accommodated her acts to the nature of the body, which is opposed to her own nature, then when this soul is separated from the body, she longs for those things to which she was accustomed and feels a desire for them, but has no instruments with which to obtain them. On the other hand, by reason of her own nature she will desire to unite with the higher forms and the immaterial substances, and will experience a longing for them. But she has not learned the elements, nor been accustomed to the service of God, the delight in which can not be enjoyed except by one who has accustomed and prepared himself for it, as the Rabbis say: The Lord gives wisdom to him only who has wisdom, for it says: "He giveth wisdom unto the wise." Accordingly, the soul will be drawn in two directions at once, upwards and downwards, the one by reason of her nature, the other by reason of her habit and custom. But she will have no instruments for obtaining the lower desires and no preparation to obtain the higher. This will cause her great pain and suffering, greater than any pain in the world or any kind of fracture - more pain than the burning of fire or cold and terrible frost, more than the wounds of knives and swords or the stings of snakes and scorpions. When a person is burned by fire, he feels pain, but it is not the body that feels the pain, but the soul. And the soul feels pain not because the fire has any effect upon the soul - fire can not affect a spiritual thing - but because the vital power is a corporeal power residing in the body when its parts are united to each other. Now when the soul becomes aware of the separation of the parts of the body one from another through fire or cold or a sword or any other agency having a similar effect, and perceives the pain which the vital power feels when the parts of the body which are its seat are divided, and the grief which it suffers on account of the dissolution of the body upon whose integrity it depends - then the soul feels pain on account of the pain of the vital power which is the seat of the soul, and is grieved on account of the separation of their union. In a similar way when the soul herself is separated from the body and is drawn in two opposite directions, as said before, by her own nature upward and by habit downward, she experiences great pain as if her parts were torn asunder. To be sure, the soul has no parts, but we use this expression to give an imaginary idea, the point being that she has two contrary desires and can not follow either one of them alone. This is the meaning of the rabbinic statement: Rabbi Eliezer said: "The souls of the righteous are hidden under the Throne of Glory, as is said: 'The soul of my lord shall be bound in the bundle of life with the Lord thy God.' As to the souls of the wicked, one angel stands at one end of the world and another at the other end and they throw it to each other, as is said: 'And the souls of thine enemies, them shall he sling out, as from the hollow of a sling.'" This is an allusion to the two contrary desires which she has. But the soul of the righteous has no downward desire, hence she is united at once with that which is akin to her nature, namely the Throne of Glory under which she dwells. As the pleasure is greater than any that can

Sefer Halkkarim BOOK [Maamar] FOUR

be imagined, as we said before, so is the pain greater than any imaginable pain.

We have already explained above that though the soul is not in place, not being a corporeal thing, nevertheless she is confined by direction, so that she can feel pain, as she is confined by the body, though she is not in place. This is the meaning of the rabbinic statement: "Antoninus said to Rabbi: The body and the soul can both evade the day of judgment. The body can say: It is the soul that has sinned, for since she has parted from me, I am lying in the grave like a stone. The soul will say: It is the body that sinned, for since I parted from it, I am like a bird flying in the air. Said Rabbi to Antoninus, I will give you a parable. This is similar to the case of a human king ... So, God takes the soul, throws her into the body and judges them together, as is said: 'He calleth to the heavens above, and to the earth, that He may judge His people.' 'The heavens above,' signifies the soul, 'And to the earth, that He may judge His people,' refers to the body."

It seems to me that they mean to say that though the soul is a spiritual thing which can not be held in place, God does confine her in a place, which they call body, in order that she may receive punishment and be afflicted with pain for her conduct. This place is called Gehenna. They call it body to indicate that just as the body confines the soul in a place - for though the soul does not occupy space, nevertheless since she is not outside of the body she is necessarily confined by the body - so the place of Gehenna, which is called body, also confines the soul in order that she may receive her punishment there. Note carefully that they make this statement only concerning pain and punishment, for we can not conceive of the soul receiving punishment unless she is confined in a place. But the statement does not apply to spiritual reward and delight. For we can conceive the soul receiving this without being confined to a place. Perhaps this is the error of those who say that the bodies must be purified to receive their reward and that the soul is not rewarded without the body. They think that just as a definite place is mentioned for judgment, i.e., punishment, so is a definite place necessary for reward. But it is not so, for both punishment and reward are given to the soul alone, but a definite place is necessary for punishment, not for reward, as we have explained.

Chapter 34

The punishment of which we have been speaking, which is inflicted

Sefer HaIkkarim — BOOK [Maamar] FOUR

upon the body and the soul together or upon the soul alone, differs according to the different degrees of the individuals. If a person has a few good deeds to his credit and is also guilty of a few transgressions, he can not be continually punished in the extraordinary manner that we mentioned, for a limited period will make him forget his habit [of committing sins]. According to the Rabbis, this period lasts twelve months. After twelve months of punishment, the individual attains to some degree [of reward] according to the number of good deeds which he has to his credit. Then there are individuals who, after they have forgotten their habits through twelve months' punishment, have no good deeds to entitle them to any degree of reward, and so they become non-existent, since they have no preparation at all for receiving spiritual reward. This is what the Bible means when it speaks of the soul being cut off. In reference to these the Rabbis say that after twelve months their body is destroyed, their soul is burned, and they are scattered by the wind under the soles of the feet of the righteous.

Then there are other wicked men who are punished eternally for their misdeeds, those, for example, who deny the principles of the Torah, as we shall see later with the help of God. The souls of these men must be confined in a place that they may receive continuous punishment, as we explained before. There are others who after twelve months attain a great degree, as the Rabbis say concerning Samuel, who was a perfectly righteous man, that the entire twelve months his soul went up and down, and that this was the reason the witch was able to bring him up, because it was within the twelve months, as she said: "I see a god-like being coming up out of the earth." But after twelve months the soul goes up but does not come down. This shows that even perfectly righteous men find it hard to give up the material things to which they have been accustomed, until they have been purified for a certain length of time. This purification lasts twelve months, a period embracing the four seasons, which include all temporal changes. This is the meaning of the passage in which we are told concerning Rabbah bar Nahamani that shortly before his death, when he was fleeing from a horseman, an officer of the king who wanted to capture him, he saw or heard in a dream or in a vision that after death the souls study the laws of the plagues as they used to do in life, and he heard them discussing: "If the bright spot comes before white hair … If it is doubtful, the celestial college said, the man was unclean and God said, he was clean. Then he heard them say: Who shall decide the matter? Answer: Rabbah bar Nahamani, who is an expert in the subject of clean and unclean ..." From the entire context there it is clear that the souls after death are eager to occupy themselves with the things to which they were accustomed in life, for even the souls of the righteous are engaged in studying the laws of the plagues and of the clean and unclean with which they occupied themselves in life. This desire, they say, disappears after twelve months.

The Rabbis speak of this frequently in different places. Concerning Rabbi Yehuda ha-Nasi they say that he came to his house every Friday evening and pronounced the Sabbath benediction, thus indicating that even after death the souls of the righteous are eager to perform the commandments which they were accustomed to perform during life, so much so that Rabbi Yehuda ha-Nasi came home every Sabbath eve to pronounce the Kiddush. We find the same thing in a few other pious men, but it never lasts more than twelve months, as the Rabbis say: After twelve months the soul goes up but she does not come down. The case of Eliyahu, who goes up and down all the time, is unique even now among the righteous men, as we find in the Zohar on the section "Vayakhel:" "We find a mystery in the book of Adam, which says that among the generations of the world there will be one spirit that will go down to the earth and clothe itself in a body. His name is Eliyahu. In this body he will go up, put it off and leave it in the storm. Then he will put on another body of light, in which he will remain among the angels. Later he will go down again and put on the body which remained in the storm, and appear in it down below. With the other body he appears above. This is the mystery contained in the words: 'Who hath ascended up into heaven, and descended?' There is no human being whose spirit ascended to heaven and then came down, except Eliyahu. He it is who ascended above and then descended." This is also the mystery of the "garment," which is mentioned in the works of the Cabalists, but I can not say more.

Chapter 35

Belief in the resurrection of the dead is obligatory according to the tradition of our people, as we explained above. Logic does not require it, but since it is something, whose existence is rationally conceivable, we are obliged to believe it, as we explained in that place. Particularly is this the case, since it is confirmed by experience. Eliyahu brought back to life the son of the widow of Zarephath, while Elisha revived the son of the Shunammite woman, and a thing to which experience testifies must be believed, even if it

Sefer HaIkkarim — BOOK [Maamar] FOUR

is not required by logic. For example, it is absolutely true that there is a stone which attracts iron, because experience shows it, though logic does not require it. We must therefore believe that God will revive the dead, even after they turn to dust, because it is something the mind can conceive.

To understand why this is a resurrection and not a new creation, we must bear in mind that a thing which has once received a higher influence or power and has lost it, is more prepared to receive it a second time than it was in the beginning. For example, wood which has once been kindled and has received the form of fire, which was later extinguished, is more ready to receive the form of fire a second time than in the beginning. Also, a person who once received the spirit of prophecy and lost it, is more prepared to receive it a second time than he was in the beginning. The reason is because when a thing receives any higher influence or power, though it loses it later, there remains in it an impression of the influence which it once received. Hence the Rabbis say: " 'And I will bring your sanctuaries unto desolation' - they are sacred even in their desolation." They also say: an article which was used in connection with holy things should be hidden. The reason is because it retains an impression of the divine object for which it served as a seat or in some other capacity. In the same way, therefore, we say that the body, which was the seat of the soul, a higher power, retains an impression of the divine power which it received in the beginning, even after the soul leaves it at the time of death.

And the proof of this is found in the case of the man who died and was buried in the grave of Elisha. The bones of Elisha had sufficient power to bring him back to life by coming in contact with him, although the soul of Elisha had long departed from the body, for he had been dead more than a year, as the Bible testifies. Nevertheless, as soon as the dead man came in contact with the bones of Elisha, he rose and stood on his feet. This was due to the impression which remained in the bones of the divine object of which they were the seat. This is the reason also why in time of trouble we prostrate ourselves upon the graves of the righteous. For on account of the impression, in those bones, of the divine spirit which they lodged, they are more prepared to mediate the divine influence than others. This may be illustrated also in the rod of Moshe. It was nothing but dry wood, nevertheless, since it was in the hand of Moshe when the prophetic inspiration began to rest upon him, it was always used in the performance of the signs, as we read: "And thou shalt take in thy hand this rod, wherewith thou shalt do the signs." And Elisha said to Gehazi: "And lay my staff upon the face of the child."

The resurrection must be explained in the same way. The body of the righteous man, by reason of the impression remaining in it of the divine spirit which it lodged, is more prepared without doubt to receive the same divine spirit a second time than it was at first, as the Rabbis say: "If those who never had been came to life, surely those who once had been would come to life again." In other words, a thing which was not fit to receive a higher power and yet received it once, is surely fit to receive it a second time, because it retains an impression and preparation for receiving it a second time more easily than at first.

Moreover the object which has the fitness to receive some power or influence, has the power, as it were, to compel the giver to bestow the influence or power upon it, as, for example, though fire does not by nature move downward, yet when we take a lamp which has been extinguished and is still smoking and put it under another lamp that is burning, the smoke rising from the extinguished lamp will force the fire of the burning lamp to let down its flame through the smoke to the extinguished lamp and it will burn again as before. This is the reason why the Bible compares the human soul to a lamp: "The spirit of man is the lamp of the Lord." The soul of man is like the light of a burning lamp. Just as the light of a burning lamp, even after it has left the wick, will burn a second time more easily than at first because of the impression of the fire which it retains, so the light of the soul which has left the body can return to the body and dwell in it, by reason of the preparation which it retains, more easily than it came to it in the beginning. This takes place when the divine Wisdom decrees that it should.

Seeing, however, that this thing is very far from being a natural phenomenon, the men of the Great Synagogue, in composing the benedictions, ascribed this thing to the power of God: "Thou art powerful forever, O Lord, Thou revivest the dead." The meaning is: Thou art powerful and canst do everything which the mind can conceive. Thy power is not like that of a human being. A human being has power to put to death the living, but the power of God is the reverse - He can revive the dead. In this benediction they mention God's kindness to His creatures during life: "He supports the living with kindness;" and after death: "He reviveth the dead with great mercy." Then they say: "He supporteth the fallen, He healeth the sick, He looseth the bound ...," to show that the power of God is not like that of a human being. A human being has power to bring men low and subdue them, while the power of God is the reverse - He supporteth the fallen. A human being has power to strike and bruise and make sick; God, on the contrary, healeth the sick. A human being has power to punish his fellow by imposing a fine or by imprisonment, God, on the contrary, looseth the bound. A human being has power deliberately to make a false promise, for who would dare to tell him to keep his promise? God, on the contrary, keeps His faith. And not merely does He keep His faith with the living, who supplicate Him, as the Psalmist says: "Remember the word unto Thy servant, Because Thou hast made me to hope;" but also with those who sleep in the dust, the dead, who have no power to supplicate Him, does He keep faith, and He revives them, as the Torah says: "I kill, and I make alive." The Rabbis, commenting on this verse, say: You might suppose it means, He kills one and gives life to another, hence the sequel says: "I have wounded and I heal." As the one wounded is the same as the one healed, so the one killed is the same as the one brought to life.

Since this belief is the most remarkable of the beliefs accepted by our people, it was placed right after the benediction of the Fathers. The expression, "abundant mercies," is applied to resurrection, because the life of man is divided into three parts, the years of growth, the stationary years and the years of decline. In all these three periods God nourishes man and supports him in life with grace, kindness and mercy. Hence these three expressions are mentioned in Grace after Meals, which Moshe composed for Israel, to correspond to the three periods mentioned. In the years of growth, when the assimilation of the food is great and exceeds the dissolution, there is no need of extraordinary kindness to keep the individual alive. Still, inasmuch as the assimilated food is altogether unlike the original fluid, some divine help is necessary, and the grace [hen] of God is sufficient. In the stationary years, when the dissolution is equal, or approximately so, to the assimilation, greater help is needed of divine kindness [hesed] to maintain life. Finally, in the years of decline, when the dissolution is much greater than the assimilation resulting from the food, man needs God's **Rahamim** [mercy] to maintain him alive. After death, neither grace, nor kindness, nor mercy is sufficient to bring man to life again, but there is need of great mercy, hence they say, "He reviveth the dead with great mercy."

As to the manner of resurrection, the Rabbis say that there is a certain dew with which God will revive the dead. It seems, therefore, that the dew which God will cause to descend upon the earth will have in it the virtue of the semen of the male, which gives the form of the person, while the earth at that time, by reason of its preparation, will have the virtue of the seed of the female, which gives the matter of the newly born individual. The prophecy of Ezekiel concerning the dead which he brought back to life disagrees with this opinion, if we interpret the text literally. Be this, however, as it may, whether after the resurrection the people will eat and drink and beget children and die in the usual manner [or not], we have already explained that it is a matter of dispute among the great men of more recent times. Maimonides and a great many distinguished men who follow him say that the persons resurrected will use all their sense functions in the natural way, and then will die again and return to dust. Rabbi Meir Halevi and Nahmanides are of the opinion that after resurrection, the persons in question will live as long as their natural capacity permits them, and then their bodies will be transmuted by purification and will become like the body of Eliyahu. And thenceforth they will continue to exist as body and soul, but will no longer use any sense functions, will not eat or drink or die and will remain forever without eating and drinking. It seems too that this latter is the opinion of some of the Rabbis of the Talmud, for they say that the righteous whom God will resurrect will not return to dust.

Although this opinion seems strange, nevertheless it may be believed, since the mind can conceive it and experience testifies in its favor, for Moshe lived forty days and forty nights without eating and drinking, though Moshe did not exist forever in his body, since he died when his time came. They hold that the individual will exist forever, and prove their point from Eliyahu. The best solution in this and similar cases is the answer Rabbi Yehoshua ben Hananiah gave to the Alexandrians - "When they come to life again, we will consult about the matter."

An important question in connection with the resurrection is whether it embraces the whole world, as some nations think, or the whole of our nation, or only a few of them. It is a matter which is not clearly alluded to in Scripture. The expression in Daniel: "And many of them that sleep in the dust of the earth shall awake," if it refers to the resurrection, indicates that not the whole world, nor the whole of our nation, nor even the majority of them, will be resurrected, but only a few. For the word "many" does not denote the majority of those that sleep in the dust, but only a few, like the expression: "And many from among the peoples of the land became Jews," which does not signify a majority of the peoples of the land, but only a few - three or five or ten or a hundred or a thousand, for

Sefer HaIkkarim — BOOK [Maamar] FOUR

example. Another similar expression is: "Many will entreat the favour of the liberal man." Moreover, our Rabbis say: "The power of rain is for the righteous as well as the wicked, the resurrection of the dead is for the perfectly righteous only."

If we say that the entire world will be resurrected, or the whole of our people, i.e., that they will all come back to life and stand in judgment on the day announced for the judgment of the world, and that the righteous will remain forever enjoying delight, while the wicked will live forever and suffer, then the passage in Daniel does not refer to resurrection, but must be understood in the way in which some literalists interpret it, as referring to the exaltation of the lowly nation in the days of the Hasmoneans or in the days of the Messiah. At that time, they say, the lowly nation, or many of the survivors, who are like those who sleep in the dust, will awake and rise to a degree which will be permanent and from which the nation will not again descend, but which it will occupy forever; while the other nations and their wicked men will always remain low and subdued under Israel: "Some to everlasting life, and some to reproaches and everlasting abhorrence."

Some of the later writers confirm the opinion of these commentators by saying that the incident of the dead being revived by Ezekiel took place in a prophetic vision, as we read: "The hand of the Lord was upon me, and the Lord carried me out in a spirit ..." The whole chapter is an allegory, typifying the misery of the Israelitish people in the Babylonian exile, where they were like dead men buried and devoid of all hope. But at the time of the second temple, in the days of the Hasmoneans, they rose again to a high degree, and rooted out the worship of idols. Then all those who came up from the Babylonian exile recognized and knew that the Lord is God. This is expressed in the biblical text in the words: "These bones are the whole house of Israel; behold, they say: Our bones are dried up, and our hope is lost; we are clean cut off." And at the end he says: "Behold, I will open your graves, and cause you to come up out of your graves, O My people; and I will bring you into the land of Israel." All this is an allusion to the return from captivity and settlement in the holy land, which led the Israelites to acknowledge God, as we read further: "And ye shall know that I am the Lord, when I have opened your graves, and caused you to come up out of your graves ..., and I will put My spirit in you, and ye shall live, and I will place you in your own land ..."

This is also the final opinion of the Talmud: "Rabbi Yehuda says: It is really [beëmet] an allegory." It is true that there is a dispute

Sefer HaIkkarim   BOOK [Maamar] FOUR

concerning the matter in the Talmud, where some one says: "I am a descendant of those people and these are the phylacteries which my great-grandfather left me," but this is merely a hyperbole, for it is an accepted rule that the expression 'really' [beëmet] indicates that the statement for which it vouches is authoritative. If, then, the passage in Daniel above mentioned does not refer to resurrection, then it is possible that resurrection embraces the whole world or the entire Jewish people, but there is no allusion to it in the Bible. The verse: "Awake and sing, ye that dwell in the dust," has the same meaning as: "He raiseth up the poor out of the dust," and other passages. The belief in resurrection is therefore merely traditional, and the verse: "I kill and I make alive; I have wounded, and I heal," concerning which the Rabbis say that just as the wounding and the healing concern the same person so the killing and the making alive also concern the same person, is not a promise of resurrection, but a statement that God is able to do this thing.

But even if we say that resurrection is for the purpose of rewarding the body, which suffered pain in the service of God, and that it is appropriate, in view of God's justice, to reward the identical thing that did the service and punish the same thing that was guilty of disobedience and not something else [though this is not a good argument, because punishment is inflicted upon the transgressor and not upon the instrument - we do not punish the sword, but the homicide], at any rate it follows that the resurrection will not take place at the time of the Messiah [according to the one who says that there is no difference between the present day and the Messianic age except freedom from political subjection] and that only a few persons will enjoy it at that time, like Moshe and Aaron and others, who will rise up at that time miraculously to publish to the world the belief in God. The main resurrection will

take place on the day of judgment and it will embrace the whole Jewish people or the greater part thereof, or the whole world or the greater part thereof, for they all deserve reward and punishment. But this opinion is hard to accept. For if we say that the body will be resurrected in order to be rewarded for the pain it endured, and that it will enjoy pleasure forever without eating and drinking, and will not change from day to day as our bodies now change, the question is: which body will rise at the time of the resurrection? The body of man changes continually from day to day with the food that comes in from outside. There would have to rise with any individual, say Reuben, any number of bodies belonging to the different periods of his life, so that they may all enjoy the pleasure. And if we say that

Sefer HaIkkarim   BOOK [Maamar] FOUR

Reuben will rise with a matter and a temperament similar to his original temperament, in order that his soul may dwell in that matter and temperament, and that this matter, being similar to the original matter, may enjoy pleasure, as we said above in the name of Rabbi Aaron Halevi, then the divine justice which, on this theory, resurrects the dead in order to pay them for the trouble they suffered, fails, for it is not proper to reward Simeon for a service done by Reuben. We have already explained before the thought that led to the idea that reward and punishment must include the body as well as the soul, and we made it clear that reward and punishment are not in the same case. The nature of punishment is such that it requires the existence of a body or of something to confine the soul, so that the soul may receive its punishment therein, but there is no such necessity in reward. Hence Maimonides agrees that the main reward that God bestows upon man is conferred upon the soul and not upon the body.

It seems, therefore, that the purpose of resurrection is not in order to reward the body, but either to give the individual an opportunity to acquire greater perfection than he acquired before, prevented as he was by external hindrances, exile, poverty and the like, and not through evil choice or any condition in the individual himself; or to make known in the world the great power of God and to publish the true faith. In this case resurrection may be confined to the righteous alone, as the Rabbis say, and will take place in the Messianic age. We can find a confirmation of this view in Daniel, where we read: "But go thou thy way till the end be; and thou shalt rest, and shalt stand up to thy lot, at the end of the days." The word **Kez** [end] when used without qualification, applies to the redemption from exile. "And thou shalt rest," means that he will die before the end. "And shalt stand up," alludes to the resurrection which will take place in the Messianic age, and which will be for the perfectly righteous only. And if we say that "end" refers to death, which is "the end of all flesh," the words: "shalt stand up," would likewise denote a promise that he will live again in the resurrection. For if he were thinking of the "world to come" after death, he could not say that after he rests, he will stand up to the lot at the end of the days, there being no connection between the end of days and the world to come. There is no doubt, therefore, that the text refers to the resurrection of the righteous in the Messianic age.

But there is no reference in the Bible to the general resurrection, which will take place on the day of judgment. The passage in the Bible: "I will gather all nations, and will bring them down into the

Sefer Halkkarim   BOOK [Maamar] FOUR

valley of Jehoshaphat; and I will enter into judgment with them there for My people and for My heritage Israel," does not refer to resurrection at all, as we can see from the context. This resurrection, therefore, is believed in as a result of tradition only. This is the best interpretation of these matters that I have selected.

Those who say that at the time of the resurrection the bodies will have everlasting delight or everlasting pain, without eating and drinking, and that they will not die again after resurrection in order that they may receive eternal reward or punishment for their deeds, and that this resurrection does not embrace the whole world, nor a majority, nor the whole Jewish people, nor yet a majority of them, but is limited to a few, the perfectly righteous men, can be compared to a person who affirms and denies a thing in the same breath without knowing it. For if the resurrection is intended for a few only and not for the rest, its purpose can not be to reward the body, but either to publish to the world the belief in God by means of the wonderful miracle that can be seen by every one, or to give the righteous man an opportunity to earn happiness and a degree of existence which he was not able to attain the first time on account of the yoke of the exile and the other troubles and hindrances which prevent a man from attaining the perfection of which his nature permits.

Chapter 36

Having explained the subject of reward and punishment, some of which is spiritual bestowed in the world to come upon the soul alone or upon body and soul together, we must now investigate whether justice requires that reward and punishment should be temporary or eternal.

Now, according to real justice and equality, reward and punishment should correspond to the act for which the reward or the punishment is received. And since the act is of finite duration, the reward or the punishment should also be of finite duration, corresponding to the finite act, without regard to the quality of the server or of the served. Thus, if one strikes his neighbor and blinds him, or breaks his arm, he should have his eye blinded or his arm broken, and similarly if one causes his neighbor pain lasting an hour, his punishment should be such as to cause him an hour's pain, no more and no less, according to strict equality and justice. In the same way if one causes his neighbor a little pleasure, his reward should also be little, corresponding to the pleasure or enjoyment which the other person received. How then can an ordinary mortal deserve eternal reward and everlasting enjoyment, whether given to the soul alone or the soul and body together, as the religionists say, and as we explained? We may, however, say that reward is not measured in this way, but that it is estimated according to the worth of the person for whom the service is performed, as is the case in political justice and the customs of men. In a political society reward and punishment are measured by the worth of the person served and not by the value of the service. One who serves a great prince gets a greater reward than one who serves an ordinary person, and one who serves the king, gets a greater reward than one who serves a prince. The greater the dignity of the person served, the greater the reward. From this it would follow that if the worth of the being served is infinite, the reward should be infinite. This is the point of view adopted by the religionists, who promise eternal reward for the service of God, because God's worth is infinite. It would follow from this also that the punishment of him who disobeys God should also be infinite, and for the same reason.

If, however, we examine carefully this human custom in the matter of measuring reward by the worth of the person served, we shall find that a different method should be used in relation to the service of God. Service done to a human king does indeed deserve greater reward than service done to any other person according to the measure of the benefit received from the service. Now since the benefit which the king receives has more value than the benefit received by an ordinary person, the reward must be greater. But God does not receive any benefit from man's service at all, as Elihu said: "If thou be righteous, what givest thou Him, or what receiveth He of thy hand?" We must say, then, that the reward should be commensurate not with the person served, but with the service, i.e., with the trouble endured by the one who does the service; and since the service is done in time, the reward should also be temporary. And similarly, punishment should be temporary, as Elihu said: "If thou hast sinned, what doest thou against Him? And if thy transgressions be multiplied, what doest thou unto Him?"

But if we consider this mode of measurement in punishment, we find that it is not proper, for punishment should be determined in accordance with the dignity of the person who is offended. Although God is not affected in any way by a person's disobedience, nevertheless inasmuch as the intention of the sinner is to do contrary to the command of God, who is infinite in worth, and to rebel against

Sefer HaIkkarim BOOK [Maamar] FOUR

Him, his sin should be regarded as very serious because of his intention. The distinction in the Torah between wilful and unintentional sin shows that sin is to be judged by the intention of the sinner and not by the mere act as such. For example, a person who disobeys the command of a great king, deserves death, even though the king did not suffer any damage on that account. Since his intention was to slight the king's honor, he should be punished for his intention and not merely for the resulting act. Hence the punishment of the wicked should be eternal, as God is eternal and infinite.

It seems also to be the opinion of the Rabbis that eternal punishment is sometimes inflicted upon the wicked for an act done in time. Thus they say that wicked men of a certain class go down to gehenna and are judged there for ever and ever. From this it appears that there is eternal punishment which is measured in relation to the person to whom the service is due, not in relation to the person who owes the service. It seems, therefore, from our argument that while reward should not be eternal according to strict justice, nor should it be measured in relation to the person served, as we have explained, punishment sholud be eternal and should be measured in relation to the dignity of the person to whom the service is due and the intention of the sinner, as we explained above. We must, therefore, make a distinction between reward and punishment. Reward must be paid simply in accordance with the benefit received. And since the server himself knows that no benefit accrues from his service to the person served, his reward should be of limited duration, corresponding to the act which was of limited duration or the trouble which the act cost him. On the other hand, punishment should be eternal, according to the intention of the sinner to disobey the command of God, who is eternal and infinite.

That this is the correct conception of the matter appears also from Onkelos' interpretation of the verse: "And repayeth them that hate Him to their face," which he translates: "He repays the wicked for the good deeds which they have done before Him during their lifetime, in order to destroy them." His meaning is that God repays those that hate Him in their lifetime, giving them a temporary reward for their good deeds, so that they may be punished with eternal destruction for their transgressions. Now if justice required that reward should be eternal and bear a relation to the person receiving the service, how is it conceivable that God would deprive any creature of its reward and give it a small temporary reward instead of the eternal reward which is its due? In the same way if strict justice required that punishment should be temporary and finite, how can we suppose that God would pervert judgment and punish the wicked eternally, as the Rabbis say that the unbelievers [minin] and informers go down to gehenna and are judged there for ever and ever, instead of giving them temporary punishment, as they deserve? It seems therefore that the truth is as we have explained, namely that in accordance with justice reward should be temporary and punishment eternal. The original question therefore comes back - How does a mortal deserve to attain eternal reward and everlasting happiness, as we said before? The religionists also promise eternal reward as well as eternal punishment, and the tradition of the Rabbis is in agreement with the same idea. For, referring to the verse: "They shall inherit the land forever," they say it alludes to spiritual reward, which is eternal, as they say: "All Israel have a share in the world to come, as is said: 'Thy people … shall be all righteous, they shall inherit the land forever.' "

My opinion is that strict justice requires that reward should be temporary, nevertheless God in His abundant kindness gives to those who do His will eternal and infinite reward, as He is eternal and infinite in worth. This is the hint that was given to Abraham in the vision, when God said to him: "Fear not, Abram, I am thy shield, thy reward shall be exceeding great." Abraham thought that reward is temporary, as justice requires, and hence he was afraid that his merits were diminished or suffered deduction by reason of his victory over the five kings. Therefore, God said to him: Fear not, Abram, I am thy shield, i.e., fear not that thy merits shall be deducted from, for I am the one who pay thy reward, and My power is unlimited. Therefore, thy reward will be very great, i.e., infinite, for the reward will be given in relation to Me and not in relation to thee and thy act, which are finite. The conversation concludes with the words: "And he believed in the Lord; and he counted it to Him for righteousness." The meaning is, Abraham believed God's promise of great reward and thought that it signified God's charity and kindness, for strict justice required that reward should be temporary and finite, but by reason of God's charity and kindness it is infinite. This is also stated in the Torah: "Who keepeth covenant and mercy with them that love Him and keep His commandments to a thousand generations." The last expression denotes infinite time, like the verse: "The word which He commanded to a thousand generations." For we find in another place: "And showing mercy unto the thousandth generation of them that love Me …," and there is no doubt that the words, "unto the thousandth generation," refer to an infinite time. The word "mercy" is used to indicate that the eternal reward is due to mercy. But punishment is eternal by strict justice, as we have explained.

Chapter 37

The idea that punishment bears relation to the being to whom service is due and not to the person who owes the service, and hence is eternal, seems to be indicated in the words which God said to Moshe: "And I will send an angel before thee ... for I will not go up in the midst of thee; for thou art a stiff-necked people; lest I consume thee in the way." Here we see that He feared they would be destroyed if God Himself with His great name should go up among them, but if an angel would go up with them, they would be saved from destruction, though some other punishment would come upon them, as we read: "Behold, I send an angel before thee ... Take heed of him, and hearken unto his voice; be not rebellious against him; for he will not pardon your transgression; for My name is in him." The words: "For he will not pardon your transgression," do not indicate that they will get greater punishment by rebelling against the command of the angel than by rebelling against God, for the text says: "For I will not go up in the midst of thee ... lest I consume thee in the way." The meaning is this: If they disobey God, there is, indeed, the fear that they may be punished very severely - with destruction. But there is an advantage on the other hand, for God has the power to pardon them, but the angel has not this power. Despite this, however, God said that it would be better for them to be guided by an angel, for though he will not forgive their transgression, their punishment, if they disobey the angel, will not be as great as it would be if God went with them and guided them without an intermediary and they disobeyed Him, for then they would be in danger of destruction.

It is clear, therefore, that the punishment of the one who disobeys God is greater than the punishment of him who disobeys an angel. This shows that in justice punishment bears relation to the master or commander or the one to whom service is due, and not to the person owing the service. We find also Moshe complaining of this characteristic in the "Prayer of Moshe." Moshe was praying to God concerning the people in captivity and was deploring the length of the exile. Wishing to complain of the characteristic above mentioned, he begins by way of apology: "Lord, Thou hast been our dwelling-place in all generations." The meaning is: Although I

Sefer Halkkarim   BOOK [Maamar] FOUR

complain of Thy principle of measuring punishment in relation to Thee and not in relation to us, nevertheless I acknowledge that all Thy ways are just and I can not quarrel with Thee, either so far as we are concerned, or so far as Thou art concerned, or so far as the punishment itself is concerned.

So far as we are concerned, I recognize and acknowledge that we are the recipients of Thy benefits, that Thou hast shown us very great kindness and we should not have sinned against Thee. And since we should not have sinned before Thee, we have no reason to complain of Thy justice so far as we are concerned, having been benefited by Thee, for Thou hast been our dwelling place and refuge and hiding-place in all generations. Nor can we complain of Thee in relation to Thyself, for Thou art eternal and infinite: "Before the mountains were brought forth, or ever Thou hadst formed the earth and the world, Even from everlasting to everlasting, Thou art God," eternal and infinite in worth. Hence he who disobeys Thee should be punished severely and we can not complain of Thy judgment so far as Thou art concerned. But neither can we complain of Thee so far as the punishment itself is concerned, for I know that all which Thou doest, the sufferings which Thou bringest upon man, when "Thou turnest man to contrition," are for a good purpose, viz. that man may turn to Thee in repentance: "And sayest: 'Return, ye children of men.'"

Nevertheless, I complain of, and am grieved by the evil which accrues to us on account of this method, in that Thou measurest the punishment in relation to Thee, who art infinite, instead of measuring it in relation to the sinner, who is finite. For if Thou measure it in relation to Thy worth, man will be destroyed in a moment, "For a thousand years in Thy sight are but as yesterday when it is past, and as a watch in the night. Thou carriest them away as with a flood; they are as sleep." The meaning is: If Thou shouldst sweep away the whole world with a flood of water, as Thou didst to the generation of the deluge, they would all be like a sleep before Thee, and in the morning, they would pass away like grass before Thee - like grass which springs up in the morning, and the time of its growth passes quickly away, "For in the evening it is cut down, and withereth." From this we get much evil, "For we are consumed in Thine anger, and by Thy wrath are we hurried away," because, "Thou hast set our iniquities before Thee," i.e., because Thou measurest our iniquities in relation to Thee - this is the complaint - and also because Thou hast set "our secret sins" ['alumenu], i.e., the sins that are hidden ['alam] from us, or it may mean the sins which

Sefer Haïkkarim   BOOK [Maamar] FOUR

we committed in our youth [biyeme 'alumenu], "in the light of Thy countenance," i.e., before Thee, so that Thou dost not forget them. It follows from this that "all our days are passed away in Thy wrath," because Thou measurest punishment in relation to Thee, and "we bring our years to an end as a tale that is told." That is, our years, which are time and belong to the category of continuous quantity, pass away like speech [hegeh], which belongs to the category of discrete quantity, whose parts are not continuous with one another. This is due to the many changes and vicissitudes that come upon us from day to day, so that our time does not flow continuously like a continuous quantity, but changes from day to day and from moment to moment like discrete quantity. Thou oughtest to measure our punishment in relation to the days of our life, which are short, for, "The days of our years are," on the average, "Three-score years and ten; or even by reason of strength four-score years," and not more, for if they extend beyond that limit, they are, "travail and vanity," and not worth counting as life. I see that the time of our life is very short, "For it is speedily gone, and we fly away," i.e., it is quickly cut off and we fly, as it were, because the years of our life pass away so quickly, for our days are like a shadow of a flying bird, which does not stand still for a moment, or like a lengthening shadow in the evening, when the sun sets quickly, and therefore I wither like grass.

All this is because Thou measurest punishment in relation to Thee, whereas Thou shouldst measure it in relation to us, who are finite beings. If Thou art going to measure it in relation to Thee, who can calculate the proper punishment, since Thou art infinite? Hence he says: "Who knoweth the power of Thine anger?" since it is infinite, "And thy wrath according to the fear that is due unto Thee," i.e.: According to the fear which is due to Thee, who art infinite, so is Thy wrath against us infinite. But it ought not to be so, but "according to the number of our days, so should the punishment be," i.e., the punishment should be measured in accordance with the number of our days. The word limnot is an infinitive used for a noun, and the word Hoda'means punishment or suffering, like, "And with them he taught [punished] [vayyoda'] the men of Succoth," as David Kimhi wrote in The Book of Roots, s. v. yada', in the name of Ibn Janah.

The meaning of the text is, therefore, as follows: As the number of our days is small, so Thy punishment for our sins should also be small; and similarly, according to the number of our days, which is small, "we may get us a heart of wisdom." But since the exile is extended for a long time, and we are laden with contempt, "Return, O Lord; how long? And let it repent Thee concerning Thy servants. O satisfy us in the morning with Thy mercy," i.e., in the time of our youth, so "that we may rejoice and be glad all our days." And if not in the time of our youth, then, "Make us glad according to the days wherein Thou hast afflicted us, according to the years wherein we have seen evil." And if Thou say that those who come after us will inherit the land, it is more proper that we should see our share in that good: "Let Thy work appear unto Thy servants," and the result will be, "Thy glory upon their children." "And let the graciousness of the Lord our God be upon us and the work of our hands," that we may prosper in all our doings, so that we may attain the delight which is found in divine works, as we explained in the introduction to this book.

Then he adds to this: "O thou that dwellest in the covert of the Highest …," as though by way of reply to the difficulty. The answer is that though the exile is long for the nation as a whole, because they are not as a whole perfect enough to deserve redemption, yet every righteous man is provided for by special Providence and delivered from trouble.

He divides the righteous into three or four classes.
    1. "He who dwells in the covert of the Highest, and abides in the shadow of the Almighty." This embraces all those Israelites who believe in the Torah and fulfil the commandments.
    2. The righteous man who trusts in God: "For thou hast made the Lord who is my refuge, even the Highest, thy habitation."
    3. He who loves God and longs for Him: "Because he hath set his love upon Me, therefore will I deliver him; I will set him on high, because he hath known My name, He shall call upon Me, and I will answer him …"
    4. "Because he hath known My name," probably represents the fourth class, who is referred to in the words: "He shall call upon Me, and I will answer him."

The Psalmist begins: "I will say of the Lord, who is my refuge and my fortress, my God in whom I trust, that He will deliver thee from the snare of the fowler, etc." That is, thou who dwellest in the covert of the Highest, and abidest in the shadow of the Almighty, fear not trouble, for I say to thee in the name of God, who is my refuge and my fortress, my God, in whom I trust, that He will deliver thee from the snare of the fowler … and from all the troubles that come upon the world. He concludes his remarks to the men of this class in the words: "And see the recompense of the wicked." Then he begins with the men of the second class, who say: "For Thou, O Lord art my refuge, etc." Concerning them he says: "There shall no evil befall thee ... The young lion and the serpent shalt thou trample under feet." The words: "I will say of the Lord, who is my refuge and my fortress, My God in whom I trust ...," which Moshe uses in the beginning, refer to this class also and to the other classes. But in place of the words: "That He will deliver thee from the snare of the fowler ...," which he said before, he says in relation to the second class: "There shall no evil befall thee ...," i.e., thou who sayest that the Lord is thy refuge, I say to thee, in the name of God, who is my refuge and fortress, and in whom I trust, that there shall no evil befall thee, that He will deliver thee from natural and unnatural accidents, so that "Thou shalt tread upon the lion and asp; the young lion and the serpent shalt thou trample under feet." Similarly, I say to you in the name of God that he who desires Him will be delivered from all evil in the world. He represents God as saying: "Because he hath set his love upon Me, therefore will I deliver him; I will set him on high ..." And if he reaches a still higher degree, namely: "That he hath known My name," then: "He shall call upon Me, and I will answer him; I will be with him in trouble; I will rescue him and bring him to honour." The meaning is that he who knows My name stands higher than all other righteous men.

The gist of Moshe' words in this Psalm is that the righteous men are taken care of and delivered from trouble in different ways, depending on the degree which they attain. We see from this that Moshe is complaining of God's method of punishing in accordance with God's being, to whom service is offered, whereas he thinks the punishment should be accommodated to the number of years of human life, which are few. This shows that the punishment which comes from God in accordance with strict justice is not computed in relation to the disobedient and the sinner, but in relation to the Being sinned against, whose spirit is defied.

Chapter 38

We have now explained that according to justice the punishments inflicted by God should be eternal, and that reward is either eternal, through divine grace, or not eternal, as strict justice demands. But there is a very important difficulty in the matter of punishment, as follows:

Since "there is not a righteous man upon earth, that doeth good and

Sefer Halkkarim   BOOK [Maamar] FOUR

sinneth not," it follows that all men should be punished eternally for any sin they have committed or for disobedience of God's command of which they are guilty, though the nature of the punishment be different. How then can any one escape eternal punishment according to this mode of determination, and how can a mortal merit spiritual reward, whether temporary or eternal? A still greater difficulty arises from the statement of the Rabbis that the punishment of the wicked in gehenna lasts twelve months, indicating that punishment is not eternal. And, on the other hand, they say that reward is eternal, inferring it from the words: "They shall inherit the land forever."

It seems to me that the difficulty may be solved by saying that just as reward is made eternal by divine grace, though according to strict justice it should be temporary, so punishment is made temporary by divine grace, though according to strict justice it should be eternal. The Bible indicates this very thing: "God hath spoken once, twice have I heard this: that strength belongeth unto God; also, unto Thee, O Lord, belongeth mercy; for Thou renderest to every man according to his work." The meaning is that the statement in the Torah that God does not hold the wicked guiltless but punishes them for their iniquities, contains two statements in it. One is that strength belongeth unto God to do justice to the wicked and to pay to every man according to his ways, as the Bible says: "The strength also of the king who loveth justice." But in this very justice which He does to the wicked we also find that God has mercy, "Also unto Thee, O Lord, belongeth mercy, for Thou renderest to every man according to his work," i.e., in the fact that Thou punishest the wicked in a temporary way, in accordance with the sin he committed, which is temporary, we can see that Thou conductest Thyself mercifully toward man in this regard, for according to strict justice, a person should receive eternal punishment for his sins in accordance with the infinity of God against whom he rebelled, as we explained above. The Psalmist says, therefore, that in the punishment which comes upon the wicked man in this world for the transgressions of which he is guilty, we see two things, viz. that God has power to do justice to those who transgress His will, and that He conducts Himself mercifully in this very justice, in that He inflicts temporary punishment, in accordance with the act of transgression, which is temporary. God does this in order that the person in question should be saved from eternal punishment in the world to come.

Some say that the words: "Also unto Thee, O Lord, belongeth mercy," refer to the spiritual reward which God bestows by grace.

Sefer HaIkkarim — BOOK [Maamar] FOUR

For man does not deserve any reward, as the Bible says: "If thou be righteous, what givest thou Him?" and granting that he does deserve reward, it should be temporary, as his good deeds are temporary, but not eternal, except by divine grace, as we said before. This statement, taken by itself, is true and in agreement with what we said, that temporary reward is made eternal by God's mercy. But it bears no relation to the contents of the passage and has no connection with the words: "God hath spoken once, twice have I heard this." Moreover, the words: "For Thou renderest [teshallem] to every man according to his work," show that he is speaking of punishment, like the words: "And recompensest [meshallem] the iniquity of the fathers into the bosom of their children after them," and: "Yea, I will requite [veshillamti] into their bosom."

It should be noted that this mercy of which we are speaking, by virtue of which the punishment which should be eternal, in accordance with the eternity of the Being to whom service is due, is made temporary by way of accommodation to the person owing the service, is shown only to those who love God and keep His commandments, as the Torah says: "For I, the Lord thy God, am a jealous God, visiting the iniquity of the fathers upon the children unto the third and fourth generation of them that hate Me; and showing mercy unto the thousandth generation of them that love Me and keep My commandments." The meaning of this passage is that in the case of those that hate Him, He visits the iniquity of the fathers upon the children to the third and fourth generation, so that they may be destroyed thoroughly and forever, as justice demands, but to those that love Him and keep His commandments He shows mercy, not visiting their iniquity upon them all at once, but distributing it over a thousand generations, so that they should not be completely destroyed, but that they may get a little punishment during a long time, in order that they may exist forever.

The Rabbis say in this connection: If a man has a thousand **zuz** owing to him and the debtor is his enemy, he collects the whole debt at once. But if he is his friend, he collects it little by little. Since, however, not every one can attain to the degree of perfect love, of which we spoke before, the Bible says that Israelites generally, who keep God's commandments, receive this mercy. Hence the Bible adds: "And keep My commandments." From this we infer that those who hate the Lord and do not keep His commandments will receive eternal punishment. Hence the Rabbis say that the Minim, the unbelievers [Apikorosim], those who deny the Torah and the resurrection, and the others that the Rabbis enumerate in the

Sefer HaIkkarim BOOK [Maamar] FOUR

Mishnah and the Baraita, persons who deny the fundamental principles or some of them or the secondary principles derived from the former, being excluded from the community of Israel and the seed of those who love God and keep His commandments, are treated in accord with strict justice and suffer eternal punishment. These are the men of whom the Rabbis say that they go down to gehenna and are judged there for ever and ever. Those, however, who believe in the principles of the Torah but are guilty of some transgressions, deserve to enjoy the mercy which is shown to those who keep the divine covenant, and to the seed of those who love Him. For just as reward is made eternal through the divine mercy that was shown to Abraham, as we explained before, so punishment is made temporary through divine mercy, as we said before.

Micah explains this when he says: "Who is a God like unto Thee, that pardoneth the iniquity, and passeth by the transgression of the remnant of His heritage? He retaineth not His anger forever, because He delighteth in mercy." The meaning is that God does not punish man according to his sins, but He pardoneth the iniquity and passeth by the transgression by way of mercy, but not for every man, only for the remnant of His heritage. The words: "He retaineth not His anger forever," indicate that according to strict justice, He ought to retain His anger forever. For it is clear that we do not say to a person: "The judge showed you mercy in not sentencing you to death," unless he deserved death. Hence if the prophet says: "He retaineth not His anger forever," it follows that strict justice demands that He should retain His anger forever, if not for His mercy. Hence, he concludes: "Because He delighteth in mercy," and adds: "He will again have compassion upon us; He will subdue our iniquities, … Thou wilt show faithfulness to Yaakov, mercy to Abraham …" The meaning is: Even if He should subdue our iniquities and hide them, or if eternal punishment should be made temporary, we would still be in need of mercy, in order that temporary reward should be made eternal. This is the mercy shown to Abraham when he was told: "Thy reward shall be exceeding great," as we explained above. Hence the prophet says: "Thou wilt show faithfulness to Yaakov, mercy to Abraham," i.e., wilt show and make permanent; and the mercy which Thou didst show to Abraham in making his reward eternal will become true for Yaakov, just as eternal punishment is made temporary by God's mercy, as we explained before.

The Psalmist also explains this, namely that eternal punishment is made temporary and temporary reward is made eternal through grace. In reference to punishment, he says: "He will not always

Sefer HaIkkarim   BOOK [Maamar] FOUR

contend; neither will He keep His anger forever," as should be the case, but, "He hath not dealt with us after our sins, nor requited us according to our iniquities." He explains then that this is due to God's mercy: "For as the heaven is high above the earth, so great is His mercy toward them that fear Him." For to give eternal reward for a temporary act shows great mercy, as great as the heavens are high above the earth. The word height signifies worth, as in the verse, "But the Lord of hosts is exalted [made high] through justice," because the heavens are eternal, as David said: "He hath also established them for ever and ever," while the earth is temporary and destined to destruction. God's mercy in giving eternal reward for a temporary act is similar. But in order that a person may deserve this reward, it is necessary to remove our transgressions from us far away, as far as the east is from the west, and to inflict temporary punishment upon the righteous in this world in order that they may merit eternal reward in the world to come. For if He should inflict eternal punishment, as justice demands, no person would merit eternal reward. Hence he says: "Like as a father hath compassion upon His children, so hath the Lord compassion upon them that fear Him," to show that it is an act of compassion on the part of God to inflict temporary punishment upon the righteous in this world for the few transgressions of which they are guilty, in order that they may merit eternal reward in the world to come, as a father chastises and punishes his son by way of compassion so as to lead him to a good end and enable him to attain a high degree for his own ultimate good.

Then he explains the reason of this mercy: "For He knoweth our inclination; He remembereth that we are dust." That is, since He knows that by reason of our inclination we are destined to sin, "For the imagination of man's heart is evil from his youth," if He should not show us this mercy in punishing a man temporarily instead of eternally, no man would escape the judgment of gehenna, and what would the righteous then do, who can not but commit some sin in this world? In the same way if God did not convert temporary reward into eternal through mercy, no man would attain eternal happiness, for man is a temporary being: "As for man, his days are as grass; as a flower of the field, so he flourisheth, for the wind passeth over it, and it is gone ..." What, then, would Moshe and Abraham and the other righteous men do in order to merit eternal reward, since they are temporary beings, and can only do temporary acts, unless they merit this reward through God's mercy? Hence, he concludes: "But the mercy of the Lord is from everlasting to everlasting upon them that fear Him ...," i.e., even though man's days are like grass and his acts are temporary, for he can only do a temporary act, his reward is eternal through God's mercy, which is from everlasting to everlasting upon them that fear Him.

In the beginning of the Psalm, he also refers to these two kinds of mercy. "Who forgiveth all thine iniquity," refers to the mercy which converts eternal punishment into temporary. "Who healeth all thy diseases," refers to the mercy which converts temporary reward into eternal. Then he explains the matter further and says: "Who redeemeth thy life from the pit," which surely refers to redemption from the eternal punishment of gehenna, for no one is redeemed from the natural death of the body. Then he says: "Who encompasseth thee with loving-kindness and tender mercies," to indicate that by making eternal punishment temporary, it becomes possible to attain eternal spiritual reward, which is a crown of beauty to the soul and a diadem of glory on the head of every righteous man. The attainment of this reward is designated as mercy and compassion.

At the end of the Psalm, he explains that these two kinds of mercy extend only to those who love God and observe His commandments: "But the mercy of the Lord is from everlasting to everlasting upon them that fear Him ... To such as keep His covenant, and to those that remember His precepts to do them." All this is due to the fact that the divine providence extends over all existing things above and below: "The Lord hath established His throne in the heavens; and His kingdom ruleth over all." This much we have desired to explain concerning reward and punishment.

Chapter 39

We must now endeavor to solve the problem which has caused no end of difficulty to the ancients as well as the moderns, namely, why are spiritual promises not mentioned explicitly in the Torah, as well as material promises?

Some have attempted to solve the difficulty by saying that spiritual reward is a profound conception, hard for the human mind to grasp. And since the Torah was given to the masses of the people as well as the wise, it was proper to promise corporeal reward, which they can grasp and conceive. For if the Torah had promised spiritual reward, which can not be perceived by the senses nor imagined and conceived by their limited minds, they would not have believed it. And this would have led to the failure and nullification of the Torah

Sefer HaIkkarim — BOOK [Maamar] FOUR

as a whole. Therefore, the Torah made corporeal promises, so that when the people see that the corporeal promises are fulfilled, they will without doubt also believe the spiritual promises mentioned only by allusion.

But this solution is not satisfactory at all. For how can the fulfilment of the corporeal promises be evidence of something which is not mentioned in the Torah at all, according to their idea? Moreover, incorporeality and the existence of a separate immaterial intellect are also matters that can not be perceived by the senses and yet the Torah did not hesitate to say: "For ye saw no manner of form …;" "Thou shalt not make unto thee a graven image, even any manner of likeness …," and so on, in order to remove corporeality and corporeal attributes from God. In another place, on the other hand, we read: "And they beheld God," which, taken literally, is absolutely untrue. But the Torah relies in this matter on the intelligence of the reader, so that the masses understand it literally and the wise interpret it in the true sense. This being so, the Torah should have mentioned spiritual reward also, and every one would understand it according to his powers and ability.

Others have said that the reason the Torah does not mention spiritual reward explicitly, is because the Torah mentions only those things which come through a miracle or sign or wonder, like the promises of material reward for fulfilment of the commandments, which comes supernaturally, for example: "Then I will command My blessing upon you in the sixth year, and it shall bring forth produce for three years." It is not natural that every sixth year the land should produce enough for three years. Also: "Thy raiment waxed not old upon thee, neither did thy foot swell, these forty years." It is well known that even a garment hanging on a line can not last forty years, and the phenomenon was supernatural. We also read: "That He might make thee know that man doth not live by bread only, but by everything that proceedeth out of the mouth of the Lord doth man live," and many other similar statements. But the immortality of the soul is something which follows by necessity from the nature of the soul, hence the Torah did not have to promise it, since it is a natural phenomenon.

This explanation, too, is weak, for immortality is no more natural in the soul than freedom of choice in man, and yet the Torah says: "See, I have set before thee this day life and good … therefore choose life …" Since immortality is not something well known, the Torah should have told us about it, as it tells us about freedom or creation or the various other ideas and beliefs which are mentioned in the

Torah. Moreover, according to those who say that spiritual reward is conferred upon body and soul together, it is not a natural phenomenon, for perpetual existence is not natural to body. Hence the Torah should have mentioned it explicitly. We must, therefore, find a more adequate solution. The most difficult part of the matter is this: If the Torah does not mention spiritual promises, which are the essence of reward, why does it mention corporeal promises, which are not the essence of reward?

Chapter 40

If we examine the corporeal promises mentioned in the Torah one by one, we shall find that spiritual promises could not have been made in those cases. For all the promises in the Torah embrace the nation as a whole. As for the promises in the section "Behukkotai," it is clear that they are all spoken in the plural and refer to the nation as a whole. But even those promises made in the section "Ki Tabo," which are expressed in the singular, refer to the nation as a whole. This is proved from the fact that at the end of those curses we read: "The Lord will bring thee and thy king whom thou shalt set over thee ... The Lord will bring a nation against thee from far, from the end of the earth ...," statements which, though made in the singular, clearly refer to the nation as a whole. Similarly, the promises of material prosperity mentioned in the Torah in section " 'Ekeb" refer to the nation as a whole.

Now it is clear that promises referring to the nation as a whole can not be spiritual, for even if the nation as a whole is righteous and deserving of life in the world to come, we can not say that the wicked man in it deserves future life for the sake of the fifty righteous men. It would be unjust to bestow future life on an absolutely wicked man and treat alike the righteous and the wicked. It is clear, therefore, that the promises which refer to the nation as a whole must necessarily be material. That is, if the majority of the country or of the nation are righteous, the country or the nation will escape exile or famine or pestilence and universal punishments in general, because good or evil decress pronounced upon nations or countries depend upon the character of the majority of the population. If the majority are righteous, the decree is good, and if the majority are wicked, the decree is evil. Hence the Rabbis say that the world is judged according to the character of the majority. Sometimes the country or the nation is saved even if the majority are not righteous, for the sake of fifty or even fewer righteous men found therein, if

Sefer HaIkkarim — BOOK [Maamar] FOUR

they are fit men to shield the majority from suffering. Accordingly, if it is true that all the corporeal promises in the Torah refer not to the individual but to the nation as a whole, there can be no question why the Torah mentions corporeal promises. For they are mentioned only where there can be no mention of spiritual promises, namely in general promises referring to the nation as a whole, which can not be spiritual, as we have explained.

But individual reward is mentioned in the Torah only in a few places. For example, in connection with the precept not to take the mother bird with the young, we read: "That it may be well with thee, and that thou mayest prolong thy days," which the Rabbis interpret as follows: " 'That it may be well with thee' - in a world which is wholly good; 'And that thou mayest prolong thy days' - in a world which is wholly long." Similarly in connection with charity we find: "Because that for this thing the Lord thy God will bless thee." This, however, is not necessarily the main reward, but the meaning is that the Lord will bless him in addition to the main reward.

The principal individual reward which is conferred on each person separately, whether spiritual or corporeal, is not mentioned explicitly in the Torah but only allusively and in a few places. One passage is found in section "Ahare Mot": "After the doings of the land of Egypt, wherein ye dwelt, shall ye not do ... neither shall ye walk in their statutes." This is not only an admonition to the nation as a whole but also to the individual, not to follow the customs of the idolaters. At the end of the section, we read: "Ye shall therefore keep My statutes, and Mine ordinances, which if a man do, he shall live by them." This no doubt refers to the individual spiritual reward, which is conferred on each individual separately, and is to be explained as follows: God admonishes the people that they should observe His statutes and His judgments, even though they entail more trouble than keeping the statutes of the land of Egypt and the land of Canaan, because, although those nations as a whole prospered by observing their respective statutes, nevertheless the individual did not attain through them his main perfection, namely the eternal life of the soul, which he can attain through the ordinances of God. Hence, we read: "Ye shall keep My statutes and Mine ordinances ...," i.e., keep them, even if there is trouble in doing so, for they have advantage and superiority over others. For these statutes help the individual also to obtain future life. This is the meaning of the expression: "Which if a man do, he shall live by them," meaning that the statutes of the other nations have not this effect. Onkelos translates it, "That through them he may live the life

Sefer HaIkkarim — BOOK [Maamar] FOUR

of eternity." The context shows that it must have reference to the life of the soul. For how can he say that by keeping the statutes and ordinances of the Torah, the person will live longer than by keeping the statutes of the other nations? This is obviously untrue, for the man who observes the Torah does not live longer corporeally than the others. But there is no doubt that he is referring to the life of the soul and not to the life of the body, hence Onkelos translates it, "That through them he may live the life of eternity." This is a clear proof to any intelligent man who will listen to reason and acknowledge the truth.

There is also another proof in section "Reëh," where Moshe says to the Israelites: "Ye are the children of the Lord your God: ye shall not cut yourselves, nor make any baldness between your eyes for the dead. For thou art a holy people unto the Lord thy God." This seems at first sight strange. How can he say: Ye shall not cut yourselves for the dead, "For thou art a holy people unto the Lord thy God, and the Lord hath chosen thee to be His own treasure out of all peoples that are upon the face of the earth?" The contrary would seem to be the case, namely that for the reason given, one should grieve and mourn the more for the dead. For one should mourn more for the death of a king's son than for an ordinary person. It is like saying to a person, don't worry about the loss of your ring, for it had a fine pearl in it. The meaning of the text is this: Since you are sons of God and a holy people and a treasure above all peoples, you must not mourn unduly for the dead, for this would indicate that you think the person has ceased to exist, and therefore you mourn for him as for a potsherd that is broken and can not be repaired. But it is not so. He is like a vessel of silver or gold which can be repaired when it is broken, for he will come into the treasury of the Lord. Hence one should not mourn unduly, but only as one is grieved at parting from a friend or from one who goes on a long journey. Hence he concludes: "For thou art a holy people unto the Lord thy God," i.e., since God is holy and His servants are holy and thou art a holy people, equals unite with equals and the soul of the departed will therefore without doubt unite with the Separate Intelligences, because it is holy and the angels are holy attendants of God. Hence it is not proper to cut oneself and mourn unduly for the dead. This shows that the soul survives after death.

There is another proof from the words of Moshe at the end of the section, "Ha'azinu," when he is about to close the Torah: "Set your heart unto all the words wherewith I testify against you this day … For it is no vain thing for you; because it is your life, and through

Sefer HaIkkarim   BOOK [Maamar] FOUR

this thing ye shall prolong your days upon the land …" In every document intended to establish a fact, the subject-matter must be repeated in the last line. So, Moshe wrote down these things here to allude to the two kinds of reward which may be attained through the Torah, spiritual and material. Spiritual reward is referred to in the words: "Because it is your life." Material reward is alluded to in the words: "And through this thing ye shall prolong your days upon the land." To indicate the difference between spiritual reward and material, he says about the spiritual: "For it is no vein thing outside of thee," i.e., do not think that it is something distinct from you, for it is your own life, namely the essence of life surviving after death. This is in order to indicate that the intellect which is acquired through understanding of the service of God, as we explained above, is itself the life and the existence of the soul after death. The word hu [=it] is an indication of this, as we explained above, when we analyzed the meaning of the expression hu hu. Material reward is referred to in the words: "And through this thing ye shall prolong your days upon the land," indicating that the material reward that is attained through fulfilment of the Torah and the commandments is not the main reward but something incidental that goes with the fulfilment of the Torah. Similarly, the words: "Because that for this thing the Lord thy God will bless thee," which are mentioned in connection with charity, do not represent the main reward, as we explained above.

We can also cite proof from the Hagiographa. David, speaking of the reward of the individual who fears God, says: "What man is he that feareth the Lord? Him will He instruct in the way that he should choose," i.e., He will instruct him in the way he should choose in order to attain the human purpose, namely, that "His soul shall abide in prosperity; and his seed [who remain] shall inherit the land." Now if the soul ceased to exist with the death of the body, he should not say that his soul shall abide in prosperity when his seed shall inherit the land. He indicates, therefore, that there is a specific good in which the soul will abide after death. This is a clear proof beyond all cavil. Solomon also says: "When a wicked man dieth, his expectation shall perish," alluding to the destruction of the soul of the wicked. But in referring to the righteous he says: "But the righteous, even when he is brought to death, hath hope," which shows that there is hope for the soul of the righteous after death.

We can also cite evidence from the Prophets. Isaiah, referring to a penitent who died, says: "I have seen his ways, and will heal him; I will lead him also, and requite with comforts him and his mourners."

Sefer HaIkkarim — BOOK [Maamar] FOUR

Since he speaks of "his mourners," it is clear that the man is dead, and yet he says that having seen his ways He has healed him and led him in the way of all the earth so that He requited with comforts him and his mourners. But there is no comfort to him and his mourners, nor healing, if the soul perishes and goes to destruction. There is comfort to him if his soul survives, and there is comfort to his mourners if they all know that the hope of the dead one is not destroyed and that he has spiritual immortality. This shows that immortality of the soul was known in those days and derived from the Torah, and therefore the prophet promises the penitent that God will heal him of his iniquities and, in consideration of his penitence, will reward him with immortality, so as to give comfort to him and his mourners. Also, in the prophecy of Zechariah the angel promises Yehoshua the son of Jehozadak, the high priest: "If thou wilt walk in My ways, and if thou wilt keep My charge ... then I will give thee free access among these that stand by." This denotes the permanent existence of the soul, as we explained before. We could cite many passages of a similar nature from the Prophets, but those that we have cited are sufficient to show the nature of the evidence that may be adduced from the Bible in favor of spiritual reward. It is also clear from what we have said that the Torah does not mention individual corporeal reward, as many have thought, but individual spiritual, and universal corporeal.

Chapter 41

There is still another philosophical and more profound way of proving immortality of the soul from the Torah, as follows:
We have shown that the various powers or faculties result from various principles. Hence if we know that man has a faculty which is common to him and the animal, and another faculty in which he differs from it, we know that the faculty in which he differs from the animal comes from a principle different from that which gives animality to the animal. In the same way verdigris contains a power of burning and a power of corroding, which are distinct. We know that the burning function comes to it from the power of copper, and we infer that the corroding power comes to it from another principle, namely vinegar. In the same way, we see that the faculty by which man is distinguished from the lower animals has a specific and peculiar function in which the corporeal powers do not participate, namely the conception of the separate substances and of immaterial and abstract ideas, which is indestructible. Hence, we infer that this

Sefer Haikkarim — BOOK [Maamar] FOUR

faculty can exist by itself without body and is not destroyed with the destruction of the body.

Accordingly, when Adam apprehended the separate substances, abstracted from matter - this is the meaning of the verse: "And the man gave names to all cattle, and to the fowl of the air …" - he inferred that he had a psychic power independent of matter and not destroyed with the destruction thereof. But he did not understand how to maintain that power. But when God revealed Himself to him and commanded him: "But of the tree of the knowledge of good and evil, thou shalt not eat of it; for in the day that thou eatest thereof thou shalt surely die," it became clear to him that the preservation of the soul is brought about by doing the will of God, and the death of it by transgressing His words.

Now the earlier divine laws, like those of Adam and of Noah, knew of this spiritual reward we mentioned, namely the separate existence of the soul through the command of God; they knew it from their own ratiocination and from Adam's knowledge, acquired by himself and received from God, which they learned from Adam himself. Hence, they threatened the loss of this spiritual reward to any one who rebelled against the command of God and transgressed His words, like a master who says to his servant: If you disobey my command, I will take away all that you have, from which we infer of course that if he does not disobey, he will retain what he has.

In this way we understand the statement God made to Adam in reference to transgressing His command: "For in the day that thou eatest thereof thou shalt surely die." The double death [mot tamut] no doubt means a special punishment for the body and a special one for the soul. Before he ate of the tree of knowledge, his natural power was adequate to supply the body with as much material as was dissolved, so that the matter that was dissolved did not exceed the new matter supplied by the food which came into the body from the outside, and hence it was possible in this way that the body should exist forever. But after he had eaten of the tree of knowledge, dissolution exceeded assimilation, as is the case to-day, and death became inevitable, as is explained in the first book of the Canon. Hence the expression: "For in the day that thou eatest thereof thou shalt surely die," referring to the body, i.e., in that day dissolution will get the better of assimilation and death will be inevitable. Now the tree of life had the power to re-enforce the natural power of the individual and to enable it to make assimilation equal to dissolution or even to exceed it. Hence the text says: "And now, lest he put forth his hand, and take also of the tree of life, and eat, and live forever."

Sefer HaIkkarim — BOOK [Maamar] FOUR

That is, he may correct the error he has made in eating of the tree of knowledge, and live forever. This is the way we must understand the text taken literally, in reference to the death of the body as a result of eating of the tree of knowledge.

The punishment of the soul consisted also in her destruction and death. The text mentions death twice, referring to the death of the body and the death of the soul. Now since the punishment of him who transgresses the commandment of God is the death of the soul, the reward of him who fulfils the commandment of God is without doubt the permanent existence of the soul.

From all this it is clear that the immortality of the soul was known to Adam and Noah and those who observed their laws. In fact, our opponents admit that the punishment announced to Adam had reference to the soul, but they say that it had reference to the soul only, whereas we say that it had reference to the body also, as the meaning of the text shows. As long as the punishment of the body has not been remitted, there is no proof of the remission of the punishment of the soul except by keeping the commandments of God. However, since we all agree that the punishment promised to the soul is without the body, reward will also be bestowed upon the soul without the body.

And this is precisely the manner in which the Torah announces punishments to the soul if she transgresses the commandments of God. Some of the things forbidden are articles of food which are good for the body and not injurious at all. For example: "For whosoever eateth leavened bread ... that soul shall be cut off ...;" also in relation to fat, we read: "For whosoever eateth the fat of the beast ... even the soul that eateth it shall be cut off from his people." But it is well known that leaven during Passover and fat at any time are not deadly poison to cut off the one who eats them before his time, for experience shows that it is not so. The expression that the person will be cut off must therefore refer to punishment of the soul of the sinner.

There are indeed instances in which the punishment of being cut off extends also to the children of the sinner, as our Rabbis say that in this particular punishment both he and his children are cut off. But it is not true of all cases, for it would not be fair. Reuben, for example, a man of eighty, eats a piece of fat, the size of an olive, and all his children and descendants die before their time, but the sinner himself is not punished, for he has lived his eighty years. This shows, therefore, that in the punishment of being cut off the soul of the sinner is also punished. Now since the punishment mentioned in

Sefer HaIkkarim — BOOK [Maamar] FOUR

the law of Moshe under the term of being cut off, necessarily refers to the soul without the body, it follows that the soul which does not sin will not be cut off and the reward will come to the soul without the body.

This conception of the punishment of being cut off, which is mentioned in the Torah in various places, is precisely the one that was accepted by Adam, Noah, Shem, Eber, and other distinguished persons, like Abraham, Yitzhak and Yaakov. This is the reason why Abraham was ready to give up his own life and the life of his only son and all the material prosperity which had been promised to him, - the possession of the land of Canaan and his children's possession of the gate of their enemies: "For in Yitzhak shall seed be called to thee," - and was going to kill his only son, because he knew that if one fulfils the commandments of God, the soul will exist forever and enjoy eternal bliss, whereas if one transgresses the commandments of God, the soul will not prosper and will be cut off from that bliss. Of what good would have been to him his family after his death and all the material promises if he had lost that eternal good, the immortality of the soul? To be sure, we may say here that Abraham served God from pure love and was not concerned with reward at all, but only with the fulfilment of the will of God whom he loved. Nevertheless, our argument as a whole is correct and compels every intelligent person to admit that from the punishment which is mentioned we infer that there is reward of the soul, which survives after death.

One may ask, however, why does not the Torah speak at length about this matter instead of relying on the inference which we made from the punishment of cutting off and death that is announced to the soul? The answer is this: He who gave the Torah was concerned about healing the ills of the soul, as an expert physician is concerned about healing the ills of the body. The physician is interested in curing the cause of the disease and not in curing the other attendant and incidental ailments, for if he cures the cause, all the other ailments will be cured. In the same way the Healer of souls is interested in curing the cause of the disease.

But it is clear that there can be no spiritual reward and punishment unless there is Providence.

The ancients, however, all the seed of Adam and all the descendants of Noah, except a few distinguished individuals, like Shem and Eber and Abraham and others, worshipped idols, denied Providence and followed sense experience only. Hence, they paid no attention to the spiritual promises which they knew from the laws of Adam and

Sefer HaIkkarim — BOOK [Maamar] FOUR

Noah. They rejected them and did not believe in them because they could not be perceived by the senses. Therefore God, who knows the hidden things of the heart, chose another way. He promised in the law of Moshe corporeal and physical rewards, supernatural in their character, to show that he who serves God and keeps His commandments is looked after by God, who provides for all the details of his existence, and is not subject to the regular course of nature. Thus the Rabbis say, commenting on the biblical verse: "Get thee out of thy country ... and I will make of thee a great nation, and I will bless thee, and make thy name great:" "A journey diminishes three things - children, money and fame - therefore God said: 'I will make of thee a great nation,' to assure him of children; 'And I will bless thee,' to assure him of money; 'And I will make thy name great,' to assure him of fame." This is in order to show that he who serves God is not subject to the laws of nature and is not injured by the natural causes of harm, but treads upon the lion and asp, and tramples under feet the young lion and the serpent.

In the Law of Moshe, God followed exactly the same method as in the law of Abraham. He performed signs and wonders in the presence of all in order that it may be clear to them that he who serves God and keeps His commandments is not subject to the things of nature, but all the things of nature are subject to him. Now we find that there is not one of the things of nature that has not some value or purpose. We also find that certain acts and practices produce results which do not logically follow from those acts. Surely, then, the commandments of the Torah must have certain valuable results, though reason can not show it.

The Rabbis mention certain practices which produce certain results that do not follow logically from the acts, as for example in treatise Shabbat: "If one has a bone in his throat, he should take a bone of the same kind, put it on the back of his head and say: 'Had had nehit, bela' bela' nehit, had had,'" and other matters of the same sort which are mentioned there. Also, in Talmud Sanhedrin it is told in the name of Rabbi Eliezer the Great that he said: "I said a word and the whole field was filled with cucumbers; I said another word and they were all collected in one place;" from which it appears that by doing certain apparently irrelevant things, or even merely by saying certain words without doing anything, certain results follow which have no logical relation to the act or word.

So, we say that the divine Wisdom knows that certain acts and practices, namely the commandments of the Torah, are followed by certain results, reward and punishment of the soul, even though we

Sefer HaIkkarim   BOOK [Maamar] FOUR

do not know how the result follows from the act. Neither do we know why certain results follow from certain acts or words mentioned by the Cabalists, where there is no logical relation between the two. In the same way the rewards and the punishments mentioned in the Torah follow upon a deliberate doing of the commandments or prohibitions and are connected with them and result from them as an effect follows from its causes.

Take as an instance Nebuchadnezzar. He was an absolutely wicked man and God decreed that he should lose his reason, abandon mankind and live among the beasts. But the decree was delayed twelve months in consideration of an act of benevolence which he had to his credit. The Rabbis even say that Daniel was punished because of a certain advice which he gave to Nebuchadnezzar: "Wherefore, O king, let my counsel be acceptable unto thee, and break off thy sins by almsgiving, and thine iniquities by showing mercy to the poor ..." It is clear, therefore, that almsgiving has the effect of annulling a decree, and that such effect follows even if the recipient is not deserving. This is why Rabbi Ammi refused to take alms from idolaters.

In reference to punishment also the Rabbis say: Since the temple was destroyed, the four modes of capital punishment inflicted by the court have been annulled, but the law of the four kinds of capital punishment still holds: If one is guilty of an act punishable by stoning, he either falls down from the roof or a wild beast tramples him under foot. If he is guilty of a sin punishable by strangulation, he either drowns in the river or he dies of suffocation. The same thing holds of the other commandments of the Torah. Even though it may not be logical we must believe it is so, since experience shows that nature is subject to the control of the righteous, the pious and those who observe the commandments of the Torah. This is an important principle of the Torah.

A case in point is Marah. Moshe cast a tree into the water and it became sweet. According to tradition the tree was the wall ivy, whose wood is very bitter and not apt to make water sweet. The Bible says: "There He made for them a statute and an ordinance, and there He proved it." The correct interpretation of the trial is that given by Rabbenu Nissim. The pronominal suffix of the verb **Nissahu** [proved it] refers to "statute" and "ordinance," and the meaning is as follows: God made for the people there a statute and an ordinance, as the Rabbis say that the laws of Sabbath and of civil justice were given in Marah, "and there he proved it," i.e., Moshe proved this statute and ordinance before the people when he showed

them that nature is subject to those who keep the commandments of God, so that bitter water is made sweet by means of bitter wood. Hence it says in the sequel: "And He said: 'If thou wilt diligently hearken to the voice of the Lord thy God, and wilt do that which is right in His eyes, and wilt give ear to His commandments, and keep all His statutes, I will put none of the diseases upon thee, which I have put upon the Egyptians; for I am the Lord that healeth thee.' "
He says here that he who hearkens to the voice of the Lord and does the things which are right and agreeable to Him and observes His commandments and His statutes, is not only delivered from accidental illnesses and those deliberately inflicted, like the diseases of the Egyptians, but is healed also from natural diseases which come upon a person at the change of the seasons of the year by reason of his temperament.
There are two kinds of diseases:

1. Natural diseases, which come to a person on account of the change of the season, and are due to his temperament, for example, a person of sanguine temperament gets sick in the spring, while a person of choleric temperament gets sick in the summer.

2. Diseases which come upon a person by reason of changes which take place in the atmosphere, like epidemics and other diseases of this sort, which are due to changes in the nature of the atmosphere and bring diseases upon a person either by chance or by divine punishment. These diseases do not come upon a person by reason of his nature, they come from outside and by deliberate imposition, like the diseases of the Egyptians. These are referred to in the words: "I will put none of the diseases upon thee which I have put upon the Egyptians;" whereas the first kind of diseases, which come upon a man by reason of his nature, is referred to in the words: "For I am the Lord that healeth thee."

Similarly, Moshe promises in Deuteronomy: "And the Lord will take away from thee all sickness; and He will put none of the evil diseases of Egypt, which thou knowest, upon thee." This statement also indicates that if one hearkens to the ordinances of the Torah and observes them and does them, he will be delivered from both kinds of diseases. Those that are due to man's nature are indicated in the words: "And the Lord will take away from thee all sickness." While those diseases which are intentionally inflicted are referred to in the words: "And He will put none of the evil diseases of Egypt, which thou knowest, upon thee."

All this is in order to show that he who observes the Torah is saved from plagues and accidents, natural or unnatural, because he stands

Sefer HaIkkarim   BOOK [Maamar] FOUR

above the things of nature, as was proved in Marah, as we explained. The suffix of the word nissahu refers to "statute" and "ordinance." The verb can not refer to the people, meaning that they proved the Lord, for we find no such thing. They merely cried to Moshe, saying: "What shall we drink?" And God would not have been angry because they asked that which was necessary to them. Nor can the verb refer to God, meaning that God proved the people, for no useful purpose was served by this trial as by the other kinds, which we explained in this Book of our treatise. Therefore, we say that the suffix of nissahu refers to "statute," and the meaning is that God showed them by an experiment that he who observes the Torah is not subject to the things of nature.

God had the same purpose in sending down the manna, which came right after the event at Marah, as Moshe explains in Deuteronomy: "And He afflicted thee, and suffered thee to hunger, and fed thee with manna," and then it says: "That He might make thee know that man doth not live by bread only, but by everything that proceedeth out of the mouth of the Lord doth man live." From this it seems that the manna and all the miracles that took place in connection with it were for the purpose of showing Israel that he who observes the Torah is above the things of nature, and that God can keep man alive without them and without bread.

Now since it was proved conclusively through all the signs and wonders which were performed in the wilderness that God changes the course of nature for those who perform His will, and that He provides for them in all their affairs, they would certainly be convinced about spiritual reward, which is the main result of providence, as they knew by tradition from the earlier laws of Adam and Noah, through Abraham, Yitzhak and Yaakov, that the soul is immortal, which is the absolute truth. The promises made through the patriarchs of the possession of the land and of corporeal benefits to all the people were in order that the people might be able to understand what spiritual happiness means if they lived in peace and tranquillity. For if they were living as exiles in a strange land, they would not be able to serve God properly, so as to attain to spiritual happiness.

This is an adequate argument according to the opinion of Maimonides, who says that the main reward in the future world is conferred upon the soul alone. According to Nahmanides, who holds that reward is conferred upon soul and body together, we must say that as we inferred punishment for body and soul together from the words: "For in the day that thou eatest thereof thou shalt surely die

Sefer HaIkkarim   BOOK [Maamar] FOUR

[mot tamut]," we likewise infer that reward is for both body and soul after the resurrection. This is what we desired to explain in this investigation, and may God deliver us from error.

Chapter 42

Every adherent of the Law of Moshe is obliged to believe in the coming of the Messiah, as we explained above. The Torah expressly commands us to believe the words of the prophet: "Unto him ye shall hearken." But the prophets announced the coming of the Messiah, hence it is clear that any one who does not believe in the coming of the Messiah denies the words of the prophets and transgresses a mandatory precept. But the belief in the coming of the Messiah is not a fundamental principle, denial of which would nullify the entire Torah.

Belief in reward is indeed obligatory upon every adherent of a divine law, and he who denies it denies a fundamental principle. But if one beieves that the soul alone is rewarded in the future world or that reward is corporeal at the time of the resurrection, he does not deny a fundamental principle even though he does not believe in reward in this world, as long as he believes in the principle of reward and punishment generally, though he has a different opinion as to one of the kinds of reward. In fact, some of the Rabbis say that there is no reward in this world for obedience to the commandments, believing that the principal reward is in the future world: "That it may go well with thee," they say, means, "in the world which is wholly good;" and "that thy days may be long," refers to "the world which is wholly long."

We say, therefore, that belief in the coming of the Messiah is not such a fundamental principle that he who denies it should be called an infidel. But it is a true belief which every adherent of the Mosaic law must believe. We do not intend in this part of our treatise to mention the specific prophecies which refer to his coming, as that would take too long, for the commentators differ as to which are the Messianic prophecies, though they all agree that the Messiah will come. Some of the sages of the Talmud hold that all the prophecies which refer to the Messiah have already been fulfilled - according to some they were all fulfilled in the days of Hezekiah, king of Yehuda: "Israel has no Messiah, for they consumed him in the days of Hezekiah king of Yehuda." Rab Ashi contradicts this opinion, and cites Zechariah in his favor: "Behold thy king cometh unto thee …," but this was not at the time of the second temple. Since he does not

Sefer HaIkkarim   BOOK [Maamar] FOUR

cite Isaiah, it seems that according to Rab Ashi too there is no conclusive refutation of the former statement in the prophecies of Isaiah. Our Rabbis agree that the prophecies were said concerning Hezekiah, but were not fulfilled in him: "God wanted to make Hezekiah the Messiah, etc." The passage in Ezekiel: "And I will make them one nation in the land, upon the mountains of Israel, and one king shall be king to them all," is also interpreted as referring to the second temple. A proof of this is the statement by Rabbi Akiba that the ten tribes are not destined to return, etc. Now if the prophecy of Ezekiel referred to the distant future, how could Rabbi Akiba say that the ten tribes will not return, when Ezekiel says the opposite? It seems, therefore, that Rabbi Akiba referred the words of Ezekiel to the time of the second temple. The words: "And one king shall be king to them all," may refer to Zerubbabel, the satrap of Yehuda, or to Nehemiah, if he was a different person from Zerubbabel, or to the Nasi, or to the reigning king of the Hasmoneans.

Some of the commentators also say that all the prophecies of Isaiah were fulfilled at the time of the second temple, which Cyrus ordered to be built: "And let the expenses be given out of the king's house." The passage in Isaiah, beginning: "And kings shall be thy foster fathers …," and the whole section there refers to Cyrus and the kings of Media and Persia. In the beginning of the second commonwealth they were poor, while later in the days of the Hasmoneans they became very rich, thereby fulfilling the prophecy: "For brass I will bring gold …" In the beginning they were so poor that they made the candelabrum of tin and covered it with brass, while the other vessels were made of brass. When they became rich, they made them of gold, as the Rabbis say about king Yannai that he ate with the Pharisees at tables of gold. In Herod's temple, which was more beautiful than that of Solomon, was fulfilled the prophecy: "And I will make thy pinnacles of rubies …"

They also say that in the second commonwealth was fulfilled the prophecy: "And they shall bring all your brethren out of all the nations for an offering unto the Lord," because Cyrus, king of Persia, commanded: "And whosoever is left, in any place where he sojourneth, let the men of his place help him with silver, and with gold …" Similarly, the words: "Shall all flesh come to worship before Me," do not refer to all the nations, but only to Israel, as we explained above, where we discussed the different meanings of the word **Kol** [all]. The words: "From one new moon to another," do not denote infinite time, for if they did, then the sequel: "And they shall go forth, and look upon the carcasses of the men that have

Sefer HaIkkarim — BOOK [Maamar] FOUR

rebelled against Me; for their worm shall not die ...," would be a promise of eternal life to the worms. But the meaning is that the sinners of that generation will be a scorn and a mockery to their neighbors and to all that see them, so that all the men of that generation will profit by example when they see the punishment of those wicked men, hence they will come "from one new moon to another, and from one Sabbath to another," to worship before the Lord.

Rabbi Hayim Galipapa also writes in an epistle called, Epistle of Redemption, that all the prophecies of Daniel refer to the second temple only. The words in Daniel: "And [he] shall wear out the saints of the Highest; and he shall think to change the seasons and the law; and they shall be given into his hand until a time and times and half a time," all refer to Antiochus. Also, the words: "But the saints of the Highest shall receive the kingdom," refer, he says, to the Hasmoneans. As for the words: "And possess the kingdom for ever, even for ever and ever ['ad 'alma ve'ad 'alam 'almaya]," he says that 'olam means one jubilee, a short and definite time during which the Hasmoneans ruled. The words: "And one that was ancient of days did sit," he refers to Mattathias the high priest, who was the head of the Hasmoneans, a very old man, all of whose sons reigned after him. He supports this interpretation by citing a statement of the Rabbis in reference to the words: "For the day of vengeance that was in My heart and My year of redemption are come" - "If the heart has not revealed it to the mouth, to whom can the mouth reveal it?" From this it appears that even the angels do not know when the redemption will come, because God did not reveal it to them; whereas in the words which the angel says to Daniel it seems that the angel knew the time, but Daniel did not understand him.

According to this writer's words the four beasts which Daniel saw do not signify the things that all the commentators write about, but the first one denotes the kingdom of Babylon; the second the kingdom of Media; the third, Persia and Media; the fourth, the kingdom of Greece, all of which existed in the time of the second temple. Therefore, it says in reference to the second beast: "And it raised up itself on one side and it had three ribs in its mouth between its teeth," because Darius the Mede, who conquered Babylon and destroyed it, ruled only over Media, Babylonia and Assyria, which latter was under the power of Nebuchadnezzar, who conquered Nineveh and became king of Assyria, but Darius did not rule over Persia and all the kingdoms that were subject to Persia.

When Cyrus the Persian, the son-in-law of Darius, who was king of

Sefer HaIkkarim — BOOK [Maamar] FOUR

Persia, came to the throne and inherited the kingdom of Media from Darius, the reign of the third beast began, which embraced the whole world, as he says: "All the kingdoms of the earth hath the Lord, the God of heaven, given me." In reference to the third beast it says: "Which had upon the sides of it four wings of a fowl; the beast had also four heads." This is an allusion to the four kings who ruled over both Persia and Media, as the text itself says: "There shall stand up yet three kings in Persia; and the fourth shall be far richer than they all; and when he is waxed strong through his riches, he shall stir up all against the realm of Greece."

Then began the kingdom of Greece, which is the fourth beast. The expressions in the text support this interpretation: "Then I desired to know the truth concerning the fourth beast, which was diverse from all of them, exceeding terrible ..." This he refers to the rule of the Greeks, which began with Alexander of Macedon, concerning whom it is said: "And the rough he-goat is the king of Greece; and the great horn that is between his eyes is the first king." All that comes after is an account of the rule of the fourth beast in the time of the second commonwealth until the time of Antiochus.

These commentators, therefore, say that the belief in the Messiah is mainly traditional in character, and there is no prophecy in the Torah or in the Prophets which must necessarily refer to the Messiah, for they can all be interpreted in accordance with their context as referring to an event that is past. Thus, the words: "The sceptre shall not depart from Yehuda," may be interpreted: "The greatness and the dignity of the tribe will not depart from Yehuda," for Yehuda will always be the first to fight the battles until Shiloh is destroyed. [The verb yabo in ki yabo shiloh, has the same meaning as in uba hashemesh vetaher, i.e., until the setting of Shiloh, namely its destruction.] The reason is because after the destruction of Shiloh, when Saul was anointed king, that rule departed from Yehuda, who no longer went first to battle. Hence the words: "Until the setting of Shiloh." Or the words may be translated, "Until his son [shiloh] comes," alluding to David [shiloh having the same meaning as **Ubeshilyatah** [after-birth]]. The meaning would then be, "The scepter will not come to Yehuda" [yasur having the same meaning as surah adonai surah elai - turn in, my Lord, turn in to me], i.e., the rule and the law-giver will not come from Yehuda until David comes, to whom all the tribes will gather [the word 'ammim in the expression velo yikhat 'ammim having the same meaning as in the phrase 'ammim har yikrau, which Onkelos translates, "the tribes of Israel"]. And the words may be interpreted in still another way in

Sefer HaIkkarim   BOOK [Maamar] FOUR

agreement with the other interpretations, as Ibn Ezra explains it.

Similarly, they refer the words: "Rejoice greatly, O daughter of Zion, Shout, O daughter of Yerushalayim; Behold, thy king cometh unto thee, he is triumphant and victorious, lowly, and riding upon an ass ...," to Zerubbabel, concerning whom it says: "Will I take thee, O Zerubbabel, my servant, the son of Shealtiel, ... and will make thee as a signet; for I have chosen thee ..." There are many such prophecies in Zechariah which, as the context shows, refer to him. Similarly, the words of Malachi: "And he shall sit as a refiner and purifier of silver, and he shall purify the sons of Levi, and purge them as gold and silver; and there shall be they that shall offer unto the Lord offerings in righteousness. Then shall the offering of Yehuda and Yerushalayim be pleasant unto the Lord," all refer to Ezra, who purged all the families and purified the priests and separated them and the Israelites from the daughters of the stranger. In the same way they explain all the prophecies in this manner and refer them to the past, maintaining that the belief in the coming of the Messiah is mainly traditional. Onkelos, the proselyte, a disciple of Shemayah and Abtalyon, who lived in the time of the second temple, refers the words: "The sceptre shall not depart from Yehuda ..." to the Messiah. This is the traditional interpretation to this day and we can not deny tradition, because if we were to deny tradition, then we could deny even the fundamental principles of the faith and interpret the texts differently. But the basis of all is tradition.

Our opinion is, however, that if there is no conclusive evidence in the text, tradition alone is not decisive, because one may say that even though he had not yet come in the time of Onkelos, may be he came later, as the Rabbis say: "If they deserve it, he will come 'with the clouds of heaven;' if they do not deserve it, then, 'Lowly and riding upon an ass.' " One might therefore say that he came after the time of Onkelos, but because of our sins the good things which were promised to come through him were not fulfilled and the people did not regard him as the Messiah.

The truth of the matter is that there are in the Torah and in the Prophets, passages definitely indicating the growth of Israel's dignity, which have never yet been fulfilled in whole or in part, for example: "There shall step forth a star out of Yaakov, and a sceptre shall rise out of Israel, and shall smite through the corners of Moab, and break down all the sons of Seth." The Rabbis say: "Shall smite through the corners of Moab," refers to David; "and break down all the sons of Seth," refers to the Messianic king. And their

Sefer Halkkarim BOOK [Maamar] FOUR

interpretation must be true, for David did not rule over all the sons of Seth and there has never been in all Israel a king who ruled over the whole world, who are the sons of Seth. Again, in Isaiah we read: "For this is as the waters of Noah unto Me; For as I have sworn that the waters of Noah should no longer go over the earth, so have I sworn that I would not be wroth with thee ...," and yet we are still in exile to-day, which shows that the prophecy has not yet been fulfilled. We also read in Isaiah: "For as the new heavens and the new earth, which I will make, shall remain before Me, saith the Lord, so shall your seed and your name remain," a promise which without doubt points to the permanent existence of the whole nation and to its ultimate grandeur.

There are nations, like the Philistines, the Ammonites, the Amalekites and others whose name has disappeared from the world, although their descendants are still existing, for there is no Philistine or Amalekite or Ammonite or Moabite nation. On the other hand, there are other nations whose name remains but not their descendants, like Egypt, which was destroyed several times, as Ezekiel prophesied. And when it was settled again, all those who came to live there were called Egyptians, although they were not of Egyptian descent - the name remained but not the race. There is no nation which continues to exist both in name and in race except that of Israel, of whom this thing was foretold: "Shall your seed and your name remain." The prophet connects it with the continuance of the new heavens and the new earth, for otherwise one might say that everything that comes into existence also passes out of existence. The other nations came into being and then disappeared and Israel too will necessarily disappear, since it came into being. To anticipate this notion, he says that it is not necessarily true that whatever is subject to genesis is also subject to destruction, for the heavens and the earth are new, that is, have come into being, according, to the opinion of those who adhere to the Torah and believe in the creation of the world in time, and yet they exist before the Lord continually, i.e., they are eternal, as David says: "He hath also established them for ever and ever; He hath made a decree which shall not be transgressed." Hence the seed of Israel as well as their name will also remain forever and will not disappear.

Jeremiah also says: "Thus saith the Lord, who giveth the sun for a light by day, and the ordinances of the moon and of the stars for a light by night ... If these ordinances depart from before Me, saith the Lord, Then the seed of Israel also shall cease from being a nation before Me for ever." This is also a promise of Israel's continuance

Sefer HaIkkarim   BOOK [Maamar] FOUR

and grandeur, for if the promise were that Israel will remain forever in exile, it would be a curse and not a blessing. The same thing applies to the prophecy of Ezekiel containing a description of the temple. Some portion of it was indeed fulfilled in the second temple, as appears from the words of the Rabbis in Talmud Menahot. Commenting on the verse: "Thus saith the Lord God: In the first month, in the first day of the month, thou shalt take a young bullock without blemish; and thou shalt purify [vehitteta] the sanctuary," they say, "Why a sin offering? It should be a burnt-offering." Said Rabbi Yohanan, "Eliyahu will explain this passage," thus indicating that it refers to the Messianic period. Rabbi Ashi said: "They offered installation sacrifices in the days of Ezra as they offered them in the days of Moshe," indicating that this prophecy was fulfilled in the days of Ezra. In Talmud "Middot", it also appears that in building the second temple they followed Ezekiel as far as they were able. Nevertheless, it is clear that there are many things in Ezekiel that were not fulfilled in the days of Ezra or in the second commonwealth, for example the division of the land into tribes was not carried out in the second commonwealth. They were all mixed up and there was no special possession for each tribe or prince as Ezekiel describes.

The prophecy concerning Gog was not fulfilled at any time. To judge from the account given by Joseph ben Gorion, the priest, of the war of Antiochus king of Greece against Yerushalayim and his defeat by the Hasmoneans, it does not agree with the prophecy concerning Gog at all. We also find in Spanish history an account of the coming of the Goths, who are descendants of Gog, to Spain, having conquered Rome and all Italy from the Greeks. But the rule of the Goths did not extend at that time over Palestine, nor did they subdue it, nor did Israel dwell at that time in their own land, as is stated in the prophecy concerning Gog. The words of Jeremiah in Lamentations: "The punishment of thine iniquity is accomplished, O daughter of Zion, He will no longer carry thee away into captivity," must refer to the last exile, that is, the exile after the second temple, for after the Babylonian exile at the time of the first temple, we were exiled again by Titus. To this reference is made in the words: "He will punish thine iniquity, O daughter of Edom," which surely refers to the Roman exile, which is the last one.

Although the Kittim are descendants of the Greeks, it is possible that they are the fourth beast, because they ruled the world after the Greeks. The Bible calls them, "Daughter of Edom," because they were converted to their new faith by an Edomite priest. The

Sefer HaIkkarim — BOOK [Maamar] FOUR

Edomites were the first to accept the religion of Jesus, and all the other nations go by the name of that one with which they identify themselves [whose religion they adopt]. Thus those who are converted to the religion of Israel are called Israelites or Jews, although they come from other nations. In the same way the Romans are called Edomites, and those who adopted the faith of the Mohammedans are called Ishmaelites, because the first converts were descendants of Ishmael. The meaning of the text, therefore, is that after this last exile God will no more carry the daughter of Zion into captivity, but will punish Edom. In order to prevent the reader from referring this to the original Edom, who were then living in Mount Seir, the text says: "Daughter of Edom, that dwellest in the land of Uz," the grandson of Shem. The Edom that dwelt in Mount Seir was destined to disappear before the exile of the second temple, having been destroyed by the Hasmoneans, just as the early kingdom of the Greeks was destroyed and its power passed to the Kittim, who are descendants of the Greeks and are now called the Edomite nation. Nor is it possible to refer all the statements mentioned in Daniel in connection with the rule of the fourth beast to any events in Israel's past or to the sinners of Israel so as to account for all the details. And there are many other prophecies of the same kind that can not be referred to the past, especially that of Malachi, the last of the prophets, who says: "Behold, I will send you Eliyahu the prophet before the coming of the great and terrible day of the Lord. And he shall turn the heart of the fathers to the children, and the heart of the children to their fathers," an event which has not been fulfilled.

Chapter 43

There are two kinds of existence, potential and actual. We perceive actual existence in two ways:

1. By means of our senses, like seeing with the eye and hearing with the ear. This mode of perception is defective because our senses perceive only the accidents of a thing, like whiteness, blackness, width, length, etc. Hence these perceptions are often erroneous, the straight appears crooked, the square appears round, and vice versa, as is explained in the Optics of Euclid. The sense of hearing also perceives things not as they are, and there are other defects besides.

2. The perception of conceptual existence. This is the idea which the intellect conceives of a thing perceived by sense, by stripping it of its accidents and apprehending the essence of the thing, which is the actual existence of things. Hence the Bible characterizes God's seeing things as a vision of the intellect. Thus when Samuel went to anoint David and, seeing Eliab, said: "Surely the Lord's anointed is before Him," God said to him: "Look not on his countenance, or on the height of his stature ... For it is not as man seeth: for man looketh on the outward appearance, but the Lord looketh on the heart." Samuel thought that Eliab was fit for a king because he was handsome and tall. But God told him not to look on his countenance, i.e., redness and whiteness, which belong to the category of quality, or on the height of his stature, which is quantity, "For man looketh on the outward appearance," i.e., man perceives things through their accidents, for it is characteristic of the eyes that they perceive only accidents. "But the Lord looketh on the heart," i.e., He perceives things in the manner characteristic of the heart, i.e., the mind, which perceives the true substance of things and their real existence.

The perception of potential existence is also divided into two kinds:

1. The perception of the existence of a thing in its causes. This is a real perception. If the causes exist, the thing must necessarily exist.

2. The perception of the existence of a thing in God's knowledge. This is the most important perception of all, for God's knowledge of a thing is the absolute cause of the existence of the thing, as God is the cause of all causes. The other causes may fail through God's will, but the perception which is due to God's knowledge can never fail. Hence the knowledge of a prophet is truer than any other, because it emanates from God, whereas the knowledge of other persons emanates from causes other than God, which may fail. Hence Isaiah, in his prophecy concerning Babel, says: "Thou art wearied in the multitude of thy counsels; Let now the astrologers, the star-gazers, the monthly prognosticators, stand up, and save thee from the things that shall come upon thee." The Rabbis say: "From some [me'asher], but not from all [kol asher]." The reason is because the stargazers can not know things as they really are, for two reasons:

A. Since their knowledge emanates from the knowledge of the causes of things which are ordered by the stars, they are dependent upon a particular time for their knowledge; whereas the prophet is not dependent upon any particular time, for all times are the same to God. This inadequacy is declared by the prophet when he says concerning the diviners, the stargazers and the false prophets: "Therefore it shall be night unto you, that ye shall have no vision;

Sefer Haikkarim   BOOK [Maamar] FOUR

and it shall be dark unto you, that ye shall not divine; and the sun shall go down upon the prophets, and the day shall be black over them. And the seers shall be put to shame, and the diviners confounded; Yea, they shall all cover their upper lips; for there shall be no answer of God. But I truly am full of power by the spirit of the Lord ..." His meaning is that the diviners and the star-gazers must have sun and stars to observe their altitudes in order to determine the hour, to know what star is in the ascendant, and to foretell the future. Therefore, he says that the sun will set upon the prophets and the day will grow dark for them, i.e., the night, for night is also called day, as in the expression: "On the day that I smote all the first-born." And without sun and stars when the night is dark and the day is cloudy, they can not tell the rising star, and hence the seers shall be put to shame and the diviners confounded, for there shall be no answer of God to their questions. The prophet, on the other hand, since he prophesies by the spirit of God, which has no relation to any definite time, can prophesy whenever he wishes, for he does not have to take the altitude of sun and stars, because his knowledge emanates from a higher cause. Hence, he says: "But I truly am full of power by the spirit of the Lord," i.e., since I prophesy through the power of the spirit of the Lord, I am not dependent upon any definite hour; I can prophesy at any time, without any one to prevent, because all things depend upon the will of God alone and nothing else.

B. The second cause which prevents the stargazers from knowing things as they are is that they are not capable of knowing correctly all the causes which determine the future, and hence they can not judge correctly. Their intellect is too weak to judge correctly even of things past, all of whose causes have been completed and realized. An apt illustration is the case of the mother of Sisera. She was grieved because of her son's delay in the battle, and sought to know, "Why is his chariot so long in coming?" attempting to get the desired information through divination or astrology or geomancy, information about an event the causes of which were all completed, the battle having been fought. She saw that her son was struck in the head by a woman. Her wise princesses saw blood in the camp of Sisera, the battle completed, and the strong men, and particularly Sisera, covered with blood at the hands of two women, Deborah and Jael. And yet they could not interpret the vision correctly and turned it to their liking. Hence Deborah said: "The wisest of her princesses answer her, yea, she returneth answer to herself. 'Are they not finding, are they not dividing the spoil? A damsel, two damsels to every man; to Sisera a spoil of dyed garments, a spoil of dyed garments of embroidery, two dyed garments of broidery for the neck of every spoiler.' " They could not understand how victory in battle could be won by women, hence they assumed that the delay was due to the fact that they had found and were dividing the spoil; and the weakening of the heroes by two women was because they found a damsel or two for the head of each man, who were weakened by overindulgence in coition. The blood which they saw as Sisera was struck in the head by a woman, could be nothing else than dyed garments of embroidery. And seeing the blood caused by two women, they cleverly guessed that there were "two dyed garments of broidery for the neck of every spoiler."

All this shows how incapable the minds of the astrologers are to interpret a thing correctly even in reference to the past, whose causes are all completed. Surely, then, they are unable to know correctly all the causes of the future. For even though they may know all the causes determined by the stars, they can not know what is determined in the knowledge of God, who is above all causes and brings to nought all causes in carrying out His will. Thus we find that Eliyahu withheld the rain when he wanted, and then caused rain to come down, by the decree of God's will, though there was a great drought at that time, and caused by his prayer a small cloud like a man's hand to rise up, though the natural causes tended in the opposite direction. This shows that the prophet has a true knowledge of things, which can not in any manner fail, because it emanates from God, who is the cause of all causes, and can bring to nought the other causes or maintain them as He pleases and as His wisdom dictates.

Chapter 44

The knowledge which we get to-day from the words of the Prophets is undoubtedly correct and can not fail. For error in a statement derived from hearsay or from a written source may be due to three causes. The original informant may not be truthful or he may not be well informed. The intermediate person who received the information from the original informant may not have understood correctly what he had been told or he may have added something of his own which was not told him; or the messenger of the intermediate person or the one who brought the writing from the intermediate person may lie. But no error can attach in any of these ways to the words of the Prophets which we now have.

Sefer HaIkkarim   BOOK [Maamar] FOUR

So far as the original source is concerned, who is God, the statement is absolutely true, because He is the cause of all causes, and no cause can be hidden from Him. Hence there can be no error as far as He is concerned. Nor can there be any error as far as the intermediate person is concerned. For if the prophet were not a man of truth, God would not have given him the prophetic inspiration, as Solomon says: "Lying lips are an abomination to the Lord; but they that deal truly are His delight." But all things associate with their like and avoid their opposite. Hence it is clear that if the prophet were not a man of truth, God would not have bestowed upon him the prophetic inspiration, and the spirit of God would not have rested upon him. One might say that the prophet misunderstood what he saw, like Hananiah the son of Azur, if the words of the prophet have not been verified, but if the words of the prophet, who is the intermediate person, have been verified several times, he can not be mistaken. Nor can error attach to the words of the prophet so far as the messenger or the one who brought the writing is concerned, i.e., the continuous tradition which we have to this day. For tradition which is transmitted from father to son can not be false in any manner, seeing that no father would want to transmit falsehood to his son as an inheritance. Now the first father who heard from the prophet, if he did not know that the prophet was a man of truth, would not have handed down the information to his son and his son to his son, and so on to this day. Hence if the original statement is true, no error can occur in it as far as tradition is concerned, which is handed down from father to son. Now if the thing is true from the point of view of the giver, the receiver and the transmitter, it can admit of no doubt at all.

This is the sign of the covenant which God made with us through Isaiah concerning the coming of the redeemer: "And a redeemer will come to Zion, and unto them that turn from transgression in Yaakov … And as for Me, this is My covenant with them, saith the Lord; My spirit which is upon thee, and My words which I have put in thy mouth, shall not depart out of thy mouth …" His meaning is that a sign of the covenant that this promise of the coming of the redeemer will be fulfilled, is that the words are absolutely true considered from every angle. The author of the promise is God and His spirit, who can not fail, as we said in the preceding chapter, because no one can prevent Him, seeing that He is the cause of all causes, hence the words: "My spirit that is upon thee." The transmitter to whom the words were told can not lie, nor err, because his words have been tested many times and found true. Isaiah prophesied the coming of

Sefer HaIkkarim — BOOK [Maamar] FOUR

Sennacherib and foretold his defeat, which came true. He prophesied the captivity of Yerushalayim through the king of Babylon, and it came true; the fall of Babylon, and it came true; the success of Cyrus, and it came true; the building of Yerushalayim through Cyrus, and it came true. Hence if he prophesies the redemption of Israel, that will come true. Hence he says: "And My words which I have put in thy mouth," i.e., inasmuch as all the words that I have put in thy mouth have been fulfilled, they are all a sign of the covenant that the redeemer will come, for from them it is known that thou art a man of truth. Finally tradition can not lie, because He promises that the tradition will be continuous from father to son, without interruption: "Shall not depart out of thy mouth, nor out of the mouth of thy seed …" This is a great sign that the covenant of the coming of the redeemer, promised by the prophets, stands.

Chapter 45

The word **Berit** [covenant] is applied to affirmation or oath or something firm which is performed by two persons to bind them to each other in love and friendship. They make a certain sign the existence of which points to the covenant, like a witness who testifies to a thing. Laban said to Yaakov: "And now come, let us make a covenant, I and thou; and let it be for a witness between me and thee." Then he raised a heap of stones and said: "This heap is witness between me and thee this day." Similarly, the rainbow is a permanent sign pointing to the existence of the covenant which God made with Noah and his sons.

The method of making a covenant, as we find in the Bible, was that they cut an animal into two parts and the covenanting parties passed between the pieces. The prophet says: "When they cut the calf in twain and passed between the parts thereof." Similarly, when God made a covenant with Abraham, He said to him: "Take me a heifer of three years old, and a shegoat of three years old, and a ram of three years old … And he took him all these and divided them in the midst, and laid each half over against the other." In the sequel it says that Abraham saw in a porphetic vision the glory of God passing between the parts, as a sign that he had made a covenant with Abraham: "Behold a smoking furnace, and a flaming torch that passed between these pieces." And further we read: "In that day the Lord made a covenant with Abraham."

The reason for this practice in making a covenant is because a covenant is a permanent bond between the two parties for the purpose of cementing and binding their friendship that they should be like one body and each should take care of the other as of himself. For this reason they cut an animal in two and pass between the parts, as a sign that just as those two parts formed one body in the animal when it was alive and each felt the pain of the other, so that when disease or injury affected one part the other felt the disease or injury and nothing but death separated those two parts, so the two parties making the covenant are to be as one body while living and nothing but death shall part them. It follows, therefore, that if the one sees any harm or grief coming to the other party to the covenant, he should do his utmost, risk danger, if necessary, to save him, as he would do for himself. Also, he must not keep from the other any knowledge or suspicion he may have that there is an evil plot to harm him; and should, moreover, reveal to him his secrets and innermost thoughts, as he reveals them to himself, for a friend is like a person's self. And he must love him as himself, as we read in the Torah: "Thou shalt love thy neighbour as thyself." The meaning is, just as in loving thyself there is no sense of otherness, so in loving thy neighbor thou must not think that he is other than thou, for the essence of perfect love is that the lover becomes one with the loved. Hence you will find that the numerical value of the word **Ahabah** [love] is the same as that of **Ehad** [one], signifying that the loved is not different from himself. Hence, he should trust him and reveal his secrets to him, as he reveals them to himself. This is true provided he has confidence in his friend's loyalty to the covenant, otherwise one should not reveal his secrets to every friend. If a friend is not proved and tried, he should not reveal his secrets to him, for he may turn into an enemy and do him great harm if he knows his secrets. Especially would it be serious if he thinks the other is a friend and he is not, because he would not be on his guard against him.

So, we find David saying that he is more afraid of his friends who know his secrets than of his enemies: "For it was not an enemy that taunted me, then I could have borne it; neither was it mine adversary that did magnify himself against me, then I would have hidden myself from him." He means to say: I would not have endured the taunt of the enemy and the wilful acts of the one who magnified himself against me, without quickly having a fight with him or hiding myself from him. But against thee, who art "Mine equal, my companion, and my familiar friend" - alluding to Ahithophel and his company, who knew his secrets: "We took sweet counsel together" - I am not able to guard myself, and am afraid that harm will come

Sefer HaIkkarim   BOOK [Maamar] FOUR

to me because thou knowest my secrets. Then he says that he does not know any remedy, but he prays to God that they should die suddenly: "Let them go down alive into the nether-world," so that they may not be able to reveal his secrets to any one: "May He incite death against them, let them go down alive into the nether-world."

But if he is a true friend in whose love he trusts, he should reveal his secrets to him and be jealous for him as he would for himself, and disclose to him any evil plots against him that he may know and assure him of his help. Hence as soon as God made a covenant with Abraham, He revealed to him all that He knew of the evil that was destined to come to his descendants: "Know of a surety that thy seed shall be a stranger in a land that is not theirs, and shall serve them; and they shall afflict them four hundred years; and also, that nation, whom they shall serve, will I judge." The meaning is: Since I have made a covenant with thee, I can not in any way conceal from thee the evil which is destined to come upon thy seed. Therefore, know of a surety that thy seed shall be a stranger, that they will be subject to others and afflicted, and that this condition of being strangers will last four hundred years. "And also, that nation, whom they shall serve, will I judge," i.e., I will strengthen the hands of those who enslave them, as though I consented to and assisted in their subjection. The words dan anoki [will I judge] have the same meaning as danani elohim ["God hath judged me"], which means, He has taken my part, pleading my cause, for He is on my side and has heard my voice, like the words: "Be Thou my judge [shofteni], O God, and plead my cause." So here dan anoki [will I judge] means: I, as it were, plead their cause and strengthen their hands in the subjection of thy seed, but "afterward shall they come out with great substance." The expression, "afterward," supports the interpretation here given. It is not connected with the words: "will I judge," but introduces another matter which has not been mentioned so far. Then, in the immediate sequel, we read: "In that day the Lord made a covenant with Abram, saying: 'Unto thy seed have I given this land.'"

Having revealed to him the decree which had been made concerning him, whether by way of punishment or by the stars, as some of the sages believe, He promised him that He would help him and deliver his seed from the hand of all those that will rise against them. Hence the Rabbis say that in that vision Abraham was shown all the instances of the subjection of Israel to other nations. Having made the covenant, it was proper that He should reveal to him all that was destined to come to his seed. And the meaning of the covenant is

Sefer HaIkkarim — BOOK [Maamar] FOUR

that He would be with him in his distress and sympathize with him in his trouble; even as the whole body shares in the pain of one of its limbs, as our Rabbis say: "The Shekinah suffers in the suffering of Israel, as is said: 'I will be with him in trouble,' " just as a person, suffers when his friend with whom he has a covenant is in trouble.

Since, however, it was possible that Abraham's seed might not attain that degree of perfection which would make them fit to enjoy continually the divine providence through this covenant, the divine Wisdom determined to make a permanent covenant with Abraham and his seed that they should be His people and the lot of His inheritance and that He should be their God always. Hence you will find that in the vision which he had after the vision of the parts he was at once given the commandment of circumcision for him and all his seed after him, in which commandment it is expressly stated that it is a sign of a covenant between God and the seed of Abraham: "And I will establish My covenant between Me and thee and thy seed after thee throughout their generations for an everlasting covenant." It is thus made clear that the commandment of circumcision was given as a sign of the covenant, signifying the bond of union between God and the seed of Abraham who maintain His covenant. And hence since that sign exists continuously in our nation, it shows that the divine bond is still with us.

Hence the men of the Great Assembly, in composing the benediction for the rite of circumcision, used the words: "And He sealed his offspring with the sign of the holy covenant." Then they explain the purpose of the covenant which is, to be delivered from the judgment of Gehenna - the pit of destruction - as is specifically stated in the benediction: "Therefore as a reward for this, O living God, our portion, our Rock, command that our beloved relative shall be delivered from destruction." And the reason given is: "For the sake of His covenant which He placed in our flesh." The "deliverance from destruction" that is mentioned here does not refer to death, for in this respect the circumcised and the uncircumcised are alike, but undoubtedly to the punishment of gehenna.

And our Rabbis say in the Midrash that Abraham sits at the door of gehenna and saves the circumcised from going in. Therefore, as long as we see this sign of the covenant maintained in the nation, we must not despair of redemption even though we see great trouble coming upon us continually, for we are to-day like a sick man neardeath, whom everybody has given up. As long as there is some sign of life remaining, we do not give up hope that he may recover. So here, although all the nations say concerning us that we are without hope and that our expectation is lost and we are cut off, still when we see this sign of the covenant maintained among us, which points to the bond existing between the divinity and our people, we know of a certainty that we still have strength to live, and that through this bond the nation will return to its original strength and will cleave to God, as was the case before in the period of prophecy.

Chapter 46

One can not be sure of the permanence of his faith, though he keeps the covenant and the law and serves God, so long as he enjoys peace and tranquillity at home and prosperity in his business affairs, his flax not being damaged nor his wine souring. He can be sure only if he maintains his integrity when his fortune changes and poverty and affliction come upon him and press him to the last degree. This is the test whether the righteous man serves God from love, namely if he maintains the strength of his faith in time of trouble and distress and does not weaken nor induce others to weaken, but trusts in God at all times, acknowledging in time of tranquillity and prosperity that everything comes from God, instead of saying: "My power and the might of my hand hath gotten me this wealth," [for it is God who gives man power to acquire wealth], and entreating Him to continue His benefits, and increasing the strength of his faith in time of trouble and trusting that God will release him from trouble and give him relief, and praying that God should give him peace, as the Psalmist says: "Trust in Him at all times, ye people," i.e., in time of prosperity as well as in time of distress; "Pour out your heart before Him," and say: "God is a refuge for us."

The sons of Korah praised Israel for this quality in the forty-fourth Psalm, beginning: "O God, we have heard with our ears, our fathers have told us; a work Thou didst in their days ..." The entire Psalm is a laudation of the people of Israel, who trusted in God in the day of prosperity and happiness and acknowledged that all things come from Him; nor did their heart turn away from trust in Him and loyalty to His covenant in time of trouble. And this too, though they had not seen with their own eyes the great signs and wonders, but only heard them from their fathers. Hence the Psalmist begins: "O God, we have heard with our ears," i.e.: although we have not seen with our own eyes, we have heard with our ears from trustworthy persons. For, "Our fathers have told us," That "a work Thou didst in their days ...," showing that Thou art in the habit of doing miracles and wonders, for "Thou with Thy hand didst drive out the nations,

Sefer Halkkarim   BOOK [Maamar] FOUR

and didst plant them in … For not by their own sword did they get the land in possession …" If, therefore, in the beginning all the prosperity of our nation was through Thee, it is not fitting now that Thou shouldst withhold Thy compassion from us, and therefore Thou, who "art my King, O God; Command the salvation of Yaakov," for there is no obstacle either from Thy side or from mine, for Thou art my King, and as a king helps his servants whether they deserve it or not, simply in order to acquire a glorious name, so Thou shouldst help us. And since Thou art God also, i.e., all-powerful, and there is no one to prevent Thee, "Command the salvation of Yaakov," for we always trust in Thee and know that "through Thee do we push down our adversaries;" and "through Thy name do we tread them under that rise up against us," and we have no other trust except in Thee. "For I trust not in my bow, neither can my sword save me," but we have always put our trust in Thee, in time of prosperity as well as in time of adversity.

This is described as follows: "But Thou hast saved us from our adversaries, and hast put them to shame that hate us," i.e., when Thou didst save us from our adversaries and puttedst them to shame that hate us, namely in the time of our prosperity, we did not become proud and haughty but "in God have we gloried all the day, and we will give thanks unto Thy name for ever," if we are again prosperous as before. Thou shouldst not therefore refrain from helping us because Thou fearest that our heart will grow proud and we will forget the Lord our God.

Having said that in time of prosperity they always put their trust in God, he says again that in time of trouble also they trusted in Him: "Yet Thou hast cast off, and brought us to confusion," i.e., even when Thou didst cast us off and didst bring us to confusion, i.e., in time of trouble, when Thou didst not go "forth with our hosts, and madest us to turn back from the adversary; and they that hate us spoil at their will, and didst give us like sheep to be eaten; and didst scatter us among the nations, and selledst Thy people for small gain … All the day is my confusion before me, and the shame of my face hath covered me, for the voice of him that taunteth and blasphemeth …" i.e., apart from the troubles which come upon me, I am confused and ashamed all the day because of those who taunt me and say: Such is your confidence and trust! He does not help thee even though He has power to do so. For a person who trusts in some thing that does not do him any good feels ashamed, as David says, complaining, as it were, in the name of every man in exile: "My God, my God, why hast Thou forsaken me?"

Sefer HaIkkarim — BOOK [Maamar] FOUR

Then he explains that he is not complaining of local abandonment, for the whole earth is full of God's glory, but his complaint is that God is far from help, and though I call, yet, "O my God, I call by day, but Thou answerest not; and at night, and there is no surcease for me," no one answers me and no one pays attention. This is not due to any change in Thee, for I know that "Thou art holy," and free from corporeal changes, and "Thou sittest," i.e., Thou art eternally the same without any change. He uses the word yosheb [sittest] because the sitting posture is the most stable of positions, as Maimonides shows in explaining the homonym yashab.

Then he says, "The praises of Israel," i.e., Israel praises themselves and boast of Thee continually, saying that Thou savest them in the time of their distress. Why, then, hast Thou forsaken me now? It was not so in the time of the patriarchs, for "in Thee did our fathers trust," and Thou didst not turn their faces back empty, but "they trusted, and Thou didst deliver them. Unto Thee they cried, and escaped; In Thee did they trust, and were not ashamed" of their trust, since they trusted in Thee, who art stable and unchanging, as David says: "O my God, in Thee have I trusted, let me not be ashamed." If one trusts in some thing that is not stable, he is ashamed of his trust, for he is not sure that his expectation will come, as Job said about those who trust in pools of rain water, which dry up in the summer: "They were ashamed because they had hoped; They came hither, and were confounded," i.e., when they found it dry. The same is true of one who trusts in his wealth, which is not stable. Hence the Bible says: "He that trusteth in his riches shall fall." The same thing is true of trusting in man: "Cursed is the man that trusteth in man."

But he who trusts in God, who is eternal, is not ashamed of his trust: "In Thee did they trust and were not ashamed." Hence, I complain of my shame when I see that "I am a worm, and no man; a reproach of men, and despised of the people. All they that see me laugh me to scorn," saying: "Let him commit himself unto the Lord! let Him rescue him; Let Him deliver him, seeing He delighteth in him." For this is the way the wicked scorn the man who trusts in God, as the Bible says: "Ye would put to shame the counsel of the poor, because the Lord is his refuge," i.e., they say that the counsel of the poor is foolish because he puts his trust in God. I am very much ashamed of this. In the same way we must explain the words: "And the shame of my face hath covered me, for the voice of him that taunteth and blasphemeth ..." For they taunt me and say: "Where are their gods, the rock in whom they trusted ... Let him rise up and help you, let him be your protection." They do this because they doubt Thy ability, Heaven forbid!

Then he says: "All this is come upon us; yet have we not forgotten Thee, neither have we been false to Thy covenant," i.e., even though all these troubles we mentioned have come upon us, we have not forgotten Thee, but have always been firm in Thy covenant and faith and have not been false to Thy covenant either in thought or in deed. Not in thought, for "Our heart is not turned back;" not in deed, for "Neither have our steps declined from Thy path." He says further: "Though Thou hast crushed us into a place of jackals, and covered us with the shadow of death," i.e., though Thou hast made the yoke of exile heavy upon us and hast covered us with the darkness of trouble, which might have led us to forget Thy name, yet we did not do this. Search Thou, O Most High, "If we had forgotten the name of our God, or spread forth our hands to a strange God," for it is God who searches this, for He knows the hidden things of the heart and to Him alone is this search fitting.

Having mentioned the praises of Israel, who endured troubles and the yoke of exile for the love of God, he mentions his complaint of God by way of prayer: "For Thy sake are we killed all the day; we are accounted as sheep for the slaughter. Awake, why sleepest Thou, O Lord?" The meaning is: even though we bear all these troubles for love of Thee with all our soul, nevertheless, since we are killed for Thy sake all the day, so that we are accounted as sheep for the slaughter, how canst Thou refrain and be silent? "Awake, why sleepest Thou, O Lord?" and, "Wherefore hidest Thou Thy face" from us? And even if Thou forget "our affliction and our oppression," still when "our soul is bowed down to the dust, and our belly cleaveth unto the earth," when we are in the lowest stage of poverty and lowliness, "Arise for our help, and redeem us," not for our own sake, but "for Thy mercy's sake," for mercy extends to those who trust in God, as the Bible says: "But he that trusteth in the Lord, mercy compasseth him about." Even if he is not worthy for his own sake, trust has the effect of extending gratuitous mercy to those who trust in God.

Chapter 47

Hope and expectation are essential to a believer in order to obtain the mercy which follows upon trust. The prophet says: "The Lord is good unto them that wait for Him." David takes credit to himself when he says: "For Thee do I wait all the day."

Hope is of three kinds:

1. Hope of mercy. The man hopes that God will help him by way of mercy and not as a matter of obligation.

2. Hope of glory. The man hopes that God will help him because He has been in the habit of helping him before, and if He failed him now His glory would suffer. For if a master who has been in the habit of helping his servant fails to deliver him from trouble in a given instance, the people say that it is because of the master's inability.

3. Hope due to a promise. This is the hope of truth, the individual hoping that God will verify His promise.

The most praiseworthy of the three is the hope of mercy, except that one is not so certain that he will get all that he desires. Thinking that he has not attained such a degree as to be worthy of God's gratuitous mercy, he believes that God will not desire to grant his request and therefore he does not hope properly, whereas if he hoped properly, mercy would not be withheld by God, for God always desires to bestow His benefits upon the one who has real hope, as the Psalmist says: "The Lord taketh pleasure in them that fear Him, in those that wait for His mercy." It is clear therefore that the failure to obtain mercy is due to the lack of real hope.

The hope of glory is more certain. For if a person has been in the habit of helping some one and has not done so in a given instance, he must, in order to prevent people thinking that his failure to help in the given instance is due to weakness or incapacity, bestir himself to help the person for the sake of the glory of his name, as the Psalmist says: "Help us, O Lord of our salvation, for the sake of the glory of Thy name." "God of our salvation," means: who hast been accustomed to save us. "For the sake of the glory of Thy name," means that we do not request aid by reason of any claim that we have against Thee, nor by reason of any merits that we have to our credit, but for the sake of the glory of Thy name, that the nations should not say that Thou art not able to do now what Thou wast able to do before. Hence the words in the sequel: "Wherefore should the nations say: 'Where is their God?'"

This is the method Moshe followed in his prayer on the occasion of the incident of the spies, when he said: "When the Egyptians shall hear - for Thou broughtest up this people with Thy might from among them - they will say to the inhabitants of this land, who have heard that Thou Lord art in the midst of this people; ... now if Thou shalt kill this people as one man, then the nations which have heard the fame of Thee will speak, saying: Because the Lord was not able to bring this people into the land which He swore unto them, therefore He hath slain them in the wilderness." And God said to him: "I have pardoned according to thy word," i.e., I will pardon for the reason that you mentioned, namely that My name may not be profaned, but I will take My revenge upon them in some other way, so that My glory will remain intact: "But in very deed, as I live - and all the earth shall be filled with the glory of the Lord - surely all those men that have seen My glory ... surely they shall not see the land ... neither shall any of them that despised Me see it."

The hope that is based upon a promise is the surest of all. If one hopes on the basis of a promise, oral or in writing, and the author of the promise is a man of truth, the person hoping is sure that the other will fulfil his words. Thus, David says: "Remember the word unto Thy servant, because Thou hast made me to hope." The meaning of these words is that an inferior or a servant has no claim against his superior or master except on the basis of a promise if there was such. And hence any hope which is based upon some of the sayings of the prophets - which are undoubtedly true, as we explained above - is sure to be fulfilled. For although the promised things as such pertain to the category of the possible or contingent, nevertheless since they are the result of God's promise, they are as good as necessary, and the person to whom they were promised may be as sure of them as if they were things which had to be by natural necessity.

Future events pertain to the category of the possible because they are not always in actuality. In some cases, the two alternatives of being and not being are equally balanced, as for example tomorrow's rain, it may either rain or not rain with equal possibility. Similarly, the recovery of a sick person may or may not come to pass with equal possibility. But there are things which, though they are future, are not equally situated with reference to the alternatives of being and not being, but are virtually necessary. For example, tomorrow's rising of the sun is necessary, although it is future. The same is true of all future events whose causes are completed.

Now the hope of a man who trusts in God and waits for the realization of the words of the prophets, must be of the same kind as that of a person who waits for a future event whose coming is necessary. Hence the Psalmist says: "I wait for the Lord, my soul doth wait, and in His word do, I hope. My soul waiteth for the Lord, more than watchmen for the morning; Yea, more than watchmen for the morning." The meaning is as follows: Those who guard the walls at night are divided into watches, one keeps guard until the cock crows, and another until the morning. Now he who is on guard until the cock crows waits for the crowing of the cock with some doubt in his mind because the two alternatives of being and not being are equally possible. But the "watchmen for the morning," i.e., those whose watch lasts until the morning, wait for morning with great certainty of its coming, for it is something that must come. Hence the Psalmist compares his hope in God with the sentinels on the walls who are in the morning watch and says that he waits for God and His word which He promised through the prophets with more assurance than the sentinels in the morning watch feel in the coming of the morning, which is something that must come.

He does not say that he waits for God as the sick man for health. For although the sick man waits for health with great eagerness, nevertheless he is in doubt whether it will come or not, because the two alternatives are equally possible, like the coming of rain, but one who waits for the morning, waits with assurance that it will come because it must, for the going forth of the morning is sure. Hence the prophet says: "Let us know, eagerly strive to know the Lord, His going forth is sure as the morning," i.e., as something that must necessarily be. "And He shall come unto us as the rain," i.e., we do not expect reward as of right, but as something which may or may not come, like rain. In the same way we must explain the words: "They shall fear Thee while the sun endureth," i.e., as a matter of obligation and necessity like the rising of the sun. But the hope of reward is like something that is contingent, viz. rain: "May he come down like rain upon the mown grass."

Hope like this, which is based upon a promise, is called hope of truth, because a person entertains this hope with the confidence that God is true and His word is true. The hope of mercy is entertained merely on the basis of God's mercy, the hope of a promise is based upon God's truth, both of them are for the benefit of the recipient. The hope of glory, on the other hand, has to do with the interest of the giver alone - the Lord is, as it were, constrained [to aid] for His own sake, out of consideration for His glory. Hence the Psalmist says: "Not unto us, O Lord, not unto us, but unto Thy name give glory," i.e., we do not ask this of Thee as a reward for our virtues, for wherein can mortal man born of woman be meritorious? Nor as a benefit to us, but for the sake of the glory of Thy name, and besides Thou must do this, "For Thy mercy, and for Thy truth's sake," i.e., the hope of mercy and the hope of promise.

Chapter 48

Hope and expectation of the kinds we mentioned may be general or particular. General hope means that a person must always hope that God will save His entire people and make their lot pleasant. The Rabbis say concerning this form of hope that the first question a man is asked on the day of judgment is, "Did you hope for salvation?" This means the salvation of the whole nation.

Particular hope means that a man should hope that God in His compassion and abundant mercy will make his way straight, will deliver him from harm and will choose what is good and suitable for him, by putting it in his heart to choose the good and reject the evil. For even in the work of his hands and the things he takes pains in doing a person does not know to reject the evil and choose the good except with the help of God, as Solomon says: "There is a way which seemeth right unto a man, but the end thereof are the ways of death;" also: "A man's goings are of the Lord; How then can man look to his way?" And he must not despair of hoping in the Lord in all his doings on account of fear of his sins, for God's providence always comes to those who hope for mercy, not to those who hope for reward, as the Bible says: "Behold, the eye of the Lord is toward them that fear Him, toward them that wait for His mercy." Then he makes clear that he is referring to particular hope by adding: "To deliver their soul from death, and to keep them alive in famine."

And when great and severe afflictions come upon him, he retains his integrity, strengthens his hope in God, and thinks and knows and understands that there is no one who can prevent God from granting his request, for His power is infinite and He can give him relief from trouble in His compassion and great mercy, which are infinite. Thus he continues to hope in God.

The prophet Jeremiah explains this in the book of Lamentations, where he speaks of the great suffering which every Israelite endured in exile: "And my soul is removed far off from peace, I forgot prosperity." The meaning is: The troubles coming upon me are so severe and so many in succession that I have forgotten what peace looks like, and the form of prosperity is no longer known to me, and hence, "I said: 'My strength is perished, and mine expectation from the Lord.'" He goes on to explain the cause of his thinking that his hope had perished, because even to "remember mine affliction and mine anguish is wormwood and gall." The word zekor is an infinitive like zekor in the passage: "Do not think [zekor] any more of the battle." Jeremiah continues: "This I recall to my mind, therefore have, I hope. Surely the Lord's mercies are not consumed, Surely His compassions fail not." That is, what I recall to my mind in the midst of my great troubles is that the Lord's mercies are not

Sefer Halkkarim BOOK [Maamar] FOUR

consumed and that His compassions fail not, for they are infinite, and therefore, "the Lord will not cast off forever. For though He cause grief, yet will He have compassion according to the multitude of His mercies." Therefore, I do not lose hope that I shall survive my troubles.

David explains the same thing in reference to general hope, when he says: "O Israel, hope in the Lord; for with the Lord there is mercy, and with Him is plenteous redemption," i.e., do not give up hoping in the Lord on account of your many sins, for you will not be redeemed for your virtues - there are not enough of them - your redemption from the depths of distress will be due to God's mercy alone. Therefore, you must hope in the Lord alone and in no one else, "for with the Lord there is mercy," and there is no other being that can do mercy outside of Him, as was explained above. And even if your iniquities are many, "With Him is plenteous redemption," for the power of the sinner to sin can not be greater than the power of God to forgive, hence, "He will redeem Israel from all his iniquities."

There is a difference, however, between the two kinds of hope. Particular hope is fulfilled through prayer, as David says: "I waited patiently for the Lord; and He inclined unto me, and heard my cry. He brought me up also out of the tumultuous pit, out of the miry clay; and He set my feet upon a rock ..." This is because particular hope depends upon the individual alone, therefore if it is of the proper kind, there is no reason why it should not be fulfilled, since there is no niggardliness in the giver, and when one prays for the thing, he hopes for he shows that his hope is real, therefore he is prepared to receive the hoped-for mercy. It is different with general hope. For though it may be real and genuine on the part of one or a few persons, the thing hoped for may not be realized, since every recipient, the entire nation, has not a genuine and real hope. And if the recipient is not prepared in respect of his hope, the hope can not be fulfilled. Therefore the Rabbis say that the final redemption of Israel is a matter of time or of merit. Commenting on the words: "I, the Lord, will hasten it in its time," they say: "If they are deserving, I will hasten it, if not, then in its time." Particular hope is not affected by time, but if the recipient prepares himself to receive mercy through hope, it will be realized by means of prayer.

Chapter 49

One might say that hope and expectation are not good for man, because they disturb the power of thought, weaken one's strength and make the mind sick and stupid. For as a result of hoping and expecting a thing, the mind is busy thinking of obtaining the thing hoped for, and this continual preoccupation with the object desired quenches at length the light of the intellect and the mind remains dimmed, as we read: "Hope deferred maketh the heart sick." Hence every intelligent person should remove from his mind hope and expectation. If one ceases to hope for something that is hard to get and contents himself with what he can get, his mind is not preoccupied with the thing and he can think of things of knowledge and understanding and of subjects which develop the intellect and illumine it. How then can we say that hope and expectation are good for a believer, so much so that the prophet urges hope above all things? Thus, we read: "Therefore turn thou to thy God; keep mercy and justice, and wait for thy God continually," from which it seems that hope is as essential to a believer as mercy and justice or even more so.

The answer to the question is this: Hope for something about which one is in doubt whether it will come or not, does disturb the soul, preoccupying it with thoughts of how to obtain it, but hope for a thing which one is sure will come as, for example, the hope for the light of the morning, does not disturb the soul but makes it glad, because it conceives the good which is sought and is confident that it will come. This is the kind of hope one must have in God. One must trust implicitly that God will fulfil one's hope without doubt, since He has the power and there is no one to prevent Him. But one must not have the kind of hope in which one doubts whether the thing will come or not. Such hope as we have described strengthens the heart and makes it glad, as we read: "Be strong, and let your heart take courage, all ye that wait for the Lord." Hope in God, far from weakening the heart, strengthens it, for if one hopes in God and his heart truly relies upon the Holy One of Israel, trusting that He will grant his request, he gets stronger and more courageous, as we read: "Even the youths shall faint and be weary, ... But they that wait for the Lord shall renew their strength." That is, even the youths, who do not usually become faint and weary, and the young men, who usually renew their strength, will all stumble and faint and be weary, but those that wait for the Lord shall renew their strength, and the more strength they have the more they will be able to hope, and the hope in turn which has God for its object, who is a permanent being, will further increase their strength, the two mutually reacting upon each other, hope causing strength and strength in turn causing hope.

The Psalmist alludes to this when he says: "Wait for the Lord; be strong, and let thy heart take courage; yea, wait thou for the Lord." This shows that hope is the cause of strength, and that strength in turn is a cause for more hope. The prophet had this hope in mind in his admonition: "Therefore turn thou to thy God; keep mercy and justice, and wait for thy God continually." For hope and waiting for God are better than all the praises that one can give Him, as the Psalmist says: "But as for me, I will hope continually, and will add to all Thy praises."

Now this seems a very strange remark indeed. How can he say that he will add to all the praises of God, when we read in the Psalms: "Who can express the mighty acts of the Lord, or make all His praise to be heard?" A person can not even enumerate the infinite praises of God, not to speak of adding to them. But the meaning of the verse is this, that by waiting continually for the Lord he adds to all the praises which a person can give to God. David explains the same thing in another place also, saying that hope and waiting for God are like praising God in the choicest of places and like the most acceptable offering, namely one that is not brought for a sin but as a vow or freewill offering: "Praise waiteth for Thee, O God, in Zion; and unto Thee the vow is performed." Now it seems to me that the word dumiyah means hope, like the word domu in the expression: "Wait [domu] until we come to you," and the word dimminu in the verse: "We have waited [dimminu] for Thy loving-kindness, O God." The meaning of the verse is therefore as follows: Hope and waiting for Thee, O God, are like praising Thee in Zion, which is the best of all places; and it is likewise to be compared to the payment of an offering that is vowed to Thee, which is the best of all offerings, since it is not brought for a sin. And by reason of our hope, "Thou hearest [our] prayer," for prayer resulting from hope is the best; and because Thou hearest prayer, "unto Thee doth all flesh come," to pray. And by reason of the prayer that comes from hope, "The tale of iniquities which are too heavy for me," and even "our transgressions," i.e., defiant acts, "Thou wilt pardon them." This shows the great value of hope, as we explained above. The Rabbis indeed explain the word dumiyah as meaning silence, when they say: "The best remedy of all is silence, as we read: 'To Thee silence [dumiyah] is praise,' " nevertheless the sequence and connection of thought suggest rather the meaning of hope.

The value of hope being so great, David urged the people to hope in God continually, without ceasing: "O Israel, hope in the Lord from this time forth and for ever." As a reward for hope he promises spiritual reward in the world to come: "Wait for the Lord, and keep His way, and He will exalt thee to inherit the land." He makes it clear that as a reward for hope in particular and for keeping the way of the Lord in general, a person will inherit the land of life. According to the Rabbis, "inheritance of the land," means the land of life, as they say: "All Israel have a share in the world to come, as is said: 'Thy people also shall be all righteous, they shall inherit the land for ever.' " Habakkuk also urges hope: "Though it tarry, wait for it; because it will surely come, it will not delay." If it tarries how can he say that it will not delay? The meaning is that though it tarries, one must always wait for redemption and hope that it will come without delay. Isaiah also says: "Happy-are all they that wait for Him."

Chapter 50

The complaint that we find in the Hagiographa concerning the long duration of our exile is not the same as the complaint that we find in the Prophets concerning the adversity of the righteous and the prosperity of the wicked. Our complaint about the exile is not that we think it is unjust; but it may be analyzed into three parts, corresponding to the three kinds of hope –
1. Complaint of mercy,
2. Complaint of promise,
3. Complaint of glory.

1. In showing mercy it is clear that the less fit the recipient is to receive the mercy shown him, the greater is the degree of the mercy. And since we are in the last stage of lowliness and poverty, having almost reached the end of dissolution, we are in need of the greatest mercy possible. But God's mercy is the greatest possible, hence now is the time when it should come to us, when we are stripped of all good, like a slave who is in the last degree of lowliness and misery. This is what David had in mind when he said: "Behold, as the eyes of servants unto the hand of their master, as the eyes of a maiden unto the hand of her mistress; so, our eyes look unto the Lord our God, until He be gracious unto us."
Now this verse seems strange. How can he say that we look to God as a servant to his master and a maiden to her mistress? The master is never willing to let his servants go free, nor does the servant look to him to save him from his trouble and let him go free. But the

meaning of the verse is as we said before. The Psalmist is complaining to God of His attribute of mercy. The duration of the exile has been so long, he says, that we have been reduced to the position of a servant - not a servant who looks for freedom through his friends or relatives, for whom he is waiting to come and redeem him, but like a servant who is without hope and despairs of ever obtaining his freedom, a slave in the hand of a cruel master, deprived of all good, who is not his own master even to be able to maintain his religion and belief, having neither children nor honor nor wealth - "The possession of the slave is the possession of the master" - nor any other hope at all. He merely looks to the hand of his master to give him a piece of bread to live by, and similarly the maiden looks to the hand of her mistress. We are in a similar position. The exile has lasted so long, troubles have come upon us thick and fast, that we have almost given up hope of redemption [Heaven forbid!] and been reduced to the position of the slave who despairs of obtaining his freedom. All we ask for is to remain in exile with our poverty and humility. This is the meaning of the words: "So our eyes look unto the Lord our God until He be gracious unto us." And hence he continues: "Be gracious unto us, O Lord, be gracious unto us; for we are full sated with contempt." The meaning is: If Thy purpose is to make Thy mercy as extraordinary as possible, which will be the case when the recipient is devoid of all good, we are full sated with contempt, we have already been reduced to the last degree of misery, and Thou oughtest to have pity upon us in Thy great mercy.

Heman the Ezrahite also complains of the long exile in the same way: "For my soul is sated with troubles, and my life draweth nigh unto the grave. I am counted with them that go down into the pit." The meaning is: So many troubles have passed over us that we are accounted like dead, and therefore Thou shouldst have pity upon us in Thy great mercy, before we reach the last degree of destruction. Why should we die before Thine eyes and our name be cut off from the earth? "Wilt Thou work wonders for the dead?... Shall Thy mercy be declared in the grave?" The meaning is, we have already reached the limit where the extraordinary mercy of God should be shown to us, for it is impossible to descend any lower, unless it be the grave, but, "Shall Thy mercy be declared in the grave?" It would not be mercy then, but a new creation. The entire Psalm is expressed in the style of a sick man who is grieved on account of his sickness although he knows that he brought it on himself by his evil conduct.

2. In the eighty-ninth Psalm by Ethan the Ezrahite, we have the two other modes of complaint, viz. the complaints of promise and of glory. An example of the complaint of promise are the words: "Where are Thy former mercies, O Lord, which Thou didst swear unto David …?"

3. Complaint of glory is expressed in the words: "Remember, Lord, the taunt of Thy servants; How I do bear … wherewith Thine enemies have taunted, O Lord …"

In order to explain these two forms of complaint according to the words of the Psalmist, I will interpret the Psalm to show the connection of thought. He begins by saying: "I will sing of the mercies of the Lord for ever," as Jeremiah said: "Right wouldest Thou be, O Lord, were I to contend with Thee; Yet will I reason with Thee," as we explained above. So the Psalmist says: I know that I can not deny the mercies of God which extend continually over His creatures, those above as well as those below, and therefore I will always sing the mercies of God and publish them and make them known to mankind forever: "To all generations will I make known Thy faithfulness with my mouth," i.e., I will make known their permanence and continuance, for I can not deny it. Nevertheless I can not forbear from complaining, not basing myself on God's mercy, but upon His faithfulness. My complaint is based upon God's promise. I see that affirmation and truth are not equal in all things: "For I have said: 'The world is built with mercy; in the very heavens Thou dost establish Thy faithfulness.' " That is, I thought that the whole world exists in its dependence on God, through mercy, the celestial as well as the terrestrial beings. Therefore it follows that as all depends upon God's mercy, God's faithfulness and fulfilment should also come to them all alike. But I see that Thy faithfulness, namely the fulfilment of Thy mercy, is in heaven alone, i.e., in the celestial beings, whereas the mercy which extends to the terrestrial beings, for example such as Thou hast expressed in the words: "I have made a covenant with My chosen, I have sworn unto David My servant; For ever will I establish thy seed, and build up thy throne to all generations," is different. The fulfilment of mercy here is not the same as it is in the celestial beings.

He goes on to explain how the mercy of bringing into being and maintaining them is extended to the celestial beings: "So shall the heavens praise Thy wonders, O Lord," i.e., the wondrous mercy which Thou hast shown them by bringing them into being in the last degree of perfection; "Thy faithfulness also," i.e., the permanence which Thou givest to them, they will praise "in the assembly of the holy ones," i.e., among the Separate Intelligences, which are the causes of the spheres and make them move, for they all acknowledge and recognize that Thou art, "a God dreaded in the great council of the holy ones," and that there is none like Thee among the celestial beings, who can do mercy like Thee, "For who in the skies can be compared unto the Lord, who among the sons of might can be likened unto the Lord?" for they all know that Thou art God above them all, and that Thou art "Lord God of hosts," of the heavens and the earth, and that there is none who "is a mighty one like unto Thee, O Lord," and I see that "Thy faithfulness is round about Thee," i.e., that permanence exists only among the celestial beings.

This is so not because Thou art the God of heaven alone and not the God of the earth, for, "Thine are the heavens, Thine also the earth; the world and the fulness thereof, Thou hast founded them. The north and the south, thou hast created them … Thine is an arm with might," to do whatever Thou desirest and to change nature according to Thy will, for "righteousness and justice are the foundation of Thy throne." That is, all those things which happen by necessity, like the things of nature which can not change - the things which he calls here "righteousness and justice" - all of them come from heaven, which is the foundation of Thy throne. But those things which take place by way of "mercy and truth," can not come from any one other than Thee, unless they "go before Thee," and pray Thee to grant them, for there is no one in the world who can do mercy except Thee, as was explained above.

He then goes on to explain that the mercy which extends to the terrestrial beings should come to the best people, viz. the people who know to praise God: "Happy is the people that know the joyful shout," i.e., know how to praise Thee. The word teru'ah [shouting] has the same meaning here as the word nari'ah [we will shout] in the verse: "Let us shout for joy [nari'ah] unto Him with psalms." This people deserve to walk "in the light of Thy countenance," i.e., to get the mercy and truth which come from the light of Thy countenance, as we said before, because "in Thy name do they rejoice all the day; and through Thy righteousness are they exalted." They boast of Thy holy name and acknowledge that Thou art the cause of their prosperity, recognizing that "Thou art the glory of their strength, and that in Thy favour our horn is exalted." Hence they always say: "For of the Lord is our shield …," i.e., that the king of Israel, who is their shield and the captain of their host, is from God and no one else. For "then Thou spokest in vision to Thy godly ones," i.e., Samuel and Nathan the prophet, "and saidst: 'I have laid help upon one that is mighty,' " i.e., David, for David was mighty before he was anointed king, as he said of himself: "Thy servant smote both the lion and the bear."

Then he tells how after He had given him the kingdom in His mercy, a covenant was made with him concerning it through Nathan the prophet, assuring him of its permanence: "My faithfulness and My mercy shall be with him; and through My name shall his horn be exalted … For ever will I keep for him My mercy, and My covenant shall stand fast with him … His seed shall endure for ever, and his throne as the sun before Me," i.e., his kingdom will be eternal among terrestrial things, as the sun among the celestial and, "As the moon establishes the world," i.e., as the moon establishes the sublunar world, so will the kingdom of the house of David establish it.

So far he speaks of the covenant which was made with David and his seed. In the sequel he mentions the complaint. He begins by saying: "And the witness in the sky is faithful," i.e., the witness which Thou didst place in the sky, viz. the sun and the moon, is, I see, faithful and permanent. But the thing to which it bears witness, viz. the kingdom of the seed of David, is not so, for, "Thou hast cast off and rejected, thou hast been wroth with Thine anointed. Thou hast abhorred the covenant of Thy servant; Thou hast profaned his crown even to the ground." He concludes this complaint, which is based upon a promise, speaking as it were in the name of the complainant: "O remember how short my time is; for what vanity hast, thou created all the children of men!" i.e., I do not wonder on my own account, for I bear in mind how short my time is, which is as nothing before Thee. Any individual man's exile lasts only his life-time which is very little, for, "What man is he that liveth and shall not see death, that shall deliver his soul from the power of the grave?" Hence, I am not complaining for myself at all. My complaint is in relation to Thy mercy and Thy faithfulness. "Where are Thy former mercies, O Lord, which Thou didst swear unto David in Thy faithfulness?"

There is possibly a hint here that if He will not fulfil the merciful promise, He made to David that the Messiah will come in order that through him the human race may be perfected and attain its purpose, the whole race will have been created in vain, since it will not attain its destiny. Hence, he says: "Remember how short my time is; for what vanity hast, thou created all the children of men! i.e., their creation will have been in vain, since they will all die in the end, for, "What man is he that liveth and shall not see death?" And if he does not perfect his soul in life, it will not survive after death. "Where, then, are Thy former mercies, O Lord, which Thou didst swear unto

David in Thy faithfulness?" This purpose can be attained only through the coming of the Messiah, when the Lord will "turn to the peoples a pure language, that they may all call upon the name of the Lord, to serve Him with one consent." But if the Messiah does not come, the existence of the human race is in vain.

Having concluded the complaint based upon God's promise, he takes up the other complaint, which is based upon God's glory: "Remember, Lord, the taunt of Thy servants," i.e., besides Thy mercy and Thy truth remember what we are enduring from all the nations. Thou shouldst be concerned about the glory of Thy name, which "Thine enemies have taunted, O Lord," and all the many peoples which "have taunted the footsteps of Thine anointed." The word **Ikebot** [footsteps] denotes the delay of his coming, as in the expression: "And he stayeth [ye'akkebem] them not when. His voice is heard." Or the word may mean the end or fate, the reference being to the kingdom of the house of David which did not have a good end. It is possible also that the words asher herefu oyebeka adonai may be translated, "who taunted Thine enemies, O Lord," and that the expression is a euphemism for "taunted Thee, O Lord," like the expression: "The Lord even require it at the hand of David's enemies," which is a euphemism for David, to whom he was speaking, as though he had said: "The Lord require it at the hand of David." So here the meaning is: many nations have taunted Thee, saying that Thou art not able to save Israel. Hence, he concludes: "Blessed be the Lord for evermore. Amen, and Amen," meaning, God is exalted far above the taunts of these men, as one should say, God forbid that such a defect should be ascribed to Him! Or the meaning may be simply that God is blessed and the source of good for ever, i.e., infinitely, and we must bless Him for evil as we bless Him for good. The reason is because since God is the source of good, everything which comes from Him is good or for a good purpose.

If we see an agent whose work is ordered in the best possible manner of perfection and good, we must assume that any evil that we find in any work of his must be for a good purpose. For if not, then it must be due either to weakness or inability to correct the evil, or to ignorance of the evil, or it may be that having both the knowledge and the power, he has not the will and caused the evil deliberately. But in a work of God, we can not impute anything to weakness or ignorance, for, "Great is our Lord, and mighty in power; His understanding is infinite." We must assume then that whatever He does is deliberate. But since He is absolutely good and all His works are absolutely good and perfect, we must say that any evil which we see in His works [God forbid!] is for a good purpose, though we do not understand it. Hence the Psalmist says, "Amen, and Amen," Amen for the evil and Amen for the good, for undoubtedly all is for a good purpose even if we do not understand it.

Chapter 51

Perfect good can not change nor receive diminution or increase. For if it can change, it must change either to evil or to good. If it changes to evil, it is not a perfect good if it can so change, and if it changes to good, then it was not a perfect good in the first place. It is clear therefore that it can not receive increase or diminution.

Now all the sublunar existences are continually being affected and changed because they have opposite principles in them, and change and affection come only from the opposite. A thing can not be affected by itself or by its like, but only by its opposite. The opposite may be in the thing itself, as in things composed of the elements, in which the elements are opposed to each other, or it may be outside, like fire and air, which are simple, but each of them is affected by the other if it comes in contact with it, because it is the nature of opposites that each prevails over the other as far as it is able. Hence the sublunar existences change continually because they are composed of opposites. One of the ancients even thought that by reason of the change which takes place in composite things, we can not say about anything that it is the same thing that it was yesterday, as it is impossible to point to the flowing water of a river and say this is the same water that was here yesterday, for it may be that the water of yesterday was sweet and to-day's is bitter, or vice versa.

In the same way an individual, say Reuben, changes constantly and his temperament to-day may be different from what it was yesterday, his qualities changing accordingly, for qualities follow temperament. A person the temperament of whose heart is warm is undoubtedly susceptible to anger and is irascible; and the same thing is true of the other qualities. Accordingly, Reuben to-day is not the same that he was yesterday. Hence perfect good can not exist in any of the composite sublunar things because they are constantly changing, whereas the perfect good can exist only in a thing that is permanent.

Hence all the prophets and the pious men, like Eliyahu, Rabbi Hanina ben Dosa and others, despised the goods of this world because they are changeable and there is not a permanent thing among them; and they cared only about the spiritual good promised to the soul, which is a permanent thing without any change. They preferred to endure pain in this world in order to obtain the delight of the spiritual world, because they knew that pleasure naturally comes after pain, as one of two opposites naturally comes when the other disappears. Thus, genesis comes only after dissolution, and dissolution only after genesis. Similarly, gladness comes only after sorrow, elevation only after a low state. Therefore, when Israel were in Egypt in the last degree of poverty and humility, God bestowed upon them the state of elevation and honor, as we are told in the Bible: "I have surely seen the affliction of My people that are in Egypt ... And I have said: I will bring you up out of the affliction of Egypt ..." It is like genesis which naturally comes after dissolution. The genesis of the bird takes place only after the dissolution of the form of the egg, and the sprouting of the seed comes only after the dissolution of the form of the seed grain. Similarly, the salvation and happiness of a nation come only after the nation has reached the last degree of lowliness, which is similar to dissolution.

This is the meaning of the biblical text: "For as the earth bringeth forth her growth ...," i.e., when the form of the seed grain has been decomposed, "so the Lord God will cause victory and glory to spring forth ...," after they have been reduced to the last stage of humility and poverty, which are similar to dissolution. Similarly rest comes only after fatigue. The wise man says: "If one seeks rest through rest, he loses rest and inherits weariness." This idea is expressed in reference to Issachar: "For he saw a resting-place that it was good, and the land that it was pleasant; and he bowed his shoulder to bear ..." The meaning is that Issachar, being desirous of rest and pleasure and seeing that the land was good to enjoy pleasure in, bowed his shoulder to bear, i.e., toiled continually so as to earn money and be able to rest afterwards. In order to be able to have pleasure later, he also leased land to till and paid a tax on it, as we read: "And became a servant under task-work." The Rabbis say in "Rabbah de Rabbah": " 'For he saw a resting-place that it was good' - 'resting-place' is nothing else than the world to come, as is said: 'And there the weary are at rest.' **Land** means the land of life, as is said: 'They shall inherit the land for ever.' 'And he bowed his shoulder to bear' - the Torah and the commandments."

It seems to me that they said this because we find that among the men of Issachar there were men of great wisdom, as we read: "And of the children of Issachar, men that had understanding of the times, to know what Israel ought to do." Hence, they said that the resting-place which Issachar selected for himself as a possession, can refer

Sefer HaIkkarim BOOK [Maamar] FOUR

to nothing else except the rest of the world to come. And since Issachar was very eager to have rest and enjoyment and he saw that there is no true rest except in the world to come and no real enjoyment except in the land of life, and that this rest and enjoyment can not be obtained except by laboring in wisdom and in the Torah and its commandments, as is true of all pleasure that it can be obtained only after labor and pain, he bowed his shoulder to bear - wisdom and Torah and commandments, for this is the labor that brings to that pleasure, the real pleasure and rest which do not change, and the absolute good in which there is no evil whatever.

All the pleasures and goods of this world always have some evil in them, because everything has its opposite in it or near by, as Solomon says: "There is a way which seemeth right unto a man, but the end thereof are the ways of death," i.e. what seems to a person good is not always so, for sometimes a person thinks that a certain thing is good, and at the end of that good he will find evil immediately following it. He gives an example when he says: "Even in laughter the heart acheth; and the end of mirth is heaviness." The meaning is: even laughter which every one regards as a good, since every one finds pleasure in it, causes heart-ache, and the end of joy is sorrow, because when one is glad and laughs, the spirits expand and go outside, causing the heart to cool off, which results at once in sorrow.

But the pleasures of the world to come are not followed by any pain or evil or change, because they are spiritual things and have no opposites. Hence there is no dissolution in them nor change nor privation. For dissolution and privation and change and diminution are due to opposites and to things composed of opposites, because every opposite seeks to prevail over and conquer the other, and when it does prevail over it, it does not rest until it destroys it completely. But at the same time the composite is destroyed, for the composite can not maintain itself or receive the form of perfection and life unless it be far from opposition. The spheres have a permanent existence and receive the form of perfection and life because there is no opposition in them. But the elements, being themselves opposites, can not exist permanently, but change into each other and do not receive the form of perfection and life. The things which are composed of the elements maintain themselves and receive the form of perfection and life as long as they are far from opposition. The more the composite approximatese quality, the greater is the degree of the life form it receives. This form persists and remains in the composite as long as it is far from opposition, i.e., when the opposite elements in it neutralize each other by their equality, so that the heat and the cold in the composite are equal. If the heat predominates, it destroys the cold, and vice versa. Similarly, the relation of the other opposites must also be such that the one does not predominate over the other, but that each should have as much power to conquer the other as the latter has to conquer it. If they are mutually related in this harmonious way, the composite endures, but when the harmony disappears and the one predominates over the other, the composite is destroyed. We find, therefore, that if the power and strength of one of the opposite elements in a composite to conquer the other is equal to the power of the other to conquer it, the composite endures, while predominance of the one opposite over the other causes destruction and dissolution.

In this way we explain the verse: "I make peace, and create evil." Harmony of the opposites is called peace, and is the cause of the existence and duration of the composite, as long as that equality exists, as society exists when men of various opinions agree. For if there is harmony between the irascible and the patient, the niggardly and the extravagant, and similarly in the other opposite qualities, there is virtue. This results when each of the extremes has as much power to predominate over the other as the other has to predominate over it. This is the cause of permanence and peace. Hence the Bible says: "The Lord will give strength unto His people; the Lord will bless His people with peace." The Psalmist is praying that God should give His people strength, but not so much strength to enable one to prevail over the other and destroy him, which would be the cause of quarrel and strife. He prays that God should give them strength so as to bless His people with peace, i.e., that there should be agreement between them, that one of the extremes should not predominate over the other so as to destroy virtue and produce vice. Such agreement is called peace. And the spiritual pleasure of the soul is called peace to indicate that there is no opposition in that pleasure and hence it will not be destroyed, just as peace is a name that is given to agreement among men who do not oppose one another.

The Rabbis say: "When a righteous man departs from the world, three groups of angels come out to meet him, one says: 'May he come in peace,' as we read: 'But thou shalt go to thy fathers in peace.'" The meaning is this: As peace is the cause of permanence in things composed of opposites, so when the soul is prepared to cleave to the celestial beings without opposition, the pleasure of the soul is called peace, to indicate eternal existence. We find also that

Sefer HaIkkarim   BOOK [Maamar] FOUR

the promise God makes to the righteous to give them continued existence is called peace. Thus, God says concerning Phinehas: "Behold, I give unto him My covenant of peace."

According to the tradition which says that Phinehas is Eliyahu, peace will mean permanent existence of the soul in the body. This will result if the harmony between the opposite elements continues so that the one does not predominate over the other. If there is such harmony, which is peace, the cause of dissolution disappears. This interpretation is proved by the literal meaning of the words concerning him: "My covenant was with him of life and peace." And the words: "Behold, I will send you Eliyahu the prophet," show that Eliyahu still exists in body and soul.

According to those of our Rabbis who have a different opinion and say that Phinehas is not Eliyahu, the peace that is promised to Phinehas alludes to the peace of the soul's rest in the world to come, in which there is no opposition. This is proved by the words of the Bible in reference to the punishment of the wicked: "There is no peace, saith my God, concerning the wicked." Now the life of the wicked in this world is not devoid of quiet and tranquillity any more than is that of the righteous. The reference is undoubtedly to the peace of the soul in the spiritual world, in which there is no opposition, and concerning which we read: "Great peace have they that love Thy law."

And since the word peace denotes essentially a thing in which there is no opposition, our Rabbis apply it to God, as in the statement: "Great is peace, for it is the name of the Holy One, blessed be He, as is said: 'And called it "Adonai-shalom" [The Lord is peace].' "

All existing things outside of God being effects, may have some opposition in them, for example the first effect is both a necessary and a possible existent; it is a necessary existent in relation to its cause, and a contingent or possible existent in relation to itself. Hence it can not be termed peace from every point of view. But God has not in Him any possibility of existence at all, He is a necessary existent from every point of view. Hence, He is called peace, because no form of opposition is conceivable in Him. His existence is therefore peace and truth.

Now inasmuch as peace denotes both the spiritual delight in the celestial world which is far from opposition, viz. the world to come, the essential reward of the soul, and the peace of the body in this world, which is the cause of reward in the world to come, the text says at the end of the priestly benediction: "And give thee peace," alluding to both kinds of peace, in this world and in the world to come. In the beginning it says: "The Lord bless thee, and keep thee," referring to material prosperity and material acquisition. Then it says: "The Lord make His face to shine upon thee, and be gracious unto thee," referring to the happiness of wisdom and the perfection of the Torah, which are called "light:" "For the commandment is a lamp and the Torah is light;" and: "A man's wisdom maketh his face to shine." "And be gracious unto thee," refers to intellectual perfection, as Moshe said: "That I may know Thee, to the end that I may find grace in Thy sight."

But inasmuch as these two kinds of happiness are opposed to each other, i.e., material prosperity is opposed to perfection of wisdom and Torah, which are the causes of the perfection of the soul and of reward in the world to come and of finding grace in the eyes of God, it says at the end: "And give thee peace," as an indication that peace is necessary in order to obtain spiritual peace. For since man is composed of two opposite powers, a material and a spiritual, human perfection can not be attained unless there be peace and harmony between them, each one being given its proper share. In this way spiritual peace may be attained.

And since eternal spiritual reward of the soul can not be obtained except through absolute mercy, as was said before, it was necessary to mention lifting up of the countenance: "The Lord lift up His countenance upon thee." Then in order to indicate the spiritual reward which comes from the lifting up of countenance, he adds: "And give thee peace," to indicate that the final good of all for the human race is the spiritual reward of the soul, which is called peace. David also says: "Mark the man of integrity, and behold the upright; for there is a future for the man of peace."

We have now completed what we intended to say in this book. Praise be to God, the giver of power and strength, who has helped us until now. He is raised and exalted above all blessing and praise.

www.ingramcontent.com/pod-product-compliance
Lightning Source LLC
Chambersburg PA
CBHW070123080526

44586CB00015B/1529